Rethinking Domestic Violence

Rethinking Domestic Violence

DONALD G. DUTTON

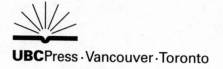

UBCPress · Vancouver · Toronto

15 14 13 12 11 10 09 08 07 06   5 4 3 2 1

Printed in Canada on acid-free paper that is 100 percent post-consumer recycled, processed chlorine-free, and printed with vegetable-based, low-VOC inks.

Library and Archives Canada Cataloguing in Publication

Dutton, Donald G., 1943-
   Rethinking domestic violence / Donald G. Dutton.

Includes bibliographical references and index.
ISBN-13: 978-0-7748-1304-4 (bound); 978-0-7748-1015-9 (pbk.)
ISBN-10: 0-7748-1304-0 (bound); 0-7748-1015-7 (pbk.)

   1. Spousal abuse. I. Title.

HV6626.D885 2006   362.82'92   C2006-901261-X

Canadä

UBC Press gratefully acknowledges the financial support for our publishing program of the Government of Canada through the Book Publishing Industry Development Program (BPIDP), and of the Canada Council for the Arts, and the British Columbia Arts Council.

UBC Press
The University of British Columbia
2029 West Mall
Vancouver, BC V6T 1Z2
604-822-5959 / Fax: 604-822-6083
www.ubcpress.ca

TO MARTA, MY WIFE AND LIFE COMPANION

The tragedy for me is that I had a vision whereby people who were infected by dysfunctional and violent parenting could find a place that would give them a chance to learn how to live in peace and harmony. This dream was destroyed along with all my evidence and projects. The feminist movement resolutely refuted any argument that women should be allowed to take responsibility for their choice of relationships. The image of women as victims, as helpless childish dependents upon brutal men worldwide, has damaged relationships between the sexes.

> – Erin Pizzey (founder of the first women's
> shelter in England), "Domestic Violence Is
> Not a Gender Issue"

Contents

Contents

Preface

> Lastly, there are idols which have immigrated into men's minds
> from the various dogmas and philosophies, and also from wrong laws
> of demonstration. These I call idols of the theatre, because in my
> judgment all the received systems are but so many stage-plays,
> representing worlds of their own creation.
>
> — Francis Bacon, *Novum Organum*

Two major social phenomena concerning gender have occurred during the latter part of the twentieth century in most North American and Western European countries. Women's rights have finally been acknowledged after centuries of religion-based political repression. Also, the violence occurring against women in intimate relationships has finally been exposed.

In patriarchal countries, violence against women still persists as a "right" that men believe they have. I was reminded of this during a recent speech in Rome where a therapist told me of cultural practices in Sardinia, which include a man's "duty" to kill his wife if he believed she was cheating on him (and destroying family honour). "Family honour" societies are typically highly religious.

For these historical reasons (see Chapter 1), it has been tempting for feminists to view intimate violence as part and parcel of the domination of women. This is true for societies that remain truly patriarchal. In North America, however, a different data pattern has begun to emerge, one that also follows from a feminist model but not from a woman-as-victim model. In Canada and the United States, women use violence in intimate relationships to the same extent as men, for the same reasons, and with largely the same results. As will be described in Chapters 5 and 6, this notion was originally dismissed as fictional, the violence thought to be self-defensive, or the consequences trivial. The data strongly suggest otherwise, despite a research agenda that can only be described as attempted "dogma preservation."

What has occurred in North American governments at national and local levels has been a simplistic conceptualization of intimate-partner violence (IPV) that has resulted in a denial of violence against men and also of bilateral complicity in violent couples. This has led to a prohibition on treatment that could better benefit victims of intimate abuse – both males and females – and a reliance on superficial "psychoeducational" models that are limited to "attitudes." Because of a need to find a "bad guy" – generated from adaptation of the Marxist view of the bourgeoisie to fit "men in general" – considerable distortion of the data of IPV has occurred. This conceptualization has generated arrest policies (see Chapter 12) and treatment policies (Chapter 14) that forbid treatment. Yes, that's correct, *forbid* treatment, replacing it with what is called "intervention," which is really no more than "thought reform" as described in Robert Lifton's great work, *Thought Reform and the Psychology of Totalism.* The mindset of "women as victims" is enshrined in legal and government policy structures, where homeostasis now operates against effective policy.

Despite this political myopia, some impressive research has charted abusiveness in both genders and over long periods of time. We now know from the work of Terrie Moffitt and her colleagues (discussed in Chapter 7) that we can predict perpetration of IPV as early as age fifteen in both genders. Some of my own retrospective work on convicted male abusers and that of others (especially the groundbreaking work of Alan Schore on "affective neurodevelopment") suggests much earlier origins (see Chapter 4). Neglect of essential conditions for secure attachment and child rearing is a huge contributor to adult abusiveness.

In this book I have limited policy issues to "after the fact" intervention for intimate abuse. It is most obvious, given these early developmental antecedents, that prevention of abuse must start at birth. In fact, according to the work of Schore (described in Chapter 4), the first eighteen months of life allow healthy or unhealthy development of neural structures that govern emotion. Intimate relationships inevitably generate emotion, and behaviour in these relationships is being shaped from birth. Schore's work also shows how "maturational windows" recycle and provide therapeutic opportunities into adulthood.

It may be that public policy for adult IPV regulation is following a dialectical course. The thesis would have been the period of neglect of the topic up to the early seventies; the antithesis is surely the simplistic paradigm that exists today: that all perpetrators are male and all victims female. The evidence is overwhelmingly against this view, and the phenomenon of interest now is the slavish adherence to an ineffectual ideology to the point of suppressing its very goal: diminution of IPV. One hopes for a synthesis in which the complexities of subtypes of couple violence patterns, motives, sexual orientation, and personality disorders are assessed by professionals, replacing the "one size fits all" monolithic model currently in practice. Intimate-partner violence exists in heterosexual, gay, and lesbian couples and across cultural groups and social strata. Whatever variations are introduced by these group memberships rest on top of a universal issue: intimacy and how to handle it. Ernest Becker's insightful words in the epigraph at the beginning of this preface point to the dyadic and problematic nature of "relationship" in the human condition.

Existing approaches to "family violence" intervention are examined in this book (Chapters 12, 14, and 15) and found lacking. The research evidence from the best-designed studies – those that use representative community samples and study them longitudinally (see Chapters 6 and 7) – finds a personality disorder in the majority of people who abuse intimates. The success of intervention strategies rests largely on the type of person to whom they are applied. This is true regardless of whether a couple is heterosexual or homosexual. In cultures where intimate abuse is not normatively acceptable (as is the case in North America), personality disorders represent the complex of ideas that generate counter-normative behaviours. This reality has been concealed by misleading theories that wife assault is normatively acceptable, an absurd assertion without empirical support.

Public policy must be driven by recognition of attachment-based personality disorder as central to therapeutic change. Psychoeducational groups do not address this issue and, according to independent outcome studies, have been a total failure. Cognitive-behavioural treatment can address personality disorder, and some steps have been taken to include it in perpetrator treatment. Intimate Abuse Circles (Chapters 15 and 16) may work under certain prescribed circumstances (as an alternative for those who do not wish criminal justice system intervention), but they probably would not work with personality-disordered persons.

This book is obviously about more than the domestic assault of women. It is a modern history of social intervention on a specific problem that shows how such intervention can be misguided by the political conceptualization of the problem. It would be preferable to see policy made by pragmatists and "dust bowl" empiricists who are willing to set and undo policy on the basis of what the data tells them about success and failure, rather than on attempts to prolong an ideological view. If we really want women (and men) to be safe, we must take a broader and more enlightened view of this complex problem.

I owe a huge intellectual debt to the following people. First and foremost, Murray Straus has been the consummate social scientist, asking the tough questions, carrying out methodologically sound research, and not flinching from the answers suggested by his data, even under unwarranted personal attacks. J.Q. Wilson and Ivan Illich shaped my thinking about the limits of legal policy, reinforced by the studies by Lawrence Sherman and his colleagues and by Laura Dugan (discussed in Chapter 12).

John Bowlby and Alan Schore are geniuses who are just starting to get their due. Bowlby integrated psychoanalysis with sociobiology. Schore is.integrating Bowlby's attachment theory with developmental neuropsychology. Ernest Becker always presides over any discourse on the problems of the human condition.

Among personal colleagues, I would like to thank Kim Bartholomew for always goading me into asking tougher questions of my own data and that of others. She is super-smart and a great colleague. Daniel Sonkin has always been supportive and has rescued me in prior projects that were dying on the vine. Along with Kim, he has kept my interest in attachment research alive and has generated a whole new approach to incorporating this issue into abuse treatment. Ehor Boyanowsky taught me to never turn away from the tough, if politically incorrect, data sets. In this Murray Straus has also been a consistent examplar of what a social scientist should do: report the data that will be unpopular as well as the rest.

I was pleasantly surprised at the solid studies of Terrie Moffitt, Miriam Ehrensaft, Marilyn Dugan, and John Archer, among others. These were real additions to a research field that is variable in quality at best. For the benefit of future researchers, this book not only points out the methodologically best work but also singles out some of the worst.

There are several other people who helped enormously on this book. Jessica Broderick did all the detective work, finding articles in journals both obscure and mainstream. Rene Lane brought me back from the brink of computer psychosis on several occasions. Laura Devlin and Makenzie Chilton helped in the pinch. Last, but not least, my cyber think-tank: Lisa Scott, Grant Brown, Ken Corso, Mariel Davison. Thanks for engaging and debating ideas from a variety of perspectives.

Rethinking Domestic Violence

1 The History of Spouse Assault

> How vast is the number of men, in any great country, who are a little higher than brutes ... This never prevents them from being able, through the laws of marriage, to obtain a victim ... The vilest male-factor has some wretched woman tied to him against whom he can commit any atrocity except killing her – and even that he can do without too much danger of legal penalty.
>
> – John Stuart Mill, *The Subjection of Women*

First, let us get our terms straight. "Domestic violence" refers to any violence occurring between intimate partners (same sex or other sex, married or un-married) and against children. Our focus is on intimate partner abuse, not child abuse. The abuse can take many forms: physical, sexual, or emotional.

This book examines mainly physical violence (with a view to improving system intervention). Some of the research also covers emotional violence, but usually associated with and measured by physical violence as the crite-rion. The terms "wife assault" and "spouse abuse" will be confined to mar-ried relationships. The term "intimate partner violence" (IPV) will be used for violence that occurs in a variety of intimate relationships: married, cohabitating, gay, and straight. The important common factor is that these relationships are emotionally bonded. Historically, feminists have focused on wife assault to the neglect of violence perpetrated by women and vio-lence in same-sex relationships.

Researchers usually define "severe" assault as actions with a relatively high likelihood of causing injury to the victim.[1] Hence, kicking, biting, hitting with a fist or object, beating up, or using a weapon against a victim are all actions regarded as constituting severe assault. These actions not only are likely to carry medical consequences for the victim but also are in practice considered "arrestable" by police. Other assaultive acts (e.g., slapping, push-ing, shoving, grabbing, throwing objects at the victim) are less likely to evoke medical or criminal justice consequences. The term "battering" denotes repeated forceful blows, although the term is frequently and inappropriately used to describe the actions of anyone charged with assault, even if they never "battered" anyone. Technically and legally, you can assault someone just by placing your hands on their body. The problem with this imprecision in the language is that it confounds less serious actions and perpetrators (for example, a man who has physically pushed his wife – the most frequent act of spousal aggression) with the more severe (a man who has literally held captive, repeatedly beaten, and injured his wife). The difference in severity requires correspondingly different explanations (the minor act may be situational or bidirectional, the latter more likely to connote serious psychological problems) and different criminal justice system policies.

Some might object that this classification system neglects the effects of the actions it classifies. Shoving someone down a flight of stairs, for example, may have more serious consequences than hitting them with a rolled up newspaper. However, a definition of spouse assault that focuses on severe abuse allows us to connect our understanding of the psychology of violent actions to the criminal justice policy used to reduce their likelihood and enables this book to make use of research that classifies violent acts according to severity (for example, by using the Straus Conflict Tactics Scale; see Chapter 3). Nevertheless, the section on measurement considers "outcome of assault" issues such as injury or psychological trauma. Many assessment scales now assess outcome as well as action.

A second objection against basing the study of violence toward intimate partners on discrete physical actions is that these actions constitute only the "tip of the iceberg." Physical assault frequently is accompanied by verbal abuse, psychological abuse, and threats or actions of destruction toward children, pets, and personal property. This constellation of destructive actions, some would argue, more fully represents a continuum of coercive control and therefore constitutes the proper subject matter for a psychology of interpersonal violence. This argument is an important one and will be considered at various times in this book. Indeed, in the development of "assaultiveness" physical abuse and psychological abuse combine to form a toxic environment.

However, a level of explanation for IPV directed at social intervention must focus on behaviours that society agrees are unacceptable and require the intervention of agents from outside the family. While some disagreement exists over how far society should go to control IPV, there would probably be little agreement whatsoever over the appropriate degree of social intervention into "family coercion." The law focuses on physical (or sexual) assault, not on psychological abuse. Whatever our philosophical and political beliefs tell us about the pathological component of coercion in social systems, society rarely becomes involved in altering the use of coercion in families until that coercion involves physical force or threats.[2] As we shall see, physical assault provides the most effective focus for policies of intervention into family dysfunction. At the same time, IPV may of course have a common psychological substratum with other, less dramatic coercive actions. Chapter 9 on psychological causes of IPV describes research that used both physical and psychological abuse as outcome measures, matched up with psychological profiles of the perpetrators.

In summary, the definition of IPV used in this book is chosen with a view to intervention, and the questions that arise about the causes of such assault will bear on the strategies a society might invoke to reduce its incidence.

A Brief Social and Legal History

The development of social history methodology in the last twenty years has provided the means for studying the life of average citizens in various historical periods. We now have available studies of the social evolution of love, sex, sex and power, manners, folly, even torture.[3] A comprehensive social history of IPV remains to be written, largely because the private nature of the event creates problems for historians in gaining access to adequate data. Typically, feminist historians have focused on the history of misogyny permitting wife assault. Other forms of IPV have not been studied historically.

What little historical work has been done has focused on attitudes of misogyny, especially in theological tracts such as the Malleus Maleficarum, Gratian's Decretum, or the writings of St. Paul and St. Augustine, and on legal sanctions (or lack thereof) on wife assault.[4] The theological tracts are relevant because of the great influence they exerted in both guiding and exonerating behaviour, especially during the Middle Ages. The Decretum (c. 1140), for example, the first "enduring systematization" of church law, specified that women were "subject to their men" and needed castigation or punishment for correction. This punishment was made necessary by women's supposed inferiority and susceptibility to the influence of devils. Jacob Sprenger's Malleus Maleficarum and the extreme views of St. Paul and St. Augustine carried misogyny to an extreme. Women's susceptibility to diabolic influence was the rationalization for murdering women during the Middle Ages in order to suppress witchcraft.[5] It is interesting to note that one basis for suspecting a woman of witchcraft was male impotence.

Modern concepts of personal responsibility for violent behaviour were foreign to the medieval mind, in which violence was excused as part of a great cosmological scheme or justified as being in the best interest of the victim (to help her avoid the influence of devils). As we shall see in later chapters, this tendency to externalize the causes of violent behaviour is still common in males who assault women, although cosmic influences as a favourite excuse have been replaced by alcohol and by attributing the cause of the violence to the female victim. Female susceptibility to diabolic influence has been replaced as an exonerative cause of male violence by the concept of female masochism, or provocation.[6] Until the 1990s, Brazil had a legal defence for spousal homicide that only required the man to suspect his wife was having an affair. Given the attachment distortion known as "conjugal paranoia" (discussed below), this is tantamount to arguing that misguided beliefs excuse violence.

Unfortunately, we know little about the prevalence of wife assault during the Middle Ages. In sixteenth-century France, community members would dress in carnival costumes and impose pranks and mocking serenades called *charivaris* upon members of the town whose actions deviated from the local norms.[7] This dramaturgical social control sometimes focused on any husband who allowed his wife to beat him. The unfortunate male was dressed up, seated backwards on a donkey, draped with kitchen paraphernalia, and punched in the genitals. That no such derision descended upon battered women suggests to Davidson that wife beating was normative, since only counter-normative behaviour was punished by the charivaris. George describes a similar practice in England called "riding Skimmington" used by the towns and communities to satirize and deride the beaten husband.[8] George, too, views such ritual as ridiculing those who transgressed against the social order (such as violent wives, victimized husbands). Hence the inference that wife beating was accepted while husband beating was not.

Davidson also cites the eighteenth-century Napoleonic Civil Code, which influenced French, Swiss, Italian, and German law, as vesting absolute family power in the male and as recognizing violence as a ground for divorce only when the courts decided that it constituted attempted murder.[9] Hence the male had a legal right to use violence up to the point of attempted murder to protect his absolute power within the family.

This situation also apparently existed in England, prompting John Stuart Mill in 1869 to write his famous essay *The Subjection of Women*, which Davidson cites as the "first significant document to spark the raising of public consciousness about the plight of battered wives."[10] In this essay, Mill decried "bodily violence towards the wife," which he viewed as arising from men's "mean and savage natures," which were checked and resisted in public transactions but went unchecked at home because their wives could not repel or escape them and because they viewed their wives as chattels "to be used at their pleasure." Mill ascribed these actions, in the paradigm of the time, as being perpetrated by lower-class men. He found it impossible to believe a well-bred upper-class British gentleman would resort to such behaviour. The French had no such illusions. Their term for wife-beating was "le vice anglais." However, in England they knew wife abuse was "caused" by social class. Now, we believe that gender is the "cause."

Mill's essay helped spark controversy about family violence and a report to the British Parliament in 1874. At that time British Common Law allowed a man to beat his wife with a rod no bigger than his thumb. This "rule of thumb" was believed to be humane because it replaced an older law that allowed beating "with any reasonable instrument."

By the end of the nineteenth century, wife assault even by the "rule of thumb" had become illegal under British Common Law and in many American states.[11] However, in practice, the criminal justice system in England, the United States, and Canada routinely ignored family violence unless a murder occurred. This discrepancy between the law and legal policy was made clear by the actions of the women's movement in the 1970s to identify wife assault as a social problem of considerable magnitude and incidence and to point out the lack of action by the criminal justice system to punish wife assaulters.

The New Protest against Wife Assault

The history of sociolegal policy to control family violence is eloquently described by Elizabeth Pleck in her book Domestic Tyranny, from which much of the following information is drawn.[12] Sociolegal policy to control family violence appears to have been implemented first by the Puritans in the colony of Massachusetts (1640 to 1680), which had laws against wife beating and "unnatural severity" to children. The Puritans considered wife-beating to be a sin and believed in strong community intervention (a "holy watching" of saintly people). Their courts developed a post called "tithingman" who was to visit ten families and report "stubborn and disorderly children and servants, prostitutes, drunkards, and Sabbath breakers" to a magistrate for punishment. Initially, Puritans were required to undergo a religious conversion much like today's Christian evangelicals. The notion of "punishment for correction" was derived from a religious base: that the father was the head of the family and could punish his wife and children with impunity. After 1670, Pleck noted, historical anecdotes indicate an increasing reluctance by the Puritans to become involved in domestic problems.

Puritans believed child abuse was a sin, too, but had a far broader concept of acceptable corporal punishment than we currently hold in North America. Anything that did not cause permanent physical damage was acceptable. This rule also applied to corporal punishment of servants. That being said, the Puritans revered the two-parent, father-dominant household. Neglect of a child's "Christian education" was more likely to get a child removed from a home than corporal punishment and physical abuse.

In non-Puritan society at that time, wife beating was punished informally. Pleck cites an example from Boston in 1707 when nine men tore the clothes off a neighbour and flogged him for having beaten his wife. In the 1750s the Regulators of Elizabethtown, New Jersey, painted their faces, dressed up like women, and whipped reputed wife beaters. More typically, the man, if he belonged to a church denomination, was brought to trial within the church community.

The last quarter of the nineteenth century also saw an increase in the use of tort protection for battered wives resulting from advocacy by both feminists and the Women's Christian Temperance Union. The WCTU believed that men were morally inferior to women and more susceptible to alcohol, which was seen as the cause of wife beating. They succeeded in passing legislation in twenty states to expand tort protection for victims of violence so that saloon keepers or saloon owners could be sued for damages caused from injury inflicted by an intoxicated person. Pleck points out that women usually won in court, although few could afford to sue.[13] The WCTU, famous for its opposition to alcohol as the root cause of wife abuse, also fought to make drunkenness a ground for divorce and to secure property settlements for drunkard's wives. Antebellum feminists believed wives had a moral duty to divorce drunkards and placed the emancipation of women ahead of duty to preserve the family. They argued that a mother and child were better off living alone than remaining bound to a drunk. Similar arguments are made in divorce courts today regarding physical abuse apart from alcohol abuse. The exact causal role between alcohol abuse and wife abuse is not clear. Most likely, as we shall see below, both are symptoms of identity issues and concomitant emotional reactions in abuse perpetrators.

Pleck argues that the history of the criminalization of family violence reflected widespread contemporary social attitudes about the family.[14] Historically, when the rights and privileges of the family (e.g., family privacy, freedom from government interference) were viewed as paramount, interest in criminalizing family violence waned. However, when family violence was seen as threatening not only its victims but the social order as well, support for criminalization increased.

Attitudes that develop during periods of disinterest in criminalizing family violence include an idealization of the family and a typical set of beliefs: that parents have the right to physically discipline children, that a husband has the right to have sexual access to his wife, that nagging women or disobedient children often provoke the beatings they receive, that wives and children need a male economic provider, and that the law should not disrupt this traditional pattern of support except in extreme circumstances.

As the eighteenth century progressed, legal thinkers distinguished between public and private behaviour. Sir William Blackstone's *Commentaries on the Laws of England* expressed the view that crimes were acts that produced mischief in civilized society, while private acts that produced moral disapproval were deemed vices and were not considered a legitimate subject of law.[15] Hence, the family came to be considered a private institution, beyond the purview of legislation designed to enforce morality (which had been the reason for the Puritan interest in legislating against family violence).

In her review of nineteenth-century court decisions, Pleck concluded that courts decided to punish husbands when permanent injuries were inflicted and to treat other wife assaults as "trifling cases" where the court would not interfere with "family government."[16]

John Stuart Mill in 1850-51 published a series of newspaper articles on the plight of women, sparked by the concerns of his mistress, Harriet Taylor. The ensuing publicity helped spark controversy about family violence and a debate in the British Parliament in the 1850s. In 1853 and 1856 the British Parliament twice considered flogging wife assaulters. These proposed "whipping post" laws were voted down as "cruel and unusual punishment" (although whipping posts were routinely used by the British navy for insignificant offences).[17]

In the United States from 1858 to 1870, Elizabeth Stanton and Susan B. Anthony wrote, spoke, and demonstrated against wife abuse.[18] Both activists sought to reveal the "darker side of marriage" and both were discredited in the usual way, through character assassination (in this case, guilt by association with presumed adulterers). Stanton argued that abuse stemmed from a man's presumed ownership of his wife and children.[19]

A wave of interest in reform occurred between 1874 and 1890 in England, the United States, and Canada. At this time societies for the prevention of cruelty to children were founded.

After the Civil War, American judges and lawyers campaigned to have wife assaulters flogged. President Theodore Roosevelt, in his annual message to Congress in 1904, decried "brutality and cruelty toward the weak" and said: "The wifebeater, for example, is inadequately punished by imprisonment, for imprisonment may often mean nothing to him, while it may cause hunger and want to the wife and children who have been the victims of his brutality. Probably some form of corporal punishment would be the most adequate way of meeting this crime."[20] At the same time, female advocates of temperance helped pass laws giving tort protection to the wives and children of drunkards. Since many of these men also abused their families, these laws often benefited victims of abuse. Pleck attributes this revival of interest in judicial sanctions to an upswing in interest in the state's responsibility to enforce public morality. Family violence was taken seriously because it was believed to lead to other forms of crime. Pleck sees this generalized fear of crime as emanating from the chaos and upheaval and increase in violent crimes that followed the American Civil War. As after most wars, intra-societal violence increased in the postwar era. In this case the violence was blamed on the "dangerous classes," which included blacks, immigrants, and homeless men. Abused children were viewed as potential members of these "dangerous classes."

By 1899, in the United States there were hundreds of societies to protect children but only one to protect women. While Victorians believed that women were abused by drunken men, they still believed (despite Stanton's and Anthony's lectures) that women should sacrifice themselves for the sake of the family. Strong support existed, however, for the flogging of wife beaters to "give them a taste of their own medicine." This idea was proposed unsuccessfully four times in the British Parliament between 1854 and 1875. In the United States, flogging bills were proposed in twelve states and in the District of Columbia. Most supporters were eminently respectable – mainly Republican male lawyers, district attorneys, and grand juries. (In the 1980s, Republicans and feminists joined forces again to combat pornography.)[21] They were supported by suffragist leaders. Congress (in 1906), and most state congresses that considered the matter, defeated whipping post legislation on the ground that it was cruel and barbaric. Where the whipping post existed (e.g., Maryland, Delaware, and Oregon), it was used disproportionately against black males convicted of wife beating. In Delaware, six whites and fifteen blacks were flogged for wife beating between 1901 and 1942.[22] Eventually, public opinion turned, and the whipping post began to be seen as cruel and unusual punishment, even in the states that had enacted it.

By the end of the nineteenth century, wife assault even by the "rule of thumb" had become illegal under British common law and in many American states.[23] However, in practice, the criminal justice system in England, the United States, and Canada routinely ignored family violence unless a murder occurred. This discrepancy between the law and legal policy was made clear by the actions of the women's movement in the 1970s to identify wife assault as a social problem of considerable magnitude and incidence and to point out the lack of action by the criminal justice system to punish wife assaulters.

During the first quarter of the twentieth century the perception of family violence as a serious crime began to diminish. With the creation of family courts and social casework, criminal justice system sanctions for family crime came to be viewed as inhumane and outmoded. The attitudinal shift was toward rehabilitation and family privacy. This era could be called the Age of Denial: families did not talk publicly about intimate violence any more than they talked about sex. Police didn't want to get involved when they received "domestic disturbance" calls. Typically couples were told to keep the peace for the remainder of the evening, that if the police had to come back they would arrest. As we shall see below, this strategy underestimated the violence potential in intimate relationships.

The Age of Denial

In Chapter 12 we will see some of the earliest studies of police handling of "domestic disturbance" calls. One study found that battered women had been assaulted thirty-five times on average before calling the police. (Actually, it was a self-selected sample of 28 percent of all women who called the police who supplied this statistic. It is reasonable that, given their willingness to be interviewed, they constituted an extreme group even among women who called police with domestic violence problems.)

The gist of the problem at that time (up until the 1980s) was that police wanted no part of violent domestic disputes, nor did judges. Family violence was a "dirty little secret" exemplified by the title of Erin Pizzey's groundbreaking book on the topic (see below) called *Scream Quietly or the Neighbours Will Hear.*[24] Several studies of police handling were performed during this "Age of Denial," and they basically revealed that police at that time rarely made arrests during violent domestic disputes. The one exception was when the male challenged their authority.

Two methods were used to study police handling of "domestics." Loving and Farmer used the first method, giving questionnaires to 130 police officers of assorted ranks from sixteen police agencies.[25] Police responded that they would make an arrest in domestic violence situations if a crime had been committed or the likelihood of recurring violence was high. In rating the importance of factors influencing their decision to arrest, they mentioned the following in decreasing order of importance: commission of a felony, serious injury to the victim, use of a weapon, use of violence against the police, likelihood of future violence, previous legal action against the assailant, previous injury to victim or damage to property, and alcohol/drug intoxicated assailant. Factors that would lead them not to arrest in decreasing order of importance were a refusal by the victim to press charges, a victim's tendency to drop charges, and lack of serious injury. Of course, as Loving and Farmer point out, there is no way of knowing, on the basis of this study, whether these factors would be given similar weight under actual intervention conditions.[26] In Chapter 12 the problem of police intervention will be revisited.

Waaland and Keeley devised simulated police reports (seventy-one descriptions of cases) containing seven informational cues: the man's occupational status, history of wife assault, assailant's behaviour toward the officers, extent of the victim's injuries, drinking by the assailant, drinking by the victim, and verbal antagonism of the assailant by the victim. With the exception of occupational status, three levels of each cue were presented in fifty-six unique combinations (order of information was randomized with a few restrictions).[27] Police (twenty-six patrol officers in Oregon) were asked to make judgments of both the husband's and wife's responsibility for the incident and to assign one of four possible legal outcomes for the offender.

The authors found that officers believed an abusive husband to be more responsible for the violence than his wife but varied extremely in these judgments. Victim antagonism and victim drinking influenced attribution of responsibility, but attribution of responsibility did not influence police decisions to arrest. Decisions to arrest were most strongly influenced by victim injuries (which accounted for 85 percent of the variance in composite arrest decisions). The assailant's behaviour toward investigating officers and his assaultive history made smaller but significant contributions to arrest decisions.

Not coincidentally, at the time the data were collected the State of Oregon had recently adopted legal standards for domestic intervention, potentially influencing officers to appear to be "going by the book." Interestingly, despite the high probability of social desirability influences, very low arrest rates were obtained in this study. Although 36 percent of the victims were depicted as severely injured, half the officers did not prescribe arrest under these conditions. Multiple bruises and blackened eyes were not considered sufficient causes for legal action, although they are explicitly evidence of unlawful assault under Oregon law.[28]

Ford provided a hypothetical example of a domestic disturbance to 439 law enforcement officers in Indiana and correlated their self-reported likelihood of arrests to a variety of attitudes and stereotypes about victims of wife assault.[29] Ford's hypothetical example contained sufficient grounds to establish probable cause (in the opinion of judges, prosecutors, and defence attorneys). Only 20 percent of officers, however, indicated a greater than 50/50 chance that they would arrest under these circumstances. Since the state policy mandated arrest where reasonable and probable grounds existed, this 20 percent rate certainly did not represent police as providing a researcher with a procedurally correct answer. Factors that contributed most heavily to the disinclination to arrest were police perceptions that the couple was in a continuing relationship and that the woman had not made a serious effort to leave (and their belief that she should take action on her own to leave). In weighing the conflicting stories given by the hypothetical man and woman at the scene, the notion that "if things were as bad as she says, why doesn't she leave?" influenced police beliefs of whether probable cause existed. Police who were most likely to report they would arrest tended to do so because they expected the violence would recur.

Observational Studies

The most obvious method to circumvent the social desirability issues raised by hypothetical studies is direct or indirect observation of actual police practice. Indirect observation means the examination of police records and the reconstruction of their arrest decisions through multivariate analysis of the information provided in the records.

Using this method, Berk and Loseke examined 262 official police reports on domestic disturbance interventions and generated a multiple regression model to predict whether police would arrest or not in these reported cases.[30] The variable that had the greatest weight in predicting whether or not the police would arrest was the victim's willingness to sign a citizen's arrest warrant. The next most powerful predictors were (1) alcohol use or intoxication by the male and (2) allegations of violence by the victim. Neither injury to the victim nor property damage had any significant effect on arrests. In addition, when the victim was the person who called the police, arrest rates dropped. Berk and Loseke do point out that the "injuries" variable approached significance ($p = .08$) and that a more sensitive measure of severity of victim injuries might have produced a significant result.[31]

To a certain extent, before the officer arrives at the scene a police "theory" of the case begins to develop, fuelled by personal beliefs about male-female violence and the dispatcher's descriptions of the current situation. Berk and Loseke suggest that when the police arrive they begin to look for signs that verify their theory of what caused the conflict.[32] Berk and Loseke propose, as have others, that police intervention decisions are not pure products of legal

requirements or departmental policy but rather are the result of an admixture of personal attitudes and occupational, informal norms that combine
with more formalized policy.[33] Hence, altering police intervention practice
would require not only specific policy directives but also changes in recruit-
ment and training that have attitudinal objectives and are buttressed by systemic support from prosecution and judges.[34] In fact, as we shall see, the
by-passing of line officers in states that went to "mandatory arrest" produced resentment and subversion of the policy by police.[35]

An early field observation of police intervention was conducted by Black
on data collected in 1966. Field observations of 108 domestic dispute interventions involving married couples revealed that, although sixty-five cases
involved violence, only thirteen arrests were made.[36] Black reported that police acted more coercively with black and working-class couples and in a
more conciliatory fashion with white middle-class couples. Again, this finding is of great relevance when combined with studies on the effects of race
on recidivism reported in Chapter 12.

Worden and Pollitz examined direct reports of trained observers who witnessed 167 domestic disturbances in twenty-four different police departments as part of a Police Services Study conducted at Indiana University.[37]
The authors corroborated results from Berk and Loseke's "indirect" study.
Both studies found that the probability of police arrest increased substantially with the woman victim's promise to sign a warrant, with the male's
appearance of having been drinking, and with the woman's allegations of
violence. Both studies found that arrest did not increase if one disputant
had been injured. Worden and Pollitz also confirmed the finding that disrespectful behaviour toward the police increases the likelihood of arrest. Observers coded citizens' behaviour into categories such as "apologetic, sarcastic,
disrespectful and hostile." The "disrespectful" category increased the probability of arrest by 43 percent.

Smith and Klein had trained civilians to ride on 900 patrol shifts, and
they observed 5,688 police-citizen encounters in twenty-four American metropolitan areas.[38] Of these, 433 involved an interpersonal dispute where the
dispute was in progress when the police arrived. For methodological reasons, 100 of these cases were omitted, leaving a data base of 333. It should
be pointed out that these were not all husband-wife or even male-female
disputes. For these 333 cases, arrests were made by police 15.3 percent of the
time. The main determinants of arrest in this study were: (1) the complainant's
statement that they wanted an arrest, (2) the demeanour of the offender, (3)
whether the offender had been drinking, and (4) the socioeconomic status

of the area where the house was located. The arrest rates by socioeconomic status were as follows: high status 5.5, middle status 1.9, low status 21.2 percent. Among factors that had no effect on the decision to arrest were: (1) the race of the parties involved, (2) whether or not one party was injured, and (3) whether weapons were involved. There was no significant difference in arrest rate between domestic disputes and non-domestic disputes. The authors concluded that the police appeared reluctant to arrest in both domestic and non-domestic disputes.

The police decision about arrest versus other alternatives initiates a chain of criminal justice policy decisions about wife assaulters. The objective of these decisions is to prevent wife assault from recurring. How might this objective best be achieved? What constellation of decisions by police, prosecutors, and judges might operate to reduce recidivist assault? It is to these questions that we now turn our attention. To find out what is commonly done in cases of wife assault, we will begin by reviewing available empirical studies that bear on the criminal justice response to wife assault discussed in Chapter 12. One thing that will become apparent is that arrest has different effects on different people (by race, socioeconomic status, and even psychological makeup), so we need to know something about the perpetrators.

The Rediscovery

The "rediscovery" of family violence in the 1970s is usually attributed to the pioneering work of C.H. Kempe, who first identified the "battered child syndrome."[39] His description of x-ray evidence of young children with multiple fractures at various stages of healing cast doubt on parents' explanations that the children had been injured in a single mishap. At this time, laws were passed requiring professionals to report child abuse to police or social agencies, and now mandatory reporting laws exist in virtually all states and provinces.[40] However, the intervention of choice has been rehabilitation, not punishment. Pleck argues that the domination of child assault reform by medical and social work professionals has resulted in the problem being defined as psychological illness in the parent requiring social services and mental health treatment.[41]

In contrast, wife assault reform advocates were mainly lawyers and feminists who saw social inequality and a lack of proper law enforcement as major contributors to the problem. The battered women's movement viewed marital rape and wife assault as crimes and sponsored legislation to increase criminal penalties and make it easier for women to file criminal charges and gain access to civil remedies.

The Shelter Movement

The first "whistle blower" in the age of denial was Erin Pizzey, who also established the first women's shelter in England in 1971 for women fleeing abusive relationships. Her landmark book, *Scream Quietly or the Neighbours Will Hear*, documented the collusion in covering up domestic violence.[42] Ironically, Pizzey ran afoul of the shelter movement when her later book, *Prone to Violence*, was published in 1982. In that book Pizzey argued that repeat victims of abuse develop a type of addiction to being battered.[43] The women's movement viewed this as victim-blaming and shunned Pizzey. Research by Harlow and Harlow, as well as by Solomon, which we shall review below, lends credence to Pizzey's theory that initially repulsive experiences can later become addictive, especially when they involve the frustration of the attachment system.[44] Lenore Walker mentioned Pizzey briefly in her own classic, *The Battered Woman*.[45] It is indicative of the paradigm that developed about domestic violence that Pizzey's landmark book was not

---

1.1 Erin Pizzey's philosophical stance

The premise of our work is that every baby needs to feel love and happiness. A baby will bond these instinctive feelings to whatever people and situations are available. It is the birth-right of every child to be surrounded by nurturing and loving parents in an atmosphere of peace. In a non-violent family, a child grows up in such an atmosphere, and then, working from the secure base of being loved, will develop an independent and choosing self that is able to recreate happy love both in future relationships and with its own children. In a violent family, however, this birth-right to love and peace is betrayed, because from the moment of conception the child lives in a world where emotional and physical pain and danger are always present. The child then bonds to pain. This bonding becomes an addiction to pain. The child then cannot grow to form an independent self, because he or she is slave to this addiction. Throughout life, the person then recreates situations of violence and pain, for those situations stir the only feelings of love and satisfaction the person has ever known.

　　Whether the children of violent families learn to find satisfaction through the inflicting or the receiving of emotional and physical pain, the violence that these people live on is merely an expression of pain. The role of the caring community is to undo this fundamental betrayal of people who have been emotionally disabled by their violent childhoods. By creating a loving environment in which deep internal work can be done to help violence-prone people to understand and to overcome their addiction to pain, these people can then learn to trust and be happy in love instead of pain.

Source: Erin Pizzey, from the preface of *Scream Quietly or the Neighbours Will Hear.*

even mentioned in Linda MacLeod's *Battered but Not Beaten: Preventing Wife Beating in Canada*.[46]

The Research Studies

Murray Straus was as important to research on domestic violence as Erin Pizzey was to the shelter movement. Dr. Straus, professor of Sociology at the University of New Hampshire, performed many early studies of the incidence of family violence (which we will see in detail in coming chapters). Over time he answered such questions as: how frequent is family violence, what are the most violent family relationships, what role does alcohol play in increasing the risk for family violence, are there racial differences, what about family power structure, what is the most "at-risk" age, are there gender differences, what is the impact of physical punishment of children on their later use of violence? Although this book will address many of these questions, the reader is advised to read Straus and Gelles' *Physical Violence in American Families*, for a complete picture.[47] In that encyclopedic work, Straus and Gelles report data from 8,145 American families in one of the most comprehensive data sets ever developed on family violence. Straus and Gelles' work has produced controversial results. Their finding that being spanked as a child was a risk factor for later violence in a dating relationship is one of the most cited studies in child development.[48] Similarly, his finding that on surveys using the Conflict Tactics Scale (more about it below) women used violence in intimate relationships more than men led to his lectures being picketed by feminist activist groups and extreme attacks on his methodology (more about this below).

Our culture has historically exhibited certain patriarchal values observable in religion and social custom. Working against the backdrop of this history, feminism quite naturally saw an antidote in ending social oppression of women. Wife assault, kept largely out of the public view and tolerated by prevailing attitudes, was regarded by feminists as an evil symptom of patriarchy. This argument will be examined in detail in Chapters 4 and 5.

2 Nested Ecological Theory

A point of consensus that developed among family violence researchers by the late 1970s was the need for more sophisticated, multifactor theories that took into account both the intrapsychic features of the violent offender and the interpersonal context in which the violence occurred. Gelles and Straus reviewed the contribution of fifteen theories to an understanding of wife assault and described the contributions and limitations of each.[1] Sociology, psychiatry, psychology, and sociobiology had all made theoretical contributions, and, as Gelles and Straus point out, their contributions tended to be complementary rather than competitive. Some theories of family violence, such as sociological ones, seek to explain the rates or incidence of violence in target populations. Psychological, psychiatric, and sociobiological theories seek to explain the violence of an individual, or of a group of individuals with similar qualities.

Since theories of family violence are so varied, attempts to disentangle their contributions are necessarily cumbersome and lead the reader into areas of metatheory and philosophy of science. Even single theoretical contributions can be very complex. For example, in the time since Straus published the "general systems" cybernetic model, adequate empirical testing of it has not been possible.[2]

I start with a social psychological perspective to incorporate both individual features and social contexts. Social psychological theories concentrate on the individual as a unit of analysis. Hence our interest will be in building a theory to explain the behaviour, feelings, and beliefs of the individual spouse assaulter. The approach examines both internal or intrapsychic events and those interpersonal or social relationships that influence assaultive behaviour.

Instead of analyzing social relationships in the "top-down" fashion of sociology, which begins with broad macrosystem analysis, social psychology determines first which social relationships are of relevance to the individual whose behaviour is to be explained. Theories are then built from the "bottom up," that is, from the context of the lifespace of this individual.[3]

This approach allows social psychological analysis to be sensitive simultaneously to differences in sociopolitical context affecting behaviour and to differences in individual behaviour in a common sociopolitical context. Rather than argue that a "norm" exists that allows wife assault to occur (as some have done), we are interested in empirical questions:

1 How much violence toward wives is considered "acceptable" by various social groups and under what circumstances?
2 How does this vary from one social group to another?
3 Does an assaultive male's behaviour fall within this range of acceptability?
4 If not, how does he justify his behaviour to himself?
5 How do broader social values shape individual experience?[4]

Originating inquiry at the psychological level makes "fine tuning" of sociological perspectives possible. Straus, Gelles, and Steinmetz state that "predictive checklists" based on economic, demographic, and family power measures make too many "false positive" identifications: these measures predict that many more males will assault their wives than actually do so.[5] Straus, Gelles, and Steinmetz point out the "obvious need to include data on the psychological characteristics." In selecting these psychological characteristics, care must be taken not to return to the reductionism of the psychiatric explanations of wife assault. Characteristics should be chosen that have prima facie relevance for male-female interaction (such as power motivation) in intimate relationships (i.e., intimacy anxiety). Certain psychological characteristics would interact with situational features to produce violence. It is a combination of the two levels that produces the violent outcome.

The theoretical structure into which these social and psychological characteristics are fitted is called a nested ecological theory.[6] Such theories were developed primarily by developmental psychologists and ethologists and are so-called because more precise variables (e.g., individual development) are viewed as "nested in" (operating within) broader variables (e.g., cultural norms, subcultures).[7]

Belsky integrated Bronfenbrenner's analysis of the social context in which individual development takes place with Tinbergen's emphasis on individual development, which he called ontogeny.[8] Bronfenbrenner divided this social context or "ecological space" into three levels: (1) the macrosystem, (2) the exosystem, and (3) the microsystem. The macrosystem refers to broad cultural values and belief systems that influence both ontogenetic development and the exosystem and microsystem. For example, patriarchy as a macrosystem value might influence both the development of individual expectations about appropriate levels of authority in a male-female relationship and the nature of social interaction at the family level. Archer found, in a cross-cultural study described below, that gender empowerment of women was correlated significantly (and negatively) with incidence of wife assault.[9] This would be a macrosystem variable.

The exosystem refers to "social structures both formal and informal that impinge upon the immediate settings in which that person is found and thereby influence, delimit or determine what goes on there."[10] Hence, work groups, friendships, peer groups, support groups, or any other groups that connect the family to the larger culture represent the exosystem (for an interesting example, see Figure 2.1). Work stress or the presence or absence of social support might also increase or decrease the likelihood of spouse assault and constitute an exosystem factor.

The microsystem refers to the family unit or the immediate context in which wife assault occurs. The interaction pattern of the couple, the conflict issues affecting them, and the antecedents and the consequences of assault

---

2.1 Football games as instigators of assault

Part of the folklore of wife assault is that assault rates go up dramatically after football games. When a team loses, as one story goes, its male fans take out their frustrations on wives and girlfriends. Another story is that when a team wins, the contagion of power feelings brings increases in wife assault.

Only one published systematic study of this question has come to light. White, Katz, and Scarborough examined all emergency-room admissions in northern Virginia over a two-year period.[1] Admissions were counted for both male and female victims of gunshot wounds, stabbings, assaults, falls, hits by objects, and lacerations. The largest football-related significant increase (about 52 percent above normal) was for male admissions on the day when the local NFL team (the Washington Redskins) lost. The second largest increase (38 percent above normal) was for female admissions the day after the team won. Of all effects on admission rates, the largest was for female admission on New Years' Day (240 percent of normal), followed by male admissions on Thanksgiving Day (150 percent of normal).

An attempt to replicate these results in Norfolk, Virginia, was not successful, a failure the authors attribute to the presence near the hospital of a large number of military men with affiliations to a variety of football teams. No significant relationships were found between football and emergency-room admissions in these data.

NOTE: 1 G.F. White, J. Katz, and K.E. Scarborough, "The impact of professional football games on violent assaults on women," *Violence and Victims* 7, 2 (1992): 151-71.

(how the man felt, how the woman acted after it was over), would constitute the microsystem level of analysis. Chapter 11 examines studies that break videotaped marital interaction down into five-second bits and analyze the reciprocal interactions that precede violence.

To Bronfenbrenner's three levels Belsky added a fourth: the ontogenetic level, which refers to individual development and defines what a particular individual's unique developmental history brings into this three-level social context. Chapters 4 and 8 through 10 will examine ontogenetic factors contributing to intimate violence. By examining the interaction of ontogenetic characteristics with social context features, we can begin to make predictions about individual behaviour patterns. Hence, two men may have been raised with the same cultural beliefs (macrosystem), have similar work and support networks (exosystem), and experience equal amounts of conflict in the home environment (microsystem), yet in the same social context one reacts with violence while the other does not. The basis of the difference in reactions is sought in the different learning experiences of the two men (ontogenetic): different exposures to violent role models, different response repertoires for handling conflict, different emotional reactions to male-female conflict.

Conversely, these individual characteristics are not viewed as existing in a vacuum but require a particular social context in which to manifest themselves. Two persons who grew up to be ontogenetically similar would behave differently with different micro-, exo-, or macrosystems. It is in this sense that the levels of explanation are said to be "nested" one within another. Figure 2.2 demonstrates the types of variables associated with each level of analysis, the scales used in this kind of research, and the types of questions these scales attempt to answer about causal variables affecting the likelihood of wife assault.

The profile of an assaultive male produced by a nested ecological theory borrows factors from all four levels in predicting risk for assault. For example, wife assault would be viewed as likely when a male with a strong need to dominate women (ontogenetic) and exaggerated anxiety about intimate relationships (ontogenetic), who has had violent role models (ontogenetic) and has poorly developed conflict-resolution skills (ontogenetic), is currently experiencing job stress or unemployment (exosystem), is isolated from support groups (exosystem), is experiencing relationship stress in terms of communication difficulties (microsystem) and power struggles (microsystem) and exists in a culture where "maleness" is defined by the ability to respond aggressively to conflict (macrosystem).

2.2 Nested ecological model

Level of analysis	Variable	Scale	Question	Sample study
Macrosystem	Women's socioeconomic power	Gender Empowerment Index	How much sociopolitical power do women have in a given country?	Archer found that religion was related to women's equality (see Chapter 2). Of the fifteen most egalitarian countries in the world, none were either Muslim or Catholic. Archer also found violence toward women was negatively related to their degree of sociopolitical power.
	Women's political power	Gender Development Index		
		Religion (e.g., Muslim or Catholic)		
		National acceptance of wife assault		
Exosystem	Isolation/stress	Demographic information sheets	Are stressed/isolated individuals more likely to perpetrate intimate partner violence?	DeKeseredy and Schwartz examined both stress and peer support on dating violence and reported evidence for both (see Chapter 2).
		Subcultural affiliations	Are there specific sub-cultures whose values tolerate greater amounts of intimate partner violence?	
		Sociometric questionnaire		

Microsystem	Couple conflict pattern	Physiological "linkage measures"	Are there specific cyclical patterns of communication in abusive couples?	K.E. Leonard, G. Margolin, and J.M. Gottman have all examined interactions of abusive couples and found spiralling negativity precedes violence (see Chapter 11).
Ontogenetic	Individual characteristics of abusers	Personality measures Anger measures Measures of cognitions during intimate conflict	Are there certain types of individuals who are "prone to intimate violence"?	D.G. Dutton's research on borderline traits in male spouse abusers (see Chapters 8, 9, 10), and Moffitt's studies on negative emotionality in female abusers (see Chapter 7).

To Belsky's four-level interactive system I would add a fifth level called the "suprasystem" (because it is deeper than the cultural attitudes of the macrosystem), encompassing power conflicts between groups in society. Historically, aggression is typically used between unequal power groups.[11] De Reincourt suggests that, in gender relations, sex and power have been traded across all cultures and at all historical times. He documents his thesis with an encyclopedic historico-cultural examination of gender relations, from Australopithecus to the present. Sex, de Reincourt argues, has always served as a power base for women despite economic subservience. At the suprasystem level, I argue, social disparities in power themselves breed conflict and violence. This occurs regardless of what group is in power. Power, in other words, is unrelated to the characteristics of the group holding power. It is the holding of absolute power that leads humans to act abusively. However, the powerless group will always attribute the abuse to characteristics of the powerful group because that is all they know.

The suprasystem could only be empirically filled by showing that the structure of conflict, at various levels and in disparate groups, produces the same effects; that power imbalances coupled with group delineation and between-group conflict produces violence; and that this occurs at any level, microsystemic or macrosystemic, and regardless of the groups involved. It is a historical absolute. It is in this sense that it constitutes a suprasystem; it describes an abstract and absolute reaction to a social arrangement that will occur with any groups at any time so long as they are in the conditions set out above. We would find the same result by looking at power dynamics in a couple (see, for example, Coleman and Straus),[12] in a nation (see, for example, the genocide in Rwanda),[13] or in international strife.

This hypothetical "profile" using ecological levels combines both sociodemographic and family interaction factors with psychological characteristics in the form of response repertoires, relevant motives, and anxieties. The combination produces a more finely tuned profile of a hypothetical assaultive male that remains sensitive to the social factors described by sociologists. One way of testing such a theory would be to investigate representative samples of assaultive males with samples that were not assaultive but who shared a variety of common characteristics (e.g., same demographics, similar degree of marital conflict). By so doing, the search for essential characteristics associated with assault could be more finely focused. The long-term objective would be to ascertain which of the several "ingredients" suggested by a nested ecological approach plays the major role in determining wife assault. An ultimate objective would be like a chemical "formula" that could tell us what amounts or "weights" to give to each factor in contributing to the likelihood of wife assault. Some of the stronger methodological studies reviewed in the chapters to follow have approximated this approach using longitudinal studies of representative community samples.[14] We now consider some factors at each level that might increase the likelihood of assaultiveness.

The Macrosystem

Broad sets of cultural beliefs and values relevant to wife assault constitute the macrosystem level of analysis, which has been the main focus of sociological investigation. Dobash and Dobash, for example, focus on patriarchy and claim that "the seeds of wife beating lie in the subordination of females and in their subjection to male authority and control."[15] The ideology of patriarchy holds that male supremacy is "natural" and that control of women and strong reactions to their insubordination are vital. Dobash and Dobash trace the history of this ideology and its buttressing via legal and religious dogma. The impact of this macrosystem belief on the family unit historically was to increase the power of the husband in order to focus power on nuclear families and the Crown while disenfranchising large feudal households. At the same time the belief was encouraged that hierarchy is the natural order. The patriarchal belief system presumably contributes to the incidence of wife assault by simultaneously creating in a husband the expectation that his wishes will not be opposed by his wife and justifying the use of violence to obtain this "natural right." Societies that regard women as chattels and maintain a strong double standard should, according to this view, demonstrate higher rates of wife assault (to the extent that male authority is occasionally resisted).

Archer has found some support for this view across nations.[16] By assessing equality of access to legal, health, educational, and other resources, Archer calculated a "gender empowerment index" for women in fifty-one countries. Gender empowerment was significantly and negatively related to incidents of violence towards women. Interestingly, religion appeared to play a large negative role in women's social power, the presence of a patriarchal religion strongly reducing women's power. Of the fifteen countries in the world rated highest for women's equality, none was Muslim or Catholic. Also of interest is the fact that the countries that supply the bulk of data on wife assault (e.g., the United States, Canada, New Zealand, Britain) are at or near the top for women's empowerment and hence may not be representative of causal factors in other countries where women have less social power.

In countries where women have low social power, social factors and patriarchy seem to explain violence toward women and lack of violence toward men in intimate relationships. In countries of relative equality, women's violence toward men exceeds men's violence towards women in intimate relationships. For both genders, violence is predicted better by psychological factors than by social-structural factors (see Chapter 5).

It is not known whether the cognitive and behavioural aspects of patriarchal ideology occur together or are somewhat independent. Bugenthal, Kahn, Andrews, and Head report that a majority of North American males approve of the use of violence to achieve "political ends." However, Stark and McEvoy reported that only a minority (25 percent of North American males) approved of slapping a wife under "appropriate circumstances."[17] That question was badly worded and the study is dated. Simon et al. found only 2.5 percent of American males approved of slapping a wife "to keep her in line."[18]

One relatively unexplored consequence of hierarchical systems is their influence on subjective emotional states. When someone claiming a position of authority has their authority challenged, might this challenge produce an enhanced arousal-anger reaction? Would the same conflict generate less anger if that person did not define him- or herself as an authority with associated expectations? I suggest, and will explore below, that one psychological mechanism that may connect patriarchy to wife assault is the shaping of a male emotional response to male-female conflict. Specifically, I suggest that men are more likely than women to become angry. Anger does not lead inevitably to violence, but it may increase the probability of violent behaviour.[19]

The Exosystem

Exosystem factors that could contribute to wife assault include job stress, unemployment, and the presence or absence of social support systems and peer group influence. Straus, Gelles, and Steinmetz reported that wife abuse rates increased with the number of stressful events a family experienced (as measured by a modified version of the Holmes and Rahe stress scale).[20] However, as the authors concluded, "counting stressful events and relating the tally to percentages of violent families does support the theory (that stress increases wife assault) but it does not convey the reasons for the relationship." Similarly, low income, unemployment, and part-time employment were also related to violence among spouses. The mechanisms that connect unemployment to wife assault include increased contact, greater likelihood of conflict over financial matters, lowered self-esteem in the unemployed husband, and redirected aggression whereby frustration from an unsatisfying work situation is expressed as aggression toward his wife.[21] These exosystem factors considered alone would lead to the prediction that economic downturns would be followed by increases in wife assault, via some or all of the above mechanisms.

An alternative view is that exosystem factors interact with microsystem and ontogenetic factors so that increases in unemployment produce violence only in families with dysfunctional interaction patterns or in men with learned dispositions to react to stress with violence. DeKeseredy and Schwartz attempted an examination of an exosystem variable (male peer support) on violence rates.[22] They examined "social support theory," which posits that "male peer group processes conducive to sexual, psychological and physical assaults on female dating partners may be the micro-level [sic] expressions of a dominant social structure and ideology that is based on the male hierarchical ordering of society."[23] DeKeseredy and Schwartz's data did not prove their hypothesis. Only 3-4 percent of their sample used serious violence items (from the Conflict Tactics Scale, explained in the next chapter), and only 3.9 percent had friends who "told them to use physical force for sexual rejection." Yet DeKeseredy and Schwartz concluded that "woman abuse in the context of dating is a serious social problem."[24] They did not report female violence rates nor consider whether couple violence was bilateral or even whether violent people seek each other out, as Moffitt et al. found.[25] After stating that sexual abuse was also a significant social problem, DeKeseredy and Schwartz found only 1.3 to 2.3 percent of their sample engaged in sexual abuse.[26] This was based on only four men! Despite what DeKeseredy and Schwartz claimed, peer group influence was not proven by this study. This is our first example of the "woozle effect" (see Figure 2.3)!

Dooley and Catalano point out the difficulty in testing the relationship between exosystem economic factors and pathological behaviours.[27] Tests founded on aggregate measures of unemployment and pathological behaviours (such as wife assault) commit what they term the "ecological fallacy": they attribute individual symptoms to individual economic circumstances based on aggregate data. Dooley and Catalano avoided this methodological problem by taking both economic and psychological measures of individuals as well as aggregate economic measures. Via this type of analysis they discovered that unemployment had a significant relationship to symptoms of psychological problems, but the relationship was much stronger when unemployment rate was considered *in combination with* a person's being in the work force (that is, looking for work, rather than retired, a student, etc.) and with education level. Unemployment rates do not affect everyone

2.3 The woozle effect

Gelles and Straus (*Intimate Violence*) described the "woozle effect" as based on a children's story by A.A. Milne, where Winnie the Pooh and Piglet hunt a "woozle" whose existence they know only from tracks on the ground – tracks they themselves have made. Gelles and Straus used the term to describe certain myths that developed in the domestic violence field without solid evidence.[1] This typically happens when crucial qualifiers from an original article are dropped to make the statements more certain than the original author intended. Gelles and Straus supply several examples, including Kempe et al. on "battered child syndrome," from which speculations about child abuse's lethality potential were exaggerated in subsequent articles by other writers. Another example was a statistic that Gelles and Straus reported themselves, that 55 percent of a selected experimental group of families reported conjugal violence. This sample came from the police department domestic disturbance files and a private social service agency, so the members were not representative but selected because of prior problems. A subsequent book (Langley and Levy, *Wife Beating: The Silent Crisis*) reported that half the women in the United States were abused, citing the Gelles and Straus study as the basis for their inappropriately extrapolated statistic.[2]

This book will use the term "woozle" for any claim or conclusion that is not proven by the researcher who conducted the original study or any flagrant error in citing a research finding.

Other examples exist. In 1980, Linda MacLeod (*Wife Battering in Canada: The Vicious Circle*) claimed that every year one in ten Canadian women in a relationship is battered.[3] Not until 2000 was the first Canadian domestic violence incidence survey done. MacLeod's figure was apparently based on the proportion of women that one shelter said they had to turn away. Coney and Mackey applied the woozle concept to the argument that all perpetrators were men and victims were women.[4]

DeKeseredy contains numerous instances of presenting data and misinterpreting them.[5] For example, his study examined "social support theory" that posits that "male peer group processes conducive to sexual, psychological and physical assaults on female dating partners may be the micro-level expressions of a dominant social structure and ideology that is based on the male hierarchical ordering of society." DeKeseredy's data indicated that only 4 percent of his male college sample endorsed acts of serious violence (from the Conflict Tactics Scale), and that only 1.3-2.3 percent of his sample (a maximum of seven men) reported having engaged in sexual abuse. In spite of these low rates of abuse perpetration, DeKeseredy concluded that "woman abuse in the context of dating is a serious social problem." He did not report female violence rates nor consider whether relationship violence was bilateral. Perceptions of male peer support for abuse against dating partners were also generally low. For instance, only 3.9 percent of participants reported that their male friends had "told them to use physical force" against a dating partner and 3.2 percent said they "use force for sexual rejection." Therefore, it is difficult to understand how DeKeseredy could conclude that "male social networks may reinforce wider patriarchal social relations by perpetuating and legitimating woman abuse." Though these data do indicate an association between perceptions of peer support for dating abuse and reports of abusive behaviour, DeKeseredy fails to consider that correlations are not causes.

As described later, DeKeseredy and Schwartz asked college women who reported having *perpetrated* dating violence whether their use of violence was in self-defence.[6] They considered levels of severity of violence used by women (according to their self-reports) and the women's reports of the extent to which their violence was motivated by three reasons, including self-defence. Only 6.9 percent of women reporting non-severe violence and 8.5 percent of women reporting severe violence said that they "always" used violence in self-defence. By comparison 62.3 percent and 56.5 percent of the non-severe and severe groups respectively reported that they "never" used violence in self-defence. In fact, women were as likely to report that they had initiated the attack as to report that their violence was self-defensive. Moreover, though women were asked to report on both perpetration and receipt of partner violence, these reports were never directly compared. Thus, the authors fail to indicate the extent to which the violence reported by these college women took place within mutually violent relationships.

DeKeseredy and Schwartz do not even acknowledge in their conclusions that, consistent with many prior findings, more women reported having acted violently toward a male partner (46.1 percent) than reported having been the victim of male violence (almost 35 percent) (see also Douglas and Straus).[7] In spite of the well-documented high prevalence rates among young adults of women's violence toward men, the college men who were sampled ($N = 1300$) were asked about their own abuse perpetration but not about their victimization. Needless to say, men were not asked whether their violence was self-defensive in nature. This study seems designed to minimize women's violence and to avoid the possibility of discovering and reporting men's victimization, or even the extent to which male violence is self-defensive. Nevertheless, the data in this study and others indicate that more college women are violent than college men, and that most of women's violence is not self-defensive.

Woozles are usually not simply a matter of authentic misreporting. They also reveal a desire to read into the data an a priori position that is really not there, what Bacon calls "idols of the theatre" (see page ix in this volume). All the data reporting mistakes I have found in the literature, without exception, were made in the direction of supporting feminist preconceptions.

NOTES: **1** R.J. Gelles and M.A. Straus, *Intimate Violence* (New York: Simon and Schuster, 1988) 39-41. **2** R. Langley and R.C. Levy, *Wife Beating: The Silent Crisis* (New York: Pocket Books, 1977), cited in Gelles and Straus, 41. **3** L. Macleod, *Wife Battering in Canada: The Vicious Circle* (Ottawa: Canadian Advisory Council on the Status of Women, 1980), 21. **4** N.S. Coney and W.C. Mackey, "The feminization of domestic violence in America: The Woozle goes beyond rhetoric," *Journal of Men's Studies* 8, 1 (1999): 45-58. **5** W.S. DeKeseredy, *Woman Abuse in Dating Relationships* (Toronto: Canadian Scholars' Press, 1988). **6** W.S. DeKeseredy and M.D. Schwartz, *Woman Abuse on Campus: Results from the Canadian National Survey* (Thousand Oaks, CA: Sage, 1998). **7** E.M. Douglas and M.A. Straus, *Corporal Punishment Experienced by University Students in 17 Countries and Its Relation to Assault and Injury of Dating Partners* (Helsinki: European Society of Criminology, 2003).

equally but have their greatest impact on middle-status groups in the work force. (Low-status groups already have high rates of undesirable individual economic events.) Hence, these authors caution against simplistic application of exosystem "main effects" on behaviour.

A form of reverse "ecological fallacy" occurred with the case of Marc Lepine, whose very unusual situation and actions were taken to represent those of men in general (see Figure 2.4). Lepine was a very extreme and non-representative case, both in having been raised as Arab-Canadian and in having been severely abused. Yet the date of his mass femicide (the Montreal Massacre) is used as representative of "violence towards women" in intimate relationships.

2.4 Marc Lepine: What does he represent?

Marc Lepine is well known in Canada as a mass murderer who killed fourteen women and wounded thirteen others at Montreal's Ecole Polytechnique in 1989. Because of this act and because he specifically targeted women, Lepine became for many people a Canadian icon of misogyny. The day of the massacre, 6 December, has become an annual "white ribbon day," a reminder of male violence to women.

This is a mistake. The evidence presented in this book shows that the actions of Marc Lepine are not representative of the behaviour and attitudes of Canadian or American men in general, or even of men who assault their spouses. Canadian men do not support the use of violence against women. The mass murder committed by Marc Lepine was not a form of domestic violence and does not resemble it. To use this mass murderer to represent intimate violence between men and women in North America is to mislead for the sake of a political agenda.

Lepine was raised with a mixed cultural background (Arab-Canadian, his birth name was Gamil Gharbi). He was severely physically abused by his father but never received any form of psychological treatment for the deep wounds. Despite what feminists say, abuse of this extreme degree does generate rage. In Lepine's case the rage was directed at women (whom he may have seen as getting favours he didn't get – the usual motive in workplace and mass killings). However, nowhere in the forensic literature are mass killers said to be "representative" of anyone. A mass killing took place in the Quebec National Assembly in May 1984, but the killer, Denis Lortie, was regarded as insane, not as representing Canadian views toward provincial governments. The spree killers at the high school in Columbine, Colorado, in 1999 (Harris and Klebold) were seen not as representative of teenagers' feelings about other teenagers or their teachers but instead in terms of teenage cliques, "Goth culture," heavy metal music, problems with weapon availability, and teenage abuse of antidepressants.

What political factors determine whether violence will be attributed to factors internal to the killer(s)?

Unemployment and job stress represent exosystem instigators that increase the likelihood of wife assault. Informal support groups, on the other hand, represent a potential ameliorative variable. By providing emotional support, corrective feedback, and so on, friendship groups can prevent individuals from acting out their worst excesses. Isolation has been found to be associated with child abuse, a correlation Belsky attributes to "the crucial assistance that members of one's social network can contribute in times of stress."[28] This explanation, however, assumes people to be motivated to make use of support systems when under duress. An alternative possibility is that people with available social support systems fail to utilize them out of either a belief that they should be able to handle their problems on their own or an inability to perceive that they have a problem. An exosystem view of wife assault would predict wife assaulters to be either more isolated or less capable of using available support groups under duress (or both).

The Microsystem
The microsystem refers to the interaction pattern that exists in the family itself or to structural elements of that family. Coleman and Straus, for example, refer to structural elements such as marital power as being related to incidence of abuse.[29] They used the Blood and Wolfe power index, which measures who has final authority in six common household decisions (e.g., buying a car, having children, money spent on food, etc.) and relates this measure of marital power to marital violence.[30] They found that acts of violence toward wives were most common in husband-dominant households, second most common in wife-dominant households, and least in "democratic" households. The explanation they provide for this relationship is that violence occurs when a power imbalance coexists with a lack of consensus about the imbalance. In these couples, conflict and violent acts are most frequent and are highest for both members of the couple. That is, both husband-to-wife and wife-to-husband violence are highest in female-dominant couples, next highest in male-dominant couples. Both violence and conflict are lower in egalitarian couples.

Psychological studies of the microsystem have tended to focus on the interaction process as a contributor to eventual assault (see Chapter 11). Some of this research has focused on verbal and non-verbal communication patterns in conflicted vs non-conflicted couples.[31] Gottman's intriguing work on "interpersonal psychophysiology" indicates that marital satisfaction is closely related to "physiological linkage" during discussions of problem areas in the marriage. Specifically, conflicted couples communicate negative affect, reciprocate the negative affect, and produce "parallel patterning of physiological responses between the spouses." Gottman sees this process as the basis for the subjective state of being "trapped" or locked into a destructive, self-sustaining interaction pattern.

Margolin reviews the assessment of marital interaction procedures and its use in predicting marital distress.[32] Comparing physically abusive couples with verbally abusive, withdrawn, and non-conflicted couples (see Chapter 11), Margolin reports that physically abusive and withdrawn couples are quite similar in certain communication styles such as low assertiveness and conflict avoidance.[33] Margolin's work suggests the potential already developed by researchers studying parent-child interaction.[34]

Patterson and his colleagues at the Oregon Social Learning Center have concentrated on reducing children's aggressive behaviours (tantrums, disobedience, acting out, etc.) by altering parent-child interaction patterns. Specifically, Patterson focuses on interaction as a communication process in which expectations for behaviour and rewards or punishments for fulfilling those expectations are communicated well or poorly. One conclusion from Patterson's work is that violent intrafamily behaviour has its roots in the mismanagement of banal daily routine.[35]

A "coercion trap" develops when a child demands an act of compliance from a parent by performing behaviour that is aversive to the parent (by whining, screaming, etc.), the parent provides punishment (by doing something that is aversive to the child), and the child (in response to the punishment) either stops its demands or acts defiantly by repeating the original aversive demand. When these three-part interchanges become a characteristic feature of the parent-child relationship, both parties are "trapped" into using frequent coercive interchanges frequently in their daily interaction.[36] Some parents respond to the child's aversive demands with their own set of behaviours (which are aversive to the child) intermittently accompanied by a reinforcer. This periodic positive/negative reinforcement and punishment keeps the "coercion trap" functioning. Eventually the reinforcement value of each person's actions begins to diminish and a form of social insularity develops.

Wahler reports that coercive interaction patterns generalize for some parents so that the parent becomes "multiply entrapped."[37] Patterson's and Wahler's studies demonstrate the advances that have been made in interaction analysis and show how aggressive behaviour can be produced by dysfunctional interaction. Margolin's work applies such analysis to wife assault. Furthermore, Margolin's finding that the interactional characteristics of physically assaultive and withdrawn couples are similar presents the possibility that assaultive behaviour is a joint function combining microsystem processes, ontogenetically learned traits, and response hierarchies to conflict. While microsystem processes may produce conflict and anger, the individual's behavioural response to this anger (withdrawal, depression, aggression, etc.) may be ontogenetically learned.

Giles-Sims has also developed an interactive approach to understanding wife assault.[38] Her model accepts that predispositional factors exist but views repeated violence as being a system product (i.e., a product of the interaction of two individuals). Giles-Sims views family processes as evolving in stages. Stage 1 requires analysis of the following questions: How do patterns established in other social systems affect the family system? How does the commitment that establishes family boundaries evolve? What rules concerning power relationships and the use of violence are part of the family system in the initial stage?

Stage 2 begins with the first incident of violence and focuses on questions such as how the couple's interaction at the time of the first violent incident affected the possibility of future incidents. For example, to what extent were the goals of the violent person satisfied? How did the victim respond? Giles-Sims found that, of thirty-one battered women she studied, 86 percent felt angry after the first incident but did not respond in an angry, retaliatory, or rejecting way, while 64 percent sought no intervention and did not leave the house. Giles-Sims then goes on to analyze how this victim response "feeds back" to the batterer, stabilizing an interactive pattern that includes rewards for violence and, hence, intermittent violence.

Ontogenetic Level

Ontogenetic level factors focus on features of the individual's developmental experience that shape responses to microsystem or exosystem stressors. From an interactive perspective, both the cognitive appraisal of what is stressful and the emotional and behavioural reactions to the stressor are learned predispositions shaped by the unique experience of the individual. Hence, one obvious area of interest in wife assault has been the male's own developmental experience with violence in his family of origin.

Straus, Gelles, and Steinmetz correlated reports of own violence with reports of parental violence on the Conflict Tactics Scale.[39] They reported that "men who had seen parents physically attack each other were almost three times more likely to have hit their own wives during the year of the study."[40] Straus et al. are careful to point out, however, that in wife assault many males had not experienced violence in their family of origin. (Also, many men who witness father-mother assault are not violent themselves.) The experience of violence used as a conflict tactic in the family of origin was one model for learning violence. Similarly, being a victim of parental violence increased the likelihood of wife assault: males who were physically punished as teenagers had a rate of severe violence toward females four times greater than that of those whose parents did not hit them. We will discuss this "intergenerational transmission" of violence below. Finally, Straus et al. report the "double whammy" effect: where physical punishment was both observed (i.e., father-mother violence) and experienced (father-son violence). The men who both observed and experienced such violence were five to nine times (depending on the specific violence measure) more likely to be violent.[41]

What the Straus et al. survey did not reveal was exactly how this modelling mechanism operates: do sons in violent families learn to define potential conflict issues as more serious (i.e., do they perceive more "causes" for anger?). Do they react to conflicts with more anger? Do they "automatically" use violence as a means of dealing with conflict? The answers to these questions await comparison studies using violent and non-violent men with matched experiences of violence in their family of origin. Is modelling of behaviour all that transpires in abusive families? Are there chronic, dysfunctional sets of emotions, cognitions, and actions that self-reinforce and constitute abusiveness? Chapters 4, 8, and 10 delve into these questions in detail.

The Straus et al. survey reported that people fought most frequently over "money, housekeeping, social activities, sex and children."[42] In treatment groups, assaultive males frequently reveal the emotional meaning of such conflict sources in the course of therapy. Money, housekeeping, and child-raising issues often involve beliefs and expectations about power and authority in the household. These beliefs may be shaped in part by macrosystem notions about family and patriarchy, but they also indicate a variety of expectations shaped partly by experience in the family of origin and partly by individual needs for power and control over family processes. Issues arising from social activities and sex often involve anxieties about too little or too much intimacy with one's spouse. Power and intimacy needs represent another constellation of perceptions and affective responses learned in the family of origin. Thus they represent another ontogenetic feature that could interact with stress and conflict at micro or exosystem levels. A "conflict event" such as a wife's desire for increased independence from her husband could trigger vastly different reactions in men with different power and intimacy needs.

An Empirical Test: As Close as We'll Get

Stith et al. used a nested ecological framework to organize risk factors for perpetrators and victims of abuse.[43] Their study used factors from each level of the original nested ecological model. Because Stith et al. performed a meta-analytic study, results from numerous studies are standardized and comparative effect sizes can be reported. We will report the stronger effect sizes here, and the interested reader is referred to the original article. For perpetrators the following were calculated at the *exosystem* level: employment, education, career/life stress, age and income. At the *microsystem* level these were calculated: history of partner abuse, jealousy, forced sex, marital satisfaction. The *ontogenetic* variables were: illicit drug use, anger/hostility, attitudes condoning violence, depression, and alcohol use. (Why emotional verbal abuse is not ontogenetic is not clear.)

For victims, the following were assessed: *exosystem:* employment, education, age, and income; *microsystem:* violence to partner, number of children; *ontogenetic:* fear, depression, and alcohol use. The authors point out that "at least four studies using different samples, which contain appropriate statistical data, are needed to calculate a composite effect size for any risk factor; therefore, we were unable to calculate any composite effect sizes for male victims."[44] For male perpetrators, exosystem effect sizes ranged from −.08 to .26 (very small to medium). Microsystem risk factors were much more important, with emotional abuse and sexual abuse having the highest effect sizes recorded ($r = .49$ and $.45$). It is debatable, however, whether these are really "risk factors" or simply co-occurring forms of abuse. Overall, husband's illicit drug use had the highest effect size of all factors for male offenders (after these two questionable abuse factors). For female victims, being violent towards her partner was the biggest predictor, followed by depression.

In summary, nested ecological approaches to explaining wife assault do not decide a priori whether to focus exclusively on individual or cultural determinants of assaultive behaviour. Rather, contributions from four levels of analysis are assessed, and specific interactions observed between levels are viewed as likely causal models. At our present stage of knowledge about wife assault, most research proceeds within one particular level of analysis. In the near future, however, we may see more sophisticated causal modelling techniques that allow us to test the "weights" of each level in determining the likelihood of assaultive actions.

Explanations and Policy

What is done about wife assault depends in part on how wife assault is explained: that is, how it is seen to be caused. Elliott, who views "explosive

2.5 Tautological prediction

A number of studies resort to what I call "tautological prediction," where the "predictor" and the "criterion" are different aspects of a single thing. For example, Stith et al. use emotional and sexual abuse to "predict" the presence of physical abuse.[1] But all these are variations of abusiveness. Since they appear together, they are of course "highly correlated." The "prediction" is redundant.

In another example, Gondolph and Heckert observe that "the strongest determinant of [women's] perceptions of safety was the woman's perception that the man would re-assault."[2] These are simply two different ways of saying the same thing, that she feels (emotionally) afraid because she believes (cognitively) he will re-assault her. The emotion and the belief are two sides of the same variable. Some risk prediction scales reviewed below "predict" assault from a lengthy history of assault. This is like "predicting" which horse will win a race three seconds before it does. Prediction is more useful the more remote (or "distal") are the predicting factors.

A more important point is made by Brown.[3] In examining the results of the Canadian General Social Survey, which assessed fear and victimization, Brown found that, of women who said they feared for their lives as a result of an intimate partner dispute, only one in seven hundred was actually killed. Yet some spousal homicide studies (such as Campbell)[4] have substituted a woman's "fear that she will be killed" for actual homicide. Fear cannot substitute for an act of violence.

NOTES: 1 Stith et al., "Intimate partner physical abuse perpetration and victimization risk factors: A meta-analysis review," Aggression and Violent Behavior 10, 1 (2004): 65-98.   2 E.W. Gondolph and D.A. Heckert, "Determinants of women's perceptions of risk in battering relationships," Violence and Victims 18, 4 (2003): 383.   3 G.R. Brown, "Gender as a factor in the response of the law-enforcement system to violence against partners," Sexuality and Culture 8 (2004): 12.   4 J.C. Campbell, Assessing Dangerousness: Violence by Sexual Offenders, Batterers and Child Abusers (Newbury Park: Sage, 1995).

rage" as stemming from an "episodic dyscontrol" syndrome, recommends pharmacological and psychiatric treatment.[45] Shainess, who sees wife battering as a "personality problem," recommends counselling and self-esteem building for wives.[46] Straus, who views wife assault as being supported by culture norms condoning "normal" violence, suggests a radical restructuring of society to alter those norms.[47]

Caplan and Nelson distinguish between "person-blame" and "system-blame" as causes assigned to social problems.[48] Person-blame views the problem as "caused" by individual characteristics (e.g., ontogenetic factors), while system-blame views the problem as caused by social system characteristics (e.g., macro- or exosystem factors). Person-blame explanations lead to inherently conservative solutions: change the individuals who "cause" the problem. An example of a policy oriented to person-blame would be the practice of tertiary intervention into wife assault, whereby identified offenders (typically men convicted by the courts) are ordered into "cognitive-behaviour modification" programs as a condition of their probation.

System-blame explanations are more consistent with radical solutions requiring a basic restructuring of societal institutions (such as the patriarchal family). Hence Straus calls for elimination of the husband as head of the family in law, religion, and administrative procedure.[49] This policy, described as "primary prevention," is aimed at lowering the incidence of wife assault in a general population by removing a societal structural cause.

A "mid-range" policy between these two is secondary prevention involving programs that seek to identify high-risk groups through improved diagnosis and "treatment." Since treatment typically still involves the alteration of individuals as opposed to social structures, secondary prevention is philosophically closer to tertiary prevention.

If one were to establish an intervention strategy on purely pragmatic rather than political grounds, then prevention would be based on (1) an assessment of the major contributors to wife assault across all levels (individuals, family, societal) and (2) an appraisal of the ease with which any of those levels could be changed. A nested ecological approach lends itself particularly well to the first of these criteria in that it does not decide a priori whether the problem lies inherently in a person or the system. If social-structural factors accounted for most of the statistical variance in measures of wife assault, then these factors would be the likely causes of wife assault. If considerable variance were unaccounted for after relevant societal factors had been assessed, then psychological-individual factors must be considered. If the inclusion of these factors accounted for a significant amount of the variation in incidence of wife assault, then tertiary intervention solutions should be considered. If neither societal nor individual factors adequately accounted for variance, alone or in interaction, then social science analysis is not yet prepared to suggest policy. From a reading of the current literature, it appears that cross-culturally societal factors are prominent, but in North America psychological factors are prominent.

Maiuro and Avery provide a three-level strategy of intervention that aims at the societal, psychological, and neurological levels, making unnecessary a final answer from a nested ecological perspective (see Chapter 14, Figure 14.1.).[50]

Since wife assault is a topic that arouses passions and political opinions, a dispassionate analysis of the causes of wife assault is not easy. Early psychiatric explanations of wife asssault occasionally "blamed the victim" for triggering the assault.[51] As a reaction to this type of explanation, feminist analyses baulked at any line of research that attributed some responsibility to the assaulted female.[52] Consequently, examination of "dysfunctional" interaction patterns was discouraged because such an examination would attribute at least some responsibility to females.

Reid, Patterson, and Loeber describe some abused children as "instigators" in that they provide a high number of aversive behaviours that make parents irritable and that they are inept at terminating.[53] Reid et al. found significant correlations between the rate of "aversive/oppositional" acts and the likelihood of the child getting hit. Reid et al. conclude that "most children are at serious risk of instigating their own abuse at some time during their development."[54] An "instigator" means any act or statement by a person that increases the likelihood of their being hit. Judgments of blame can be independent of "instigations": we might not blame a woman who refuses to run an errand for her husband at midnight after working all day, although such refusal can constitute an "instigation." Our own judgments about what constitutes acceptable behaviour or level of compliance enter into such determinations. We now present two brief case studies of men in our own treatment group called the Assaultive Husbands Project. These cases show how wife assault can have widely different etiologies and provide concrete examples of the difficulty with single perspectives in explaining all cases of wife assault.

Case #1: Robert

Robert was referred to our treatment group while his wife was still hospitalized for injuries sustained from his beating. He appeared tense and volatile, making other men in the group nervous. He would rock back and forth in his chair and clench and unclench his fists repeatedly; he looked to be on the verge of tears. Robert reported no feelings and was surprised to find out that other men viewed him as tense and angry.

The incident that led to his being in the group occurred at his wife's office party. About thirty people were drinking and chatting when, according to Robert, his wife disappeared (i.e., he could not find her in a large, unfamiliar house). After ten to fifteen minutes he saw her and insisted that they leave the party. He recalled feeling nothing at this point. They drove home, she went to bed, and he began to watch television.

His next memory was of seeing her lying in a pool of blood and realizing that he had severely beaten her. He called relatives and the police.

During treatment, Robert revealed that he believed his wife was having an affair and that, when she disappeared at the party, she was having sex with a co-worker. (In fact she was talking to two female co-workers on an outside balcony.) Two months into treatment Robert phoned me in a panic and said that he was "about to kill [his] wife." He had returned from an out-of-town business trip to find "a key with a man's name on it." (It was the name of the key manufacturer.) He again assumed that his wife was having an affair and became enraged. It took him three days to completely calm down, despite my pointing out his erroneous assumption.

Subsequent therapy revealed that Robert had been put up for adoption at age two. Whenever he failed to comply with the wishes of his adoptive parents, they threatened "to send him back." He experienced strong arousal states at the prospect of abandonment. His delusional beliefs about his wife and his chronic anxiety mutually reinforced each other, spiralling upwards into an extreme state of arousal and panic. The outburst of rage temporarily reduced this aversive state. A psychiatric label for Robert would be conjugal paranoia.

Case #2: Dan

Dan came into treatment on a court order, having been convicted of assault. He was articulate and intelligent, if a little disorganized. The incident that led to his being in the group occurred when Dan was phoning a movie theatre to find out when a film started. His wife called to him from another room and he somewhat curtly told her to be quiet because he couldn't hear the telephone announcement.

His wife became enraged and began screaming, smashing furniture, striking Dan, and verbally berating him. The colour in her face turned to purple. Dan tried to leave but his wife threatened (a) to follow him and publicly embarrass him and (b) to kill herself. After five hours of abuse, Dan "lost it" and struck his wife. She called the police.

Dan's wife had been sexually and physically abused by her stepfather and would fly into rage states when she felt dismissed or neglected. She went through extreme fluctuations in mood and was "unpredictable" according to Dan. She promised to seek treatment after these episodes were over but subsequently reneged. Dan was strongly attached to her but felt powerless to either change or leave her.

As the case examples show, highly varied causal patterns can produce wife assault. Stereotypes of assaultive males as pathological bullies are as incomplete as the early psychiatric theories based on incarcerated males convicted of wife assault. Social scientists attempt to find "common threads" that link wife assaulters and differentiate them from other males. Therapists working with wife assaulters are impressed with the variety and idiosyncrasy of each client's background and use of violence. As a therapist trained as a social scientist, I have attempted to reconcile these two opposing views. The result has been the adoption of a theoretical framework that allows for individual differences in the client population while seeking a common set of background "causes."

3 Measurement and Incidence of Abuse

Intimate abuse occurring in families may not be publicly visible. Government surveys attempt to assess its incidence to establish the size of the problem in a given country. Typically these estimates are made by surveys of citizens. One form of survey is the crime victim survey, focused on people who define themselves as "crime victims." The methodology and wording of these crime victim surveys filter out many people who may have been victims of abuse or assault in the home but who do not view the event as a crime. Straus showed that crime victim surveys seriously underestimate the incidence of family violence for this reason.[1]

Crime Victim Surveys

The Canadian Urban Victimization Survey (CUVS) generated a subsample of 10,100 incidents of wife assault.[2] Of these, 6 percent were "series" assaults (five or more) by the same offender, and 45 percent were reported to police either by the woman or a third party. In these incidents, 51 percent of the women were injured, 27 percent required medical treatment, and 52 percent lost time from their jobs. The 6 percent "series" assault rate is very close to the 6.8 percent rate generated for repeat severe violence by the studies of Straus and Gelles and of Schulman.[3]

The National Crime Survey (NCS) in the United States used a stratified multi-cluster sample design. The Bureau of the Census selected a rotating sample of 72,000 households that were representative of the entire population of the United States.[4] Of these, 60,000 yielded interviews. Sample households were interviewed every six months until seven interviews had been completed in each household. At each interview, respondents were asked to recall incidents of crime that had occurred during the previous six months.

As with the CUVS, the NCS was not specifically designed to answer certain questions that are especially important to family violence research.

3.1 Intimate violence against women: Incidence rates found in US and Canadian surveys (percentages)

	American rates			Canadian rates
	Schulman (1979)[1]	Straus, Gelles, and Steinmetz (1980)[2]	Straus and Geller (1985)[3]	Kennedy and Dutton (1989)[4]
Any violence ever	21.0	28.0	22.0	19.0
Severe violence ever	8.7	12.1	11.3	7.8
Repeat severe violence ever	5.9	8.0	7.7	5.4
Severe violence/past year	4.1	3.8	3.0	2.3
Repeat severe violence/ past year	2.5	2.5	2.0	1.5

NOTES: **1** M. Schulman, *A Survey of Spousal Violence against Women in Kentucky* (Washington, DC: US Department of Justice, Law Enforcement, 1979). **2** M.A. Straus, R.J. Gelles, and S. Steinmetz, *Behind Closed Doors: Violence in the American Family* (Garden City, NY: Anchor Press/Doubleday, 1980), data collected in 1975. **3** M.A. Straus and R.J. Gelles, *Is Family Violence Increasing? A Comparison of 1975 and 1985 National Survey Rates* (San Diego: American Society of Criminology, 1985). **4** L.W. Kennedy and D.G. Dutton, "The incidence of wife assault in Alberta," *Canadian Journal of Behavioural Science* 21, 1 (1989): 40-54, data collected in 1987.

"Spouse or ex-spouse" was a single category used to define the victim's relationship to the offender, so no reliable distinction could be made between assaults that occurred while the victim was married to the offender and those that occurred after separation.[5] The NCS survey revealed that 32 percent of assaults by a spouse or ex-spouse were repeated three or more times, but it did not ask questions about the victim reactions that may have accounted for repeater/non-repeater differences.

For a total of 1,058,500 victimizations, injuries resulted in 56.8 percent, medical care was required for 23.7 percent, and hospitalization for 14.3 percent. As a result of the attacks, 21 percent of the victims lost one or more days from work. In 55 percent of cases the victimization was reported to the police. In surveys such as the CUVS and the NCS, which are defined to the victim as "crime" surveys, report rates to police for assaults by husbands are relatively high (CUVS = 37 percent, NCS = 55 percent) and are comparable to report rates for other types of assault.[6] Given that these are defined by the respondent as crimes, this is not surprising. What is left unmeasured though, is the "*chiffre noire*" (hidden statistic) of IPV: assaults that are not defined as crimes and not reported to police. In fact, one of the reasons Straus used the

Conflict Tactics Scale (CTS) in the surveys in Figure 3.1 was to get around the "crime victim" filter that suppressed reporting of IPV because it was not defined as a crime. The US National Violence against Women Survey (NVAWS) found that, of 8,000 men and 8,000 women, 22.1 percent of the women and 7.4 percent of the men reported some physical assault by an intimate partner across their lifetime; 1.3 percent of the women and 0.9 percent of the men reported a physical assault by a partner in the previous twelve months.[7] As an assessment of the lifetime incidence of victimization of women, the survey agrees with the "conflict tactics survey" (reported below) that 22 percent seems to be a best estimate for the United States.[8] Rates are higher in countries where women have less sociopolitical power.[9] Conversely, violence against men drops in countries where women have less sociopolitical power. It is important to note that this study was presented as a study of criminal victimization of women, so findings may be based on the extent to which respondents define actions as criminal and themselves as being victimized. It was also presented as a study of the victimization of women.

Statistics Canada attempted to overcome the underdetection of IPV in earlier crime victim surveys by specifically asking questions about IPV victimization to a sample of about 26,000 people over the age of fifteen in an annual random-digit telephone survey called the General Social Survey

3.2 Incidence of family violence in Canada as reported by women and men in the General Social Survey (percentages)

	Women	Men
"Kicked, bit or hit by a current or previous spouse in the previous 5 years"	33	51
"Hit with something"	23	26
"Beaten"	25	10
"Choked"	20	0.4
"Used or threatened to use a knife or gun"	13	7
Overall (five-year) victimization rates	8	7
Repeat victimizations	61	54
Report to the police	37	15

NOTE: *N* = 26,000
SOURCES: General Social Survey 1999, Table 3.1, 12; GSS 1999, Table 2.4, 14; GSS 1999 Table 2.5, 14, 19. See also Statistics Canada, *Family Violence in Canada: A Statistical Profile* (Ottawa: Canadian Centre for Justice Statistics, 2000, 2003, 2004), and Statistics Canada, *A Profile of Criminal Victimization* (1999).

(GSS).[10] Statistics Canada's rationale was given in their 2000 report: "Because the GSS asks a sample of the population about their personal crime experiences, it captures information on crimes that have been reported to the police as well as those that have gone unreported"[11] (see Figure 3.2).

The response rate for this survey was 81.3 percent.[12] Despite the government claim above, it must be noted that the GSS does not entirely circumvent the problem of whether a respondent defines an action as a crime and hence worthy of being reported. There are probably three categories of assault events as follows: (1) victimizations defined as crimes and reported to the police; this was 48 percent of all crimes (44 percent of all assaults reported to the survey by women and 32 percent of all assaults reported to the survey by men); (2) victimizations defined as crimes but not reported to the police; and (3) intimate violent acts not defined as a crime. According to Straus, and based on an analysis of his survey data, category 2 is about 4.5 times the size of category 1. However, category 3 is about 16 times the size of category 2.[13] Hence, any "crime victim" survey will be of limited value in assessing the true incidence of family assaults.

Hence, what this rationale overlooks is that government action relevant to abuse in intimate relationships has focused on defining wife assault as a crime and downplaying violence against men, even to the point of police reluctance to arrest.[14] When this police reluctance is coupled with men's reluctance to acknowledge victimization, it becomes questionable whether men would view female assaults against them as crimes. Brown reported that data from the 1999 GSS survey showed men were less willing to respond to the survey than were women.[15] Despite these concerns, the results of the survey showed much higher rates of male victimization than had prior government surveys. The five-year prevalence rates for intimate violence victimization was 70 per 1,000 females and 63 per 1,000 males.[16] The overall victimization rates were 8 percent for women and 7 percent for men.

Hence, in the Canadian survey, victimization rates by gender were quite similar. This led to attempts to show the violence against women, although as prevalent as that against men, was far more serious. To do so, women but not men were asked about injuries, medical care needed, etc. The data show an incomplete pattern of outcome reports for men but complete reports for women.[17] From the incomplete data provided, it appears that 13 percent of male victims were injured (compared to 40 percent of female victims).[18]

Brown has shown numerous data errors and anomalies in the Canadian GSS survey data and has pointed out that, for reasons unknown, Statistics Canada never provided raw data totals but instead projected estimates to the entire Canadian population.[19]

In the United Kingdom, a recent survey of 22,000 people by the Home Office asked whether respondents had been victims of domestic violence in the previous year.[20] Of the respondents, 2.8 percent said yes in a self-report, whereas 0.6 percent said yes in a face-to-face interview. Of victims subjected to more than four incidents, 89 percent were women and 11 percent were men. As a result of the "most serious incident," 20 percent of women suffered moderate injuries (such as severe bruising) and 6 percent suffered severe injuries (such as broken bones). Male injuries were not reported. Of those surveyed, 64 percent did not think what had happened to them was a crime (this dropped to 33 percent if they had been subjected to multiple attacks). Men were less likely to have told anyone about the victimization than were women, while 31 percent of women had not told anyone.[21]

In Washington State, 3,381 persons were surveyed as part of an ongoing Risk Factor Surveillance System survey.[22] Using items from the Conflict Tactics Scale (see below), the authors found that 23.6 percent of women and 16.4 percent of men reported lifetime experiences with intimate partner violence; 21.6 percent of women and 7.5 percent of men reported injuries. These injuries could be classified as minor (sprain, bruise, small cut) or severe (broken bone, knocked unconscious). Women reported minor injuries 18.8 percent of the time, men reported them 6.2 percent; women reported severe injuries 7.4 percent of the time, men reported them 1.7 percent.[23]

Hence, four large sample government victim surveys in the United States, Canada, and the United Kingdom have found women to be more victimized, to use violence less, and to be injured more, than men. In the Canadian survey, presented as a study of "perception of crime," the differences were less than in the other two national surveys, which were presented as surveys of "victims of crime." In contrast to this finding, 159 independent, peer-reviewed studies have found women to use violence (even serious violence) to about the same extent as men, to be somewhat more likely to be injured than men, and to be arrested less often than men. A meta-analytic study by Archer, combining results from 426 independent studies of intimate partner violence reported by gender, also found women to be more violent but injured somewhat more.[24]

Note that because of differential tendencies to report to police, as well as differences in police willingness to answer calls from men and women, all data based on criminal justice system statistics may misrepresent actual assault rates, especially for men.

The Conflict Tactics Scale Surveys

To circumvent the filtering problem with crime victim surveys, Straus, Gelles, and Steinmetz devised the Conflict Tactics Scale (CTS),[25] which attempts to obtain more complete estimates of the incidence of domestic assault in a general population. This is obtained by a survey that interviews a representative sample drawn from a general population about any experiences they have had with being victimized by violence during family conflicts. Presenting the survey in the context of normal conflict rather than crime reduces filters against reporting. The preamble to the CTS states:

> No matter how well a couple gets along, there are times when they disagree on major decisions, get annoyed about something the other person does, or just have spats or fights because they're in a bad mood or tired, or for some other reason. They also use different ways of settling their differences. I'm going to read you a list of some things that you or your partner might have done in the past when you had a dispute and would like you to tell me for each one how often you did it in the past year.[26]

The time frame (one year) can be changed (six months, entire marriage) as can the relationship (parent, child, sibling, or any other dyadic family relationship). Generally, six- to twelve-month recall periods are best. Yoshihama et al. developed the Life History Calendar method to enhance recall.[27] Respondents are asked to provide information of a personal nature (e.g., children's birth dates) and then use this information to recall less memorable events. This is sometimes called autobiographical memory. The calendar was only used with women, so no data exist for males. It has been used to obtain information on women with multiple partners. Unfortunately the sample of Yoshihama et al. was small ($N = 40$) and predominantly African-American (38/40), although I know of no published reports of racial differences in autobiographical history. I mention it here because of its potential threat to external validity. Respondents were asked to rate the difficulty in remembering events in specific domains. Respondents were eighteen to fifty years old (average 33.4). "Reliability" as reported by the authors was merely test-retest reliability. Interviewers made a subjective rating of the respondents' "interest in the questionnaire. There is no way to validate the truthfulness of the memories. The authors seemed to treat all recollections as truthful. If we treat the reports as true, the average respondent had six partners (range one to fourteen), with an average of two being abusive.

Fals-Stewart, Birchler, and Kelley also used a "timeline followback spousal violence interview" survey in which 104 men in a spousal violence

3.3 Straus's Conflict Tactics Scale

No matter how well a couple gets along, there are times when they disagree on major decisions, get annoyed about something the other person does, or just have spats or fights because they're in a bad mood or tired or for some other reason. They also use different ways of trying to settle their differences. I'm going to read a list of some things that you and your (spouse/partner) might have done when you had a dispute and would like you to tell me for each one how often you did it in the past year.

Frequency of:	You							Partner						
	1	2	5	10	20	20+	Ever?	1	2	5	10	20	20+	Ever?
(a) Discussed an issue calmly	1	2	5	10	20	20+	Ever?	1	2	5	10	20	20+	Ever?
(b) Got information to back up (your/his/her) side of things	1	2	5	10	20	20+	Ever?	1	2	5	10	20	20+	Ever?
(c) Brought in or tried to bring in someone to help settle things	1	2	5	10	20	20+	Ever?	1	2	5	10	20	20+	Ever?
(d) Argued heatedly but short of yelling	1	2	5	10	20	20+	Ever?	1	2	5	10	20	20+	Ever?
(e) Insulted, yelled, or swore at each other	1	2	5	10	20	20+	Ever?	1	2	5	10	20	20+	Ever?
(f) Sulked and/or refused to talk about it	1	2	5	10	20	20+	Ever?	1	2	5	10	20	20+	Ever?
(g) Stomped out of the room or house (or yard)	1	2	5	10	20	20+	Ever?	1	2	5	10	20	20+	Ever?
(h) Cried	1	2	5	10	20	20+	Ever?	1	2	5	10	20	20+	Ever?
(i) Did or said something to spite the other one	1	2	5	10	20	20+	Ever?	1	2	5	10	20	20+	Ever?
(j) Threatened to hit or throw something at the other one	1	2	5	10	20	20+	Ever?	1	2	5	10	20	20+	Ever?
(k) Threw or smashed or hit or kicked something	1	2	5	10	20	20+	Ever?	1	2	5	10	20	20+	Ever?
(l) Threw something at the other one	1	2	5	10	20	20+	Ever?	1	2	5	10	20	20+	Ever?
(m) Pushed, grabbed, or shoved the other on.	1	2	5	10	20	20+	Ever?	1	2	5	10	20	20+	Ever?
(n) Slapped the other one	1	2	5	10	20	20+	Ever?	1	2	5	10	20	20+	Ever?
(o) Kicked, bit, or hit with a fist	1	2	5	10	20	20+	Ever?	1	2	5	10	20	20+	Ever?
(p) Hit or tried to hit with something	1	2	5	10	20	20+	Ever?	1	2	5	10	20	20+	Ever?
(q) Beat up the other one	1	2	5	10	20	20+	Ever?	1	2	5	10	20	20+	Ever?
(r) Threatened with a knife or gun	1	2	5	10	20	20+	Ever?	1	2	5	10	20	20+	Ever?
(s) Used a knife or gun	1	2	5	10	20	20+	Ever?	1	2	5	10	20	20+	Ever?
(t) Other _____	1	2	5	10	20	20+	Ever?	1	2	5	10	20	20+	Ever?

NOTE: e-k: verbal aggression; j-k: direct verbal and symbolic aggression; l-n: physical aggression; o-s: severe aggression.
SOURCE: Straus, Gelles, and Steinmetz, *Behind Closed Doors: Violence in the American Family* (Garden City, NY: Anchor Press/Doubleday, 1980).

treatment program and their partners were interviewed at pre-treatment, post-treatment, and quarterly thereafter for one year and asked to identify both male-to-female and female-to-male aggression.[28] By using both partners, the authors were able to develop concurrent validity (within-couple agreement about frequency of occurrences). The interview used CTS items but was re-administered over time. The sample, drawn from a male treatment group, was mostly white and averaged thirty-two years of age.

Respondents were asked to identify days in which physical aggression had occurred in their relationships and then to keep a weekly diary. In addition, men and their partners were asked to keep a daily CTS checklist for violence and then to bring the diaries to a follow-up interview to assess memory at that time. Hence, this study provided a much better assessment of validity (assuming the daily diaries were accurate) than the Yoshihama et al. methodology. Respondents also completed a scale of conflict (the Dyadic Adjustment Scale) and one of test-reporting honesty (the Marlowe-Crowne Social Desirability Scale 1960).[29] Scores on the Marlowe-Crowne (MC) were low, indicating a lack of socially desirable responding. Male to female agreement on "violence days" was better after treatment than before, perhaps because couples were aware of tracking. Interestingly, given this was a treatment group for males, the women were violent on more days than the men, regardless of whose report was read. We could interpret this as "payback," assuming the male was the predominantly abusive person before treatment. The Fals-Stewart method is promising but requires considerable investment by respondents in completing the questionnaires. However, it would be a recommended assessment procedure for treatment providers. An even better method of obtaining violence data will be reviewed below: "peer cohort" data from selected same-age cohorts, collected longitudinally at time intervals.

Straus found reported violence incidence rates with the CTS that were sixteen times greater than with crime victim surveys (see Figure 3.4).[30] The annual assault rate according to the NVAW study was 1.1 percent, whereas according to CTS surveys it was 16 percent. Hence, it appears that lifting the "crime victim" filter and replacing it with a "we all get into conflict" prologue greatly enhances the sensitivity of the scale.

Moffitt et al. confirmed Straus's point.[31] In one of the best methodological studies of intimate violence, the Dunedin study (reported in Chapter 6), they found that, when they asked respondents about "assault victimization," the rates of male-perpetrated violence appeared much higher than did female, and both rates were quite low. When they asked the same respondents about "relationships with partners" the rates reported by both genders were much

3.4 Comparison of CTS family conflict results with "crime victim" surveys

	Family conflict studies	National crime survey	National crime victim survey	Police call data	NVAW study
Annual assault rate	16%	0.2%	0.9%	0.2%	1.1%
Conflict rate					
Injury rate	1-3%	75%	52%	unknown	76%
Male rate	12.2%	0.4%	0.76%	90%	1.3
Female rate	12.4%	0.03%	0.11%	10%	0.9
Male-to-female ratio	1:1	13:1	7:1	9:1	1.4:1

NOTE: Annual assault rate means proportion of families surveyed in which physical assaults occurred. Injury rate is the proportion of assaults resulting in visits to the hospital. Male rate means proportion of all males surveyed who perpetrated assaults (or in the middle column were victimized by assaults). Female rate means proportion of all females surveyed who perpetrated assaults (or in the middle column were victimized by assaults). Male-to-female ratio is male rate to female rate.
SOURCE: Adapted from M.A. Straus, "The controversy over domestic violence by women: A methodological, theoretical and sociology of science analysis," in X. Arriaga and S. Oskamp, eds., *Violence in Intimate Relationships* (Thousand Oaks, CA: Sage Publications, 1999), 17-44, 23.

higher and were equivalent.[32] This was a representative population sample, studied longitudinally. Several such CTS surveys have been completed.[33]

Surveys of Incidence: Conflict Tactics Surveys

As described above, two general types of incidence surveys exist: what I shall term "conflict tactics surveys" and "crime victim surveys." The former ask people what actions they have taken to resolve family conflicts; the latter ask by what crimes they have been victimized. The often-cited Straus survey, the Kentucky survey, and the Alberta survey used the Straus Conflict Tactics scale as a measure of the type of actions used to resolve family conflicts.[34] This common measure enables some direct comparison between these surveys.

The Straus, the Kentucky, and the Alberta surveys, for example, use Straus' definition of severe assault as anything from item O on the Straus Conflict Tactics Scale (kicked, bit, or hit you with a fist) to item S (used a knife or fired a gun) as shown in Figure 3.3. Using this definition, the victimization rates for husband-to-wife violence on the Schulman and the Straus et al. survey reports were 8.7 percent and 12.6 percent.[35] Corresponding rates, using the more inclusive measure of any (as opposed to severe) violent husband-wife acts, including slapping, pushing, shoving were 21 percent and

27.8 percent.[36] These rates refer to the use of violence at any time in the marriage. In Chapter 7 we will examine the results of the 1985 national survey, which indicated a decrease in incidence of wife assault from the 1975 data.[37]

The Kentucky survey reported single versus repeat assault in its data, specifically asking respondents the number of times they had been assaulted in the past twelve months.[38] These data bear on an issue we will consider in more detail throughout this book: IPV as a repeated, self-sustaining habit. Both the Straus and Schulman surveys found that if a woman was victimized by spouse assault at any time in the marriage, this was likely to be repeated in about 63 percent of cases.

Kennedy and Dutton used a combination of face-to-face and random-digit dialing techniques to survey 1,045 residents in Alberta, Canada.[39] Since this survey also used the Straus Conflict Tactics Scale, it led to a comparison of American and Canadian rates of wife assault. These data are reported in Figure 3.1. The "minor" violence rates for the two countries are virtually identical, but the "severe violence" rates were quite different. In effect, as acts became increasingly violent, the Canadian incidence rates fell further below the American rates. For "kicking" and "hitting" (items O and P) the Canadian rates were 80 percent of the American, for "beat up" (item Q) they were 25 percent, for "threatened with or used a gun/knife" (items R and S) they were 17 percent.

Note that these data are for males and females combined. The gender of the perpetrator is not known (except for Kennedy and Dutton, who reported only female victimization; later data on male victimization reported by Kwong, Bartholomew, and Dutton showed essentially the same rates).[40] Nor is it known whether the perpetrator's partner was violent as well. Straus reported approximately equal perpetration rates by gender. More will be said about this in the next chapter.

By way of comparison with these North American data, Kim and Cho report IPV rates for Korea.[41] Since they also used the Conflict Tactics Scale, there is comparability in instrument. Respondents were asked to report violence for the year preceding the survey. Whereas, Straus et al. report 11.6 percent for wife assault (any violence) in the preceding year, the Korean rate was 37.5 percent.[42] The Severe Violence wife assault rate in the United States for the preceding year was 3.8-3.0 percent, but in Korea it was 12.4 percent.[43] Hence, Korean society appears to be more violent. In the United States in 1985, the lifetime incidence of wife assault was 22 percent; by comparison, Kumagai and Straus found a lifetime incidence of wife assault in Japan of 58.7 percent.[44]

Archer examined societal structural variables assessing the sociopolitical position of women in fifty-one countries.[45] He found that women's social power was related to the incidence of male-to-female violence. In countries where women's status was less, men were the more violent gender; when relative equality occurred in a country, women were more violent than men. Archer used two measures of women's sociopolitical power: the Gender Empowerment Index (GEM), which measures the extent to which women have attained political, occupational, and economic power, and the Gender-related Development Index (GDI) measuring women's access to health care, education and knowledge. For the fifty-one countries he examined, wife assault lifetime incidence rates were negatively correlated with both the GEM (-.69) and the GDI (-.75). Fluctuations in methodology occur from country to country, and in some countries the rates may be influenced by temporal events (e.g., Cambodia). Hence these lifetime incidence rates should be taken only as rough estimates.

If we combine the estimate of violence repeating in about two-thirds of marriages with the incidence estimates for severe violence "ever" occurring in a marriage obtained by Straus et al. and Schulman (12.1 and 8.7 percent respectively), we obtain the estimate that severe repeated violence occurs in about 7.2 percent of all marriages in the United States and 5.4 percent in Canada.[46] As we shall see, however, not all this violence is directed against wives, and not all is unilateral.

The distinction between the use and effects of violence has implications for the importance we attach to the incidence of various types of violence. As Straus points out, the national "speed limit" on IPV is that it must be severe enough to cause an injury requiring medical treatment for police intervention to lead to arrest.[47] The distinction between the Violence Index and the Severe Violence Index in the Straus Conflict Tactics Scale reflects this threshold. Actions such as slapping or shoving are less likely to produce injury than are punching, beating up, or using a weapon. Exceptions exist, of course, as in our example of shoving someone at the top of a staircase, but in general the Conflict Tactics Scale ranks actions with potentially more injurious effects. Similarly, although slapping or pushing someone is technically an assault, in practice, police in most jurisdictions would not arrest unless an action corresponding to the Severe Violence Index had occurred. Accordingly, in reviewing the incidence of IPV, we will focus on these more serious actions, which have the greatest potential for injury.

In surveys of family conflict resolution that measure spousal violence as such, rates of reporting "serious assaults" (defined by the CTS subscale) to the police are only 14.5 percent (hence the higher figure of 37 percent reported for women in the GSS in Canada may reflect the "crime victim" definition still residing in that survey).[48] One interpretation is that many interspousal acts of violence are not considered criminal by the victim.

Some criticisms have been made about the Conflict Tactics Scale.[49] Examples are that the CTS ignores the context in which the violence occurred, that differences in size between men and women make acts scored the same on the CTS quite different in reality, and that impression management or social desirability factors may preclude people from answering the CTS accurately.

Straus' rejoinders to these criticisms are as follows: the assessment of context should be done separately because there are so many context variables that they could not all be included on the CTS.[50] The CTS is designed so that any special set of context questions can be easily added. This would also be true for questions about the consequences of assault (e.g., whether anyone was injured, the nature of the injury, whether the police were called).

The issue of gender differences in size is as follows: if a 180-pound man hits a 120-pound woman, the act is different from when a 120-pound woman hits a 180-pound man. But both get counted the same on the CTS. A similar problem, Straus notes, is that repeated slapping is highly abusive and dangerous but gets counted as Minor Violence on the CTS. Straus argues that while it is possible to weight actions by differences in size between perpetrator and victim, or to construct an upper limit after which slapping gets counted as Severe Violence, such weightings have rarely led to changes in research results.[51]

The social desirability criticism was answered, in part, by a study by Dutton and Hemphill that correlated scores on two measures of social desirability (the tendency to present a "perfect image" on self-report tests) and scores on the CTS.[52] Social desirability is measured by the Marlowe-Crowne (MC), the test-reporting honesty test, which assesses the tendency to present the self in a socially acceptable manner. MC scores did correlate significantly (and negatively) with perpetrators' self-reports of verbal abuse. The higher their social desirability score, the lower their reported rates of verbal abuse. However, their MC scores did not correlate significantly with their reports of physical abuse, nor with any reports of abuse (verbal or physical) made against them by their wives. Hence, it seems that reports of physical abuse are largely uncontaminated by socially desirable responding. This means that the incidence survey rates are probably fairly accurate as far as image management is concerned. Other studies indicate that women report higher levels of both perpetration and victimization than do men.[53] However, increases in base

3.5 When do survey respondents try to improve their images? Correlations of perpetrators' self-report measures with the Marlowe-Crowne Social Desirability Scale

	Marlowe-Crowne Social Desirability Scale	
	Perpetrators	Victims
Straus' Conflict Tactics Scale		
Verbal aggression	-.38*	.01
Physical aggression	-.20	-0.9
Multidimensional Anger Inventory	-.44*	n/a
Psychological Maltreatment of Women Inventory		
Emotional abuse	-.50*	-.05
Dominance/isolation	-.57*	-.08

NOTE: The higher the correlation, the more likely the self-reporting in this category is influenced by image. The lower correlation on physical aggression means self-reports in this category tend to be more reliable. Note that these are convicted perpetrators who have something to feel guilty about.

*$p < .01$

SOURCES: From D.G. Dutton and K.J. Hemphill, "Patterns of socially desirable responding among perpetrators and victims of wife assault," *Violence and Victims* 7, 1 (1992): 29-40; D.P. Crowne and D.A. Marlowe, "A new scale social desirability independent of psychopathology," *Journal of Consulting Psychology* 24 (1960): 349-54; J.M. Siegel, "The multidimensional anger inventory," *Journal of Personality and Social Psychology* 5, 1 (1986): 191-200; R.M. Tolman, "The development of a measure of psychological maltreatment of women by their male partners," *Violence and Victims* 4, 3 (1989): 159-77.

level rates have not affected studies of gender use of violence, which are consistent whether male or female reports are used.[54] Whether or not respondents remember all abuse continues to be an issue.

A further criticism of the CTS is that it assesses violence occurring in a conflict and may miss "out of the blue" violence. However, the vast majority of violent acts are perceived as emanating from conflict.[55] While the CTS may miss an "out of the blue" attack, it more than makes up for this with its increased sensitivity over crime victim surveys.

The CTS-2

To answer some criticisms of the CTS, the CTS-2 was developed.[56] The CTS-2 added four items to the "psychological aggression" scale of the CTS, added three items to the severe aggression scale and modified five others, added seven sexual coercion items, and added six injury items (see Figure 3.6).

In summary, two types of surveys of family violence exist. The "crime victim" surveys (CUVS, NCS, NVAWS) find rates of reporting wife assault to the police that are comparable to the reporting rates for other assaults. However, these surveys probably fail to detect violent acts used by one spouse against the other that are not defined as criminal by the victim. A second type of survey, which uses the CTS and asks respondents to report modes of conflict resolution in the family, avoids this question of whether the respondent defines the action as criminal or not.

The Severity of Violence against Women Scale

Some other scales have been developed that are of central importance to family violence researchers. One is the Severity of Violence against Women scale (SVW) developed by Linda Marshall (see Figure 3.7).[57] A parallel form, the Severity of Violence against Men (SVM) scale, also exists.[58] The SVW assesses forty-six acts in the following categories: symbolic violence, threats of violence (mild, moderate, severe), acts of violence (mild, minor, moderate, severe), and sexual violence. For each action, Marshall had two groups of women (university undergraduates, community sample) rate the severity of each action for both physical and emotional harm. University men rated the acts against men. The resulting weightings can be used to multiply frequency scores. As a result, more finely honed scores in each of the nine subscales can be obtained. Interestingly, acts against women are rated as more severe than the same actions against men. For example, "burned her with something" gets a physical harm rating from students of .91 and an emotional harm rating of .91, "burned him with something" gets a physical harm rating of .81 and an emotional harm rating of .77. "Physically forced her to have sex" was rated at .82 for physical harm and .93 for emotional harm. "Physically forced him to have sex," was rated at .43 and .64, respectively. In a chapter below, we will explore the societal view of pain caused to

3.6 Revised Conflict Tactics Scale (CTS-2)

Item	Item-total r
Negotiation (alpha = .86)	
Explained side of argument	.74
Suggested compromise to argument	.70
Showed partner cared	.69
Said could work out problem	.63
Agreed to try partner's solution	.62
Respected partner's feelings	.58

Item	Item-total r
Psychological aggression (alpha = .79)	
Insulted or swore at partner	.66
Shouted at partner	.65
Stomped out of room	.61
Threatened to hit or throw something at partner	.52
Destroyed something of partner's	.47
Did something to spite partner	.46
Called partner fat or ugly	.42
Accused partner of being a lousy lover	.35
Physical assault (alpha = .86)	
Kicked, bit, or punched partner	.70
Slapped partner	.70
Beat up partner	.65
Hit partner with something	.62
Choked partner	.61
Slammed partner against wall	.60
Grabbed partner	.56
Threw something at partner that could hurt	.52
Used knife or gun on partner	.52
Pushed or shoved partner	.51
Twisted partner's arm or hair	.47
Burned or scalded partner on purpose	.39
Sexual coercion (alpha = .87)	
Used force to make partner have sex	.74
Used threats to make partner have anal sex	.73
Used force to make partner have anal sex	.70
Insisted on anal sex (no force)	.69
Used threats to make partner have sex	.58
Insisted on sex (no force)	.54
Insisted on sex without a condom (no force)	.34
Injury (alpha = .95)	
Partner was cut or bleeding	.92
Partner went to doctor for injury	.92
Partner needed to see doctor but didn't	.86
Partner felt pain the next day	.79
Partner had sprain or bruise could see	.77
Partner's private parts were bleeding	.74

NOTE: Internal consistency reliability is calculated for descriptive statistics for self-reports of perpetration and an approximation to the CTS-2 scales in which some items differ from the final CTS-2 scales. The correlations are corrected, meaning they exclude the correlation of the item shown from the total r. All correlations are significant at $p < .001$.

SOURCE: M.A. Straus, S.L. Hamby, S. Boney-McCoy, and D.B. Sugarman, "The revised Conflict Tactics Scale (CTS-2)," *Journal of Family Issues* 17, 3 (1996): 282–316.

men. Because the SVW and SVM scales cover all forms of abuse and the individual acts are weighted, they are particularly useful to researchers.

The Psychological Maltreatment of Women Inventory

The Psychological Maltreatment of Women Inventory (PMWI) is designed to focus more comprehensively on emotional abuse.[59] The version of the CTS

3.7 Severity of Violence against Women Scale (SVW)

You have probably experienced anger or conflict with your partner. Below is a list of behaviors you may have done during the past 12 months. For each statement, describe how often you have done each behavior by writing the appropriate number in the blank.

1 – never; 2 – once; 3 – a few times; 4 – many times

_____	1	Hit or kicked a wall, door, or furniture
_____	2	Threw, smashed, or broke an object
_____	3	Drove dangerously with her in the car
_____	4	Threw an object at her
_____	5	Shook a finger at her
_____	6	Made threatening gestures or faces at her
_____	7	Shook a fist at her
_____	8	Acted like a bully towards her
_____	9	Destroyed something belonging to her
_____	10	Threatened to harm or damage things she cares about
_____	11	Threatened to destroy property
_____	12	Threatened someone she cares about
_____	13	Threatened to hurt her
_____	14	Threatened to kill yourself
_____	15	Threatened to kill her
_____	16	Threatened her with a weapon
_____	17	Threatened her with a club-like object
_____	18	Acted like you wanted to kill her
_____	19	Threatened her with a knife or gun
_____	20	Held her down, pinning her in place
_____	21	Pushed or shoved her
_____	22	Grabbed her suddenly or forcefully
_____	23	Shook or roughly handled her
_____	24	Scratched her
_____	25	Pulled her hair
_____	26	Twisted her arm
_____	27	Spanked her

_____	28	Bit her
_____	29	Slapped her with the palm of your hand
_____	30	Slapped her with the back of your hand
_____	31	Slapped her around her face and head
_____	32	Hit her with an object
_____	33	Punched her
_____	34	Kicked her
_____	36	Choked her
_____	37	Burned her with something
_____	38	Used a club-like object on her
_____	39	Beat her up
_____	40	Used a knife or gun on her
_____	41	Demanded sex whether she wanted it or not
_____	42	Made her have oral sex against her will
_____	43	Made her have sexual intercourse against her will
_____	44	Physically forced her to have sex
_____	45	Made her have anal sex against her will
_____	46	Used an object on her in a sexual way

SOURCE: Adapted from L.L. Marshall, "Development of the severity of violence against women scales," *Journal of Family Violence* 7, 2 (1992): 103-21.

shown in Figure 3.3 has only six items that count in the Verbal/Symbolic Abuse Scale (e, f, g, i, j, k). The PMWI, on the other hand, has sixty-two items, which fall into two distinct factors: Dominance/Isolation and Emotional/ Verbal Abuse. The former is made up of items such as "monitored her time," "did not allow her to leave the house," "did not allow her to work," and "restricted use of car." In general, these have to do with male control of the woman's use of space, time, and social contacts. The second factor is made up of items such as "blamed her when upset," "said something to spite her," "treated her like an inferior," and "swore at her." These really have to do with acts designed to hurt the woman's feelings. Often part of the context for physical abuse is a background of accompanying emotional abuse. The PMWI was used in my research with male perpetrators. A gender-neutral version was written by Kasian and Painter.[60] In the chapter on the domestic assault of men, we will see how specific items are judged very differently (in terms of whether they constitute abuse), depending on the gender of the perpetrator.

The net or cumulative effect of repeated physical and emotional abuse can be great. Briere and Runtz review several self-report scales for trauma

3.8 Psychological Maltreatment of Women Inventory (PMWI)

For each of the following statements please indicate how frequently *your partner* did this to you during the last year by circling the appropriate number.

0 – not applicable; 1 – never; 2 – rarely;
3 – occasionally; 4 – frequently; 5 – very frequently

1	My partner put down my physical appearance.	0 1 2 3 4 5
2	My partner insulted me or shamed me in front of others.	0 1 2 3 4 5
3	My partner treated me like I was stupid.	0 1 2 3 4 5
4	My partner was insensitive to my feelings.	0 1 2 3 4 5
5	My partner told me I couldn't manage or take care of myself without him.	0 1 2 3 4 5
6	My partner put down my care of the children.	0 1 2 3 4 5
7	My partner criticized the way I took care of the house.	0 1 2 3 4 5
8	My partner said something to spite me.	0 1 2 3 4 5
9	My partner brought up something from the past to hurt me.	0 1 2 3 4 5
10	My partner called me names.	0 1 2 3 4 5
11	My partner swore at me.	0 1 2 3 4 5
12	My partner yelled and screamed at me.	0 1 2 3 4 5
13	My partner treated me like an inferior.	0 1 2 3 4 5
14	My partner sulked or refused to talk about a problem.	0 1 2 3 4 5
15	My partner stomped out of the house or yard during a disagreement.	0 1 2 3 4 5
16	My partner gave me the silent treatment, or acted as if I wasn't there.	0 1 2 3 4 5
17	My partner withheld affection from me.	0 1 2 3 4 5
18	My partner did not talk to me about his feelings.	0 1 2 3 4 5
19	My partner was insensitive to my sexual needs and desires.	0 1 2 3 4 5
20	My partner demanded obedience to his whims.	0 1 2 3 4 5
21	My partner became upset if household work was not done when he thought it should be.	0 1 2 3 4 5
22	My partner acted like I was his personal servant.	0 1 2 3 4 5
23	My partner did not do a fair share of household tasks.	0 1 2 3 4 5
24.	My partner did not do a fair share of child care.	0 1 2 3 4 5
25	My partner ordered me around.	0 1 2 3 4 5
26	My partner monitored my time and made me account for where I was.	0 1 2 3 4 5
27	My partner was stingy in giving me money.	0 1 2 3 4 5
28	My partner acted irresponsibly with our financial resources.	0 1 2 3 4 5
29	My partner did not contribute enough to supporting our family.	0 1 2 3 4 5
30.	My partner used our money or made important financial decisions without talking to me about it.	0 1 2 3 4 5

31	My partner kept me from getting medical care that I needed.	0 1 2 3 4 5
32	My partner was jealous or suspicious of my friends.	0 1 2 3 4 5
33	My partner was jealous of friends who were of his sex.	0 1 2 3 4 5
34	My partner did not want me to go to school or other self-improvement activities.	0 1 2 3 4 5
35	My partner did not want me to socialize with my same sex friends.	0 1 2 3 4 5
36	My partner accused me of having an affair with another man/woman.	0 1 2 3 4 5
37	My partner demanded that I stay home and take care of the children.	0 1 2 3 4 5
38	My partner tried to keep me from seeing or talking to my family.	0 1 2 3 4 5
39	My partner interfered in my relationships with other family members.	0 1 2 3 4 5
40	My partner tried to keep me from doing things to help myself.	0 1 2 3 4 5
41	My partner restricted my use of the car.	0 1 2 3 4 5
42	My partner restricted my use of the telephone.	0 1 2 3 4 5
43	My partner did not allow me to go out of the house when I wanted to go.	0 1 2 3 4 5
44	My partner refused to let me work outside the home.	0 1 2 3 4 5
45	My partner told me my feelings were irrational or crazy.	0 1 2 3 4 5
46	My partner blamed me for his problems.	0 1 2 3 4 5
47	My partner tried to turn our family, friends, and/or children against me.	0 1 2 3 4 5
48	My partner blamed me for causing his violent behavior.	0 1 2 3 4 5
49	My partner tried to make me feel like I was crazy.	0 1 2 3 4 5
50	My partner's moods changed radically, from very calm to very angry, or vice versa.	0 1 2 3 4 5
51	My partner blamed me when he was upset about something, even when it had nothing to do with me.	0 1 2 3 4 5
52	My partner tried to convince my friends, family, or children that I was crazy.	0 1 2 3 4 5
53	My partner threatened to hurt himself if I left him.	0 1 2 3 4 5
54	My partner threatened to hurt himself if I didn't do what he wanted me to do.	0 1 2 3 4 5
55	My partner threatened to have an affair with someone else.	0 1 2 3 4 5
56	My partner threatened to leave the relationship.	0 1 2 3 4 5
57	My partner threatened to take my children away from me.	0 1 2 3 4 5
58	My partner threatened to have me committed to a mental institution.	0 1 2 3 4 5

SOURCE: R.M. Tolman, "The development of a measure of psychological maltreatment of women by their male partners," *Violence and Victims* 4, 3 (1989): 159-77. Used by permission of Springer Publishing Company, Inc., New York 10036.

3.9 The Trauma Symptom Checklist (TSC-33)

How often have you experienced each of the following in the *last two months?*
(Please circle the appropriate number.)

0 – never; 1 – occasionally; 2 – fairly often; 3 – very often

1	Insomnia (trouble getting to sleep)	0	1	2	3
2	Restless sleep	0	1	2	3
3	Nightmares	0	1	2	3
4	Waking up early in the morning and can't get back to sleep	0	1	2	3
5	Weight loss (without dieting)	0	1	2	3
6	Feeling isolated from others	0	1	2	3
7	Loneliness	0	1	2	3
8	Low sex drive	0	1	2	3
9	Sadness	0	1	2	3
10	"Flashbacks" (sudden, vivid, distracting memories)	0	1	2	3
11	"Spacing out" (going away in your mind)	0	1	2	3
12	Headaches	0	1	2	3
13	Stomach problems	0	1	2	3
14	Uncontrollable crying	0	1	2	3
15	Anxiety attacks	0	1	2	3
16	Trouble controlling temper	0	1	2	3
17	Trouble getting along with others	0	1	2	3
18	Dizziness	0	1	2	3
19	Passing out	0	1	2	3
20	Desire to physically hurt yourself	0	1	2	3
21	Desire to physically hurt others	0	1	2	3
22	Sexual problems	0	1	2	3
23	Sexual overactivity	0	1	2	3
24	Fear of men	0	1	2	3
25	Fear of women	0	1	2	3
26	Unnecessary or over-frequent washing	0	1	2	3
27	Feelings of inferiority	0	1	2	3
28	Feelings of guilt	0	1	2	3
29	Feelings that things are "unreal"	0	1	2	3
30	Memory problems	0	1	2	3
31	Feelings that you are not always in your body	0	1	2	3
32	Feeling tense all the time	0	1	2	3
33	Having trouble breathing	0	1	2	3

SOURCE: J. Briere and M. Runtz, "The Trauma Symptom Checklist (TSC-33): Early data on a new scale," *Journal of Interpersonal Violence* 4 (1989): 151-62.

symptoms. Consequences include injuries and health problems, days lost from work, and general social withdrawal.[61] A variety of trauma symptoms also develop with chronic abuse.

The third related scale, the Trauma Symptom Checklist (TSC-33) can be used to assess these long term consequences.[62] The TSC-33 is a scale of thirty-three items that assess Depression, Anxiety, Sleep Disturbance, Dissociation ("spacing out"), and other experiences that can result from trauma in the family. Below we will examine the short- and long-term effects of trauma. Repeated exposure to extreme abuse (credible life threats accompanied by extreme abuse such as choking to the point of losing consciousness) can generate high chronic trauma scores (now measured on the newer Trauma Symptom Inventory) and can generate "Complex PTSD (Post Traumatic Stress Disorder)" triggered by stimuli not apparently similar to the original stressor.[63] Trauma can also contribute to the generation of violent reactions in perpetrators as we shall see below. Although the TSC-33 has been replaced by the Trauma Symptom Inventory (TSI), I show the earlier TSC because that is the scale used in my research.[64]

4 Theories of Wife Assault: Psychiatric Contributions

Evidence is accumulating that the alarm reaction initiates a cascade
of cellular and molecular processes that alter brain structure and
function to create an adaptive record of survival-related information.

  – E.D. Schwartz and B.D. Perry, "The post-traumatic response
  in children and adolescents"

John Stuart Mill's attribution of wife assault to the "mean and savage natures" of some men exemplifies nineteenth-century explanations of human
behaviour: actions were attributed to an inferred construct called "nature"
residing within the person. Such reasoning was clearly circular: the construct was used as "cause" for the behaviour, yet the only proof of the
construct's existence was the behaviour itself. Considerable credence was
given to the belief that "human nature," be it savage or superior, was the
product of "breeding." Good "breeding" was found in the upper classes.
Psychiatric studies of wife assault view assaultive males as different from the
normal population, unlike the feminist view that abuse by men is "normal."[1] The survey data from Chapter 3 indicated a lifetime prevalence of
intimate assault victimization of 22 percent. However that was for a single
experience, and the assault may have been bilateral or less serious (pushing
and shoving counted on that survey). As we shall see in a chapter to follow,
the likelihood that a person will be repeatedly unilaterally assaulted by an
intimate in a serious (potentially injurious) fashion is closer to 4 percent.
We will "do the math" below. For now, if 4 percent of persons is accurate,
then perpetrators of these acts are not "normal" but are performing relatively rare actions – actions that might set them apart from the "norm,"
actions that require a special psychological explanation.

Early psychiatric attempts to explain wife assault (there were no attempts
to explain husband assault that I could find) in the twentieth century were

based on case studies of men who had been incarcerated for the crime. Those cases were exceptional in the extent of their violence (since nothing short of extreme assault or attempted murder led to conviction) or else were revealed in psychiatric treatment of individuals who presented with other psychological problems.[2] These few exceptional case studies served as a basis for the questionable conclusion that all men who assault their wives did so because of a psychiatric disorder. Clinical syndrome explanations of wife assault attributed it to pathological dependency, brain lesions such as temporal lobe epilepsy, or sadistic character.[3] Such explanations helped reinforce the view that any form of wife assault was rare and that the men who committed it were unusual, atypical, and pathological. Nevertheless, we still find that the more extreme and chronic the kinds of intimate violence, the more frequently psychiatric diagnostic categories may apply.

The psychiatric "explanation" of wife assault was based on an overgeneralization from small clinical samples obtained under extremely selective circumstances. Faulk, for example, discussed the "psychiatric disturbance of men who assault their wives" based on a sample of twenty-three men "remanded in custody for charges of seriously assaulting their wives."[4] The extreme nature of this sample is indicated by the fact that all men in it had either murdered their wives (eight), or tried to murder them (nine), or wounded or seriously injured them (six). Faulk reported that sixteen of these twenty-three men had "psychiatric disorder," but seven of these were suffering from anxiety or depression, which might have been a consequence of their violence and the ensuing incarceration.

Faulk's methodology exemplifies the problems associated with early clinical views of wife assaulters: the sample is small and non-representative. The extremity of the violence is not considered in generalizing to less-violent perpetrators. The empirical basis for the psychiatric diagnoses is not fully described but seems to be based on prison records, depositions, and an unstructured interview. What these early studies lacked was a large sample of perpetrators drawn not just from prison populations but more representative of the typical non-incarcerated perpetrator. Nor did they consider whether there were several subpopulations of perpetrators. Faulk had distinguished overcontrolled types (whom he called passive-dependent) from undercontrolled ones (whom he called violent and bullying), but the differentiation was rudimentary and unsystematic. Also, there was never any comparison with appropriate control groups.

Some early psychiatric studies of "domestic violence" are fascinating period pieces reflecting the views of the day. In 1964, Snell, Rosenwald, and

Robey put forward the following explanation of why women who had put up with being battered for many years suddenly had their husbands arrested:

The husbands, for their part, had much complaint about their sons and about the relationships between their sons and wives. The relationship between father and son was reported to be distant and/or troubled in each of the nine families with eldest sons over ten years of age, and the sons' sympathies were universally reported by both parents to be with their mothers. The consistency of these observations throughout the group studied gave rise to our speculation that a common significant factor in determining the timing of the court appearance may be the presence in the family of an adolescent child (commonly male) whose intervention in the parents' struggle disturbs a marital equilibrium that had been working more or less satisfactorily.[5]

The authors went on to compare abusive families with alcoholic families and saw the "trend" in these dynamics as being a depressed, domineering, and masochistic wife: "We see the husband's aggressive behavior as filling masochistic needs in the wife's (and the couple's) equilibrium."[6] In other words, a woman stays in an abusive relationship because it fills an unconscious need in her. This viewpoint was quickly seen as victim-blaming and was responded to by Hilberman, citing the emerging literature of the day, including her own study of sixty battered wives. Hilberman pointed out that pervasive patterns of sex discrimination, alcohol abuse, and jealousy by the husband as well as an attitude of male privilege defined abusive relationships, and the depression or masochism that Snell et al. described was a consequence of years of abuse not a cause.[7] Hence the die was cast for a paradigm clash between sociological-feminist views of wife assault and conventional psychiatric views. Judged by the standard of subsequent research, Hilberman was correct, and her paper was important in challenging the paradigm of the day.[8] She rightly pointed out that most women left abusive relationships because of credible threats to their lives and pressures to keep the family intact. There was, in fact, no evidence in the Snell et al. paper for the assumption of masochism on the part of battered women.

The *Diagnostic and Statistical Manual of Mental Disorders* (DSM) is a five-axis system of categorizing client disorders. It contains a variety of disorders that share symptomatologies with descriptions of wife assaulters given by their wives, by clinicians working with the wife assaulters, or by the men themselves.[9] These include "conjugal paranoia" with delusions of sexual in-

fidelity by one's spouse, intermittent explosive disorders, including temporal lobe epilepsy with intense acceleration of autonomic activity and post-
episode amnesia, and borderline personality disorders with intense mood
swings, interpersonal disturbances, anger, and suicidal gestures.[10] Also, both
Rounsaville and Gayford reported substance abuse syndromes in approximately half of an assaultive population, although Rounsaville reported that
only 29 percent had been drinking at the time of the assault.[11] Furthermore,
Rounsaville found that only six of thirty-one wife assaulters had a history of
psychiatric contact (although eleven of the wives had had "prolonged contact" for unspecified reasons).

Rounsaville's study represented one of the groundbreaking studies on violent relationships at that time. Rounsaville took up the challenge of pitting
sociological against psychiatric explanations in light of the data he collected
on thirty-one battered women contacted in a hospital emergency room and
a mental health centre. Rounsaville's sample reported abuse starting in the
first year of the relationship (two-thirds were married), and 71 percent reported having their life threatened if they left, supporting Hilberman's argument above. However, Rounsaville did find some evidence for masochism,
namely, that some women deliberately escalated arguments in which they
expected violence. The reasons for this were not obtained. Some later inter-
preters would talk of "pre-emptive strikes" to get the violence sequence fin-
ished. Rounsaville also found evidence against masochism, noting that in
his sample 65 percent of battered women had called police but only 10
percent were satisfied with the response they received. Also, there was no
evidence for a life-long pattern of seeking abuse. Only 26 percent had been
abused as children, and only four of thirty-one had been in a prior violent
relationship. Rounsaville concluded that the key element in abusive relationships was a relational one: the "intense and exclusive dyadic system in
which the couple is enmeshed."[12] As he put it: "The most striking phenomenon ... was the tenacity of both partners to the relationship in the face of
severe abuse sustained by many of the women."[13]

Rounsaville noted the possessiveness of the males in his study and saw
both partners as having unmet dependency needs, manifested in the women
through depression and in the men through possessiveness and alcohol
abuse. Rounsaville took an "interactionist" position, seeing both partners as
contributing to the abuse; "a particularly volatile combination seems to be a
jealous, possessive man with paranoid tendencies and a counter-dependent,
indomitable, passive-aggressive woman."[14] The anger was viewed as arising
from these unmet dependency needs.

In making this observation, Rounsaville was ahead of his time. Later research would show "preoccupied" attachment styles (discussed below) to be frequent in both male abuse perpetrators and female abuse victims. Rounsaville also noted that although 26 percent of women and 39 percent of male perpetrators in his sample had been beaten as children, 66 percent of the women and 78 percent of the men had experienced "death or separation from either parent or serious school difficulties." (Later, in Chapter 6, we shall see that "death or separation from a parent" can lead to later "serious school difficulties" and subsequently to abusiveness.) Rounsaville observed that the sample "may have been sufficiently stressed as to be unable to develop self control or a healthy view of family relations." This observation foreshadowed the later work connecting attachment disruption to intimate violence.[15] Although he was a psychiatrist and described attachment phenomena in his findings, as in the quotes above, there was no reference to John Bowlby or attachment theory in Rounsaville's references. The connection of insecure attachment to domestic violence would not be made for another sixteen years.

Another early psychiatric study of note was by Bland and Orn who presented data from an urban random sample (N = 1,200) of an adult population that used the Diagnostic Interview Schedule, which asks 259 questions related to "diagnostic criteria" from the DSM-III and the use of violence.[16] Only 20 percent of contacted persons refused to participate (295/1495). The authors reported only three diagnostic categories: antisocial personality disorder, major recurrent depression, and alcohol abuse/dependence. For respondents with any one of these three diagnoses there was a 54.5 percent chance of "violent behaviour" (hitting or throwing things at their partner). For respondents with no diagnosis based on the Diagnostic Interview Schedule, the self-reported violence rate dropped to 15.5 percent. When alcoholism was combined with either or both of antisocial personality disorder or depression, the violence rate jumped to 80-93 percent. In terms of initiating the physical aggression, 59 percent of males and 74 percent of females said they were the first one to hit or throw things at their partner. The study was largely actuarial (simply counting risk contingencies) and descriptive and did not seek to causally disentangle family violence from the other diagnoses reported. Hence, the reader does not know whether depression "causes" violence to the spouse or whether both are produced by some unreported third factor, or what the relationship might be among depression, alcohol abuse, and spouse abuse. This was a common problem with the actuarial method used in these community psychiatry studies. However, Bland and

4.1 Personality disorder

Having a personality disorder means that you have a continuous pattern of internal experiences and behaviour that is very different from the expectations of your culture.

It can be seen in two or more of the following ways:
- cognition (perception and interpretation of self, others, and events)
- affectivity (range, intensity, lability, and appropriateness of emotional response)
- interpersonal functioning
- impulse control.

This pattern must be continuous and inflexible across a long time and across a range of personal and social contexts. The pattern must lead to disruption of life (social, occupational, etc.) or to clinically significant distress. In addition to being stable and continuous for a long period of time, the onset of the pattern can be traced back to adolescence or early childhood.

SOURCE: Based on diagnostic criteria from the DSM-IV. This is not intended as a substitute for the more extensive DSM diagnoses.

Orn had introduced a new explanatory concept to the mix: personality disorders.

Personality disorders are chronic, dysfunctional ways of seeing the world, ways of feeling and behaving that are atypical within the ambient culture. They constitute systems that are homeostatic but where emotion, cognition, and behaviour are mutually reinforcing of dysfunction (see Figure 4.1).

Hamberger and Hastings report clinical assessments of 105 men attending a wife assault treatment program.[17] Using the Millon Clinical Multiaxial Inventory (MCMI) to assess personality disorders (a broad-based psychological self-report scale that attempts to draw profiles consistent with DSM diagnoses), Hamberger and Hastings factor-analyzed the protocols, identifying three orthogonal factors that they labelled as schizoidal/borderline, narcissistic/antisocial, and passive-dependent/compulsive. Their assaultive sample fell about equally (ten to sixteen men each) into these three categories, four categories that combined various aspects of the first three "pure" categories, and one category that had no aspects of the clinical pathology indicated in the first three categories. These seven pathological subgroups made up 88 percent of the entire wife assault subject sample. Subsequent comparison of assaultive males with a non-assaultive population indicated that the former had greater difficulty in modulating affective states and feeling comfortable in intimate relationships. The authors reported that subject selection factors may have influenced their results. They did not explain in detail how these particular personality disorders would lead to assaultiveness or even what sense one could make of their factors. Schizoids, for example, present a very different clinical picture from borderlines, yet the two are combined in one factor in the Hamberger and Hastings study. What common thread leads both groups to a common factor and to assault their wives? Despite the unanswered questions raised by this study, however, the implication that assaultive males tend to exhibit personality disorders suggests one way that assaultive men may be different from other men and that, as personality disorders are notoriously difficult to change via short-term therapy, treatment programs that do not address personality disorders will have little success.

Other studies found incidence rates of personality disorders to be 80 to 90 percent in both court-referred and self-referred wife assaulters, compared to estimates in the general population, which tend to range from 15 to 20 percent.[18] As the violence becomes more severe and chronic, the likelihood of psychopathology in these men approaches 100 percent.[19] Across several studies, implemented by independent researchers, the prevalence of personality disorder in wife assaulters has been found to be extremely high.

Hamberger and Hastings began in 1988 to report the existence of an expanded non-personality-disorder group emerging from their data. What caused personality disorders to diminish in frequency in comparison with the results of earlier studies? Lohr, Hamberger, and Bonge cluster-analyzed the eight personality-disorder scales on the MCMI-II in a sample of 196 men.[20] This time, a cluster was found that showed no elevations on any personality disorder scale (39 percent of the sample, compared to 12 percent in the 1986 paper). A second cluster (35 percent) was termed Negativistic (Avoidant-Overcontrolled), while a third (26 percent) was labelled Aggressive (Antisocial-Narcissistic-Paranoid).

A later study by Hamberger and his colleagues used a large sample of 833 court-referred men – though unfortunately this study relied on self-reports of relationship violence, which typically is underreported by men in criminal justice proceedings.[21] Using a two-stage clustering technique, they again obtained three large clusters and three smaller clusters. Cluster 1 (Overcontrolled and Dependent–Passive Aggressive) composed 18 percent of the sample. Cluster 2 (Instrumental) accounted for 26 percent of the sample; this group showed elevations of Antisocial and Narcissistic subscales. Cluster 3, the no-personality-disorder group, composed 40 percent of the sample, an increase from the original 12 percent. The Borderline and Emotionally Volatile cluster seemed to have disappeared. There are several possible explanations for this disappearance; one is that socially desirable responding increased as treatment groups became more punitive.[22] That is, court-mandated clients would begin to try and "fake good" on psychological tests so as to not be required to take even more treatment by the courts. There is some evidence that social desirability increased in research results. Dutton pointed out how a study by Gondolf showed "out of range" desirability scores for the treatment group, which should have the effect of suppressing the reporting of personality disorder.[23] However, if this were the the case, why were the antisocial scores not also suppressed? Some other selection factor may be at work, influencing the type of clients entering treatment groups and the research pool. We will come back to this issue after examining the incidence of unidirectional and bidirectional violence in a later chapter, as well as changes in arrest policy that might influence the composition of a treatment population.

Early psychiatric studies had a common epistemological problem: the association between clinical categories was too frequently used as a substitute for systematic explanation. A systematic explanation might account for the co-occurrence of personality disorders, substance abuse, dysphoric moods, and the use of violence toward one's spouse. Psychiatric explanation, as it was offered in these early studies, substituted reference to a clinical category for explanation. The appearance of similarity between descriptions of assaulters and some DSM-III categories is not a substitute for a systematic analysis. By systematic explanation, we mean an examination and integration of the causal origins of intimate rage, coupled with cultural shaping of expectations about intimacy and the use of violence, and the immediate antecedents and consequences of adult assaultiveness.

Neurobiology

Psychiatry has searched for propensities to impulsivity and aggression in both neural structures and neural functioning. Daniel Goleman's book, *Emotional Intelligence*, argues that the startle responses of fear and rage (fight or flight) are generated by sensory messages proceeding first to the limbic system (thalamus and amygdala) before their subsequent processing by the neocortex.[24] The processed, "reasoned," reaction comes too late to stop the initial impulsive rage. However, Goleman does not view limbic reactions as purely a function of "nature." Aspects of the "nurture" side of the equation also influence limbic function. Drawing on Schore's work on early experience and brain maturation, Goleman argues that early emotional messages from parental treatment influence the development of the amygdala. Psychiatrist Bessel van der Kolk had argued in a similar vein that separation and attachment disruption produced changes in the number and sensitivity of brain opioid receptors as well as permanent changes in neurochemistry and that "certain childhood experiences make people vulnerable to disorders of the neurotransmitter systems, which may later be activated under stress, particularly after the loss of affiliative bonds."[25] The etiology of the neurological disturbance was secondary in the theory of early psychiatry. What was essential was that neurological electrical storms caused impulsive outbreaks of rage.

An example of the original line of thought was an article published in the medical journal *The Practitioner* in 1976 by Frank Elliott, a psychiatrist at the Pennsylvania Hospital.[26] The article describes something called the "episodic dyscontrol syndrome," a term coined first by Karl Menninger, founder of the clinic named after him. Menninger had originally described episodic dyscontrol as an unconscious bodily reaction to chronic stress. It referred to episodes where a person suddenly and inexplicably went out of control and ran amok. It was beyond rational "ego" control and was explosive in nature. In this sense it stood out as a different level of reaction to stress, as compared to the other types of stress adaptation, such as anxiety, neurotic symptoms, and psychosis. Episodic dyscontrol was listed in the DSM-IV as one of the impulse-control disorders called Intermittent Explosive Disorder (IED) and given the official notation number 312.34. The diagnostic criteria included several discrete episodes of loss of control of aggressive impulses resulting in serious assaultive acts or destruction of property, where the degree of aggressiveness expressed was "grossly out of proportion to any precipitating psychosocial stressor (trigger)." There were no signs of generalized aggressiveness between episodes and the episodes did not occur during the course of a psychotic disorder or other disorders (e.g., psychopathy). In other words, the person is not psychotic and is generally not aggressive at all between "episodes" but then bursts into an uncontrolled rage out of all proportion to whatever preceded it.

Elliott believed these episodes were caused by neurological firing, activity in the limbic system, that "ancient" part of the brain, situated in the brainstem, underneath and behind the cerebral hemispheres. The limbic system is called ancient because it is believed to have developed far back in humanity's evolution, prior to the later development of the neocortex. It contains structures like the amygdala, the hippocampus, and the temporal lobe. These areas are believed to be the "seat of emotion." Stimulation of the amygdala in animals using microelectrodes produces rage or pleasure, depending on the exact location of the implant. Some locations will cause monkeys to press a bar repeatedly to keep the stimulation turned on. They will press

4.2 Selected brain structures relevant to domestic assault

Amygdala	A structure of the medial temporal lobe that plays a role in the memory for the emotional significance of experience.
Brain stem	The part of the brain on which the cerebral hemispheres rest and which, in general, regulates reflex activities that are critical for survival (e.g., heart rate and respiration).
Cingulate cortex	A large area of the neocortex.
Fornix	The major tract of the limbic system.
Hippocampus	A structure of the medial temporal lobes that plays a role in memory for spatial locations.
Hypothalamus	Located below the thalamus, and important in the regulation of several motivated behaviours.
Limbic system	A collection of interconnected nuclei and tracts that circles the thalamus and is widely assumed to play a role in emotion; also involved in the regulation of motivated behaviours, particularly the "four Fs" of motivation: fleeing, feeding, fighting, and sexual activity.
Prefrontal lobes	The large areas, left and right, at the very front of the brain.
Reticular formation	A complex network of nuclei in the core of the brain stem that contains, among other things, motor programs for complex species-common movements such as walking and swimming.
Septum	A midline nucleus located on the tip of the cingulated cortex; part of the limbic system and connected by several tracts.
Thalamus	A two-lobed structure that constitutes the top of the brain stem, and an important relay station in the visual, auditory, and somatosensory systems.

until they drop from exhaustion. Other locations cause monkeys to bare their teeth and attack.

Almost every psychology student has sat through the riveting film of Spanish neuropsychologist Jose Delgado, dressed like a matador and being charged by a bull with a microimplant in its limbic system that Delgado could activate by remote control. When Delgado flips the switch in a small control box, the bull stops in its tracks. Obviously, electrical activity in this area can have extensive effects on behaviour associated with aggression. One kind of internally generated electrical activity in the brain is an epileptic seizure. Hence, to neurologists, this kind of epilepsy was a potential cause of uncontrollable aggression.

Elliott believed that temporal lobe epilepsy was the most common "organic" condition associated with explosive rage. Temporal lobe epilepsy, in turn, can be caused by any early trauma such as "an anoxic incident in early infancy" (the air supply is cut off) or "traumatic scars." Elliott never described his thoughts on the origin of these traumatic scars, nor did he speculate that temporal lobe epilepsy might be a consequence of childhood abuse victimization. Recent research is far more suggestive of a link. The excellent cross-generational studies by Byron Egeland and his colleagues find a "transmission rate" of maltreatment from one generation to the next of 40 percent (meaning that 40 percent of adults who maltreat their children were themselves maltreated as children) and psychologist Alan Rosenbaum would find that 61 percent of men assessed for outpatient treatment for wife assault had received prior head injuries. The suggested causal pathway was early physical trauma (such as blows to the head) causing temporal lobe epilepsy, which in turn caused Intermittent Explosive Disorder. Was head trauma leading to temporal lobe epilepsy the source of these outbursts?

My own clinical experience has been that men come into our treatment group who do have the obvious "soft signs" of neurological disorder. These sometimes include pronounced nystagmus (jerky or saccadic eye movement) and attention deficits. One such man completed the treatment and then went on to reoffend six more times (one-sixth of all the post-treatment assaults in a group of 156 men!). However, these men constitute a very small proportion of all clients.

Metabolic disorders can also cause explosive rage. Elliott described a case of matricide triggered by hypoglycemia in a man who had suffered brain damage at birth or infancy. Elliott characterized the features of dyscontrol as being episodes of intense rage "triggered by trivial irritations and accompanied by verbal or physical violence." The individual usually has a "warm, pleasant personality" but may have "a history of traffic accidents resulting from aggressive driving." More recent psychiatric explanations have maintained this focus. A study by Felthous and Bryant in 1991 is typical.[27] The authors found a subgroup of fifteen men (out of 443 studied) whom they diagnosed with Intermittent Explosive Disorder. The typical victim of their outburst was "a spouse, lover, or boyfriend/girlfriend."[28] In study after study, these neurological "explanations" seem to avoid the fact that the violence only occurs in the context of intimacy and typically in private. These contextual features suggest certain specific triggers for aggression that are overlooked by the focus on "uncontrollable" violence.

A literary example provided by Elliott unintentionally underscored this problem with the entire concept of impulse disorder. Elliott cites Emile Zola's character named Jacques in his novel La bête humaine, whom Elliott describes as "a man with the symptoms of temporal lobe epilepsy who could not always control an urge to kill women who attracted him."[29] How does a neurological disorder lead one to only attack attractive women? Or, to re-state our earlier question, why would these men only attack their wives and only in private? There appears to be something else going on besides neural firing. Some neurological disorders, such as Tourette's syndrome, can be con-trolled by the afflicted person under specific, focused circumstances. Does this model also describe the abusive male? Or is there something in the specificity of intimacy that triggers rage? Clearly, some higher-order process of mental association, some associations of the meaning of the target person to the perpetrator and the context, must direct and influence the act of vio-lence. What does the man's wife mean to him? What symbolic baggage does this man carry from his earlier days, which gives shape to this meaning? Is there something special about intimacy that alters the meaning of the other person?

The insufficient nature of the activation of neural mechanisms to explain behaviour is demonstrated by another classic study by Jose Delgado. In this study, stimulation of an area of the temporal lobe in a dominant male mon-key produced a rage response: teeth baring and attack. Stimulation of the same area in a subordinate monkey produced withdrawal: cowering and huddling in the corner of the cage.[30] To social psychologist Albert Bandura, this finding of Delgado's suggested that direct stimulation of brain systems was never a direct cause of aggression but that aggression always had learned aspects to it. The "prepotent" or most used response at the time of the brain stimulation was the response that was evoked by the stimulation. Habitual responses would change with the circumstances. The dominant monkey had learned to attack; attack was at the top of its hierarchy of responses, the one most likely to be used when neural mechanisms were kicked into action by any triggering event. Submissive monkeys had learned that any attempt to attack would be met by severe punishment. Their response hierarchies were different; they had learned to supplicate. The dominant monkeys and sub-missive monkeys made opposite responses to stimulation of the same brain area. The "neural mechanism" did not have functions that were permanently fixed, and the decision to attack or to curl into a ball or show the jugular vein (in an act of submission) seemed to be based in part on what expecta-tions were generated at that time by being in a particular social status.

Neuroanatomy

Davidson, Putnam, and Larson review the activity of brain circuitry regulat-ing emotion: the orbitofrontal cortex (OFC), amygdala, hypothalamus, an-terior cingulated cortex, and prefrontal cortex (PFC).[31] The amygdala appears crucial for learning to associate stimuli with intrinsic punishment and reward. In human neuroimaging studies, the amygdala is activated in response to cues connoting threat (such as facial signs of fear). In contrast, increasing intensity of angry facial expressions is associated with increased activation of the orbitofrontal cortex (OFC), a cerebral structure that is located in the anterior undersurface and interior of the cortex and is especially developed in the right hemisphere. Using functional MRI scans, Davidson et al. found that impulsive-aggressive individuals do not show normal glucose metabolic functioning in the PFC area. Furthermore, lesions in the PFC or OFC areas produce syndromes characterized by impulsivity and aggression. Also, impulsive-aggressives (Temporal Lobe Epilepsy: TLE) diagnosed with Intermittent Explosive Disorder have left PFC areas that are 17 percent smaller than TLE's without a history of aggression. The authors conclude that these neuroanatomical areas and the interconnections among them are central in the generation of impulsive aggression. Further, they argue that the structure and function of this circuitry is affected by both genetic and early environmental factors.

Studies of the development of these neuroanatomical areas have been extensively reviewed by Schore, who concludes that the infant's affective interactions with the early human social environment (interactions with the mother) directly and indelibly influence the postnatal maturation of brain structures (especially right hemispheric structures) that will regulate all future socioemotional functioning.[32] The system that regulates this functioning is composed of the orbitofrontal cortex (OFC). Because of its unique and extensive interconnections to other subcortical systems, the OFC represents a hierarchical apex of the limbic system that regulates emotional regulation. The critical period for maturation of the OFC occurs at the same temporal interval that interests attachment researchers such as John Bowlby and psychodynamic theorists such as Melanie Klein (i.e., the "rapprochment subphase" or Pre-Oedipal stage of development, occurring around age one and one-half to two years). In other words, there is a profound connection between mother-infant attachment and neural development.

Schore describes the development of impulse control or "automodulation of rage" as occurring because of "structural transformation [rewiring] of the [OFC], a system governing internal inhibition ... This anatomical locus with its far-reaching cortical and subcortical connections is equivalent to the frontal functional system that inhibits drive ... Its mature function is expressed in the braking mechanism of shame, which leads to inhibition and 'drive restraint.'"[33] Schore meticulously detailed the elements of maternal-infant interaction that lead to "attunement" and to optimal neural development in the right hemisphere (which governs emotion, the self concept, trust, and holistic patterned thinking) during the first eighteen months of life.[34] Dysregulation in this interaction produces non-optimal neural development during this maturational window, leading to problems with emotion regulation and impulse control late in life. Schore views the brain as a "self-organizing system" that "matures in discontinuous discrete stages."[35] His work is of utmost importance in understanding the full significance of attachment and the basis for all later emotional regulation. These interactive and maturational events occur before the acquisition of language and "autobiographical memory." Hence, we have no memories (just feelings and bodily sensations) of the most important relationship of our lives.[36] We describe more of Schore's groundbreaking work below.

Perry argues that "the structural organization and the functional capabilities of the mature brain develop throughout life, with the vast majority of the critical structural organization taking place in childhood ... Due to the sequential development of the brain, disruptions of normal developmental processes early in life (e.g., during the perinatal period) which alter the brainstem or midbrain will necessarily alter the development of limbic and cortical areas because the critical signals these areas depend on for normal organization originate in these lower brain areas."[37] In a study of hyperaroused, reactive boys who had been exposed to prolonged domestic violence, Perry found that a subset of the boys developed predatory behaviour. The boys described a soothing, calming effect when they began "stalking" a victim. Perry views aggressive acting out as a means of attempting to control an inner aversive arousal and a persistent fear response developed through exposure to domestic violence. He posits that a neural network of interconnected synapses that all fired simultaneously during the initial exposure to trauma became the pathway for "malignant memories" of trauma. In some persons this firing produces aberrant behaviours, even violence, as a learned method of reducing the aversive arousal produced. As Schwartz and Perry put it "malignant memories rooted in early developmental trauma are likely to manifest later as disorders of self, personality or ego functions, including cognitive development and regulation of object relations, attention, affect, and arousal and are not usually recalled as deriving from discrete events."[38] Chapter 10 shows that trauma symptoms are common among abusive men and that their trauma symptom scores are related to negative experiences in childhood. Figure 4.3 summarizes some of the key findings of neuropsychology on the development of neural structures governing violence.

Functional imaging studies (Positron Emission Tomography, or PET, scans) of violent psychiatric patients have demonstrated decreased brain

4.3 Neural structures and development influencing violence

There is clear evidence from several independent researchers that the early years are a critical period for a neural development:

- Perry (1995), Schore (1994), Pynoos et al. (1996) in van der Kolk (1996), Seigel (2003), among others, show that secure attachment is essential for normal development especially during early maturation (birth-3).[1]
- Neural structures, such as the hypothalamus, which regulates emotion and the prefrontal and orbito-frontal cortex, develop rapidly at this time.
- Siegel (2001) observes that "when certain sub-optimal attachment experiences occur, the mind of the child may not come to function as a well integrated system."[2]

NOTES: 1 B. Perry, "Incubated in terror: Neurodevelopmental factors in the 'Cycle of Violence,'" in J.D. Osofsky, ed., *Children, Youth and Violence: Searching for Solutions* (New York: Guilford Press, 1995); A.N. Schore, *Affect Regulation and the Origin of Self: The Neurobiology of Emotional Development* (Hillsdale, NJ: Erlbaum, 1994); R.S. Pynoos, *Post-traumatic Stress Disorder: A Clinical Review* (Lutherville, MD: Sidran Press, 1994); B. Van der Kolk, A.C. Mcfarlane, and L. Weisaeth, *Traumatic Stress: The Effects of Overwhelming Experience on Mind, Body and Society* (New York: Guilford Press, 1996); 2 D. Siegel, "Toward an interpersonal neurobiology of the developing mind: Attachment relationships, 'mindsight,' and neural integration," *Infant Mental Health Journal* 22, 1-2 (2001): 67-94.

metabolism in prefrontal and medial temporal cortices, along with a high incidence of structural abnormalities seen on Computerized Tomography (CT) scans and increased serotonin activity post-synaptically in impulsive-aggressive individuals.[39] These findings lend support to a theory that prefrontal regions are involved in containing affective reactions and inhibit limbic regions normally involved in the expression of aggressive drives. Further evidence comes from a study by Raine et al. that tested the notion that impulsive, affectively aggressive individuals differed from predatory reactive-aggressive persons.[40] Citing past studies showing that the prefrontal and subcortical areas played a role in aggression, they did brain imaging studies (PET scans) of forty-one subjects in prison for murder or attempted murder and forty-one non-violent controls. Affective murderers relative to controls had lower left and right prefrontal functioning, higher right hemisphere subcortical functioning, and lower right hemisphere prefrontal/subcortical ratios. In contrast, predatory murderers had prefrontal functioning that was more equivalent to comparisons, while also having excessively high right subcortical activity. The authors argued that the prefrontal areas acted as a brake, and the subcortical areas as an accelerator, for violence.

Hence, the relative balance of activity between the two areas was important and consistent with Schore's developmental emphasis on the OFC area as a braking mechanism. Schore attributes the development of stress-regulating strategies to practising "distress-relief sequences" that "facilitate a transition from distress to quiet alertness ... Relief is neurophysiologically expressed in the diminution of sympathetic and activation of parasympathetic activity ... Distress-relief sequences, which are composed of sequential periods of sympathetic hyperaroused distress (separation protest, narcissistic rage) followed by parasympathetic relief thus reflects a shift of limbic system predominance."[41] Pine concludes that, "as a result of particular experiences with a reliable caregiver, the infant develops an expectation of relief which allows for delay in the face of need and acts to regulate inner states ... Prefrontal cortical structures are known to mediate the highest control of bridging temporal gaps."[42] Schore argues that the research evidence shows that relational traumas affect the development of the orbitofrontal-amygdala relationship and that this produces rage states and contributes to infant, adolescent, and adult aggression.[43] We will describe Schore's groundbreaking work in more detail below.

Raine, Buchsbaum, and Lacasse found brain abnormalities in murderers who had pleaded NGRI (Not Guilty by Reason of Insanity).[44] Using PET scans and a continuous performance challenge task, they found that forty-one murderers (compared to matched controls) showed reduced glucose metabolism in the prefrontal cortex, superior parietal gyrus, left angular gyrus, and corpus callosum. Abnormal asymmetries were also found for the murderers (left hemispheric function lower than right) in the amygdala, thalamus, and medial temporal lobe. The authors speculated that a "network of abnormal cortical and subcortical brain processes may predipose to violence in murderers – pleading NGRI."[45]

Neurobiological Functioning

Coccaro and Coccaro and Kavoussi have examined the role of monoamine transmitters (serotonin, norepinephrine, and dopamine) in human aggression and violence, using postmortem brain studies of individuals who had committed suicide or had been killed in accidents.[46] Suicide victims tended to have lowered serotonin levels compared to accident victims. Furthermore, individuals who had used a violent means of committing suicide had even lower levels of serotonin (5-HT) in their cerebrospinal fluid (CSF). Coccaro and Kavoussi also report studies linking low serotonin levels with histories of aggressive behaviour in naval recruits. As the authors put it: "This suggested that, in some populations at least, reduced CSF 5-HIAA (a metabolite of serotonin) concentration predisposes humans to aggression directed both at the self and the other."[47] Studies of brain receptors generally support the

hypothesis that self-directed aggression is associated with reduced serotonin activity. Suicide victims typically have lower numbers of receptor sites
than accident victims. Comparisons of groups low or normal in serotonin
(5-HT) levels revealed that 5-HT function is specifically associated with physically assaultive behaviours as measured by the Buss-Durkee assault scale.
Stanley et al. assessed whether serotonin dysfunction was related to aggression in the absence of a history of suicidal behaviour.[48] They did a median
split for aggression on sixty-four patients with no suicidal history. The aggressive group had significantly lower levels of a serotonin metabolite drawn
from cerebrospinal fluid (CSF 5-HIAA) concentrations than did the non-
aggressive group. Aggressive individuals also scored higher on self-report
measures of hostility, impulsiveness, and sensation-seeking. Stoff and Vitiello
examined the role of serotonin in adolescent aggression.[49] They noted that
animal behaviour studies indicated that increasing or decreasing serotonin
(5-HT) activity produced concomitant decreases or increases in aggression
and that these results were consistent with the human data collected by
Coccaro and Kavoussi.[50] Stoff and Vitiello reviewed twenty-five studies and
noted that aggressive tendencies and cerebrospinal serotonin concentrations
(obtained by lumbar puncture) are both highly stable over the life cycle.[51]
Decreased levels of CSF concentrations of 5-HIAA were obtained in children
and adolescents with Conduct Disorder, and low 5-HT levels were generally
related to aggressiveness in adolescent populations.

Coccaro and Kavoussi also review animal studies for other neurotransmitter systems such as norepinephrine (NE), dopamine (DA), and endog-
enous opioids.[52] These include findings that increased NE function in the
brain correlates positively with the number of shock-induced aggressive episodes in rodents.[53] Agents that enhance NE function (i.e., tricyclic/MAOI
antidepressants) increase shock-induced fighting in rodents.[54] Stimulating
post-synaptic noradrenergic receptors in the hypothalamus facilitates aggression in cats.[55] In humans, clinical treatment with these agents is associated
with agitation and irritability, especially in subsets of patients with borderline personality disorder.[56] Similarly, agents that diminish noradrenergic function diminish aggression.

In humans, CSF and plasma measures of NE are positively related to a
scale measuring impulsivity.[57] Coccaro and Kavoussi hypothesize that a neuropsychological model of impulsive aggression in humans is modulated by
serotonin system function; the lower the functional status of the serotonin
system, the more likely the individual is to respond to "threat, frustration or
aversive circumstances with an aggressive outburst."[58] The role of other neurotransmitter systems (NE, DA, opiates) lies in their role in perceiving threat

or frustration and in activating the cognitive and motor systems necessary for aggression. This model seems to represent a person who generally reacts to threat with aggression. However, most spousal killers have no record of conviction for aggression outside an intimate relationship.[59] Dutton has suggested that insecure attachment is a trauma source for both lethal and non-lethal spouse abusers.[60] Insecure attachment would indicate an inability to self-soothe and a consequent reliance on the intimate other to provide soothing. In addition, in men who experienced traumatic childhoods, attachment loss or threat of lost attachment may produce a variety of psychobiological reactions similar to Post-Traumatic Stress Disorder (PTSD) reactions.[61] If the threat of attachment loss is a distinct stressor in these men, then the psychobiological reactions described by Coccaro and Kavoussi would occur with greatest intensity in perceived abandonment. Another line of research has shown that separation in itself produces alterations in neurotransmitter function.[62] To most readers with a background in psychology, attachment was something studied in infant development classes while neurobiology was part of biological psychology. In the real world of domestic violence, the two are inextricably linked.

In short, numerous studies performed by independent researchers indicate differential brain functioning in impulsive-aggressive individuals and also raise the possibility that this altered reactivity is a by-product of faulty attachment. The impact of faulty attachment is to alter crucial neural development during critical periods of brain development. The brain grows from an average of four hundred ounces at birth to one thousand ounces at the end of the first year. Dysfunction in families occurring during this critical time can generate neurological deficits that impact on emotion regulation and the ability to curb impulses.

4.4 Early development of the right hemisphere according to Schore

The right hemisphere of the brain:
- governs non-verbal and emotional reactions
- develops before the left hemisphere (in the first two years of life)
- develops through emotional communication with the mother in a joint regulation of psychobiological states (arousal)
- having developed prior to speech, is best repaired therapeutically using non-verbal methods.

SOURCES: A.N. Schore, *Affect Dysregulation and the Disorders of the Self* (New York: Norton, 2003); B. Perry, R.A. Pollard, T.L. Blakeley, W.L. Baker, and D. Vigilante, "Childhood trauma, the neurobiology of adaptation and the 'use-dependent' development of the brain: How states become traits," *Infant Mental Health Journal* 16, 4 (1995): 271-91; D.J. Siegel, *The Developing Mind: How Relationships and the Brain Interact to Shape Who We Are* (New York: Guilford Press, 2001).

Attachment Theory

It may turn out that psychiatry's most influential theoretical contribution to understanding human behaviour will be made not by Sigmund Freud but by John Bowlby. Ironically, though, after Bowlby's original writing, almost all critical research has been done by psychologists.

As Shaver and Mikulincer argue, psychodynamic explanations of personality had largely fallen out of research attention, and neither Freud nor the neo-Freudians (Sullivan, Horney, Fromm) are well known today.[63] One reason was that it was difficult to develop valid measurement techniques to test psychodynamic concepts, and research turned away from psychopathology to focus on "normal" college student populations who were available as subjects. Attachment theory is also psychodynamic but has a stronger and more verifiable motivational base (survival) than classical Freudian theory. What's more, attachment theory has lent itself to research testing, first with infants and later with adults. Finally, attachment relates to notions of identity and personality, describing the part of the personality that functions in intimate relationships.

John Bowlby

Bowlby, a psychiatrist, became disenchanted with the intrapsychic dynamic teachings of his mentor, Melanie Klein. Bowlby believed that attachment to a powerful other had survival value and thus was a much stronger motive than any other previously preferred by psychoanalysis. Bowlby united psychoanalysis with sociobiology. He developed his theory through observing infants in England during the bombing raids of the Second World War. He became fascinated by the emotional displays that occurred when infants were separated from their mothers. These "attachment patterns" seemed to fall into one of three categories: Secure, Fearful, or Dismissing. The Secure infant seemed untroubled by separation and appeared to have a "mental model" of a safe base in mind that allowed it to set forth into the uncharted waters of the "strange situation." The Fearful infant constantly visually checked to ensure that its secure base was still present. The Dismissing infant appeared aloof. Bowlby pointed out that these attachment patterns correlated with patterns of social and play behaviour with adults other than mother and were long-lasting. More recently, attachment styles have been related to adult romantic attachment styles, risk for suicide, depression, and, in my research, adult abusiveness.[64] The power of attachment stems from its survival value. A human child is dependent on another longer than infants of any other species. Successful attachment is literally "life and death" to humans. Bowlby, in a landmark series of books entitled *Attachment and Loss*,

developed the notion that human attachment was of paramount importance for human emotional growth, serving a vital biological function in-
dispensable for the survival of the infant.[65] In his view, the human need for
secure attachment is the result of a long-term evolutionary development
that rivals feeding and mating in importance.

Bowlby argued that attachment is a sociobiologically determined cultural
universal. With humans, who have a protracted period of dependency on
food, shelter and basic safety needs, this process of attachment is of the highest importance, and its emotional consequences are strong. Indeed, Bowlby
offered a powerful alternative grounded in sociobiology to Freud's paro-
chial "sexual repression" as a fundamental human motive.

Bowlby and Ainsworth indicate that there are three important principles
that drive infant attachment behaviour:

1 First, an alarm of any kind, stemming from any source activates an
   "attachment behavioural system" of the infant.
2 Second, when this system is intensely active, only physical contact with
   the attachment figure will serve to terminate it.
3 Finally, when the attachment system is activated for a long time without reaching termination, angry behaviour is regularly observed in the
   infant.[66]

Hence, a fundamental principle of attachment research is that *anger follows unmet attachment needs*. Anger's first objective is to get a missing attachment object to return. An anger display that increases the emotional distance
between the self and the attachment other is dysfunctional. Anger can acquire other functions later in development – it can attract attention or serve
as a means of expression – but this is its original motive.

Bowlby defined attachment as a bond developed with "some other differentiated and preferred individual who is conceived as stronger and/or wiser."[67]
Proportional to this sense of the other as having absolute and unrestricted
power over the infant, threats to or separations from that secure attachment
should produce emotional responses that are extremely strong, responses
such as terror, grief, and rage.

Bowlby emphasized the importance of the relationship in the first years
of life between the infant and the primary caretaker for the development of
the self and for later social behaviour. During the first six months the infant
develops many behaviours (e.g., smiling, crying upon caretaker leaving) that
function to bring closer proximity and interaction with the caretaker. In the
second six months, proximity and interaction-promoting behaviours are

integrated into a coherent system organized around a particular figure. At nine months, the goal of proximity/security regulation includes locomotion towards attachment figures and away from strangers. All of the behaviours that serve to generate proximity to the caregiver during times of threat form the general attachment system.

Bowlby reported observations of the reactions of children (aged fifteen to thirty months) in nurseries who were separated for the first time from their parents. This reaction can be broken into three distinct phases he called Protest, Despair, and Detachment. It is instructive to hear Bowlby's own description of these reactions:

[In] the initial phase *(Protest)*, the young child appears acutely distressed at having lost his mother and seeks to recapture her by the full exercise of his limited resources. He will often cry loudly, shake his cot, throw himself about, and look eagerly towards any sight or sound which might prove to be his missing mother. All his behaviour suggests strong expectation that she will return ... During the phase of *Despair* .... his behaviour suggests increasing hoplessness. The active physical movements diminish or come to an end, and he may cry monotonously or intermittently. He is withdrawn and inactive ... and appears to be in a state of deep mourning ... [In] the phase of *Detachment,* when his mother visits it can be seen that all is not well, for there is a striking absence of the behaviour characteristic of strong attachment normal at this age. So far from greeting his mother, he may hardly seem to know her; so far from clinging to her he may seem remote and apathetic; instead of tears there is a listless turning away.[68]

In other words, the actions associated with the first phase of the separation cycle can be construed as angry. They all involve outward actions on the world generated to produce a result (in this case the return of the mother). Loud crying and shaking of the cot are prototypical forms of later physical acts we would call aggressive. With the infant, it is only after prolonged failure to have these outward actions on the world lead to a successful recreation of the mother's presence that the subsequent emotions of depression (mourning) and eventual detachment appear. With adult males, the realization that a wife or lover is leaving or has left produces deep depression and suicidal ideation (or threats/actions) where previously anger and violence were used to control the female's emotional proximity to the male.

While developing a relationship with a primary caregiver and through repeated transactions in which the consistency and adequacy of the primary caregiver's responses are crucial, an infant forms an "internal representation" of the self and others. This is "a set of conscious or unconscious rules for the organization of information relevant to attachment, attachment related experiences, feelings and ideations."[69] This internal representation directs feelings and behaviour related to attachment as well as memory, attention, and cognition. It is a model of the self as worthy or unworthy of care and love, generating unconscious expectations about the consequences of attachment and providing a context for later social relationships. Although this model of the self can be restructured, to do so is difficult since once it is organized it tends to operate outside conscious awareness and resist dramatic change (see Figure 4.4).[70]

Bowlby pointed out that attachment patterns (secure, avoidant, resistant) correlated "with the patterns of social and play behavior with adults other than mother,"[71] and this correlation continued "during both the second and subsequent years of life."[72] Research evidence available at the time of his writing already indicated continuity to ages five to six. Attachment issues have now been related to behavioural problems at ages three to six and to adult romantic attachment styles.[73] Conversely, evidence is very weak for longitudinal attachment effects due to temperament.[74]

Mary Ainsworth began the empirical study of specific differences in responding to attachment and to separation from the caregiver. These responses were first noted in what has come to be called the Strange Situation, in which a child is experimentally separated from its parent and its behaviour observed. On the basis of these observations, infants were assigned to one of three categories: Secure, Anxious-avoidant, and Anxious-ambivalent. Secure infants greeted their mother with pleasure when she returned, stretching out their arms and moulding to her body. They were relatively easy to console and were distinguished from other groups by the frequency with which they sought emotional sharing with the caregiver and by their ability to be comforted and calmed by her when distressed. About 62-75 percent of a North American middle class population fit this category. They have caregivers who readily perceive, accurately interpret, and promptly and appropriately respond to their needs as infants. These caregivers (predominantly mothers) provided a predictable and controllable environment that promoted the infant's regulation of arousal and sense of efficacy.[75] Sometimes referred to as "attunement," the essential feature of this maternal responsiveness is that the parent matches through expression the emotional state expressed by the infant. There are vast differences in mothers' abilities to do this. The importance of attunement, however, cannot be overemphasized.[76]

Anxious-avoidant infants (also called "dismissing") give the impression of independence. They explore a new environment without using their mother as a base, and they don't turn around to be certain of their mother's presence (as do Secure infants). When separations occur, Anxious-avoidant infants do not seem affected, and when mothers return they are snubbed or avoided. Infants who exhibit avoidant attachment communicate with their caregiver only when they are feeling well. When distressed, these infants do not signal the primary caregiver or seek bodily contact. At six years of age, many of these behaviours are still evident. Anxious-avoidant children direct attention away from their mother upon reunion, move away from her physically, seem ill at ease discussing separation, and turn away from family photographs.[77] This set of responses then defines the Anxious-avoidant style: displays of minimal affect or distress in the presence of the caregiver and an avoidance of the attachment figure under conditions that with Secure children elicit proximity-seeking and interaction. Anxious-avoidant behaviour attends to the environment while actively directing attention away from the parent. Robert Karen describes this group as follows: "The avoidant child takes the opposite tack [to the ambivalent child]. He becomes angry and distant (even though he becomes no less attached). His pleas for attention have been painfully rejected, and reaching out seems impossible. The child seems to say, 'Who needs you – I can do it on my own.' Often in conjunction with this attitude, grandiose ideas about the self develop: I am great, I don't need anybody ... Bowlby believes that avoidant attachment lies at the heart of narcissistic personality traits, one of the predominant psychiatric concerns of our time."[78]

About 32 percent of Ainsworth's sample were Anxious-avoidant infants. Their mothers were insensitive, unresponsive, and understimulating, and had an aversion to physical contact.[79] "Dismissing" mothers reject their babies' bids for comfort and reassurance, using comments to override the baby's emotional displays. If these don't succeed in quelling the baby's affect display, they are followed by "sadistic misattunement" (i.e., the expression of misaligned feelings). Such mothers tend to be unable to remember details of their own childhoods or to idealize their relationship with their parents, even though they could remember contradictory rejecting memories.[80]

Psychologist Kim Bartholomew has observed that, although avoidant children's behaviour could be interpreted as reflecting a lack of need or desire for contact, there is compelling evidence to the contrary. For example, avoidant children exhibit cardiac acceleration in response to separation in spite of a lack of overt distress.[81] Bartholomew concludes that their apparently innocuous focus on inanimate objects may be a form of displacement behaviour. Furthermore, although avoidant children show little aggression in the Strange Situation, they show considerable anger directed toward their mother at home.[82] Moreover, the greater the avoidance upon reunion with mother, the greater the display of anger and dependent behaviour toward her over the ensuing weeks – again underscoring Bowlby's argument that anger is a protest behaviour aimed at increasing proximity with a caregiver. Hence, the anger that avoidant children express towards their mother in less stressful circumstances (presumably in response to her rejecting or unresponsive treatment) can be taken as evidence of their lack of indifference. In response to separation, avoidant infants feel angry with their mother, but the expression of anger in this situation risks decreased proximity, so angry impulses are suppressed and replaced with "cool" detached avoidance.[83] The angry impulses are expressed later when conditions are less stressful or safer.

Chronically rejected infants experience particularly strong angry impulses with high avoidance of anger display. Again, in less stressful circumstances the anger is expressed indirectly. Kim Bartholomew argues that strong and unresolvable approach/avoidance may underlie the behaviour of chronically avoidant people: threats lead to tendencies to approach the attachment figure, who rejects physical contact, thus generating withdrawal accompanied by an even stronger need for attachment. The ensuing self-perpetuating feedback loop leads to chronic avoidance (presumably accompanied by chronic unfulfilled attachment needs). Hence, anger is central to the Anxious-avoidant attachment style. One wonders whether the Anxious-avoidant pattern represents the emotional origin of later withdrawal styles

---

4.5 Insecure attachment style characteristics: Fearful-Angry

Anxious-avoidant (preoccupied, fearful)	Anxious-ambivalent (angry)
• highly invested, high breakup rate	• converts anxiety to anger
• low self-esteem	• uses control to cover dependency
• feels unappreciated in work with others	• high levels of jealousy
• slacks off after praise	• abusive verbally/physically
• binges on chocolate	• externalizes blame consistently
• describes parents as unfair	• experiences depressions
• becomes emotional under stress	
• worries about rejection	

SOURCES: C. Hazan and P. Shaver, "Conceptualizing romantic love as an attachment process," *Journal of Personality and Social Psychology* 52 (1987): 511-24; R. Karen, "Becoming Attached," *Atlantic Monthly*, Feb. 1990, 35-70.

where anger is suppressed. Gayla Margolin found similarities in communication styles between physically abusive and withdrawn couples. Both were characterized by low assertiveness and conflict avoidance.

Ainsworth's third group of infants, called Anxious-ambivalent (later sometimes Fearful or Preoccupied), tended to cling to their mother and resisted exploring the room on their own. They became extremely agitated on separation, often crying profusely. An Anxious-ambivalent infant typically sought contact with its mother when she returned but simultaneously arched away from her angrily and resisted all efforts to be soothed. The implication is that these infants somehow incorporate anger into their terror at being "abandoned by the mother." The mothers of these infants tended to be inconsistent and least confident in coping with early caregiving tasks. Ainsworth's Anxious-ambivalent category was later split in two: Anxious or Preoccupied infants, who are consistently anxious in intimate relationships, and Ambivalent or Fearful infants, who exhibit the push-pull of ambivalence.

Karen describes the resulting behavioural style as follows: "The ambivalent child (ambivalent children represent about 10 percent of children from middle-class US homes) is desperately trying to influence her. He is hooked by the fact that she does come through on occasion. He picks up that she will respond – sometimes out of guilt – if he pleads and makes a big enough fuss. And so he is constantly trying to hold onto her or to punish her for being unavailable. He is wildly addicted to her and to his efforts to make her change."[84]

These ambivalent children sound similar to physically abusive men.[85] The intensity and the need for impact on the woman are reminiscent of descriptions of the "abusive personality" and of Winter's description of the power motive, which he sees as driving the "Don Juan": the sexually promiscuous male who is addicted to a successive pattern of sexual conquest-abandonment.[86]

In a longitudinal study, Allen Sroufe found that Grade 3 children with anxious attachment had the poorest social skills and clear psychiatric disturbances.[87] Anxiously attached individuals seem to have diminished capacity to form bases of social support or to seek it when needed. Hence, a life-long pattern of isolation may derive from early lessons that support from others is unreliable. Assaultive males are characteristically isolated individuals. Also, gender-specific expectations develop. For example, with an absent father and a demanding (but unavailable) mother a boy learns that males are not available for emotional support, that women appear to be supportive but are ultimately demanding and can't be trusted. As a result, he isolates and withdraws inside himself, while at the same time feeling a gnawing anger.

Faulty Attachment: Developmental Psychopathology

Intuition tells us that an infant who is intermittently abused by a parent may not form an attachment to that person. However, there is evidence that under such circumstances strong bonds do form and are characterized both by closeness and by repressed anger. As Bowlby put it, "We may presume that an attack from any source arouses some fear and withdrawal tendencies. What is peculiar to the situation in which the attack comes from the haven of safety is, of course, the arousal of conflicting tendencies. From this single threat or signal at least two conflicting messages are received: to go away from and to come toward the haven of safety."[88]

In a now-classic study by Harry Harlow, "evil surrogate mothers" exude noxious air blasts onto baby rhesus monkeys.[89] They also extrude brass spikes, hurl the infant monkey to the floor, or vibrate so violently as to make the infant's teeth chatter. None of the above disrupted the bonding behaviour of the infant monkeys, leading the authors to conclude that "instead of producing experimental neurosis, we have achieved a technique for enhancing maternal attachment."[90] In effect, the Harlows had produced an experimental analogue of child abuse where contact comfort was intermittently disrupted by noxious behaviours. To their surprise, the attachment process was strengthened, not weakened, by this process.

More recently, the effects of maltreatment on human infants' attachment systems has been examined by researchers such as Patricia Crittenden and Dante Cicchetti.[91] Most of this research has been established by studying maltreating families who have come to the attention of local social service agencies. These examinations of the attachments of abused children again show that they are characterized by avoidance-ambivalence and anger and also by excessive closeness, which appears as "compulsive compliance." The authors see this closeness-protective behaviour in abused children as a way of both maintaining closeness of attachment and denying pervasive anger with the abusive "caretaker." Those with closeness-protective behaviour could, in other words, be the overcontrolled wife assaulters of the future, while the avoidant-ambivalent could be the cyclical personalities of the future. Filled with rage, unable to express it, possessing negative representations of himself and women, but still cyclically drawn in a repetitive push-pull pattern, the avoidant-ambivalent child is a prototype for an abusive adult.

With abusive parents, the child is in a situation where he is locked into forming an attachment to his primary caregiver who is also a source of pain and injury. The rage that is experienced with such a parent is repressed. It will not be expressed until a similar intimate attachment is formed later in life. In the meantime, the child will pass into adolescence consumed by developing his public person. The intimate personality will remain dormant until an intimate attachment, later in life, triggers the emotional template developed in the original attachment experience.[92] Abusive males who experience physical violence in their family of origin are also at risk for ambivalent attachment, growing up in dysfunctional, unstable families. Although this "intergenerational transmission" of violence is initially focused on behaviour modelling, attachment theory and research suggest that something more is going on. That "something more" involves the development of faulty internal schemas, self-concepts, and expectations of attachment to others that are fraught with fear and rage. The groundwork for abusiveness is set. In other words, abusive childhood experiences produce something more than just learned behaviour patterns. They produce avoidant-ambivalent bonding styles that generate tendencies to be both overly demanding and angry in adult romantic attachments, a profile often reported by battered women about their husbands and again consistent with the descriptors of the pathology of borderline disorders.

Adult Attachment and Problem Behaviour

One intriguing bit of evidence for the longevity of attachment longings is the research reported by psychologist Robert Silverman. Claiming that there are "powerful unconscious wishes for a state of oneness with the good mother of early childhood" and that gratification of these wishes can enhance adaptation, Silverman and a variety of colleagues have presented subliminal stimuli (four milliseconds in duration) that read MOMMY AND I ARE ONE. These presentations have produced ameliorative effects on a variety of problem behaviours ranging from schizophrenia to smoking. Silverman refers to this as "activating symbiotic-like" (oneness) fantasies whereby "representations of self and other are fused and merged" which originate when "the mother is experienced very early in life as comforting, protective and nurturing."[93] Gender differences appeared in their research, with males showing the ameliorative effect more than females. Silverman has speculated that this may be so because daughters have less of a basis for differentiating themselves from their mothers than do sons. Studies using DADDY AND I ARE ONE or MY LOVER AND I ARE ONE produced ameliorative effects on schizophrenia and anxiety in women subjects. Silverman speculates that the activation of oneness fantasies alleviates anxiety and gratifies dependency-related needs, and he provides empirical results to support these notions. Although Silverman and his colleagues reported studies on forty groups of subjects with a variety of adult problems, they did not report tests of different attachment styles. Given that insecurely attached infants experienced less of the ideal nurturing mother than securely attached adults, one might expect a difference in the ameliorative effect of the subliminal stimulation in these two groups.

The bridge from infant to adult attachment was finally built by social psychologist Phillip Shaver and his colleagues in a landmark study that made the empirical leap from infant attachment to adult "attachment styles."[94] The study made the argument that adult romantic love had attachment properties that may derive from love's infantile forms. The authors state: "Personal continuity, in fact, is primarily due to the persistence of mental models, which are themselves sustained by a fairly stable family setting ... We are ready to suggest more explicitly that all important love relationships – especially the ones with parents and later ones with lovers and spouses – are attachments in Bowlby's sense. For every documented feature of attachment there is a parallel feature of love, and for most documented features of love there is either a documented or a plausible feature of attachment."[95] Shaver et al. found that in an adult population of over seven hundred subjects, self-described attachment styles fell into approximately the same proportions as Ainsworth had found for infant populations: 56 percent Securely attached, 25 percent Avoidant, and 20 percent Anxious/ambivalent. (These findings are summarized in Figure 4.6.) The Anxious/ambivalent lovers experienced love as involving obsession, desire for reciprocation and union, emotional highs and lows, and extreme sexual attraction and jealousy. Anxious/ambivalent respondents claimed that it was easy to fall in love and said that they frequently feel themselves beginning to do so, although they rarely find what they would call "real" love. They reported more self doubts and more feelings of being misunderstood than did the other groups.

Attachment history was assessed by asking respondents to describe how each parent had generally behaved towards them (and towards each other) during childhood. Anxious/ambivalent respondents described their mothers as more intrusive and unfair (than Secure respondents did) and their fathers as unfair and threatening. The term intrusive was the main one used by Ainsworth et al. in their description of mothers of Anxious/ambivalent infants. Descriptions of mothers paralleled Ainsworth's characterization of the mothers of Avoidant infants as more thoroughly negative than were the less-consistent mothers of Anxious/ambivalent infants. Hazan and Shaver's research was an important first step in relating early attachment to adult relationship functioning.

Since this seminal research was conducted, attachment in adults has exploded as a research topic. Although debate continues, it is generally accepted that four distinct adult attachment styles exist, called Secure,

4.6 Adult attachment types and their frequencies

Question: Which of the following best describes your feelings?

Answers	Newspaper sample	University sample
Secure:		
I find it relatively easy to get close to others and am comfortable depending on them and having them depend on me. I don't often worry about being abandoned or about someone getting too close to me.	56%	56%
Avoidant:		
I am somewhat uncomfortable being close to others; I find it difficult to trust them completely, difficult to allow myself to depend on them. I am nervous when anyone gets too close, and often, love partners want me to be more intimate than I feel comfortable being.	25%	23%
Anxious/Ambivalent:		
I find that others are reluctant to get as close as I would like. I often worry that my partner doesn't really love me or won't want to stay with me. I want to merge completely with another person, and this desire sometimes scares people away.	19%	20%

SOURCE: Adapted from P. Shaver, C. Hazan, and D. Bradshaw, "Love as attachment: The integration of three behavioral systems," in R.J. Sternberg and M. Barnes, eds., *The Psychology of Love* (New Haven, CT: Yale University Press, 1988).

Dismissing, Preoccupied, and Fearful.[96] The self-explanatory names constitute adult versions of the infant attachment patterns described above. The Secure people had positive self schematas (complex images of the self) and positive expectations about intimate relationships; they expected the best would happen and were untroubled by closeness. The Dismissing people, as Hazan and Shaver had described them, had "signed off" from close relationships. They were independent to a fault. They didn't need anybody.

The Preoccupied were the clingy types, the ones who worried a lot about being rejected by the other person and were falling over themselves to please and gain approval. The Fearful group is, from my perspective, the most interesting because these people seem simultaneously drawn and repelled by intimacy. As Kim Bartholomew put it, the Fearful "desire social contact and intimacy but experience pervasive interpersonal distrust and fear of rejection."

The connection of attachment style to abusiveness is made through the chronic feelings generated by insecure attachment and the way those feelings might translate into behaviour for men who had the double dose of abusive role models in their early life and social conditioning into the "masculine role" later on. Men with early attachment problems are more likely to experience anxiety about intimacy regulation. The arousal, anxiety, and anger these men experience originates in deep-seated anxiety about the original attachment object.

Abusive males have exaggerated needs for control in intimate relationships because their need corresponds to a felt anxiety and such control represents behaviours designed to lower the anxiety/anger. These men try to diminish their anxiety about being abandoned through exaggerated control of their female partners.

As developmental psychologist Patricia Crittenden argues, anxious attachments may occur at any age. Some of the indications of anxious attachment in older children and adults resemble the indications of anxious attachment in infancy: undue preoccupation with the whereabouts of the attachment figure and undue difficulty in separating from him or her, lack of trust in the attachment figure, chronic anger and resentment toward him or her, inability to seek or use support from the attachment figure when such support is needed, or absence of feeling toward him or her.[97] Crittenden goes on to suggest that other attachment disorders are less frequent but seem to be generated by "traumatic or depriving separation from the attachment figure."

Attachment and Neural Development

Bowlby's work replaced Freud's outmoded motivational theory with the more supportable notion of survival. In doing so, it combined psychoanalysis with sociobiology. In the 1990s, however, with the invention of Magnetic Resonance Imaging (MRI) and brain scans, the major new area of research became the combination of attachment theory with neural development. Using this new technology, Allan Schore has clearly demonstrated relationships between dysfunctional early attachment and neural development – especially in the right hemisphere of the brain, which develops earliest and before speech. We can now say that *faulty attachment creates problems with neural structures that govern emotion and self-control.* This conclusion provides the foundation for understanding and developing therapies for intimate violence.

In an encyclopedic series, Schore has described how maternal "protocommunication" (communications from the mother to the child that are minutely attuned to microreactions in each) are essential for the normal development of brain structure.[98] Maternal communications generate endorphins in the infant and stimulate the arousal level into an optimal zone necessary for neural development. Schore shows how mother-infant attachment communications are accompanied by the strongest feelings and emotion and occur within a context of facial expression, posture, tone of voice, physiological changes, tempo of movement, and incipient action.[99] In fact, these "non-verbal" aspects of communication are the only important aspects at an age when emotional abilities have developed but verbal abilities have not. Schore refers to this as "affect synchrony" (others call it attunement) and sees it as paramount in healthy development of interpersonal trust, attachment bonds, and development of right hemisphere (RH) neural structures regulating emotion (e.g., the RH limbic areas). Schore calls this "experience dependent maturation," because, for example, if the proper experience does not occur, the brain structures do not mature. The orbitofrontal area of the right brain, as it turns out, becomes important in the development of empathy, the ability to cope with stress, the regulation of negative affect, and the emergence of a concept of self. In a child whose right-brain neural structures are underdeveloped, these abilities and concepts are impeded.

As Schore puts it "I believe that every type of early forming primitive disorder involves, to some extent, altered orbital prefrontal function ... Indeed, there is now evidence for impaired orbitofrontal activity in such diverse psychopathologies as ... drug addiction, borderline and psychopathic personality disorders. Because the orbital system is centrally involved in the executive functions of the right cortex, these studies underscore the importance of the role of the right hemisphere dysfunction in psychiatric disorders."[100] By "primitive" he means, pre-oedipal, related to early development. The right hemisphere, which governs emotion, develops before the left hemisphere, which governs language. For this reason, disorders related to the right hemisphere may require non-verbal intervention. Hence, secure attachment is essential in the development of those brain structures that regulate emotion throughout life. In a later chapter we will examine insecure attachment as a risk factor for abusiveness in adults.

Schore also presents evidence for a neuropsychological basis for borderline personality disorder. According to empirical studies of neural development, borderlines have an unresponsive mother and an emotionally unavailable father. The "provocation rage" characteristic of borderlines reflects an orbitofrontal system that poorly modulates limbic arousal and is unable to regulate neural inhibition. The result is a neural inability to self-soothe.[101]

That a psychological process such as feeling of rejection can have powerful neurological consequences is indicated by Figure 4.7, summarizing the

4.7 The neurology of rejection and pain

A study of a part of the brain that registers pain measured the neural reactions of people who thought they had become outcasts in a game. The study found that social rejection causes as much distress as a poke in the eye. So the need to be accepted as part of a social group may be as important to humans as the need to avoid other types of pain.

In the experiment at UCLA, researchers monitored blood flow in the brains of people who had been led to believe that other players in a computer ball game were intentionally excluding them and refusing to let them play with the group. The shock and distress of this rejection was registered in the same part of the brain that also responds to physical pain, the anterior cingulate cortex.

The significance of the findings was explained by Naomi Eisenberger, a UCLA researcher and first author of the study, which appeared in the journal *Science* in 2003, in an interview with a reporter: "There's something about exclusion from others that is perceived as being as harmful to our survival as something that can physically hurt us, and our body automatically knows this ... You can imagine that this part of the brain is active any time we are separated from our close companions. It would definitely be active when we experience a loss" (such as a death or the end of a love affair).[1]

The tendency to feel rejection as an acute pain may have developed in humans as a defensive mechanism for the species, she said. "Because we have such a long time as infants and need to be taken care of, it is really important that we stay close to the social group. If we don't we're not going to survive ... The hypothesis is that the social attachment system that makes sure we don't stray too far from the group piggybacked onto the pain system to help our species survive ... If it hurts to be separated from other people, then it will prevent us from straying too far from the social group."

NOTE: 1 The report in question is N. Eisenberger, M.D Lieberman, and K.D. Williams, "Does rejection hurt? An MRI study of social exclusion," *Science* 302 (2003): 290-92.

work of Eisenberger and colleagues, who used functional Magnetic Resonance Imaging to find that pain and rejection were processed identically by brain systems.[102] At a neurological level, being excluded from a group through "indirect aggression" hurts as much as being pricked or burned.

The upshot of this review is that psychiatric theories, although they may have started in a naïve, context-ignoring way, subsequently developed into two major breakthroughs in our understanding of dysfunctional behavior. First, Bowlby's brilliant substantiation of survival-based attachment as a prime human motive and, secondly, Schore's uncovering of a basis for attachment and its dysfunction in neural development. These twin advances lay the groundwork for understanding human emotional dysregulation, especially in intimate relationships resembling the primal relationship in which the dysfunctions first occurred. It is ironic that we cannot remember this relationship, arguably the most important of our lives.

5 Feminist and Sociobiological Explanations for Intimate Partner Violence

Sexuality is to feminism what work is to Marxism ... the molding, direction, and expression of sexuality organizes society into two sexes: women and men. This division underlies the totality of social relations.

– Catharine MacKinnon, *Toward a Feminist Theory of the State*

Given the history of mistreatment of women outlined in Chapter 1, it's not surprising that certain scholars evolved explanations of wife assault based on gender analysis. These explanations saw wife assault as normal violence used by males to sustain the oppression of women and motivated by a male sense of entitlement. Feminist explanations were essentially sociological, viewing wife assault as generated by social-structural conditions. They tended to resist psychological explanations of wife assault because these psychological explanations insisted that assaultive men had personal inadequacies and that these personal issues rather than the general culture caused the violence. The essential flaw in feminist "gender analysis" is contained in MacKinnon's above quote. Sexuality cannot be mapped onto an economic relationship because sexuality is governed by attachment, a sociobiologically determined, neurologically supported motive of utmost importance in all intimate relationships. The failure of MacKinnon and of radical feminism to understand this point originates in ideological ignorance of the psychology of intimacy and of the multilayered levels of power between men and women.[1]

Sociological explanations for wife assault that were developed in the 1970s endeavoured to correct the impression, created by psychiatric explanations, that wife assault was a rare event committed only by men with diagnosable psychiatric disturbances. Rather, sociologists viewed wife assault as a common event, generated by social rules that supported male dominance of women and tacit approval by society.[2]

The Straus, Gelles, and Steinmetz survey revealed what psychiatrists had ignored: that wife assault was far more "normal" violence than had been previously recognized.[3] As Straus claimed, society actually has rules and values that make "the marriage license also a hitting license."[4] The feminist claim was twofold: that society was patriarchal and that the use of violence to maintain male patriarchy was accepted. As Dobash and Dobash put it "men who assault their wives are actually living up to cultural prescriptions that are cherished in Western society – aggressiveness, male dominance, and female subordination – and they are using physical force as a means to enforce that dominance."[5]

According to Bograd, there are some defining features that are central to most feminist analyses of the phenomenon of woman assault.[6] Feminist researchers, clinicians, and activists try to address a primary question: "Why do men beat their wives?" This question "directs attention to the physical violence occurring in heterosexual relationships" and distinguishes feminists from others who ask, "What psychopathology leads to violence?" or "Why are people involved in violent interactions in families?" Since the phrasing of a question always directs attention toward something and away from something else, the causes of "beating of wives" must perforce reside in "men." As Bograd goes on to write: "Feminists seek to understand why men in general use physical force against their partners and what functions this serves for a society in a given historical context." Bograd describes the four dimensions of analysis that are common to feminist perspectives on wife abuse: the explanatory utility of the constructs of gender and power, the analysis of the family as a historically situated social institution, the crucial importance of understanding and validating women's experiences, and the employment of scholarship for women.[7]

From the first of these analytic dimensions, wife assault is seen to be a systematic form of domination and social control of women by men. As Serran and Firestone recently asserted, "battered women have little reason to believe the criminal justice system will protect them. The law and patriarchal hierarchy have legitimized wife beating and control, resulting in unequal power relationships between men and women."[8]

This view has implications such as the following. All men can potentially use violence as a powerful means of subordinating women. Men as a class benefit from how women's lives are restricted because of their fear of violence. Wife abuse reinforces women's dependence and enables all men to exert authority and control. The reality of domination at the societal level is the most crucial factor contributing to, and maintaining, wife abuse at the individual level. In other words, the maintenance of patriarchy and patriarchal institutions is the main contributor to wife assault. Wife assault is mainly "normal" violence committed, not by madmen who are unlike other men, but by men who believe that patriarchy is their right, that marriage gives them unrestricted control over their wives, and that violence is an acceptable means of establishing this control.[9] The claim from a feminist analytical perspective, therefore, is twofold: that society is patriarchal and that the use of violence to maintain male patriarchy is accepted. This feminist argument indicates patriarchy as a direct cause of wife assault rather than an inducement that interacts with other causes. Hence the feminist distrust of psychological causes of male violence as potentially "exonerative" and the lack of empirical studies of possible interactive causes conducted within a feminist perspective.[10]

Thus stated, feminist theory renders implausible the notion of therapy for wife assaulters. If assaultive males are simply carrying out the prescriptions of the culture, it seems pointless to focus on individuals and expect them to change. Nor is there much point in trying to alter a pervasive societal phenomenon through therapy with a small group of highly selected individuals. Indeed, much feminist analysis argues that an emphasis on psychopathology in explaining wife assault is misguided because wife assault results from "normal psychological and behavioral patterns of most men" and that "trait theories tend to excuse the abusive man through reference to alcohol abuse or poor childhood histories."[11]

In contrast, I present evidence below that psychopathology and abusive histories are important in the background of abusive men (and women) but that these factors do not excuse behaviour. I shall insist that the same rules of analysis be applied to both sexes. Thus I do not accept that violence is justified from a woman as a member of an oppressed class, though it might be justifiable as self-defence by an individual victim of battering.

The result of the feminist analysis of wife assault has been the acknowledgement of the powerful and complex role of social factors in creating the context in which violence occurs. As Walker points out, feminist analysis puts research findings back into the context out of which they were lifted by scientific abstraction.[12] For example, as Rosewater has shown, MMPI scores on battered women were typically read out of context and misdiagnosed.[13] Post-event tests that indicated anger, anxiety, and confusion in response to battering were misinterpreted as indicating a pre-existing "personality problem" such as paranoia. Similarly, Dutton and Painter demonstrated how contextual features of battering promoted paradoxical attachments that made it difficult to leave a battering relationship and led to erroneous interpretations of battered women as masochistic.[14] Further, Browne and Williams

---

5.1 Bedrock beliefs in feminist theory

Certain "bedrock" beliefs about domestic violence have developed from feminist theory:

1 Domestic violence is used by men against women, and men are violent whenever they can get away with it.[1]
2 Women are never violent except in self-defence.[2]
3 Male violence will escalate if unchecked by criminal justice intervention.[3]
4 Males choose to be violent and have a gender-based need for power.[4]
5 The victims of intimate violence are overwhelmingly women.[5]
6 When a man is injured by a woman, she is acting in self-defence.[6]

NOTES: **1** M. Koss, L. Goodman, A. Browne, L.F. Fitzgerald, G.P. Keita, and N. Russo, *No Safe Haven: Male Violence against Women at Home, at Work, and in the Community* (Washington, DC: American Psychological Association, 1994).   **2** D.G. Saunders, "Wife abuse, husband abuse or mutual combat: A feminist perspective on the empirical findings," in K. Yllo and M. Bograd, eds., *Feminist Perspective on Wife Abuses* (Beverly Hills: Sage, 1988), 90-113.   **3** L.E. Walker and A. Browne, "Gender and victimization by intimates," *Journal of Personality* 53 (1985): 175-95.   **4** Ibid.   **5** P. Tjaden and N. Thoennes, *Prevalence, Incidence and Consequences of Violence against Women: Findings from the National Violence against Women Survey* (Washington, DC: US Department of Justice, 1998).   **6** L. Walker, "Psychology and violence against women," *American Psychologist* 44, 4 (1989): 695-702; Koss et al., *No Safe Haven*; P. Tjaden and N. Thoennes, *Prevalence, Incidence and Consequence of Violence against Women: Findings from the National Violence against Women Survey* (Washington, DC: US Department of Justice, 1998).

demonstrated how female-perpetrated homicide decreased when criminal justice system resources became more available to women in abusive relationships, a pattern that was distinct from that of male homicide.[15]

These beliefs have now been codified in law in several states, specifying how intervention with "batterers" must be treated for state certification to be maintained by treatment providers (at the time of writing forty-three states had family violence certification committees).[16] Since male violence is considered a choice, for example, any therapy is ruled out that addresses the perpetrator's psychological profile (differences in impulsivity, attachment style, substance abuse history, exposure to violence in the family of origin) or suggests that different subgroups of batterers may exist. (As we shall see below, there is considerable evidence for both assertions.) These laws have been drafted and codified by "commissions" made up of feminist activists, lawyers, and judges. The cause of domestic violence is now legally prescribed. In addition, several government surveys of "crime victimization of women" have been conducted, further emphasizing the claim that intimate violence is one-way. Interestingly, this "woman-as-victim" position seems an extreme version of feminism. Many feminists reject this view as bizarre and non-feminist.[17]

Government Incidence Surveys

As described in Chapter 3, several government surveys found higher rates of intimate partner abuse perpetration by males than by females. For example, in the US National Violence against Women Survey (NVAWS), Tjaden and Thoennes reported that women experience significantly more partner violence than men do.[18] The report indicates that, of 8,000 men and 8,000 women, 22.1 percent of women and 7.4 percent of men reported any physical assault by an intimate partner across the lifetime; 1.3 percent of women and 0.9 percent of men reported a physical assault by a partner in the previous twelve months. This 3:1 ratio of male-perpetrated to female-perpetrated violence is typical of government surveys that present themselves as surveys of "crime victimization of women," as the US NVAWS did.[19] This "crime toward women" filter acts to lower report rates by males who define victimization differently (after government programs have emphasized female victimization and named the survey accordingly). As we saw in Chapter 3 (see Figure 3.4), such surveys are insensitive, obtaining report rates far lower than those obtained by surveys of "conflict tactics" and by filtered male reports of "abuse victimization."

Gender Reporting Differences

Men are less likely to define themselves as victims, less likely to view an assault by a woman as a crime, and less likely to report victimization (either to a researcher or to the police) than women.[20] Straus and Gelles broke down violence rates by whether men or women did the reporting on the survey. The largest discrepancy is for males under twenty-five years who under-report violence by their wives compared to their wives' reports of their own violence. Husbands' reports of their own victimization are only 72 percent of wives' perpetration reports for all assaults. Conversely, husbands' perpetration reports for all assaults are 79 percent of wives' victimization reports.[21] If we assume that wives' perpetration reports may themselves be an under-representation, then men's victimization reports are a gross under-representation. (The alternative is to view the women's reports as an exaggeration of their own violence, which is unlikely, or as accurate accounts, in which case the men are still under-reporting.) For severe assaults, wives' own perpetration reports are 208 percent of husbands' victimization reports. These data suggest that men grossly under-report both perpetration and victimization by severe violence.

Like most crime surveys, the government surveys reviewed above may have implicitly affected the response by emphasizing "personal safety," "violence," and "criminal victimization." In government surveys, the sex of the interviewer is not always specified, although it too could influence reporting. Where specified, the interviewer is usually female. Moreover, Archer noted the NVAWS was presented to respondents as "a survey of violence toward women, thus giving the message that men's victimization was not a concern."[22] The NVAWS, Home Office, and the Statistics Canada government surveys described above either present the survey as a "crime victim survey," a perceptions of crime survey (Canada), or, worse, rely on police data that are then cited as evidence for a greater incidence of violence against women.[23] (Since Stets and Straus found that women are ten times as likely as are men to report assault victimization to the police, police data are problematic.) The reporting biases of the original Uniform Crime Reports are repeated, despite the methodological improvements Straus and colleagues made in developing and using the CTS and in collecting data about conflict resolution tactics from representative samples.[24] These methodological biases limit the reporting of intimate violence rates by both women and men, but especially by men.[25]

What can we conclude from these crime victimization surveys? First, despite the filters that operate to reduce male victimization reporting, substantial numbers of men do report being victims of both minor and severe violence. As we shall see in the next chapter, women tend to be more violent than men and to get injured slightly more.[26] As we shall also see, this edge in female perpetration over male perpetration becomes more pronounced in younger samples.

Cross-Cultural Studies of Patriarchy and Violence

Feminist analysis implies greater violence directed toward women in intensely patriarchal cultures. Campbell reports that "there is not a simple linear correlation between female status and rates of wife assault."[27] Female status is not a single variable. For example, "spousal violence" rates for Mexican and American white populations from a study by Sorenson and Taylor indicate that, although Mexican culture is more patriarchal, spousal assault rates are lower.[28] Rates of spousal assault by American-born Hispanics are higher than for American-born non-Hispanic whites, but this may reflect both stress and acculturation.

Levinson found family-related female status (economic, decision-making, and divorce restrictions) to be more predictive of wife beating than societal level variables (control of premarital sexual behaviour, place of residence, property inheritance).[29] The exception to this finding was female economic work groups, whose presence correlated negatively with wife assault incidence. Campbell also points out that the notion that male sexual jealousy is an expression of a cultural norm, that women are male property, is not supported by cross-cultural studies of jealousy and wife assault.[30] Except in extreme cases, jealousy varies widely between cultures and appears unrelated to variations in wife assault incidence.

Archer has completed the most extensive study ever done on cross-cultural rates of domestic violence, examining the relationship of women's sociopolitical power to wife assault (relative to husband assault) rates in fifty-one countries.[31] The former was measured by what Archer called the Gender Empowerment Index (GEM), measuring the extent to which traditional patriarchal values are lessened in a nation, and a Gender-related Development Index (GDI,) reflecting equality in access to health care, education, and knowledge. Archer also examined cross-national studies of attitudes to wife beating. Much of the data came from the World Health Organization (WHO).[32] The study found that women's victimization was inversely related to gender empowerment for three periods – the previous year, a current relationship, and throughout adult life. Countries with low gender empowerment of women and general acceptance of wife assault had relatively high rates of victimization of women. The highest overall victimization rates were in Muslim countries (e.g., Turkey, Egypt, Pakistan), Hindu countries (India, Bangladesh), and Catholic countries (especially in Central America). North American and Western European countries had the highest empowerment of women and the lowest overall victimization rates. The highest lifetime rates of victimization of women were found in Papua New Guinea, Sri Lanka, Chile, Japan, Nicaragua, and Costa Rica. The lowest lifetime rates were in Norway and Finland. One critical point that must be raised is that Archer depended on WHO data for the country studies, but data collection efficacy varies by country. Random-digit dialing does not work well in countries with few phones (or for that matter, in countries where everyone has unlisted cell phones). In general, we might expect better data collection methods in countries with better communication systems. These countries might also be ones that have been more progressive with respect to women's roles.

Archer concluded that the best theoretical explanation of the relationship between women's power and victimization was "social role theory."[33] This theory is based on the premise that sex differences in social behaviour are not innate but, rather, reflect different social roles, such as that of homemaker or of outside worker. Expectancies associated with the role of outside worker include "agency" (acting outwardly against demands), instrumental traits, and direct aggression. Eagly and Steffen used social role theory to explain sex differences in aggression but Archer discovered that it also accounted for societal differences in intimate violence.[34] In societies where women are

5.2 The meaning of violence

Can male intimate violence and female intimate violence ever be compared through "hit counts?" Psychologist Angela Browne argues that equating the two is like equating head-on collisions with fender-benders.[1] When a larger and stronger man uses violence that is potentially injurious against a woman, its function and consequences will be different than when a smaller women uses violence against a man. So it makes little sense to count hits by gender. In this sense the gender paradigm is overblown.

In contrast, I argue that to understand we must look at motivation and not consequences. If the perpetrator knows the potential consequences of the violence, these become part of his motivation in being violent – part of what is called the function of violence. But if the consequences are not foreseen, or if the perpetrator is too physiologically aroused or dissociated to care about consequences, then they may not be part of his motivation. To a certain extent, this is the difference between instrumental and impulsive violence.

Furthermore, while men have 40 percent more upper body strength than women, they have less of an advantage in lower body strength. Violence in the form of kicking or using a knife or gun can be equally injurious regardless of the gender of the perpetrator. In examining the prevalence of specific acts on the NVAWS (see Chapter 2), Morse reported that "severe violence" acts by females (14 percent) were more frequent than by males (6 percent).[2] Of those acts reported, "kicking/biting/hitting with fist" by females was about double the male rate. Threatening with a knife or gun was done by 1.8 percent of females and 0.7 percent of males (see also Figure 7.1).

Being bigger is meaningless unless someone is willing to use force. Some men will simply "not hit a women" even when hit themselves. This is a norm in western culture that Archer describes.[3] Finally Pimlott-Kubiak and Cortina showed that the amount of exposure to trauma and not gender determines long-term negative psychological effects in both males and females.[4]

NOTES: 1 A. Browne, "Violence against women by male partners," *American Psychologist* 48, 10 (1992): 1077-97.   2 B. Morse, "Beyond the Conflict Tactics Scale: Gender differences in partner violence," *Violence and Victims* 19, 4 (1995): 251-72.   3 J. Archer, "Sex differences in aggression between heterosexual partners: A meta-analytic review," *Psychological Bulletin* 126, 5 (2000): 651-80.   4 S. Pimlott-Kubiak and L.M. Cortina, "Gender, victimization, and outcomes: Reconceptualizing risk," *Journal of Consulting and Clinical Psychology* 71, 3 (2003): 528-39.

empowered, they work outside the home more and are less subject to narrow expectations about "female" behaviour. However, they become more like "males" in that their use of direct aggression increases as their victimization decreases. Ironically, one of the weaknesses of the feminist model as applied to North America comes from its strength cross-culturally; it just cannot account for the high rates of intimate violence perpetrated by women in North America.[35] Social role theory, however, may provide the explanation: as women in North America have become agents in the work world, their violence rates have increased. We will explore this issue in the next chapter.

However, some research by Follingstad and her colleagues, presented below, indicates that some acts performed by a man against a woman are perceived as more injurious and abusive than are the same acts performed by a woman against a man. They include psychological abuse and controlling behaviours.

Feminist activists have had a powerful effect on social policy in North America. Criminal justice intervention is much more aggressive than it was in the early 1970s. Feminists have also influenced court-mandated handling of arrested perpetrators. Eschewing psychological explanations for wife assault, feminists have opted instead for "interventions" based on a "psycho-educational model" developed in Duluth, Minnesota.[36]

The initial effect of the feminist paradigm in practice was to focus so exclusively on male intimate violence that female violence was overlooked entirely; not denied, just never discussed. Corvo and Johnson outline the bedrock view of feminist thought: "that battering (by males) is NEVER provoked, hereditary, out of control, accidental, an isolated incident. It is not caused by disease, diminished intellect, alcoholism/addiction, mental illness or any external person or event. It is a means for men to systematically dominate, disempower, control and devalue women ... It is greater than an individual act, it supports the larger goal of oppression of women."[37]

It is enlightening to contrast this view of male abusers, which allows no "excuses" (some would call them risk factors) for their violence, with studies of female perpetrators, reviewed later. The latter initially seek explanations of the woman's behavior from environmental causes, the very ones denied to men, and including, as a first explanation, the perspective that her violence must have been "self-defensive."[38]

Strange Bedfellows: Feminism and Sociobiology

Sociobiologists have extended Charles Darwin's notion that physical characteristics and behaviours of species develop over time through the process of natural selection.[39] Characteristics and behaviours that enable a species to function in a specific environment are maintained and gradually evolve to enable the species to survive. In more recent years, the evolutionary point of view has been extended to account for the social behaviour of animals and humans.[40]

In extending evolutionary ideas to human social behaviour, sociobiologists attempt to account for cooperation, competition, and aggression from the standpoint that each behaviour has an evolutionary function; that is, it maximizes the likelihood that individuals who demonstrate the behaviour will survive, as will their offspring, maximizing their contribution to the gene pool.[41]

In making their argument, sociobiologists tend to focus on social behaviour that is common to humankind across all cultures (rather than on cultural variations, as do anthropologists). They regard these common types of social behaviour as part of an evolutionary heritage. So, for example, groups and individuals who developed aggression in early hunting cultures would be more likely to compete successfully for territory and mates, thus maximizing the survival of themselves and their offspring.

Sociobiological theory comes in for strong attack by most social scientists, who claim that it underestimates the impact of sociocultural factors on contemporary social behaviour and overestimates the biological or inherited aspect of such behaviour.[42] It is not necessary to get into the current controversy, however, in order to raise a question that is difficult for sociobiologists to answer: How does one explain domestic violence and, in particular, the killing of one's spouse? It seems a less-than-optimal way to "increase one's contribution to the gene pool"; in fact, it seems evolutionarily unsound, and yet it has occurred with alarming frequency since the beginnings of recorded history.[43]

Even Wilson concedes that the evolution of aggression has been jointly guided by three forces: (1) the genetic predisposition toward learning some form of aggression, (2) the necessities imposed by the environment in which a society finds itself, and (3) the previous history of a group that inclines it toward adopting one cultural innovation over another.

Wilson views humans as disposed (1) to respond with "an unreasoning hatred to external threat" and (2) to escalate hostility sufficiently to overwhelm the source of threat by a wide margin of safety. If we apply this analysis to cases of sexual threat, it seems the sociobiologists would predict an inherited predisposition of aggression against invading males, but there is nothing in the sociobiological argument to account for jealousy based on sexual threat resulting in violence toward the intimate partner. Simeons, for example, argues that men have a genetic predisposition to react with rage to sexual threat.[44] However, the stimuli that constitute "sexual threat" are often socially determined, as we shall see, and the emotional response to such stimuli, while most certainly a form of physiological arousal, is itself often labelled (as rage, hurt, anxiety, etc.) in ways that vary across cultures.

Finally, the behaviour that follows from the emotion is again directed by what the culture deems more or less acceptable. Indeed, most recently, sociobiological writers on the evolution of human sexuality have argued that human behaviour (with the exception of simple motor patterns) "is too variable and too far from the genes."[45] Indeed, Symons states: "I imagine that many psychological systems are involved (in uxoricide) – emotional goals, cognitive abilities to appreciate the relations between various events (real and imagined), and goals, anger, and the like."[46] I think the strongest statement that can be made on sociobiological grounds is that men have an inherited tendency to secrete adrenalin when they believe themselves to be sexually threatened and that they will experience this state as emotionally arousing. The label applied to this arousal, however, will be socially determined, and the tendency to label this arousal as anger, the behavioural response of acting out anger aggressively, and the choice of a target for aggression, are all shaped by societal values and learned dispositions.

The above arguments notwithstanding, a major empirical work on intimate violence has been produced from a sociobiological perspective: *Homicide* by Daly and Wilson.[47] This book argues that intimate homicides follow patterns that are uninterpretable without the aid of a sociobiological perspective. The book does provide an impressive array of statistics. For example, Daly and Wilson examine 212 homicides in Detroit categorized by motive (in 164 homicides a male killed a male, in nineteen a male killed a female, in eighteen a female killed a male, and in eleven a female killed a female).[48] A sociobiological perspective argues, for example, that males would be far more likely to experience extreme sexual jealousy: they have no guarantee of paternity in the way a female has a guarantee of maternity. Hence, jealousy as a motive for homicide should be more frequent with male perpetrators. The Detroit data found that 13.6 percent (25/183) of male homicides were jealousy-driven. By comparison, they found that 31 percent (9/29) of female homicides were jealousy-driven. A comparable study in Canada found that 24 percent (195/812) of male and 7.6 percent (19/248) of female homicides were jealousy-driven.

Daly and Wilson view these data as supporting their claim that males are far more likely than females to experience extreme sexual jealousy. To me, the data say something else. They say that the relationship between gender, jealousy, and homicide varies considerably in different races and cultures. The Detroit homicides are largely black, the Canadian mainly white. The jealousy-driven rate for the female homicides in Detroit is four times that of the Canadian rate, while the male rate for Detroit is little more than half the Canadian rate (the reason being that a much larger number of homicides in Detroit fall into other categories). These data are not inconsistent with Darnell Hawkins' study of homicide among African-Americans.[49] What this exemplifies to me is the inability of sociobiological explanations to account for cultural variability. In fact, Daly and Wilson don't even attempt to account for it. Instead, they talk about "male proprietariness" and argue that cross-cultural studies show "no exceptions to this dreary record of connubial coercion" – even though their own reported data suggest the contrary.[50]

From a sociobiological perspective, jealousy motives should influence the homicide rates of various age categories as well. For example, so-called "May-December" (younger woman-older man) relationships should be at higher risk because of greater jealousy. Daly and Wilson cite statistics that show that marriages with high age disparities have four times the risk of marriages with a small (two-year gap).[51] The highest risk for homicide victimization is for wives ten or more years younger than their husbands.

As Daly and Wilson themselves admit, there are alternative interpretations for these data. One alternative that they do not include is this: that identity issues are bound up with intimacy in relationships in a way that is naturally confounded with what sociobiologists call kinship; the closer the person, the more our personal identity is founded upon our relationship with them. Hence, if our identity is unstable and the relationship is troubled, the greater may be the risk of anger and violence. Older men (Decembers) have more to lose in the potential loss of a younger female partner (Mays). They may perceive themselves as too old to replace her; their vulnerability is greater. Hence, it is my argument that this data provided by sociobiologists does not prove what is claimed. It may not be kinship or zealous protection of the gene pool that drives rage; it may be an aspect of threatened loss of identity that is heightened when intimacy is imperilled. Older men may kill younger women because they have more at stake through the loss of the relationship. Among the cases of jealousy-precipitated homicides in Detroit cited by Daly and Wilson as evidence for their sociobiological position are two cases of homosexuals killed by lovers for alleged infidelity.[52] Can protection of genetic fitness be a motive for homosexual men? I think not. Sociobiology ignores phenomena that it cannot explain, such as homosexuality.

Buss laid out the sociobiological case for abuse (which he assumed was exclusively male to female).[53] It is about "coercive control," which culminates in jealousy. Although Buss speculates that although "the abuser may be seeking an increased commitment and investment" (through fear, one supposes), "the tactic may backfire and produce a defection instead." Peters et al. hypothesized that, from an evolutionary perspective, since spouse abuse is control over female sexuality, abuse rates should vary with the woman's age.[54] Younger women should be most at risk. In a study of almost four thousand cases this is just what the authors found. The trouble is that all impulsive crimes of violence peak during early years (the perpetrator's most common age was thirty-five, the victim's thirty-two). Even if the perpetrator is older, aren't younger women a socialized sexual ideal? (One that changes with fashion: but do sociobiologists examine changes in age risk as that fashion changes?) Even if one could prove sexual jealousy, does this occur for reproductive reasons? Or is sex a highly personal act that symbolizes attachment and love, apart from being inherently pleasurable. If reproduction is so paramount a motive, why do most men have such small families? Why has the birth rate in North American dipped below two children per male, when the sociobiological possibilities are suggested by rhythm and blues singer Screamin' Jay Hawkins, who is said to have fathered seventy-five children with numerous women.[55]

In 1992, sociobiology and feminism attempted a détente, in the form of a jointly authored paper by the major advocates of the feminist position (Dobash and Dobash) and the sociobiological position (Wilson and Daly).[56] What was it that united these philosophically different positions? After all, sociobiology essentially argues that wife assault is a dysfunctional extension of an inherited propensity for mate retention in order to maximize contribution to the gene pool. Feminism accepts no such historical-genetic mandate and sees male coercion as a primary motive of the wish to dominate females. What they have in common is a shared belief that males are more violent than females and a common enemy: the incidence surveys using the Conflict Tactics Scale.[57] Dobash et al. critiqued the CTS as representing "currently fashionable claims" and as having problems with interpretation, since almost any category on the CTS could contain acts that varied in severity. They picked an example where a woman playfully kicked at her spouse and pointed out that it would be a severe act on the CTS and qualify as a battered-husband item. However, the CTS, like any broad-based instrument, of necessity reduces data.

Dobash et al. criticized all studies using the CTS as misrepresenting intimate violence. One source of criticism is that males and females within couples do not agree on the amount of violence used. The implication is that males are under-reporting their use of violence. However, Morse showed that both sexes tend to over-report minor acts they commit, under-report serious acts they commit, and over-report serious acts they suffer.[58] In surveys using representative community samples, the same results are obtained for the relative frequency of male and female violence regardless of whether the respondent is male or female. The supposed lack of agreement is a non-issue.[59]

The ultimate criterion that Dobash et al. use for the survey data is that the "meagre case descriptions do not resemble those of battered wives and battering husbands."[60] In other words, the community sample does not resemble the extreme clinical samples upon which they have based their paradigm. From this perspective, the authors dismiss the representative samples and accuse the CTS of "inaccuracies and misrepresentations" based on their own non-representative samples and their subjective perceptions. Kahneman et al. call this the "representativeness heuristic," i.e., when people hold incorrect personal notions (stereotypes) that underestimate selective bias, the baseline incidence of characteristics, and so on, leading to erroneous social judgments.[61] Dobash et al. continue to stereotype men despite data on heterogeneity of male attitudes to women, violence use, and marital power.[62]

Dobash et al. complained that no "conceptual framework for understanding why women and men should think and act alike" exists.[63] But in fact such a framework does exist and will be reviewed below.[64] The psychological literature clearly demonstrates how intimacy produces emotional states such as anxiety and anger that are abusogenic, especially in persons with Axis II personality disorders. This occurs regardless of gender.[65] Males and females with identity disorders of a borderline variety think and feel differently than normal in intimate relationships. The framework is psychological and involves issues such as attachment, trauma reactions, and intimacy issues. Substantial literatures exist on each of these topics, and their empirical relationship to intimate abusiveness has been established.[66]

The shotgun marriage of feminism and sociobiology was based on nothing more than a futile attack on the methodology of a common enemy. The two perspectives remain philosophically at odds and equal only in their inability to explain domestic violence.

6 The Gender Debate and the Feminist Paradigm

Most research in domestic violence journals relied on samples of women drawn from shelter houses and men from batterer-treatment groups. As a result of sample selection and of the prevailing ideology of feminism, the notion evolved that spouse assault was exclusively male-perpetrated or that female intimate violence, to the extent that it existed at all, was defensive or inconsequential.

Subsequent research using community samples and showing equivalent rates of serious female violence has been greeted with skepticism, especially by the activist-research community.[1] Data surveys were dismissed as missing the "context" of IPV (i.e., the power relations of the perpetrator and victim and the motives for the use of violence), especially by feminist researchers who were committed to the view that intimate violence was the by-product of patriarchy and hence an exclusively male activity.[2] The initial dogma persevered despite data to the contrary.

This type of error in social judgment is demonstrated in research studies by social psychologists such as Kahneman, Slovic, Tversky, Janis, Lord, Ross, and Lepper that show the "confirmatory bias" (also called "biased assimilation") and "belief perseverance" that occurs when research subjects have a strongly held belief and are exposed to research findings inconsistent with the belief.[3] The subjects reconcile the contradiction by discounting the research methodology, but they do not apply the same rigorous standards to research whose findings confirm their belief. Kahneman et al. describe the tendency of humans to make premature causal judgments, often based on unconscious biases in human inference. Personal experience is an especially erroneous basis for making social judgment as we tend to give too much weight to single, salient experiences and to discount evidence contrary to the "confirmatory bias" we have established. Lord et al. show how contradictory data sets are systemically discounted. Janis demonstrated how social groups evolve a social reality called "groupthink," where group ideology is protected by and sustains itself through rationalizations for discounting contradictory data. A conjunction of the social psychological phenomena of groupthink and belief perseverance appears to account for the "paradigm" (or "worldview") and ensuing urban myth surrounding domestic violence found in academic journals specifically focused on domestic violence.

Lord et al. and Janis focused on "lay judgments" not on academic studies. The notions of scientific objectivity and falsifiable hypotheses act, at least in principle, against the formation of "groupthink" or, as it is sometimes called, a "social reality." However, social scientists frequently become aligned with contemporary notions of social justice and attempt to fit their enterprise to the objectives of achieving social change. In so doing, they increase the risk of straying from objective reporting of data. In domestic violence research, the sense that the greater good of women's rights and the protection of women should prevail over questions of scientific accuracy has directed the investigations, the data reported, and the interpretations of the data. In concert with value-laden theories, the focus of attention on male violence has deflected study and recognition from female violence. In effect, a "paradigm" has developed in the domestic violence literature in which perpetrators are viewed as exclusively or disproportionately male.[4] Any and all data inconsistent with this view are dismissed, ignored, or explained away. In some cases data are simplified, altered, or distorted to make them more consistent with the theoretical position. Gelles and Straus called this the "woozle effect" (see Figure 2.3).[5]

The function of the gender paradigm originally was to generate social change in a direction that righted an imbalance against women.[6] The result, however, has been to misdirect social and legal policy, to misinform custody assessors, police, and judges, to disregard data sets contradictory to the prevailing theory, and to misdirect attempts at therapeutic change for perpetrators.[7]

The Radical Feminist Paradigm

In an earlier paper, Dutton described feminist theory as being a "paradigm," roughly translated as a set of guiding assumptions, or worldview, commonly shared within a group and serving to ward off recognition of data that are dissonant with the paradigm's central tenets.[8] This theory views all social relations through the prism of gender relations and holds, in its neo-Marxist view, that men (the bourgeoisie) hold power advantages over women (the proletariat) in patriarchal societies and that all domestic violence is either male physical abuse to maintain that power advantage or female defensive violence, used for self-protection. When women are instigators, in this view, it is a "pre-emptive strike," aimed at inducing the inevitable male attack, perhaps in order to get it over with rather than to be caught by surprise. All blame for violence falls on the male.

The feminist paradigm supports the notion that domestic violence is primarily a culturally supported male enterprise and that female violence is always defensive and reactive. In contrast, male violence is not similarly contextualized and is always attributed to a broader social agenda. As a result of this perspective, feminists tend to generalize about violent men and about men in general and to ignore female pathology. As Dobash and Dobash put it: "Men who assault their wives are actually living up to cultural prescriptions that are cherished in Western society – aggressiveness, male dominance and female subordination – and they are using physical force as a means to enforce that dominance."[9] Bograd defined feminist researchers as asking the fundamental question "Why do men beat their wives ... Feminists seek to understand why men in general use physical force against their partners and what functions this serves in a given historical context."[10] In fact, the data demonstrate that while feminists are accurate in raising awareness about the incidence of IPV, the reality is that most often both parties engage in aggression – indicating the need for interventions different from the traditional ones. Feminism favours strong arrest policies and "intervention" rather than treatment (since treatment implies that society is less to blame).[11] Yet it is not clear how men can be held individually responsible by feminism when patriarchy is to blame, nor how feminists account for differences in male populations in regard to attitudes toward and acceptance of violence.

Disconfirming research data appear to have had little impact on supporters of this perspective over the past two decades. For instance, speaking of intimate partner homicide, Serran and Firestone recently asserted that we live in "a society where almost every major institute accepts or ignores the problems of gender inequality ... The law and the patriarchal hierarchy have legitimized wife beating and control, resulting in unequal power relationships between men and women."[12] In fact, considerable evidence suggests that there are strong social prohibitions inhibiting men from aggression against women, legal sanctions against men who do transgress, and fewer social prohibitions inhibiting women from aggression against men.[13] These legal and social policies, well intended though they might be, are based on erroneous information about both the causes and the incidence of most intimate violence. They have evolved based on the need of the small – though significant – minority of women who experience extreme and often chronic "wife battering." They do little to serve the much larger majority of men, women, and children coping with the more frequently encountered "common couple abuse."[14]

Several data sources exist that are problematic for a feminist view.

Direct Tests of Patriarchy

Some direct empirical tests of patriarchal norms on assaultiveness have been reported in the literature. Yllo and Straus attempted a quantitative analysis of the relationship between patriarchy and wife assault by assessing the latter with the Conflict Tactics Scale, and the former with American state-by-state economic, educational, political, and legal indicators of the structural inequality of women.[15] A composite Status of Women Index resulted, with Alaska having the highest status (70) and Louisiana and Alabama the lowest (28). An ideological component of patriarchy was also assessed: the degree to which state residents believed that husbands should be dominant in family decision-making (patriarchal norms).

A curvilinear (U-shaped) relationship was found between structural indicators and wife assault rates, with the lowest- and highest-status-of-women states having the highest rates of severe wife assault. Structural indicators and patriarchal norms had a correlation of near zero. Patriarchal norms were related to wife assault in that states with the most (and least) male-dominant norms had double the wife assault rate of states with the most egalitarian norms.

Yllo and Straus attempt to explain why there is a relationship between patriarchal norms and wife assault in states where the status of women is highest. They say this is due to an inconsistency between a woman's sociopolitical status and her "in family" status. The structural changes came initially while family patriarchal norms lagged behind, thus generating conflict.[16] However, no independent evidence to support this explanation is presented.

This explanation immediately faces the contrary question about why low-status states have high rates of wife assault. The authors attempt to explain this as due to "greater force being necessary to keep women 'in their place' and because women in these states have fewer alternatives to violent marriage."[17] In low-status states women are more likely to be trapped in abusive marriages, whereas in high-status states women feel free to violate the patriarchal norms of marriage. In other words, men will use violence against women when they can (in low-status states) and when they can't (in high-status states).

This explanation is confusing and contradictory. Trapping women in marriage through lessened opportunity should produce higher violence frequency scores within couples but not necessarily higher incidence scores. That is, it accounts for why women could not leave an abusive marriage but still does not supply a motive for male violence. The assumption that men will use

6.1 Woozle alert! What's an attitude?

There have been some strange attempts to compel the data to show that attitudes cause intimate partner violence. Hanson et al. administered questionnaires to 780 men from a forensic out-patient clinic and 217 men from a community-based employment centre, assessing personal history, criminal behaviour and "attitudes towards violence."[1] The sample was divided into 184 non-abusive men (based on self-report), 517 moderately abusive, and 296 severely abusive. The authors then did linear comparisons on fifty-three variables in order to find which ones differed significantly between groups. They concluded: "The single strongest group difference concerned attitudes tolerant of wife assault. Most (68 percent) of the severely abusive men endorsed one or more of the items on the scale, whereas only 22 percent of the non-abusive men endorsed any items."

This finding is undermined by the variable called "attitudes tolerant of wife assault," which was measured as follows: "An unfaithful wife deserves to be hit," "I might slap my wife to make her listen," "I could slap my wife to stop her being hysterical," "I might slap my wife if she made me really angry." These attitude measures are worded as predictions of a likelihood of violence: "I might slap my wife if ..." When "severely abusive" men endorse these statements they are not indicating their tolerance of abuse; they are merely predicting the likelihood of their own behaviour. These men indicated with some accuracy how they might react. Therapists usually want their clients to have this ability to see themselves as high-risk in certain situations so they can learn to be more vigilant in those situations.

A more general flaw is that the study turned into a fishing expedition. If one does a large number of linear comparisons between groups, some comparisons will be different by chance alone. To prevent this misinterpretation of chance, a statistician named Bonferroni invented a technique that divides the alpha level (the size needed for differences to be significant) by the number of comparisons made. Hence, when ten comparisons are made, .05 is no longer acceptable; the alpha level would then have to be .005. This procedure is called "Bonferroni-ing the alpha." Without it, researchers desperate to find a significant difference could just do unlimited comparisons of independent variables. In effect, that was just what Hanson et al. did.

NOTE: **1** K. Hanson, O. Cadsky, A. Harris, and C. Lalonde, "Correlates of battering among 997 men: Family history, adjustment and attitudinal differences," *Violence and Victims* 12, 3 (1997): 191-208.

violence when they can would lead to the prediction that most men in such social circumstances would be violent. This assumption is not supported by surveys that show the majority of males to be non-violent, even in low-status states.[18]

The explanation for high-status states is stronger. Here male violence is generated through a threat to informal patriarchal norms. The finding that structural inequality and patriarchal norms are not associated with male violence is not explored, although it raises another problem for patriarchal explanations of wife assault: namely that macrosystem (cultural) patriarchy is unrelated to microsystem (familial) patriarchy.

Smith also conducted a test of patriarchy by asking 604 Toronto women to guess their male partner's response to a series of questions about "patriarchal beliefs" and then correlating these responses with socioeconomic factors and, finally, with that woman's responses to the Conflict Tactics Scale measure of "wife assault."[19] Through this method, Smith claimed he was assessing "patriarchal ideology" and that this measure, in combination with sociodemographic factors, could predict wife assault. However, the responses that these women supplied for their male partners described a very non-patriarchal group, with the majority disagreeing with the patriarchal statements of the measure in all cases save one, that "sometimes it's important for a man to show his partner that he's the head of the house." Of course, using the modifier "sometimes" can usually increase agreement rates. One conclusion that could be drawn from Smith's attitudinal data is that the patriarchal structure of North American society has a weak effect on the "patriarchal ideology" of most men. Smith does not draw this conclusion. As Smith puts it: "When all the socioeconomic risk markers and indexes of patriarchal ideology were combined in a single model assessing the extent to which these variables predicted wife beating, the combination of husband's educational attainment, patriarchal beliefs and patriarchal attitudes parsimoniously explained 20 percent of the variance in wife beating."[20] In other words, he piggybacked the weak "patriarchal attitude data" onto other variables to make the case.

It seems to me that such a claim clearly accentuates the paradigmatic aspect of current family violence research. A predictive study by Dutton and Starzomski using women's CTS self-reports on husband violence found that brief (sixteen-item) assessments of the husbands' anger and identity problems explained 50 percent of the variance in psychological abuse and 20 percent of wife assault reported by one sample of battered wives.[21] In other words, some psychological factors have much greater predictive weight than the attitudinal and sociodemographic assessments of "patriarchal ideology" reported by Smith. Only someone working within a paradigm could find the explanation of 20 percent of the variance conclusive. In fact, no correlational study can prove that attitudes "cause" behaviour. Social psychologists have known for years that people update their attitudes to conform to recent, relevant behaviour.[22] Hence, after-the-fact measures of attitudes may be reactions to abuse, not causes.

Is Wife Assault Considered Acceptable?

Dobash and Dobash argued that wife assault was accepted in North American society, yet never offered evidence for the assertion.[23] Social acceptance of intimate violence can be measured by survey. A survey by Stark and McEvoy found that 25 percent of men and 17 percent of women approved of a man slapping his wife "under appropriate circumstances."[24]

This finding, however, hardly seems to prove a cultural norm for the use of violence against wives. First of all, only a minority of men or women approved a man slapping his wife under any circumstances. Viewed from another perspective, the survey result tells us that the large majority believe slapping is never appropriate. Second, the wording of the question was ambiguous. The phrase "appropriate circumstances" loads the question and we do not know what egregious transgressions may be conjured up by respondents as necessary before a slap is appropriate. Finally, the question tells us nothing about the degree of violence that is acceptable. While 25 percent of men may approve of slapping a wife, fewer may approve of punching or kicking a wife, and still fewer may approve of beating or battering a wife.

A more recent study of attitudes toward family violence indicates even less acceptance of men hitting women, although some acceptance was found for women hitting men. Simon et al. collected data from a nationally representative sample of 5,238 adults in the United States.[25] Although the authors concluded, based on a multiple regression analysis, that acceptance of interpersonal violence was higher among participants who were male and younger than thirty-five, were non-white, were divorced, separated, or had never been married, in fact acceptance rates were low in all samples (see Figure 6.2). Apart from reinforcing the finding that the majority of respondents do not approve of intimate violence, the Simon et al. study also underscores the importance of stating the context in the survey question, something that was missing in the Stark and McEvoy study. It also strongly refutes the feminist claim that society accepts violence towards women (see Dobash and Dobash).[26] An overwhelmingly high percentage of both males and females do not accept violence toward women under any circumstances,[27] and only two percent of men approve of hitting a woman "to keep her in line." The myth of acceptance of violence described by Dobash and Dobash turns out to have been just that: a myth.

Does the Criminal Justice System Condone Violence toward Women?

The reluctance of the criminal justice system to prosecute wife assault has also been offered as proof of patriarchal acceptance of violence toward women. However, Shotland and Straw performed a "bystander intervention"

6.2 Attitudes toward use of intimate violence

	Percentage agreeing with statement	
	Men	Women
Ok for a man to hit his wife/girlfriend:		
If she hits him first	9.8	7.2
To keep her in line	2.0	1.8
Ok for woman to hit her husband/boyfriend:		
If he hits her first	33.0	27.0
To keep him in line	5.0	4.4

SOURCE: Adapted from T.R. Simon, M. Anderson, M.P. Thompson, A.E. Crosby, G. Shelley, and J.J. Sacks, "Attitudinal acceptance of intimate partner violence among US adults," *Violence and Victims* 16, 2 (2001): 115-26.

study in which a man verbally abused and physically threatened a woman in order to investigate both third-party perceptions of this event and their behavioural likelihood of intervening.[28] Shotland and Straw had one male and one female actor engage in a verbal altercation in an elevator whose door opened across the hall from where experimental subjects awaited another study. In one experimental condition the woman yelled "Get away from me. I don't know you!" in another "Get away from me. I don't know why I married you!" In all other respects the conditions were the same, with moderately high levels of verbal abuse and low levels of physical conflict. Subjects who witnessed the fight between "strangers" took intervening actions 69 percent of the time, while those who believed the couple was married did so only 19 percent of the time.

Subsequent examination of the beliefs and perceptions of third-party witnesses to a film of a man-woman fight revealed that when the couple was believed to be married (as opposed to strangers), onlookers believed the woman to be in less danger, and less likely to want their help, though the man was perceived as more likely to stay and fight. In other words, an entire constellation of perceptions about the seriousness of the violence and the costs of personal intervention altered with the belief that the couple were intimates. Some of these perceptions may be erroneous (such as the belief that the violence is less), and some may be rationalizations of personal inaction, but the complex alteration of perception does not show mere "tacit approval of wife assault."

What is required to clarify this issue is a systematic extension of the Shotland and Straw study that varies the degree of violence and the social relationship between the third party and the couple in conflict. Some complex issues affect intervention decisions, and when professional objectives (such as arrest and conviction for police officers) are added, it becomes difficult to deduce approval for wife assault from intervention decisions alone. Some have argued that the criminal justice system is helpful to women victims but not to male victims. Stets and Straus found women to be ten times more likely than men to call police in response to a partner-initiated assault. Brown found huge discrepancies in arrest and prosecution of spousal assault as a function of gender.[29] Women were four times more likely to report partner violence to police (81 percent vs. 19 percent) and more likely to have the police arrest when reporting (75 percent vs. 60 percent) than were men reporting an assault by a woman. The higher arrest rate of men occurs despite injuries to male victims. When men are injured, female perpetrators are arrested only 60.2 percent of the time, compared to 91.1 percent of cases involving the reverse situation. A combination of men's unwillingness to report and police unwillingness to arrest female perpetrators means that only 2 percent of female perpetrators are arrested.[30] When no one was injured, men were sixteen times more likely to be charged than women.[31] This is not because male injuries are always less serious. Buzawa, Bannon, Austin, and Jackson, in a study of the police arrest policy in Detroit, found that "male victims reported three times the rate of serious injury as their female counterparts, 38 percent compared to 14 percent."[32] Hence, government surveys of intimate violence estimates based on crime report data (police arrest, etc.) appear to underestimate male victimization.

Back to the CTS

As described in Chapter 3, the Straus studies using the Conflict Tactics Scale (CTS), which focus on conflict rather than on crime victimization, obtain a fuller estimate of actual violence.[33] In the conflict surveys by Straus and his colleagues, annual assault rates reported are about sixteen times higher than those in the US National Violence against Women Survey. Mihalic and Elliott found that phrasing questions about partner assaults in the context of "criminal assaults" reduced reporting of serious partner assaults by 83 percent compared to phrasing questions about relationships.[34] Conclusion: the CTS/CTS-2, which Dobash et al. malign, is a far more sensitive measure of intimate violence than any government surveys predicated on crime victimization.[35] Straus has demonstrated that the CTS generates a violence report rate about sixteen times greater than crime survey questions (see Chapter 1).[36]

But Do Males and Females Report Differently on the CTS?

Dobash et al. criticize all studies using the CTS as misrepresenting intimate violence.[37] One source of criticism is that males and females within couples do not agree on the amount of violence used. The implication is that males are under-reporting their use of violence and women always tell the truth. As described earlier, in Chapter 5, in comparison with women, men tend to under-report both victimization and perpetration.[38]

However, whether violence rates are based on either male or female reports, intimate violence by women toward non-violent male partners is more common than violence by men toward non-violent female partners.[39]

Is Female Violence Self-Defensive?

Walker and Saunders acknowledged the presence of female violence but argued that it was defensive, or in some cases a pre-emptive strike.[40] Both the samples upon which Walker and Saunders based this argument came from women's shelters or from self-selected battered women and so, by definition, contained women who were physically abused but may not be representative of community samples of women. Saunders did not comment on this generalization problem but simply stated that as a "feminist researcher" he had an obligation to examine motives in addition to hit counts.[41] Saunders argued that social science must be a "tool for social change."[42] Saunders concluded that female violence is always self-defence, even when the woman uses severe violence and the man uses only mild violence. This, he asserted, is because of the woman's smaller size and weight. He focused this analysis on the Straus et al. data, but these data never asked who used violence first and cannot confirm self-defence.[43] Bland and Orn in a survey conducted in Canada did ask who used violence first. Of the women who reported using violence against their husbands, 73.4 percent said they used violence first.[44] Stets and Straus reported that females said they struck first 52.7 percent of the time (see below).[45]

Follingstad, Wright, Lloyd, and Sebastian asked victims about their perceptions of their assaulters' motivations and asked the perpetrators to report their own motivations.[46] In the total sample of 495 undergraduate subjects in South Carolina, 115 respondents (23 percent: 16 percent of the men and 28 percent of the women) reported they had been victimized by a partner using physical force. Women reported being victimized *and perpetrating physical aggression* twice as often as men. The authors found that there was no significant difference in the percentage of men (17.7 percent) and women (18.6 percent) who endorsed using aggression in self-defence. Furthermore, a greater percentage of women than men reported using aggression to feel more powerful (3.4 percent vs. 0), to get control over the other person (22.0 percent vs. 8.3 percent), or to punish the person for wrong behaviour (16.9 percent vs. 12.5 percent). The two perpetrator motives most commonly

6.3 Woozle alert! Facts versus conclusions

DeKeseredy and Schwartz reported levels of severity of violence used by under-graduate women (according to their self-report) and the women's own reports of whether it was never, sometimes, mostly, or always self-defence.[1] Whether the violence was severe or non-severe, these women report that their violence was rarely in self-defence. Only 8.7 percent (31/356) of women using severe violence and only 6.9 percent (47/678) of women using non-severe violence reported that they "always" used violence in self-defence. What's more, 58 percent (205/356) in the severe group and 62 percent (422/678) in the non-severe group reported that they "never" used violence in self-defence.

Amazingly, the authors state: "Our overall conclusion is that much of the violence by Canadian undergraduate women is self-defense and should not be labeled mutual combat or male partner abuse." When ideology forms the conclu-sion, not even one's own data get in the way.

NOTE: 1 W.S. DeKeseredy and M.D. Schwartz, *Woman Abuse on Campus: Results from the Canadian National Survey* (Thousand Oaks, CA: Sage, 1998), 77, 91.

reported by victims (i.e., their perceptions of their assaulter's motives) were not knowing how to express themselves verbally (cited by 32.7 percent of male victims and 28.2 percent of female victims) and self-defence (cited by 4.1 percent of male victims and 4.8 percent of female victims). Feminist views on men's abuse of women hold that the male motive is control, but this study found that few men acknowledged that motive. The authors noted that, although men might have been under-reporting this motive, they ad-mitted to many other socially undesirable motivations.

Fiebert and Gonzalez surveyed a sample of 968 California college-age women regarding their initiation of physical assaults on their male part-ners.[47] Twenty-nine percent of the women (N = 285) revealed that they had initiated assaults during the past five years. Women in their twenties were more likely to aggress than women aged thirty years and older. Women re-ported aggressing because they did not believe that their male victims would be injured or would retaliate. Women also claimed that they assaulted their male partners because they wished to engage their attention, particularly emotionally. The above studies, taken as a whole, are inconsistent with the feminist view of female violence being solely self-defensive. Women report using violence against male partners repeatedly, using it against non-violent male partners, and using it for reasons other than self-defence.

Gender Rates of Perpetration

Kennedy and Dutton collected data on intimate violence incidence in Alberta,

6.4 Self-reports of perpetrating violence against partner among couples reporting intimate violence

	Violence percentages reported								
	M-Minor F-None	M-None F-Minor	Both Minor	M-Severe F-None	M-None F-Severe	M-Severe F-Minor	M-Minor F-Severe	Both Severe	N
Dating	9.6	26.9	21.2	0.1	12.5	4.8	13.5	10.6	104
Cohabit	3.5	13.4	23.2	7.3	13.4	1.2	6.1	22.0	82
Married	7.5	18.9	28.3	5.7	9.6	2.4	7.1	10.5	736
Summed			13.1	35.5	8.4	26.7			922

NOTE: X^2 - 33.9, $p < .01$, df-14. These are CTS reports from males and females. The generation does not change as a function of sex of respondent. The 3:1 male/female ratio of severe/non-violent comes from the summed total across relationship types (35.5/13.1). Repeating this procedure with severe/minor violence (26.7/8.4) produces a similar female/male ratio of 3.2:1.

SOURCE: Based on J. Stets and M. Straus, "Marriage license as a hitting license" in M.A. Straus and R.J. Gelles, eds., *Physical Violence in American Families* (New Brunswick, NJ: Transaction Publishers, 1992), 234, Table 13.2.

reporting only the male data.[48] A decade later, two female colleagues pushed me for the publication of all the data.[49] Women reported perpetrating more violence than they received for overall, minor, and severe violence. Four other surveys in Canada that reported both male-to-female and female-to-male violence also found higher rates of female-perpetrated violence.[50] Similarly, in an American sample, O'Leary et al. found that, of 272 couples planning to marry, more women than men had been physically violent toward their partners (44 percent vs. 31 percent).[51]

Sommer, Barnes, and Murray surveyed a random sample (N = 1,257) of residents of a Canadian city between the ages of eighteen and sixty-five. Thirty-nine percent of female respondents reported "participation in some form of spouse abuse," and 16.2 percent reported severe violence perpetration.[52] The risk factors for female participation were being young, having high scores on the Eysenck psychoticism scale, the neuroticism index, and the MacAndrews alcoholism scale. In other words psychological disturbance and alcohol abuse predicted female violence.

Ridley and Feldman examined 153 respondent females in a community sample (community public health clinic) for a study of conflict and communication.[53] These women reported the following physical abuse frequencies directed at their male partners: kicked (him) 20.2 percent, choking/strangling (of male partner) 9.1 percent, physically attacked the sexual parts of his body 7.1 percent, used a knife or gun against him 7.8 percent. Those who reported these acts also reported using them repeatedly: 40 incidents of kicking (per perpetrator who reported using this action), 6.5 incidents of "physical attacks to the sexual parts," 4.25 acts of choking per perpetrator, etc. In other words, community-sample women who used violence used it repeatedly. Again, since this was a clinic sample, one must use caution in generalizing to the broader community.

Kwong and Bartholomew surveyed 596 men and 616 women in Vancouver and found equal rates (1 percent difference, males higher) for male-perpetrated and female perpetrated violence (when women reported) and higher rates (9 percent difference, females higher) of female-perpetrated violence (when males reported).[54] Women who were victimized were about twice as likely to report severe injuries (14 percent vs. 7 percent) and to feel physical pain the next day (38 percent vs. 18 percent) than were men who had been victimized. These "effects" data were for the percentage of *victims* who experienced injury or pain. When calculated as proportion of the entire sample, 2.5 percent of men and 4 percent of women had severe injuries, while 6.5 percent of men and 11 percent of women experienced physical pain. Hence, the method of reporting the proportion can increase gender differences (when calculated as effect per victim) or decrease them (when reported as sample proportions).

Stets and Straus combined the 1985 US National Family Violence Resurvey ($N = 5,005$) with a sample of 526 dating couples to generate a large and representative sample of male-female relationships, in which they reported incidence of intimate partner violence (IVP) by gender.[55] Their data table on relationship form and gender is reproduced below (see Figure 6.4). Using a subset of the 825 respondents who reported experiencing at least one or more assaults, Stets and Straus found that in half (49 percent) of the incidents the couples reported reciprocal violence, in a quarter (23 percent) of the cases the couples reported that the husband alone was violent, and a quarter (28 percent) reported that the wife alone was violent.[56] Men ($N = 297$) reported striking the first blow in 43.7 percent of cases and that their partner struck the first blow in 44.1 percent of the cases. The women ($N = 476$) reported striking the first blow in 52.7 percent of the cases and that their partner struck first in 42.6 percent of the cases. (Not all respondents answered this question.) Stets and Straus concluded not only that women engage in a comparable amount of violence but also that they are "at least as likely" to instigate violence.[57] The results also indicated that women were more likely to hit back (24.4 percent) than men (15 percent) in response to violent provocation by a partner.[58] This result is difficult to explain from the feminist argument that women are more afraid of male violence than the reverse. In all, these data do not support the argument that female violence is solely defensive. Straus has cited six studies that found equal rates of violence initiation by women and men.[59]

The Stets and Straus data contained another finding that is problematic for the self-defence and pre-emptive strike arguments; three times as many women reported using severe violence against non-violent men than the reverse pattern (compare the Female-severe/Male-none and Male-severe/Female-none columns highlighted in Figure 6.4).[60] In other words, summed across relationship styles, the proportions were 12 percent for "women more severe" and 4 per cent for "men more severe."

A comparison of the Female-severe/Male-none (severe violence defined by the CTS) pattern with its reverse (Male-severe/Female-none) reveals that the pattern of unilateral violence by the female only is about three times more prevalent (Mean = 11.8 percent) than the male only pattern (Mean = 4.3 percent) across all types of relationships. This is true whether males or females are reporting the data.[61] This predominance of the more severe violence pattern by females is also true for Female-severe/Male-minor vs. Male-severe/Female-minor patterns. Despite these data, where little or no male violence occurred, Saunders, Dobash et al., and Tutty have all continued to report that female violence is exclusively self-defensive.[62]

Patriarchal Terrorism

The argument is sometimes made that males terrorize women in a fashion that is not found with female perpetrators. The Stets and Straus data (reviewed above) notwithstanding, the argument could be made that those males who do use severe abuse against non-violent or minimally violent women generate a state of terror and domination that is not equally reflected by female perpetrators.[63] From the Stets and Straus table (Figure 6.4) we could add the Male-severe/Female-none group and the Male-severe/Female-minor group and generate a composite group where such "male terrorism" is possible. For married couples this terrorized group would be 8.1 percent (compared to 16.7 percent for the female-perpetrator pattern) and for cohabiting couples it would be 8.5 percent (compared to 19.5 percent for female perpetrators).

Johnson discussed the issue of patriarchal terrorism but mainly to show that evidence for it from community samples was scant.[64] The notion of patriarchal terrorism is based on shelter samples that are non-representative but are nevertheless regarded as viable data sources. The question becomes whether the patriarchal terrorism profile has become a stereotype that is not representative even of intimately violent men. According to the Stets and Straus data, the subgroup that could be called patriarchal terrorist represents only a minority of intimately violent men (about 33 percent) based solely on violence patterns (Male-severe/Female-none-or-minor divided by mutually severe).[65] According to surveys, two-thirds of these men would use this potentially terroristic pattern repeatedly, so of the 12.0 percent of all men who are severely violent according to surveys, one in three would be unilaterally severely violent (33 percent of the 8 per cent reporting repeat severe violence ever; see Figure 3.1). For a general population, that would be about 3 percent of all men who, in other words, met criteria as patriarchal terrorists.[66] Put somewhat differently: about 12 percent have used severe violence according to the conflict surveys, about 8 percent use it repeatedly, and one-third of these use it unilaterally, or (0.33×8) about 3 percent. These are the serious "batterers" who should draw the greatest criminal justice attention. Mutually violent cases are problematic too but may require a different intervention strategy.

This is the same number as reported in the Canadian General Social Survey (1999) by LaRoche, who analyzed both violence severity reported in this "perceptions of crime survey" and reports of partners' use of controlling actions (in a scale devised by Johnson and Leone). Instead of just asking women about partners' use of control, the GSS asked both sexes. The resulting victimization rates for combined unilateral severe violence and control by the partner was 2.6 percent for men and 4.2 percent for women. LaRoche's data revealed what Johnson overlooked – "matriarchal terrorism." Given that the Stets and Straus data (see Figure 6.4) were reported years before Johnson's false dichotomy of patriarchal terrorism vs. common couple violence, it is hard to see how Johnson could have overlooked the women using violence against non-violent men.[67]

Using a court-mandated treatment group sample, Dutton found that only about 33 percent of men in that group met criteria for terrorism (severe male violence reported by wife, plus threats and sexual violence).[68] Those that met these criteria had significantly higher likelihood of having a personality disorder than those who did not. Of the men arrested and convicted of wife assault, about one-fifth would qualify as terrorists. The sample is a subgroup (men convicted) of a subgroup (men arrested) of a subgroup (men who use violence against their spouses). However, this stereotype of male terrorism is commonplace.[69]

As a result of the gender paradigm, the debate over Johnson's study involved comparing a group (severe unilateral violent males) that constitutes about 1 percent of intimate violence per year (0.025×0.33; see Figure 3.1) with another group (mutually violent couples) that constitutes 38.8 percent of violence in married couples and 45 percent of violence in cohabiting couples. The remaining group, Female-severe violence/Male-none, never entered the debate.[70]

Lesbian Violence

Finally, the feminist viewpoint has difficulty explaining several key empirical studies. One is a fascinating study of intimate assault in lesbian relationships. The prevalence of violence in homosexual relationships, which also appear to go through abuse cycles, is hard to explain in terms of men dominating women.[71] Bologna et al. surveyed seventy homosexual male and female college students about incidence of violence in the most recent relationship. Lesbian relationships were significantly more violent than gay relationships (56 percent vs. 25 percent).[72] Another study, by Lie and Gentlewarrier, surveyed 1,099 lesbians, finding that 52 percent had been victims of violence by their female partner, 52 percent said they had used violence against their female partner, and 30 percent said they had used violence against a non-violent female partner.[73] Finally, Lie, Schilit, Bush, Montague, and Reyes, in a survey of 350 lesbians (most of whom had had

6.5 Types of abuse experienced by lesbian respondents in prior relationships with male and female partners

	By male partner (%)	By female partner (%)
Physical abuse	34.0	45.0
Sexual abuse	41.9	51.8
Verbal/emotional abuse	55.1	64.5
Overall abuse	65.4	73.4

SOURCE: Adapted from G. Lie, R. Schilit, J. Bush, M. Montague, and L. Reyes, "Lesbians in currently aggressive relationships: How frequently do they report aggressive past relationships?" *Violence and Victims* 6, 2 (1991): 121-35.

prior lesbian and heterosexual relationships), found that reported rates of verbal, physical, and sexual abuse were all significantly higher in the lesbian relationships than in the heterosexual relationships.[74] Of this sample of women, 78.2 percent had been in a prior relationship with a man. Reports of violence by men were all lower than reports of violence in prior relationships with women (see Figure 6.5).

This finding is difficult to accommodate from the perspective of patriarchy: why are violence rates so high in lesbian relationships, and why are they higher for past relationships with women than past relationships with men? Keep in mind that the women in this sample reported past abuse victimization rates for both lesbian and heterosexual relationships. Hence, each woman served as her own control, and issues about whether this is a representative sample are reduced in importance.

It might be argued that lesbians adopt the values of the dominant patriarchal culture and that a dominance-submissiveness relationship may exist in a lesbian relationship, whereby the "functional male" (i.e., the dominant member) is the abuser. The problem with this argument is that even in heterosexual relationships, a variety of power relations exist. The "functional male" theory maps onto lesbian relationships a stereotype that has no data support. The Lie et al. data are difficult to explain in terms of male domination. Homosexual battering seems more consistent with other views on intimate violence: that intimacy generates anger that is sometimes expressed violently.

The variety in heterosexual relationships is demonstrated in a study by Coleman and Straus.[75] In an American nationally representative sample of 2,143 couples, respondents reported on their power-sharing arrangements in terms of who had the "final say" on family decisions in six major areas. Couples were classified as equalitarian, male-dominant, female-dominant, and divided power. Degrees of consensus about marital power arrangements

6.6 Power structure, marital conflict, and minor violence rates

			Percentages		
Power type	N	Of N	High conflict	High consensus	Violent
Male dominant	200	9.4	39.0	22.0	27
Female dominant	160	7.5	33.1	26.3	31
Divided power	1,146	54.0	33.8	30.7	21
Equalitarian	616	29.0	20.5	47.7	11

SOURCE: Adapted from D. Coleman and M.A. Straus, "Marital power, conflict, and violence in a nationally representative sample of American couples," in M.A. Straus and R.J. Gelles, *Physical Violence in American Families* (New Brunswick, NJ: Transaction, 1992), Tables 17.1 and 17.2.

were also assessed, as were the degree of conflict and violence in each couple. Coleman and Straus's data table (Figure 6.4) shows the proportions of couples falling into each power category, reporting high degrees of conflict, and agreeing about their power arrangement. Only 9.4 percent of couples qualified as male-dominant, and of these, 22 percent exhibited consensus about this arrangement. The largest contributor to conflict was not the specific power arrangement but the *level of agreement* over the power-sharing (the Power Norm Consensus). Where consensus was low, conflict increased by a factor of 2.5 independent of the power arrangement, which only marginally increased conflict. Husband-to-wife minor violence rates were highest in the female-dominant group (31), followed by male-dominant (27), divided-power (21), and equalitarian (11).

The notion of a male-dominant marriage where both parties agree to that power-sharing arrangement may be reprehensible to some, but it is not a strong cause of violence. When we compare the survey results in the preceding section with the Coleman and Straus results above, we see that 90 percent of men are non-assaultive (by the criterion of using severe violence against a wife), and only 9.4 percent are dominant. In other words, the large majority of men raised under patriarchal norms are non-assaultive and non-dominant. Clearly, some individual difference factor must operate to discriminate unilaterally assaultive men from non-assaultive men.

Power and Control and Violence

Another tenet of feminist thought is that male violence is part of a wider repertoire of control tactics by which men dominate women. In the literature on "feminist therapy," emphasis is placed on "male control and domination."[76] However, in one of the few studies to examine controlling behaviours and psychological abuse, Kasian and Painter found that females were more jealous, more verbally abusive, and more controlling than males in a sample of 1,625 dating undergraduates.[77] Use of controlling behaviours and verbal abuse appears to be bidirectional in intimate relationships. Certainly in the LaRoche analysis of the GSS sample of 25,876, each gender reported controlling behaviours by the other. If controlling behaviours are bidirectional, and if "feminist therapy" seeks to reduce "control tactics" in men who already feel powerless in intimate relationships, a positive therapeutic outcome may be contra-indicated.

O'Leary et al. make the point that power and control as measured by the Tolman Domination scale on the Psychological Maltreatment of Women Inventory does not differ between maritally distressed and physically aggressive groups.[78] O'Leary et al. do not comment on female use of power and control in these groups.

The entire debate about power and control demonstrates a profound misunderstanding of the psychology of power. McClelland showed that power motivation could be realized in four general ways, only one of which applies to abuse.[79] One can seek to have power over another person through controlling them, persuading them, taking care of them, any method in which one is in the superior position. This is the category that applies to abuse, but it also includes motives of nurses, salesmen, and social workers. The other ways of feeling power involve being attached to a powerful person or group. This is the power motivation that applies to cult members and women who propose marriage to serial killers or sports fans. Still another has nothing to do with other people but involves strengthening the self through bodybuilding or collecting. Hence, McClelland found that stamp collectors felt more power when they had increased their stamp collection. Finally, seekers of political or religious office satisfy power in a fourth way. In one sense, power is too broad a motivational category to have any meaning when applied to abuse. Feminist activists who seek to control criminal justice system function are motivated by power and control no less than male perpetrators of violence.

Powerlessness means different things for a politicized woman and a non-politicized man. For such a man, sociopolitical comparisons with women or with a woman are irrelevant. What is experienced, especially in intimate relationships, is the power advantage women appear to have in their ability to introspect, analyze, and describe feelings and processes. Transference from early relationships in which a female (mother) had apparently unlimited power still affects male assessments of power in adult relationships.[80] Hence, assaultive males report feeling powerless with respect to their intimate partners.[81]

One is reminded of Eric Fromm's definition of sadism as the conversion of feelings of impotence to feelings of omnipotence.[82] While batterers may appear powerful in terms of their physical or sociopolitical resources, they are distinctly impotent in terms of their psychic and emotional resources, even to the point of depending on their female partners to maintain their sense of identity.[83]

The sociological analysis of wife assault has revealed the complex role of social factors in creating the context in which violence occurs. The shortcoming of the sociological approach has been its inability to explain why men exposed to the same normative context behave so differently. If social licence determines violent behaviour, we would expect a majority of men to be violent, but only a minority are. Also, as the violence becomes more extreme, the size of this minority group of perpetrators shrinks. In any given year, only about 2 percent of men commit repeat severe violence against their wives in the manner of the stereotypical wife beater. Two groups consistently overestimate this percentage. If men in treatment are asked how many men are as violent as they are, they guess about 60 percent (the correct answer is the 2 percent cited above). Feminists who see patriarchy as the cause of wife assault also tend to overestimate the incidence of assaultiveness. A complete explanation for wife assault must distinguish men who repeatedly and severely assault their wives from men who do so sporadically and in a less serious way. It must explain why many wife assaulters commit wife assault only once.[84] Where psychiatric theories erred by setting their focus too narrowly and overlooking the context of wife assault, sociological theories have set their focus too broadly and miss the variations in assaultive behaviour in common contexts. A complete theory of wife assault must avoid both shortcomings; it must locate a man's violence in the "normal" learning environment to which that man has been exposed, and it must be able to differentiate assaultive from non-assaultive males on the basis of differences in that learning environment.

Inevitable Escalation

Feminists argue that violence tends to escalate if left unchecked and that this is a risk factor for spousal homicide.[85] However, Feld and Straus found that for husbands assessed in the 1985 national survey, more were likely to de-escalate violence than to escalate.[86] The survey also found that one-third of victims report no repeat victimization even without criminal justice intervention.

Hence, while sociological theories provide important analyses of the social context of wife assault, this context has to be combined with characteristics of the assaultive male in order to explain variation in behaviour. Gender analyses of domestic violence simply do not pass the data test. Nevertheless, it was a heavily influenced feminist paradigm that influenced the shape of domestic policy from criminal justice response to treatment choice. To summarize the paradigm's collapse:

- Male violence is general: *not so*. About 4 percent of men each year commit repeat severe unilateral violence.[87]
- Female violence is self-defensive: *not so*. Stets and Straus found that more females use severe violence against non-violent or minor-violent males than the reverse pattern.[88]
- Wife assault escalates: *not so*. According to the research of Feld and Straus, de-escalation is more likely than is escalation.[89]
- Only women are injured: *not so*. Archer and others find males are injured too.[90]

Johnson argued that population surveys suffered from a sampling bias due to large rates of non-response. However, the General Social Survey (1999) cited by LaRoche in a 2005 study proved this false. Furthermore, as LaRoche says: "The data from the GSS do not seem to corroborate Johnson's hypothesis that intimate terrorism is almost the exclusive domain of male perpetrators."[91] In other words, data from large representative samples indicate the presence of female violence, even in relationships where the male is not violent.

7 The Domestic Assault of Men

With respect to personal safety, women victims were five times as likely to fear for their lives.

        – P.G. Jaffe, N.D. Lemon, and S.E. Poisson,
        Child Custody and Domestic Violence

- Proportion of female victims who feared for life in intimate terrorism relationships – 83 percent
- Proportion of male victims who feared for life in intimate terrorism relationships – 77 percent

        – Canadian General Social Survey[1]

The last chapter reviewed data that have been troubling for feminists since the first US National Survey of 1975: women are as violent as males. Because this finding contradicts feminist theory, it has been suppressed, unreported, reinterpreted, or denied. The female violence rates have been portrayed as self-defensive violence, less serious violence, or a result of reporting differences. In fact they equal or exceed males rates, they include female violence against non-violent males, and they have serious consequences for males.[2]

Violent Femmes: New Studies of Dating Aggression

New data from dating violence studies are remarkably consistent with the adult partner abuse literature. Watson, Cascardi, Avery-Leaf, and O'Leary sampled 475 high school students (266 males and 209 females) from a large, metropolitan area on Long Island.[3] Using a modified Conflict Tactics Scale, of students with past or current romantic relationships ($N = 401$), 45.6 percent reported at least one incident of physical aggression by their current or former partners but just 9 percent reported exclusive victimization (i.e., had been victim but not perpetrator of physical aggression). Using

a measure they developed, Watson and colleagues also studied gender differences in responding to aggression by a dating partner. Female students
were significantly more likely than male students to report an aggressive
response. Specifically, girls (42 percent) were significantly more likely to
fight back than boys (26 percent). Male students (24 percent) were more
likely than female students (6 percent) to do nothing in response to abuse
by a partner. There was also a trend for female students (28 percent) to be
more likely to report breaking up with an abusive partner than male students (21 percent).[4]

Katz, Kuffel, and Coblentz studied intimate violence in two samples of
undergraduates at an American university.[5] In the first study (N = 184 women,
103 men) participants had been in exclusive heterosexual dating relationships of at least three months' duration (Mean = 1 year, Standard Deviation
= six months). Dating abuse, assessed with the CTS, was common, with 47
percent (N = 133) of the sample reporting a current relationship in which
their partner had used physical aggression against them.[6] Male victims sustained higher levels of moderate violence than did female victims. Severe
violence was rare for both women (N = 6) and men (N = 4). The frequency
data also showed few gender differences: 55 percent of the women and about
50 percent of the men had non-abusive partners, 18 percent of women and
13 percent of men had partners who had been abusive once, and 26 percent
of women (N = 48) and 38 percent of men had repeatedly abusive partners.[7]

Callahan, Tolman, and Saunders studied dating violence in a sample of
190 high school students (53 percent boys, 47 percent girls).[8] Dating violence was evaluated by severity, frequency, and injury. For girls, increasing
dating violence was related to PTSD and dissociation. Contrary to the assertion that abuse by females against males is unlikely to result in significant
harm, increasing levels of dating violence were associated with increasing
levels of anxiety, depression, and PTSD in boys, even controlling for demographic, family violence, and social desirability items.

In a recent study of intimate abuse among college students, Hines and
Saudino used the CTS-2 with 481 college students (302 females, 179 males)
in romantic relationships during the previous six months.[9] Twenty-nine percent of males and 35 percent of females reported perpetrating physical aggression; 12.5 percent of the males and 4.5 percent of the females reported
receiving severe physical aggression; 14 percent of females reported that they
were the sole perpetrators of aggression. There were no significant gender
differences in the perpetration of either psychological aggression or severe
physical aggression. Injuries were sustained by 8.4 percent of males and 5
percent of females. The study was designed to counter criticisms of the

original CTS: that its physical aggression scale was too limited and that it did not include psychological aggression. With these criticisms answered, females were still more aggressive than males. Since reporting was anonymous, response biases were minimized.

Follingstad and her colleagues conducted a particularly well designed study of dating violence.[10] They developed a structural equation model (which delineates primary and moderator variables) to best connect psychological causes to dating violence in a sample of 412 college students. Since the authors assessed both members of the couple, individual characteristics could be statistically connected to couple variables. They also used subjects with a history of IPV (30 percent of the class contacted) and a subsample of those without a history (about 15 percent of the remainder). Psychological variables measured included anxious attachment and angry temperament. The "outcome variables" included controlling behaviour and physical violence. Their resulting model found that anxious attachment related to angry temperament that, in turn, generated control. Control, in turn, generated violence.[11] As the authors put it: "The primary path leading to the use of force in dating relationships was initially due to the presence of anxious attachment influencing the development of an angry temperament that then leads to behaviors to control one's partner. The controlling behavior is, however, the significant mediator between the angry temperament and greater frequency and severity of dating violence."[12] This study was conducted on 233 males and 199 females combined. No gender differences were reported. Attachment seems to be predictive of control and physical abuse in either gender.

The largest and most comprehensive of all dating violence studies was a cross-cultural study of partner violence in a sample of 6,900 university students from seventeen nations by Douglas and Straus.[13] They found adolescent girls were 115 percent more likely to assault male partners than adolescent boys were to assault female partners, regardless of whether overall assault or severe assault rates were considered. Severe assault was much more likely to be female-perpetrated in Scotland (552 percent of male rate), Singapore (457 percent), and New Zealand (296 percent). In this study, male-perpetrated injury rates were 8.1 percent (serious injury 2.6 percent), while female-perpetrated injury rates were 6.1 percent (serious injury 1.2 percent).

Some have argued that dating relationships are different than cohabiting and married relationships. However, while they differ in terms of commitment and ease of exit, all are intimate relationships. Recalling the Stets and Straus data table reported in Chapter 6, it could be said that the predominance of female severe/non-violent male patterns found in their study is even more pronounced in dating relationships than in the other two forms of relationship. Dating violence studies indicate that female IPV is common in dating relationships, is related to attachment insecurity, and generates depression in male victims.

Longitudinal Cohort Studies

Longitudinal cohort studies are methodologically the soundest design for studying a variety of problem behaviours. The samples are large and representative of an age cohort, not self-selected through their presence in a shelter or a court-mandated group (or even a college). Hence, the external validity (the degree to which results can be generalized to an entire population) is higher. Also, since the cohort is followed over time, cause-and-effect relationships can be deduced. Unlike "snapshot" studies that freeze behaviour to one time sample and rely on correlations at that time, the protracted longitudinal study can examine effects from a measure taken years before. Three major peer-cohort longitudinal studies have been done.

The Concordia Longitudinal Risk Project

One of these studies, the Concordia Longitudinal Risk Project in Montreal, used data collected in a longitudinal study of 4,109 French-speaking school children in 1976.[14] The children were categorized into Aggressive and Withdrawn categories using a French version of a systematized peer-rating scale called the Pupil Evaluation Inventory. Extremes in Aggression and Withdrawal were developed by taking children who scored above the ninety-fifth percentile on Aggression and below the seventy-fifth percentile on Withdrawn. This sub-sample yielded 101 girls and 97 boys. (Similarly, reverse criteria yielded a Withdrawn group of 129 girls and 108 boys). Age-matched comparisons were developed by taking children who were average (between the twenty-fifth and seventy-fifth percentiles) on both Aggression and Withdrawal. Serbin et al. describe their sample as "community based" and therefore "avoiding biases inherent in clinic-referred samples."[15] Aggressive children of both sexes had lower IQs and academic achievement than comparison controls. Both were more physically aggressive during play.

Girls' aggression was associated with a preference for male partners who were also aggressive. As they approached adolescence, these Aggressive girls had elevated rates of smoking, alcohol, and illicit drug use and "continue[d] to seek out behaviourally compatible peer groups, probably comprised of boys and girls with similar aggressive or 'predelinquent' behavioural styles."[16] They had elevated rates of gynecological problems, were more likely to go on birth control sooner, had higher rates of sexually transmitted diseases between ages fourteen and twenty, and became pregnant sooner and more frequently (girls who scored above the seventy-fifth percentile on both Aggression and Withdrawal had a teen pregnancy rate of 48 percent).

The Aggressive group had elevated levels of depression and anxiety disorder by their late teens. When they married, their children had higher health risks, and the Aggressive girls had become Aggressive mothers, exhibiting maternal childhood aggression and having children who had more visits to hospital emergency rooms for treatment of injuries. These risk factors for women are completely overlooked in the advice given by domestic violence experts to custody evaluators.[17] These experts concentrate solely on male intimate partner violence and warn evaluators of this risk. The Concordia study and the Dunedin study (below) present clear examinations of the development and independent expression in women of aggression to others (i.e., aggression that develops not in reaction to male aggression but independently of the behaviour of the male partner). They show the developmental trajectory and the "trait" character of this aggression. Both studies indicate that these women will select aggressive men and contribute to ongoing intra-couple aggression.

The Dunedin Study

Magdol et al. followed a birth cohort of 1,037 subjects in Dunedin, New Zealand.[18] The original cohort was "a complete cohort of births between April 1972 and March 31, 1973 in Dunedin, New Zealand (population 120,000). The group has been studied every two years since its inception for a variety of health, development and behavioural measures. The sample is predominantly of European ancestry and is representative of the social class distribution of New Zealand."[19] The study of partner violence took place when the group was aged twenty-one and was embedded among other questions about mental health issues. Of the original cohort of 1037, 941 provided data. Respondents had to have had "a relationship with a romantic partner during the last twelve months that lasted at least one month," and 861 of the 941 qualified. Partner violence was assessed using the CTS, each respondent reporting for both self and partner. Measures were also reported of the following: socioeconomic status, social ties, substance abuse, criminality, and mental health (anxiety, depression, mania, and psychosis). Criminality focused on self-reports of crimes against strangers, using the DSM measure of antisocial personality.

The 425 women and 436 men who were in intimate relationships from the Magdol et al. cohort indicated that both minor and severe physical vio-

7.1 Perpetration of intimate violence: The Dunedin (New Zealand) study and the National Youth Survey (United States)

	New Zealand (N = 861)		United States (N = 2002)	
	Females (%)	Males (%)	Females (%)	Males (%)
Female perpetration was higher for the following:				
Kick/bite/hit with fist	14.4	4.4	13.8	3.6
Hit with object	8.3	1.1	8.8	3.5
Threaten with a weapon	0.5	0	1.8	0.7
Use a weapon	0.2	0	0.7	0.1
Verbal aggression	9.4	8.6	n/a	n/a
Violence to stranger	3.6	2.5	n/a	n/a
Male perpetration was higher with the following:				
Choke/strangle	0	1.4	n/a	n/a
Beat up	0.9	1.1	0.9	2.0

NOTE: n/a means not available.
SOURCES: L. Magdol, T.E. Moffitt, A. Caspi, D. Newman, J. Fagan, and P.A. Silva, "Gender differences in partner violence in a birth cohort of 21 year olds: Bridging the gap between clinical and epidemiological approaches," *Journal of Consulting and Clinical Psychology* 63, 1 (1997): 68-78, Table 1; B.J. Morse, "Beyond the Conflict Tactics Scale: Assessing gender differences in partner violence," *Violence and Victims* 4 (1995): 251-71, 261, Table 3, most recent (1992) data.

lence rates were higher for women whether self-reported or partner-reported. The female severe physical violence rate was more than triple that of males (23.4 percent vs. 5.5 percent). Based on this same sample, Moffitt et al. reported that pre-existing characteristics of the women (at age fifteen) predicted (1) their choice of an abusive male partner by age twenty-one and (2) their own use of violence at age twenty-one apart from the male's violence (see below).[20] As Magdol et al. put it: "Early studies of partner violence assumed that men's perpetration rates exceeded those of women, in part because these studies relied almost exclusively on clinical samples of women who sought assistance or of men in court-mandated counselling programs."[21]

A comprehensive analysis of the Dunedin data was done by Moffitt et al.[22] Based on the data from the other measures, these authors reported that the following characteristics predicted intimate violence in females: approval of the use of aggression, excessive jealousy and suspiciousness, a tendency to experience intense and rapid emotions, and poor self-control. As we shall see, these are the same characteristics found in male abusers.

Moffitt et al. found that antisocial traits measured in females at age fifteen (1) made them more likely to be involved in a relationship with an abusive man at age twenty-one, and (2) even after controlling for their partners' physical abuse, "women with a juvenile history of conduct problems were still more likely to commit violence against their partners."[23] Antisocial behaviour in women through their teens made them likely to be assaultive to intimate partners at age twenty-one. A similarly designed study in the United States found the same gender equality of violence (see Figure 7.1).[24]

Chapter 12 will examine an in-depth study of male perpetrators that describes an "abusive personality." The abusive personality has the same profile as Moffitt et al. described for women as "negative emotionality": jealousy, impulsivity, rapidly fluctuating emotions, and poor self-control. With the men, these were related to independently assessed borderline traits.[25] These psychological aspects, in fact, are central to definitions of borderline personality, which unfortunately was not formally assessed in the Dunedin women. From the descriptors given by Moffitt et al., however, it seems that a

---

7.2 Negative emotionality

Moffitt et al. found that "negative emotionality" predicted abusiveness in both genders. Negative emotionality was measured by forty-nine selected true/false items from the Tellengen and Waller's Multidimensional Personality Questionnaire. These questions measured:

1 Reactions to stress: "I often get irritated at little annoyances."
2 Experience of emotion: "Sometimes I feel strong emotions like anxiety or anger without knowing why."
3 Expectations of others: "Most people stay friendly only so long as it is to their advantage."
4 Attitudes towards using aggression: "When someone hurts me, I try to get even."

High scorers describe themselves as nervous, vulnerable, prone to worry, emotionally volatile, and unable to cope with stress. They say that they have a low threshold for feeling tense, fearful, hostile, angry, and suspicious. They see the world as peopled with potential enemies and seek revenge for slights, enjoy frightening others, and could remorselessly take advantage of others.

Negative emotionality measured in women at age fifteen predicted their use of violence towards an intimate other at age twenty-one regardless of whether that person fought back or not.

SOURCES: T.E. Moffitt, A. Caspi, M. Rutter, and P.A Silva, *Sex Differences in Antisocial Behavior* (Cambridge: Cambridge University Press, 2001); A Tellengen and N.G. Waller, "Exploring personality through construction: Development of the Multidimensional Personality Questionnaire," in S.R. Briggs and J.M. Check, eds., *Personality Measures: Development and Evaluation* (Greenwich, CT: JAI Press, 2001).

similar "abusive personality" may exist for male and female intimate abuse perpetrators. Chapter 9, which examines personality assessments done on female perpetrators of intimate partner violence, shows that borderline features are prominent in this group.

In sum, Moffitt et al. found that antisocial behaviour measured in females at age fifteen predicted their use of intimate aggression against male intimates at age twenty-one. A woman's conduct problems correlated +.44 with her later use of violence against her partner (with his violence partialled out). It also correlated +.36 with his use of violence toward her. The antisocial female sample had earlier puberty, earlier initiation of intercourse, more older friends, and more delinquent friends.[26] Essentially, the pattern of correlations between early conduct problems and later intimate violence and partners' use of violence was similar for both sexes. The correlations were roughly similar, certainly not significantly different. Moffitt et al. emphasize the importance of puberty as a developmental crossroads for these girls. The authors also make a provocative argument, based on their impressive data set, that males form two types of antisocial behaviour, one against strangers (which may be neurologically based) and another against intimate females. Females form only one type of antisocial behaviour: against intimate males. The sophisticated path analysis (a statistical method of differentiating independent, moderator, and dependent variables) used by the authors on this huge and representative sample gives added weight to their findings. However, the reader is reminded that other studies (including Serbin et al.) found a broader array of antisocial actions by women, including physical abuse of children. Antisocial personality is assessed by both behavioural criteria (crimes) and psychological criteria (lack of empathy and remorse, tendency to lie). The DSM-1V diagnostic criteria for Antisocial PD are shown below.

Ehrensaft, Moffitt, and Caspi studied the Dunedin birth cohort, finding 9 percent to be in "clinically abusive relationships," defined as those that required intervention by any professional (e.g., hospital, police, lawyers).[27] The authors found comparable rates of violence: 68 percent of women and 60 percent of men self-reporting injury.[28] *Both male and female perpetrators evidenced signs of personality disturbance.* The authors noted, for instance, that the women had "aggressive personalities and/or adolescent conduct disorder."[29] As the authors put it: "These findings counter the assumption that if clinical abuse was ascertained in epidemiological samples, it would be primarily man-to-woman, explained by patriarchy rather than psychopathology."[30]

The US National Youth Survey

This preponderance of female stranger aggression was replicated in the

---

7.3 Antisocial Personality Disorder (ASPD)

A person with antisocial personality disorder will have a pervasive pattern of disregard for and violation of the rights of others. This is indicated by three or more of the following. The person:

- fails to conform to norms in society with respect to breaking the law, which is indicated by repeated arrests
- is deceitful, indicated by lying, using aliases, and/or conning others for profit or pleasure
- cannot plan ahead and is impulsive
- is irritable and aggressive, seen in repeated physical fights or assaults
- has reckless disregard for self and other's safety
- is continuously irresponsible, failing to maintain consistent work behaviour or honour financial obligations
- has a lack of remorse, seen in the indifference or rationalization that occurs when the person mistreats, hurts, or steals from another.

The person must be at least 18 years old but with evidence of conduct disorder onset before the age of 15 in order to be diagnosed with antisocial personality disorder.

SOURCE: Based on diagnostic criteria from the DSM-IV. This is not intended as a substitute for the more extensive DSM diagnoses.

United States Youth Survey reported by Morse.[31] This survey used a national probability sample of 1,725 respondents, began in 1976, and provided nine waves of data over seventeen years. Respondents were interviewed annually using structured, face-to-face, confidential interviews. Violence was measured using the eight-item subscale from the CTS; injury was also assessed. For the years 1983, 1986, 1989, and 1992, female-to-male violence and severe violence was about double the rate of male-to-female violence and severe violence. Data were not collected every year.

To demonstrate, in 1992 female-to-male severe violence was reported by 13.8 percent of respondents, male-to-female by 5.7 percent.[32] At this stage the respondents were twenty-seven to thirty-three years old. On the intimate violence scale, females were higher than males on the following acts: kick/bite/hit with fist, hit with object, threaten with knife or gun, and use knife or gun. (On the latter, identical victimization rates were reported, but higher perpetration rates were reported by women.)

Men were higher than women on the following acts: beat up, and choke/strangle. Morse also reported data from this survey, finding little or no change in the ratio of female-to-male vs. male-to-female violence over the years, with slightly over twice as much female-initiated as male-initiated violence. This pattern remained unchanged in all years for which data were collected. When the most serious fight had involved one-sided violence that was not reciprocated, both men and women were twice as likely to report that the perpetrator was female (see also Stets and Straus).[33]

As with many other studies, to get a clear picture the reader has to examine the data tables, not the conclusion or abstract. In her abstract, Morse reports that "men were more likely than women to repeatedly beat their partner during the course of a year"; in her conclusion, she states that "men beat up their female partners an average of three to four times annually, or at least three times as often as women engaged in such violence." The data on which these claims are based are in Morse's Table 3. They show that in 1992, 2 percent of men "beat up" their partners an average of 3.3 times while 0.9 percent of women beat up their partners an average of 1.3 times. Here we have tiny minorities of each gender being compared to keep the "gender paradigm" alive (see Figure 7.1).[34]

The New York Children in the Community (CIC) Study

Ehrensaft et al. followed a randomly selected cohort sample of 543 children over twenty years to test the effects of parenting, exposure to domestic violence between parents (ETDV), maltreatment, adolescent disruptive conduct disorders, and substance abuse disorders on the risk of violence to and from an adult intimate partner.[35] Conduct Disorder (CD) was the strongest predictor of perpetration for both sexes, followed by ETDV. Essentially, the CD in some individuals failed to disappear but developed into a variety of adult personality disorders. Ehrensaft et al. call these "personality disorder trajectories." A failure of personality disorders to diminish from adolescent to adulthood predicted intimate violence in both sexes. Women with a pattern of distrust, interpersonal avoidance, unusual beliefs, and constricted affect were more likely to assault intimate male partners. This pattern was similar for males and will be discussed in Chapter 8. *It was personality disorder, not gender, that predicted violence.* As the authors put it: "It was personality functioning measured prospectively from adolescence to early adulthood (that) can distinguish individuals who will go on to perpetrate partner violence."[36]

The US National Comorbidity Survey (NCS) was a nationally representative household survey completed between September 1990 and March 1992 to assess mental illness.[37] The NCS involved face-to-face interviews with 8,098 people between the ages of fifteen and fifty-four. A probability subsample was then generated to assess the social consequences of mental disorders. Of that sample, 3,537 participants (N = 1,738 men, 1,799 women) were cohabitating or married and completed the CTS. Kessler et al. reported there was no significant gender difference in the prevalence of minor physical victimization reported by women (17.4 percent) and men (18.4 percent). Similarly, for minor violence, victimization exceeds perpetration in reports of both men and women (18.4 percent of men report victimization and 17.7 percent report perpetration; 17.4 percent of women report victimization and 15.4 percent report perpetration). For severe violence, reports of victimization did not differ significantly by gender (6.5 percent of female respondents and 5.5 percent of male respondents), but reports of perpetration did differ, with men reporting significantly less perpetration (2.7 percent) than women (6.5 percent).[38]

Kessler and colleagues also examined reciprocal aggression (i.e., couple aggression, in which both partners perpetrate aggressive acts and are victimized by their partner). As in prior studies, reciprocity was the norm.[39] Similar proportions of women (10.5 percent, SD = 1.2 points) and men (11.7 percent, SD = 1.2 points) reported both partners engaged in the same amount of minor violence. Of the participants reporting reciprocal minor aggression, "70.7 percent of the women who reported minor violence victimization and exactly the same percent of comparable men (70.7 percent) said that they reciprocated minor violence."[40] Of those reporting reciprocal minor violence, by far most women (85.4 percent) and men (90.0 percent) reporting reciprocal minor violence described the frequency by each partner as the same. Among those who reported committing severe aggression, each gender was more likely to report their partner as reciprocating than was the partner likely to report this. Of those reporting reciprocal severe aggression, again by far most men (96 percent) and women (80.4 percent) stated that the abuse frequency was the same for both partners. In this study, Kessler et al. replicated Stets and Straus's findings on this issue of reciprocity.[41]

Williams and Frieze recently analyzed the National Comorbidity Survey data. They reported several different violence patterns (as did Stets and Straus) based on a sample of 3,519, concluding that the most common was "mutual and mild violence" followed by "mutual severe violence." In terms of reactions to the violence, the similarities by gender outweighed the differences. More women than men reported perpetrating violence, and slightly more men than women reported being the victim of severe violence. The authors conclude that this "may challenge assumptions about women's victimization in relationships."[42]

The Oregon Youth Study

Capaldi, Kim, and Shortt examined data from an ongoing community-based longitudinal study of youth in Oregon (Oregon Youth Study, OYS).[43] By young adulthood, 9 percent of men and 13 percent of women were identified as engaging in frequent partner violence. Consistent with prior findings, frequent violence was most common in relationships with bidirectional abuse. As far as injuries were concerned, 13 percent of the young men and 9 percent of the women indicated they had been hurt at least once by partner violence, and again injury was also likely to be mutual.[44] No gender differences were found in fear of partner's abusive behaviour.[45] Women's prior antisocial behaviour and depressive symptoms predicted both their own abusive partner behaviour as well as their male partners' abuse. Notably, the women's characteristics were predictive over and above the contribution of their male partners' antisocial characteristics. These findings suggest "assortative mating" (people choosing partners like themselves) for antisocial behaviour, as well as the independent contribution of women's risk factors to the development of violent relationships. Stability of aggression was found for both genders. As Capaldi et al. concluded "aggression thus appears to be predominantly bidirectional"[46] and based on "assortative mating" (i.e., that aggressive people choose each other).

The results of several longitudinal developmental studies of women, all based on large community samples, generate a common conclusion: that female violence is common, occurs at about the same rate as male violence, and is generated independently of the actions of the "current boyfriend" or husband. The female violence has a long developmental history preceding the current adult relationship and so cannot be dismissed as self-defence. When violence does occur, the most common form is mutual, followed by female more severe, followed by male more severe. As Moffitt et al. say: "The argument that women's abuse perpetration in the community is too trivial to research could prove to be tantamount to arguing that smoking in the community is too trivial to research and scientists should focus on cases of lung cancer."[47]

The Archer Meta-Analytic Study

The most comprehensive study on gender differences in intimate violence was conducted by Archer.[48] This meta-analytic study examined combined results from eighty-two independent studies (including the US Violence against Women Survey) from which data were available for comparing gender rates of abuse perpetration. Based on combined data across studies (a combined data sample of 64,487), women were slightly more likely than men to use physical abuse (defined using the CTS) against an intimate partner (effect size or $d' = -.05$).[49] This was true whether or not outliers were removed and whether or not studies with a ceiling N of 800 were considered to offset swamping of the outcome by studies with huge samples. Samples from shelters were unrepresentative of community samples, since, by definition, they were male-violent/female-victim samples. This was not true of community samples. As with the dating samples reported above, the younger the sample, the higher the level of female violence relative to male violence.

Medical treatment for injuries across studies revealed an effect size of +.08, with women being slightly more likely than men to seek treatment.[50] Neither the use of violence nor medical treatment resulted in a large effect size. (An effect size of $d' = .08$ is a difference between genders of less than one-tenth of one standard deviation.) Archer's main results are reproduced here in Figure 7.4. Given the methodology employed by Archer, his work has to be considered the "gold standard" of studies in gender usage of violence.

Archer cites the norms regarding use of violence: the so-called "acceptance norm" repeatedly cited by Dobash and Dobash (for which no evidence has been reported) and the contrary "chivalry" norm (against males using physical aggression towards women).[51] A subsequent analysis of the data that disaggregated the violence into discrete acts found that women were more likely than men to slap, bite, kick, punch, or hit with an object. Men were more likely to beat up or choke and strangle, although "a substantial minority of endorsements of 'beat up' and 'choke or strangle' involved women perpetrators."[52] Gender differences ranged from "very small to medium." Samples selected for marital problems showed large effects in the male-perpetrator direction; student samples showed effects more in the female-perpetrator direction than community samples. Patterns of findings did not differ depending on whether perpetrator or victim was reporting. Archer concluded that "concern with the (female) victims in such cases is certainly not misplaced but regarding them as the only victims of partner violence is too narrow a view of the problem according to the present findings."[53]

Fiebert has amassed a bibliography of 159 peer-reviewed publications finding equal or greater aggression by females than males.[54] The total collected sample is greater than 109,000. An earlier version was published in 1997.[55]

In sum, across several large sample studies, with varying demographic compositions, dating violence is more likely to be perpetrated by female than male youths. The literature reviewed above demonstrates that this abuse

7.4 Meta-analytic study of sex differences in intimate aggression

	Number of men	Number of women	Effect size
Violence perpetration	30,434	34,053	-0.05*
Injured	7,011	7,531	+0.15
Medical treatment received	4,936	6,323	+0.08

* Women slightly more likely to be violent, by 1/20 of a standard deviation, women also more likely to be injured (by 1/6 of an SD, and to require medical assistance by 1/12 of an SD.). All values are from the perspective of the perpetrator.
SOURCE: Adapted from J. Archer, "Sex differences in aggression between heterosexual partners: A meta-analytic review," *Psychological Bulletin* 126, 5 (2000): 651-80, 657, Table 3.

results in injuries in an important minority of young men and women and further supports the original findings of Stets and Straus, obtained from the 1985 US National Survey.[56] These findings clearly run counter to the common assertion that female aggression in intimate relationships is uncommon and inconsequential. They also lead us to query, first, whether the rate of intimate abuse is at risk of increasing rather than decreasing with the next generation; and, second, to note that large social changes have been made in other relevant areas (e.g., smoking, drinking and driving, bullying). It might be the case that similar strategies, aimed at least in part at youth, through school education and public information campaigns, for instance, might be an effective strategy for reducing the prevalence of this serious public health issue.

Effects More Severe for Women

It is widely supposed that women's aggression against male partners is less likely than male aggression against female partners to result in serious physical or psychological harm. The Archer study (cited above) revealed a much smaller effect size for injuries by gender (one-sixth of one standard deviation) and hospitalization (one-eleventh of one standard deviation) than had been claimed by prior feminist theory. Other studies also have supported this finding. Felson found evidence that size and strength are important in explaining gender differences in violence generally.[57] Men were much more likely than women to injure their adversaries, and women were more likely to be injured, at least in incidents where the offender was unarmed. Gender differences were reduced when physical size and strength were controlled. In addition, physical power was unrelated to whether the respondent was injured in incidents involving guns or knives. These results suggest that physical differences between men and women are important in explaining gender differences in injury.

Cascardi et al. examined physical injuries and depressive symptomatology in 109 couples drawn from a clinic (ninety-three) and a community sample (sixteen).[58] In a severe aggression group, 11 percent of wives reported broken bones compared to zero percent of husbands. Women were somewhat more depressed in the clinic group. The representation problem addressed above in regard to clinical groups applies to this study.

Felson and Cares reanalyzed the NVAW data and compared patterns of intimate violence with stranger violence. They found that violence occurs more frequently between people who are living together than with strangers.[59] Assaults are more much more frequent when they involve spouses, cohabiting partners, and family members than when they involve strangers or other known offenders. Felson and Cares also found that men are more likely than women to produce minor injuries, but they are not particularly likely to produce severe injuries. Women are more likely than men to suffer minor injuries, but men are more likely to suffer serious injuries. Felson and Cares conclude: "We also observe evidence that contradicts the idea that violence by male partners tends to be more serious. First, the injuries to female partners tend to be less serious than the injuries to male partners. Second, violence by male partners is just as likely to be victim-precipitated as violence by female partners ... However, prior research also suggests that the frequency of men's violence against their partners is low relative to the frequency of verbal conflict among partners."[60]

Felson and Cares comment further: "Some factors are apparently inhibiting men, who are generally much more violent than women, from using violence against their female partners. The results in the current study show that those men who do engage in violence against their spouse and those women who engage in violence against their family members are more likely than other offenders to do so with high frequency. It is surprising that this result was obtained in what was essentially presented to respondents as a study of violence against women."[61] Felson and Cares are arguing that men's levels of violence in intimate relationships are actually inhibited, as compared to their non-intimate levels.

Coker et al. reanalyzed data from the NVAW survey (N = 6,790 women and 7,122 men) to assess associations between physical, sexual, and psychological abuse and current and long-term physical and psychological effects in men and women.[62] Results indicated that psychological and physical abuse were associated with much the same outcomes and had similar effects for men and women. The authors cautioned that it is possible that male victims were also perpetrators and that their mental health status resulted from inflicting abuse rather than from being victimized. Interestingly, they did not present this hypothesis for women.

The reanalysis of the Canadian GSS data by LaRoche, based on a sample of 25,876, also strongly refutes the idea that males do not suffer ill effects from intimate partner violence.[63] It is of interest that, though not all "victim" data in that survey were available for men, what was available indicated great similarity in male and female victimization. LaRoche reports that 83 percent of men who "feared for their life" did so because they were unilaterally terrorized by their female partners while 77 percent of women were unilaterally terrorized. Of the terrorized men, 80 percent reported having their everyday activities disrupted (compared to 74 percent for the terrorized women), 84 percent received medical care (the same rate as for terrorized women), and 62 percent sought psychological counselling (63 percent for women). Hence, in a nationally representative and huge sample, victim reactions for abused men were virtually identical to those of abused women. It was simply that earlier research was driven by a paradigm that avoided asking the right questions of men.

When these questions are asked, the results are surprising. An emergency clinic in Philadelphia found that 12.6 percent of all male patients over a thirteen-week period (N = 866) were victims of domestic violence. These patients reported having been kicked, bitten, punched, or choked by female intimate partners in 47 percent of cases, and in 37 percent of cases reported having a weapon used against them.[64] The authors observe that the numbers would have been higher except they had to stop counting after midnight and screened out "major trauma" cases, which could have upped the proportion injured by female partners. Note that many emergency clinics ask women but not men about possible domestic violence origins for injuries.

An emergency clinic study in Ohio found that 72 percent of men admitted with injuries from spousal violence had been stabbed.[65] The most frequent cause of admission for women victims was assault (53 percent). The authors report that burns obtained in intimate violence were as frequent for male victims as for female victims. As this study demonstrates, community samples, unless they require subjects to self-report as crime victims, show a different and more equivalent pattern of violence by gender than that alleged by the radical feminist perspective.

Finally, men have rarely had their fear of female violence assessed (the LaRoche analysis of the Canadian National GSS data is one exception). A study by Hines, Brown, and Dunning examined calls from men to the American national domestic violence helpline for men.[66] As the authors pointed out, it would be unlikely for male perpetrators or co-perpetrators to use this line. When the line opened, it received one call a day. When it was advertised in state telephone directories, it began to receive 250 calls a day. Given that 2.6 million American men are victims of severe violence, further usage increase is expected.[67] All but a few callers experienced physical abuse from their female partners (only 4 percent were gay), and a substantial minority feared their partners' violence and were stalked. Over 90 percent experienced controlling behaviours, and several men reported frustrating experiences with the domestic violence system; 52.4 percent of males who were currently in an abusive relationship indicated that they were fearful that their female partners would cause serious injury if they found out that they had called the helpline. Hines et al. state that "according to qualitative accounts, several physical attacks were reported to have occurred to the groin area" (17). Callers reported forms of violence that are not measured in surveys, such as having a partner try to drive over them with a car. Twenty-nine percent reported being stalked by their female partners. Callers' reports indicated that their female abusers had a history of trauma, alcohol/drug problems, mental illness, and homicidal and suicidal ideations. Hines et al. concluded that the "system in place to prevent IPV (interpersonal violence) re-victimizes these men and hence, no help is available for half the population."[68] Violent actions reportedly experienced by these men are listed in Figure 7.5

In the United Kingdom in 2005, "calls to domestic violence helplines by male victims have more more than doubled over the past five years."[69]

Types of Female Violence Reported by Callers to a Domestic Abuse Hotline for Men

Feminist theory alleges that females are universally more vulnerable to abuse by men than men are to abuse by women. This perspective has found little support in the data. Several studies indicate male victims are as likely as, or significantly more likely than, female victims to experience assaults involving the use of weapons.[70] George separated kicking and punching in his nationally representative sample and recommended what might be an important methodological improvement. Since women have less upper body strength than men, they may be more likely to use their legs than their arms during an altercation.[71] This was exactly what was found by Moffitt et al. and Morse in the cohort studies reported above.[72]

Pimlott-Kubiak and Cortina carried out a large-scale ($N = 16,000$) study of gender differences in traumatic reactions to violence victimization, intimate violence, stalking, and emotional abuse.[73] Arguing that earlier studies

7.5 Types of female violence reported by male callers to a domestic abuse hotline for men after having been asked a series of questions

Type	Percentage who experienced it	(N)
Physical aggression (N = 158 men)		
Slapped/hit	43.7	(69)
Pushed	41.8	(66)
Kicked	39.2	(62)
Grabbed	31.0	(49)
Punched	24.7	(39)
Choked	22.2	(35)
Spit on	9.5	(15)
Stabbed	1.9	(3)
Scratched	1.3	(2)
Controlling behaviours (N = 155 men)		
Does your partner try to control you?	94.8	(147)
Of those who were controlled, how were they controlled? (N = 147)		
Coercion and threats	77.6	(114)
Emotional abuse	74.1	(109)
Intimidation	63.3	(93)
Blaming, minimizing, and denying	59.9	(88)
Manipulating the system	50.3	(74)
Isolation	41.5	(61)
Economic abuse	38.1	(56)
Through the children (N = 107)	64.5	(69)

NOTE: The types of controlling behaviours were coded according to the Power and Control Wheel of the Duluth Model.
SOURCE: Adapted from D.A. Hines, J. Brown, and E. Dunning, *Characteristics of Callers to the Domestic Abuse Helpline for Men* (Durham, NH: University of New Hampshire, Family Violence Lab, 2003), Table 2.

had focused too specifically on PTSD, the authors broadened their assessment of trauma reactions and found eight distinct combinations of exposure profile, gender, and mental and physical health. The only thing that predicted the severity of psychological consequences was the degree of exposure, not gender. The authors concluded that their findings argued against theories of greater female vulnerability to traumatic outcomes.

Regardless of the variation in the studies, two conclusions seem reasonable: (1) women are injured more than men but (2) men are injured as well and are not immune to being seriously injured. Simply because the injury rates are lower, men should not be denied protection.

7.6 Victims by type and gender found in the United States National Violence against Women Survey

	Distribution by gender (percentages)	
	Men	Women
Victimized by multiple forms of violence (without sexual violence) (*N* = 509)	66.2	33.8
Victimized by child physical abuse (*N* = 1,713)	67.1	32.9
Victimized by adult physical abuse (*N* = 1,802)	56.4	43.6

NOTE: Total sample was 8,000 men and 8,000 women.
SOURCE: Adapted from S. Pimlott-Kubiak and L.M. Cortina, "Gender, victimization, and outcomes: Reconceptualizing risk," *Journal of Consulting and Clinical Psychology* 71, 3 (2003): 528-39, 533, Table 2.

The argument is sometimes made that men use threats more frequently than women, but Straus and his colleagues found that women reported using somewhat more psychological aggression than did men.[74] The "threatened to hit or throw something at partner" item correlated .52 with this scale, of which it is a part. Also, Giordano et al. in a study of 721 young adults found that women were more likely than men to threaten to use a knife or gun.[75]

Underestimating Male Victimization from Criminal Justice Statistics

Male victimization is not taken seriously, in part because of the gender paradigm described earlier and partly because of a cultural belief that men should be able to defend themselves or a disbelief in female violence. The item "burned him with something" is rated less serious by males than the item "burned her with something" is rated by females.[76] Law enforcement is lax when men are injured in domestic violence disputes.[77] When Dwayne Bobbit had his penis cut off by his wife in 1993, it became material for late night comedy routines, and his wife was found not guilty by reason of temporary insanity. This reaction would have been unthinkable with the genders reversed.

Buzawa and her colleagues, in a study of the police arrest policy in Detroit, found that "male victims reported three times the rate of serious injury as their female counterparts, 38 percent compared to 14 percent."[78] The police rarely arrested a female perpetrator. As Buzawa et al. put it: "Not one male victim was pleased with the police response. They stated that their preferences were not respected by the officers, nor was their victimization taken seriously. The lack of police responsiveness occurred regardless of the degree of injury. For example, one male reported requiring hospitalization for being stabbed in the back, with a wound that just missed puncturing his lungs. Despite his request to have the offending woman removed (not even arrested), the officers simply called an ambulance and refused formal sanctions against the woman, including her removal. Indeed, all the men interviewed reported that the incident was trivialized and that they were belittled by the officers."[79]

Brown studied differences in responses by the criminal justice system to assaults committed by males and females equated for severity.[80] Using police and prosecutorial case files, Brown examined 2,044 cases where the man was charged, 155 where the woman was charged, 118 where both were charged, and 617 where a complaint was filed but neither was charged. There were 206 cases where only the male partner was injured, and the female was charged in 60.2 percent of those. However, when the female partner was injured, the male was charged 91.1 percent of the time.[81] In no-injury cases, the male was charged 52.5 percent of the time, the female 13.2 percent of the time.[82] Hence, injuries made little difference to charging rates for female offenders (52.5 percent vs 60.2 percent).[83] Brown found that women were more likely to have used weapons and caused injuries and also to have received more serious charges (more than twice as likely to be charged with aggravated assault or assault with a weapon). Self-defence arguments by men tended to be disbelieved by police.[84]

Women who were prosecuted tended to have inflicted higher levels of injury against their victim than had prosecuted men and, as with arrested women, were more likely than men to have used weapons (knives and clubs).[85] In severe injury cases, 71.4 percent of men and 22.2 percent of women were found guilty.[86] The low percentage of women found guilty was due to "witness problems" (few men being willing to testify).[87] More than half the male victims refused to testify, and female perpetrators of severe injuries had charges withdrawn 77.8 percent of the time. This pattern was reversed for woman victims; the more seriously injured, the more likely they were to testify. Brown commented that "all of the evidence indicates that abused men fit the theory of the 'battered woman' better than abused women do."[88] In a similar study, Henning and Renauer found the same thing: almost one-half (47 percent) of the cases involving women arrested for domestic violence against a heterosexual intimate partner were rejected by prosecutors, and another 16 percent were dismissed by a judge.[89] Legal factors, such as a defendant's prior criminal arrests, use of a weapon, victim injury, and, most importantly, the type of arrest (i.e., dual vs. single arrest), all affected prosecutors' decisions to take these cases. Female defendants arrested for offending against a male intimate partner were treated more leniently than either male defendants or women arrested for domestic offences involving other types of relationships (i.e., familial, homosexual).

When we examine the Buzawa et al. study or the Brown study, it becomes apparent that the criminal justice system under- responds to male victimization. The situation for males in 2005 is much the same as it was for women in 1965. Hence, government "victim" surveys of intimate violence based on crime report data (police arrest, etc.) underestimate the incidence of male victimization. For this reason, the Straus studies using the CTS, which focus on conflict rather than on crime victimization, provide a fuller estimate of actual violence.[90] As Brown concludes:

> After laying charges, police are significantly more likely to take a man into custody than a woman, even when factors such as the level of injury inflicted and prior criminal record are taken into account. Nor do prosecutors tend to mitigate this disparately harsh treatment of men. On the contrary, prosecutors appear to pursue cases involving male suspects more vigorously than those involving female suspects. Thus men are more likely to be found guilty and are less likely to benefit from withdrawn charges, even though they are suspects in proportionately more of the no-injury cases. Men are also less likely to benefit from favourable plea bargains, despite the fact that they have committed, on average, less grievous offences. And men are significantly more likely to receive harsher sentences than women, even when all other relevant factors are taken into account. Indeed, gender is often *the most significant factor* in predicting how the law-enforcement system responds to incidents of partner violence."[91]

How We See Abuse

What constitutes "abuse" varies considerably according to the gender of both the perpetrator and the victim.

Sorenson and Taylor implemented a random-digit dialled survey in four languages of 3,769 adults in the Los Angeles area.[92] Respondents were presented with five vignettes in which characteristics of the victim, assailant, and incident were experimentally manipulated. The vignette variables (assailant's motive, type or intensity of abuse, whether alcohol was involved, presence of weapons, presence of children, frequency of abuse) and respondent characteristics were examined using a multivariate log regression. Respondent characteristics turned out to be unrelated to their judgments.

Judgments about women's violence against male intimates (versus the opposite) were less harsh and took contextual factors into account. The type of violence and the presence of a weapon played a central role in respondent judgments. Across vignettes, male violence was seen as more likely to be illegal, that the police should be called, that the assailant should be arrested and should serve jail or prison time, that a restraining order should be issued. It is important to note that while some of the abuse types were physical, others were psychological, involving control or humiliation. Physical abuse (slap, forced sex) was more likely to be perceived as illegal by women when the assailant was a man. In general, the genders agreed more than they disagreed, whatever the event. To test the hypothesis that social norms about female abuse are less clear, Sorenson and Taylor examined the standard deviation of the residuals (a measure of response variability); it was 36 percent greater when the assailant was a woman, suggesting much greater diversity of opinion or lack of a clear-cut norm.

Not only the general public but also professional psychologists rate aggression as less serious when it is performed by females and even when it is psychological aggression, according to a study by Follingstad and her colleagues.[93] Two scenarios describing the context and psychologically abusive behaviours with the genders reversed were given to 449 clinicians (56 percent male) whose median age was fifty-two. Psychologists rated male-perpetrated behaviour as more abusive and severe than they rated the wife's use of the same actions. Contextual factors (frequency, intent, and perception of recipient) did not affect this tendency.

As Follingstad et al. concluded that "the stereotypical association between physical aggression and males appears to extend to an association of psychological abuse and males."[94] Unfortunately this sometimes leads to serious problems. Coontz, Lidz, and Mulvey found that clinical predictions of dangerousness made in psychiatric emergency rooms consistently underestimated female dangerousness.[95] Predictions that a male would not be violent were correct 70 percent of the time, but for females, they were correct only 55 percent of the time.

Custody Evaluations

In many high-conflict divorces, custody evaluations are required. Two new books to assist evaluators in assessing for domestic violence, by Jaffe et al. and Bancroft and Silverman, both view domestic violence from within the gender paradigm described earlier.[96] Jaffe et al. devote a paragraph to dismissing violence against men and then proceed to focus on the abusive male throughout their book, citing high overlap between spouse abuse and child abuse rates of 30-60 percent. The "abuse assessment" is designed to be given to the woman only. Both Jaffe et al. and Bancroft and Silverman use the term "he" as synonymous with "perpetrator." The connection of male-perpetrated wife assault to child abuse stems from a paper by Appel and Holden, who reported a 40 percent overlap based on reviews of studies of women and children in shelters.[97] In their "representative community samples," by contrast, the overlap was only 6 percent. Appel and Holden present a graphic of various patterns of the flow of family violence. Female-perpetrated violence toward a male spouse is not included among the five separate patterns of family violence they present.

Custody assessors should be aware of the largest study of child abuse and neglect that, to my knowledge, has ever been conducted. This is a study of 135,573 child maltreatment investigations conducted by Health Canada and published by the National Clearing House on Family Violence.[98] The study designates the abuse type as physical abuse, sexual abuse, neglect, emotional maltreatment, "multiple categories." The investigations are further divided into substantiated, suspected, and unsubstantiated categories. Substantiation rates do not, in general, vary by gender of perpetrator and run from 52 to 58 percent. Biological mothers (as compared to biological fathers) are the more likely substantiated perpetrator of physical abuse (47 vs. 42 percent), neglect (86 vs. 33 percent), emotional maltreatment (61 vs. 55 percent), and multiple categories (66 vs. 36 percent). The biological father is the most likely perpetrator of sexual abuse (15 vs. 5 percent). For physical abuse the substantiation rate was 6 percent higher for fathers, bringing the total perpetration rates to equality (see Table 4, page 49, in the report). These data, based on a huge nationally representative sample, tell a very different picture than that represented by Jaffe et al. or Bancroft et al., both of whom over-rely on shelter samples to draw erroneous conclusions about risk to children.

Chapter 12 below presents a study by Dugan that examines the long-term effect of criminal sanctions on subsequent wife assault. One of the sanctions Dugan examines is the giving of child custody to a woman when a man has violated a restraining order. The unintended effect of this sanction was negative: it led to increases in subsequent violence. As Mills describes, the violation of restraining orders is often by mutual consent, but this concurrence is overlooked by a custody evaluation that is swayed by a male-blaming paradigm. Men who feel that an injustice has occurred and that contact with their children is being jeopardized may become enraged. The unintended effect of increased violence may therefore be a result of heavy-handed application of the law. Dugan found that, in states where men with a restraining order automatically lost custody of their children, recidivist assaults against women increased (compared to states where this sanction was not in effect; this is discussed further in Chapter 12).

How Did It Happen?

How mainstream governments came to support domestic violence policy based on radical feminism is an intriguing question. I think most people, including governments, think of liberal feminism when they think of feminism and they see the domestic violence issue as related to liberal feminism. Most women who call themselves feminists don't know about Catharine MacKinnon's radical argument that women "cannot" give consent for sex (because of false consciousness) or the Marxist notions behind radical feminist ideas of the "male oppressor." Feminism was liberal when the laws and policy were instituted (women's rights issues that everyone agreed on), but then women's groups became increasingly radical because of group polarization.[99] When groups with a "dominant tendency" (i.e., a political leaning on one side of an issue) discuss that issue within the group, they become more extreme in the direction of the dominant tendency (measured across a wide variety of opinions and policy decisions).[100] This occurs because the individual members gain status within the framework of the group reality by taking increasingly radical positions to the extreme of the group leaning. It also occurs because more arguments are amassed in the direction of the group leaning, while arguments against the group leaning are censored. Hence, liberals become radicals through group discussion. This historical point in gender politics is where people like Erin Pizzey were ostracized by radical feminists. Once domestic violence policies have been drafted, government bureaucrats just enforce homeostasis without really knowing what ideas they are supporting, and both left- and right-wing governments support feminist domestic violence laws. These policies are not challenged because there is no public forum for the alternative discussion of ideas.

Conclusion

In the best studies, with the largest and most representative samples (i.e., community or epidemiological), presented without a "crime victim" filter on the data, female violence rates are higher than male rates.[101] Also, in the largest study done on effects of abuse, no gender differences were found.[102] The best predictor of intimate partner violence is not gender but personality disorder.

There are cases of wife abuse so extreme that it is difficult to imagine the abuse occurring with genders reversed. These cases usually involve a form of hostage-taking or captivity of the victim and are, fortunately, very rare. However, they receive a great deal of publicity and have a huge impact on our judgments of gender and IPV. Nevertheless, Chapter 6 gave reasons to believe that female IPV and even terrorism exist as well (if defined by unilateral severe violence and instrumental uses of violence). Also, it is not the case that men do not suffer from intimate abuse victimization. The LaRoche data analysis clearly refutes this idea.[103] However, police treatment differs in the extreme by gender. Judgments about violence and abuse differ according to the genders of the assailant and the victim. While this is easily understood for some acts (such as punching or beating up), where the consequences may be greater for women victims, the results also apply to actions where the consequences are the same (e.g., being stabbed or burned). But the view that women are more vulnerable is shared not only by the general public but also by psychologists. A question raised by the above data is this: what happens to these men? No shelter houses exist and the problem is neither recognized nor sympathized with. A man who presents to the police with an injury is likely to be viewed as having brought it on himself. Ironically the situation for these men is identical to that of abused women during the Age of Denial.

8 The Social Psychology of the Perpetrator

The interested reader is referred to an excellent overview of the research on violent husbands by Holtzworth-Munroe, Bates, Smutzler, and Sandin.[1] In providing an overview of psychological factors associated with abusiveness, Holtzworth-Munroe et al. review psychopathology (personality disorders, depression), borderline personality disorders, attachment disorders (dependency, jealousy), anger, hostility, alcohol abuse, social skills deficits, head injuries, biochemical correlates (one study suggesting higher testosterone is associated with intimate violence), attitudes toward women (concluding the results are "mixed and contradictory"), relationship standards, desire for power (an inconsistent risk marker for intimate violence), feelings of powerlessness, lack of resources, and stress. Of course, many of these risk markers are interrelated in real life. This chapter and those to come will review many of the causal factors in domestic violence and try to develop a theory that takes account of the crucial ones.

A Social Learning Theory of Intimate Violence

In 1963, a small sample of nursery school children took part in an experiment that subsequently changed psychology. They were divided into groups that did different things: watched an adult aggressively attack an inflatable "Bobo Doll," watched a film of an adult doing the same thing, watched an animated cartoon with an aggressive character in it, or experienced no prior aggression at all. Soon after, all the children were mildly frustrated by the experimenter. The frustrated children who had watched any prior exhibition of aggression behaved more aggressively than the children in the control group. Follow-up studies by psychologist Albert Bandura showed that high-status adults were the most effective "models" for aggression and that dependent children were the most effective learners. Punishing the child for acting aggressively only inhibits the aggression in the presence of the punitive parent. It goes underground and is displayed when that parent is not around. Aggressive adolescent boys had fathers who punished them severely for aggression at home. The paradox was that the parents may have produced the very thing they tried to stamp out.[2]

Any habitual strategy can be shaped by cultural expectations, as well as by an individual parent. Examples include anorexia, based on cultural tastes for slim women, or *hikikomori*, which is occurring with increasing frequency in Japan, involving young boys (age 13-15 usually), who withdraw to their rooms for long periods of time, watch DVDs, surf the internet, and play computer games, venturing out in the middle of the night to pick up bento boxes (with the day's food supplies) to take back to their rooms. The phenomenon is thought to be related to the enormous pressures put on Japanese youth (and especially first-born males) to "succeed" by excelling in increasingly competitive academic pursuits and in the corporate world, coupled with pressure to uphold the family name. One Japanese psychiatrist reported boys with this "affliction" as being lethargic and noncommunicative.[3] Few cultures, including our own, have a vocabulary for learned dysfunctional strategies caused by societal pressures. We are more familiar with a vocabulary for "crime" or "disease."

Derived from earlier learning experiments with animals, social learning theory (SLT) analyzes the acquisition of habits, defined as chronic, repeated ways of doing things. Taking learning into the human realm, social learning discovered that the principal means of human learning was through observation. From the perspective of social learning theory, physical abuse is a habit, a learned means of coping with stress. Every time it succeeds in reducing the stress or eliminating the circumstances that produced the stress, it becomes more fixed, more entrenched. That success provides the "reward" that sustains and deepens the habit.

By understanding the circumstances contributing to this acquisition, the habit can be "undone" or altered. Social learning principles, as will be seen in a later chapter, formed the basis for the first treatment groups for assaultive males. The goal of treatment was to get the males to analyze their use of anger and abuse and learn other ways of expressing anger.

SLT views our reactions to "aversive life events" (events we would like to change or avoid) as learned habits based on two perceptions: (1) the "controllability" of the event and (2) our personal capacity for enacting that control (see Figure 8.1). Note that aggression is in the left-hand column along with more positive reactions. That is because these reactions all have in common a tendency to act outward on the event to alter the external world. The actions in all other columns involve avoidance, withdrawal, or "learned helplessness" (passive acceptance).

8.1 Social Learning Theory: Responses to aversive life events

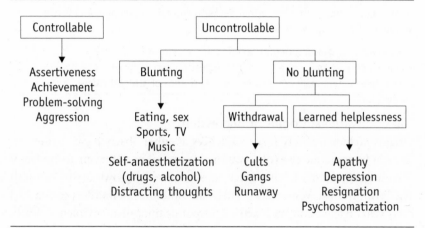

All habits have three aspects or components that help us to understand why they persist: origin, "instigator" (the event that triggers the habitual action), and "regulator" (reactions to the habitual action that either extinguish it or sustain it). One origin of a habit can be the very body we inherit. Large men are more likely to be rewarded for physical actions, including violence. They might learn while still boys that conflicts can be resolved through aggression. Conversely, people who do not have this inherited means of aggression may learn indirect ways to act aggressively.[4] But origins such as physical capability simply set limits or create an opportunity for reward. Reward is defined as obtaining what you want or achieving your objectives. The large person does not inherit the tendency to be physical (or violent) but rather the body that makes physical actions more likely to succeed. Someone who finds rewards for using physical actions is likely to repeat them.

Experiments in both animal and human learning show that we unconsciously repeat the actions that are rewarded. Occasional reward strengthens the tendency to use violence, and a habit develops. Activity level and physical stature, for example, are inherited and are viewed as setting limits on the types of aggressive responses that can be developed and influencing the rate at which learning progresses. The inherited characteristic will not by itself determine aggression but only create a learning-reward opportunity. In this way, social learning theory acknowledges biological influences on behaviour. Learning can be guided by physical endowment, which can influence the probability of rewards for aggressive responses.

8.2 Social Learning Theory: The origins of aggression

In SLT, aggression is a response that seeks to control or eliminate an aversive situation. It develops with three factors:

- observational learning (e.g., observing aggression in the home)
- reinforced performance (e.g., trying aggression successfully)
- structural determinants (e.g., genetic inheritance of strength, size)

The Observational Origins of Aggression

Origins include our very first experiences at either observing an action carried out by someone else (observational learning) or testing an action (reinforced performance). Of course, everyone who grows up in modern "civilization" observes violence. There are thousands of murders committed every year on television, and "action" adventure films involve violence, death, and mayhem. The observational learning aspect of acquiring a habit remains one of the major contributions of social learning theory and has been used extensively to support arguments that television can increase aggression, the basis being that men who watched violent television as boys were more likely than were others to have been convicted of a serious criminal offence by the time they were thirty.[5]

Others argue that the television preferences and criminal behaviour are not necessarily cause and effect but might both result from a predisposition to violence, which might be genetic. In response, social learning advocates point out that even in cases where exposure to observed aggression is not self-selected, subsequent violent behaviour still increases. This may be due to what Rowell Huesmann calls the acquisition of aggressive cognitive scripts, which are blueprints or programs for aggressive behaviour learned through observation.[6] These blueprints include evaluations of whether or not the other person can be controlled, the chances of success, and whether or not rewards or punishments might follow the use of aggression. In the case of wife assault, rewards typically would mean "winning a power struggle" or "blowing off steam," while punishments could include such consequences as police intervention, one's wife leaving permanently, or one's own guilt or shame for the use of violence.

There are some questions left unanswered by this approach. For example, why would observation and subsequent acting out be needed when hitting someone is so obvious and easy that making a habit of it should not require an elaborate learning process? Moreover, the "blueprint" for aggression may get distorted when someone is truly enraged. But the research on social learning, typically done only with the approval of university research ethics committees, has not been able to infuriate subjects in a way that resembles the reality of intimate rage.

However, witnessing violence in one's own home between one's parents has an impact that goes beyond the impersonal violence of television. Straus, Gelles, and Steinmetz found from the national survey data that both males and females who had observed their parents attack each other were three times more likely to have assaulted their spouses.[7] The reported rates jumped from 10.7 percent to 35 percent for those who had been child witnesses of violence. If the parents had been observed hitting each other, the adult's chances of being a perpetrator (or victim) of violence against a spouse more than tripled. The analysis of Straus et al., however, simply reported a correlation or association between the two. The kids who witnessed violence also had other potential causes for their adult violence: their families were poorer, they were more likely to be struck themselves by parents, and their families had little social support and were generally more "dysfunctional." Such other factors were more likely to have been experienced in homes where the parents struck each other and hence are said to be confounded (or mixed up with) with the child's observation of violence. Nor could the child's own inherited predisposition be ruled out as a possible cause.[8] To the scientist who likes to narrow the possibilities, this natural "confounding" of potential causes for adult violence was a problem. The result was a debate over the rate and meaning of what is called "intergenerational transmission," that is, the transmission of an abuse rate from one generation to the next. Do violent parents produce violent offspring by having their abusive actions observed or overheard? What if the children are the victims of abuse? Are they then more likely to become perpetrators of abuse?

Apart from observational learning, habits may be acquired through self-teaching, or trial and error. Gerald Patterson runs the Oregon Learning Center, which specializes in managing unruly kids through the systematic application of social learning principles. Patterson and his colleagues have studied aggressive boys in detail. In one study they observed boys who were initially passive at school.[9] Some of these boys just stayed out of trouble by avoiding others. They remained passive, avoidant, and non-aggressive. Other passive boys were occasionally forced into battle. Some lost, got beaten up, and remained passive and submissive. Others occasionally succeeded in halting attacks on themselves by fighting back. Something strange then happened with these successful resisters: not only did they learn to use aggression as a defensive tactic but also they then went on the offensive, looking for fights. They became predatory where once they had been avoidant. This type of learning is called trial and error. It gradually "shapes" behaviour and gets it to take a narrow form that we might call habitual. The action becomes fixed and rigid. The learner's repertoire of problem-solving strategies atrophies to the narrow band where success was found. All conflicts lead "automatically" and quickly to the learned habit: to anger and a threat of aggression.

Of course, trial and error learning is not the only origin or "acquisition mechanism," as Albert Bandura called it. A popular advertisement in boy's comics in the 1950s and 1960s was the "Charles Atlas" bodybuilding ad. Set up like a comic strip, the ad showed a skinny guy at the beach who gets sand kicked in his face by a muscular adversary. He goes home, builds himself up using the Charles Atlas training system, and on his return punches out the bully. His girlfriend is impressed; she feels his bicep. The original stimulus here is observational, but the practising aspect is trial and error. Today, female "action heroes" function much the same way for women (and as we have seen, female violence has increased in incidence with younger groups); they are typically young, beautiful, and adept at the martial arts.[10] Female action heroes in the 1940s, such as "Wonder Woman," had magical powers and rarely needed to use violence.

The evidence for social learning processes at work focuses on the question of what proportion of abused children go on to become abusing spouses or parents. The answer to this question, based initially on retrospective studies, is about 40 percent. Psychologist Catherine Widom reviewed all available evidence bearing on this question and concluded that being abused as a child did increase one's chances of being an abusive parent but the pathway between the two was not simple or direct.[11] Too many of the studies done had been retrospective in nature. Starting with a group of abusive parents, they had worked backwards to ascertain what percentage of them had been abused as children. The rates were typically quite high. However, such an approach cannot indicate how many abused children go on to become non-abusive parents. Since retrospective studies start with abusive parents as their sample population for study, non-abusive parents are "selected out" of the research. They don't qualify for the study. As a consequence, rates of being victimized in their childhood are unknown. To rectify this problem, Widom did a "prospective" study in which known victims of child abuse were traced years later to see whether they were more at risk for adult violence. Abused children turned out to have higher subsequent rates of violent crime, especially abused male children.

Developmental psychologist Byron Egeland at the University of Minnesota also did a prospective study to answer this question.[12] In this study, an identified group of abused children was followed *before* they became abusers

8.3 Abused children are less astute socially

Abused children are:

- less likely to see situational causes of another's behaviour during conflict
- more likely to see conflict as generated by a character trait in the other
- more likely to think of aggressive responses
- less likely to think of bargaining and negotiating strategies.

SOURCE: Based on K. Dodge, G.S. Petit, J.E. Bates, and E. Valente, "Social information-processing patterns partially mediate the effect of early physical abuse on later conduct problems," *Journal of Abnormal Psychology* 104, 4 (1995): 632-43.

as adults. This is important because it eliminates the retrospective bias described above. That is, if researchers choose abusive adults to trace back retrospectively, they never get to find out what percentage of abuse victims go on to become non-abusive adults. Egeland found that 40 percent in his prospective sample went on to maltreat their own children.

Ken Dodge and his colleagues also performed a prospective follow-up of children who were known to be abused before kindergarten age.[13] In Grade 5, these children were given a hypothetical conflict scenario and asked about the motivations, actions, and best solutions to the conflict. As Figure 8.3 summarizes, they were more likely than non-abused children to attribute the problem to the character of the "other," to think of aggressive responses, and to believe these would successfully resolve the problem.

Two conclusions are typically drawn from these findings: one is that the experience or witnessing of abuse increases one's chances of being abusive, and the other is that the majority of abused children do not go on to be abusive. This is not a contradiction, because the modelling or observation influences, but does not decide, whether someone will become abusive. Social learning theorists argued that people could acquire a capacity to act aggressively through observation but that this capacity would not be translated into action unless violence served some function for them as adults. Many abused children may not have had the need or adult opportunity to engage in violence. Others may have had long lists of what are called protective factors: positive events that could militate against early negative experiences. By now a number of such protective factors have been identified – having one supportive adult in an otherwise hostile early environment, being in an emotionally supportive family as an adult, or involvement in psychotherapy as an adolescent or young adult.[14] And yet I have seen cases where abuse had been going on for at least three generations, which is as far back as most families' oral history extends.

The learning of physical violence seems relatively straightforward, in that exposure to the violent act provides a learning opportunity. However, when we come to apply social learning processes to the learning of intimate abusiveness, some problems arise. For one thing, how is the information learned? While it is relatively simple to learn how to make a fist and strike a blow, the intricacies of emotional abusiveness seem much more complex. How does one "model" how to find a particular partner's emotional weak point, when such vulnerabilities vary from one person to the next? Did the child observe the father exploiting similar vulnerabilities in the mother? Why do virtually all abusive men everywhere in English-speaking countries use the same sexually derogatory words to abuse their partners? Why do most of these men never use these words in public? Why is abusiveness so often accompanied by extreme jealousy and blame-avoidance? Are these personality qualities also learned? The available evidence doesn't provide answers to these questions.

Another problem is motivation. There is no evidence that men learn abusiveness to women in order to fend off physical attacks. Is there some set of feelings common to a young victim of a schoolyard bully and a man arguing with his wife? Powerlessness? In fact, in intimate conflict men appear to feel generally powerless, threatened, and out of control. But to say that an inner feeling rather than a measurable external event can trigger violence takes one step beyond the original social learning formulation. Nevertheless, it is instructive to "line up" the findings of prospective studies on children exposed to abuse with the men studied because of their use of intimate violence.

The Instigators of Aggression

The instigators of aggression include all the triggering events in the current or adult social milieu. For example, that abused boy, now grown up, gets into barroom fights because someone makes fun of his weight. That insult triggers an inner state of discomfort in him called "aversive arousal." Aversive arousal is a state of excitement that feels unpleasant, uncomfortable. This state is something he would like to get rid of (the aversive aspect). The perceived insult creates a felt tension that the person has an urgency to reduce or remove. Just how it gets removed depends on the learning history of the person. That learning history is likely to make them respond to aversive arousal in one of two ways: either they see the event that caused the arousal as controllable or not. If they see it as not controllable, they try to reduce aversive arousal by escape or withdrawal from the event. Let's say, for example, that the aversive triggering event is the actions of an abusive father who comes home late, yelling and being abusive. He startles the kids and threatens his wife. He smashes things. The kids are in no position to control him. If they tried to confront him, things would get worse. Maybe on one occasion they did try this, and quickly learned not to. What options do they have to reduce the aversive arousal they feel in the face of their father's abusiveness? They might try to escape from the room, to somehow blunt the aversiveness of their father's abuse. If they succeed, they might try to escape further by listening to music on a Walkman. They try to tune out the father's yelling. But if he won't let them escape, if he demands their attention, their route to quiescence is blocked. The only remaining resort is to dissociate, "tune out" or self-hypnotize. These choices are outlined in Figure 8.4.

If they see the father's abuse as controllable, however, the aversive arousal is converted into feelings of anger, which prepare them to take action and override other feelings that might interfere with action. Psychologist Raymond Novaco describes anger as an "emotional response to provocation" that serves a function of overriding less acceptable emotions such as guilt or fear.[15] Anger can carry built-in rewards and so be difficult to alter or change. "Arousal will be probably construed as anxiety if the person withdraws from or avoids the provocation and as anger if he or she approaches. In another sense, whether one experiences anger or anxiety is a function of one's coercive power relative to the provoking person. As the perception of personal control diminishes, the arousal of anxiety during a provocation has increased probability."[16] In another sense, whether one experiences anxiety or anger is a function of one's coercive power relationship to the provoking person. As

---

8.4 Social learning theory: Instigators of aggression

Situational modelling influences are:
- disinhibitory
- facilitative
- arousing
- stimulus-enhancing

Aversive treatment through:
- physical attacks
- verbal threats and insults
- adverse reductions in reinforcements

Incentives (e.g., killing for gain)

Instructional control (e.g., the sergeant orders you to kill)

Bizarre symbolic control (e.g., the cat orders you to kill)

the perception of personal control diminishes, the arousal of anxiety during a provocation becomes more likely. Indeed, anger can be aroused to generate a sense of personal control.[17]

At some point in the developmental reward history of the abusive man, anxiety and anger lead to acting out or coercive behaviours that were occasionally rewarded. When this occurred, a habit of reacting with anger and coercive or punitive behaviours began to develop. This habit will become remarkably durable for several reasons. First, having been established by intermittent reward, it will be notoriously difficult to extinguish. For proof of the tenacity of habits formed through intermittent reinforcement, think of people pulling hopelessly away at slot machines that reward only every thousandth pull, or "hackers" still pursuing the perfect golf shot (which may occur only once in one hundred shots). Second, the *expression* of anger can be intrinsically rewarding. It feels good because it releases bodily tension, and it generates actions consistent with the man's notion of what "manliness" entails.

Novaco lists a series of functions that anger serves for the angry person: the energizing of behaviour, expressive and communicative functions, and defensive functions. The energizing function increases the vigour with which we act and may increase the chances of being rewarded (termination of aversive events), especially when it enables the person to assertively confront provocation or injustice. Interpersonal problems in intimate relationships may never reach the discussion stage until one person becomes demonstrably angry. A break into cold anger can lead to problem resolution if the anger is expressed in a problem-solving way rather than in a way that blames, hurts, and escalates a sequence of antagonism. Anger not only acknowledges that a problem exists but also has a self-promotional function in advertising potency, expressiveness, and determination. To the extent that these qualities are part of one's sex role or self-definition or are thought to be valued by the immediate group, then anger expression enhances self-image. The defensive function of anger works by short-circuiting anxious feelings of vulnerability. It is less distressing to be angry than to be anxious. In fact, one represses anger because of anxiety about its consequences. When that anxiety is overcome, anger is expressed. If this function operates successfully, angry people should feel less anxious, although this may depend on the active expression of anger, its being acted out. In this sense, anger also externalizes the conflict by directing attention to the other and hence to the non-self.

Novaco describes two other functions of anger; anger arousal generates a sense of potency. To borrow a phrase from Eric Fromm, it converts *a feeling of impotence into a feeling of omnipotence.*[18] Through this process, the entire experience of the self and the anger-provoking stimulus are transformed. For example, in either the personal or the political arena one's feelings of alienation and self-blame are reversed into feelings of power, self-worth, and conviction, while the erstwhile oppressor is vilified and becomes a worthy target for anger and violence. "The feeling that one has little control over his own destiny may lead to attempts to restore oneself as an active agent. This may involve attacking those who appear to be influencing and controlling the individual."[19] Anger arousal and the thoughts associated with it can instigate aggressive actions that are expected to change the situation to remove the aversive stimulus.

All these aspects of emotional life are shaped by culture; men are programmed to ignore fear and act anyway, to be "agentic," that is, active rather than passive. When men feel a situation is going out of control, they tend to react with anger. However, the form that anger takes – its target and its means of expression – vary enormously from man to man. In these ways, the emotional response to provocation is learned and a habit of anger sustained. Both the amount of anger and the way it is expressed are problems for abuse perpetrators.

When abuse by a parent is chronic, it wears down the defences of the victim so that "active strategies" to reduce the aversiveness feel beyond the will. Many children who grow up in abusive households learn passive withdrawal as a tactic for blunting the aversiveness they experience. They retreat into other worlds – television, computers, music, and books – and begin to inhabit those worlds exclusively. The body is still present in everyday reality, but the mind is somewhere else.

In the studies of trauma victims, one response to repeated trauma that shows up repeatedly is something called dissociation. Dissociation means that the person has learned to split off their thought processes from their body. A sexual abuse victim who cannot escape the abuse learns to "watch" her own victimization from a spot on the ceiling. She dispassionately sees her uncle performing sexual acts on her. When you interview her about her "adult" life of prostitution, she describes her tricks in the same dissociated manner. No affect, no feeling. "I was going down on him," she says matter of factly, "and the cops were cruisin' by." She has learned to blunt all feeling associated with her sexuality. The split was forced upon her by the trauma of the early sexual violation. Some therapists refer to this as "psychic numbing."

When "blunting" or evasive tactics don't succeed in reducing the aversiveness of existence, victims try something more radical like running away, getting ill, or suicide – anything to get rid of the constant aversive arousal, the sickening tension that won't disappear. The main reason why many abuse victims don't become abusive is that they have learned other, more passive, strategies for dealing with aversive arousal. In fact, using aggression against an abusive parent is likely to be punished in the extreme. The action sequence may be stored in memory, but the impulse is stifled whenever circumstances do not seem controllable. Abusers do not seem controllable; they seem to have all the power. When abuse victims do successfully fight back, they are often amazed that their former perpetrator was vulnerable.

In the social learning view, both aggression and achievement start from the perception that circumstances are controllable. They both involve direct action designed to change those circumstances. Aggression, however, is designed to control and change people. Social learning places less emphasis on "expressive aggression," viewing aggression instead as instrumental. The aggressor has learned to reduce tension by being violent. If you yell, stomp and scream, and threaten and hit, things will fall into place. If the violence gets rid of the tension state by changing the actions of the offending person, it is rewarded, and a habit of violence is becoming entrenched.

Social learning theory sees aversive arousal as being generated by current events called "aversive experiences," by external "stimuli" such as arguments, or by criticisms from another person. But could aversive arousal be generated internally in the absence of aversive experiences? Could it, like water behind a dam, build up with time? If so, the person experiencing internally generated aversive states would be in a serious predicament. They would feel bad and yet would lack an explanation for their bad inner feeling. To what could it be attributed? Since the male orientation is to what is "out there" rather than to interior states, the chosen explanation for the aversive arousal will probably hinge on something or somebody else. It will involve blame. Blaming someone else has another advantage; it facilitates getting angry with, maybe even yelling at, that person. This allows the tension to be discharged through anger display.

Males in particular, by virtue of sex role conditioning that discourages inner awareness, are unlikely to view aversive arousal as internally caused.[20] Of course, male sex role conditioning, whatever its shortcomings, cannot be blamed for female IPV.

Jealousy and Conjugal Paranoia

Abusive men are frequently irrationally jealous about their wives. They monitor their wives' use of space and time, questioning all contact with other men. They are suspicious about any other man's interest in their wife, as if all anyone would see in her would be a sex object. Some men question their wives' choice of clothes as "too sexy." A female client of mine had a husband who checked her soiled underwear for signs of intercourse! Martin Daly and Margo Wilson found jealousy to be the motive most frequently cited by police for spousal homicides.[21] Sociobiologists would be tempted to see this behaviour as directed to control over reproduction. At some point, however, one has to ask how genetic fitness could possibly be maximized by acting on irrational perceptions. Are baseless suspicions genetically sound? Perhaps it is possible for a jealous husband to be too careful. Sociobiology, adopting the widespread view that all domestic violence is male-perpetrated,[22] has trouble explaining the evidence for female jealousy or violence (see Chapter 6).[23] In social learning terms, unfounded jealousy is called a "delusional instigator." Apart from supplying this title, however, social learning has little to say about how delusional instigators develop and how changes in intimacy can become an "aversive stimulus."

Assaultive males in our treatment groups talked about jealousy and abandonment a great deal in treatment even while trying to maintain a distanced "cool" or dismissing tone about their emotional dependence on their wives. Men in the beginning of treatment complain a lot about their wives' behaviour, in part as a way of deflecting the focus from their own abusiveness. It was not unusual for a man who had been complaining at length about his wife's worst habits to be asked, "so why do you stay with her?" and to draw a blank. It was as though he had never asked himself that question. And the answers he tried to give would be typically flimsy and transparent. What he would never say was that he needed her, found himself irreparably bound to her, and regarded as terrifying the prospect of being alone. This process is described as "masked dependency" and helps maintain control over the other person. With abusive men, the abuse would allow the man to overlook his own masked dependency needs. Of course, many of the same control motives have been shown to operate for abusive women as well.

The Videotape Simulation Study

To test these intimacy-related issues with abusive men, Jim Browning and I concocted an ambitious study, which I will describe in some detail here.[24] We endeavoured to capture, on videotape, the essence of the conflict issues described by men in treatment. We thought that if we could have professional actors play out couples in conflict in scenarios scripted by the issues of treatment, and then measure men's reactions to these videotapes, we might have some evidence for the role of intimacy issues in generating fear and anger, the forerunners of abuse. We thought of a variety of ways of measuring reactions to the videotapes, ranging from self-reports in which the men fill out lists of emotion scales to represent what they are feeling to complicated psychophysiological measurement. The latter involved strapping research subjects into a form of polygraph, popularly known as a lie detector, which measured psychophysiological indices associated with emotion, such as "galvanic skin response" (electrical conductivity in the skin), pulse transit time, and respiration.

The first problem was to get the conflict scenarios right. We wanted one scenario to reflect "abandonment" themes as described by the men, another to reflect "engulfment" themes, and the third to be neutral with respect to intimacy change. We also wanted one scenario to be male-dominant and the other female-dominant. The abandonment themes included the woman telling her husband that she wanted to visit a nearby town (Seattle) for a long weekend with female friends. He reacts with outrage, telling her that they will be "sitting ducks" in the singles bars he imagines them to be frequenting. She doesn't believe this and soon informs him that she will be joining a woman's "consciousness-raising" group. In the engulfment tape, the woman complains that the couple has no quality time anymore and that the man spends too much time on solitary pursuits. He says to her, in effect, "get a hobby." In the neutral scenario, the couple argues over where to spend their holidays, but since they will be spending them together in any event, the scenario is neutral with respect to changes in amount of intimacy. Each scenario had to be emotional and believable for it to have its desired impact on the subjects who watched it. Fortunately, once the tapes were made, everyone saw them as realistic.

The second challenge was to get a subject sample. While men were sent by the courts for mandatory treatment, there was nothing in their probation order that said they had to participate in research studies. The generally violent men were no problem; they came from our treatment group. The maritally conflicted men were recruited from local couple-counselling programs. The happily married men proved to be the biggest obstacle. We ran advertisements on the sports pages of the local paper, and many men responded.

The study itself involved two lab sessions. The first was spent entirely on collecting data through questionnaires and self-reports. This session showed that the wife assaulters had attitudes toward women that were no different from those of the men in the other groups. They did, however, have one set of characteristics that could contribute to their abusiveness: they had both a stronger need for power over others and poorer verbal assertiveness skills. In other words, they lacked the verbal capacity to satisfy their power needs. The second session was used to show the videotaped scenarios to each subject individually, each time recording his self-reports of emotion and his perceptions of the conflict.

The emotional self-ratings showed a difference between the groups of men. The wife assaulters reported the greatest anger and anxiety from the scenarios in general, and the highest ratings of all from the abandonment scenario. There was something about this group that made them especially emotionally reactive (about two and one-half times as reactive) and more sensitive to rejection or abandonment than the happily married men, the generally violent men, and the maritally conflicted men. For some reason, none of these differences showed up in the physiological measures. But the wife assaulters reported themselves to be more angry and anxious. They also said they would be more likely to use violence to resolve the conflict presented if they had been the man in that situation. They perceived the husband as being humiliated by the wife's demands. The other men hardly even saw them as demands. The wife assaulters also saw the intimacy issues portrayed in the videotapes as being more relevant to their relationships than did the other men.

Cognitive Distortions and Anger

Eckhardt and his colleagues have improved on our dependent measure using something called the "articulated thoughts in simulated situations technique."[25] This approach stemmed from the work of Beck, who outlined cognitive biases associated with extreme anger.[26] These include "arbitrary inferences" (making assumptions or drawing conclusions in the absence of supporting evidence), "selective abstraction" (understanding an experience on the basis of one detail taken out of context while ignoring salient aspects of the situation), "overgeneralization" (constructing a general rule from one or a few isolated incidents and applying the rule generally), "magnification" (overestimating the incidence of events and reacting incongruously to the situation), "personalization" (the tendency to engage in self-referent thinking when presented with situations having little to do with the self), "dichotomous thinking" (categorizing an event in one of two extremes). Eckhardt, Barbour, and Davis had men listen to anger-arousing audiotapes and articulate their thoughts during tape stoppages. These thoughts were then coded for the above cognitive distortions. Eckhardt et al. also had abandonment themes in their experimental conflicts (jealousy and an overheard conversation in which a wife plans to leave her husband). Reactions to a control conflict situation were compared to reactions to the experimental situations.

8.5 Cognitive biases associated with extreme anger

Arbitrary inferences	making assumptions or drawing conclusions in the absence of supporting evidence.
Selective abstraction	understanding an experience on the basis of one detail taken out of context while ignoring salient aspects of the situation.
Overgeneralization	constructing a general rule from only one or a few isolated incidents and applying the rule generally.
Magnification	overestimating the incidence of events and reacting incongruously to the presenting situation.
Personalization	the tendency to engage in self-referent thinking when presented with situations having little to do with the self.
Dichotomous thinking	categorizing an event as one of two extremes.
Hostile attributions	blaming the cause of an event on another's malicious and hostile intentions.

SOURCE: Adapted form C. Eckhardt, K.A. Barbour, and G.C. Davidson, "Articulated thoughts of maritally violent and non-violent men during anger arousal," *Journal of Consulting and Clinical Psychology* 66, 2 (1998): 259-69.

Maritally violent men articulated a significantly greater degree of cognitive biases than did non-violent men in response to the experimental tapes but not to the control tapes.

Irrational Beliefs

Ellis and Dryden outlined four "core irrational beliefs" that they targeted in rational-emotive therapy.[27] These were "awfulizing" (an exaggerated rating of the badness of an aversive event), "low frustration tolerance" (severe intolerance for discomfort [I can't stand, can't tolerate, can't take]), "demandingness" (rigid, absolute beliefs that events or people must be a certain way and that conditions such as success and approval are absolute necessities), and "self/other rating" (evaluations of the total worth of a human being on the basis of a specific behaviour or attribute). Dutton showed how faulty attachment led abusive men to have deficits in their ability to "self-soothe" – they would catastrophize an event, experience extreme arousal, and be unable to lower their arousal level.[28] Often, the catastrophized events had an abandonment theme, hence, the psychiatric term "conjugal paranoia."[29] Eckhardt et al. found an increase in irrational beliefs for maritally violent men exposed to experimental anger conflicts.[30] In distinguishing mild from severe aggression groups, demandingness, magnification, and awfulizing were all pronounced and were significantly correlated with the discriminant function. Hence, a combination of two irrational beliefs and one cognitive distortion typified the thinking of violent men, although other distortions and irrational beliefs were involved to a lesser extent.

These studies were an important first step in getting "inside the head" of the wife assaulter. We now knew that he saw intimate conflict differently from other men, men who had been raised under the same socializing culture as he had. The abusive man saw more threat, felt more anxious and humiliated, and reacted with more anger than other men, even men who were violent outside relationships. There was a distinct emotional and perceptual response from the men whose violence was relationship-specific.

It began to appear that more than mere imitation of actions sustained abusiveness. At that time, we could not account for the origin of these differences, and we did not know that they might be part of a larger psychological picture. We could only say that they existed. We knew nothing then, as we do now, of what we call the "abusive personality." Instead, we couched our description of wife assaulters in the vernacular of the day: social learning theory.

Neutralizing the Conscience and the Regulation of Violence

The last category in social learning analysis is what is called the regulators of aggression. Since behaviour is shaped by the immediate reactions it generates, the regulators include the external rewards and punishments that occur after aggression (i.e., the reactions of others) and "self rewards and punishments" (i.e., the way we think about what we have just done). In this category is what some would refer to as conscience. Two learning principles in the regulation of violence are especially important. First, in the absence of overt punishments from others, the violence is rewarded. Males who act violently are automatically rewarded through the means described above: ending aversive tension and producing a feeling of autonomy and domination. These feelings are enough to regenerate the violence on another occasion. Second, these feelings have to occur only occasionally to sustain the habit; if the violence is intermittently rewarded, the habit will be entrenched. Nevertheless, according to Straus's surveys, about one-third of men who assault their wives do stop being violent without the police getting involved. What happened in these cases to generate this "spontaneous desistance" is unknown. The woman may have convinced the man that if he ever did that again, she would leave, or the man may have been upset by his own reaction to what he did.

With assaultive men, aggression evokes a variety of responses from their partners, including calling the police, leaving, staying away for some time, threatening to leave the relationship, being fearful and sexually guarded,

---

8.6 Social Learning Theory: regulators of aggression

External   *Reinforcement*
- tangible rewards
- social and status rewards
- acknowledgment of injury
- alleviation of aversive feelings

Vicarious reinforcement
- observed reward
- observed punishment

Punishment
- inhibitory
- informative (e.g., the teaching value of the law)

Internal   *Self-reinforcement*
- self-reward
- neutralization of self-punishment
- moral self-justification
- palliative comparison
- euphemistic labelling
- displacement of responsibility
- diffusion of responsibility
- attribution of blame to victims
- dehumanization of victims
- downplaying of consequences

Self-punishment
- guilt, shame
- acceptance of responsibility

---

etc. Many of these responses, if taken seriously, generate punishment to the abuser. They may not be taken seriously, however, if they have been made before without follow-up action. They become "idle threats" without sanctioning power.

There are great differences in conscience, the self-punishment aspect of abuse. Psychopathic men do not suffer pangs of conscience. Most normally socialized men who are not psychopathic do go through some remorse if they abuse their wives. The remorse feels bad, and to avoid it, men go through what Bandura called the "neutralization of self-punishment." In social learning terms, conscience is the ability to punish the self for violating one's own standards of conduct. In men with conscience, feelings of guilt or shame would follow the use of aggression against a loved one. The "contrition phase" that Walker described would be generated by conscience. Since pangs of conscience are painful, a sufferer finds ways to "neutralize" them by mentally reconstructing a more acceptable version of a reprehensible action one has committed. Perhaps the most famous neutralization is Adolph Eichmann's proclamation at his Jerusalem trial, "I was only following orders," so thoughtfully described by Hannah Arendt.[31]

In the case of intimate aggression, this mental reconstruction of the act includes blaming the victim for having provoked the aggression ("If she hadn't nagged me so much, this wouldn't have happened ... I told her not to make me angry"), ascribing the aggression to external factors such as alcohol consumption ("I only get that way when I drink"), and minimizing the severity of the act both through the language used to describe it ("the night we had our little incident") and the comparisons made ("most men are as violent as I am"). I have routinely asked court-mandated men to estimate what proportion of the men in the general population are as violent as they are. Their average estimate is 85 percent (the real incidence is about 3 to 4 percent). Ironically, abusers and feminists agree in ascribing wife assault to social factors. For the wife assaulter, this exonerates him from personal responsibility for his violence. He uses the inflated incidence as "evidence" that he is only following social dictates. Figure 8.7 shows some frequently used excuses.

While all or some of these aspects of denial may be present in most wife assaulters, victim-blaming is by far the most prominent. Men arriving in treatment groups regularly introduce themselves by a list of their grievances with their wives.

Effects of Observing Violence on the Child Witness
In their study of the 1975 US National Survey, Straus, Gelles, and Steinmetz describe what they call the social heredity of family violence. By this term

---

8.7 Neutralizing self-statements

"The Bible (Koran, etc.) says I am the head of the household and she must submit."
"I'm not a real batterer because I never used a weapon."
"I was so drunk, I didn't know what I was doing."
"It happens in every marriage."
"It's no big deal in my culture."
"My old lady deserves everything I dish out."
"She drove me to it. If she didn't keep nagging me none of this would have happened."
"I got mad at her only once."

they refer to the learning of violence in the family of origin. In order to ascertain whether such learning occurred, Straus et al. compared husbands whose parents had not been violent toward each other to husbands who reported at least one incident of violence between their parents. Men who had seen parents physically attack each other were almost three times more likely to have hit their wives during the year of the study. In fact, about one out of three had done so (35 percent) compared with one out of ten (10.7 percent) of the men with non-violent parents. These statistics were virtually identical for women: daughters of violent parents had a much higher rate of hitting their husbands (26.7 percent) compared to daughters of non-violent parents (8.9 percent). The scale of violence toward spouses rose steadily with the violence these people observed between their parents. Sons of the most violent parents had wife-beating rates ten times greater than those of sons of non-violent parents, and daughters had a rate of spouse-beating six times greater.[32]

Straus et al. argue that the family of origin is the place where people experience violence first and learn the emotional and moral meaning of violence. For most, this experience occurs through being a victim of violence; for some it is the observation of parental violence. Straus et al. describe the "unintended lessons" of such violence: (1) that those who love you are also those who hit you, (2) that hitting other members of the same family is morally acceptable, and (3) that violence is permissible when other things don't work. Being hit as a teenager clearly makes people more prone to spouse-assault: people who experienced the most punishment as teenagers had spouse-beating rates four times greater than those whose parents did not hit them. Straus et al. concluded by reporting a "double whammy" effect: when people both experience violence from a parent themselves and witness parent-parent violence, they are five to nine times more likely to be violent than are people who experience neither.[33]

Rosenbaum and O'Leary obtained comparison data for twenty "maritally dysfunctional" couples (receiving therapy for problems related to marital violence) with a group of twenty non-violent couples.[34] The authors reported that abusive husbands were more likely to have been victimized by parental physical abuse and to have witnessed parental violence. They did not report covariation between the two. The significant between-group difference for witnessing violence appeared whether using the husbands' self-reports or the wives' reports of their husbands' family backgrounds.

Kalmuss reviewed prior studies on the effects of observing father-mother violence and found mixed results that she attributed to methodological inconsistencies in the research.[35] Some studies, for example, examined

attributional consequences of witnessing parental violence rather than effects on violent actions as such. Others failed to distinguish behavioural
effects due to victimization from those due to witnessing and also failed to
disentangle the two dependent behavioural variables involved: likelihood
of aggression and likelihood of victimization.[36]
    Furthermore, effects of parent-parent aggression may be contingent upon
the role of the same sex parent. If children model the behaviour of the same
sex parent, we would expect sons to show increased aggression when they
witnessed father-mother aggression. We would expect daughters who witnessed such aggression to be at increased risk for victimhood. These effects
should be reversed for mother-father aggression. Using the data from the
1975 US National Survey, Kalmuss established that 15.8 percent of her respondents had witnessed parental hitting, and 62.4 percent had themselves
been hit by parents while in their teens.[37] By correlating these responses
with CTS scores for their adult relationships, Kalmuss was able to generate
the following findings: witnessing parental hitting and being hit as a teenager are both related to severe husband-wife (and wife-husband) aggression. However, for both types of aggression, the stronger effect comes from
witnessing parental hitting (which doubles the chances of aggression toward a spouse). As with the Straus et al. study,[38] Kalmuss reports a double
whammy effect: the odds of IPV increase dramatically when sons both observe and are victimized by parental aggression.
    Kalmuss concludes that two types of modelling occur for parental aggres-
sion. "Generalized modelling" communicates the acceptability of aggression
between family members and increases the likelihood of any form of family
aggression in the next generation. "Specific modelling" occurs when individuals
reproduce the particular types of family aggression to which they were exposed. Intergenerational modelling, Kalmuss concludes, involves more specific than generalized modelling in that severe marital aggression was more
strongly related to witnessing than to being victimized by parental aggression.
    It is not clear how Kalmuss arrives at the conclusion that witnessing in-
volves more the specific than the general modelling mechanism, especially
given a further finding from her study that there is no evidence for sex-
specific learning of aggression. Exposure to fathers hitting mothers increases
the likelihood of both husband-wife and wife-husband aggression in the
next generation, and neither is specified by sex. That is, both sons and daughters are more likely to be victims and perpetrators when they have witnessed
parental hitting. This latter finding is consistent with social learning findings that challenge the notion that children are more likely to imitate same
sex parents.[39] As Kalmuss points out, however, her study has two limitations:

first, as with most studies of this sort, it is based on retrospective accounts, which may be reconstructed to justify current use of marital aggression. Second, the data report on only one member of a current relationship. It is not known whether the results would change by including the current partner's experience with parental violence.[40]

A later study by Kalmuss and Seltzer partly rectified the latter problem. This study examined continuity in the use of violence across relationships (first and second marriages), and concluded that evidence supported the notion that individual characteristics rather than current family structure better accounted for use of violence. The authors also concluded, however, that a repertoire of marital violence was not necessarily rooted in early childhood experience but frequently originated in the first marriage and maintained itself in new relationships.[41]

How can we sum up these findings? The weight of evidence, it seems, suggests that witnessing violence in the family of origin strongly increases the chance that violence will be used in the adult relationship. This learning is not sex-specific but occurs about equally for men and women and independently of the sex of the aggressor parent. Also, witnessing violence increases the chances of becoming a victim or a perpetrator of violence.[42] Very little is known about factors that determine which direction one takes. Self-taught aggression also occurs and carries over from the relationship in which it was learned to new relationships. However, witnessing violence never occurs in a vacuum. Rather it occurs in a dysfunctional family where other stressors affect the child as well, including a lack of a secure base and emotional abuse directed at them. These, in turn, may produce an "emotional template" that increases the probability of abuse perpetration, victimization, or reciprocity. The specific direction may depend on factors experienced later. Recall the longitudinal studies of abusive women described in Chapter 6. There was little report of early family influences in their lives, but adolescent conduct problems predicted later IPV. Were the conduct problems produced by experiencing abuse at home? We will further explore this triad of events in Chapter 10 on the formation of the abusive personality.

Immediate Effects of Witnessing Parental Violence

We do not know whether the "modelling effects" described above are examples of simple imitation or whether witnessing parental violence produces other negative psychological consequences that act as mediating variables for adult aggression. Carlson estimated in 1984 that about 3.3 million children in the United States witnessed interparental violence every year.[43] The research of Peter Jaffe and David Wolfe, among others, has indicated a variety of adjustment problems for children who witness violence. Wolfe, Jaffe, Wilson, and Zak evaluated behavioural problems of 198 children from violent and non-violent families.[44] The CTS was used to assess violence, and the Achenbach Child Behaviour Checklist to assess the children's behavioural problems. Half of the children were from transition houses. Interviewers established via interviews with the mother whether the children had witnessed the violence, but the study did not report scales for extent of exposure. Amount of violence had significant effects on diminished social competence and behavioural problems, but this effect was mediated by maternal stress. Over one-quarter of the children assessed had behavioural problems falling into the clinical range on the measurement instrument, and these children tended to have been exposed to a higher frequency of violence and to have experienced more negative life events. Additionally, the maternal stress variable accounted for 19 percent of the variance in child behaviour problems. Relevant here is the work of Schore, demonstrating the impact on the child's neuro-emotional development of attachment signalling from the mother.[45] If the mother is stressed, that communication has to be altered.

Jaffe, Wolfe, Wilson, and Zak later reported that adjustment problems seemed more severe for boys than for girls exposed to parental violence.[46] Boys displayed a higher degree of both externalizing symptoms (e.g., argumentativeness, bullying, temper tantrums) and internalizing symptoms (e.g., withdrawal, attention deficits). General social competence was impaired, and all the above problems were significantly associated with the degree of violence witnessed. Girls from abusive homes were described as demonstrating internalizing symptoms related to depression and anxiety. Boys, however, also showed heightened signs of inadequacy, dependency, anxiety, and depression. The authors raised the question of whether these behaviours were modelled by abusive fathers in addition to violence.

Jaffe, Wolfe, Wilson, and Zak also compared victims of child abuse with children who had witnessed parental violence (defined as having been in visual or auditory range of the parents during conflict where violence occurred at least once in the previous year).[47] The profiles of behavioural problems in the two groups were quite similar. Child Behaviour Checklist scores indicated that witnessing parental violence was as harmful as suffering physical abuse. However, as the authors point out, common factors existed for both groups such as family stress, abrupt home changes, inadequate child management, and parental separations. Most of these samples were drawn from shelters, so they may be an extreme and non-representative group. However, they conclude that, for this group, exposure to family violence is a major factor determining children's problem behaviour.

Interestingly, some of the problem areas identified by Jaffe et al. for this sample of children from violent homes, such as exaggerated dependency and impulse control problems, have also been identified as common in populations of wife assaulters.[48]

Several studies on the effects of witnessing parental battering found a constellation of behavioural problems to be associated with witnessing interparental abuse.[49] These included lower social competence, shyness, depression, conduct problems (irritability, impulsivity), school phobia, poorer academic performance, and attention deficits. Hilberman and Munson found a variety of health-related issues for children who had witnessed interparental abuse, including headaches, stomachaches, diarrhea, ulcers, intestinal difficulties, asthma, enuresis, insomnia, sleepwalking, and nightmares.[50] Many of these trauma symptoms are also found in abusive males.[51]

Dutton argued that witnessing abuse or experiencing abuse can have two broad effects on the child.[52] First, it can provide the opportunity to model physical aggression, as described by Kalmuss, leading to a behavioural repertoire of actions. Second, it can lead to the development of what Dutton calls the "abusive personality," by generating trauma reactions.[53] Of course, not all children who witness or experience abuse become either traumatized or abusive. For example, Lehmann found that the development of PTSD symptoms in children who witnessed violence in the family was associated with the child's witnessing at age nine or earlier, seeing violence for more than four years, and violence perpetrated by multiple perpetrators.[54] This suggests that their mother may have been in multiple abusive relationships. Other factors must somehow interact with these early experiences.

Even for more extreme experiences, the differential "resilience" factor applies. Rind, Tromovitch, and Bauserman found that many lay persons and professionals believe that child sexual abuse (CSA) causes intense harm (regardless of gender) pervasively in the general population.[55] The authors examined the basis for this belief by reviewing fifty-nine studies based on college samples. Meta-analyses revealed that students with CSA were, on average, only slightly less well adjusted than controls. However, this poorer adjustment could not be attributed to CSA, because family environment (FE) was consistently confounded with CSA and explained considerably more adjustment variance than CSA, while CSA-adjustment relations generally became non-significant when studies controlled for FE. Self-reported reactions to, and effects from, CSA indicated that negative effects were neither pervasive nor typically intense, and that men reacted much less negatively than women. Basic beliefs about the effects of CSA in the general population were not supported. If "family environment" interacted with childhood sexual abuse, it would certainly also interact with witnessing maternal abuse, especially in samples from transition houses.

Dutton, van Ginkel, and Starzomski, and Dutton showed that being shamed by a parent, in conjunction with being physically abused, significantly increased the likelihood of acting abusively as an adult.[56] The shaming and abuse acted in a synergistic fashion to greatly increase the effects of physical abuse. Having an abusive personality sets the stage for intimate abusiveness by creating repeated dysphoric states or internal aversive stimuli that the man learns to extinguish through abusive explosions. However, cultural and relationship factors interact with this personality in a fashion not unlike a chemical formula.

The Douglas and Straus study of cross-cultural effects of corporal punishment on dating aggression (see Chapter 6) probably constitutes the most comprehensive study ever conducted of learning effects.[57] In this study, 6,900 university students in seventeen countries reported CTS scores for violence by their parents directed toward them when they were children or adolescents. They also reported their use of violence in a current dating relationship and whether violence had been used against them. Finally, they reported whether they had ever injured a partner. The findings indicated that with other variables controlled for (such as social desirability or response bias), corporal punishment was a risk factor for (1) approving of partner violence, (2) committing partner violence, and (3) injuring a partner. These results applied to both male and female students. Women were somewhat more violent (115 per cent) than men summed across cultures.

Douglas and Straus point out that corporal punishment is used by parents to "correct" misbehaviour by their children and that respondents reported using violence to "correct" perceived misbehaviours by their partner (such as sexual infidelity). In other words children learn that violence is the appropriate way of punishing misbehaviour by others. Corporal punishment may be the least severe form of parental violence. It is not even considered abuse in many countries (although some Scandinavian countries have moved to make it illegal). Despite the perceived innocuous nature of corporal punishment, it is a risk factor for later dating aggression. Straus argues that what is learned by being spanked is that when someone does something wrong, you hit them. Not that the specific action is mimicked, but the main effect is on acceptance of violence as a means of generating compliance.

Limitations of Social Learning Theory

Social learning theory had one big advantage over previous theories of wife assault: it could account for individual variation. For a long time social learning theory seemed to be the best way to think about explaining wife assault. With its extensive research base, it could relate wife assault to a large body of general studies on aggression. However, there were persistent problems with a social learning analysis. For one thing, social learning, largely as a result of its reliance on lab research methods, views people as "responding to stimuli," so that violence is always triggered by an external event. Like a rat in a cage (the context from which social learning theory developed), the wife assaulter is viewed as responding to external events (conflict, an aversive stimulus, etc.). The person has no "inner life," apart from deciding whether or not an "aversive stimulus" is controllable and having conscience-like reactions to their own behaviour.

This portrait is very unlike the one offered by battered women. Their descriptions portray the man as generating tension and arousal in the absence of objective changes in his environment. He "becomes irritable for no apparent reason" and reacts with escalating verbal abuse and then physical abuse. He is pathologically jealous, drawing ludicrous conclusions about non-existent affairs. He externalizes blame for everything. He is never wrong. He experiences sleep disturbances, anxiety, and depression. He goes through tension cycles that are unrelated to his surroundings. These cycles of tension suggest an inner life that is much more complex than social learning depicts, one that can scarcely be "modelled" because it is interior and private. Batterers do not merely react to external stimuli; they create a different view of the world where emotional bumps become earthquakes. Neither social learning nor feminist theory nor the psychiatric labels we have seen so far can account for these syndromes of rising and falling tensions, or the shifting phases of emotion, perspective, and attitude. A deeper, more pervasive form of personality disturbance seems to be at work.

This is suggested too by the difficulty social learning theory has in predicting whether someone who experiences abuse in the family of origin will become a perpetrator, a victim, or both. Similar experiential variables seem to predict what appear to be divergent pathways. Surprisingly, little is known about the differentiation into the victim and perpetrator roles. Victims and perpetrators have more background experiences in common than they do with non-victims/perpetrators.[58]

Attitudes and Violence

Feminist theory emphasized attitudes as purveyors of patriarchy. Hence, the attitudes of individual men were viewed as causes of violence. "Intervention" systems like the Duluth model were focused on confronting "sexist attitudes" or male entitlement. The problem was that there was no evidence that batterers had "sexist attitudes." It might simply be, as Bandura stated, that batterers "violated their own self standards" when it came to using abusive behaviour. Certainly, the research on acceptance of violence did not support the idea of sexist attitudes driving violence. As reported in Chapter 6, a study by Simon et al., using data from an American representative sample of 5,238 adults, found only 2.1 percent of males (and 1.5 percent of females) believed it was acceptable for a man to hit a women "to keep her in line."[59] The mythical "acceptance of violence norm" described by Dobash and Dobash was just that, a myth.[60]

Holtzworth-Munroe et al. reviewed the studies of attitudes towards women.[61] On the whole, the evidence suggests no relationship between attitudes and intimate violence. One study by Stith and Farley did find a relationship (a correlation of $r = -.33$ between husband violence and sex role egalitarianism).[62] Several other studies found no relationship.[63]

Smith also tested "patriarchal beliefs" by asking 604 Toronto women each to estimate her partner's response to a series of four questions tapping this attitude and then correlating the projected attitude with her reports of his violence on the CTS.[64] (Women were not asked about their own use of violence). Smith argued that he was assessing "patriarchal ideology," but the responses supplied looked very non-patriarchal. The women said their partners would disagree that a man has a right to decide (1) whether his partner has a right to work outside the house (64 percent), (2) whether she should go out for the evening (68 percent), and (3) whether to have sex without a consenting partner (80 percent). The only statement that did not get a majority disagreement was "sometimes it's important for a man to show his partner that he's head of the house" (47 percent). The women also said that 90-96 percent of their husbands would not approve of violence toward them. Even if he learned she was having an affair or she hit him first, the majority (75 percent) said he would not approve of violence. The most obvious conclusion from Smith's data would be that "patriarchal ideology" simply did not exist for these men and was not related to use of violence. Instead, Smith lumped the attitude measure in with educational attainment and other "socioeconomic risk factors" and claimed he had "parsimoniously explained 20 percent of the variance in wife beating." Of course, it's impossible to tell what proportion of that is accounted for by projected attitudes since Smith offers no proof that people can accurately interpret the attitudes of others, and the precise contribution of "attitudes" is not given. Instead,

Smith hypothesizes about a "violent sub culture" made up of low-income, violent men. A reader of his paper might ask: where's the violence? What the Smith study shows is how a variable that was part of feminist mythology about abuse is uncritically assessed by domestic violence researchers. The bottom line is that one cannot assess an attitude after the fact of violence having occurred and then claim that the attitude "caused" or was a risk factor for the violence. It's an impossible conclusion to draw. Why? Evidence from numerous social psychological studies shows that attitudes change to become consonant with behaviour. This is done to reduce "cognitive dissonance" about an inconsistency between acts and attitudes.[65] A study cited by Holtzworth-Munroe et al.[66] provides a clear example: Crossman, Stith, and Bender found that "18 percent of the variance in men's scores on a measure of sex role egalitarianism was accounted for by the men's use of severe violence." The attitudes are brought into line with the preceding behaviour, which is often inexplicable to the perpetrator.

What is measured after the violence occurs may not have existed beforehand. The infamous woozle effect appeared for reports of attitudes to violence. Stith et al. performed a meta-analytic study of risk factors for assault perpetration and concluded (on the basis of four studies) that the effect size for attitudes was .30.[67] That would have made attitudes more important than anger as a risk factor for abuse. However, one of the four studies they cite as evidence for attitudes is the Smith study described above. Stith et al. assure the reader that all studies in their meta-analysis were methodologically sound.[68] I disagree. Moreover, if you remove the Smith study, the meta-analysis no longer contains the requisite four independent studies. Despite the lack of evidence for attitudes as risk factors for male abusiveness, attitudes constitute the central focus of "psycho-educational" models of intervention.[69]

A final note on the learning of abusiveness: while the evidence is quite strong that growing up in an abusive family increases the likelihood of using abuse as an adult, the fact remains that the majority of people growing up in abusive households do not go on to become abusive.[70] Kaufman and Zigler point out that "transmission rates" fluctuate from 18 to 70 percent partly as a function of research design.[71] Retrospective studies and studies using identified abusers understandably produce higher transmission rates. Studies based on national representative samples produce lower rates (e.g., Straus and Smith).[72]

These considerations raise the question of whether different people react differently to being abused or witnessing abuse. Chapters 9 and 10 argue that certain personality disorders form early in life, including borderline personality disorder (BPD) and antisocial personality disorder (ASPD). There is some evidence that exposure to parental violence in persons predisposed to these personality disorders presents a multiplicative effect, a sort of "double whammy."[73] Moffitt et al. found that persons exposed to parental violence who went on to develop conduct problems were most likely both to choose violent partners and to perpetrate violence in intimate relationships. Ehrensaft et al. found that persons exposed to parental violence were more at risk to develop personality disorders.[74] Those in whom these disorders did not resolve were more likely to use intimate violence. This happened for both males and females. Ehrensaft et al. argued that the presence of a personality disorder rather than gender was the main predictor of intimate violence.

Dutton outlined the specific ways that abuse contributed to borderline traits, which in turn contributed to abusiveness in male batterers.[75] Data being gathered by Babcock and Dutton suggest the same is true for females.[76] People predisposed to attachment disorders or personality disorders with an attachment aspect may be especially reactive to experiencing violence in the family of origin. Seeing their security base attacked may carry symbolic value more psychologically destructive than mere modelling of aggression. The insecure attachment resulting from this experience may provide a faulty sense of self from which aggression is used in an illusory attempt at regaining power. In any event, research now indicates that far more than specific behaviours is transmitted intergenerationally – that entire dysfunctional personality constellations can be transmitted.[77]

9 Subtypes of Perpetrators

We begin with the subtypes of violence patterns. As described in Chapters 6 and 7, Stets and Straus found that mutual violence was the most common pattern within a couple, followed by Female more severe, followed by Male more severe.[1] Personality disorders in either or both parties appear to contribute to both the choice of an abusive partner and the tendency to be abusive.[2] It is possible to find personality disorders in both mutually violent relationships and in relationships where one person terrorizes the other. Studies of the terrorizing type of perpetrator have been done on male abuse perpetrators. Some early work is beginning to be done on female abuse perpetrators.[3] (I avoid the term "batterers" because many of the men in these studies have not battered anyone. On the other hand, "battered women" are typically known to have been battered.)

"Personality disorders" are defined as self-reproducing dysfunctional patterns of interaction.[4] In some cases, they affect all social relationships; in others, they manifest primarily in intimate relationships. Dutton described an "abusive personality" as being characterized by shame-based rage, a tendency to project blame, attachment anxiety manifested as rage, and sustained rageful outbursts, primarily in intimate relationships.[5] This "abusive personality" was constructed around a fragile core called "borderline personality" (see the definition of personality disorder in Chapter 4).

In a direct test that pitted gender vs. personality disorder as causes of IPV, Ehrensaft et al. studied a peer cohort for twenty years in a large-sample, longitudinal study.[6] They found that minorities of both men and women developed personality disorders that, in some, failed to dissipate after the teenage years. As described in Chapter 7, these lasting personality disorders best predicted violence in intimate relationships. Ehrensaft et al. call these enduring patterns "personality disorder trajectories." A failure of personality disorders to decline predicted intimate violence in both sexes. Women with a pattern of distrust, interpersonal avoidance, unusual beliefs, and constricted affect were more likely to assault intimate male partners. As the authors put it: "It was personality functioning measured prospectively from adolescence to early adulthood [that] can distinguish individuals who will go on to perpetrate partner violence."[7]

A variety of researchers have found an extremely high incidence of personality disorders in assaultive populations. Studies have found incidence rates of personality disorders to be 80-90 percent in both court-referred and self-referred wife assaulters, compared to estimates in the general population ranging from 15 percent to 20 percent.[8] As the violence becomes more severe and chronic, the likelihood of psychopathology in these men approaches 100 percent.[9] Across several studies, implemented by independent researchers, the prevalence of personality disorder in wife assaulters has been found to be extremely high. These men are not mere products of male sex role conditioning or "male privilege"; they possess characteristics that differentiate them from the majority of men who are not repeat abusers.

The MMPI and Assaultiveness

According to Groth-Marnat, the MMPI is "a standardized questionnaire that elicits a wide range of self descriptions scored to give a quantitative measurement of an individuals' level of emotional adjustment and attitude toward test taking."[10] The test-taking measure is composed of three scales: the L Scale, designed to detect a naive, global attempt to present oneself in a favourable light; the F Scale, whose items are infrequent and suggest deviant attitudes; and the K scale, indicating clinical defensiveness. Obviously, in a forensic assessment (including assessment for inclusion into an abusers' treatment program), consideration of response defensiveness is an issue. The MMPI also contains ten original clinical scales that include Hypochondriasis, Depression, Psychopathic Deviate, and paranoia, among others. Computerized printouts will show corrected elevations for these groups (generated originally in 1943 by comparison of mental patients in Wisconsin with community controls), a variety of supplementary scales, content scales, and breakdowns of the clinical scales into "Harris-Lingoes" Subscales. Clearly, a full description of the development and interpretation of the MMPI or the MMPI-II is beyond this review. The interested reader is referred to Groth-Marnat for an excellent description of the most widely used self-report scale in psychology.[11]

Hale and his colleagues administered the MMPI to sixty-seven abusive males.[12] The composite profile revealed an elevation on the Psychopathic deviate (Pd) subscale and, more specifically, a 24/42 two-point code (Pd plus D [Depression]). The authors suggested this indicated an antisocial personality with impulse control problems and depressive features that are usually situationally produced and short-lived. Measures of alcohol addiction were also high. Additional analyses of the MMPI research scales indicated that the group obtained low scores on Ego Strength (Es) and Dependency in close relationships. Interestingly, the abusers scored low on a general measure of Dominance (Do) associated with social competence or effectuality. The authors also noted that three clusters could be extracted from the composite profile and that these clusters indicated that no single profile for abusers existed. Only 15 percent of the entire sample had no clinical elevations.

Flournoy and Wilson administered an MMPI to fifty-six male abusers and also found a 24/42 generic profile.[13] Forty-four percent of their sample demonstrated a 42 profile in the clinical range. Else and her colleagues compared twenty-one perpetrators with matched non-abusive controls on the MMPI.[14] Abusers scored higher on the borderline and antisocial MMPI personality disorder scales.

A cautionary note is relevant here. The Pd Scale on the MMPI can generate elevations because of family discord, poor peer relations, alienation from the self or society, or acting out because of legal difficulties. When I appeared as an expert witness for the prosecution in the case of *California* v. *O.J. Simpson*, on a charge of killing his wife, Mr. Simpson had omitted eight items from the MMPI assessment done by the defence psychologists. Apparently he said he did not know whether to answer them from his current state or from "before any of this happened." All eight items were from the Pd scale of the MMPI. Since abusers typically have high scores on what is called "familial discord" and frequently are angered by being arrested, some elevations on this scale are virtually a given.

The Millon Clinical Multiaxial Inventory

In an attempt to devise a scale more closely connected to the DSM taxonomic categories, Millon developed a scale called the Millon Clinical Multiaxial Inventory that has now gone through three versions.[15] The Millon provides several personality disorder scales (Axis 2) as well as Severe Disorder scales and reporting measures (Disclosure, Debasement, and Desirability).

Maritally violent men have consistently been found to show higher levels of psychopathology on the MCMI than non-violent men. For example, Hastings and Hamberger found that abusers scored higher than non-violent men on most of the MCMI mood scales (e.g., anxiety, depression) and on the psychotic depression scales.[16] Hamberger and Hastings compared the MCMI scores of abusers in treatment, abusers recruited from the community, and non-violent comparison groups; abusers scored higher than the non-violent subjects on the anxiety, hysteria, neurotic depression, alcohol and drug scales, as well as on the borderline, psychotic thinking, and psychotic depression scales.[17] Hart, Dutton, and Newlove administered the MCMI (version II) and the Personality Disorder Examination (PDE, a semi-structured interview) to eighty-five men in treatment for wife assault.[18] Eighty percent to 90 percent of the men met criteria for personality disorder on the MCMI, 50 percent on the PDE. Both frequencies are far above population baselines. The most frequently diagnosed disorders were aggressive-sadistic, antisocial, and borderline. Figure 9.1 shows scores for each of the personality disorders measured by the MCMI-II (scores above 75 are considered "clinically significant," those above 85 "clinically central"). Response-style scores refer to various scales that assess honesty in reporting.

Gondolf recently published the results of a multi-site study assessing MCMI-III results of men in treatment for wife assault.[19] Gondolf found lower rates of personality disorder than did previous studies.[20] He attributes this finding to the superiority of the MCMI-III over previous versions of the MCMI and to his sampling from "major metropolitan areas with well-developed court and referral services" and to the possibility of higher refusal rates in prior studies.[21] It is unclear how "high percentages of refusals" would inflate the incidence of personality disorder. If anything, it should suppress the rate, because those with personality disorder would be more likely to be aware they were "different" and not participate. In any event, Gondolf could have easily deconfounded many explanatory problems by simply giving the MCMI-II to half his subjects and the MCMI-III to the others.

Gondolf also overlooked a more obvious explanation for his low scores on personality disorder subscales. Fully 55 percent of his sample was above the seventy-fifth percentile criterion for Desirability, and although he does not report means or standard deviations for the Disclosure and Debasement scales, they appear low from the percentile data. Gondolf drew his sample from "psychoeducational" treatment groups (typically, the Duluth Model). The setting and treatment of this particular model creates a shaming atmosphere for clients, one that instantly puts them on the defensive.[22] Gondolf's low scores could simply have occurred because men were underreporting on any item they read as signifying psychological pathology.

Finally, Gondolf never tried to ascertain which men in treatment came from bilaterally abusive relationships and which were unilateral abusers. One would expect less psychopathology in the bilateral group, where the

9.1   Millon Clinical Multiaxial Inventory - II (MCMI - II) score
comparisons between court-referred and self-referred samples

	Referral source			
Scales	Court (N = 38)	Self (N = 40)	t	ñ
Response-style scales				
Debasement	52.0 (20.5)	67.0 (20.0)	3.2	.002*
Disclosure	65.0 (23.6)	72.0 (20.0)	1.4	.18
Desirability	53.8 (19.2)	50.7 (16.3)	0.8	.44
Personality-style scales				
Schizoid	53.8 (23.2)	63.7 (25.7)	1.8	.08
Avoidant	55.1 (33.2)	75.7 (32.1)	2.6	.01*
Dependent	39.7 (31.7)	36.5 (28.6)	0.5	.63
Histrionic	70.8 (17.3)	57.3 (24.8)	2.8	.01*
Narcissistic	77.0 (22.0)	69.7 (18.8)	1.6	.11
Antisocial	84.2 (22.1)	84.2 (20.0)	0.02	.99
Aggressive/sadistic	80.9 (25.8)	90.0 (21.8)	1.6	.11
Compulsive	48.7 (21.9)	61.8 (15.6)	3.1	.003*
Passive/aggressive	80.0 (32.6)	87.0 (28.9)	1.0	.32
Self-defeating	60.2 (27.2)	78.0 (24.3)	2.5	.01*
Clinical syndromes				
Anxiety disorder	41.8 (31.0)	58.0 (30.0)	2.4	.01*
Somatoform disorder	49.5 (18.5)	52.3 (14.6)	0.7	.46
Bipolar disorder	61.1 (18.5)	52.8 (18.6)	2.0	.05
Dysthymia	45.0 (29.5)	62.7 (28.3)	2.7	.01*
Alcohol dependence	62.1 (23.7)	67.0 (20.3)	1.0	.33
Drug dependence	72.1 (19.0)		0.1	.89
Severe syndromes				
Thought disorder	49.4 (21.1)	58.5 (18.9)	2.0	.06
Major depression	48.0 (21.4)	59.7 (17.2)	2.7	.01*
Delusional disorder	46.8 (19.2)	49.6 (18.0)	0.7	.50

* Denotes significance at Bonferroni-adjusted level (ñ = .015)
SOURCE: D.G. Dutton and A.J. Starzomski, "Psychological differences in court-referred and self-referred wife assaulters," *Criminal Justice and Behavior* 21, 2 (1994): 203-22, 214.

abuse has interactional considerations. This is a general problem with studies done on the "psychology of batterers": it is rarely ascertained whether the person is a "batterer" (see Chapter 6) or in a bilaterally abusive relationship. There is no item that captures "battering" on the CTS or CTS-2. It would have to read, "I repeatedly struck or kicked a person who was not resisting."

Depression in Violent Men

Using other questionnaire measures of psychological functioning to compare violent and non-violent men, one consistent finding is that violent husbands report more depression than non-violent men. Maiuro et al. administered the Beck Depression Inventory (BDI) to four groups of men: maritally violent, generally assaultive, maritally violent and generally assaultive (mixed), and non-violent men.[23] Significant differences in BDI scores existed between the four groups, with the highest median score being found among the maritally violent group. Similarly, Julian and McKenry found that a sample of violent husbands reported more depression than a comparison sample of non-violent men.[24] In a study of over ten thousand men in the military, Pan, Neidig, and O'Leary found that men who were physically aggressive toward their partners reported more depressive symptomatology than men who were non-aggressive.[25] Babcock and Dutton found depression in partner-violent women to be related to their own use of aggression (but unrelated to their partners' aggression).[26]

Anger, Hostility, and Assaultiveness

Another consistent finding is that violent husbands experience higher levels of anger and hostility than other men. Maiuro and his colleagues compared maritally violent men's scores to non-violent men's scores on the Buss-Durkee Hostility Inventory (BDHI).[27] Violent men had significantly higher mean scores on the Overt (motoric aggression) and Covert (internal affective experience) scales and on six of the seven subscales. Maiuro et al. compared maritally violent, generally assaultive, maritally violent and generally assaultive (mixed), and non-violent men on the Buss-Durkee Hostility Inventory (BDHI) and the Hostility and Direction of Hostility Questionnaire (HDHQ).[28] All the violent groups were significantly higher than the non-violent group on a variety of subscales. Barnett, Fagan, and Booker asked men to complete the Buss-Durkee Hostility-Guilt Inventory (BDHGI).[29] Violent men not in treatment scored significantly higher than the other groups on the Resentment scale, and higher than all but the violent offender group on the Assault and Indirect Hostility scales. (See also Eckhardt's work cited in the last chapter.)

McKenry, Julian, and Gavazzi recruited aggressive and non-aggressive couples from the community and assessed men's scores on three subscales of the Psychiatric Symptom Checklist 90 (SCL-90): anxiety, hostility, and paranoia.[30] While they found that both hostility and paranoia were positively correlated with the level of husband physical aggression, only hostility was a significant predictor of it.

Leonard and Blane, using the Buss-Durkee Hostility Inventory, found that men's hostility was related to their reports of having hit a female partner, even after controlling for sociodemographic factors.[31] Leonard and Senchak similarly found that hostility was related to premarital husband aggression, again after sociodemographic variables were controlled.[32] Dutton, Saunders, Starzomski, and Bartholomew have used the Multidimensional Anger Inventory (MAI)[33] to compare the general anger levels of maritally violent and non-violent men. They found that men in treatment programs for marital violence scored higher on the MAI than a demographically matched non-violent comparison group.[34]

Dutton found that abusive men reported more anger than did control subjects.[35] Dutton and Starzomski found that MAI scores of violent men were positively correlated with wives' reports of husbands' psychologically abusive behaviour, and that husbands' MAI scores correlated significantly with wives' reports of the husbands' use of severe violence.[36] In other words, abusive men appear to have elevated levels of depression, anxiety, and anger, and these reveal themselves as "peaks" on psychological assessment tests such as the MMPI or MCMI. Nevertheless, there exist certain subtypes of perpetrators of intimate partner violence. Four different laboratories have arrived at the same tripartite division as a result of cluster-analyzing psychological test scores of court-mandated abusers (see Figure 9.2).

9.2 Batterer classifications compared

Hamberger and Hastings[1]	Holtzworth-Munroe and Stuart[2]	Saunders[3]	Tweed and Dutton[4]
Antisocial/ Narcissistic	Generally violent/ Antisocial	Type 2 (Generally violent)	Instrumental/ Undercontrolled
Schizoid/ Borderline	Dysphoric/ Borderline	Type 3 (Emotionally volatile)	Impulsive/ Undercontrolled
Dependent/ Compulsive	Passive/ Dependent (family only)	Type 1 (Emotionally suppressed)	Impulsive/ Overcontrolled

NOTES: **1** L.K. Hamberger and J.E. Hastings, "Personality correlates of men who abuse their partners: A cross-validation study," *Journal of Family Violence* 1 (1986): 323-41. **2** A. Holtzworth-Munroe and G.L. Stuart, "Typologies of male batterers: Three subtypes and the differences among them," *Psychological Bulletin* 116 (1994): 476-97. **3** D.G. Saunders, "A typology of men who batter women: Three types," *American Journal of Orthopsychiatry* 62 (1992): 264-75. **4** R. Tweed and D.G. Dutton, "A comparison of instrumental and impulsive subgroups of batterers," *Violence and Victims* 13, 3 (1998): 217-30.

Early Research on Personality Disorders

By the 1980s the Millon Clinical Multiaxial Inventory (MCMI) had joined the Minnesota Multiphasic Personality Inventory (MMPI) as a broad assessment instrument able to detect personality disorder.[37] The MCMI was intended to configure closely to DSM-IV definitions of Personality Disorder (PD). Having a self-report instrument allowed lengthy structured interviews to be avoided and generated more attention to PD. The initial studies investigating the incidence of PD among abusive males were conducted by Hamberger and Hastings.[38] These researchers identified eight subgroups composed of various combinations of three factors that could account for 88 percent of the entire wife assault subject sample.

Dutton argued that repeat offenders were personality-disordered and that three specific forms of PD were most prevalent among wife assaulters: Antisocial, Borderline, and Overcontrolled.[39] Hamberger and Hastings refined their eight clusters to three groups corresponding to their initial factors: Schizoid/Borderline, Narcissistic/Antisocial, and Passive/Dependent/Compulsive. Each subgroup scored high on one factor and low on the other two factors. This "three factor solution," or set of three subtypes of batterers, has been found repeatedly (albeit under different labels) in various studies (see Figure 9.2).[40]

Hamberger and Hastings began to report the existence of an expanded non-PD group emerging from their data in 1988.[41] Whether or not this was the result of a more aggressive criminal justice response catching less serious abusers is not known. Lohr, Hamberger, and Bonge cluster-analyzed the eight PD scales on the MCMI-II in a sample of 196 men.[42] This time a cluster was found that showed no elevations on any PD scale (39 percent of the sample, compared to 12 percent in the 1986 paper). A second cluster (35 percent) was termed Negativistic/Avoidant (Overcontrolled), while a third (26 percent) was labelled Aggressive (Antisocial/Narcissistic-Paranoid). The non-disordered group is, in my opinion, a result of changes in arrest policy (see Chapter 12). I don't think there is a sudden increase in non-disordered men becoming abusive. Male-perpetrated spouse abuse declined between 1975 and 1985.[43]

A study by Hamberger, Lohr, Bonge, and Tolin used a sample of 833 court-referred men, but unfortunately relied on self-reports of relationship violence, which typically are under-reported by abusers.[44] Using a two-stage clustering technique, they again obtained three large clusters and three smaller clusters. Cluster 1, Dependent/Passive-Aggressive (Overcontrolled), composed 18 percent of the sample. Their average MCMI scale elevations exceeded baseline (> 75: clinically present) on the Dependent/Passive-Aggressive/

Negativistic, and Avoidant subscales. Cluster 2, Instrumental, accounted for 26 percent of the sample; this group showed elevations of Antisocial or Narcissistic subscales. Cluster 3, no PD, composed 40 percent of the sample, an increase from the original 12 percent. The Borderline or Emotionally Volatile cluster seemed to have disappeared. This could have been due to either of two factors: increasing self-protectiveness among research participants as criminal justice sanctions increased, or arrests of non-PD men who were part of a dyadic violent couple. Why else would personality-disordered men suddenly disappear from research profile studies using criminal justice samples? The reason is more likely a change in the system of collection than in the sample itself.

Hart, Dutton, and Newlove investigated the incidence of personality disorders in court-referred and self-referred wife assaulters using the MCMI-II and a structured interview called the Personality Disorder Examination (PDE).[45] The PDE results were more modest than were the MCMI results, with a prevalence rate around 50 percent. The MCMI-II results indicated that 80-90 percent of the sample (court-referred and self-referred, $N = 85$) met the criteria for some personality disorder. The most frequent PD was what came to be called "Negativistic" (Passive-Aggressive + Aggressive-Sadistic). Almost 60 percent of the sample achieved base rate scores equal to 85 or higher, signifying that this particular PD was central and prominent in the psychological makeup of these men. In contrast to that of Gondolf's sample, the mean Desirability score for court-referred men was 53.4, for self-referred 50.7.[46] Hart et al. argued that the court-ordered men approximated a random selection of spouse assaulters (compared to self-referred), because the criminal justice system operated somewhat capriciously.[47]

Saunders performed a cluster analysis of 182 men being assessed for wife-assault treatment.[48] He also found a trimodal set of patterns described as Family Only (overcontrolled), Emotionally Volatile (impulsive), and Generally Violent (instrumental). The Generally Violent group (26 percent of the sample) reported severe abuse victimization as children but low levels of depression and anger. They were violent both within and outside the marriage. The Emotionally Volatile group (17 percent of the sample) was the most psychologically abusive and had the highest anger and depression scores. The Family Only group accounted for 52 percent of the sample.

Murphy, Meyer, and O'Leary compared batterers with non-violent men in discordant relationships and with well-adjusted men in non-conflicted relationships, using the MCMI-II.[49] Each sample contained twenty-four men. Abusers had significantly higher elevations on Borderline, Narcissistic,

9.3 Characteristics of Overcontrolled personality pattern among wife assaulters

- *Tries to avoid conflict*
- *High masked dependency*
- *Attachment: Preoccupied*
- *Chronic resentment*
- Flat affect or constantly cheerful persona
- Attempts to ingratiate therapist
- High social desirability scores
- Overlap of violence with alcohol use
- Some drunk-driving arrests
- Lists "irritations" when told to keep anger diary (anger denial)
- MCMI Peak Scores: Avoidant, Dependent, Passive-Aggressive

NOTE: Clinical keys in *italics.*

Aggressive-Sadistic, and Passive-Aggressive PD than non-batterers. More important, Desirability scores did not differ among groups, although Debasement was higher among batterers, possibly reflecting a pervasive remorse about their violence. Severe physical abuse in the family of origin was related to the presence of psychopathology.

One conclusion that emerges from this review is that, when social desirability scores are equivalent, batterers exhibit significantly more psychopathology than controls. When they differ, groups emerge that show significantly higher social desirability scores while appearing to have no PD elevations. Personality pathology, it seems, is something that respondents attempt to conceal when they are assessed for wife assault.[50]

Holtzworth-Munroe and Stuart reviewed previous studies clustering men involved in domestic violence, reiterating the tripartite typology of batterers, and again describing instrumental and impulsive batterers.[51] The impulsive batterers (whom they labelled Dysphoric/Borderline), primarily confine violence to their families, carry out moderate to severe violence, and engage in sexual and psychological abuse. These abusers are emotionally volatile (and were so labelled by Saunders), psychologically distressed, and have Borderline and Schizoid personality disorders, elevated levels of depression, and substance abuse problems.[52] Holtzworth-Munroe and Stuart estimate that impulsive abusers make up 25 percent of the treatment samples.[53] The instrumental cluster (called Generally Violent/Antisocial) abusers engage in more violence outside the home than the other abusive men, carry out moderate to severe violence, and engage in psychological and sexual abuse. They may have an antisocial personality disorder or psychopathy and may abuse alcohol and/or drugs. Their use of violence is frequently instrumental. Holtzworth-Munroe and Stuart suggest that the instrumental group also makes up 25 percent of all abusers in treatment. A third group (which they called Family Only) appears to be Overcontrolled, and to make up 52 percent of the sample. It is important to note that the authors were not insisting on respondents' achieving criteria on a test such as the MCMI to make these determinations.

Holtzworth-Munroe, Meehan, Herron, and Rehman conducted an empirical confirmation of their earlier work, comparing 102 maritally violent men.[54] This time four clusters were observed, the difference being that the Antisocial (Instrumental) cluster was subdivided into two groups, depending on level of antisocial behaviour. Consistent with Dutton's findings, Borderline/Dysphoric exhibited the highest level of fear of abandonment and had the highest scores on Fearful Attachment and Spouse-Specific Dependency.[55] Their wives reported them to be the most jealous of all groups. They also had significantly higher scores on the BPO (Oldham et al.)[56] scale (Mean = 74, SD = 14.3) than did non-violent males (M = 48, SD = 12.2). Their BPO score was also higher than those of any other abuser groups. Dutton found BPO mean scores of 72 for abusers and 74 for independently diagnosed borderlines.[57] As in the Dutton research, violent men in Holtzworth-Munroe et al. had the highest reports of parental rejection.[58]

Impulsive versus Instrumental Violence

Jacobson et al. recruited a "severely violent sample" of couples in which male-perpetrated abuse was occurring.[59] The psychophysiological responding of these men was monitored *in vivo* while they argued with their partners in a laboratory conflict. Two distinct patterns of psychophysiological responding were obtained. Type 1 abusers demonstrated unexpected heart rate decreases during intimate conflict. They were also more likely to be generally violent and to have scale elevations on the MCMI-II for Antisocial and Aggressive-Sadistic behaviour. Type 2 abusers showed psychophysiological increases during intimate conflict.

Tweed and Dutton examined these two groups, which they called Instrumental (Type 1) and Impulsive (Type 2), on a variety of psychological measures.[60] Note that a third group (Overcontrolled) was obtained, but its number was too small for analysis. The Instrumental group showed an Antisocial-Narcissistic-Aggressive-Sadistic profile on the MCMI and reported more severe physical violence. The Impulsive group showed elevations on Borderline,

9.4 Characteristics of Impulsive/Undercontrolled personality pattern among wife assaulters

- Cyclical phases
- High levels of jealousy
- Violence predominantly/exclusively within intimate relationship
- Attachment: Fearful/Angry
- High levels of depression, dysphoria, anxiety-based rage
- Ambivalence to wife/partner
- MCMI: Borderline

SOURCE: R. Tweed and D.G. Dutton, "A comparison of instrumental and impulsive subgroups of batterers," *Violence and Victims* 13, 3 (1998): 217-30.

Avoidant, and Passive-Aggressive, higher scores on the Oldham et al. BPO measure of borderline personality organization (more about this below), higher chronic anger, and a fearful attachment style on the Relationship Style Questionnaire (RSQ).[61]

The Impulsive group will be described in Chapter 11 on the abusive personality. With its basis in BPO and with its clinical signs of impulsiveness and hyper-emotionality in intimate relationships, the abusive personality described by Oldham et al. seems more closely aligned with Impulsive or Type 2 abusers. Tweed and Dutton confirmed this in a comparison of "instrumental" and "impulsive" abusers; impulsive men had BPO mean scores of 75 (identical to Oldham et al.'s reported mean for borderlines), while instrumental and control abusers had significantly lower BPO scores.[62]

More recently, Edwards and his colleagues also found that measures of Borderline and Antisocial Personality Disorder were significantly correlated with physical aggression (spouse assault) in a forensic sample (forty-three men convicted of wife assault and forty convicted of non-violent crimes).[63] Their high-violence groups had higher scores on all pathology scales of the Personality Assessment Inventory (PAI).[64] The authors related personality disorder to spousal violence via the mediating variable of impulse control.

The Impulsive group also had a high (84) Antisocial PD score but it was accompanied by high scores on Passive-Aggressive PD, Avoidant PD, and Borderline PD. The Instrumental group was self-absorbed and lacking empathy. The Impulsive group had problems with self-esteem and assertiveness. In all, the results reinforced the evidence that two main peaks of personality disorder exist for abusive males: antisocial and borderline. The former engages in instrumental violence, the latter in impulsive violence.

9.5 Means for clusters of abusive men and controls on trauma attachment and other variables with ANOVAs for the two larger clusters and controls

	1 Instrumental/ Undercontrolled N = 32	2 Impulsive/ Undercontrolled N = 38	3 Controls N = 44	ANOVA p	Significant pairwise contrasts	Impulsive/ Overcontrolled N = 9
Attachment						
Secure	15.6	13.7	16.3	.001	1, 3 > 2	17.3
Fearful	14.0	16.1	13.3	.007	2 > 1, 3	14.0
Preoccupied	12.0	13.1	10.3	<.001	2, 1 > 3	12.1
Dismissing	15.6	15.1	15.8	.802		14.9
Conflict Tactics Scale						
Severe physical corrected	2.58	1.19	-0.08	<.001	1 > 2 > 3	0.84
Severe physical	2.56	1.16	0.22	<.001	1 > 2 > 3	1.00
Physical total corrected	7.08	4.41	1.04	<.001	1 > 2 > 3	2.53
Physical total	7.06	4.37	1.27	<.001	1 > 2 > 3	2.67
Age	34	36	36	.263		38
Education	12	14	12	.075		14
BPO	63	75	62	<.001	2 > 3, 1	47
Anger	78	86	75	.006	2 > 3	60
Marlowe-Crowne*	13	13	16	.030	3 > 2, 1	15
Trauma Symptoms	19.6	34.0	17.4	<.001	2 > 1, 3	11.2

SOURCE: R. Tweed and D.G. Dutton, "A comparison of instrumental and impulsive subgroups of batterers," *Violence and Victims* 13, 3 (1998): 217-30, 225, Table 3.

In Chapter 10, the Impulsive abuser described in the Tweed and Dutton article above will be outlined in more detail. Several researchers have found impulsivity to be a problem for a subgroup of batterers. Saunders' "emotionally volatile" batterers had impulsivity problems. In Edwards et al.'s study of forty-three wife assaulters and forty men convicted of non-violent crimes in Sacramento, both groups were assessed using a battery of psychological tests.[65] These included the MCMI-II and the Barrett Impulsiveness Scale. Impulsive Aggression was measured as shown in Figure 9.6.

Impulsive Aggression Scale

Edwards et al. hypothesized that a cluster analysis of the scales used would yield two groups of spouse abusers, Instrumental and Impulsive, similar to those described by Tweed and Dutton. The Impulsive group would have the highest scores for impulsivity, borderline personality, and fearful attachment. This cluster was found, and high scorers (Impulsives) correlated with spousal violence. Two groups were indeed produced by the cluster analysis and were roughly similar to the Instrumental and Impulsive groups described by Tweed and Dutton. Like Tweed and Dutton, Edwards et al. found high levels of psychopathology and personality disorder in their spouse-abuse sample. The authors were unable to confirm the abuse scores reported by the men as their ethics committee felt that contacting the men's wives would put the wives at risk. (In the 160-plus men I studied who were court-ordered for treatment, wives reports were used as confirmatory data, and no woman was ever put at risk as a consequence. We know this because we collected the data about the third week of the group, and checked back constantly with wives until at least six months after group completion.) They concluded that Impulsiveness and Impulsive Aggression and Antisocial and Borderline personality disorder were significant predictors of spousal violence.

9.6 Impulsive aggression questionnaire

---

1 Have you tried to kill yourself?
2 Do you have a problem with impulse control?
3 Do you do bad things without thinking?
4 Do you have problems with your temper?
5 Do you have rages where you lose control?
6 Have you been told that you have a bad temper?

SOURCE: Adapted from D.W. Edwards, C.L. Scott, R.M. Yarvis, C.L. Paizis, and M.S. Panizzon, "Impulsiveness, impulsive aggression, personality disorder and spousal violence," *Violence and Victims* 18, 1 (2003): 3-14.

Research in neurobiology, on personality disorders, by Zanarini and her colleagues, and direct studies of abusers all verify the existence of an impulsive group who need therapeutic help in controlling their impulsivity.[66] Zanarini's work suggests that the instability and impulsivity may appear and exacerbate when borderlines enter into a sexual relationship.[67] As we saw in Chapter 4, according to Schore, impulsivity arises from a failure of the right orbitofrontal lobe to develop during the first year after birth.[68] Familial stress, such as that deriving from abuse, could cause neurological impairment in this location. Hence, while observational learning, such as described in Chapter 8, can provide one vehicle for "intergenerational transmission" of abusiveness, neurologically derived inability to control impulses can be another (recall Chapter 4).

Psycho-Social Histories of Female Abusers

Using a non-experimental design in a convenience sample, Abel compared sixty-seven female abusers attending a court-ordered abusers' intervention program with fifty-one female abusers receiving partner-abuse counselling services.[69] Both groups reported similarly high rates of victimization. There was some evidence of a trend, with abusers reporting more experience as victims (e.g., being threatened, threats, coercive sex, etc.), though in four of the six areas of exposure the differences did not reach significance. Women in victim programs (67 percent) were twice as likely to have previously used domestic violence victim services than were women in abusers programs (33 percent).

The female victims in Abel's study reported significantly more trauma symptomology than the female abusers. Using the Trauma Symptom Checklist (TSC-33, Briere and Runtz),[70] Abel did not report significance testing when comparing Briere and Runtz's non-abused women with their abuser group. But TSC-33 scale and subscale comparisons for anxiety (5.73, 6.00), depression (10.10, 8.11), sleep disorder (4.35, 4.52), and overall trauma (28.25, 25.13) indicated small differences, suggesting the female abusers in this sample were similar to non-abused women in their trauma symptomology. In contrast, the women in Abel's victim programs had scores very similar to those of Briere and Runtz's abused group and substantially higher than those of Briere and Runtz's non-abused group. In addition to the lack of an experimental control and small sample size, a limitation of Abel's study is that the "abuser" group was composed primarily of African-American women and the "victim" group primarily of Caucasian women. As the authors noted, cultural differences might have implications for help-seeking. This study provides evidence to suggest that female abusers are unlike female victims and probably present with different treatment needs. Interestingly, whereas male perpetrators were never asked about their partners' violence, female perpetrators are routinely asked.

Holtzworth-Munroe and Stuart asserted there are three types of male batterers: family-only, dysphoric/borderline, and generally violent/antisocial.[71] Building on their work, Babcock et al. examined the contexts and motivations of abuse reported by fifty-two women referred to a treatment agency for abusive behaviour.[72] They divided the women in their sample into two a priori categories: Partner-Only (women who reported using aggression only against their romantic partners since age eighteen) and Generally Violent women (women who reported using violence in a variety of circumstances since age eighteen: fights with at least four different people). The Generally Violent (GV) women had committed significantly more physical and psychological abuse, and also inflicted more injuries during the previous year than had the Partner-Only (PO) women. Notably, there were no significant differences between the PO and GV groups' experiences of abuse by their partners. As the authors hypothesized, according to the Trauma Symptom Checklist, GV women reported more current trauma symptoms than the PO women. (Elevated levels of trauma symptoms are part of the profile of male abusiveness as well, as will be seen in the next chapter.) The GV women more frequently reported a desire to hurt themselves, a desire to hurt others, and interpersonal problems.

Both the GV and PO women in Babcock's sample reported high rates of childhood physical and sexual abuse. The only significant difference between the women's backgrounds was that the GV women more often reported seeing their mothers aggress against their fathers. Babcock et al. concluded that female intimate abusers, like their male counterparts, are a heterogeneous group. Adding further evidence to Abel's results presented above, this study demonstrated that, as with women who might be primarily identified as partner-abuse *victims* and partner-abuse *perpetrators* presenting with some unique characteristics, GV and PO violent women likely have several overlapping traits but perhaps will present with some diverse needs as well.

Henning, Jones, and Holford reported demographic, childhood family functioning, and mental health characteristics for a large sample of male (2,254) and female (281) domestic violence offenders.[73] They found few demographic differences between men and women arrested for domestic violence. Women were more likely to have attended college but were less likely to work outside the home. A similar proportion of men and women had low (borderline to mentally deficient) IQs according to the WAIS-R. Analyses comparing childhood experiences (e.g., physical abuse, interparental physical aggression, parental criminal behaviour, or substance abuse) that might result in adulthood adjustment difficulties or psychopathology revealed few gender differences. Men were more likely than women to report corporal punishment by primary caregivers ($p < .01$), and women were more likely to report severe interparental abuse ($p < .01$). More gender differences were evident with regard to the subjects' mental health histories and current mental health status. Men were more likely than women to report prior treatment for substance abuse/dependence, to be rated high-risk for substance dependence currently, to have had child conduct problems prior to age sixteen, and to have a desire to continue the relationship with the victim. The women were more likely than the men to have been prescribed psychotropic medication and to have a prior suicide attempt. Men and women were equally likely to report clinically significant distress. Females were about five times more likely to have elevations on a borderline scale. In

9.7 Male and female domestic violence offenders: Clinical and personality functioning results on MCMI-III

	Percentage whose MCMI-III Base Rate Score ≥ 75	
	Male (N = 1,158)	Female (N = 112)
Clinical syndromes (Axis 1)		
Delusional disorder	4.2	11.6**
Major depression	1.6	10.7**
Bipolar	3.6	9.8**
Somatoform	0.3	3.6**
Thought disordered	0.7	3.6*
One or more elevated scales	35.2	33.0
Personality patterns (Axis 2)		
Compulsive	17.2	50.0**
Histrionic	3.1	36.6**
Borderline	2.8	11.6**
Antisocial	18.1	3.6
One or more elevated scales	69.8	94.6**

*$p < .01$, **$p < .001$.
SOURCE: Adapted from K. Henning, A. Jones, and R. Holford, "Treatment needs of women arrested for domestic violence: A comparison with male offenders," *Journal of Interpersonal Violence* 18, 8 (2003): 839-56.

a later chapter on treatment, the issue of treating borderline functioning in abuse perpetrators is explored in more detail. In all, the Axis 2 personality disorder patterns found by Henning et al. indicated high levels of psychopathology in female offenders. Bear in mind that personality disorder generally develops over long "trajectories" and is unlikely to be a reaction to current relationship problems.

Psychopathology among Female Abusers

Dutton has asserted that personality factors, rather than "maleness" as such, generated emotional and physical abuse in males. In a series of empirical studies of court-mandated treatment participants, Dutton showed that combinations of fearful attachment, borderline traits, and chronic trauma symptoms generated what he called an "abusive personality" in males.[74] Recent research has begun to explore the role of these features among female perpetrators of partner abuse.

Follingstad, Bradley, Helff, and Laughlin generated a model for predicting dating violence in a sample of 412 college students.[75] They found that anxious attachment resulting from early life experiences led to the development of an "angry temperament," which in turn related to attempts to control and use abuse against an intimate partner. The model predicted abusiveness for both genders.

Ehrensaft, Cohen, and Johnson followed the community sample described in Chapter 6 for twenty years to study the associations among childhood exposure to family violence, personality disorder symptoms, and perpetration of intimate violence in adulthood.[76] They found that the formation of personality-disorder clusters, as described in the DSM-IV, mediated intergenerational transmission of family violence, and, again, this occurred for both genders. The presence of a personality disorder was better than gender as a predictor of partner violence. The authors also asserted that personality-disorder clusters, which usually decline after adolescence, decline more slowly in abusive men and women. Hence, there appears to exist across genders an abusive personality, which they describe as "having an early pre-existing pattern of distrust, interpersonal avoidance, unusual or bizarre beliefs and constricted positive affect."[77] These traits remain more stable in abusive people regardless of gender. As Ehrensaft et al. put it, "studies suggest that this single-sex approach is not empirically supported, because both partners' behaviours contribute to the risk of clinically significant partner abuse, and both partners should be treated. Women's partner abuse cannot be explained exclusively as self-defence against men's partner abuse, because a woman's pre-relationship history of aggression toward others predicts her abuse toward her partner, over and above controls for reports of his abuse towards her."[78]

Henning et al. found that women arrested for domestic violence had more symptoms of personality dysfunction and mood disorders than men arrested for domestic violence (see Figure 9.7).[79] Women were significantly more likely to score in the clinical range for delusional disorder, major depression, bipolar disorder, somatoform disorder, and thought disorder. Female offenders were more likely than male offenders to score in the clinical range on the MCMI-III Axis 2. These findings were perhaps the most notable, with 95 percent of the women compared to 70 percent of the men having one or more elevated personality subscales. The authors concluded that many women convicted of abuse against intimate partners are likely to have stable personality disorders that complicate their intimate relationships and may affect treatment.

In a recent study of female undergraduates at a large university in western Canada, Spidel et al. found a high rate of personality disorders according to self-reports on the SCID-II.[80] In this sample of women who had committed abuse against an intimate male partner, 13.2 percent exhibited enough traits to meet the criterion for one personality disorder, 16.9 percent had two personality disorders according to their self-report, and 33.1 percent met criteria for three or more personality disorders. The most prevalent PD diagnoses included Obsessive Compulsive (34.6 percent), Antisocial (33.8 percent), Passive-Aggressive (28.7 percent), Narcissistic (22.8 percent), and Borderline (22.1 percent). Although the high prevalence rates may be due in part to self-report, the findings are in line with other samples of males who commit spousal assault.

Magdol et al. found that the female severe physical violence rate (18.6 percent) was more than triple that of males (5.7 percent).[81] Perpetrators and victims of both genders presented the same demographic profiles: unemployed (compared to non-perpetrators and non-victims), limited education, more alcohol dependence, and higher scores on all mental illness and criminality scales. The risk factors for female violence were high scores on a scale of psychoticism, neuroticism, and the MacAndrew Scale for alcohol abuse. Both the psychoticism and neuroticism scales as described in the study were composites of measures assessing poor ego strength and may have been correlated with borderline features in this population. Substance abuse is also a problem behaviour for individuals with borderline personality disorder. Dutton's work had hypothesized a borderline personality structure as a risk factor for intimate violence in male perpetrators.[82]

Moffitt et al. obtained the same finding (see Chapter 7). In their study of the Dunedin sample, they found that antisocial traits in females (1) made them more likely to become involved in a relationship with an abusive man, (2) and even after controlling for their partners' physical abuse, "women with a juvenile history of conduct problems were still more likely to commit violence against their partners."[83]

Some studies have also found Bipolar Disorder (BPD: extreme high and low mood swings) predictive of intimate violence in female perpetrators. Zanarini found that BPD symptomatology increased with sexual relations and included intimate abusiveness for both male and female subjects.[84] Fortunata and Kohn found that lesbian batterers were also more likely to report both borderline and antisocial personality traits on the MCMI-III (as well as substance abuse problems).[85] Similarly, Renzetti found jealousy and dependency to be the two strongest psychological factors predicting lesbian violence.[86] Babcock (personal communication) reported a peak on the Borderline Scale of the MCMI-II given to women in the University of Washington study of male batterers (40 percent of these women reported using severe violence themselves). Babcock and Dutton found two spikes on MCMI-II scores for self-identified female intimate abusers.[87] The two spikes were on the antisocial and borderline personality disorders.

Hence, as studies begin to assess psychological factors predicting female intimate violence, a pattern similar to that of male violence emerges: personality disorders (especially those affecting intimacy), attachment style, and constricted affect all appear. These manifest themselves, as did the same profile in males, with an "angry temperament," substance abuse, conflict-generating beliefs, and intimate violence. This finding holds, regardless of whether dating violence is studied cross-sectionally, lesbian violence is studied, or longitudinal studies are done on community groups.

In sum, women who are victimized by their partners can be distinguished from women who have been identified primarily as abusers. Further, as we have seen from research on male abusers, women who are violent only in their relationships appear to be quite different from women who also commit aggression in other contexts. Finally, female abusers share many of the same traits as their male counterparts, especially antisocial and borderline personalities.

Antisocial Personality Disorder

One "peak" that showed up on personality tests of abusers (whether male or female) is Antisocial Personality Disorder (see DSM-IV diagnostics above). The DSM-4R has a set of diagnostic criteria for habitual criminals who lie, cheat, and feel no remorse for their victims. These persons think nothing of using violence to obtain instrumental ends. This will apply to intimate relationships as well, although "intimacy" as normal people experience it (a bonded, attached relationship with concerns for the welfare of the other) does not exist for either psychopaths or those with Antisocial Personality Disorder (ASPD). Instead, these people tend to view others as objects who exist for their own needs. Their "attachment style" is dismissing; people can easily be replaced. This is a disorder characterized by low-empathy people who frequently break the law and feel entitled to do so. They are the Instrumental-Undercontrolled group. As can be seen from Figure 9.8, these people do not really attach to others. Instead, they view others as objects who can be used for their own self-serving needs.

For this reason, ASPDs are unlikely to engage in "abandonment killings." It's too easy to replace the person since no deep emotional bond formed anyway. However, they do kill for money or insurance claims (see below).

Dutton and Kerry examined ninety men in prison for killing their wives, examining the differences in motive between ASPD men and men with identity disturbance (Dependent, Avoidant, and Self-Defeating PD).[88] The former engage in "instrumental" violence to get financial gain; the latter kill in a futile reaction against abandonment. Edwards et al. found that ASPD, which is similar to but not synonymous with Psychopathy, was a significant predictor of wife assault in their sample.[89] A key moderating variable between ASPD and violence seems to be a lack of empathy and a sense of entitlement (the so-called Factor 1 characteristics; see below).

More recent work is focusing on the lifestyles of "white collar" psychopaths, fraud artists, and market manipulators. Too many of these "white collar" criminals would be missed by the DSM-IV's "antisocial personality" criteria.

9.8 Characteristics of Instrumental/Undercontrolled personality pattern among wife-assaulters

---

- violent inside and outside the home
- history of antisocial behaviour (car theft, burglary, violence)
- high acceptance of violence
- negative attitudes to women (macho)
- attachment: Dismissing
- usually victimized by extreme physical abuse as a child
- low empathy
- associations with criminal/marginal subculture
- MCMI: Antisocial, Aggressive-Sadistic

The problem with the DSM definition of ASPD is that it relies heavily on behavioural and lifestyle characteristics (Factor 2), which vary with social class and circumstances, whereas in actual cases psychological characteristics (Factor 1) are more important.[90]

Psychopathy

As Robert Hare, the world's top expert on psychopaths, says, "psychopaths are social predators who charm, manipulate, and ruthlessly plow their way through life, leaving a trail of broken hearts, shattered expectations, and empty wallets."[91] Hare cites serial killers John Gacy, Ted Bundy, Richard Ramirez (the Nightstalker,) Ken Bianchi (the Hillside Strangler), and Jeffrey Macdonald (who staged the murder of his family and Diane Downs). Hare also lists Kenneth Taylor, a philandering New Jersey dentist who abandoned his first wife, tried to kill his second wife, savagely beat his third wife on their honeymoon in 1983, battered her to death the next year, hid her body in the trunk of his car while he visited his parents and his second wife, and later claimed he killed her in self-defence when she attacked him following his discovery that she was sexually abusing their infant child. Clearly, lying, deceit, and casual violence are central to psychopathy.

Psychopathy, by definition, is determined as scoring above thirty on an assessment test developed by Hare called the Psychopathy Checklist-Revised or PCL-R,[92] though people with scores below thirty can still have psychopathic traits. Psychopathy is characterized as a personality disorder that involves a variety of distinct interpersonal and affective characteristics and socially deviant behaviours.[93]

Hare has developed two factors that define psychopathy through careful statistical methods (factor analysis and multiple regression). Hare's PCL-R, the primary assessment tool for this disorder, generates two factors for psychopathy: one is psychological, involving ways of viewing or feeling about the world; the other is behavioural and reflects a common lifestyle of most but not all psychopaths. Factor 1 is composed of interpersonal and emotional features, including shallow affect, grandiosity, lack of empathy, glibness, and manipulation. Factor 2 characterizes the behavioural pattern that presents for most psychopaths as one of irresponsibility, impulsivity, violence or aggression, and promiscuity. Since psychopaths are notorious liars, the PCL requires corroboration for each one of the traits it measures. Figure 9.9 shows features similar to those assessed by Hare.

Features of Psychopathy Assessed by Hare's Psychopathy Checklist

In spouse abuse, psychopaths who use violence would tend to use it in

---

9.9 Features of psychopathy

---

1. Psychological features: cognitions, lack of affect
   - glibness, superficial charm
   - grandiose sense of self (belief: I have to look out for number one)
   - pathological lying (belief: lying and cheating are okay so long as you don't get caught)
   - a general lack of empathy and remorse (belief: if people don't take care of themselves, that's their problem)
   - conning, manipulative style (belief: cunning is the best way to get things done)
2. Behaviours and lifestyle features
   - a "parasitic" lifestyle (lives off others)
   - juvenile delinquency or early run-ins with the law or authority
   - general irresponsibility
   - impulsivity, poor behavioural controls
   All of the above are based on these beliefs:
   - We live in a jungle and only the strong survive.
   - People will get me if I don't get them first.
   - Keeping promises and paying debts is for suckers.

SOURCES: Adapted from: R.D. Hare. *Without Conscience: The Disturbing World of Psychopaths among Us* (New York: Pocket Books, 1993); A. Beck, *Cognitive Therapy for Personality Disorder* (New York: Guilford Press, 1990); H. Cleckley, The Mask of Sanity (New York: Mosby, 1976).

general, both within and outside an intimate relationship. They would use it instrumentally as described above. In fact, psychopaths tend not to form strong emotional attachments, so they don't typically experience abandonment panics. They may just routinely use violence as a form of control. The feminist view of all abusive males seems to have been generalized from psychopaths.

As Langhinrichsen-Rohling and her colleagues point out, even though a particular abuser may not meet the statistical cut-off on the PCL-R, and thus may not be classified as a psychopath, the presence of a significant number of the more severe interpersonal and affective characteristics could still be important for discriminating this class of abuser.[94] Finally, the generalized and instrumental violence identified in the generally violent abuser is also quite characteristic of offenders with psychopathic personalities.[95]

Langhinrichsen-Rohling et al. argue that psychopaths who score high on Factor 1 of the PCL commit more instrumental violence with less provocation and arousal and tend to have a more distant relationship with the victim than do other assaulters.[96] Hence, the quintessential psychopath seems defined more by Factor 1 scores (lack of empathy, manipulativeness, shallow affect, pathological lying, glibness) than by the social deviance scores generated by Factor 2. Thus, similar to the batterer typologies, the most common type of violence across all batterers is reactive or impulsive. Those who are capable of committing planned acts of violence for control or gain, however, are more likely to be psychopathic.

Notwithstanding the other similarities, it is this pattern of generalized and instrumental violence identified in the generally violent abuser that most clearly demonstrates the likelihood that these men are psychopathic. Waltz et al. found that generally violent abusers were more violent both within and outside their relationships.[97]

Subgroups of Psychopaths

Hervé performed a cluster analysis (actually several different types of cluster analysis) on several large samples of incarcerated men (combined $N = 2,000$) to ascertain whether several subtypes of psychopath existed.[98] He found evidence of subgroups he termed classic, macho, manipulative, and pseudo-psychopaths and argued that they differed in anxiety and the extent to which they scored high or low on four different facets of psychopathy. The subgroups who experienced more anxiety might be more amenable to treatment. As Hervé put it: "With regard to the fourth facet (i.e., Antisocial), the classic, macho, and pseudo-psychopaths scored high in this domain and the manipulative psychopath scored relatively low, as predicted by clinical wisdom, theory, and research."[99]

Hervé's conclusion was as follows (referencing omitted):

Theoretical accounts, for example, have highlighted the possibility of both genotype (i.e., idiopathic, primary, fundamental) and phenotype (i.e., symptomatic, secondary, pseudo) versions of psychopathy, with the former being the product of nature and the latter of nurture. In addition, several different sightings of the genotype have been reported as well, including one that embodies all aspects of the disorder (i.e., classic), one that manifests itself in parasitic ways (i.e., manipulative), and one whose aggressive impulses predominate (i.e., the aggressive) ... The goal of the present investigation was to provide empirical support for the notion that subtypes of psychopaths can be distinguished based on their characteristic presentation. As predicted, three psychopathic subtypes and a pseudopsychopathic subtype were identified across both clustering methods and samples, each of which varied

---

9.10 Psychopaths are not all alike

Hervé found empirical evidence for three distinct psychopathic subtypes and one pseudopsychopathic subtype. These four subtypes were reliable and generalizable to diverse samples.

First subtype	The "classic" psychopath scored high on all three factors (affective, interpersonal, behavioural) and also had the highest overall scores on the PCL-R.
Second subtype	The "macho" psychopath scored second highest on the PCL-R, higher on affective and behavioural than on interpersonal.
Third subtype	The "manipulative" psychopath scores higher on interpersonal and affective than on behavioural. Interpersonal plays a larger role than behavioural in defining the type.
Fourth subtype	The "pseudopsychopath" scores less than 30 on the PCL-R and higher on interpersonal and affective than on behavioural. This subtype lacks the core affective traits of the true psychopath.

SOURCE: H.F.M. Hervé, "The masks of sanity and psychopathy: A cluster analytical investigation of subtypes of criminal psychopathy," PhD dissertation, Department of Psychology, University of British Columbia, 2002.

from the others in the extent to which it displayed the interpersonal, affective, and behavioural characteristics of the disorder.[100]

Psychopaths, Sociopaths, Dissocial Personalities

Hervé's ground-breaking work shows that psychopathy may be a catchall phrase for different subtypes that have different prognoses regarding treatability. That research has yet to be done, as has research on the relation of these subtypes to propensity for intimate abusiveness. The implications are far-reaching. As Hervé put it (again, his extensive references are omitted):

The current findings support the clinical and behavioural observations that offenders who meet criteria for psychopathy may exhibit different patterns of defining characteristics, particularly those associated with the interpersonal and lifestyle features of the disorder. Of the four clusters or subtypes that emerged, three were of particular significance to the construct of psychopathy. As compared to the pseudopsychopaths, the classic, macho, and manipulative psychopaths all possessed high levels of the core affective traits thought to underlie the disorder and, therefore, these subtypes could be viewed as "primary" or "idiopathic" psychopaths.

Unlike these three idiopathic types, the *pseudopsychopaths*, while similar to other psychopaths in many respects, did not seem to have the prerequisite constellation of emotional traits thought to underlie the disorder. These individuals might represent what others have termed "secondary" or "symptomatic" psychopathy, a disorder related to but not the same as the primary type. This type of individual may not be a psychopath per se (i.e., is a false positive) but an individual who either reacts to the injustices of society (e.g., the sociopath), mimics his/her delinquent sub-culture (e.g., the dyssocial), suffers from a longstanding dissociative and/or posttraumatic stress response, or has another disorder altogether (e.g., borderline and/or antisocial personality disorder. Future research may even investigate the notion that several of these conditions may manifest as pseudopsychopathy.

That only one mask of psychopathy was identified within the current study does not negate the possibility that different types of individuals wear this mask ... While dyssocial individuals and socio-paths may have learnt to suppress their affective experiences in light of long-term environmental demands (i.e., emotional reactions could be viewed as a sign of weakness in antisocial subcultures), trauma-induced conditions, as well as those reflecting borderline personality disorder, may have limited affective experiences, not due to environmental demands, but as a result of the underlying pathology. The end result is that each of these nonpsychopathic emotionally constricted (not barren) conditions should score highly on the affective facet of psychopathy but lower than those individuals who have greatly attenuated or impaired affective experiences (i.e., idiopathic psycho-paths).[101]

Development of Psychopathy

The current findings also imply that psychopathy has multiple sources, with nature and nurture having different influences across the various subtypes. For example, one might speculate that the idiopathic and symptomatic psychopaths have different biological predispositions, the former being much more biologically weighted than the latter.

Another implication of these findings for the criminal justice system is that these subtypes may differ in both the type and frequency of crime and violence in which they engage. Hervé hypothesizes that, while the classic psychopath may become involved in all types of antisocial behaviours, the manipulative psychopath (the "talker") may specialize in fraud and embezzlement, the macho psychopath (the "doer") may be more prone to commit armed robberies and assaults, and the pseudopsychopath (the "distressed") may be most likely to engage in crimes of anger and destruction. As noted by Hervé, preliminary research appears to support these hypotheses; each subtype appears to have a unique criminal profile.[102] In addition, the pseudopsychopath may display a pattern of offending, especially with violence, unlike his idiopathic counterparts. Specifically, the pseudopsychopath, whose conscience presumably is in a state of chaos and whose system is likely highly aroused, may be much more violently reactive than an instrumentally motivated peer.[103] Recent research also suggests that macho psychopaths, who engage in destructive crimes to the same extent as pseudopsychopaths, may be the most reactive of the idiopathic psychopaths, possibly due to an increased sense of frustration at not being able to communicate effectively.[104] Further research is needed to investigate the extent to which these subtypes differ in various criminal history variables. Such research could potentially increase the sensitivity and specificity of risk prediction in a group of individuals who account for a disproportionate amount of crime.[105]

Hervé's study is important for another reason. In the everyday world of forensic corrections, psychologists are called upon to decide who is treatable and who is not. Forensic psychology is not a precise science, but the view has developed that no psychopath is treatable. Hervé's study raises another possibility, a finer distinction that would suggest treatability for, say, pseudopsychopaths but not the other subtypes.

There are not only subgroups of abusers but also subgroups within subgroups. There are bilateral abusers and unilateral abusers. Within unilateral abusers there are antisocial (generally violent) types, impulsive types, and overcontrolled types. Within antisocials there are psychopaths and pseudopsychopaths. This attempt at classification is not merely an academic exercise; it has implications for treatment. It may surprise the reader that, in most jurisdictions where court-ordered interventions are a condition of parole, only "one size-fits-all" treatment is available. It may surprise the reader even more to know that in some jurisdictions any psychological treatment of those convicted is illegal.

10 The Cycle of Violence and the Abusive Personality

In her 1979 book, Lenore Walker described a "cycle of violence" based on descriptions of battered women interviewed in Colorado.[1] These women described their husbands, starting at a neutral mood "baseline," as becoming increasingly withdrawn and abusive. Verbal abuse would increase; the man's mood would be "prickly" and tense; he would be "moody." Any substance abuse problem would exacerbate the tension. The escalating verbal abuse would turn to yelling. Eventually, destruction of property would occur. Frequently, the man would smash something of value to the woman. O.J. Simpson, in his rapid cycle moods, would smash family pictures of Nicole Simpson, hurling them from the top of a staircase. This first phase is hence characterized by escalating anger and outbursts on the part of the man, accompanied by his sense that his wrong behaviour is justified (through blaming and negatively perceiving his partner), by a fear of the woman's leaving, and by increasing oppression, jealousy, and possessiveness to keep the woman captive.

Women reported trying anything and everything to calm the man: focusing attention on him, neglecting her friends, cooking his favourite dinner. These women were working on the everyday belief that something in the man's environment was causing his upset. They did not realize that it was something internal to the man himself that was influencing his mood. No environmental "bandaids" were going to change his slide into fury.

Inevitably (in a few seconds to a few months), the man would cycle to the second phase, a rage state, and begin serious physical and (sometimes) sexual abuse. At this point, the woman's focus was on protection of herself and her children. The police might be called and the man arrested. In some cases he would receive a restraining order, barring him from the house. In other cases, the woman would move in with friends or into a transition or shelter house. This second phase "is characterized by the uncontrollable discharge of tensions that have built up during phase one."[2] The trigger for moving into the second phase, as Walker's respondents reported it, was either "an external event or the *internal state of the man.*[3] This uncontrollable rage generates acute battering until the batterer becomes "exhausted and emotionally depleted," typically within two to twenty-four hours.[4] Victims report that the battering occurs in response to anything that they do (e.g., both staying quiet and answering back escalate anger).

At this point something strange occurred with many of the men. Having "blown out" the accumulated tension during the Battering Phase, they now became docile and contrite. Many would become obsessed with "winning back" their estranged partner. They would send her gifts and try to elicit support from others (friends, priests, anyone who believed the marriage could be rescued). One man in our treatment group had married his girlfriend when she was in the hospital recovering from a beating. The man makes lots of promises at this contrition phase: to stay sober, go into therapy, join Alcoholics Anonymous, go to church regularly, never again be violent, etc. Hence the beginning of Walker's third phase is characterized by exhaustion, contrition, confession, promises of reform, and attempts to convince the victim and others that the abuse will not recur.

It's a confusing time for the women. She may have reasons for wanting to keep the family together if the violence can be stopped. She is also traumatically bonded if the violence has been intermittent and thus is in the grasp of a strong attachment bond that she barely understands.[5] When I ran treatment groups for court-mandated men, their wives would often call to get their husband into treatment, though I would insist that he call before anything else transpired. It is essential in working with these men that a complete list of everything he has promised to change be obtained while he is still in the contrition phase and that he agree to these terms and sign a contract to honour them.

Walker's respondents depicted these phases as predictable. Until recently, little attention has been paid to the dynamics generating cyclical abuse by males. My recent work has searched for a personality basis for cyclical male-initiated abuse. I believe such a basis exists in borderline personality organization (BPO).

Borderline Personality Organization and Assaultiveness: The Theoretical Connection

The Walker descriptions, rich as they were, came from observers of an abuse cycle. I was interested in explaining the inner workings of such men. What could possibly account for the contrast between the first phase man and the third phase man, who seemed to be two different people. I could find nothing to account for such variation in standard personality texts, which emphasized consistency in personality rather than swings in behaviour. A book by Gunderson describing a "borderline personality" caught my interest.[6] It described people (believed by psychiatrists to be mostly women) who went through extreme personality shifts, from loving to the point of idolizing to hostile to the point of rage. Gunderson called this Borderline Personality Organization (BPO).[7]

BPO is a clinical category characterized by intense, unstable interpersonal relationships, an unstable sense of self, intense anger, and impulsivity, characteristics that seem likely to increase the chance of violence in intimate relationships.[8] BPO is a less severe form of the more rare Borderline Personality Disorder (BPD).[9] The difference is that BPO is characterized as a continuum running from low to high borderline traits, whereas BPD is a distinct category.

As Gunderson describes the Borderline Personality (BP), the essential characteristics (in order of importance) are as follows: a proclivity for intense, unstable interpersonal relationships characterized by intermittent undermining of the significant other, manipulation, and masked dependency; an unstable sense of self with intolerance of being alone and abandonment anxiety; and intense anger, demandingness, and impulsivity, usually tied to substance abuse or promiscuity.[10]

Gunderson described a three-stage defence sequence of Borderline Personality that produces sudden shifts in "phenomenology," affect, and behaviour.[11] This defence sequence could theoretically produce the kinds of behaviour depicted by Walker's "abuse cycle" description of some wife assaulters.[12] Gunderson described the BP as existing in a "dysphoric stalemate" in relationships, where intimacy needs are unmet but where the requisite motivation and skills to assert the needs were non-existent. Gunderson's first stage resembled the "tension-building" phase of Walker's abuse cycle, during which frustrations increase. Gunderson's second stage occurred when the BP perceived an intimate relationship as possibly lost. Defensive behaviour at this stage was expressed as anger, devaluation of the significant other, or open rage. This appeared to correspond to Walker's second "battering" phase of the abuse cycle. Gunderson's third stage occurred when the significant other was lost. At this point, the BP engaged in behaviours designed to ward off the subjective experience of aloneness. Impulsive substance use and promiscuity were the examples offered by Gunderson. Reading Gunderson, I thought that possibly another example might be the exaggerated "appeasement" behaviours that assaultive husbands engage in after their wife has temporarily left the relationship. These behaviours persist until the woman has emotionally returned, when the cycle begins again.

Phasic Personality Structure as a Defence against Shifting Anxiety Sources

In a similar description of homicide perpetrators, Revitch and Schlesinger described a "catathymic personality" which underwent three stages: incubation, violent act, and relief.[13] The primary affect during incubation is depression, accompanied by a constant sense of tension build-up. When the violent act was homicide, it appeared to be preceded by a period of brooding. Retrospective accounts reveal that, during this incubation period, the perpetrator viewed the tension build-up as being "caused" by the victim who acted in a perceived malevolent and persecutory manner toward the perpetrator. The relief experienced after catathymic violence came from a release of stored affect: specifically, a release from depressive and anxious symptoms and muscular tension. Although Revitch and Schlesinger's analysis was meant to be applied to intimate homicides, it also appears to describe the abuse cycle. Both wife assault and borderline personality have been empirically linked to being a victim of childhood abuse.[14] Hence, there is a prima facie case for systematically examining the relationship between wife assault and the BP.

10.1 Borderline personality disorder

Having borderline personality disorders means that there is a continuous pattern of unstable interpersonal relationships, self-image, and affects. There is also marked impulsiveness beginning by early adulthood and present across a variety of situations. Pattern must include five or more of the following:

- frantic efforts to avoid real or imagined abandonment (not including suicidal or self-mutilating behaviour)
- patterns of inconsistent and intense interpersonal relationships, alternating between extremes of idealization and devaluation
- identity disturbance: markedly and persistently unstable self-image
- impulsivness in at least two areas that are potentially self-damaging (e.g., spending, sex, substance abuse, reckless driving, binge eating) (not including suicidal or self-mutilating behavior)
- recurrent suicidal behavior, gestures, threats, or self-mutilating behaviour
- unstable affect due to a marked reactivity of mood (e.g., intense episodic dysphoria, irritability, or anxiety usually lasting a few hours only rarely more than a few days)
- chronic feelings of emptiness
- inappropriate, intense anger or difficulty controlling anger
- transient, stress-related paranoid ideation or severe dissociative symptoms.

SOURCE: Based on diagnostic criteria from the DSM-IV. This is not intended as a substitute for the more extensive DSM diagnoses.

Diagnostic Criteria for Borderline Personality Disorder

A more complete list of borderline traits was developed by Westen and Shedler, who asked therapists to do Q sort ratings on borderline and non-borderline clients.[15]

10.2 Westen and Shedler's new definition of borderline personality disorder

---

- tends to feel he/she is inadequate, inferior, or a failure
- tends to feel he/she will be rejected or abandoned by those who are emotionally significant
- is unable to soothe or comfort self when distressed, requires involvement of another person to help regulate affect
- tends to feel helpless, powerless, or at the mercy of forces outside his/her control
- emotions tend to spiral out of control, leading to extremes of anxiety, sadness, and rage
- tends to be angry or hostile (whether consciously or unconsciously)
- tends to be anxious
- tends to react to criticism with feelings of rage or humiliation
- tends to be overly needy or dependent; requires excessive reassurance or approval
- tends to feel misunderstood, mistreated, or victimized
- tends to become irrational when strong emotions are stirred up; may show a noticeable decline from customary level of functioning
- tends to get into power struggles
- tends to "catastrophize": is prone to seeing problems as disastrous, unsolvable, etc.
- emotions tend to change rapidly and unpredictably.

SOURCE: Adapted from D. Westen and J. Shedler, "Revising and assessing Axis II," *American Journal of Psychiatry* 156, 2 (1999): 258-85, 265.

Borderline Personality Organization and Assaultiveness: The Empirical Studies

In a series of studies, Dutton and his colleagues have examined personality profiles of assaultive males.[16] The overall strategy of this work has been based on self-report scales, filled out by abusive men as part of an assessment procedure for treatment and used to establish correlations with their female partners' reports of the men's abusiveness. Both self-referred and court-referred men have been compared to demographically matched controls.[17] Extensive analyses of the men's reporting tendencies have been made through the use of both the Marlowe-Crowne scale and the Balanced Inventory of Social Responding and through the use of the Disclosure, Debasement, and Desirability Scales of the Millon Clinical Multiaxial Inventory-II (MCMI-II).[18] An extensive report on the relationship of social desirability to all self-report scales described below is available in Dutton and Hemphill and Dutton and Starzomski.[19] Self-reports of a man's anger, jealousy, experience of trauma symptoms, and abusiveness, and reports of his abusiveness (both physical and psychological) made by his female partner, have constituted the dependent variables in these studies. Dutton and Starzomski argued that self-referred assaulters constituted a "purer" group of abusive personality (typically self-referring during the contrition phase of an abuse cycle) while court-referred samples were more heterogeneous.[20] Consistent with this view was the finding that 45 percent of self-referred but only 27.5 percent of court-referred wife assaulters reached the eighty-fifth percentile on the borderline scale of the MCMI-II.[21] Self-reports were made on a scale measuring borderline personality organization (BPO).[22] This scale has three subscales: Identity Diffusion (a poorly integrated sense of self), Primitive Defences (projection and splitting), and Reality Testing (transient psychotic states). The scale has good psychometric properties, with Cronbach's alphas for its subscales in the range of 0.84-0.92.

In an initial sample of eighty wife assaulters and forty demographically matched controls, Dutton found BPO scores to be similar to those for diagnosed borderlines.[23] The mean BPO score for the sample of wife assaulters was 71.3 (SD = 17.1), whereas the mean score for diagnosed borderlines was 74.8. By comparison, Oldham et al. reported a mean score of 61.3 for a non-borderline sample,[24] and our controls scored 60.0 (SD = 17.0) on the BPO scale.[25] Furthermore, BPO scores were significantly related to chronic anger, jealousy, use of violence, and experience of adult trauma symptoms in the wife assault group. High-BPO scorers reported significantly more anger, of greater frequency, magnitude, and duration. They also reported greater jealousy and more trauma symptoms: dissociation, anxiety, sleep disturbance, depression, and post-sexual abuse trauma. Finally, they reported significantly more abuse toward their wives: both verbal-symbolic and physical as measured on the Conflict Tactics Scale (CTS).[26] Correlations of BPO to other measures were significant. Analysis of response styles indicated that these associations were not merely effects of disclosure or social desirability.

Dutton and Starzomski evaluated these findings by focusing on wives' reports of abusive treatment by their husbands through assessment of both physical abuse using the CTS and emotional abuse using the Psychological Maltreatment of Women Inventory (PMWI).[27] The latter's fifty-eight item

10.3 The centrality of Borderline Personality Organization in an assaultive group of men

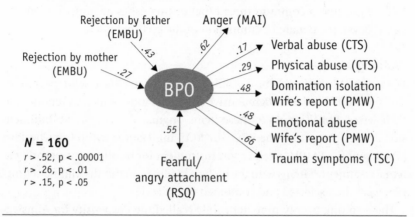

NOTE: BPO is "central" because it is a form of personality organization in which anger, trauma symptoms, and abusiveness are consequences, and parental treatment the demonstrated precursors. SOURCE: D.G. Dutton, *The Abusive Personality* (New York: Guilford, 1998, 2003).

scale yields two factors called Dominance/Isolation and Emotional Abuse. Correlations of men's self-reported BPO scores with women's reports of the men's abusiveness are shown in Figure 10.3. Strong associations of men's BPO scores with women's reports of male abusiveness were found. A multiple regression indicated that BPO scale scores combined with scores from a self-report for anger (MAI) accounted for 50 percent of women's reports of Dominance/Isolation (PMWI Factor 1) and 35 percent of Emotional Abuse scores (PMWI Factor 2).[28] This is a sizable amount of the variance by social science standards.

Saunders developed a three-part typology of wife assaulters.[29] Using behavioural descriptors, essentially the three groups were overcontrolled, antisocial, and borderline. The latter group constituted about 30 percent of all assaultive males. I am not attempting to account for all assaultive behaviour on a personality basis. Rather, I argue that men who are violent only in intimate relationships and who repeatedly initiate the violence appear to have borderline features. Both the borderline personality and the abusive behaviour may have a common origin. Interestingly, the empirical relationship between BPO and women partners' reports of abusiveness was maintained for psychological abuse in non-physically abusive control groups, implying that BPO and anger scores may define a general profile for intimate abusiveness that is differently manifested in different groups of men, possibly as a function of abuse styles learned in the family of origin. As described in Chapter 9, other studies confirmed this tripartite division, although the names used were somewhat different.[30] My aim in this chapter is twofold: (1) to find a common thread that distinguishes all abusive men and (2) to develop a detailed examination of the cyclical batterer.

Profiling Abusiveness

Dutton established an "abuse profile" by combining those self-report items that most differentiated high-abusive from low-abusive men as reported on their wives' PMWI scores.[31] These items originated from the Multidimensional Anger Inventory, the BPO, the MAI, the Trauma Symptom Checklist (TSC), and the EMBU, a self-report instrument for recollections of early parental treatment.[32] Items with the highest loadings on this discriminant function were then selected and combined into a scale.

The resulting twenty-nine item scale (called the Propensity for Abusiveness Scale, PAS) correlated +.51 ($p < .001$) with wives reports of Dominance/Isolation on the PMWI, and +.37 ($p < .001$) with the Emotional Abuse scale from that same inventory.[33] Predictive validity was again assessed by using the scale to discriminate high-abuse from low-abuse groups. Using the criterion of one standard deviation from the mean, the PAS correctly identified 82.2 percent of men on Dominance/Isolation and 81.3 percent of men on Emotional Abuse.

The scale has been cross-validated successfully and has also been found to identify abusiveness in populations of clinical outpatients, blue collar workers, gay males, and college students.[34] In effect, the same constellation of personality features (BPO, high anger, fearful attachment, chronic trauma symptoms, and recollections of paternal rejection) accounts for reports of abusiveness by one's intimate partner in all of the above groups.

Dutton expanded social learning theory's notion of "instigators of aggression" to include perceived abandonment and control of intimacy.[35] The control of intimacy seemed to define a special category of aversive stimuli frequently mentioned by assaultive males in treatment groups. Dutton proposed that changes in socioemotional distance between the man and his wife could serve as instigators of wife assault.[36] In an empirical test of these notions, Dutton and Browning found that wife assaulters reacted with more anger than did control males to videotape scenarios depicting uncontrollable abandonment of a male by his female partner.[37] The anger was significantly greater than that reported for equally conflictual arguments without abandonment themes.

10.4   Propensity for abusiveness (PAS) questionnaire

PART 1

For each of the statements below, please circle the number to the right of the statement that most accurately describes how it applies to you, from 1 (completely undescriptive of you) to 5 (completely descriptive of you).

1 – completely undescriptive of you; 2 – mostly undescriptive of you;
3 – partly undescriptive and partly descriptive; 4 – mostly descriptive of you;
5 – completely descriptive of you

1. I can make myself angry about something in the past just
by thinking about it.   1 2 3 4 5
2. I get so angry, I feel that I might lose control.   1 2 3 4 5
3. If I let people see the way I feel, I'd be considered a hard
person to get along with.   1 2 3 4 5

PART 2

For each of the statements below, please indicate how true it is about you by circling the appropriate number.

1 – never true; 2 – seldom true; 3 – sometimes true; 4 – often true; 5 – always true

4. I see myself in totally different ways at different times.   1 2 3 4 5
5. I feel empty inside.   1 2 3 4 5
6. I tend to feel things in a somewhat extreme way,
experiencing either great joy or intense despair.   1 2 3 4 5
7. It is hard for me to be sure about what others think of me,
even people who have known me very well.   1 2 3 4 5
8. I feel people don't give me the respect I deserve unless I put
pressure on them.   1 2 3 4 5
9. Somehow, I never know quite how to conduct myself with
people.   1 2 3 4 5

PART 3

Please read each of the following statements and rate the extent to which it describes your feelings about *romantic relationships* by circling the appropriate number. Think about all of your romantic relationships, past and present, and respond in terms of how you *generally* feel in these relationships.

Not at all like me		*Somewhat like me*		*Very much like me*
1	2	3	4	5

10. I find it difficult to depend on other people.   1 2 3 4 5
11. I worry that I will be hurt if I allow myself to become too
close to others.   1 2 3 4 5
12. I am somewhat uncomfortable being close to others.   1 2 3 4 5

PART 4

How often have you experienced each of the following in the *last two months*? Please circle the appropriate number.

0 – never; 1 – occasionally; 2 – fairly often; 3 – very often

13. Insomnia (trouble getting to sleep)	0	1	2	3
14. Restless sleep	0	1	2	3
15. Nightmares	0	1	2	3
16. Anxiety attacks	0	1	2	3
17. Fear of women	0	1	2	3
18. Feeling tense all the time	0	1	2	3
19. Having trouble breathing	0	1	2	3

PART 5

Beside each statement, please circle the number of the response listed below that best describes how often the experience happened to you with your mother (or female guardian) and father (or male guardian) when you were growing up. If you had more than one mother/father figure, please answer for the persons who you feel played the most important role in your upbringing.

1 – never occurred; 2 – occasionally occurred; 3 – often occurred; 4 – always occurred

	Father or Guardian	Mother or Guardian
20. My parent punished me even for small offenses.	1 2 3 4	1 2 3 4
21. As a child I was physically punished or scolded in the presence of others.	1 2 3 4	1 2 3 4
22. My parent gave me more corporal (physical) punishment than I deserved.	1 2 3 4	1 2 3 4
23. I felt my parent thought it was *my* fault when he/she was unhappy.	1 2 3 4	1 2 3 4
24. I think my parent was mean and grudging toward me.	1 2 3 4	1 2 3 4
25. I was punished by my parent without having done anything.	1 2 3 4	1 2 3 4
26. My parent criticized me and told me how lazy and useless I was in front of others.	1 2 3 4	1 2 3 4
27. My parent would punish me hard, even for trifles.	1 2 3 4	1 2 3 4
28. My parent treated me in such a way that I felt ashamed.	1 2 3 4	1 2 3 4
29. I was beaten by my parent.	1 2 3 4	1 2 3 4

Note: The test is scored by adding the item scores.

NOTE: The note on scoring above appears in the questionnaire as here.
SOURCE: D.G. Dutton, "A scale for measuring the propensity for abusiveness," *Journal of Family Violence* 10, 2 (1995): 203-21.

A limitation of social learning theory is its emphasis on immediate external stimuli producing "aversive arousal." This somewhat passive view of perpetrators sees them as responding to proximal stimuli with rage and abuse. However, based on certain descriptive features of batterers provided by their victims, these men appear to respond to internal stimuli, which seem to increase over time in the absence of any increase in real "aversive stimuli" and to disappear temporarily upon catharsis.[38] There is no systematic explanation within a social learning framework for the development of these apparently cyclical internal states.

The Origins of Abusiveness

Having developed this assessment of the abusive personality, I attempted to ascertain the etiology of this personality. First a discriminant function analysis was performed on abusive personality scores themselves. Family of origin factors (CTS + EMBU) correlated +.41 ($p < .001$) with scores on the PAS. The largest contributor to a discriminant function on abusiveness was paternal rejection, correlating +.87 with the discriminant function.[39]

Next, composite scores were developed for abusive personality, abusive behaviour, and abuse experiences in the family of origin.[40] Figure 10.5 gives

10.5 Contributions of early experience factors to the abusive personality

	Discriminant function
EMBU	
Paternal rejection	.87
Paternal warmth	-.63
Maternal rejection	.39
Maternal warmth	-.39
Conflict Tactics Scale (FOO)	
Physical abuse (father to you)	.64
Verbal abuse (father to you)	.41
Physical abuse (mother to you)	.34
Verbal abuse (mother to you)	.34
Physical abuse (father to mother)	.24
Verbal abuse (father to mother)	.36
Physical abuse (mother to father)	.27
Verbal abuse (mother to father)	.38

NOTE: EMBU is "Egna Minnen Beträffande Uppfostran" (Memories of My Upbringing); FOO is "family of origin."
SOURCE: D.G. Dutton, "The origin and structure of the abusive personality," *Journal of Personality Disorders* 8, 3 (1994): 181-91, 187.

factors contributing to the abusive personality. Note that paternal rejection is the strongest contributor, an effect emphasized by the strong opposite contribution of paternal warmth.

The association of abuse in the family of origin with abusive personality (+.41) is stronger than its association with abusive behaviour (+.22). This result suggests a more complex pattern than the direct modelling of abusive behaviours suggested by social learning theory. Both borderline personality and wife assault have been empirically shown to have childhood origins.[41] The possibility exists that some common set of early experiences serves as a common cause for both.

Attachment and Abusiveness

If early experiences influenced adult abusiveness, attachment theory might provide a valuable perspective on how abusiveness develops. Bowlby asserted that "attachment behaviour is held to characterize human beings from the cradle to the grave," that confidence in the availability of attachment figures is built during the years of immaturity – infancy, childhood, and adolescence – and that "whatever expectations are developed during those years tend to persist relatively unchanged throughout the rest of life."[42] Bowlby viewed interpersonal anger as arising from frustrated attachment needs and functioning as a form of "protest behaviour" directed at regaining contact with an attachment figure.

In turn, chronic childhood frustration of attachment needs may lead to adult proneness to react with extreme anger (which I refer to as "intimacy-anger") when relevant attachment cues are present. Thus, attachment theory suggests that an assaultive male's violent outbursts may be a form of protest behaviour directed at his attachment figure (in this case, a sexual partner) and precipitated by perceived threats of separation or abandonment (as with the argument made by Dutton and Browning).[43] A "Fearful" attachment pattern may be most strongly associated with intimacy-anger. Fearful individuals "desire social contact and intimacy but experience pervasive interpersonal distrust and fear of rejection."[44] Figure 10.6 shows how each attachment style is associated with features of abusiveness and wives' reports of emotional abuse.

The Fearful attachment style manifests itself in hypersensitivity to rejection (rejection-sensitivity) and active avoidance of close relationships where vulnerability to rejection exists (hence extreme jealousy and "conjugal paranoia"). While anxiety over abandonment is shared by the Fearful with another insecurely attached group (Preoccupied), their avoidance orientation may lead to more chronic frustration of attachment needs. Subjects were

10.6 Association of types and features of abusiveness with different attachment styles

	Secure	Fearful	Preoccupied	Dismissing
BPO	-.35***	-.58***	.42***	-.04
Trauma symptoms	-.28***	.50***	.34***	-.03
Anger	-.36***	.49***	.20	.02
Jealousy	-.16*	-.34***	.18	-.015
Verbal Abuse (PMWI):				
Dominance/isolation	-.30*	.46**	.27*	.06
Emotional abuse	-.09	.52***	.26	-.20

* means p < .05, ** means p < .01, *** means p < .001
NOTE: Correlations of RSQ attachment styles with total scores on other measures for entire sample (N = 160).
SOURCE: D.G. Dutton, A. Starzomski, K. Saunders, and K. Bartholomew, "Intimacy-anger and insecure attachment as precursors of abuse in intimate relationships," *Journal of Applied Social Psychology* 24, 15 (1994): 1367-86, 1376.

assessed using the Relationship Style Questionnaire (RSQ), a thirty-item self-report measure.[45]

Fearfully attached men experience high degrees of both chronic anxiety (as measured by the TSC-33) and anger (as measured by the MAI). In addition, the Fearful group had the highest scores for both trauma in general and dissociation in particular. Fearful attachment alone accounted for significant proportions of variance in both emotional abuse criterion factors. Fearful attachment was also strongly correlated with borderline personality organization. Since anxiety (+.42) and anger (+.48) are both strongly associated with Fearful attachment, one could argue that an emotional template of intimacy-anxiety/anger is the central affective feature of the Fearful attachment pattern. These correlations are maintained in the control sample (fearful-anxiety +.53, fearful-anger +.52), suggesting that this emotional template does not only reside within physically abusive men.

A prominent feature of BPO is intimacy-anger.[46] The correlation of Fearful attachment to BPO is so strong (+.62) that one could argue BPO is a personality representation of this particular attachment style.[47]

Attachment Perspective on Partner Abuse

Relationship abuse has been conceptualized, drawing on theorizing by Bowlby, as an exaggerated and dysfunctional form of protest behaviour.[48] Thus, anger toward a partner is expected to be precipitated by attachment-related threats, such as interpersonal conflict and fears of rejection, separation, and abandonment. Individuals high in attachment anxiety are expected to be hyper-sensitive to such threats because they are more likely than those low in anxiety to perceive ambiguous partner behaviours in threatening terms. Anxious individuals who have failed to effectively communicate their need for reassurance to a relationship partner in more functional ways may then strike out in abusive anger or even violence to gain or regain proximity to an attachment figure. In intimate relationships, the attachment figure is the partner against whom the protest is directed. This perspective on partner violence is consistent with the finding that relationship violence typically takes place in the context of couple conflict, and that perpetrators of partner violence are characterized by high dependency and psychological vulnerability.[49]

An attachment-based conceptualization of partner violence is not gender-specific. However, this reasoning has typically been applied to understanding male violence against women. As expected, studies have demonstrated links between anxious attachment (assessed in various ways) and male-to-female partner violence.[50] Moreover, those studies, which have also considered other forms of partner violence, have found similar patterns of findings. For example, attachment anxiety (and especially a Preoccupied orientation) is associated with women's violence toward male partners and with men's violence toward male partners.[51]

Holtzworth-Munroe, Stuart, and Hutchinson did two studies to compare the attachment patterns, dependency, and jealousy of violent husbands with that of maritally distressed and non-distressed controls using the Relationship Style Questionnaire (RSQ) and the Adult Attachment Interview.[52] Violent husbands had more insecure, preoccupied, and disorganized attachments, more anxiety about abandonment, more discomfort with closeness, more dependency, jealousy, and obsession with the woman. Dutton and Kerry proposed that, in the extreme, attachment-related identity issues characterized men who murdered women who were leaving them.[53]

Babcock et al. examined attachment styles in three groups of men (non-violent, unhappily married, and violent husbands) using a structured interview, the Adult Attachment Interview (AAI).[54] Violent husbands were most likely (74 percent) to be classified into one of the insecure categories on the AAI. The authors found, however, that different wife behaviours triggered violence in men with different attachment styles. Preoccupied men were triggered by wife withdrawal. Dismissing husbands were triggered by wife defensiveness. The authors speculated that Preoccupied husbands used expressive violence in response to abandonment fears. Dismissing

husbands, on the other hand, used instrumental violence to assert authority and control.

Henderson et al. examined how individual differences in attachment were
associated with women's and men's relationship abuse.[55] A telephone survey assessed levels of psychological and physical abuse in 1,249 Vancouver
residents. Of these, 128 completed an attachment interview exploring their
interpersonal relationships. Hierarchical regressions revealed that attachment
variables contributed significant variance to the prediction of both receipt
and perpetration of psychological and physical abuse, with Preoccupied attachment acting as an independent predictor. There was no evidence that
gender moderated these associations. The findings suggest that attachment
preoccupation in either partner may increase the likelihood of abuse in
couples.

Bond and Bond examined predictive factors for aggression in forty-one
discordant couples, some of whom reported intimate partner aggression.[56]
They found that an Anxious attachment style was a predictor of females'
being victims of violence. The combination of Anxiously attached females
with Dismissive males was a potent predictor of violence.

Bookwala and Zdaniuk compared the attachment styles of individuals
who reported that they were engaged in a reciprocally aggressive dating relationship with those who reported that they were involved in a mutually
non-aggressive relationship.[57] They found that after controlling for relationship satisfaction, length of relationship, and interpersonal problems, individuals who described themselves to be involved in reciprocally aggressive
relationships scored higher on the Preoccupied attachment style than those
who reported being involved in non-aggressive romantic relationships. Like-
wise, in a study on the links between relationship aggression and the two
underlying dimensions of attachment styles – discomfort with closeness and
anxiety over abandonment – Clulow found that higher scores on anxiety
over abandonment (most typical of Preoccupied individuals) were associated with the expression of more aggression by men and women in intimate
relationships.[58] Moreover, women were more likely to report aggression
against a partner who scored higher on anxiety.

Mauricio and colleagues tested this notion in a sample of 192 men in a
court-mandated treatment program for spouse assault.[59] The men completed
a battery of questionnaires assessing attachment style (Experiences in Close
Relationships Questionnaire), antisocial and borderline personality disorders (Personality Disorder Questionnaire), and abusiveness (CTS and PMWI).
The researchers found that anxious attachment and borderline personality

disorder scores were highly correlated. Surprisingly, anxious attachment was also correlated with antisocial personality scores. The authors used a sophisticated statistical technique called path modelling to develop a model of abusiveness (both physical and psychological) that included attachment and personality disorder variables. In doing so they found that anxious attachment was related to abusiveness through two pathways: antisocial and borderline personality. In other words, the personality disorder mediated the effects of attachment insecurity on abuse. The insecure attachment had crystallized into a personality disorder. Since personality disorder is a major risk factor for abusiveness, studies that obtained this finding may have captured a masked attachment disorder.

Correlations of Abuse and Attachment Style in Gay Relationships

Bartholomew, Oram, and Landolt found attachment was associated with abuse in gay relationships. Forty-one percent of gay men ($N = 192$) reported having been the recipient of at least one act of violence from a male partner, and 35 percent reported that they had acted violently toward a partner on at least one occasion in the past. There were strong associations between receipt and perpetration of various forms of abuse (ranging from .57 to .79), suggesting reciprocity of abuse in many relationships. For example, there was .79 correlation between men's reports of receipt of violence (ever in the past) and perpetration of violent acts (using a variety of scores).[60]

Preoccupied attachment (characterized by attachment anxiety and very active seeking of support and intimacy) was consistently associated with reports of both perpetration and receipt of relationship abuse. Dismissing attachment showed small, but significant, negative associations with physical abuse (perhaps because Dismissing individuals would not be expected to stay in highly dissatisfying relationships). Finally, there were no significant correlations between Fearful or Secure attachment and experiences of abuse.

Landolt and Dutton examined abuse in fifty-two gay male couples, finding higher-than-heterosexual levels of abuse despite the relationships' being relatively egalitarian.[61] Abusive personality measures still predicted abusive perpetration in these relationships.

Attachment Disruption and Trauma

In abused boys, another prominent sequela of abuse victimization is hyperaggression. Carmen, Reiker, and Mills suggested that abused boys are more likely than girls to identify with the original aggressor and eventually perpetuate the abuse on their spouse and children.[62] In the authors' view, an

10.7 The centrality of Borderline Personality Organization in a sample of gay men

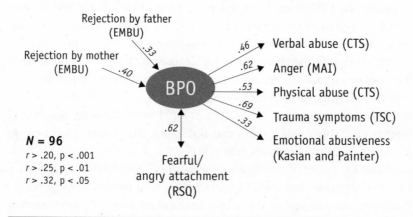

SOURCE: M. Landolt and D.G. Dutton, "Power and personality: An analysis of gay male intimate abuse," *Sex Roles* 37, 5/6 (1997): 335-59.

effect of physical maltreatment by a parent is to exaggerate sex role characteristics, possibly as a means of attempting to strengthen the damaged self. Van der Kolk noted that children who were traumatized had trouble modulating aggression, and he included being physically abused as a child as a trauma source.[63] Schore also noted the traumatic impact of attachment disruption realized through alteration of right hemispheric functioning.[64] This occurs during the first year of life when right hemispheric development has a maturational spurt. Hence, abuse stressors during this period can have long-lasting impact on neural development, especially the parts of the brain that regulate emotion. The right orbitofrontal cortex, which acts as a brake to curb impulsivity (see Chapter 4), develops rapidly during this time. Moreover, in households where abuse is occurring, the failure of Secure attachment to buffer the child from stress reactions to abuse amplifies trauma.

The Trauma Model for Impulsive Perpetrators

Some evidence shows abuse in the family of origin to be a risk factor for the development of post-traumatic stress disorder (PTSD). Herman and van der Kolk noted how PTSD included poor affect tolerance, heightened aggression, irritability, chronic dysphoric mood, emptiness, and recurrent depression, and was "described in patients who have been subjected to repeated trauma over a considerable period of time."[65] Hence, the possibility is presented that

PTSD may be another link or mediating variable between childhood abuse victimization and adult perpetration of intimate abuse.

In order to test this notion, Dutton compared wife assaulters to two groups of diagnosed PTSD men from independent studies.[66] In the wife-assault sample, 45 percent of all men met criteria for PTSD (75 percent on the MCMI-II on the "82C profile" [avoidant-passive-aggressive-borderline]). On the MCMI-II, wife assaulters and men diagnosed with PTSD (Vietnam veterans from two separate, independent studies) were similar on all profile peaks with the following exceptions: wife assaulters had significantly higher scores on antisocial personality, and PTSD men had higher scores on anxiety and dysthymia.[67] This result implies that the acting out of aggression by wife assaulters may dispel pent-up dysthymia.

What is the source of trauma for these men? Is it the childhood experience of abuse, rejection, and disturbed attachment seen in their self-reports? At this point, the data suggest the answer in the affirmative. The most traumatized men in the assaultive group were the ones with the greatest exposure to physical abuse while growing up, the greatest exposure to emotional abuse in the form of shaming, and the least secure attachment base to buffer these assaults on their systems.[68] We may recall from Chapter 3 the research by Schore on attachment disruption and brain reaction.[69] The result of attachment disruption was essentially a trauma reaction in which emotion-regulating structures in the right hemisphere became malformed. In abusive households, more happens than the witnessing of or being victimized by physical violence. Shaming and emotional assaults also occur on the sense of self and on the mother's capacity to provide a safe haven.

Projection and Attribution

How are chronic abuse habits maintained? One mechanism appears to be cognitive. Starzomski and Dutton replicated the BPO results reported above with a non-clinical population of college students.[70] Fearful attachment in this group was again strongly associated with anger (+.58, $p < .001$), as with the wife assault group.[71]

Furthermore, one mechanism was unearthed in this study that contributes to the maintenance of chronic intimate anger. Fearfully attached college males make attributions for intimate events differently than do other attachment groups. Fearful attachment is correlated +.33 ($p < .01$) with a tendency to make blaming attributions to the partner on the Relationship Attribution Measure.[72]

This finding is again consistent with a feature of BPO described in the clinical literature. Gunderson and others had identified the tendency to

10.8 Attributions for intimate anger by non-clinical college males by attachment type

Negative attributions about	Attachment dimensions			
partner behaviour	Secure	Fearful	Preoccupied	Dismissing
Her fault	-.05	.20	.20	.23*
Stable in future	-.30	.48***	.07	.36
Generalizes	-.12	.19	.03	.14
Intentional	-.17	.26*	.11	.25*
Selfish motives	-.05	.30*	.27	.14
Blameworthy	-.13	.43***	.31	.17

* $p < .05$, ** $p < .01$, *** $p < .001$ two-tailed, $N = 72$
SOURCE: A. Starzomski, "Attachment style, anger and attribution in the intimate context" (Master's thesis, Department of Psychology, University of British Columbia, 1994).

project blame as a defining feature of BPO, and Oldham et al. included measures of projective identification as part of their measure of Primitive Defences (a subscale of the BPO self-report instrument). Although couched in attributional terms, the empirical results of Starzomski and Dutton support this clinical claim.[73] Scores on Fearful attachment also correlated significantly with the BPO subscale for Primitive Defences, which assesses the tendency to split women into ideal and devalued objects and to project angry impulses onto the devalued woman-object. This projection or blaming attributional tendency serves to maintain high degrees of chronic intimate anger and may have its origin in attempts to ward off shame. By projecting unacceptable impulses outward, their potential to threaten a weak self-concept is neutralized.

This blaming attributional style will maintain anger towards the spouse at a high chronic level.[74] We saw in Chapter 8 the work by Eckhardt et al. on articulated thoughts of intimate violent men during anger arousal.[75]

Cognitive Errors of Abused Children: Shame

Dodge et al. found that children known to have been abused made the same kind of cognitive errors as abusive men when presented with hypothetical age-appropriate conflict scenarios.[76] Tangney has presented a more focused analysis of the potential role of shame as a mediator between the early experiences of assaultive men and their adult experience of anger and abusiveness.[77] Tangney identifies shame-proneness and guilt-proneness as two moral affective styles where the former has to do with "global, painful, and devastating experience in which the self, not just behaviour, is painfully scrutinized and negatively evaluated."[78] In this sense, shame-inducing experiences that generate a shame-prone style may be viewed as attacks on the global self and should produce disturbances in self-identity. Shame-prone individuals have been found to demonstrate a limited empathetic ability, a high propensity for anger, and self-reports of aggression.[79] Dutton, van Ginkel, and Starzomski found recollections of shame-inducing experiences by parents of assaultive men to be significantly related to the men's self-reports of both anger and physical abuse and to their wives' reports of the men's use of Dominance/Isolation.[80] Miller and others have commented on the relationship of shame to anger, deriving from Helen Block Lewis' description of "humiliated fury."[81] Tangney et al. found significant correlations between TOSCA (Test of Self-Conscious Affect) shame-proneness and hostility, anger arousal, and tendencies to blame others for negative events.[82] Novaco described anger as serving the function of overriding less acceptable emotions.[83] Shame and guilt would appear to be two such emotions. Shame-proneness, as Tangney described it, is a tendency to experience global attacks on the self. Since such affective experiences are aversive, shame-prone individuals attempt to ward them off by externalizing causes for negative events, thereby avoiding personal responsibility, which they experience as shameful.

Dutton, van Ginkel, and Starzomski found three recalled sources of shame in assaultive males.[84] These were public scolding, random punishment, and generic criticism. All three were recalled as generating experiences of shame. These, in turn, were correlated with adult anger and tendencies to project blame. Not surprisingly, given these tendencies, abusive actions also correlated with recalled shame experiences. Partial correlations revealed that parental shaming still correlated significantly with measures of abusive personality after physical abuse by the parents had been partialled out. The converse, however, was not true. With parental shaming partialled out, physical abuse by parents did not correlate significantly with abusive personality measures. Dutton, van Ginkel, and Starzomski suggested that a two-step learning process may be involved in the acquisition of abusiveness. Shaming experiences appeared to contribute to the formation of the abusive personality, and physical abuse to the modelling of its behavioural manifestations. In non-assaultive control groups, abusive personality is still significantly related to verbal and emotional abusiveness. These men report fewer modelling experiences in their family of origin. Hence, abuse or rejection by parents, insecure attachment, and parental shaming all appear to contribute to the formation in males of a personality type associated with abusiveness.

The Trauma Model: A Triad of Abusogenic Family Features

A general "trauma model" is presented here to summarize these findings. Note that the "triad" of exposure to violence, shaming, and insecure attachment produces specific long-term effects. These have been demonstrated in my own work and that of others.

The "abusive personality" described is both a product of this early exposure and a constellation of mutually reinforcing beliefs, emotional reactions, and behaviours. Far more occurs in reaction to early exposure to violence than the mere modelling of behaviour as social learning theory suggests. Children who are exposed to ongoing violence also tend to be shamed by parents and to have no secure base. The three exist as a package in dysfunctional abusive families. For these reasons, treatment that fails to address the underpinnings of abusiveness is destined to fail. Elsewhere I have given a more detailed presentation of this model.[85]

Why do these men get so angry in intimate relationships? Part of the answer may lie in the meaning they ascribe to intimacy. For men high in BPO, intimate relationships serve the unenviable task of maintaining their ego integrity. With an unstable sense of self and an inability to tolerate aloneness, these men depend on their relationship with their female partner to prevent their fragile selfhood from disintegrating. Yet that very relationship is fraught with "dysphoric stalemates" (being unable to communicate intimacy needs

10.9 Trauma model of abusiveness

Family of origin	Adult deficits
Physical abuse • between parents • directed at child	Cognitive problem resolution deficits Violent response repertoire

Parental rejection
• shaming
   – public punishment
   – random punishment
   – global criticism
	Externalizing/blaming attributional style
	High chronic anger

Insecure attachment	Rejection sensitivity Ambivalent attachment style Disturbed self schema • inability to self soothe • anxiety, depression

while being extremely demanding), chronic intimacy-anger, and a tendency to project unacceptable impulses onto the significant other, while denying and masking his own unconscious dependency. The intimate relationship of the high-BPO scorer is asked to do the impossible, and when it fails, or appears in his eyes to fail, anger escalates because his very sense of self is threatened and because he projects blame on his partner for the dysphoria that he inevitably experiences during intimacy. He views her, at this phase of the relationship, as "all bad." If that impasse is resolved, he then tends to view her as "all good," and himself as bad, and so enters the contrition phase of the abuse cycle.

The unavoidable aspect of attachment-anger, the tendency to blaming, the projection of anger onto the partner, and the inability to verbalize dysphoric states defines a personality profile that generates both relationship conflict and abuse. I have come to call this personality profile the "abusive personality" and to assess it with the Propensity for Abusiveness Scale (PAS). The behavioural manifestation of abusiveness (e.g., whether it takes a physical or verbal form) may still depend on modelling and autodidactic ontogenetic experiences.[86] BPO correlates with abusiveness in our control groups, but only with emotional abuse, because men in these groups are, according to their wives, non-violent. The mood cycles that characterize Borderlines are essential features of the extreme scores on BPO (otherwise known as BPD), but the behavioural forms of abuse may be learned reactions, not just to external stress, but also to the internal cues of dysphoria. It is for this reason that victims of the abuse describe it as self-generated within the abuser.

Relationship to Socializing Culture

If early experience contributes to a propensity for assaultiveness, it may be that elements of Borderline Personality Organization seek out aspects of the culture to direct and justify abuse. The Primitive Defences of the Borderline Personality, for example, which involve "splitting" good objects from bad objects, are reinforced by cultural judgments about female sexuality. Cultures that divide women into "Madonnas" and "whores" provide a sanctioned reinforcement of the object-split in the assaultive Borderline male. Cultures that socialize men to expect the woman to be responsible for relationship outcome provide a rationale for the Borderline Personality's expectation that his intimate partner should mitigate his dysphoria. Archer found that in countries where women's status is low, abuse of women is more frequent.[87] In such countries men who do not have personality disorders are abusive too, feeling it is their right. In countries with greater equality, personality disorders contribute more to male abusiveness. From this perspective, the personality pattern contains emotional demands that it directs and justifies through drawing on the ambient culture. High-BPO men will rationalize their maltreatment of intimate partners by adopting negative sexual stereotypes of women. In a non-clinical sample, Starzomski found that BPO scores correlated +.57 with scores on a measure of hostility toward women.[88] This was replicated in our control group of blue-collar workers. In my clinical experience, abusive men frequently blame their female partners for their own behaviour. After a series of relationships in which their abusiveness continues to re-manifest itself, they "progress" from blaming a woman to blaming women in general.

11 Relationship/Interactionist Explanations

The explanations reviewed in this book to date have been located in the social structure (e.g., feminism), the individual psyche (e.g., social learning, attachment, personality disorders), even in neural development.[1] However, another line of research has examined the process of dynamic interaction in couples where abuse occurs. We saw in Chapter 6 that Stets and Straus found that 45 percent of all reports of intimate violence on conflict surveys indicated bidirectional violence, which was the most common incidence category found in that study. Similarly, analyses of data from the National Comorbidity Study found the same thing: that the most common form of intimate partner violence was bidirectional.[2] In a large sample study of the United States Army (N = 55,000+), Neidig found that 63 percent of all IPV reported was mutual.[3] Hence, bilateral IPV is the most common form in both civilian and army samples. Even when one person uses unilateral violence that gets reported in a survey, it could represent the end of an escalating interaction sequence characterized by growing negativity. Two kinds of "interactionist" studies have been done. The first examines the fit of psychological characteristics of victim and perpetrator (e.g., attachment styles in both) and predicts longitudinally how violence persists. The second examines actual interactions in a lab setting, using video recording of behavioural sequences and coding schemes.

Longitudinal Studies
Some researchers have studied couples over time to see whether the abuse ceases, remains the same, or increases. In surveys, two-thirds of people who report abuse say that it was recurring.[4] So one-third desist without outside intervention. Feld and Straus conducted one-year follow-ups of 420 respondents in the 1985 US National survey.[5] Among those that reported at least one act of minor violence, only 5.8 percent had moved up to severe violence, whereas, among those who had committed severe violence in the first year, 69.6 percent had de-escalated in the second year. Hence, the evidence supported de-escalation more than escalation. These studies are for married

persons in a representative community sample who did not receive any form of intervention by the state.

Leonard reported the Buffalo Newlywed Study (BNS) begun in 1987, a three-wave longitudinal study of couples over the first three years of marriage.[6] Couples applying for a marriage licence who indicated that it was the first marriage for both and were between the ages of eighteen and twenty-nine were solicited and paid to participate in the longitudinal study (N = 647 couples completed assessments). The first assessment took place prior to marriage, the second one year later (84 percent of the originals completed this, N = 543), and a third on their third anniversary (N = 400). There was an acceptable attrition rate. Older white couples were more likely to complete all three questionnaires.

Screening assessed demographics (age, race, religion, socioeconomic class), employment, alcohol consumption pattern, personality factors (anger, hostility), relationship functioning factors (conflict-solving strategies, intimacy), and the CTS. The main findings were that a pattern of heavy drinking among newlywed couples was associated with premarital aggression (with demographic and personality factors partialled out). Leonard and Senchak reported, based on these data, that premarital aggression (average violence, wife-to-husband and husband-to-wife) correlated significantly with both the husband's heavy drinking and the wife's heavy drinking.[7] Heavy drinking was established on the basis of self-report of frequency of six or more drinks at a time on the Alcohol Dependence Scale (never have six or more drinks at a time, do so less than monthly, monthly, weekly).

Of the 647 couples, 118 reported an episode of physical aggression. Drinking was higher for both husband and wife in this group, but husband rates exceeded wife rates. Twenty-five couples reported a severe physical episode. This group was characterized by very high rates (43 percent) of husband drinking. In an analysis of the 1985 National Survey data, Kantor and Straus found that drinking just prior to a violent event was related to frequency of drinking.[8] Binge drinkers tend to have borderline traits.[9] Leonard reported a strong association between frequency of intoxication and alcohol-related violence. Nevertheless, there were sober-abusive subjects and frequently drunk subjects who only got abusive when sober.[10] Overall, however, the data showed that acute alcohol consumption was associated with both the frequency and severity of marital aggression. This was true for drinking by both husbands and wives (frequently connected). Although he collected bidirectional CTS data, Leonard only reported husband violence, supporting the paradigmatic view that males are perpetrators. According to Leonard, the wife aggression data has never been published.[11]

However, Schumacher and Leonard did examine the violence of both males and females.[12] In a study of 634 couples, recruited as they applied for marriage licences, they examined correlations between marital dissatisfaction, verbal aggression, and physical aggression as risk factors for physical aggression during the first two years of marriage. Couples completed assessments at the time of marriage and at their first and second anniversaries. The results of a series of path analyses suggest that prior verbal aggression and physical aggression by both partners are important longitudinal predictors of marital dissatisfaction, but do not support the role of marital dissatisfaction as a unique predictor of subsequent physical aggression. Wives' and husbands' use of physical aggression correlated at .79 ($p < .001$) at Time 1 (time of marriage) of the study, and both correlated with their use of physical aggression at Time 2 (first anniversary) and Time 3 (second anniversary). Results also failed to support physical aggression by itself as a predictor of marital dissatisfaction. There were no significant relationships between use of physical aggression by either person and any ratings of marital dissatisfaction, except for one: women who were more violent were more satisfied in the marriage. By using time-lag analysis it was possible to see who was initiating the subsequent dyadic aggression. Husband verbal aggression was not predictive of wife physical aggression, either from T1 to T2 or from T2 to T3. In contrast, wife verbal aggression was significantly predictive of husband physical aggression from T1 to T2, and marginally predictive from T2 to T3. For husbands and wives, one's own verbal aggression at one time period was predictive of one's own physical aggression at the subsequent time period for both time lags. Tests to evaluate gender differences were uniformly non-significant. The path corresponding to wife physical aggression at T1 as a predictor of husband physical aggression at T2 was significant, but the parameter for husband physical aggression as a predictor of wife physical aggression during the same time lag was not significant at the .05 level. Hence, in the temporal ordering of the relationship, husbands become physically violent first.

Given the potential importance of dyadic factors in the prediction of intimate partner violence, marital researchers examined whether physical aggression by one partner predicts future aggression in the other partner, perhaps as self-defensive or retaliatory behaviour. Murphy and O'Leary found some evidence for this dyadic prediction, but only three of twelve predicted paths were significant.[13] O'Leary, Malone, and Tyree examined 393 young couples in a longitudinal study.[14] Pre-relationship predictor variables included experiencing violence in the family of origin, aggression against others in childhood and adolescence, and personality characteristics. Relationship predictor variables were marital discord and spouse-specific aggression (measured at eighteen months of marriage). Dependent variable data were collected after thirty months of marriage. Unfortunately, the authors committed the fault of making a "tautological prediction" (violence at eighteen months "predicts" violence at thirty months). This relationship was so strong that it washed out the effects of other variables when a multiple regression was done on the data. However, in constructing some recursive path models of aggression separately for males and females, the authors found that "defendence" (suspicion, hypervigilance to threat) and "aggression to other" predicted psychological aggression within the marriage, which in turn predicted physical aggression. For males and females, this was true. However, two other factors, "hit parents" and "hit peers" directly affected their use of violence in the marriage. As the authors put it, "our results suggest that men and women who have aggressive and defensive personality characteristics and who are experiencing a lack of satisfaction with their marriages tend to engage in psychological aggression. In turn, psychological aggression appears as a precursor to physical aggression."[15] The "aggressive-defensive" personalities sound like borderline or ego-related problems.

Jacobson et al. examined battering over a two-year relationship span.[16] At two years, 62 percent of the "batterers and their spouses" were still cohabitating. Of those still living together, 46 percent of the husbands had not reduced their severe violence (wife violence was not reported; more on this below). Only 7 percent of male batterers had achieved complete desistance.

Moffitt et al. studied a representative sample of 360 young adult couples from a birth cohort (the Dunedin Cohort, see Magdol et al.).[17] Moffitt et al. used couple analysis, measuring for both members of the couple their usual self-reported reactions to stress, negative emotionality, use of aggressive strategies interpersonally, and expectations of other people. Earlier chapters discussed these psychological aspects from both an attachment and a borderline personality organization (BPO) perspective. The authors refer to the collectivity of these traits as negative emotionality (NEM), as discussed in Chapter 6.[18]

In the Dunedin study, all these traits were assessed for both men and women using the Multidimensional Personality Questionnaire.[19] Moffitt et al. found that women were slightly more likely to have abused their partners, but in general there were no gender differences in either NEM or abuse. In the sample there was a range from no abuse at all in a couple (25 percent) to clinically significant abuse (9 percent), defined as having used medical or police services. Abusiveness was predicted by NEM, independent of gender. The authors tested a number of explanatory models and found that a male-dominance model was not supported by their data.[20] But a perpetrator-effects model was supported. This means that NEM in either person was significantly associated with the receipt of abuse by their partner. Consistent with Stets and Straus, 18 percent of the women in the sample committed physical abuse against a non-violent male.[21] The data were also consistent with a multiple-effects model: when both members of the couple were high in NEM, the likelihood of mutual abuse increased additively. In a prior study Moffitt et al. showed that NEM measured at age eighteen predicted abusiveness at age twenty-one. The authors conclude: "We found abuse was a dyadic process; both partners' personal characteristics increased the risk and both sexes participated ... Treating men only may not reduce risk completely for young couples."[22]

Interactional Studies

Gayla Margolin has contributed consistently to interactional studies.[23] Margolin's work started with an examination of interaction patterns in four different types of couples called physically abusive (PA), verbally abusive (VA), withdrawn but non-abusive (WI), and non-distressed and non-abusive (ND), based on responses to the CTS and the Dyadic Adjustment Scale.[24] In the early 1980s, self-report questionnaires were used to assess interaction style (questionnaires such as the Communication Apprehension Inventory or the Spouse Specific Assertivness Scale); later these would be replaced by more sophisticated techniques for videotaping and scoring marital interaction.

In the initial studies, Margolin's PA spouses were similar to WI spouses in having low assertion, high communication comprehension, and the belief that conflict was "destructive." (The latter belief may have come from observing their past violence.)[25] Interestingly, and reflecting the times, Margolin worried that her physically abusive sample was not representative of abusive couples. "These couples scored beyond 95 percent on the physical aggression scale of the CTS. Yet they have not sought treatment for the problems of abuse and thus, have not been labeled abusive by any social agency."[26] In other words, she was noticing – and using – the majority of violent couples who go undetected, even by crime victim surveys. Margolin noted that "the interactional processes of abuse and withdrawal seem to be related in some couples."[27] Men in these groups showed particularly low self-disclosure. The physically abusive group also used withdrawal, as did the group that only withdrew but was not abusive. Margolin speculated that the physically aggressive group might use withdrawal as an initial response to conflict, then become abusive when the withdrawal failed. Perusal of the screening criteria (Table 1 of Margolin's printed presentation) reveals that these were bidirectionally violent couples.[28] Both the women's and men's individual physical aggression scores on the CTS were greater than 8.

By 1988 Margolin and her colleagues had moved to assessment of *in vivo* interactions. Typically, couples would sign in for the research, undergo an initial screening/assessment, and then be asked to "discuss" two "problematic topics" (chosen from three offered in the screening self-reports of the couples). These discussions were videotaped for later coding. Experimenters observed the interaction through a one-way mirror (and later reviewed the videotapes).[29]

Coding was done by independent coders based on an interaction coding system developed by Forgatch and Weider.[30] Beep tones signalled to coders when a fifteen-second interval of interaction had transpired. Coders then assigned codes to the previous interaction into one of five summary categories: (1) offensive negative (mildly negative gestures, negative gestures, negative touch, and non-verbal command), (2) negative voice, (3) defensive negative (head hand, no eye contact, lean away, distract), (4) physical positive (positive gesture, positive touch), and (5) smile/laugh. Each discussion was independently coded by three coders. Obviously, before any conclusions can be drawn, the coders must agree with each other on their use of the coding system (exhibit inter-rater reliability). Depending on which code category was examined, inter-rater reliability ranged from .84 to .94, all highly acceptable. After each discussion, subjects reported their emotional reactions on four dimensions: sadness, anxiety, anger, and feeling attacked.

As with her previous studies, Margolin and her colleagues examined Physically Abusive (PA) couples, Verbally Abusive (VA) couples, Withdrawn but non-abusive (WI) couples, and non-distressed, non-abusive (ND) couples. Again these categories were based on self-report measures of CTS and Dyadic Adjustment by both members of the couple. The authors studied 78 demographically matched couples in the four groups. The women in these studies did not perceive themselves as battered (even in the PA group) and, according to Margolin et al., "ranged considerably in the extent to which they themselves had engaged in physical violence."[31]

Margolin et al. found the chief differentiating factor between the PA group and other groups was the husbands. PA husbands exhibited more instances of negative voice and more overtly negative behaviours than husbands in other groups.[32] PA husbands also reported more sadness, fear, anger, and feeling attacked (and somewhat more physiological arousal).

Despite the controlled and semi-public nature of the discussions, PA husbands exhibited negative affect patterns that were indicative of non-constructive approaches to conflict and could escalate into a more extreme expression of aggression. These included irate, angry, whining, yelling, sarcastic, nagging, lecturing, accusatory, mocking, and otherwise irritating voice tones. Negative behaviours included signs of dismissal, waving arms, pointing a finger at the other, threatening or mimicking gestures, and negative physical contact. The PA husbands tended not to exhibit head-hanging, no eye contact, or leaning away.

PA wives showed a greater escalation of offensive negative behaviours than did VA or WI wives during the middle portions of the discussion period and then showed a greater de-escalation in the final period. The authors concluded that, "paradoxically, the wives' backing down may negatively reinforce the husbands' behaviours and may inadvertently strengthen his attack."[33] Of course, we do not know the outcome had the women continued to escalate. To draw that conclusion, we would have to follow a group of women who never de-escalated and see what the outcome was and what group they were in. It may be that, regardless of their response at this point, violence would occur. This view is consistent with work on personality disorders in abusive men.[34] Borderline male batterers or those who have an "abusive personality" would proceed to the aggression phase of the conflict at this point based on physiological arousal and misconstrual of the woman's actions.

Burman, Margolin, and John utilized sequential analysis of couple interactions from videos taken in the couples' home, which were believed to be "more ecologically valid."[35] The PA group was again composed of bidirectionally violent couples.

Couples were instructed to recall a typical serious conflict and how it began, who said what to whom, how the conflict progressed, and how it ended. Couples then re-enacted these conflicts, and the re-enactments (which averaged ten minutes in length) were videotaped and coded. This time the coding was based not on fifteen-second intervals but instead on "floor switches" (a statement of one person bounded on either side by a statement of the other). This created a series of "lags" from one person's action to the reaction of the other and so on. PA couples turned out to exhibit more hostile affect and more contingent behaviour patterns involving anger. Non-distressed couples could "exit these negative interaction cycles quite quickly."[36] The authors conclude that "contrary to images of women in abusive relationships as passive and reticent, the women in the types of PA relationships presented here are angry with or contemptuous of husbands and are quick to respond to their husband's anger."[37]

The University of Washington Studies

As Margolin and Burman point out, "the family therapy movement is grounded on ideas that clash ... particularly with the feminist movement."[38] After all, there is no point to marital and couple therapy if violence is always male-initiated. But this book has reviewed evidence that male-initiated violence is not the only pattern. As will be seen, individual or group therapy for each member of the couple separately might be effectual, followed by therapy for them as a couple. Couple therapy has been shown effective in altering dysfunctional interaction patterns.

Interesting findings from an interactionist perspective were also reported by the University of Washington psychology lab.[39] Using techniques for assessing marital interaction that originated with Levenson and Gottman, the lab assessed three dimensions of marital interaction (positive-negative affect, reciprocity, and asymmetry) and focused on domestic violence.[40] Initially, Levenson and Gottman had focused only on marital satisfaction and had measured physiological linkage (interconnectedness in heart rate, skin conductance, and pulse transmission time) using time series techniques for physiological measurement as well as self-reports of affect using a video recall procedure. Their finding was that parallel patterning of physiological responses was related to reported marital satisfaction. In the University of Washington studies these techniques would be used, on domestically violent couples in an "experimental apartment" created in the psychology lab. Couples would re-create their most serious conflicts in that environment, and physiological reactions would be measured.

In turning to the study of domestic violence, the University of Washington lab recruited through newspaper ads. The criterion for the domestically violent group was wives' reports of husband violence on the CTS. Wives' reports were used because "we assumed husbands might under-report their own violence."[41] The focus of the study was on husband violence, using categories of violent husbands developed from a popular book on the research, classifying violent husbands as "pit bulls" (tenacious, emotional) or "cobras" (cool, instrumental). Couples were solicited as "couples experiencing conflict in their marriage." One has to read the fine print in the method section of the report to discover that "according to the wives themselves, almost half (28/57) would have qualified for the DV group if wife violence had been the criterion."[42] In other words, there were bilaterally violent couples in the mix, although the focus was entirely on the males. No measures were taken of the wives' use of violence, and all independent variables focused on male violence as though it were being produced unilaterally in all relationships (even though it clearly was not).

Babcock et al. assessed power discrepancies between husband and wife based on economic status, decision-making power, communication patterns, and communication skills.[43] Domestically violent couples were more likely than non-violent controls (maritally distressed/non-violent and happily married/non-violent) to engage in withdrawal behaviours (wife withdrawal/husband demand). Husbands who had less power were more physically abusive to their wives. The authors viewed this as "compensatory power," but this is dubious.

In contrast to the common feminist claim that as male power increases, so does violence toward women,[44] a country-by-country analysis of male power shows a curvilinear relationship. The high-power-male countries and the lowest-power-male countries experienced the most violence against women.[45] The "compensation" argument is used to explain the violence in low-power states. But that is to have it both ways: if high-power males use more violence, it is domination; if low-power males use more violence, it is compensation for a wish to dominate. Such a view is unaffected by data.

One interesting unreported piece of data from the Babcock et al. study was that male socioeconomic power was unrelated to decision-making power at home or to communication skill advantages. Power, it seems, emanates from several levels, which are mutually inconsistent or unrelated.

Cordova et al. used a Marital Interaction Coding scheme (MICS) applied to videos of couples arguing in the University of Washington lab.[46] Twenty-nine couples designated as domestically violent (DV) based on the wives' reports were compared with fifteen distressed non-violent (DNV) and thirteen happily married (HM) couples. The study was inspired by Margolin's finding on negative reciprocity and suggestion that the drop in negative reciprocity by wives may have negatively reinforced the husbands' violence. The MICS required coders to initially code interactions into three broad types of behaviour: aversive, facilitative, and neutral. (There was a 70 percent agreement among raters calibrated against Cordova's rating, although Kappa's [measures of average agreement] were lower than that.) Since the study focused on changes in aversive behaviour over time, sequential analyses were examined. Negative reciprocity was defined as the occurrence of aversive behaviour given the prior occurrence of aversive behaviour by the other. Various time-lags for this reciprocity were measured (immediate vs. delayed). As with Margolin et al.'s sample, DV husbands exhibited a higher proportion of aversive behavior than did their non-violent counterparts.[47] Similarly, the authors conclude: "The behaviour of DV wives in this sample does not suggest passivity, docility or surrender. Rather, the women are continuing in conflict engagement, even though they have histories of being subjected to physical abuse ... Although these women were being beaten, they had not been beaten into submission. They were standing up to rather than surrendering to their battering husbands."[48] Of course, this explanation overlooks the fact, reported in Jacobson et al. (on the same sample) that 28/57 wives would themselves have qualified for the DV group given the criteria used.[49] Why then depict them as "reactive victim/heroines"? Because that depiction fits the paradigm of male perpetrator/female victim. In fact the Cordova et al. data tables reveal that the DV women used more aversive acts than did the DV men (18.2 vs. 15.8) in the time assessed.[50] (That was also true for women in the other two groups).

Cordova et al. are clearly troubled that the wives in their sample used so many aversive acts. They say "these results appear to be surprising in the light of descriptions such as Walker's battered woman syndrome" and then try to explain away the female violence (the women felt safer in the lab, the women were trying to put an end to "protracted tension," and so on).[51] Not once do they state the obvious: these women were as abusive as their male partners.

Jacobson et al. studied the "affect, psychophysiology, and verbal content of arguments in couples with a violent husband."[52] Again, the same taped fifteen-minute arguments from the same couples were examined, although the sample had now increased to sixty DV couples and thirty-two DNV couples. Arguments were coded for (1) affect: affect (positive/neutral), aggression, and distress (fear or sadness), and (2) content: withdrawal, criticize, defend, demand, emotional abuse, physical aggression, positive/neutral, distress, and self-defence. In addition, the Specific Affect Coding System (SPAFF) was used to code affect in these interactions, yielding three options: neutral, positive (affection, humour, interest/curiosity, or joy/enthusiasm), or negative (anger, sadness, fear). Non-student, staff observers were trained to do the coding. In addition, psychophysiological data were obtained, including measures of cardiovascular arousal (cardiac interbeat interval, pulse transmission time, and finger-pulse amplitude). The chief finding was that "only husband violence produces fear in the partner." The authors say "this gender difference underscores one of the major differences between husband and wife violence: Only husband violence produces fear in the partner."[53] This finding was cited extensively as showing a differential effect for male vs. female abuse.

Dutton, Webb, and Ryan, studying gender differences in affective reactions to conflict, found that women used affect scales differently, reporting higher scores even in baseline controls.[54] Actually, Jacobson et al.'s data table shows female fear at 8.7 (SD = 7), male fear at 6.7 (SD = 8.6).[55] The actual comparison between husbands and wives was not on fear but on fear increases. The authors claimed the difference to be significant. However, as Jacobson et al. admit, "the men were less likely to acknowledge there was anything wrong with them."[56] The data also show that DV wives were more belligerent than their husbands and showed more contempt. The husbands showed more defensiveness. Jacobson et al. justify their interpretation by arguing "even DV husbands admit that wife violence is largely reactive to either physical or emotional abuse on their part."[57] Were the wives asked these questions as well? This is not reported. At the end of the paper the authors observe that "intense anger, combined with fear and sadness, may be part of the helplessness reported by battered women."[58] Of course that conclusion overlooks the fact that half the women were themselves physically abusive, and women in general exhibited more belligerence on the experimental tapes. A subsequent re-analysis showed that MCMI data were collected for the women but never reported, although most of the women who had peaks on personality disorder seemed to have Borderline Personality Disorder. The unpublished data show both men and women in the DV group were elevated on Antisocial, Avoidant, Passive-Aggressive, and Borderline.[59]

Gottman et al. focused on the physiological reactions observed in the conflicts: cardiac interbeat interval, pulse transmission time, finger-pulse amplitude, and skin conductance level.[60] In addition, MCMI-II Data were obtained for husbands and wives, and the laboratory interactions were coded as described above using the SPAFF. On the basis of physiological reactivity the men were classified as Type 1 (those with lowered heart rates during marital conflict) and Type 2 (those with increased heart rate). All data were reported through the filter of comparing these two groups of men (e.g., Type 1 men had significantly higher rates of Antisocial PD and Aggressive Sadistic PD than did Type 2 men). Type 1 men were more angry, belligerent, and contemptuous than Type 2 men. Type 1 men were more generally violent outside marriage and had greater problems with drug dependency.

Leonard and Roberts performed an unusually well-controlled study of the interactive mechanisms in operation.[61] Sixty maritally aggressive and seventy-five non-aggressive men received either no alcohol, a placebo, or alcohol (vodka). The couples (who had been married less than two years) were asked to discuss an issue that was a chronic source of conflict for them. Then their interactions were videotaped and coded in both a baseline interaction (before the alcohol administration and involving their second most important disagreement) and an experimental interaction (after the alcohol or placebo and involving the most important issue of disagreement). As with the Jacobson et al. and Margolin studies, aggressive couples exhibited more negative behaviour (criticism, disagreement, interruptions, disapproval, put downs, etc.) and higher levels of negative reciprocity (these behaviours are reciprocated) in their baseline interaction than did non-aggressive couples. Alcohol increased the husbands' use of negativity. This was not a placebo effect. It was a pharmacological effect of alcohol. Since baseline negativity was higher in the abusive couples, alcohol raised negativity levels still more. Leonard and Roberts conclude: "It may be that alcohol simply disrupts attempts at conflict resolution for both aggressive and non-aggressive husbands. These disruptions, in turn, may lead some husbands to behave aggressively, but may lead to different outcomes among other husbands."[62] Finally, they say, "alcohol is neither a necessary nor sufficient cause of violence but there is growing evidence that it may contribute to violent behaviour."[63] Alcohol seems to potentiate an already dysfunctional interaction sequence that is indicative of abusive couples.

Couple Therapy

Given the interactional aspect of couple violence described above, marital or couple therapy (sometimes called systems therapy) seems like a logical way to proceed. Heyman and Schlee have written a good overview of this approach in which they review the Stony Brook Treatment Project, which uses a system called Physical Aggression Couple Treatment (PACT) emphasizing the circular causality demonstrated in the research studies on couples described above.[64] In this system, each partner is held responsible for their own behaviour, but each takes a role in conflict escalation (or conversely its reduction). PACT is an extended version of Domestic Conflict Containment Program (DCCP).[65] The rationale is as follows: most acts of physical aggression in intimate relationships occur in the context of an argument between partners. Conflict escalates until one partner strikes the other or both partners strike each other (called "circular causality"). Two of the working rules are (1) the system is not used when the woman is still at risk for physical violence, and (2) the purpose of the system is not to teach women to be "non-conflictual" (i.e., acquiesce to whatever the partner wants). Rather it is to become aware of one's reaction to conflictual responses from one's partner, take responsibility for it, and control it.

Neidig and Friedman called the perpetrator/victim distinction a "therapeutic dead end" and believed people needed to learn to use assertive and nonviolent communication *in vivo*.[66] Family systems approaches regard wife assault from an interactive (microsystem) rather than an intrapsychic perspective.[67] Major contributors to family violence are seen in the rules of the family system that define what behaviour is acceptable, the power imbalances of that system, and the personal resources of individual members that provide a basis for exchange.

Giles-Sims acknowledges that "victims may inadvertently be reinforcing the violent behaviour,"[68] a perspective supported in the child abuse literature by the interactive studies of Patterson and his colleagues reviewed in Chapter 2. Patterson, Cobb, and Ray, for example, observed parents' reinforcement of the violence of their highly destructive boys.[69] These parents were not aware of the reinforcement they provided, and Giles-Sims suggests that the same may be true for battered women. Pagelow describes how some of these reinforcers include a low likelihood of retaliation, an acceptance by the weaker partner of battering as a proper response to stress, and an intense "traditional ideology" (i.e., that the woman shouldn't leave the marriage no matter how destructive it is and that she has a responsibility to "save" the man from his own excesses).[70] All these tendencies lead to the assaultive male's avoiding punishment for his violence.

Neidig and Friedman begin their description of their couples' treatment program with the statement that "abusive behaviour is a relationship issue but it is ultimately the responsibility of the male to control physical violence."[71] Their view is that approaches that attribute total responsibility to either party lead to blaming, which compounds the problem. It does so, according to these authors, by beginning a chain of retributional strategies by the victim and the aggressor whereby each tries to "get even" for the other's most recent transgression. A systems approach avoids blaming by getting couples to think of the causes of violence from a circular feedback perspective rather than a linear one. This leads to "constructive interventions in the escalating process" which permit each partner to accept a portion of the responsibility. Having said that, however, Neidig and Friedman assign "ultimate responsibility to the male for controlling violence" as a recognition that both parties are not equal in physical strength. But if a man is responsible for his violence, then why is he not to blame if he acts violently? One answer may be that his violence occurred in a state of high arousal when he perceived no alternatives to the actions he took. Therapeutically, a couple approach and an individual approach have a fundamental disagreement: the couple approach tries to reduce blame, and the individual approach tries to increase responsibility.

The decision whether an individual or a couple approach is best may depend on the client. If a man (or woman) has a history of violence in several relationships with women, he may be a conflict generator capable of creating the pattern observed by the systems therapist in his current relationship. Certainly the "abusive personality" profiled above requires extensive therapeutic work at an individual level before couple treatment seems viable. Also, as some therapists have shown, single persons are capable of generating entire interaction patterns within families on the basis of their individual pathologies. Richter describes how a paranoid personality who holds power in a family can generate a shared paranoia in the entire family system.[72]

I expect that individuals with abusive personalities are conflict generators in all intimate relationships, regardless of the personality or style of their partners. Of course, such men may also pick women with their own backgrounds of abuse victimization and personality disorders. It is desirable to obtain detailed social histories of clients and their partners prior to embarking on a systems approach, especially in view of the Kalmuss and Seltzer findings reported in Chapter 8. If a male batterer has a history of violence with women that predates his current relationship, or strong indicators of an abusive personality, couple treatment may not be advisable.[73] Where the female feels a threat from the man's violence potential or where violence is still recent, couple therapy might be delayed until the man has successfully completed an anger management program and is violence-free for a lengthy period. In general, where the violence and conflict seem specific to the present relationship, couple treatment may be more useful after the man's anger treatment.

Cascardi and Vivian found that the majority of couple-clients seeking marital therapy both engaged in aggressive acts, and the woman got the worst of it.[74] Vivian and Langhinrichsen-Rohling classified couples as follows: (1) Mild Bidirectional (about 50 percent report low-level aggression – pushes, slaps, grabs – committed by both husband and wife), (2) Moderate, and (3) Severe (30-40 percent report high levels of wife victimization and much lower levels of husband victimization).[75] This leads to the question from the Stets and Straus table: what happens in female-dominant violent couples?[76] Obviously they do not seek marital therapy. Interestingly, only a small percentage of women seeking marital therapy report physical violence as a problem. O'Leary, Vivian, and Malone found 6 percent while Ehrensaft and Vivian found 14 percent, despite CTS reports revealing higher levels of physical aggression in the marriages.[77]

Outcome Success of Couple Treatment

Heyman and Schlee assessed for levels of aggression prior to their treatment program and found that very few couples reported severe levels of aggression.[78] When someone was injured or fearful or when the husband was in denial, the couple was screened out. They did not comment on wives in denial.

Post-treatment assessment revealed significant drops in aggression and increases in marital satisfaction rated by both parties. The reduction in aggression was still significantly lower than its pre-treatment level one year after cessation of treatment. Complete cessation was found with 26 percent one year later. Reductions occurred in a substantial subgroup.

Stith, Rosen, McCollum, and Thomsen in a study of forty-two couples also found significant reductions in male violence, reduced recidivism six months after couple treatment, and cessation.[79] In this couples' group-therapy format, only 25 percent recidivated; in an individual couples' format, 43 percent recidivated; in a non-treated control, 66 percent recidivated. By comparison, in a treatment outcome study done on the Duluth model (described in Chapter 14), Shepard found a 40 percent recidivism rate in a six-month follow-up of Duluth clients, higher than most control recidivism levels.[80] Dutton found a recidivism rate of 16 percent (or 84 percent complete cessation) based on wives' reports for a court-mandated cognitive behavioural group treatment for men.[81] Stith, Rosen, and McCallum reviewed six outcome studies of couple treatment and concluded they were at least as effective as "traditional treatment."[82] The latter seemed to include both "psychoeducational" and cognitive-behavioural group therapy for males. We will expand our understanding of group treatment outcome evaluation in Chapter 14.

12 The Failure of Criminal Justice Intervention Policy

The proper design of public policies requires a clear and sober
understanding of the nature of man, and in particular, the extent
to which that nature can be changed by plan.

        – J.Q. Wilson, *Thinking about Crime*

Feminist legal scholars have argued for mandatory arrest for wife assault
and, as a result of this political pressure and some expensive civil suits against
lax police administrations, mandatory arrest became the legal policy in fifteen US states as of 1999.[1] Some of the landmark studies that preceded mandatory arrest are worth reviewing before we look at the current situation.

The Police and Wife Assault: Early Studies
Seminal psychological contributions to police intervention in family conflict were designed to improve the decision-making and communication
abilities of police officers. Morton Bard developed an experimental program
with the New York Police Department in 1967 that was designed to diminish "iatrogenic violence," i.e., violence accidentally triggered by police
(mis)handling of the conflict.[2] Ivan Illich held the view that well-intended
social intervention could have unintended consequences that produced the
opposite of the intended result.[3] He focused primarily on the health system,
but Bard used Illich's premise in investigating police intervention. As we
shall see throughout this chapter, Illich proved correct in ways he never lived
to see.

    Bard held the pioneering view that police officers served a preventive
function in that they could reduce the likelihood of future crime by proper
handling of current family conflict. His system was intended to train officers how to use arbitration, mediation, and negotiation to manage crisis
situations. The trained officers were then assigned to a high-crime precinct
in the Harlem area of New York City and responded to all the domestic

disturbance calls within it. Bard established an ongoing case discussion system between the officers and psychologists for the duration of the two-year program. At the conclusion of the program, the project managers claimed that the training had produced decreases in injuries to officers and a reduction in the incidence of domestic disturbances (presumably by diminishing repeat calls).

However, these claims have been disputed by others. Liebman and Schwartz argued that Bard's data indicated a higher percentage of repeat calls than in a control district.[4] Since effective conflict resolution was the objective of Bard's approach, repeat calls indicated that the problem had not been successfully resolved. Furthermore, family homicides and assaults increased in the experimental district and decreased in the control district. The highly publicized claim that injuries decreased for trained officers was based on no injuries to officers in the experimental district and one injury in the control district. Finally, the study was a non-equivalent design with different cultural groups in the experimental and control areas, making any results ambiguous. The controversy over the Bard project highlighted the early issues that surrounded police intervention in domestic disturbances; could such interventions be carried out so that the police would be safer, and could the police decision about how to "clear" the disturbance call reduce future repeat calls?

It is of note that arrest was not an option in the Bard studies. Instead, the preferred options for clearing a domestic violence call were negotiation or referral to social agencies.

To demonstrate a legal definition of an assault, Figure 12.1 shows the law in the State of Washington.

Can Police Intervention Prevent Repeat Wife Assault? Early Studies

A second prominent study of police response to domestic disputes was conducted for the Police Foundation in 1977 by Marie Wilt (in Detroit) and Ron Breedlove (in Kansas City).[5] This study began by analyzing the arrest records of "homicide and assault participants" for the years 1970 and 1971. The "characteristics" of the homicides and aggravated assaults, and of the participants, were analyzed based on interviews by police and project personnel and on Disturbance Profile Cards filled out by officers reponding to domestic disturbances. Recorded in addition were the number of prior police responses to the address of a participant in a homicide or assault in the two years before the arrest. Data from the Disturbance Profile Cards indicated that the best predictors of homicide/assault were the presence of a gun in the household, a history of prior disturbances, and the presence of alco-

12.1   Assault as legally defined in the State of Washington

An assault includes such things as slapping, pushing, shoving, pinching, throwing down, pulling hair, and other violent actions that are unwanted and unpermitted, or any physical action, as well as threats, which are intended to cause the victim to reasonably fear imminent serious bodily injury or death.

In Washington State, police officers are required to arrest when there is probable cause that a crime of domestic violence has occurred. If there is evidence of assault by both parties, the person who the officer believes is the primary aggressor is to be arrested. To determine the primary aggressor in the incident, an officer may look at the history of domestic violence between the parties, the comparative extent of injuries, or the fear of physical injury. An officer must arrest if the incident occurred within the previous four hours. A citation or summons to court is usually issued if the incident occurred outside the four-hour mandatory arrest period.

If the accused is charged with or arrested for a crime, a criminal "No Contact Order" may be issued to prevent the abuser from having any contact whatsoever with the alleged victim. A police officer shall also arrest a person who, with knowledge of a court order, has allegedly violated the terms of the order. If there is an assault or reckless endangerment that is in violation of an "Order for Protection" or a "No Contact Order," the abuser may be subject to felony criminal charges.

Domestic violence includes, but is not limited to, the following crimes when committed by one family or household member against another: assault, reckless endangerment, coercion, harassment, malicious mischief, stalking, kidnapping, criminal trespass, rape, burglary, or unlawful imprisonment.

Revised Code of Washington (RCW), Section 26.50, provides a civil remedy for domestic violence. A victim of domestic violence may fill out a Petition for an "Order for Protection" and file it with the court. The civil Order for Protection may be sought without police intervention. Violation of the Order for Protection may subject the respondent to arrest and possible felony charges if a subsequent assault or reckless endangerment is committed.

SOURCE: Lisa Scott, Attorney, Seattle, Washington, personal communication, September 2005.

nately, the police return rate for these cards was only 5 percent, making the generalizability of these findings questionable. Analysis of the data on prior police response indicated that 90 percent of the homicide participants and 85 percent of the aggravated assault participants had at least one prior police response to their address, and 50 percent of both homicide and aggravated assault participants had five or more police responses.

The Wilt and Breedlove study was cited as indicating the preventive policing potential of domestic disturbance calls since the possibility of avoiding the subsequent violent crime might have been realized if the police had acted more effectively on the prior calls. However, the study was retrospective in nature, working back from a crime-identified sample. Hence, it does not tell us what percentage of police responses to domestic calls do not result in repeat violence. We are, in effect, looking only at the interventions that subsequently had an undesirable outcome. To determine police policy requires prospective studies of the long-term effects of police practice that can establish the incidence of desirable/undesirable outcomes as a function of the mode of intervention.

In 1975 Lipton and colleagues reviewed published research on effectiveness of rehabilitation treatment and concluded that "nothing works."[6] Although their review was limited to treatment done in correctional settings, the conclusion was generalized to domestic violence treatment and intervention. This started a move toward arrest.

Police Decisions to Arrest for Wife Assault

Is there a prima facie case for police arrest on domestic disturbance calls? We know from an observational study by Bard and Zacker that police witness assaults in 29-33 percent of the domestic disturbances they attend.[7] Furthermore, the victims of these assaults are disproportionately women (95 percent of the time).[8] The women victims are injured in 36 percent of all domestic disturbances attended by police and require medical attention 17 percent of the time.[9] Clearly, then, domestic disturbance calls do present a category of calls for police service with a high violence potential. We also know from the Schulman and the Straus, Gelles, and Steinmetz surveys that the likelihood of repeat violence is high (66 percent without police intervention).[10] Furthermore, in a study reviewed below, Sherman and Berk found that when police attend and do not make an arrest there is a 28-37 percent likelihood of recidivist assault within six months.[11] Combining these findings, that is, assuming that arrest would lower this recidivism rate, a case can be made for police arrest for putative wife assault.

If one objective of the criminal justice system is to prevent recurrent violence, the means of handling husband-wife disputes is important, because such disputes constitute a source of considerable repeat violence. This being the case, it is instructive to examine those studies that have attempted to determine how police make the decision whether or not to arrest on domestic disturbance calls. Essentially three types of methodology have been used to examine such decisions. The first has involved having police specify how they would respond to hypothetical scenarios. A second has been to reconstruct arrest decisions from information on police reports. The third has been to examine police behaviour in real interventions. Many of these studies have already been reviewed in Chapter 1.

12.2 Kinds of deterrence

Deterrence is the ability of the state to reduce a crime level through criminal sanctions.

Specific deterrence is the ability of the state to impose sanctions on an individual on a first offence in order to discourage re-offending.

General deterrence is the ability of the state to reduce a crime level in a population by threatening severe sanctions.

A number of issues emerge in examining the police "decision matrix" (the complex of attitudes and thoughts that determine the way the call is "cleared" – whether through arrest, of which party, and so on). One issue is the apparent lack of weight given to victim's injuries by police and their indifference about ascertaining whether the assault is an isolated incident or part of a continuing series of violent incidents. If habitual assault is occurring, the likelihood increases of future violence, victim injury, and repeat demands on police service. From a decision-making perspective this information seems essential. On the other hand, the man's demeanour toward the police is largely irrelevant to likely recidivism and is probably given too much weight by police. The police decision about arrest versus other alternatives initiates a chain of criminal justice policy decisions about wife assaulters. The objective of these decisions is to prevent wife assault from recurring. How might this objective best be achieved? What constellation of decisions by police, prosecutors, and judges might operate to reduce recidivist assault?

It was because of the inconsistency in police response that was revealed in studies that many police departments made it easier for victims to get restraining orders, attached sanctions to the orders, and adopted "mandatory arrest" policies in cases of wife assault, while prosecutors adopted "no-drop" policies. These measures were viewed as "getting tough" on spouse assault. Their goal was to generate both specific and general deterrence of wife assault (see Figure 12.2).

Prosecution and Restraining Orders

Further support for the notion of giving victims a voice in system proceedings comes from a study of prosecutorial decisions. An elaborate study of the effects of prosecutorial policy was conducted by Ford and Regoli.[12] Using a randomized design with 678 cases in Indiana, they tested which of four policies – no prosecution, pre-trial diversion, prosecution, and rehabilitation – was most effective in reducing future recidivism. They found that prosecutors' actions could have a dramatic effect on future rates of re-cidivism. The simple act of accepting the charges and proceeding through the initial hearing decreased future acts of violence. Surprisingly, this effect held even if the victim was later allowed to drop the charges. Of the four treatment conditions, allowing women to drop the charges resulted in the lowest percentage of new reports of violence in a six-month follow-up pe-riod (26 percent vs. 35 percent with the other treatments). The authors specu-lated that empowering the victim may be more important than maintaining prosecution to the point of court conviction.

Ford's "power by alliance" concept is based on his findings from a domes-tic violence prosecution study.[13] A domestic violence victim can form a part-nership or an alliance with a legal actor, a police officer or a prosecuting attorney, who conveys respect and concern for her safety. The alliance itself can be a powerful resource that victims can use to prevent violence. The threat to call an ally backed by the power of the state in response to a crimi-nal code violation has a greater deterrent effect than the threat to call a stranger or a friend. The "power by alliance" concept, coupled with giving victims discretion, is the key to new notions of criminal justice described by Mills (see Chapter 16).

Mandatory Arrest

Legal power, used by victims of domestic violence, can prevent recurring violence. Threat of criminal sanction is called deterrence, and mandatory arrest was intended to generate specific and, perhaps, general deterrence of wife assault. By removing an officer's discretionary powers, the state could show itself as getting tough with wife assault. The case for mandatory arrest came in part from the studies reviewed earlier (see Chapter 1), which showed "under arrest" in arrestable circumstances because family violence was not viewed as a crime. The high number of women who would not pursue the complaint led to mandatory arrest's being coupled with "no-drop" policies by which the event became a crime against the state for which prosecutors would not allow charges to be dropped. This was to prevent men from pressuring the victims at home to abandon their allegations. Police could try to counter this by testifying to what they witnessed during the domestic disturbance call or even what the victim reported to them. However, victim-witnesses could always say they were angry and had made up the com-plaint, leaving the judge no choice. No-drop policies cannot get around this problem.

Buzawa and Buzawa call mandatory arrest "a response to political pres-sure at the inadequacy of reform efforts" and point out that mandatory arrest limits police discretion just as a "no-drop" policy limits prosecutorial discretion.[14] Buzawa and Buzawa contrast this to what they call a "presumptive" policy that guides action but allows for discretion. A presumptive policy could generate a short-form risk assessment and allow the officers to decide how to proceed. The case for mandatory arrest is based, in part, on the difficulty placed on officers in making quick decisions based on ambiguous information (conflicting testimony, etc.), the historical dislike police have had for handling domestic calls, and the possibility of gender bias (pro-male) affecting decision making. Buzawa and Buzawa reviewed evidence that might suggest implementation of mandatory arrest would affect police behaviour and lead to lower rates of identified domestic assaults. In a review of studies by the Victim Services Agency in 1988, some regional increases in the arrest rate were found.[15] For example in the state of Washington the arrest rate doubled, though much of this was due to police arresting both parties instead of the customary designated perpetrator.

Jaffe, Wolfe, Telford, and Austin reported a 2,500 percent increase in the rate of arrests after the introduction of mandatory arrest for domestic assault in London, Ontario.[16] However, this policy expanded the officers' ability to make warrantless arrests and initiated an "increasing tendency for the officers to fail to find 'reasonable and probable grounds.'"[17] In Minneapolis, when a mandatory arrest policy existed, only 20 percent of domestic violence calls resulted in arrest. Buzawa and Buzawa conclude that the mandatory arrest policy is applied unevenly, a result of not consulting rank-and-file police before instituting the policy. As they put it: "In the area of domestic violence, many policies have been formulated to appease a concerned public without altering police conduct."[18] In addition, funding for police training has been sporadic and inconsistent, while police turnover has been high (50 percent within ten years in Detroit). Police in many cities continue to believe that domestic violence is a normal part of life for some deviant groups and that intervention is futile. Such officers devise strategies to circumvent mandatory arrest policies. The authors cite a study in Phoenix where police simply did not report cases where the perpetrator had fled the scene. Finally, the chief of police personally intervened and expressed to officers his commitment to the new policy. The arrest rate then skyrocketed, leading judges to complain about "ridiculous arrests."[19]

Buzawa and Buzawa do not favour a mandatory arrest policy for misdemeanour domestic violence. They see arrest costs as too high for small departments, and manpower requirements as too substantial. They believe call screening will evolve to shut out certain groups of victims based on police attitudes. Finally, they argue that the victims' preferences should be considered. As they say, "frankly, it appears presumptuous that womens' advocates can determine what is best for an entire category of battered women."[20] Many women may not desire arrest, may want the beatings to end, but want to control the outcome of the legal process, and may feel their own autonomy is lost to the police insistence on arrest.

Deterrence

As Williams and Frieze state: "Multiple versions of deterrence theory have evolved ... but the application of deterrence theory to the study of intimate partner violence has a common theme: People will avoid violent behavior because they fear sanctions."[21] Personal or vicarious experiences of the judicial system presumably promote the prevention, reduction, or cessation of violent behaviour. This theme implies the traditional distinction between general and specific deterrence. General deterrence refers to the impact of sanctions, imposed or avoided, on all potential perpetrators of violence, that is, to the sanction experiences of others. Specific deterrence refers to the impact of sanctions, imposed or avoided, on an actual perpetrator of violence, that is, to personal sanction experience. The fundamental argument is that would-be or actual perpetrators will be less likely to engage in violence if they perceive sanctions as certain (likely to occur) and severe (costly to their lives).

The problem of individual variation is that, detached from meaningful life circumstances, arrest is not likely to prevent or reduce intimate partner violence. Deterrence may be achieved only when potential perpetrators see arrest as having damaging consequences for their relationships with others. People connected to intimate social networks, strong friendship ties, work, financial gain, and other markers of "conventional" living have much to lose by having their violence dramatically publicized through arrest. This

---

12.3 The debate over deterrence

Two perspectives are in conflict:

1 **The economic position:** Criminals are rational decision makers. If the cost of crime (e.g., the severity of punishment by the state) increases, the crime rate will decrease. This effect will be enhanced if there are acceptable alternatives with financial advantages. Deterrence should be based on these principles.

2 **The sociological position:** The causes of crime are complex and not a simple reflection of relative incentives. For example, criminals often believe they can avoid arrest and beat the system of sanctions. As with gamblers, irresistible impulses play a role. Deterrence should vary with persons and situations.

life-disrupting event can significantly alter their social world. However, people on the margins of "conventional" life may have less to lose and perceive arrest for intimate partner violence (or any other law violation) as an inevitable event, and so may attach little stigma to the sanctioning experience. Worse yet, those lacking significant social bonds may find arrest infuriating and provocative, resulting in escalated violence.

Could the criminal justice system deter wife assault through more aggressive responding? Deterrence refers to the state's ability to diminish the incidence of a prohibited action through legal threats by making the cost of the action greater than any benefits that derive from the action.[22] While considerable disagreement exists in the literature about whether criminal justice deterrence of violent crime has or has not been demonstrated by crime incidence studies, some agreement exists as to the minimal conditions required in order for criminal justice to serve as a deterrent.[23] The efficacy of legal threats in deterring prohibited actions requires that the criminal justice system generate perceived certainty, severity, and swiftness of punishment.[24] Furthermore, where gains from the prohibited action are great (as in illegal drug sales) or where the action is impulsive and not reasoned, deterrent effects are unlikely.[25]

General deterrence refers to a state's ability to control or minimize the *incidence* of a prohibited act in a general population (e.g., the total number of wife assaults in a specific jurisdiction and time period). Specific deterrence

---

12.4 Criminal sanctions

The effectiveness of criminal sanctions as deterrence depends on three aspects:

Perceived probability of being caught and punished: This perception contains three multiplied probabilities: of being arrested for the crime, or being convicted following arrest, and of being punished following conviction. This series is sometimes presented arithmetically as a process of multiplying and cancelling:

$$\frac{p \text{ arrest}}{\text{crime}} \times \frac{p \text{ conviction}}{\text{arrest}} \times \frac{p \text{ punishment}}{\text{conviction}} = \frac{p \text{ punishment}}{\text{crime}}$$

Severity of punishment: Severity is weighed according to average sentence length, minimum sentences, and likelihood of plea options.

Extra sanctions: Specific sentencing practices can add extra inhibitions: "extraordinary circumstances" (e.g., more than one person killed during a crime), "three strikes law" (perpetrator has two prior felonies), commission of crime B during commission of crime A (e.g., perpetrator has an unregistered firearm while holding up a grocery store).

refers to a state's ability to prevent or minimize *recidivism* among a subgroup that has already committed at least one prohibited act. If governments publicized new, more severe punishments for wife assault, and if large-sample victim surveys revealed a diminution in first-time offenders after the crackdown, then claims for a general deterrence effect of the crackdown could be made. If actual procedures for rendering swift and certain punishment demonstrated to first-time offenders that the state was treating their prohibited action more seriously than they had expected, with an ensuing decrease in their rate of recidivism, specific deterrence could be claimed. Clearly, for general deterrence to occur, the probability of the authorities' detecting the "event" or prohibited act must be high enough to generate the belief in the general population that ensuing punishment is highly probable. As Ross has shown, such has not been the case with the deterrence of drunk driving (see Figure 12.4).[26]

Subjective Contributors to Recidivism Reduction

As we have seen, detection of wife assault has a low probability in an objective sense, because the great majority of incidents go unreported. However, deterrence research has examined subjective perceptions of likelihood of punishment.[27]

Wilson has raised an objection to an exclusively objective approach to evaluating the criminal justice system's capacity to deter, questioning the assumption that such an analysis makes about a person's knowledge or estimate of being caught.[28] He describes how recidivist offenders frequently belong to a criminal subculture that has extensive informal knowledge of criminal justice system operation. They know, in effect, how to "beat the system."

One could argue, however, that subjective estimates of the likelihood of punishment could also operate in the opposite direction. For example, a "placebo" effect of the criminal justice system could operate if objective probabilities of punishment were low but potential lawbreakers believed otherwise. As we will see in a Sherman and Berk study, short-term specific deterrence for arrested husbands may have occurred because a sudden, conspicuous change in police behaviour acted as a salient cue for an aggressive criminal justice system response.[29] Although few of the men in this group were subsequently punished with fine or incarceration, the police action of arrest, in and of itself, may have provided a highly visible signal of future system intervention.

It is obviously difficult to ascertain the subjective perception of the wife assaulter with regard to the probability of being punished. It is reasonable to conclude, based on the Schulman and Straus et al. surveys (discussed in

Chapter 2), that, through some admixture of socialization, conscience, and general deterrence, the majority of men (89.8 percent) do not assault their wives. Furthermore, of the 10 percent of men who do assault their wives once, 33-37 percent (3.3 percent of all men) do not repeat within a year.[30] Since only 14.5 percent of women in the Schulman and Straus and Gelles samples who reported being assaulted had called the police, the 33-37 percent cessation rate is probably due to factors other than concern about punishment by the criminal justice system.[31]

Guilt, remorse, shame, or related emotional reactions produced by the assaultive event or the victim's threat to leave the relationship if assault recurs could account for the drop in recidivism.[32] If this is so, we must also account for the failure of these mechanisms in the 2.8 percent of men who are repeatedly severely assaultive. We shall return to this consideration below. The possibility of "desistance" or reduced recidivism would be restricted in any event to this very small percentage of men who are repeat wife assaulters and who are most likely to come to the attention of the criminal justice system.[33]

We do not know, at present, whether men arrested for wife assault do not repeat because of fear of re-arrest or whether the original arrest served a didactic function of demonstrating to them that wife assault was unacceptable behaviour. A step in this direction consists of data reported by Dutton, Hart, Kennedy, and Williams using a questionnaire developed by Williams and Carmody, which asks respondents to estimate the likelihood and perceived severity of each of a list of sanctions should they commit wife assault.[34] The authors compared responses for two non-arrested and one arrested sample of men.

A "sanction weight" is derived for each of such possible outcomes of assault as arrest, divorce, etc., by multiplying its perceived likelihood and severity. These sanctions are categorized as legal (arrest, etc.) and extra-legal (or informal). Men who had not been arrested for wife assault estimated extremely low sanction weights for legal sanction. Men who had been violent but never arrested estimated even lower weights for legal sanctions (for the obvious reason that they had never been arrested). Men who had been arrested estimated significantly higher weights for legal sanctions and, also, for informal sanctions if they were ever to re-offend. In other words, they thought that if they were to commit wife assault again, not only would the police likely intervene, but also their partner would pick up the phone and call the police anytime, the police would believe her, and she would be likely to leave (divorce). This effect, however, would be dependent on the man's socializing group, because peer reaction varies widely.

The finding of inflated estimates of legal sanction following arrest is, of course, not surprising. However, the evidence that inflated estimates of informal sanction follow arrest is interesting and consistent with Fagan's notion that arrest might redress a power imbalance in the family. But as we saw earlier, not all abusive couples are male-dominant.[35] This leads to the question, so far unanswered, whether arrest works best on couples that are male-dominant. In female-dominant couples, it may heighten the male's sense of powerlessness, which was an original cause of his assaultiveness.[36]

The Minneapolis Study

It is extremely rare to conduct a randomized experiment in a naturalistic criminal justice setting. Sherman and Berk set out to do just that, to have police in Minneapolis "treat" misdemeanour wife assault calls with one of three responses.[37] These responses were predetermined by colour coding in a report-call book that the officers carried. They assigned 314 cases of misdemeanour wife assault attended by the Minneapolis police to randomly assigned treatments of arrest, separation, or mediation. Only a few officers from two precincts supplied the bulk of the data. Some cases were reclassified because the alleged perpetrator challenged police authority (turning the cases designated for separation or mediation into an arrest). For a six-month period following the event, the recidivism of arrested men was significantly lower (13 percent repeated assault on police reports, 19 percent repeated assault based on interviews with wives) than of men who received separation (26 percent and 28 percent) or mediation (18 percent and 37 percent). Sherman and Berk did not report whether a trial had been completed or was pending for the arrested men during this period, how many couples had broken up, or whether the assaultive males knew their wives were being interviewed every two weeks by social scientists. If the latter were the case, a differential effect would have become a possibility: arrested men would know they were under observation that could lead to greater sanction, something that did not exist for men in the other groups. Hence, an arrest/probation effect might have been more accurate.

What makes the Sherman and Berk evidence impressive (apart from the randomized design) is that the reduced recidivism rate (if we accept that it was not produced by these unreported factors) seems to have been produced with repeat offenders. Eighty percent of the victims in their study had been previously assaulted at least once by the suspect in the prior six months. This result suggests that, for that small subgroup of all men who are repeat offenders without police intervention (probably about 3-4 percent, as calculated in Chapter 6), a possibility of recidivism reduction exists (at least for a six-month period) in that only 19 percent of this group will again assault their wives if arrest occurs.[38] The Minneapolis experiment had as great an impact on social policy as any other experiment ever conducted.[39] Within a matter of months after the data were released, police departments across North America began to adopt mandatory arrest policies for cases of marital assault. With mandatory arrest, the police officer must arrest the presumed perpetrator whenever "reasonable and probable grounds exist for believing an assault has occurred."

Garner and Maxwell make a few other observations about the Minneapolis experiment that provide "context" for the research.[40] The experiment was conducted in the context of reform and was set to have its findings released to coincide with a press release and a documentary by a Minneapolis-based domestic violence coalition. The results were based not on all of Minneapolis but on only two precincts, and from a small number of cooperative officers. These officers may not be representative of the police described by Hotaling and Buzawa who resisted policy changes implemented from above without consultation.[41] Also, the Minneapolis study used significance tests even though the criteria for these tests were not met because the subject cases were not drawn at random. The study used a "correction technique" to adjust for the failure of randomization but did not report the technique in the published paper. A recalculation by Gartin reanalyzed the Minneapolis data and found "there was not as much of a specific effect for arrest."[42] Nevertheless, Gartin did re-confirm the Sherman and Berk findings from their data. The result of the Minneapolis study was to shift the criterion for successful intervention from officer safety to victim safety.[43]

Sherman and Berk reported that in their sample of wife assaulters, 80 percent had assaulted their wives in the previous six months but only 5 percent had been arrested for it.[44] Once arrested, however, only 19 percent repeated the assault in the next six months. In the light of these aggregate data, it seems that arrest may function to signal increased state intervention above and beyond any objective probability of future detection, arrest, or punishment. However, in this study the numbers are too small to draw these conclusions (e.g., 3 percent of 314).

Furthermore, arrest may serve a didactic function in indicating that the state considers wife assault to be a crime. We do not know from the Sherman and Berk data whether the recidivism reduction observed for the arrested group is due to deterrence or to some other factor. As described above in the Dutton et al. study, arrest also serves to teach that an act is considered wrong by society, to correct a power imbalance in a family, and so forth.[45] These other functions of law could lead to recidivism reduction whether or not men believed punishment for repeat assault to be likely. Only research on the subjective estimates of consequences for future assault would disentangle these explanations. Clearly, research that relates subjective estimates of punishment to the likelihood of recidivism is required.

Some, but not all, wife assaults are impulsive acts, performed in states of high physiological and emotional arousal.[46] Such actions, by definition, do not fall under the "rational self-interest" assumptions of deterrence theory. However, many other wife assaults are deliberate, and a rational process is sometimes indicated by an assaulter's careful choice of time, place, and parts of the body to be injured.[47] That recidivism reduction may occur with some wife assaulters is supported by the Sherman and Berk study, which indicated that 81 percent of assaultive males could monitor and control their assaultive behaviour for a six-month period after arrest (regardless of whether arrest or arrest plus suspected surveillance caused the effect).[48] The remaining 19 percent of assaulters need further incentives and assistance to monitor and control their behaviour.

Fagan has argued that the central mechanism that precludes recidivism is an equalization of power in the male-female relationship.[49] Citing data from his own study and from a study by Lee Bowker, Fagan points out that fear of divorce and fear of relationship loss are mentioned more frequently than is fear of legal sanction as a factor that enabled abusers to desist.[50] Furthermore, Bowker's subjects (battered women) reported that social disclosure worked as well as legal intervention in getting their husbands to stop their assaults. This may work for male perpetrators of unilateral assaults in husband-dominant relationships, which, of course, represents only a small sub-group of all arrested men.

Cessation or desistance, Fagan concludes, occurs when legal or extra-legal factors diminish power imbalances in the family and raise the costs of repeat assault for the husband. When wife assault is disclosed to informal groups or to police, a variety of psycho-social mechanisms are initiated:[51]

1 The victim may discover that assault is more common than she formerly believed and, as a consequence, may stop blaming herself for the assault (see Chapter 6).
2 The husband may learn that others consider his assaultive behaviour illegal or unacceptable.
3 The husband may learn that his wife has the power to disclose his unacceptable behaviour to others who can sanction or punish him.

Whether or not the husband fears re-arrest, these psycho-social factors may reduce recidivist assault. Clearly, studies such as that by Sherman and Berk, which assume deterrence to be the operating mechanism in reducing recidivism, are overlooking the potential impact of psycho-social mechanisms.

Does Arrest Reduce Future Assaults? The Milwaukee Replication

The Milwaukee replication that Sherman et al. performed was the largest and most extensive of six replications of the Sherman and Berk study.[52] The arrest potential for recidivism reduction suggested by Sherman and Berk led to replications with larger samples in six American cities. In Milwaukee, twelve hundred cases of domestic violence were analyzed with a sample composition as follows: 91 percent male, 76 percent black, 64 percent never married to victim, 55 percent unemployed, 50 percent with prior arrest, 32 percent with prior arrest for domestic violence. The experiment was conducted from 1987 to 1988, when Milwaukee had a citywide policy of mandatory arrest for such assaults. Police responding to wife assault calls deemed the call eligible for the experiment if the victim was not seriously injured, the perpetrator was on the scene, and no warrants existed for his arrest. Experimental treatments included "warning" (suspect not arrested but read warning of arrest if police had to return), "short arrest" (suspect arrested, booked, and released, typically within two hours), and "full arrest" (suspect arrested, booked, eligible for release on $250 bail). These treatments were randomized within all eligible cases using colour-coded response sheets that determined the intervention to be applied in each case.

Outcome measures were subsequent "hotline" reports called in by all police to the local battered women's shelter whenever they encountered a case of wife assault (whether or not they could make an arrest). Arrests, offence reports, and victim interviews were also used as data sources (78 percent of contacted victims were interviewed). Using all of these data sources, the authors composed a "time at risk" index. They found that arrest did not cause couples to break up. The arrested men cohabitated after arrest as much as the non-arrested. The initial effects of arrest were to suppress recidivism. For thirty days after the presenting incident, the prevalence (proportion of cases with one or more incidents) of repeat violence reported in the victim interviews was substantially lower in the arrest groups. However, at about seven to nine months after the presenting incident, the arrest and non-arrest recidivism curves crossed over, and from that point on the arrest group had a higher rate of recidivism. That is, for this sample, the long-term effect of arrest was to *increase* the rate of repeat violence. This increase was small but

12.5 Relative deterrence effects of different sanctions in the Milwaukee Experiment

	Repeat Hotline calls per 10,000 suspects in six months			Relative recidivism (% difference)	
	Full arrest	Short arrest	Warning	1 vs. 3	2 vs. 3
Arrest deters more than warning					
Prior arrest	3,341	3,950	3,846	-13.3	2.7*
No prior	1,873	1,828	2,089	-10.3	-12.5
Whites	1,481	1,538	2,436	-39.2	-36.8
Employed	2,011	1,702	2,766	-27.3	-38.5
High school grad	2,278	2,958	3,235	-29.6	-8.6
Less than high school	2,327	2,000	2,466	-5.6	-18.9
Married	1,700	1,509	2,564	-33.7	-41.1
Warning deters more than arrest					
Not married	2,813	2,808	2,734	2.9	2.7
Blacks	2,656	2,721	2,633	0.8	3.3
Unemployed	2,775	3,140	2,629	5.5	19.4

* Short arrest deterred less than warning when the individual had been arrested before.
SOURCE: L.W. Sherman, J.D. Schmidt, D.P. Rogan, D.A. Smith, P.R. Gartin, E.G. Cohn, D.J. Collins, and A.R. Bacich, "The variable effects of arrest on criminal careers: The Milwaukee domestic violence experiment," *Journal of Criminal Law and Criminology* 83, 1 (1992): 137-69, 159, Table 6. Reprinted by special permission of Northwestern University School of Law.

consistent across all measures of repeat violence. The arrested group averaged 124 days before repeating, whereas the warned group averaged 160 days. Hotline data showed a statistically significant long-term escalation effect from arrest (but only for the short-arrest group). The authors conclude that police departments with policies of releasing arrestees within three hours of arrest might want to reconsider this policy.

The persons for whom arrest backfired in the long term were socially marginal (defined by the authors as unemployed and high school dropouts). While arrest deterred those who were most likely to socially conform, it escalated other groups into higher frequencies of domestic violence. When "the majority of domestic violence incidents responded to by police involve unemployed suspects, then mandatory arrest fails to produce the greatest good for the greatest number."[53]

Men with a "stake in conformity" did better than those who were marginalized. Being black, unemployed, not completing high school, or cohabitating lowers the deterrent effect of arrest. Being white, completing high school, and being married raises the deterrent effect. Unemployment and lack of a high school education predict a fairly high criminogenic effect of arrest. Hence, a policy for any police force might in part be determined by demographics of the population it serves. One conclusion that can be drawn from these data is that a society that fails to include all members in the social fabric cannot remedy this through police action, which will find less response among disenfranchised or socially marginal persons. (The same results as in Milwaukee were found in Omaha, Nebraska, and Colorado Springs, Colorado.)

In general, the authors conclude that in areas where urban problems are great and "marginality" high, arrest may be contraindicated. In other words, when general social constraints have broken down, arrest "in a vacuum" will not reduce recidivism in wife-assault cases. Arrest only works for men with something to lose by being arrested.

There is another troubling aspect to the Milwaukee results. Mills reports Sherman et al.'s conclusion that when Milwaukee police arrest 10,000 Caucasian men, they produce 2,504 fewer acts of domestic violence.[54] But when they arrest 10,000 African-American men, they produce 1,803 more acts of domestic violence. If they have a pattern of arresting three times as many black as white offenders (which is typical in many cities), they prevent 2,504 acts of violence against white women at the cost of 5,409 acts of violence against black women. In this context, mandatory arrest has policy implications based on the racial composition of the jurisdiction.

Obviously, the Sherman et al. study raises large and complex issues for those who make criminal justice system policy. If their results can be generalized, it would mean that mandatory arrest-and-release policies could endanger subgroups of women in the long term, a point raised by the authors themselves. Garner and Maxwell make the point that the main contributor to the results in the Milwaukee experiment was the hotline calls and that this measure does not prove that an assault occurred but is merely a prima facie indication of an altercation.[55] Hence, the shelter data do not prove deterrence from arrest.

A replication in Omaha found (and later studies confirmed) that when probable cause existed to make an arrest, the police did so in the 60 percent of cases when the offender was present.[56] Dunford et al. did not find a significant deterrence effect for arrest when the offender was present. The recidivism rate in Omaha was over 40 percent, whereas it had been 26 percent in Minneapolis (despite a narrower measure of new violence in Omaha).

A subsequent replication in Charlotte, South Carolina, also failed to find evidence for deterrence through arrest.[57] Hirshel and Hutchinson added police-issued citations as a fourth treatment option and employed the entire patrol division in round-the-clock and citywide sampling for the full duration of the project. The investigators' conclusion was that "arrest of spouse abusers is neither substantially nor statistically a more effective deterrent to repeat abuse than either of the other two responses (separation, mediation) examined in the study."[58]

Two other replications were performed, in Miami-Dade County and in Colorado Springs. Both studies found a statistically significant effect of arrest when re-offending was measured through victim interviews but not when it was measured through police reports. In Colorado the extensive interviewing of victims may have created a surveillance effect where the suppression of recidivism was created not by arrest alone but by the combination of arrest and surveillance. This study defect impairs policy inferences because such heightened surveillance would not be possible under ordinary probation circumstances.

Garner et al. and Garner and Maxwell pooled data across all six replication sites to standardize the methodologies and measures.[59] Using victim interviews (the more sensitive measure) as outcome measures, this reanalysis found that offenders in the arrested group were significantly less likely to repeat their "aggression" (subsequent assaults, verbal threats of assault, and property damage) than those in the non-arrest group. This result was independent of site, length of time between initial and follow-up interviews, and suspect characteristics. Moreover, the frequency of re-offending was significantly lower in the arrest group than the non-arrest group. However, no statistically significant effects of arrest were found when prevalence and frequency measures were based on police records.

Even with victim interviews, the estimated deterrence effect of arrest was modest, especially compared to the effects of suspect characteristics, such as prior arrests and age, and a general trend of cessation over time held for both the arrested and non-arrested groups. In other words, individual characteristics counted more – far more – than arrest in ending assaults, and cessation occurred independently of arrest. Garner and Maxwell report that arrest reduces future aggression by 4 percent to 30 percent depending on the data source and the measure of re-offending used. By comparison, the suspect's age and prior criminal history affected the likelihood of re-offending by 50 to 330 percent – *ten times* as important.[60]

Across all sites, most suspects did not re-offend. Arrested suspects desist from further violence unless they are young and have a record of criminality. These offenders generated about five new incidents prior to follow-up interviews. These findings confirm Sherman's admonition: "Does punishment deter crime? This question provokes fierce debates in criminology and public policy. Yet there is ample evidence that this is the wrong question in the widely varying results across a range of sanction studies. The studies suggest instead a far more useful question: under what conditions does each type of criminal sanction reduce, increase, or have no effect on future crimes?"[61]

Sugarman and Boney-McCoy did a meta-analysis of all sites combined.[62] They found, on average, no deterrence effect for arrest based on police data but a modest deterrence effect based on victim interview data. The only measure that could be used was frequency of new offending. Strange as it may seem, different data sets were collected at the various sites with little standardization. For a thorough discussion of these issues, the reader is directed to Garner and Maxwell. Gelles argued that the media ignored subsequent studies that questioned deterrence effects.[63]

Dugan reanalyzed data from the National Crime Victim Survey to ascertain whether violence is deterred by legal sanctions in state legislation against domestic violence.[64] These sanctions include (1) beyond cohabitation (states that allow victims who do not live with the offender to petition for a protection order), (2) custody (states that authorize the court to award temporary custody of children to the victim once a protection order is issued), (3) discretion index (states that make a range of sanctions available to a judge when a protection order is violated), (4) felony (states that classify protection order violations as a felony), (5) mandatory arrest (states that have mandatory arrest laws for protection order violations), and (6) states that confiscate offenders' firearms once a protection order is served. Note that these sanctions are for enforcement of protection orders, not for assault.

Dugan then calculated odds ratios estimating the effects of legal sanctions and demographic factors on subsequent spousal assault ($N = 529, 829$ households; 1.00 is baseline likelihood).[65] The base rate of reporting for any domestic violence incident was 0.5 percent, (one household in two hundred), and for the subset of spousal violence it was 0.18 percent. Dugan's odds ratios are as follows:

beyond cohabitation	0.87
custody	1.2
discretion index	0.94
felony	1.3
mandatory arrest	0.89
separated/divorced	4.3
living in public housing	0.628
white	1.9

The custody sanction had a boomerang effect, increasing the odds of spousal assault by a factor of 1.2 (significant at .05 given the sample size). Mandatory arrest generated an odds ratio of 0.885, a small effect, consistent with the Garner and Maxwell findings. No other state sanctions had significant effects on subsequent violence odds. The largest effect was for the status separated/divorced, an odds ratio of 4.3 ($p < .01$) and clearly not a state legal sanction. In this study, the gender of the victim was not reported. Public housing had an odds ratio of 0.628. In other words, living in public housing (our stereotypes aside) lowered the likelihood of repeat violence whereas imposing custody sanctions increased them. Dugan suggests that nearby apartments may serve as guardians to the victim.

Another overall problem exists with the arrest studies: they all treated arrest as an isolated event. In practice, arrest can lead to charges being laid, a guilty verdict in court, and mandatory treatment, yet none of these sequelae were examined in any of the arrest studies. As with Sherman and Berk, the authors of the arrest replications studies never report what happened to the subjects after arrest. Were the charges dropped? Did they go to court? Get convicted? Were they referred to mandatory treatment groups? As we shall see below, these criminal justice system outcomes may make a difference in long-term recidivism reduction, although two points should be kept in mind: (1) the most serious recidivists, according to Garner and Maxwell, are career criminals, men who would benefit least from therapy, and (2) the ones who would benefit most from therapy probably don't need it.

Victim Empowerment vs. No-Drop Prosecution

Another issue remains for police and prosecutors who use mandatory arrest/no-drop policies. Will the "overkill" nature of the response discourage women who want an end to a temporary conflict but don't want their husbands arrested? Some data from Colorado suggest that they might. Once a mandatory arrest/no-drop policy was instituted in Colorado Springs in 1994, 911 calls for domestic violence began to decrease, while other 911 calls increased in line with population growth. Dugan replicated this finding in her examination of post-policy recidivism in the United States. States that had brought in mandatory arrest subsequently received only 85 percent as many domestic violence calls as those who had not.[66]

A strategy of victim empowerment was supported by the study described earlier of the effects of prosecutorial policy by Ford and Regoli.[67]

A study by Hotaling and Buzawa supports the Colorado finding.[68] The authors examined the impact of case processing on the disclosure of re-victimization in the Quincy District Court (QDC) in Massachusetts. The authors chose QDC as a data collection site because it was cited by the Department of Justice as a model jurisdiction in implementing pro-intervention strategies in domestic violence cases.[69] Multivariate analysis was used to control for the impact of incident, victim, offender, and case-processing characteristics. "Re-reporters" (of subsequent violence) were distinguished from "non-reporters," to investigate whether new incidents had in fact occurred among the latter but had gone unreported.

Findings suggested the importance of victim frustration with the criminal justice system. A victim survey revealed that nearly half (58/118) the offenders had violated restraining order conditions, but of the 49.2 percent of women thus revictimized, fewer than half (22 percent) re-reported to the court. Yet the violence against women who did not report it was no greater than was that perpetrated against the re-reporters.

The decision to report revictimization was related to (1) their perception that the criminal justice system was unresponsive to their preferences (non-reporters said they had no voice or rights 55 percent of the time, compared to 12 percent for re-reporters), and (2) their being less likely to want the offender prosecuted in the first place.[70] Offender dangerousness did not differ between groups. Hotaling and Buzawa conclude: "What is troublesome is that this research has found that despite the victim's experience with a 'model' intervention program, re-reporting was still a major concern as the majority of victims did not report subsequent offenses to the police. In fact, research adds credence to earlier expressed fears that a too aggressive criminal justice response that did not reflect diversity of victim desires might have had the unintended effect of deterring future reporting."[71] The authors also suggest that because the majority of women chose to stay with their abusers, the treatment that offenders were receiving needed to be improved. Consistent with the drop in calls data already mentioned is the fact that fewer than 30 percent of abused women are turning to the criminal justice system.[72] The Colorado 911 data, the refusal to use the criminal justice system, and the Hotaling and Buzawa study tend to support an argument about criminal justice system response made by Mills, to which we now turn.

Summarizing the Arrest Results

Arrest for spouse assault is applied unevenly and has only a modest effect on deterrence. Furthermore, these effects depend almost entirely on the characteristics of the perpetrator and are short-term.[73] Not only does mandatory arrest depend on the gender of the perpetrator but it also decreases subsequent use of police by victims.[74]

Linda Mills, in a thoughtful and provocative article in the *Harvard Law Review*, argues that state intervention itself has become abusive to "victims" who don't want that intervention.[75] Battered women, she argues, are safest and feel most respected, when they willingly partner with state officials to prosecute domestic violence crimes. Mandatory state interventions do not allow clinical healing to occur. The unwanted state intervention replicates "rejection, degradation, terrorization, social isolation, mis-socialization, exploitation, emotional unresponsiveness and close confinement that are endemic to the abusive relationship."[76] In other words, current state "mandatory arrest" and "no-drop" policies constitute what Ivan Illich called "iatrogenic violence." Mills advocates what she calls a "survivor centered approach," which focuses on listening to the woman, discussing the options with her, and leaving control of the outcome in her hands. Mills states:

> I oppose mandatory interventions because they fundamentally ignore the fact that the form and substance of intimate abuse crimes are intimate. It is not the privacy of the crime that requires protection, but rather the woman's emotional relationship to the experience. These issues can be identified as "clinical." This position grows out of my awareness that most, if not all, battered women experience intimate abuse as emotional – not as legal or political. This approach is not designed to pathologize a survivor or to relegate the issue of domestic violence to the sphere of mental health, and hence to push it outside the scope of feminist or political concern. By adopting the survivor's perspective, which is fundamentally an emotional one, we should be charged with hearing her story on her terms and in ways that take into account her particular circumstances.[77]

Mills later adds:

> To assess incapacity, clinicians would consider such issues as the severity of the battered woman's injuries (is she physically capable of making a decision?); the significance of the threat the batterer poses (does he have weapons he has shown a propensity to use?); and the presence of illness (is she suffering from Complex Post-Traumatic Stress Disorder (PTSD) or other illnesses that are so severe that they prevent her from making appropriate safety decisions for herself or her children?). Clinicians would also consider whether the intervention is likely to help the battered woman (does the batterer have ties

to the community such that he may be deterred from future incidents of violence, or, regardless of his social ties, does he have a pattern of escalating violence so that he is likely to inflict serious harm?).

A battered woman who chooses to return to her abusive partner is not necessarily incapacitated. The batterer may not pose a significant threat (there are no weapons), or he may have agreed to enter counseling. Or she may previously have taken steps toward self-protection and protection of her children (removed them from the violent situation), and may appear to be grappling adequately with the difficult financial, emotional, and safety issues that she faces. Rather than assuming incapacity in all cases, professionals should limit mandatory interventions to cases in which nonconsensual state action is appropriate and necessary. If the battered woman does not want state officials to act on her behalf because she has reasonably concluded that state intervention is inappropriate or is even unwelcome in her situation, state actors should respect her desires. Seeing state actors respond to her direction is liberating to the battered woman; it indicates respect for her decision making capacity even when the state actors do not necessarily agree with her assessment.[78]

What Mills calls for is clinically informed assessment rather than a knee-jerk "one size fits all" response. This issue is important in assessing both the alleged perpetrator and the victim and should not be glossed over by a homogeneous policy. If a woman decides she may be better off without the arrest of her abuser, her wish should be honoured – provided the assessment criteria above are in effect. If a decision is made to prosecute, the victim should not be required to testify, and effective prosecution should not depend on her testimony. Hanna describes how police can be trained in crime scene investigation techniques when attending domestic dispute calls.[79] Obviously these considerations would apply to unilateral male abuse situations.

Is it time to re-think mandatory arrest and no-drop prosecutions? There are ways to increase police arrest without making it mandatory and to make conviction more probable without victim coercion.[80] Is arrest more important than victim empowerment? Should arrest be assisted by risk assessment for future violence? Should decisions about how to handle cases be re-thought? Is it viable to arrest men for misdemeanour wife assault given the ineffectiveness of arrest and the fact (from the Stets and Straus study) that 45 percent of the cases involve mutual combat?[81] Finally, what about therapy? Men who desist following arrest alone would be the ones most likely to benefit from therapy – but they will desist without it. So is therapy unnecessary? The men who will not desist, according to Garner and Maxwell, are the antisocial personalities least likely to benefit from therapy. Garner and Maxwell conclude their review of the arrest studies this way:

The contemporary policy discussion surrounding the appropriate societal responses to domestic violence includes numerous suggestions for mandating arrest, coordinated legal and social service responses, the use of protection orders, offender treatment programs, intensive responses to high-risk situations and the prosecution and incarceration of offenders. These suggestions do not appear to be derived from, nor tested by, systematic empirical research that approaches the standards of the National Academy of Sciences and met by the police arrest studies. The current discussions and policy options appear to be driven more by personal preference and ideology of the currently powerful than any real evidence about the safety of victims or behavior of suspects subjected to these plausible but untested approaches.[82]

The demand made by J.Q. Wilson, quoted at the opening of this chapter, is not being met. Since we constantly evaluate everything from automobile performance to prescription drugs (after their release), why do we not evaluate laws by assessing whether they are accomplishing their intended effect and whether they bring unintended negative side-effects?

13 Risk Assessment

From the preceding chapter, we have seen that risk for escalation of spousal violence can vary with the individual arrested. A risk assessment can be based on proximal variables such as recent abusiveness, non-compliance with a court order, or a recent escalation in substance or spouse abuse. Alternatively, it can be based on distal (more remote) variables such as early family history, personality pathology, or attachment insecurity. In general, proximal variables are better predictors, but they are also more obvious. If I hear that a man with a history of violence is high on alcohol and cocaine and has been told by his girlfriend that she is leaving him, I'm not too surprised if he hits her. On the other hand, to learn of this "abandonment violence" by someone with no prior history of violence can be a surprise. But intimate violence is something that can come "out of the blue" from someone who had not previously been violent. Risk assessment instruments are designed to take all items shown empirically to be risks for recidivism and combine them into a scale or checklist to guide assessment and preferably to generate a risk score.

Assessment of Risk

Obviously, the responses of the police and of the criminal justice personnel who handle cases after arrest (prosecutors, judges, therapists) could be more considered and better suited to the case if more were known about the potential for future violence. Kropp and Hart have developed the B-SAFER screening questionnaire for police.[1] The instrument requires no psychological knowledge, is firmly grounded in solid empirical validational studies and could resolve some of the "one size fits all" problems discussed in the previous chapter.

The B-SAFER checklist provides ten questions and two "other considerations" to be asked of complainants. The questions assess spousal violence (occurrence, threats, escalation, violation of court orders, negative attitudes) and psychosocial adjustment (other antisocial behaviour, intimate relationship problems, employment problems, substance abuse problems, and mental health problems). The instrument requires officers to provide a risk management strategy (monitoring/surveillance, control/supervision, assessment/treatment, and victim safety planning) and, in light of the victim's answers to the questions, to state their opinions on future risk, life-threatening violence, imminence of violence, and likely victims. The concept is good, though I see problems with some of the questions (e.g., asking a complainant to estimate escalation in the "ideation" of a perpetrator is to ask a victim to read the perpetrator's thoughts) and with treating all assaults equally, as if a push equalled a severe beating.

Risk Assessment Instruments

Until recently there were very few efforts to empirically validate any of the risk assessment schemes. This state of affairs is changing rapidly, with several evaluation studies under way. Roehl and Guertin, and Campbell have conducted useful surveys of dangerousness assessment instruments in current use in North America.[2] Recent years have seen a proliferation of instruments and scales, ranging in scope and degree of development. Most of these have not been validated, so their utility is unknown. The interested reader is referred to Roehl and Guertin for more information on some of these projects.[3]

The remainder of this chapter will focus on a category of instruments for which published validity data are available. We focus on five such instruments: the Danger Assessment Scale (DAS), the Spousal Assault Risk Assessment Guide (SARA), the Domestic Violence Screening Instrument (DVSI), the Propensity for Abusiveness Scale (PAS), and the Psychopathy Checklist (PCL) – Revised.

The Danger Assessment Scale

Jacquelyn Campbell developed the Danger Assessment Scale (DAS) instrument, which she described as a "form of statistical prediction, contrasted with clinical prediction, because it is based on prior research and has some preliminary evidence of reliability and validity."[4] It was based on consultation and content validity support from battered women, shelter workers, law enforcement officials, and other clinical experts on battering.[5] The initial items in the DAS were developed from retrospective research studies of intimate partner homicide or serious injury.[6]

The first portion of the DAS assesses severity and frequency of battering by presenting the woman with a calendar of the past year. She is asked to mark the approximate days when physically abusive incidents occurred, and to rank the severity of the incident on a 1 to 5 scale (1 = slap, pushing, no injuries or lasting pain, through 5 = use of weapon, wounds from weapon). The calendar portion was conceptualized as a way to raise the consciousness of the woman and reduce the denial and minimization of the abuse, especially since using a calendar increases accurate recall in other situations.[7] In the original scale development, 38 percent of women who initially reported no increase in severity and frequency changed their response to "yes" after filling out the calendar.[8]

The second part of the DAS is a fifteen-item yes/no questionnaire on risk factors associated with intimate partner homicide. The instrument as a whole takes about twenty minutes to complete. The woman can complete the DAS by herself, with professionals from the health care, criminal justice, or victim advocate systems assisting in the interpretation of the instrument for her situation. The DAS is scored simply by counting the "yes" responses, with no attempts at classification or cutoffs. A higher number indicates that more of the risk factors for homicide are present in the relationship. The DAS has published data on construct validity but no predictive validity information.[9]

13.1 Danger Assessment Scale: Self-report yes/no questionnaire

---

1 Has the physical violence increased in frequency over the past year?
2 Has the physical violence increased in severity over the past year and/or has a weapon or threat with a weapon been used?
3 Does he ever try to choke you?
4 Is there a gun in the house?
5 Has he ever forced you into sex when you did not wish to?
6 Does he use drugs? By drugs I mean "uppers," or amphetamines, speed, angel dust, "crack," street drugs, or mixtures (maybe steroids).
7 Does he threaten to kill you and/or do you believe he is capable of killing you?
8 Is he drunk every day or almost every day?
9 Does he control most or all your daily activities? For instance, does he tell you who you can be friends with, how much money you can take shopping, or when you can take the car?
10 Have you ever been beaten by him while you were pregnant?
11 Is he violently and constantly jealous of you? (For instance, does he say "If I can't have you, no one can"?)
12 Have you ever threatened or tried to commit suicide?
13 Has he ever threatened or tried to commit suicide?
14 Is he violent toward your children?
15 Is he violent outside of the home?

SOURCE: J.C. Campbell, *Assessing Dangerousness: Violence by Sexual Offenders, Batterers and Child Abusers* (Newbury Park, CA: Sage, 1995), 103.

Campbell's criterion was "women's perception of the danger of being killed by their partners." However, the relationship of a partner's fear to the actual danger is unknown. Brown found that women had higher perceptions of danger than men (even men who had self-selected for dangerous occupations) and estimated that women were twice as likely as men to fear death from a partner, adjusted for the objective probability of being killed.[10] Brown calculated the ratio of "fearing for life/being killed" for women at 700:1. For men it was 350:1. For either gender, objective probability of violence is greatly over-estimated if one fears for one's life. Furthermore, Campbell's validity data appear not to be measures of partner violence taken subsequent to the interview with the female respondent, but measures of the severity of prior partner violence. Hence, her initial study was retrospective and hence was not validated as a predictive instrument.

Goodman, Dutton, and Bennett have completed a study using the DAS to predict short-term misdemeanour wife assaults.[11] An increment of one standard deviation on the DAS was related to a fourfold increase in likelihood of repeat abuse (22 percent of the entire sample re-offended). Some methodological problems were pointed out by the authors. The sample was small ($N = 92$), and only 53 percent could be re-contacted. This smaller group ($N = 47$) may, of course, not be representative of the original sample. The authors called for replication with a larger sample and more detailed outcome measures.

Using items from this instrument, Weisz, Tolman, and Saunders studied the victims' predictions of future violence as an objective predictor.[12] Data were supplied by 177 women partnered with men in court-ordered batterer treatment. They reported their partners' violence using an expanded version of the CTS, including eight severe-violence items. The authors found that victims who predicted no violence or a strong likelihood of subsequent violence were likely to be right for a four-month period following the prediction. A bivariate analysis of women's reports found that the following items were also significantly related to recidivism: kicked, bit, or hit with a fist (from the Conflict Tactics Scale), forced sex, choked, or strangled, woman obtained protection order before man's first arrest, woman sustained injuries before first arrest, violent disputes between first arrest and court date, man threatens her to drop complaint, man tells her she cannot leave or see certain people, man restricts her use of phone or car, man accuses her of an affair.

Weisz et al. included the DAS in their prediction package. In a bivariate regression, there were two items that correlated strongly with subsequent violence. One was whether there had been more violence between the "focal incident" and the man's court date (+.29) (interviews were conducted shortly after that date). The other was the woman's prediction of violence in the coming year (+.42). A multiple regression composed of DAS and the above items yielded an R squared of .15. In other words, the combined instruments accounted for 15 percent of the variance in repeat violence. The victims' predictions of future violence, however, increased the R squared by another .10. Hence, when the prediction was added in, 25 percent of the variance could be accounted for. In other words, the victims' own predictions added significantly to the predictive ability of the scale.

Finally, the Danger Assessment Scale was used to predict female homicide victimization rather than perceptions. Since this is a low-likelihood event (measured in the range of 3 per 100,000), it is difficult to predict. Campbell et al. adopted an ingenious "case control" design using proxies (women who knew a female homicide victim well were cases; $N = 220$), while randomly identified abused women residing in the same metropolitan area served as controls ($N = 343$).[13] This is not, strictly speaking, "prediction" but rather an after-the-fact construction of differentiating items between cases and controls. (For obvious reasons, including a duty-to-warn, a homicide prediction study could not be carried out.) Data on the victims were gathered by proxy, and police and medical records from 1994 to 2000 were used to assess victim-perpetrator relationships.

Pre-incident risk factors associated with risk of intimate female partner homicide included unemployment (for the perpetrator), drug abuse, the victim's having left for another partner, and the perpetrator's having access to a gun (a risk factor of 8). (If the victim did not live with the perpetrator, her having a gun decreased the risk.) In addition, bivariate analyses indicated the following risks: stalking, forced sex, and abuse during pregnancy. Prior arrests for domestic violence lowered the homicide risk. The authors' Table 2, which lists bivariate risk factors, indicates that virtually all forms of violence and threats differ significantly between cases and controls. The final summary snapshot is of a perpetrator who has no job and abuses drugs (by inference, no meaning to life), and for whom the relationship that he has destroyed was his last hope. His irrational action, of course, does not alter his situation with the victim dead.

There is, unfortunately, a design problem with this study. The abuse controls, according to the data tables, were minimally abusive. The criterion for selection into the control group was one incident of physical assault or threat with a weapon by a current or former lover in the past two years. However, the abuse controls report no verbal abuse in 52 percent of cases, that their partner was not controlling in 75 percent of the cases, and that their partner had not threatened to kill them in 85 percent of the cases. These low rates on normally abusive behaviour account for the numerous significant "risk factors" but raise the question whether the prediction is really of killing or only of extreme abuse vs. mild abuse. A more productive analysis would have used serious non-lethal abuse cases as controls for the proxy cases.

The Spousal Assault Risk Assessment Guide (SARA)

The Spousal Assault Risk Assessment Guide (SARA) is a set of guidelines for the content and process of a thorough risk assessment. It consists of twenty items identified by a review of the empirical literature on wife assault and the clinical literature evaluating male wife abusers. The authors point out that the SARA is not a test. Its purpose is not to provide absolute or relative measures of risk using cutoff scores or norms, but rather to structure and enhance professional judgments about risk. Since the SARA is not a formal psychological test, professionals other than psychologists can use it. The authors list several potential applications of the SARA: pre-trial assessment, pre-sentence, correctional intake, correctional discharge, civil justice matters, warning third parties, and reviewing spousal risk assessments given by others.

Items selected for the SARA were carefully based on relevant factors reported in the literature. The SARA assessment procedure includes interviews with the accused and victims, standardized measures of physical and emotional abuse and of drug and alcohol abuse, and a review of collateral records, such as police reports, victim statements, criminal records, and other psychological procedures. If the user is not a psychologist, the authors recommend appropriate referrals or a review of existing psychological and psychiatric reports. The authors also recommend that any risk assessment interview should cover the areas listed in Figure 13.2.

The SARA manual describes the rationale and scoring system for each of these areas. The items have the format 0 = absent, 1 = sub-threshold, and 2 = present. The SARA has an "override" of "critical items," defined as those that, "given the circumstances of the case at hand, are sufficient on their own to compel the evaluator to conclude that the individual poses an imminent risk of harm." The SARA provides case management strategies appropriate to various risk factors. It is intended to serve as a "checklist," guiding the assessor as to what questions to ask. It provides risk ratings of low, medium, and high but leaves the final determination to clinical judgment. This is a good idea. A straight numerical approach might be misleading; for example, in Item 1, "physical assaultiveness," one would not want to equate

13.2 Spousal Risk Assessment Guide (SARA)

Part I

1 Past assault of family members
2 Past assault of strangers or acquaintances
3 Past violation of conditional release or community supervision
4 Recent relationship problems
5 Recent employment problems
6 Victim of and/or witness to family violence as a child or adolescent
7 Recent substance abuse/dependence
8 Recent suicidal or homicidal ideation/intent
9 Recent psychotic and/or manic symptoms
10 Personality disorder with anger, impulsivity, or behavioural instability

Part II

11 Past physical assault of spouse
12 Past sexual assault/sexual jealousy
13 Past use of weapons and/or credible threats of death against spouse
14 Recent escalation in frequency or severity of assault against spouse
15 Past violation of "no contact" orders against spouse
16 Extreme minimization or denial of spousal assault
17 Attitudes that support or condone spousal assault
18 Severe and/or sexual assault in index offence
19 Use of weapons an/or credible threats of death in index offense
20 Violation of "no contact" order index offence

SOURCE: Adapted from P.R. Kropp, S.D. Hart, C.D. Webster, and D. Eaves, *Manual for the Spousal Assault Risk Assessment Guide* (Vancouver: British Columbia Institute on Family Violence, 1995).

"pushing or shoving" with use of a weapon. The SARA ties to balance common sense with completeness.

Kropp and Hart have evaluated the reliability and validity of judgments concerning risk for violence made using the Spousal Assault Risk Assessment Guide. SARA ratings were analyzed in six samples of adult male offenders (total $N = 2,681$). The distribution of ratings indicated that offenders varied greatly in exhibiting individual risk factors and in their overall perceived risk. Inter-rater reliability was high for judgments concerning the presence of individual risk factors and for overall perceived risk. SARA ratings significantly discriminated between offenders with and without a history of spousal violence in one sample, and between recidivistic and non-recidivistic spousal assaulters in another. Finally, SARA ratings showed good convergent and discriminant validity with respect to other measures related to risk for general and violent criminality.[14]

13.3 Success of SARA at predicting recidivism

Prediction	Correctly predicted: no (%)	Correctly predicted: yes (%)
Low risk	36	8
Medium risk	32	33
High risk	32	60

NOTE: N = 50 recidivist and 52 non-recidivist offenders.
SOURCE: Based on P.R. Kropp and S. Hart, "The Spousal Assault Risk Assessment (SARA) guide: Reliability and validity in adult male offenders," *Law and Human Behavior* 24, 1 (2000): 101-18, 113, Table 9.

Note that Kropp and Hart reported the mean SARA score for non-recidivists in their study (N = 50) to be 15.7 (SD = 5.4) and for recidivists (N = 52) to be 17.7 (SD = 5.6).[15] This was not a significant difference (p = .068). SARA Part 2 items seemed to be better predictors than the Critical items, which are really only clinical hunches about which items apply most to a specific case. It is therefore wise of the authors to emphasize that the SARA is only a guide and is not intended as a replacement for clinical judgement. For their validation study of the SARA, Kropp and Hart reported significant (above-chance) accuracy in using scores on the SARA to differentiate low-, medium-, and high-risk offenders (see Figure 13.3).[16]

Another large-scale study involving the SARA is under way in Colorado. The Colorado group has developed and implemented a process for evaluation of domestic violence offenders. The process uses two instruments, the custom-made Domestic Violence Screening Instrument (DVSI; see below) and the SARA. The DVSI is a structured criminal history screening completed prior to an offender's first appearance in court. The SARA is completed as a pre-sentence evaluation.

The Domestic Violence Screening Instrument (DVSI)

The state of Colorado developed a Domestic Violence Screening Instrument (DVSI), a twelve-item checklist that assesses the presence of prior domestic violence convictions, prior arrests for assault, threats, or menacing, prior treatment for domestic violence, alcohol or drug abuse, a history of restraining orders, violations of restraining orders, evidence of a weapon used in commission of a crime, presence of children during the domestic violence incident, current employment status, separation from the victim in the last six months, restraining order in place at the time of the offence, and being under community supervision at the time of the offence.[17]

Williams and Houghton used a prospective design to assess the predictive validity of this instrument and the SARA, using 1,465 domestic violence offenders, collecting data on re-offending from a subsample of 125 victims over a six-month period, and examining official records for all perpetrators for an eighteen-month period.[18] They concluded that the DVSI was a reliable instrument with acceptable concurrent, discriminant, and predictive validity for serious behaviours (those most likely to generate serious injury). The authors examined the predictive accuracy of the DVSI and two versions of the SARA, including a hybrid that multiplied SARA scores by clinical judgments of "imminent risk." All three instruments performed roughly the same, with the SARA slightly outperforming the DVSI. Predictive accuracy for domestic violence re-offending was in the .60 to .65 range for predictive accuracy (total true hits, true misses, false positives, and false negatives), for any re-offending in the .68 to .71 range.[19] The "clinical" SARA did not outperform the "actuarial" SARA (total score only). The DVSI was found to predict above a chance level for total re-offending and domestic violence re-offending. A chance level would be .50, whereas the SARA was .70 (for total reoffending, .65 for domestic violence re-offending) and the DVSI .68 and .60 respectively. Since 1.00 is perfect prediction, .75 would be half way between chance and perfection.

The Propensity for Abusiveness Scale (PAS)

The PAS (see Figure 10.4) was empirically developed by assessing which items in the comprehensive assessment given to convicted batterers and non-violent controls (N = 206) best predicted their female partners' reports of abusiveness.[20] It is a self-report scale that, at face value, appears unrelated to abusiveness since it taps into background factors such as parental treatment, attachment style, anger response, trauma symptoms, and stability of self-concept. It is a scale of psychological factors only. It does not assess prior assault or substance abuse. The scale has focused primarily on emotional abuse and can correctly discriminate abusive men with 82.2 percent accuracy. Social desirability factors do not appreciably alter its relationship to women's scores of abusiveness.

The PAS has been cross-validated on men in community groups (N = 500+), and its predictive accuracy has remained at the same level as with the original sample. While the PAS is a good predictor of abusiveness, its main research focus has been on emotional abuse. The PAS correlated .51 with victims' reports of dominance and isolation by the perpetrator and .37 with emotional abuse. Using the Severity of Violence against Women Scale, the

PAS correlated .76 with use of threats toward the victim and .30 with physical violence.[21] All correlations were statistically significant. The PAS also correlated significantly with men's anger and general dysphoria ratings when listening to audiotaped abandonment scenarios.[22] It should be noted that the PAS is probably more suitable for non-criminal or pre-criminal populations (first-time offenders) where the main objective is to predict emotional abuse and risk of physical abuse. Instruments such as the SARA, on the other hand, include factors related to prior assaultive behaviour and may therefore be better suited than the PAS for assessment in a more violent population.

The Psychopathy Checklist (PCL)

Psychopathy is a personality disorder characterized by deficits in empathy and persistent, frequent, and varied antisocial behaviour starting at an early age.[23] Psychopathy is assessed using the Psychopathy Checklist, later revised to the seventeen-item PCL-R (see Figure 9.9), designed for male criminal populations, and the twelve-item PCL-SV (Screening Version), a new version designed for both criminal and non-criminal populations.[24] The PCL is included in this discussion because it has been demonstrated to be a robust predictor of violent behaviour in general, with many of its validity studies covering domestic violence perpetrators.[25] The PCL-R is a structured interview, a set of ratings based on the interview, and verifications based on case history reviews, institutional files, interviews with family members and employers, and criminal and psychiatric records. The PCL-R has generated two factors labelled Interpersonal/Affective and Lifestyle/Social Deviance. The first has to do with glibness, lack of empathy, and pathological lying; the second with antisocial behaviour.

Psychopaths have criminal careers that start early (in their teens) and generate high rates of violent offending until at least their mid-forties. They are also the most likely group to engage in violence while incarcerated, to recidivate after release, and to constitute treatment failure from prison programs.

In a meta-analytic review of prediction of recidivism, Hemphill et al. compared the predictive ability of the PCL with other predictor variables.[26] They conclude that "the PCL and PCL-R by themselves are significant predictors of re-offending. However, an important issue is their ability to add to the predictive validity of other more traditional variables."[27] The PCL, in other words, contributes unique information beyond that offered by demographic and criminal history variables.

PCL/PCL-R is also more strongly related to recidivism than is any personality diagnosis, including Antisocial Personality. Finally, the PCL/PCL-R has also shown incremental predictive validity in comparison to the following statistical risk scales: Base Expectancy Score, the Salient Factor Score, the SIR Scale, and the RAG.[28]

Dunford assessed 850 men who completed treatment for wife assault in San Diego.[29] A random sample of treatment successes (no violence reported by the wife) and treatment failures revealed that unsuccessful men were more than six times as likely to have PCL-SV scores above 12 (Scale range 0-24).

Kropp et al. included the PCL-SV in a study following back fifty spousal assault recidivists and fifty non-recidivists. Raters coded the SARA and the PCL-SV blind to outcome status. While the SARA discriminated between the two groups, the PCL-SV did not. This is an intriguing finding, given how effective the PCL has proven to be when predicting violence in general. In some ways, however, we do not expect the psychopath to be the most likely type of spousal assaulter to re-offend. Fundamental to the psychopath's personality is the tendency not to form attachments to other people; he may roam from partner to partner. Psychopaths do not form the pathological "clinging" attachments that some other batterers exhibit.[30] Nevertheless, the Kropp et al. data suggest that the PCL may not be the best instrument to use, at least not on its own, when assessing the risk of repeated spousal violence.

Conclusion

Clinicians, correctional personnel, police, and victim service workers have for many years been asked to make judgments about risk and dangerousness in spousal assaulters. Until recently, however, there were few guidelines or tools to assist them in this task. This has changed with a proliferation of spousal assault risk instruments. Unfortunately, there is still relatively little published research on the reliability and validity of these tools. This situation is likely to improve if the number of validation studies in progress is any indication. The results of these studies will be welcome, as the science and practice of spousal assault risk assessment is obviously still in its infancy. There exists no single assessment instrument that would infallibly predict recidivist domestic violence, and there never will be. Yet there are, among the instruments reviewed above, several that show promising advances in both recognizing factors relevant to domestic violence and making empirical attempts to predict based on these factors.

Empirically validated risk assessment instruments should constitute one part of the constellation of decision factors used to make determinations of risk. Quality risk assessment instruments (firmly grounded in valid empirical studies, internally and externally valid and reliable, longitudinally verified, peer-reviewed, and based on quality research) should be an important part, but again not all, of the assessment process. The quality of the information upon which the assessment is based is also critical. Assessments should use multiple methods and multiple sources – including the victims – for data collection.

Although validation studies are needed, longitudinal outcome research is difficult because of practical and ethical considerations. For example, to truly know whether "predictions" for violence are accurate, we would need to release "high risk" offenders into the community without intervention or restraints to determine whether they re-offend (that is, that they are "true positive" predictions). Such a strategy would not be defensible. Therefore, any predictive study in this area must attempt to control for level of supervision, access to treatment, and so forth. In the absence of such carefully controlled research, it might still be useful to have risk assessment guidelines that (1) improve the reliability of assessments, (2) introduce accountability into the assessment process, and (3) allow more effective communication regarding risk to the courts, victims, and other interested parties. At present, many of the reviewed instruments, especially those that offer structured guidelines for gathering and reporting information, can serve these purposes. However, any risk assessment instrument must be appropriate to the level of expertise of the assessment users, who in turn should be sensitive to legal issues that could arise from its use.

Regardless of which risk measure is used, the evaluator should always consider implications for risk management. The process of risk assessment should not conclude with a prediction of dangerousness or lethality. A prediction is only the beginning. The evaluator should then formulate a risk management plan aimed at specific risk assessment variables, particularly those dynamic variables that might change over time. Such a plan can be linked to the risk factors that are present and absent (e.g., the perpetrator's strengths or protective factors). It is important to remember that the true policy goal is to *prevent* violence, not predict it. This can only be achieved through sound planning based on a comprehensive and informed risk assessment.

The studies in this chapter addressed risk for any form of spousal violence. My definition of spousal violence, therefore, was any actual, attempted, or threatened violence in the context of an intimate relationship. As the field of domestic violence risk assessment evolves, it will be useful to make distinctions regarding risk for various forms of spousal assault. Campbell has made advances in our understanding of factors associated with the narrower issue of domestic homicide, but it might prove possible to isolate specific risk indicators for different levels of violence severity, type (e.g., emotional abuse versus sexual violence), frequency, and imminence.[31] But given the state of the literature it remains premature to make such distinctions.

Risk assessment has become a well-used term in the literature. Properly applied, the practice of risk assessment can serve as a paradigm for effective case management of spousal assaulters. It can serve as the basis for release planning, treatment placement, and safety assessment for the victim. Improperly applied, it can mislead the courts, victims, and offenders into falsely believing in an infallible "science" that does not yet exist. However, the accumulation of twenty-five years of research on domestic violence makes possible informed decisions about factors related to spousal violence. Judicious, ethical, and professional application of risk assessment instruments has a valuable role to play in the protection of spousal violence victims. Nevertheless, as the incidents described in Figure 13.4 can remind us, violence sometimes can be impossible to predict, can come "out of the blue."

Estimating Risk in Females

The risk assessment instruments described above have been developed and normed on male populations. Although there have been studies of female antisocial personalities, the assessment has been developed with males in mind.[32] Skeem and her colleagues had 147 clinicians assess 680 patients in

---

13.4 Unpredictable cases

Some murders occur "out of the blue." But they tend to follow a pattern. They usually involve (1) abandonment or expectation of an intolerable separation or rejection, (2) a perpetrator with little or no prior violence and criminal justice system involvement, and (3) annihilation of the loved person. This strange combination resembles a "scorched earth" policy where a losing army destroys its land so the "enemy" can't have it.

Since the perpetrator has no prior police record, these cases are not predictable using any instruments, such as the SARA or the DAS, which depend on prior criminal justice system involvement. Abandonment homicide is a rare event that tends to happen with perpetrators who have no criminal record. Here are two examples.

Brodie Waldrat of Port Orchard, Washington
Brodie's girlfriend had obtained a restraining order preventing him from seeing her or their forthcoming child. He left Washington State for Idaho, then turned back and drove to his girlfriend's town on the Olympic Peninsula. He slept in the car and waited until her mother left for work. Then he knocked on door and tried to convince his girlfriend to give relationship another try. She refused. He murdered her (the fetus also died).

▶

◄ **13.4**

Pre-homicide
The victim had been bound with duct tape, and he vaguely remembered doing this to stop the "sickening sound." The victim had been dragged onto her parents' bed and raped. He vaguely remembered hitting the victim but not raping her.

Post-homicide
He changed his shirt, left the victim on the bed, took a cellphone and money, and drove six hundred miles to California, where he fell asleep in a motel parking lot still wearing his bloody jeans. When awakened by police he asked: "Is she all right?"

Brodie's background
He ran away from home at the age of five and lived in a series of foster homes. He had had no prior involvement with the law, and his only prior violence was a fist fight (over a girl) at a dance. There had been some low-level abuse of his current girlfriend. She was not injured but decided to end the relationship.

The jury decision was guilty of second degree murder.

Henry White of Long Beach, California
Henry had been voted "father of the year" for carefully attending to his two children. He washed and pressed their school clothes and brought them to school every day. There was no record of prior violence.

Pre-homicide
His wife was leaving him. He was on the telephone with her, trying (unsuccessfully) to reconcile with her. The children were in the bath. He hung up the phone, went to the bathroom, and drowned both children.

Post-homicide
Seeming unable to understand what he had done, he wandered around, had lunch, then turned himself in to the police.

Henry's background
He was severely beaten by his father, according to his sisters. One of them said that his father "used to hang the defendant in the air by one leg and whip him with a belt. Sometimes this occurred as frequently as four times a week." Another said that the beatings "started when he was two years old and may have started when he was six months old." In effect he was tortured and found no safe refuge within his family.

The psychiatrists' report stated that Henry's childhood was "characterized by parental instability/abandonment."

SOURCE: These are cases in which I was an expert witness. All quotes are from reports made to the court by others.

a psychiatric emergency room for risk of future violence.[33] Mental health professionals of both genders turned out to be "particularly limited in their ability to assess female patients' risk of future violence."[34] In fact, the "false negative rate" for female patients (the rate at which one was judged to be low risk but subsequently re-offended) was double that of male patients.[35] The criterion for violence was physical violence: the patient had to have been reported to have "laid hands on another person with the intent to harm him or her, or had threatened someone with a weapon in hand."[36]

This finding was true across all professional groups and was unrelated to the type of violence. That is, the finding occurred for general violence and for severe violence. In the MacArthur Risk Assessment study of psychiatric patients released into the public, Robbins et al. found that women were just as likely as men to be violent during the first year after discharge.[37] Robbins and her colleagues attributed the underestimation of women's violence to its being less visible "since it occurs disproportionately in the home with family members."[38] When this finding (which applies to psychiatric populations) is combined with Follingstad's (see Chapter 7) and Sorenson's, the evidence is strengthening that female violence is underestimated by professionals.

One last word on risk prediction. All risk prediction instruments used in IPV prediction assess risk solely on the basis of perpetrator characteristics (the SARA, DAI, PAS, etc.). Given what we have seen about the frequency of bilateral violence (Stets and Straus found it to be the most frequent form) and about how dysfunctional interaction patterns lead to IPV (Chapter 11), assessment of risk in the future should be made on the basis of characteristics of both members of a couple.

14 Treatment Policy Issues

> Using slavery, a colonial relationship, or an oppressively structured
> workplace as an example, the facilitator can draw a picture of the
> consciousness of domination.
>
> – E. Pence and M. Paymar, *Education Groups*
> *for Men Who Batter: The Duluth Model*

Treatment for abuse perpetrators has traditionally followed two lines: the
"psychological" line has used cognitive behavioural techniques, while the
"psychoeducational line" has eschewed them. When it was recommended
that a single set of techniques should be established by a state board super-
vising intervention and treatment, Gelles argued against government standards for a court-mandated treatment format because "the standards that are
being called for, developed, and applied represent a particular ideological
commitment of those who work on behalf of battered women and who are
less tied to a therapeutic theory of philosophy."[1] Gelles presented this conclusion citing an outcome study by Levesque that found there was no effective treatment for batterers and hence no basis upon which to form "standards
for treatment."[2] Advocates of a single treatment method, Gelles suggested,
never did expect the interventions to work and never did believe men were
capable of change. They viewed the intervention as containment at best. I
remember that advocates in the 1970s said "treatment doesn't work," even
though no outcome studies had been done at the time.

Maiuro, Hagar, Lin, and Olson have investigated whether current state
standards for perpetrator treatment are adequately informed by research.
The finding was that in the majority (60 percent) of the thirty states surveyed they were not.[3] Surprisingly, as of 2000, most of the thirty states surveyed (75 percent) had no specified standards.[4] Of those that did, most had
subscribed to feminist models of the kind described by Gelles, either the
Duluth model (see below) or the Emerge model from Boston, both of which

regard psychological attributes as unimportant.[5] Adams's views represent those of supporters of these models: "Clinical approaches fail to adequately address the violence by focusing on individual psychological issues that, although important, are not the cause of violence ... Some of these approaches collude with batterers by not making violence the primary issue or by implicitly legitimizing men's excuses for violence."[6] Adams failed to understand that working on psychological issues that underlie the violence might be more effective than "making violence the primary issue." For example, there may be less resistance to addressing and correcting psychological issues that foster abusiveness. Maiuro et al., Eckhardt et al., and Novaco cite abundant research evidence on anger as central to abuse (see Chapters 8 and 9). There is too much evidence for anger as central in abuse and too much emphasis on so-called anger management treatment to dismiss it as a treatment focus. But anger is merely one treatment focus among many in Cognitive-Behavioral Treatment (CBT) for IPV. The key question is: Does violence diminish after treatment?

Figure 14.1 lists the multitude of possible targets for three broad types of intervention. Maiuro et al. surveyed the treatment modalities allowed in the state standards examined.[7] They found that of the thirty states surveyed, 90 percent dictated group therapy (mostly feminist psychoeducational approaches). Some states permitted other forms of treatment: 55 percent allowed individual treatment, 55 percent allowed couple therapy, 65 percent specified gender-specific treatment, and 35 percent specified gender-specific treatment before couple therapy. No specific comparisons of individual vs. group therapy were made, but Maiuro et al. listed the advantages of group treatment: group cohesiveness to maintain treatment, economy, and "shame detoxification" (see Chapter 15). They mentioned O'Leary's suggestion that couple treatment could be just as effective as individual treatment if proper screening for safety and risk were done first.[8] Maiuro et al. caution that "although few would question the need for employing certain methods in order to protect the safety of victims, there is danger in prematurely dismissing potentially effective approaches. The risk is magnified by the fact that such generalizations may become officially codified in standards as a 'known' basis for practice."[9] Maiuro et al. then cite the woozle effect as being a risk for limiting treatment practice on grounds of what's "known" to work. Maiuro et al. call this "the greatest risk of stunting the development of new or alternative interventions for families afflicted with domestic violence. In this respect more work is needed to assure that the existing guidelines truly protect the well-being of victims without inadvertently impeding much needed program

14.1 Types of intervention available to address spousal abuse and domestic violence

Psycopharmacological targets
  Depressed mood
  Pathological grief reactions
  Irritable temperament
  Hyperactivity
  Impulsivity
  Emotional lability
  Pathological anxiety
  Obsessiveness and compulsivity
  Post-concussive/other organic syndrome

Cognitive-behavioural targets
  Minimization and denial
  Projection of blame and responsibility
  Denigrating and abusagenic attitudes toward women
  Power and control expectancies
  Personal acceptance and justification of violence
  Lack of awareness of the destructive and self-defeating impact of abusive behaviour
  Anger management
  Assertiveness and communication skills
  Non-violent conflict resolution skills
  Enhanced stress and coping skills
  Family of origin modelling influences
  Post-traumatic sequelae
  Relationship enhancement skills
  Relapse prevention skills

Social intervention targets
  Cultural and community acceptance of violence
  Public accountability for perpetration of violence
  Mandated intervention for perpetration of violence
  Legal support for victim's right to safety and health
  Comprehensive police protection for victims
  Victim shelter resources
  Prioritization of social and health care services for victims and perpetrators
    of abuse
  Sex role conditioning conducive to spouse abuse and violence
  Gender inequality in sociopolitical power and access to resources
  Preventive education in schools
  Improved surveillance methods
  Modelling and desensitizing influences in the media

SOURCE: R.D. Maiuro and D.H. Avery, "Psychopharmacological treatment of aggressive behavior: Implications for domestically violent men," *Violence and Victims* 11, 3 (1996): 239-61, 251. Used by permission of Springer Publishing Company, Inc., New York 10036.

development."[10] Hence, Gelles and Maiuro et al. both warn against political dogma's being translated into both law and "state authorized" therapeutic practice.

Maiuro et al. also reported the alarming fact that of the states surveyed only 20 percent required a college degree for treatment providers and, of those, four-fifths required only "specialized training in domestic violence" (i.e., socialization into the prevailing paradigm). This reflects, in my view, the anti-professional perspective of feminist activists. Maiuro et al. recognize the non-professional attitudes and suggest care must be taken to avoid a state standards committee made up exclusively of activists and treatment providers. They recommend an ethicist to ensure against conflicts of interest, including "secondary gain in the form of training contracts for a particular intervention approach or an agenda to put those competitors out of business who do not adopt a particular philosophy or offer a specific for of program."[11] One method to ensure this is to have a rotating multidisciplinary board (including at least one researcher) with re-appointments every two years. Maiuro et al. also suggest a national blue ribbon panel of experts to provide consultation to state boards. The only group to put this recommendation into practice is the US Department of Defence, who set up a panel of experts to advise them on their spouse assault treatment. The panel included Roland Maiuro, Chris Murphy, Dan Saunders, and myself.

We will now examine some existing statutes or penal codes that determine what legally must transpire after arrest. I begin with what I consider to be some reasonable approaches to probation and the setting of treatment standards, then move to others that I consider questionable.

Reasonable Approaches

California

Here is part of the California penal code pertaining to state handling of domestic violence:[12]

(3) Conditions of probation for crime of domestic violence:
    (a) If a person is granted probation for a crime in which the victim is a person defined in Section 6211 of the Family Code, the terms of probation shall include all of the following:

        1 A minimum period of probation of 36 months, which may include a period of summary probation as appropriate.

        2 A criminal court protective order protecting the victim from further acts of violence, threats, stalking, sexual abuse,

and harassment, and, if appropriate, containing residence
exclusion or stay-away conditions.

3   Notice to the victim of the disposition of the case.

4   Booking the defendant within one week of sentencing if
the defendant has not already been booked.

5   A minimum payment by the defendant of two hundred
dollars ($200) to be disbursed as specified in this para-
graph. If, after a hearing in court on the record, the court
finds that the defendant does not have the ability to pay,
the court may reduce or waive this fee.

Other provisions allow the court to order community service, fees for counselling, and payment to a woman's shelter. A provision describes the following terms of a man's release from a counselling program: has participated,
performance rated as acceptable by the therapists, has been violence-free for
six months (including threats), can demonstrate positive conflict-resolution
skills, and has gotten beyond victim-blaming and coercion. Then comes the
following provision:

(12) If it appears to the prosecuting attorney, the court, or the probation department that the defendant is performing unsatisfactorily in
the assigned program, is not benefiting from counseling, or has
engaged in criminal conduct, upon request of the probation officer,
the prosecuting attorney, or on its own motion, the court, as a priority
calendar item, shall hold a hearing to determine whether further
sentencing should proceed. The court may consider factors, including,
but not limited to, any violence by the defendant against the former
or a new victim while on probation and noncompliance with any
other specific condition of probation. If the court finds that the
defendant is not performing satisfactorily in the assigned program, is
not benefiting from the program, has not complied with a condition
of probation, or has engaged in criminal conduct, the court shall
terminate the defendant's participation in the program and shall
proceed with further sentencing.

In California, the probation department receives criminal histories and
probation reports including medical history, employment, and service
records, educational background, community and family ties, prior incidents
of violence, police report, treatment history if any, demonstrable motivation, and other mitigating factors. This information is used to determine

which community programs the defendant would benefit from and which of those programs would accept the defendant. The probation department reports its findings and recommendations to the court and also contacts the victim and assesses future risk for the perpetrator.

Batterer-treatment programs in California have to meet the following criteria:

No program, regardless of its source of funding, shall be approved unless it meets all of the following standards:

1   The establishment of guidelines and criteria for education services, including standards of services that may include lectures, classes, and group discussions.
2   Supervision of the defendant for the purpose of evaluating the person's progress in the program.
3   Adequate reporting requirements to ensure that all persons who, after being ordered to attend and complete a program, may be identified for either failure to enroll in, or failure to successfully complete, the program or for the successful completion of the program as ordered. The program shall notify the court and the probation department in writing within the period of time and in the manner specified by the court of any person who fails to complete the program. Notification shall be given if the program determines that the defendant is performing unsatisfactorily or if the defendant is not benefiting from the education, treatment, or counseling.
4   No victim shall be compelled to participate in a program or counseling, and no program may condition a defendant's enrollment on participation by the victim.
5   For defendants who are chronic users or serious abusers of drugs or alcohol, standard components in the program shall include concurrent counseling for substance abuse and violent behavior, and in appropriate cases, detoxification and abstinence from the abused substance.
6   The program shall conduct an exit conference that assesses the defendant's progress during his or her participation in the batterer's program.

Note that this program establishes some treatment standards but does not try to rule out other strategies as inappropriate (when that is not known).

British Columbia

Another reasonable approach is outlined in the Province of British Columbia Guidelines on contact with women partners (Figure 14.2).

Questionable Approaches

Internet sources describe standards for court-mandated treatment in a variety of American states.[13] I will briefly discuss three whose approaches are seriously deficient: Arizona, Georgia, and Alabama.

14.2 British Columbia guidelines for contact with women partners

---

Contact with women partners is essential for a complete assessment of the abuse. It is also important to provide women with information about supportive counselling, transition houses, and legal alternatives. Ensuring the woman has a safety plan or will be referred to someone who can help her formulate one is crucial. Women need to be given accurate information about the process of the men's group and likely results. Great care should be taken to present a conservative estimate of success ("there is no guarantee with your partner") so as not to build false hopes. The woman should be encouraged to protect herself through separation or legal means even if this runs contrary to the wishes of the male client.

Women should be encouraged to participate, but their involvement should be voluntary. In addition to initial contact for assessment, attempts should be made to contact her throughout the program to monitor safety and validate abuse reports from the man. Some programs may choose to conduct parallel women's support groups with communication between group leaders taking place.

Principle #27: Ongoing contact with women partners is required for assessment purposes and assurance of her safety. Contact should be based on her willingness to participate. Provision of supportive counselling or referral for such counselling should be undertaken.

Principle #28: Women should be encouraged to protect themselves through appropriate measures, which may include separation or legal action even though these may be unpopular with the abuser.

Principle #29: Great care should be taken to be conservative in communicating expectations for change in men's behaviour so as not to bias women's self-protective decision-making.

NOTE: These paragraphs are extracts.
SOURCE: Janice Bell, Jim Browning, and Alayne Hamilton, *Violence against Women in Relationships with Men: Guiding Principles for Services in British Columbia* (British Columbia Ministries of Attorney General, Social Services, and Women's Equality, 1999).

Arizona

Figure 14.3 sets out Arizona's standards for treatment providers. While giving a workshop in Arizona, I learned that the local shelter prevented therapists from contacting the spouses of men in treatment. The "standards" read: "does not require participation of a victim"; but "participation" is being stretched to no contact even with treatment providers.

14.3 Arizona treatment standards for domestic violence perpetrators

---

A. A licensee of an agency that provides misdemeanor domestic violence offender treatment shall ensure that:

1 The agency's program description includes, in addition to the items listed in R9-20-201(A)(2), the agency's method for providing misdemeanor domestic violence offender treatment;

2 The agency's method for providing misdemeanor domestic violence offender treatment:
   (a) Is professionally recognized treatment for which supportive research results have been published within the five years before the date of application for an initial or renewal license;
   (b) Does not disproportionately or exclusively include one or more of the following:
      (i) Anger or stress management,
      (ii) Conflict resolution,
      (iii) Family counseling, or
      (iv) Education or information about domestic violence;
   (c) Emphasizes personal responsibility;
   (d) Identifies domestic violence as a means of asserting power and control over another individual;
   (e) Does not require the participation of a victim of domestic violence;
   (f) Includes individual counseling, group counseling, or a combination of individual counseling and group counseling according to the requirements in R9-20-302; and
   (g) Does not include more than 15 clients in group counseling;

3 Misdemeanor domestic violence offender treatment is not provided at a location where a victim of domestic violence is sheltered; and

4 Misdemeanor domestic violence offender treatment for a client is scheduled to be completed within not less than four months and not more than 12 months after the client is admitted into misdemeanor domestic violence offender treatment.

SOURCE: Arizona: R9-20-1101. Misdemeanor Domestic Violence Offender Treatment Standards. Batterer Intervention Services Coalition of Michigan: Alabama Certification Standards for Domestic Violence Perpetrator Intervention Programs (May 2001), Prohibited Educational Approaches, at http://www.biscmi.org/other_resources/state_standards.html.

It is essential for therapists to have direct contact with partners. Apart from getting a different history and perspective on the relationship, power dynamics, and abuse, the therapist should be assessing both partners for (1) use and receipt of both physical and psychological abuse, and (2) personality disorder. The first is essential to find out whether the client's reports are just a defence or have some basis in fact. This is important because, while the therapist is still going to hold the client responsible for his own behaviour, it is essential to know the reality being faced at home. To dismiss the statements of a client who speaks the truth will surely undermine a therapeutic bond.

Georgia
The State of Georgia adopts a strict "Duluth" model. The State of Georgia has a Commission that passed guidelines for batterer intervention programs (Figure 14.4), which seem to fall into the pitfalls described by Maiuro.

Obviously no therapist would put a victim in danger or "coerce" their participation. The State of Georgia rules out every type of therapy known, including some promising treatments (see "Inappropriate Intervention Approaches" in Figure 14.4).[14]

14.4 Georgia intervention guidelines

---

10. **Appropriate Intervention Guidelines.** The model is "psycho-educational." It addresses abuse in both a personal and social context through gender-based expectations, beliefs, and attitudes. This model acknowledges that violence is a learned behavior and can be unlearned. Group intervention for batterers is mandatory under these standards. Over the course of twenty-four weeks FVIPs must also address each of the following content areas in the intervention sessions:
    (a) assisting the batterer in taking responsibility for violent and abusive behavior;
    (b) defining domestic violence;
    (c) erasing myths and beliefs about domestic violence, including myths about provocation;
    (d) helping batterers to learn to identify behavioral, emotional, and physical cues which signal escalating danger;
    (e) improving the batterers' ability to identify and articulate feelings;
    (f) improving listening and communication skills and listening with empathy;
    (g) challenging stereotypical gender role expectations;
    (h) exploring the soci-cultural basis for domestic violence;
    (i) identifying the effects of distorted thinking on emotions and behavior;
    (j) comparing self-control versus power and dominance;

(k) learning about the relationship of alcohol and drug use/abuse with domestic violence; and

(l) exploring the role of ethnicity and culture in domestic violence.

11. **Inappropriate Intervention Approaches.** The following is a list of intervention approaches that are inappropriate for a batterers' intervention program and are specifically prohibited:

(a) Any intervention approach that blames or intimidates the victim or places the victim in any danger. Any intervention approach that suggests there is behavior on the part of the victim that causes or excuses abuse. Any intervention approach that does not state clearly that batterers bear sole responsibility for their actions.

(b) Any approach that coerces, mandates, or otherwise requires victim participation. Couples, marriage, or family therapy is prohibited.

(c) Psychodynamic interventions that link causes of the violence to past experiences and unconscious motivations.

(d) Communication enhancement or anger management techniques that lay primary causality on anger.

(e) Systems theory approaches, which treat the violence as a mutually circular process, blaming the victim.

(f) Addiction counseling models that identify violence as an addiction and the victim and children as enabling or codependent in the violence.

(g) Any approach that encourages gradual containment and de-escalation of violence.

(h) Theories or techniques that identify poor impulse control as the primary cause of the violence.

(i) Teaching fair fighting techniques.

(j) Individual therapy or treatment.

SOURCE: Batterer Intervention Services Coalition of Michigan: Alabama Certification Standards for Domestic Violence Perpetrator Intervention Programs (May 2001), Prohibited Educational Approaches, at http://www.biscmi.org/other_resources/state_standards.html.

Alabama

Like Georgia, Alabama rules out any "psychological treatment" as a condition of probation (Figure 14.5). Instead, these states (and others) opt for the psychoeducational intervention of the Duluth model. Given what we know about the psychology of assaultive men, does this make sense?

Cognitive Behavioural Treatment (CBT)

Where court-mandated treatment groups are legally allowed to exist, a variety of types have emerged based on social learning notions of the development and maintenance of aggressive behaviour patterns. Bandura describes

14.5 Alabama: Prohibited interventions

Victim Blaming
Any intervention approach that blames the victim or places the victim in danger is prohibited. There is no behavior on the part of the victim which causes or excuses abuse. Perpetrators bear sole responsibility for their actions.

Victim Coercion or Mandates
Any approach that coerces, mandates, or encourages voluntary participation of the victim is inappropriate.

Couples, Marriage or Family Therapy
Couples, marriage or family therapy is prohibited during the psycho-educational intervention.

Circular Process or Family Systems Approach
Any approach that uses a systems theory model, which treats the violence as a mutually circular process or any other model that minimizes the responsibility of the perpetrator and places responsibility for the violence upon the victim is prohibited.

Addiction Models
Addiction counseling models, which identify the violence as an addiction and the victim and children as enabling or co-dependent in the violence are prohibited.

Containment Approaches
Any approach that attempts to use containment methods in an attempt to de-escalate the violence is prohibited.

Impulse Control Models
Use of theories or techniques that identify poor impulse control as the primary cause of violence is prohibited.

Psychopathology
Any approach that identifies psychopathology on the part of either party as a primary cause of violence is prohibited.

Psychodynamic Interventions
Interventions that link causes of the violence to past experience and unconscious motivations may not be used as a program's primary educational approach. This may be used as one technique within a more appropriate educational approach (see section on theoretical approaches) outlined in these standards.

Communication Enhancement or Anger Management
These techniques may not be used as the program's primary educational approach. This may be used as one technique within an educational approach (see section on theoretical approaches) described in these standards.

Fair Fighting, Getting in Touch with Emotions
These techniques and alternatives to violence and non-threatening ventilation techniques may not be used as a program's primary educational approach. This may be used as one technique within an approach described in Standard 3 (see section on theoretical approaches).

SOURCE: Batterer Intervention Services Coalition of Michigan: Alabama Certification Standards for Domestic Violence Perpetrator Intervention Programs (May 2001), Prohibited Educational Approaches, at http://www.biscmi.org/other_resources/state_standards.html.

in detail the psychological mechanisms that allow "reprehensible conduct" to recur.[15] While these mechanisms of self-justification may be challenged by arrest, they can be further confronted through court-mandated treatment. Indeed, a primary objective of such treatment is to undermine directly the cognitive, habit-sustaining mechanisms in assaultive males.[16]

A second objective of such confrontation is to challenge the belief held by some convicted wife assaulters that their arrest was unjust. To the extent that a wife assaulter believes that his wife's injuries were minimal, or she was to blame for the conflict, or his use of violence was justified, he is more likely to view his subsequent arrest and conviction as unjust. Most treatment formats confront these beliefs as well.[17]

A third objective of treatment is to enable wife assaulters to improve their ability to detect the "warning signs" of their own violence (e.g., increased arousal, anger) and to develop an effective set of behaviours for managing situations that previously evoked violence. The empirical question for such treatment is whether these improved cognitive and behavioural abilities, when linked with the belief that future assault will lead to punishment, can decrease recidivism in a treatment population.

The Difficulties of Court-Mandated Treatment

Chapter 12 presented studies indicating that men who desisted from arrest alone were the types of men who would be most amenable to treatment

---

14.6 Basic steps in Cognitive-Behavioural Treatment (CBT)

- establish therapeutic alliance
- allow group cohesiveness
- generate acceptance of client; explain role of confrontation
- focus on unacceptability of abuse: confrontation with emphasis on attitude and choice
- generate client agreement with unacceptability of abuse: violence contract
- generate commitment to therapy
- skills training: emotional labelling, anger management (anger diaries), self-soothing (Reichian breathing), redirected power needs, assertiveness
- focus on specific "problem" emotions: anger, jealousy, anxiety, depression
- attitudinal challenge: use of violence, women
- awareness of violence potential, contact with partner: crisis strategies
- connection of learned patterns in family of origin to present dysfunctional action patterns.

NOTE: This is a synthesis based on my own experience as a therapist.

because they accept responsibility. Those who failed to desist had criminal histories suggestive of antisocial behaviour and possibly antisocial personality disorder. These men are notoriously difficult, if not impossible, to treat.

A group frequently sent to court-mandated treatment consists of men with borderline traits. Many men with these traits even self-refer to existing court-mandated groups. In any event, psychological problems will be commonplace in court-mandated treatment, as will a general reluctance to participate.

This combination of problems and reluctance presents the therapist with a difficult situation. Men who have violence problems and are in denial about them are in what Prochaska et al. called the "precontemplation" phase of the change cycle, not yet persuaded or ready to work at changing themselves.[18] To further complicate the problem, many of the men sent to court-mandated groups will be partnered with women who are themselves violent.[19] Yet if they refer to their wife's violence, they will be deemed as being in denial. Finally, in some systems the man must "confess" to his violence problem in order to fulfill his conditions of probation. This sets up an unproductive conflict between the man and the so-called therapist who is supposed to be helping him. The role of a true therapist, requiring a therapeutic bond and emotional connection, is compromised by system requirements that prevent the formation of that bond.

In North America, a typical result of arrest and conviction for a domestic violence conviction involves court-mandated treatment as a requirement of probation. Two forms of treatment are generally available: cognitive behavioural therapy (CBT) and "psychoeducational" groups, sometimes referred to as the Duluth Model.[20] The latter did not call itself therapy, because it did not want to imply that there was a psychological component in the makeup of abusive men, who were seen instead as playing out a socially predetermined and "normal" male role preoccupied with power and control.[21] The psychoeducational groups basically operated from the perspective that all abuse is generated by male power and need for control. The arguments against this position have been seen in Chapters 5 and 6.

There are two major problems with most court-mandated approaches: (1) they treat all cases alike, instead of requiring assessment of differences in severity, chronicity, mutuality, and whether personality disorders underlie the abuse; (2) they opt for superficial "re-education" of attitudes when attitudes are not the issue. Mysogynistic opinions are a symptom, not a cause. The key underlying issue has to do with personality disturbance.

Levesque, after surveying existing treatment applications and finding that they were failing, suggested applying notions of individual change stemming from the Prochaska model (which she called the Transtheoretical

Model). She attributed the failure of "potentially powerful interventions" to (1) a dogmatically sociopolitical understanding of violence rather than empirically validated theories of individual behaviour change, (2) the standardization of these models into "one size fits all," and (3) the tendency of the standardized model to be "confrontational and coercive."[22]

The Problem with the Duluth Model

The Duluth Domestic Abuse Intervention Project (DAIP) designed an intervention program to be applied to men who had assaulted their female partners but who were not going to receive jail time. The objective of the program was to ensure the safety of the female victims (protection from recidivist violence) by "holding the offenders accountable" and by placing the onus of intervention on the community to ensure the woman's safety. The curriculum of the Duluth model was developed by a "small group of activists in the battered women's movement" (including the Emerge therapists from Boston) and was designed to be used by paraprofessionals in court-mandated groups.[23] It is now one of the most commonly used court-sanctioned interventions for convicted men with mandatory treatment conditions placed on their probation. This is true in many American states and Canadian provinces.

The curriculum of the model stresses that violence is used as a form of "power and control" and a "Power and Control Wheel" has become a famous insignia of the program. Also, power and control is seen as being an exclusively male issue. As Pence and Paymar say, "they are socialized to be dominant and women to be subordinate."[24] Hence, the "educational" aspect of the program deals with male privilege that exists in patriarchal structures such as North American countries. The DAIP view of female violence is that it is always self-defensive. "Women often kick, scratch and bite the men who beat them, but that does not constitute mutual battering."[25] Male battering stems from beliefs that are the product of socialization. These include the belief that the man should be the boss in the family, that anger causes violence, that women are manipulative and think of men as income earners, that if a man is hurt it's natural for him to hurt back, that smashing things isn't abusive, that feminists hate men, that women want to be dominated by men, that men batter because they are insecure, that a man has the right to choose his partners' friends and associates, and that a man can't change if the woman won't.[26] According to the program manual, the basis for these beliefs came from a sample of five battered women and four men who had completed the Duluth program. The authors apparently do not sense any problem with this small and unrepresentative sample.

The Duluth perspective on psychological problems is outlined in the program manual: "Most group members are participating not because of a personal history of family dysfunction but rather because violence is a socialized option for men. To attach a clinical diagnosis to the batterers' use of violence provides a rationalization for behavior that may not be accurate."[27] In the rare case where "mental illness" is diagnosed, other treatment is recommended.

The Duluth model's focus on power and control has men keep "control logs" and review the socialization that leads to expectations of "male privilege." It "discusses how making women into sex objects and then defining sex objects as bad degrades women and lowers their self esteem. From there it goes on to discuss why men would want women to have low self-esteem."[28] It does not address any psychological issues or emotions that group members may have. "Negative feelings" are seen as caused by patriarchal beliefs.[29] To demonstrate patriarchy, participants draw a pyramid and ask Who is at the top? and How did he get there?[30] The facilitator is advised to use slavery or a colonial relationship as an example to "draw a picture of the consciousness of domination."[31] The Duluth model uses role-playing to show male abusiveness and to raise men's consciousness about trivializing women's anger.[32] Men are encouraged to "respond in a respectful way" when their female partner gets angry.[33]

The objective of the Duluth model – respectful and non-abusive relationships – is the same as that of other theoretical models of intervention for abusive men (such as Cognitive Behavioural Therapy or even psychodynamic treatment). However, the means to the end differ significantly from those of psychological models, and the latter have been proven to be more effective than is the pure Duluth model.[34] Many of the processes and skills that the Duluth programs utilize are in fact similar (affect regulation, assertiveness skills, negotiation skills, etc.) to psychotherapeutic models of intervention. The primary difference seems to be in an unyielding adherence to their explanation of violence, their monolithic model of male domination and instrumental violence taken as a given, and the emphasis on socialization and control of women to the exclusion of other factors contributing to abuse and the various subtypes of abuse perpetrators.

According to the model's proponents, a political model of the origins and nature of violence is incongruent with psychological and biological models. The Duluth model, for example, avoids using the term "therapy" because it implies there is something wrong with clients, whereas, in the Duluth philosophy, they are normal men simply following cultural dictates. In contrast, I believe that psychological, biological, and social/political factors

14.7 Profile of typical Duluth Model client

Based on police arrest statistics and court and treatment group data, we know the following about the statistically most likely participant in a court-mandated group. He is about 31, under- or unemployed. He resents his lot in life but has several mouths to feed. He does not hate women but in his eyes his wife "isn't pulling her weight." He drinks more than he should, but he doesn't like her telling him about it. His anger has increased lately, especially with work layoffs, but he is in denial about it. His anger is starting to generalize to other groups, groups that are "taking his work away." (Their identity varies with geographic location). He feels powerless but hates to admit it because of pride. The arrest startled him. He had no previous police record.

He is terrified about a "treatment group." He's never been in treatment; he thinks it's for sick people. When the group leader tells him he's using violence as a form of "power and control" and that he flaunts "male privilege" he is stunned. He sees himself as the last person to have "privilege." He thinks the "facilitator" is "full of shit" but knows he had better keep that opinion to himself because he has to finish this group as a condition of probation. That means the therapist has to think he's okay. If that means going along with the nonsense they're spouting, so be it. They try to tell him he's like a slave owner, but he thinks, "If anyone's a slave here, it's me!"

He mentions in group that his wife flies into rages and is sometimes violent, but his statements are dismissed as "victim blaming," so he learns not to talk about these problems. He "goes underground" in group, not revealing what he sees as marriage problems. He keeps things to himself. The facilitator tells him he must write a letter of apology to his wife. He struggles with that one. He is feeling chronic anger now: toward her for calling the cops and toward the system that is forcing him to say and do these things. Some of the guys meet outside group to discuss how to "get by and get out."

His sense of powerlessness is increased or intensified by the unfairness of how he is being dealt with by the "system." Consequently, his sense of worth plummets further, and whatever optimism he has left is dealt a further blow. In other words, all the psychological and societal dynamics that came into play in the violent domestic situation become intensified and further solidified.

SOURCE: This is a synthesis based on my own experience as a therapist.

are not inherently incongruent and that the research to date suggests that we must consider all these levels, with perpetrators, victims, and witnesses, if we truly want to intervene effectively against domestic violence,

The Duluth model's psychoeducational groups were legislated as mandatory in many American states (and Canadian provinces), and a state "domestic violence council" was put in place to "oversee," to ensure that treatment groups adhered to the model, including making group leaders "accountable" to victim advocates. In California, the policy gave leeway to therapists to add their methods onto the essential components of the Duluth model: that all abuse was a male-generated need for "power and control." In other locations service providers became disenchanted with the Duluth program, to the point that, when a recent treatment outcome study sought to compare Duluth with CBT models, only one "pure" Duluth model could be found. The others had reverted to using cognitive behavioural therapeutic techniques – blended with Duluth perspectives in order to satisfy state requirements.[35] Dutton argued that Duluth models had two major flaws that prevented effective treatment: (1) they attempted to shame clients, and (2) by taking a strong adversarial stance to clients (based on a feminist view that a major issue in domestic violence is male sex role conditioning), they failed to establish a therapeutic bond with their clientele.[36]

The Theoretical Problem

The theoretical problem has been explored above and in other papers.[37] Simply put, it is that the evidence for patriarchy as a "cause" of wife assault is scant and contradicted by several data sets showing that male-dominant couples constitute only 9.6 percent of all couples, that women are at least as violent as men, that women are more likely to use severe violence against non-violent men than the converse, that powerlessness rather than power seems related to male violence, that most men in North America do not find violence against their wives acceptable, and that abusiveness is higher in lesbian relationships than in heterosexual relationships, suggesting that intimacy and psychological factors regulating intimacy are more important than sexism.[38] We have provided evidence on all these points in previous chapters.

The research evidence has not favoured the simplistic view that male intimate violence is a form of gendered political suppression.[39] Using "slavery" as a model when men are dominant in only 9.6 percent of families makes no sense. Were only 9.6 percent of white slaveowners dominant? Studies such as the Archer meta-analytic combination of numerous studies with a combined sample size of 60,000 found women to be more violent than men, especially as the age of the sample dropped.[40] Other studies ruled out the rejoinder that this was all self-defensive violence. In fact, about 4 percent of all males (and about one-third of males in court-mandated treatment) fit the stereotype of terrorist violence put forward by the Duluth model. Many males will be arrested who come from families in which violence is reciprocal, minor, or female-perpetrated.[41] According to Duluth, all must be treated as patriarchal terrorists regardless of these differences.

Anger and Violence

One truism of the Duluth philosophy is that anger does not cause violence. This belief makes the Duluth perspective dismissive of cognitive behavioural therapy (CBT), which it frequently mislabels as "anger management," though CBT has never focused primarily on anger, and anger management would be one of about sixteen treatment objectives in CBT.[42] Duluth's view of abuse is that it is always an instrumental act and hence not a product of anger.

This view is not supported by the evidence. Maiuro et al. found that domestically violent men had significantly higher levels of both anger and hostility than controls. The authors concluded that their findings supported the "idea that anger dyscontrol is a key issue in the profile of domestically violent men" and noted that both depression and anger were elevated in this group.[43] Margolin, John, and Gleberman found that physically aggressive husbands reported significantly higher levels of anger than husbands in three control groups.[44] When Dutton and Browning showed videotaped husband-wife conflicts to wife assaulters and control males, the assaultive males reported significantly higher levels of anger than controls, especially in response to an "abandonment" scenario.[45] Dutton and Sonkin's application of attachment theory to intimate violence also contradicts this notion.[46] According to attachment theory, insecure attachment patterns are essentially maladaptive methods of regulating affect, particularly anger and other emotions stemming from loss.

Dutton and Starzomski found elevated anger scores for assaultive men as measured by the Multidimensional Anger Inventory.[47] They related the anger to certain personality disturbances, especially Borderline Personality Disorder, Antisocial PD, Aggressive-Sadistic PD, and Passive-Aggressive PD, all of which have anger as a component. Dutton et al. found elevated anger in assaultive males to be related to certain attachment disorders, especially an attachment style called "Fearful" attachment, which they re-labelled "Fearful-Angry" attachment.[48] Citing Bowlby's work on attachment, which viewed anger as having a first function of re-uniting with an attachment object and dysfunctional anger as further distancing the object,[49] Dutton et al. explored the developmental origins of elevated anger in assaultive males, viewing it as being produced by paternal rejection, exposure to abuse, and a failure of protective attachment.[50] Failure to address these underlying issues therapeutically, while focusing on symptomatic beliefs and "male privilege," would stand in the way of treatment success.

Jacobson et al. recruited physically aggressive and maritally distressed nonviolent control couples to discuss "areas of disagreement" in a laboratory setting. Maritally violent husbands and maritally violent wives both displayed

significantly more anger than controls. (Although the study focused on husbands, 50 percent of the wives committed severe acts of abuse as well.)[51]

Eckhardt, Barbour, and Stuart reviewed several anger measures and argued that anger and hostility were both elevated in maritally violent men.[52]
Eckhardt, Barbour, and Davis used an "articulated thoughts, simulated situations" technique that found maritally violent men articulated more an-
ger-inducing irrational thoughts and cognitive biases than non-violent
controls.[53] In short, numerous studies from several independent sources
have found anger to be prominent in physically assaultive males. For a review of additional studies not reported above, see Eckhardt, Barbour, and
Stuart.[54]

Beliefs and Violence

Another shibboleth of Duluth is that male intimate violence can be stopped
by altering "patriarchal beliefs." The problem is that the evidence that patriarchal beliefs cause violence has very little empirical support. A recent
meta-analytic review by Stith et al., assessing evidence for "traditional sex
role ideology," cited Hanson et al. as showing "attitudes condoning violence."[55] Actually, Hanson et al.'s measure was a predictor of future violence
by differentially violent men, not a statement of acceptance. The authors
asked men to predict the likelihood of their being violent, not whether
they thought violence was acceptable. Since some of these men had been
violent in the past, their predictions of higher likelihood were likely accurate. Stith cited a study by Smith that also sought to assess "patriarchal beliefs" but where the answers were all supplied by women partners and
depicted the men as distinctly non-patriarchal.[56] Two other studies applied
to specific groups and were non-representative. Measures of beliefs taken
after the event may simply reflect rationalizations for previous violence,
from which causation cannot be inferred. Social psychological research has
shown for years that people adjust their attitudes to reconcile attitudes with
behaviour.[57] Furthermore, irrational beliefs and thoughts increase during
anger, and despite the Duluth denial that anger is important, it is typically
a precursor of abusive episodes.

Duluth proponents fail to understand that thoughts, emotions, and
behaviours are inter-related and that this interaction is multidirectional. For
example, under the influence of strong emotions, thoughts or beliefs may
become distorted, which in turn will lead to particular behaviours. Pre-existing thoughts or beliefs may exacerbate emotions (such as "I can't depend
on anyone for love"), also leading to problematic behaviours. Behaviours
can trigger thoughts or emotions that were not present before the action was

taken. For example, one can smile and shortly afterward begin to feel happy. Additionally, many behaviours can occur in a mindless way, with little awareness in thought or emotion (walking or riding a bike, for example). In other words, the Duluth model of thoughts and behaviours is ridiculously simplistic and fails to capture the true complexity of the human mind.

Subtypes of Abusers

Men who are court-mandated for treatment for wife assault come from couples varying in their violence patterns.[58] However, men in mutual-violence couples (the most common form) who are arrested and who report their wives as also being violent are disbelieved in Duluth model groups. Their experience is invalidated and treated as rationalization and victim-blaming. Furthermore, Duluth models in most locations prohibit therapists from interviewing wives to make assessments of whether violence is reciprocal or unilateral, so the therapists cannot know when their male clients are excusing their behaviour and when they are reporting truthfully. When a client reports victimization by his partner and is disbelieved or invalidated by his therapist, it only supports the attitude that many victims of child abuse experience – don't bother telling because no one will believe you anyway. Although, in my view, men would be responsible for their own violence in either case, different treatment strategies might be invoked according to the presence or absence of reciprocal violence.

Even men who are unilateral abusers vary greatly in the personality structure that supports the use of violence, beliefs about violence, and emotional responses to intimate relationships[59] (see Chapter 9).

Dutton and Sonkin present an attachment theory conceptualization of domestic violence.[60] Studies have indicated that batterers, like the general population, consist of differing attachment categories stemming from different parenting experiences in childhood. Some batterers have learned to deactivate attachment-related emotions (Dismissing), whereas others have learned to overactivate attachment distress (Preoccupied). Persons suffering from unresolved trauma or loss have developed extremely maladaptive mechanisms for regulating attachment distress (Disorganized or Fearful), such as dissociation or extreme aggression. However, by treating all batterers the same way, the Duluth model misses the nuances that other models, such as attachment theory, capture and use for intervention.

Duluth model treatment does not assess for and cannot treat personality disturbances (including attachment insecurity), disbelieves clients who claim their partners are also violent, and does not have the flexibility to tailor therapy to fit the clients.

Couple Violence

Stets and Straus found that the most common form of domestic violence consisted of couples reciprocally using the same level of violence (mild, severe),[61] but a paper by Johnson focused on "common couple violence" vs. "patriarchal terrorism," overlooking the fact that a female severe/male non-violent pattern was *three times* as prevalent as "patriarchal terrorism."[62] Suffice it to say that the data reviewed above do not support the view that all female violence is self-defensive and not serious. The implication of this view was that the concept of couple violence was never applicable to domestic violence. In fact, couple violence is incompatible with patriarchal terrorism. However, several studies have found couple therapy effective with violent couples (see Chapter 2).[63] Obviously the form of treatment is dictated by an assessment of violence levels and danger, and ruling out a treatment *a priori*, as the Duluth model does, reduces treatment efficacy and raises the failure rate.

It is true that bias against women is a serious social problem that has required and will require many changes in both social policy and personal attitudes. Women have for centuries been blamed for the violence perpetrated against them by men and by institutions peopled by men. In reaction to this history of male oppression, there is a tendency for the pendulum to move in the opposite and equally simplistic direction – it's all men's fault. In the huge GSS 1999 survey done with 25,000+ respondents, LaRoche reported rates for severe violence with instrumental control (intimate terrorism) for male perpetrators of 4 percent and female perpetrators of 2.6 percent.[64] This is scarcely the the huge "gender disparity" that Duluth suggests. However, if one takes the stance that violence is not a valid solution to problem-solving no matter who is perpetrating the act, and that there is plenty of evidence that both men and women perpetrate violence, then our models of domestic violence intervention must acknowledge this fact and find solutions for both partners.

The Therapeutic Bond and the Group Process

The single best predictive factor for successful therapeutic outcome (realizing that the Duluth model is not therapy, though being required of many mental health practitioners) is the therapeutic relationship.[65] However, it becomes extremely difficult for therapists to form a positive relationship when they are required in the Duluth model to disbelieve acts of violence by the partner, are liable to lose their certification with probation if they don't confront their clients enough, and are considered enabling or manipulated when they advocate for their clients' continued treatment.

To develop a solid therapeutic alliance, one must balance confrontation with support, belief, and caring. Building a therapeutic alliance without colluding with dangerous acting-out behaviours is one of the greatest challenges facing treatment providers for domestic violence perpetrators. The process of building a trusting relationship is particularly difficult because so many of these individuals have experienced abuse by authority figures.

According to Lester Luborsky of the Penn Psychotherapy Project, the therapeutic alliance may be defined as "that point in the therapeutic relationship when the client on one hand elevates the therapist to a position of authority, but on the other hand believes that this power and authority is shared between them, that there is a deep sense of collaboration and participation in the process. In this way a positive attachment develops between the client and the therapist."[66]

Luborsky describes two types of therapeutic alliance. A Type 1 therapeutic alliance, which is more evident at the beginning of therapy, is based on the client's experiencing the therapist as supportive and helpful. A Type 2 therapeutic alliance, more typical of the later phases of treatment, is a joint struggle against what is impeding the client, a shared responsibility for working out treatment goals, and a sense of "we"ness.

Luborsky states: "On one hand, the clients 'clothe the therapist with authority,' but on the other hand, they also need to feel that this power and authority is shared. This sense of collaboration and participation may importantly contribute to a sense of safety that is essential for the development of trust between therapist and client and deep commitment to the therapeutic journey."[67]

Luborsky makes several recommendations to therapists on how to develop this alliance:[68]

1 Freud's suggestions, made almost 75 years ago, still hold true today. "A friendly, sympathetic attitude toward the client is beneficial for the initial development of the alliance."
2 Feeling and expressing empathy toward the client.
3 Helping clients feel invested in the tasks necessary to change (e.g., client involved in treatment planning).

Furthermore, respected therapists such as Daniel Sonkin and Allan Schore point out that the process of treatment is more important than the didactic aspect of treatment.[69] Although Schore focuses more on individual treatment and Sonkin on group treatment, both see the therapist-client relationship as an opportunity to repair attachment bonds that were not developed properly. Since, as we have described above in Chapters 3 and 10, attachment disorder is a prominent basis of IPV, the importance of this aspect of treatment cannot be overlooked.

These recommendations run counter to the Duluth model, which emphasizes confrontation and accountability. Given the inherent dangerousness of domestic violence situations, it is important for therapists to incorporate clear guidelines and structure in treatment to minimize acting-out. However, without a positive relationship with the therapist, the client is not going to truly be invested in treatment and is likely to either "fake it" (comply) or drop out altogether, being labelled as "unmotivated" (not unlike the abused child who is viewed by teachers as a problem rather than as a victim).

Many state providers use some subversion to slip in treatment under the state guidelines. A more reasonable approach is to do what the British Columbia Treatment Guidelines allow, which nicely blends the Duluth objectives into what is essentially a treatment format (Figure 14.8).

Not only the relationship with the therapist but also the relationships among the men in treatment are important for group success. These are variables that depend on processes that transpire between people rather than on the content of what is taught. In one of the few studies of court-mandated treatment to actually ask the men what worked for them (after the completion of the group), Mindy Rosenberg found that "elements that were most helpful were primarily relational ones, such as group support and therapist/facilitator alliances, and secondarily, specific strategies of handling anger and other emotions, and interpersonal communication."[70] When post-completion re-offence rates were analyzed, the offenders interviewed were not different from others not interviewed. Given the "confrontational and coercive" atmosphere (Levesque's term) of groups telling clients they are like slaveowners, the relational aspects of Duluth inhibit the formation of therapeutic bonds.

Treatment Outcome Studies of the Duluth Model

Because of the ever-present risk of findings being biased by program selection processes when studying treatment outcome success, results from experiments in which participants have been randomly allocated among alternatives are the "gold standard" for evaluation.

In a randomized treatment outcome study done on the Duluth model, Shepard found a 40 percent recidivism rate in a six-month follow-up of Duluth clients, higher than most control recidivism levels.[71] In another randomized study of a Duluth model, Babcock et al. put recidivism rates in a

14.8 British Columbia treatment philosophy

Two main approaches to conceptualizing the problem of abuse of women in relationships have developed over the years and have merged to varying degrees within individual programs. One approach views abuse of women in relationships as an anger management problem involving skill deficits remediated through cognitive-behavioural methods. The other approach arising from a feminist analysis focuses on the power and control motivation for abuse within a patriarchal system in which men are conditioned to dominate. This approach suggests a greater emphasis on changing sex role conditioning, promoting sexual equality and personal responsibility on the man's part for his violence.

While the degree of emphasis may vary, most programs incorporate aspects of both approaches. Clearly, a pure anger management approach devoid of any sex role socialization content will be insufficient and may risk creating more sophisticated abusers. Similarly, an approach which focuses only on power/sex role issues while providing no skill acquisition would seem inadequate. Therefore, an incorporation of these two approaches into a hybrid model is recommended.

The task for counsellors of abusive men is to take a strong stand against the man's use of violence and power and control while at the same time being supportive of him as a person. Without a respectful approach there is a danger of alienating the man, reducing his willingness to accept ownership of his behaviour and his responsiveness to the counselling process.

Principle #8: An approach to each individual man that demonstrates respect and care is fundamental to the process of change.

Principle #9: A treatment philosophy that combines cognitive behavioural and resocialization approaches is recommended. Changing sexist attitudes without skill development will likely be inadequate. Use of anger management without emphasizing power and control issues and the need for more equality in relationships may increase the risk of more sophisticated abuse to meet power needs.

NOTE: These paragraphs are extracts.
SOURCE: Janice Bell, Jim Browning, and Alayne Hamilton, *Violence against Women in Relationships with Men: Guiding Principles for Services in British Columbia* (British Columbia Ministries of Attorney General, Social Services, and Women's Equality, 1999).

six- to twelve-month follow-up at 35 percent according to wives and at 21 percent using arrest data.[72]

Feder and Forde randomly assigned batterers on probation to either a feminist-psychoeducational program or no treatment in Broward County, Florida.[73] In general, there were no statistically significant differences between the two groups on recidivism as measured by police records or by victim report. There was a small but significant effect on recidivism among the subset of men randomly assigned to group treatment who attended all twenty-six sessions, though of course this is a self-selected and non-representative sample. In this study, random assignment apparently failed, with an uneven number of men being assigned to the treatment and control conditions. Moreover, this study suffered from a particularly high attrition rate of men from treatment (60 percent) and a low response rate from victims at follow-up (22 percent).

In a large evaluation of US Navy personnel stationed in San Diego, Dunford compared a thirty-six-week cognitive-behavioural group and a twenty-six-week couple-therapy format to a rigorous monitoring condition and a no-treatment control (victims safety planning).[74] Neither CBT men's groups nor couple therapy had a significant impact on recidivism at a one-year follow-up based on victims' reports. This study represents the most methodologically rigorous study conducted to date in terms of sample size, length of follow-up, attrition rates, follow-up reporting rates, and assessment of treatment adherence. However, it is important to note that this sample of abusers, those employed through the Navy in San Diego, are not representative of the population of batterers who are court-mandated to domestic violence programs around the country. All of the research participants were employed, had a high stake in social conformity, and thus, were more "socially bonded." Any intervention, including arrest and being identified by authorities, may work to deter socially bonded individuals from repeat offences.[75] This may be reflected in the unusually low official recidivism rates of the non-treated batterers (4 percent).

Davis, Taylor, and Maxwell compared a long (twenty-six-week) psycho-educational group to a brief (eight-week), psychoeducational group, and to a community service control (seventy hours of clearing vacant lots, painting senior citizen centres, etc.) in Brooklyn, New York.[76] From criminal records they found a statistically significant reduction in recidivism and a small but respectable effect size of $d' = .41$ among the long treatment group only; the eight-week group was indistinguishable from the community service control ($d' = .02$). When based on victims' reports of recent offences and compared to no treatment, neither the long nor the brief intervention had a statistically significant effect on re-assault. Correspondingly, based on partners' reports of subsequent violence, the effect size due to any treatment was small ($d' = .21$). It is important to note that, as in the Broward County experiment described by Feder and Forde, random assignment may have been compromised. Nearly 30 percent of initial assignments were subjected to "judicial overrides," that is, judges reassigned defendants to different interventions.[77] Ford and Regoli designed a study that randomly assigned batterers into treatment as a pretrial diversion (i.e., defendants' criminal records would be cleared pending treatment completion), treatment as a condition of probation post-conviction, versus alternative sentencing strategies (e.g., paying a fine or going to jail).[78] Even though this study was designed to test different sentencing options rather than the effects due to treatment, one can compare batterers sentenced to treatment versus batterers not sentenced to treatment (although the type of treatment and actual attendance rates were not specified). Again, there were no significant differences or effect sizes comparing recidivism rates based on victims' reports between men sentenced to treatment and those who were not. Neither treatment as pretrial diversion (d' = .00) nor treatment as a condition of probation post-conviction (d' = –.22) was found to be superior to purely legal interventions.

The result of evaluations of Duluth interventions is therefore clear: there is no treatment success from this approach. Given the theoretical problems with the model described above, this should come as no surprise: it's hard to imagine a therapeutic case for a positive treatment result in groups where no therapeutic bond is developed.

Conducting an experiment in which judicial discretion is sacrificed and criminals are randomly assigned to treatment or no treatment can be problematic on ethical as well as practical grounds.[79] Adopting a random experimental design does not *guarantee* a more rigorous evaluation than quasi-experimental designs afford. While experimental designs permit greater confidence in conclusions regarding causal relations, it is also true that problems with differential attrition and failures in random assignment can reduce the internal validity of this design. In the case of the Dunford Navy study, despite the experimental design, it is questionable whether one can generalize from a military group, where even the control subjects were under intense scrutiny, to a civilian population. It is recommended that researchers report recidivism rates separately for all batterers who were assigned to treatment and for all who actually completed treatment (although few studies have done so).

Babcock, Green, and Robie conducted a meta-analytic study of twenty-two studies of treatment outcomes.[80] The effect size (d') for Duluth treatment was only .19. Comparisons between CBT and Duluth were not significant, but "pure" Duluth models were hard to find. As the authors state, "modern batterer groups tend to mix different theoretical approaches to treatment, combining feminist theory of power and control as well as specific interventions that deal with anger control, stress management and improved communication skill."[81] The groups that performed best were "pure" CBT groups.

The d' of .34 reported by Babcock, Green, and Robie is less than optimal for most therapeutic outcomes. The average effect size in psychotherapy studies is d' = .85, but it is substantially lower for court-mandated treatment. For comparison, the effect size of aspirin on heart attacks is d' = .41.[82] By standards of court-mandated client populations, however, this is an average result. By expanding the focus of treatment in a blended model described in the next chapter this outcome may improve.

By any reasonable standard, Duluth treatment is a failure. If one reads the great therapists, one sees that the development of a therapeutic bond is essential for treatment to have an effect.[83] The four outcome studies reported above make it clear that the Duluth model has no effect. However, as with the issue of women's violence, enthusiastic advocates do not accept refuted hypotheses; they simply redefine the issue to keep the ideology alive. This is what happened with the failure of Duluth. Gondolf interprets the failure of Duluth as a failure of the "coordinated community response" that supports the system.[84] He says that "the program's success, consequently, reflects the effectiveness of the system in establishing consistent police and court action for domestic violence cases ... and providing ongoing outreach and support to victims."[85] The program is therefore made a success by spinning the interpretation. Criminal justice system effectiveness is indeed important, but it is no more effective for CBT programs that outperform Duluth than it is for Duluth. Gondolph, like Dobash, Saunders, and other feminist advocates, seems unable to recognize that a hypothesis has been disproved and is able to find confirmation in any data whatsoever.

Stages of Change

Men who come to treatment through the court system may have no prior experience with treatment groups. They may be discomfited by the prospect of disclosing personal problems in front of other men. Denial and minimizing of abuse is commonplace, as is blaming (of the victim, of the criminal justice system, of any other convenient external source) in an attempt to ward off personal responsiblity for violence. (Recall from Chapter 8 Bandura's schema for neutralization of self-punishment.) How then to motivate these men to work at reducing their violence?

Prochaska and his colleagues present a model of the change process applied to addictive behaviours (Figure 14.9).[86] They describe empirical studies of change for a wide variety of addictive behaviours, which indicate that most people do not successfully maintain the gains made on their first attempt at change. Rather, what occurs is a type of spiral process in which

14.9 A spiral model of the stages of change from addictive behaviours

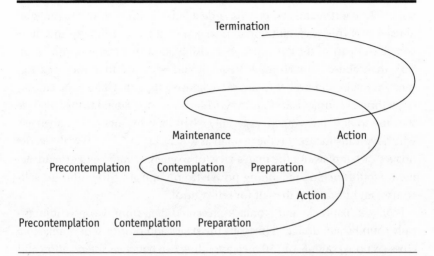

SOURCE: Adapted from J.O. Prochaska, C.C. DiClemente, and C.C. Norcross, "In search of how people change: Applications to addictive behaviors," *American Psychologist* 47, 9 (1992): 1102-14.

gains and relapses follow each other as the person progresses through four stages.

When we apply this model to wife assaulters, the following conclusions seem reasonable. Wife assault is a form of addictive behaviour that the man has learned to use habitually in ego-threatening or stressful conflict. Men who enter treatment are anywhere from the precontemplative stage to the action stage. Denial and minimizing are similar to the underawareness reported by Prochaska et al. Their conclusion is that, unfortunately, some form of relapse is almost inevitable for men who are trying to quit for the first time and have entered therapy in the earlier (precontemplation or contemplation) stages. This would describe almost all court-mandated men, so we have to wonder whether it is realistic to expect court-mandated men to become violence-free immediately following a sixteen-week treatment group. Levesque found that men in the precontemplation stage were highly likely to drop out of treatment.[87] Levesque, Gelles, and Velicer developed a scale to assess preparedness using the Prochaska model.[88] The stages and processes used by Prochaska et al. were able to predict with 93 percent accuracy which patients would drop our prematurely from therapy.

Prochaska et al. also suggest that different forms of treatment might work better at different stages. For example, consciousness-raising (sometimes called "motivational interviewing") is important at the precontemplation stage, whereas reinforcement management is more important at the action stage.[89] In court-mandated groups, a detailed examination of the range of abusive acts (physical, emotional, sexual, and abuse of property and pets) constitutes part of the consciousness-raising. Men frequently comment on how their abuse is much more frequent and pervasive than they had formerly thought and how they are more abusive than they had realized. Another form of consciousness-raising is to get the men to attend to the language they use to describe women, especially when they are angry. This language, which typically focuses on the woman as a "whore" or "slut," reveals deeper images or templates in the man's view of women. Reinforcement management would include redefining power from control of the other to self-control and rewarding the self for self-control.

Eckhardt, Babcock, and Homack presented data from two psychometrically sound scales designed to assess the stages and processes of change in a cross-sectional sample of 250 men attending two batterer's intervention and prevention programs. The URICA scale assesses movement through the stages of change, and the Processes of Change Scale (POC) assesses self-reported usage of behaviour change processes.[90]

Cross-validated cluster analyses indicated a three-cluster solution based upon URICA-DV scores: Immotive, Unprepared Action, and Preparticipation. The results indicated that individuals in more advanced stages of change reported using more behaviour change processes, although this did not appear to result from being in treatment for a longer period of time. These data were interpreted in light of recent data indicating relatively small effect sizes for batterer's treatment programs. An objective was to see how assessment of the stages and processes of change might assist in matching men to different levels of treatment. Eckhardt et al. found most men they evaluated to be in an early stage of preparation and not making much progress:

Our cluster analysis revealed that the present sample comprised men primarily in the Precontemplative and Contemplative stages only. There were clear cluster differences in process of change usage, with men in the Unprepared Action and Preparticipation clusters (i.e., Contemplative men) using significantly more of nearly all the processes of change than Immotive men (i.e., men in the Precontemplative stage). To evaluate whether stage of change is related to the battering intervention, we examined the relationship between the number of sessions attended and cluster membership, with the question being whether

URICA-DV scores were dependent upon the number of treatment sessions completed by our respondents. Surprisingly, stage of change cluster was unrelated to number of treatment sessions attended ... The reason could be due to the intervention. Although the Duluth-model intervention attempts to pierce the batterers' "denial" and motivate them to action, few if any of the batterers in our sample could be classified as being in the Action stage, despite having completed on average roughly half of their assigned sessions. Therefore, the intervention may not be adequately addressing their target population in ways that encourage readiness to change and the adoption of more change processes. Finally, it may be that the readiness-to-change construct is better conceptualized as a *trait*-based characteristic of the men rather than as a static by-product of the intervention. If men enter the program at varying stages of change, as expected, the number of treatment sessions completed is likely to be unrelated to stage of change, even if the men make some advances in readiness to change and in process of change usage. Similarly, many men are likely to remain in treatment because they feel coerced by the legal system to remain in treatment. Thus, they experience little benefit from the interventions being offered and perhaps remain in the Precontemplative stage for the duration of their legally mandated program attendance.[91]

Attrition

Scott used the stage-of-change model to predict attrition among men attending a batterer-treatment program.[92] As outlined by the transtheoretical model of change, men were classified into the precontemplation, contemplation, or action stage based on their level-of-change motivation and behaviour. It was hypothesized that men in the precontemplation stage would drop out of treatment at higher rates than men in later stages of change. Participants were 308 men who enrolled in a batterer treatment program over the course of one year, 61.4 percent of whom dropped out of treatment. Completion of treatment was significantly predicted by counsellor-rated, but not self-rated, stage of change once demographic, contextual, and personality variables were taken into account. Specifically, men identified by counsellors as being in the precontemplation stage were 2.3 times as likely to drop out of treatment as men rated in the contemplation stage and 8.8 times as likely as men rated in the action stage. Referral source, age, and history of arrest also made significant contributions to the prediction of attrition. The best combination of predictive factors led to the successful prediction of the outcome (recidivism) of 72 percent of the cases: 98 percent of the dropouts, but only 19 percent of the completers. Current discussion understandably focuses on the limitations of current findings and their implications for the use of the transtheoretical model to predict attrition from batterer treatment.

Evidence-Based Practice

In 1969, Campbell suggested that any policy reform be regarded as an experiment to be evaluated for effectivness and and altered accordingly.[93] Cournoyer and Powers have usefully suggested that such "evidence-based practice ... dictates that professional judgments and behaviour should be guided by two distinct but interdependent principles. First, whenever possible, practice should be grounded on prior findings that demonstrate empirically that certain actions performed with a particular type of client or client system are likely to produce predictable, beneficial, and effective results ... Secondly, every client system, over time, should be individually evaluated to determine the extent to which the predicted results have been attained as a direct consequence of the practitioner's actions." [94]

The body of findings that provides the groundwork for evidence-based practice is derived from investigations that test fully explicit and potentially falsifiable hypothesized relationships between variables, while attempting to control for numerous potential sources of bias and confounding influences. Such studies also are potentially replicable because their methods are explicit. To be regarded as evidence-based, "knowledge must withstand the test of possible refutation by virtue of being subjected to scrutiny in the form of some rigorous reality check."[95] Well-conducted qualitative and quantitative studies can provide important information to practitioners, although the validity and utility of a given study's findings clearly depend on the study design and implementation.

A necessary, but not a sufficient, condition for evidence-based practice is that practitioners appreciate the key role that scientific findings should play in guiding the selection and application of practice interventions and the importance of remaining current with an ever-growing scientific database. In addition, evidence-based practice, as I conceive of it, should incorporate the principles of the earlier empirical practice movement within social work, which held that practitioners should possess a broad awareness of scientifically tested and proven policies and practices in their respective practice areas and the general skills needed to deliver and evaluate their own interventions.

Is evidence-based practice being used in domestic violence intervention and treatment? I think not. How could one reconcile the rich psychological data in earlier chapters with government prohibitions against interventions that address these very issues in a therapeutic setting?

According to Holtzworth-Munroe, mandated treatment standards make four presumptions that have failed the experimental test: (1) that conjoint treatment is never appropriate, (2) that we know the best length, content, and process of treatment, (3) that one size can fit all, and (4) that doing something is better than doing nothing.[96]

15 Treatment: The Next Step

Psychoeducational intervention has been an abysmal failure. Several outcome evaluations reviewed in the last chapter have shown it to have a treatment effect of zero. It's easy to see why it failed if one considers the prerequisite for a successful group outcome: therapeutic bonds with the therapist and with others in the group. Psychoeducational intervention has an atmosphere of confrontation in which the clients, typically men who feel powerless in the world, are being likened to slaveowners. All this happens with a criminal justice "hammer" held over their heads. Compliance can be expected, but not long-term change.

Psychoeducational models do not address the associated features of abusiveness; they simply deal with hypothesized "sexist attitudes" for which the research evidence is doubtful. This style of intervention is less like therapy than like the thought reform practised by the Maoist Red Guards.[1] Therapy has to find a way to engage clients in a shared enterprise of change. This involves the client coming to see the need for change and then working to that end. Elsewhere I have described this as a "Zen" process, looking for the correct amount of acceptance and pressure to change.[2]

"Biopsychosocial" Treatment for Assaultiveness

Maiuro and Avery developed a three-stage program called "biopsychosocial" intervention with an ordering from broad to narrow.[3] The broadest *social* focus is aimed at the socializing culture. In my opinion this is the level at which activists should focus, leaving treatment to competent therapists (see Chapter 14, Figure 14.1).

The *biological* aspect involves administering pharmacological treatment for depression, irritable temperament, hyper-reactivity, emotional lability, pathological anxiety, obsessiveness, compulsiveness, and post-concussive or other related syndromes. The biological treatment intervention was based on the assumption that pharmacological agents such as antidepressants, anxiolytics, and serotonin re-uptake moderators might aid in treating certain aspects of the abusive personality. However, as the authors point out, this form of intervention cannot be substituted for social change or psychological (group) treatment. Instead, it must be viewed as an adjunct to the other forms of intervention: psychological and sociocultural.

The *psychological* aspect is aimed at the following potential treatment targets: defences against acknowledgment of responsibility (e.g., denial, minimizing, blame projection), anger management (detection and control of anger responses), assertiveness, bargaining and communication skills, attitudes toward women, family of origin modelling influences, relationship enhancement skills, and relapse prevention skills. I agree that these appear to be reasonable targets for psychological intervention. Yet both the narrower biological and psychological interventions must be set within a social context of activism concerning general cultural acceptance of violence, violence against women, women's safety, and male sex-role conditioning. I would also add that the list of targets for therapeutic intervention needs extending. In particular, in view of the research from many sources examined in this book (Holtzworth-Munroe et al., Ehrensaft et al., Moffitt et al., Magdol et al., and Dutton et al.), the central place of personality disorder in assaultiveness has to become a part of court-mandated assault treatment.

Cognitive Behavioural Treatment for Assaultiveness

Court-mandated treatment models arose in a number of locations in the early 1980s and ranged in length from eight weeks to one year. The criminal justice system needed an effective way for judges to settle wife-assault cases before them, and treatment was developed to meet that need. Maiuro and Avery defined the treatment foci of such groups as shown in Figures 14.1 and 14.6.

At intake, a man is given a "time-out" card instructing him to leave a high-risk situation, to walk away until calm, not to return until calm, and to leave again if he becomes angry again. He must inform his wife of this procedure. At this point, no training is yet done to lower anger. Typically, cognitive behavioural therapy (CBT) is done in a group format (see Dutton for a detailed description).[4] As outlined earlier in Figure 14.6, current CBT focuses on responsibility for abusiveness, cognitive reframing of abusogenic thoughts, assertiveness, and awareness of anger.

Most men sent by the courts for wife-assault treatment have had no experience with psychotherapy. Wallace and Nosko have described the opening-night ritual (in which men are asked to describe "the event that led to your being here") in such groups as a "vicarious detoxification" of shame.[5] Most men who come to these groups, assuming they are "normally" socialized, experience high levels of shame as a result of their violent behaviour (as shown by their denial and minimization of the assaultive events).[6] Hearing other men in the group discuss their own violence allows the man to "vicariously detoxify," that is, to face his own sense of shame. This sense of shame, were it not detoxified, would preclude his opening to treatment by keeping the man's anger at a high level to hold the shame at bay. Anger allows blame to be directed outwardly, preventing shame-induced internalized blame. One reason why Duluth psychoeducational models are counterproductive is that they enhance shame instead of reducing it to allow further work.

Figure 15.1 shows a sample didactic and group process structure for a short (sixteen-week) CBT group. Note that in Week 5 a "violence policy" is established. This asks men to complete the sentence "I think the use of violence is justified when ..." Most men will answer with self-defence or defence of the family. From that point on, the therapist can portray all therapy

15.1 Treatment outline for a short CBT group

Week	Didactic exercise	Group process goals
1	Describe the assault that led to your being here; participation agreement	Shame detoxification and therapeutic alliance
2	Conflict issues > emotions > actions	Group cohesiveness
3	What is "abuse"? Definitions, power wheel	Assessment of denial levels
4	Explanation of confrontation; first group check in	Authority issues
5	Violence policy	Group cohesiveness
6	Anger diaries	Shame detoxification
7	Stress management: Reichian breathing	Hierarchy in group
8	Abuse cycle	Authority issues
9	DESC scripts	Attitude confrontation
10	Family of origin: how did your mom/dad show their anger?	Authority issues
11	Continuation: how did you/your siblings feel?	Personal responsibility
12	DESC scripts: role play	Emotion detection
13	Detection of other prevalent emotion: shame, resentment, guilt, etc.	Therapeutic alliance
14	Consolidation of communication skills	
15	Preparation for the end: relapse prevention	
16	What did you learn? What continues to be a problem? What other therapies are available?	

SOURCE: D.G. Dutton, "Cognitive behavioral treatment for intimate abuse," in D.G Dutton and D.J. Sonkin, *Intimate Violence: Contemporary Treatment Innovations* (Binghampton, NY: Haworth Press, 2003).

as an attempt to allow the man to learn to live up to his own violence policy. This serves to undercut resistance to the imposed aspect of the treatment. The anger diary (Week 6) is a basic tool to improve the men's ability to detect and manage their anger. It requires them to specifically state what triggered their anger as objectively as possible (under the trigger column), to list how they knew they were angry (what physical or cognitive cues told them so), to rate their anger severity on a scale where ten is their own personal extreme, and to describe their "talk up" thoughts (their thoughts as their anger escalates) and their "talk down" thoughts (their thoughts as their anger diminishes). Most clients have some initial difficulty with the latter.

Comparison of the "trigger" and "talk-up" columns of the anger diary will assist the therapist in identifying the interpretations and assumptions that generate and sustain anger as a consequence of the client's perception of the trigger (see also Ellis).[7] Assumptions of malevolent intent or what Beck called "hostile attributions" (that the action of the other person was done intentionally, to hurt them) are frequent with angry clients.[8] We have seen that Eckhardt and his colleagues (see Chapter 8) found that the cognitive factors from Beck's analysis that were most predictive of abusiveness were (in order of importance) hostile attributions, magnification, dichotomous thinking (which is also a borderline trait), and arbitrary inference.[9]

Group discussion should help the client see that alternative interpretations of his spouse's actions are both possible and probable. This exercise can also be used to evaluate the client's ability to empathize with the other person. Lack of empathy itself sustains an anger response and has been therapeutically handled by "compassion workshops" for spousal abuse.[10]

Later sessions address "self soothing" as a stress-reduction technique that also serves to lower anger arousal. Wilhelm Reich describes character armour as the result of storing tension in the fascia or connective tissue of the body.[11] Since many assaultive men react to a build-up of physical tension, it is important to teach them how to maintain tension within acceptable levels through daily routines of breathing and stretching. A variety of useful stretching programs exist that can be combined with breathing and breath-control exercises to develop useful tension self-management techniques (see, for example, Kabat-Zinn).[12] The didactic goal here is to teach effective tension management to lessen the reliance on abusive outbursts to diminish tension.

Borderline clients can benefit from the tension management aspect of the group because cyclical tension build-ups are a major part of their abusiveness. In working with cyclical or borderline clients, it is important to ensure that the therapist is consistent from week to week. Any alterations in the client's relationship with the therapist can then be pointed out as part of the clients' changeability, and cues can be elicited to help the client track his changes (see also Dutton and Winters).[13] Once a man can recognize and chart anger (or another relevant emotion), he can then express it to his partner in an assertive way. My groups use a DESC script (Describe, Express, Specify Positive Consequences) for an assertiveness exercise and role-play it with the men, inviting them to tell us how their assertiveness might be sabotaged by their spouse. This exercise is presented as a negotiation tool, not as a control tool.

When empathic listening, anger control, and assertiveness skills have reached an acceptable level, the participants are prepared for group completion. Some men are asked to repeat the group. Relapse prevention includes listing high-risk situations and having a clear plan for management, staying in touch with "24/7 support buddies" (chosen during the group), and returning to the group voluntarily when anger or stress levels begin to increase. Excellent program guides for CBT with abuse groups include Wexler, and Murphy and Eckhardt, which are written for the therapist, and Sonkin and Durphy, which is written for the client.[14]

Treatments of this kind have tended to produce acceptable results. Dutton, Bodnarchuk, Kropp, Hart, and Ogloff, using Canadian Police Information Centre records, followed group completers and dropouts for up to eleven years looking for recidivism.[15] Group completers had a 23 percent recidivism rate for up to eleven years afterwards, whereas non-completers had a 50 percent rate. The presence of personality disorder in clients reduced treatment success.[16] Babcock et al. established a d' of .34 (one-third of a standard deviation) in quasi-experimental designs for the twenty-two treatment groups they studied, though these were mainly hybrids of Duluth and CBT.[17] Babcock et al. concluded that one type of treatment could not be shown superior to the other (since few "pure forms" were found). Techniques that enhanced treatment retention increased the effect size for a CBT group, which Babcock et al. indicated could be viewed as a harbinger of potentially powerful intervention.[18]

There are several ways to increase the treatment success of court-mandated therapy. These methods apply to court-mandated treatment some established CBT techniques that are successfully used for other problems. Moreover, a rich psychology of intimate violence perpetrators has developed since the first wave of treatment was developed. This research has unearthed the emotions, cognitions, and situational interactions that combine to generate and support abusive behaviour. Such features constitute what may be called the infrastructure of abuse.

The Associated Features of Assaultiveness

As reviewed above in Chapter 10, Dutton has shown empirically a strong relationship between borderline traits in male perpetrators and intimate abusiveness.[19] A constellation of personality features (BPO, high anger, fearful attachment, chronic trauma symptoms, and recollections of paternal rejection) were all statistically related to IPV in the studies reported above. Each of these features of abusiveness is a potential target for treatment.

Attachment and Abusiveness

If early experiences influence adult abusiveness, attachment theory might provide a valuable perspective on the etiology of abusiveness. Bowlby viewed interpersonal anger as arising from frustrated attachment needs and as a form of "protest behaviour" directed at regaining contact with an attachment figure.[20] He viewed dysfunctional anger as increasing the distance from the attachment object.

In turn, chronic childhood frustration of attachment needs may lead to adult proneness to react with extreme anger (which I refer to as "intimacy-anger") when relevant attachment cues are present. Thus, attachment theory suggests that an assaultive male's violent outbursts may be a form of protest behaviour directed at his attachment figure (in this case, a sexual partner) and precipitated by perceived threats of separation or abandonment. As reviewed above, "Fearful" attachment pattern is most strongly associated with intimacy-anger. Fearful individuals desire social contact and intimacy but experience pervasive interpersonal distrust and fear of rejection. This style manifests itself in hypersensitivity to rejection (rejection-sensitivity) and active avoidance of close relationships where rejection could occur. While the Fearful share anxiety over abandonment with another insecurely attached group (called Preoccupied), their avoidance orientation may lead to more chronic frustration of attachment needs. There are now several empirical studies relating attachment insecurity to IPV (see Chapter 10).[21] Mikulincer found (as had Dutton et al., and Schore) that attachment style was related to a failure to regulate negative emotions in intimate relationships.[22]

Bowlby had identified several therapeutic tasks for insecure attachment: creating a safe place, or Secure Base, for the client to explore thoughts, feelings, and experiences regarding self and attachment figures; exploring current relationships with attachment figures; and exploring the relationship with psychotherapist as an attachment figure.[23] What is essential for CBT in attachment therapy (as for success of CBT with other foci) is the establishment of a therapeutic bond between the therapist and client. Not until this bond is established will the client provide genuine descriptions of threat stimuli.

Attachment and Psychotherapy

Over the past ten years, a number of individuals have begun to explore how the body of knowledge of attachment theory would apply to clinical practice. Dutton and Sonkin have recently developed and applied attachment concepts to therapy. Sonkin advocates forming a secure therapist-client base from which feelings and thoughts can be safely explored.[24]

Fonagy says the hallmark of secure attachment is the ability to reflect on one's internal emotional experience and make sense of it (to introspect), and at the same time to reflect on the mind of another (to empathize).[25] One can immediately see how these capacities are imbued in the infant through sensitive attunement by the caregiver. When a caregiver reads the verbal and non-verbal cues of the child and reflects them back, the child sees himself or herself through the eyes of the attachment figure. It is through this attunement and interactive communication process that the seeds of the developing self are planted and realized. Insecurely attached individuals lack this empathetic function either because their emotional responses are so repressed, as in the case of the Dismissing attachment status, or so exacerbated, as in the case of the Preoccupied attachment status, that they are unable to understand either their own internal experience or that of the other. When either Dismissing or Preoccupied is the method of regulating the attachment behavioural system, the capacity for understanding oneself and others is compromised.

Jeremy Holmes describes the narratives of insecurely attached individuals.[26] He refers to story-making and story-breaking. In the case of Dismissing attachment, where the story is restricted to reduce the possibility of dysphoric affect, the clinician is helping the patient create a story that is coherent, full of memory, and with manageable affect. In the case of Preoccupied attachment, where anxiety over-runs the client's story so that it becomes convoluted and saturated with anger and disappointment, the therapist's role is to help break the negative cycle of the narrative, manage the affect more productively, and create a story that is balanced and coherent.

Allan Schore's two most recent books go beyond integration of developmental theory and psychotherapy to describe the neuroscience of attachment and the interaction of the brains of parent and infant.[27] Schore speaks in depth about the neurobiology of the developing mind during the first three years of life and how the right brain processes are integrally involved in attachments and the development of the self. He spells out clearly how insensitive ("misattuned") parenting leads to emotion dysregulation patterns in childhood and later in adulthood. He understands insecure attachment as emotion dysregulation and therefore sees the goal of psychotherapy as being to learn new capacities to manage attachment distress. He regards psychotherapy as the process of changing neural patterns in the brain, the right brain in particular.

Daniel Siegel, like Schore, has expanded our understanding of how attachment relationships and the brain influence each other.[28] Siegel is particularly interested in how the right and left brain work together (or don't, in the case of insecure attachment) to create a coherent life story and way of responding to relationships and life. He applies complexity theory to psychological functioning, arguing that complex systems are more adaptive and stable than are rigid systems. His book examines not only attachment but also related topics such as emotion, memory, trauma, and consciousness. He draws from numerous disciplines to help the reader understand that no single focus of study, such as psychology, will have all the answers to such questions as "what is mental health?"

Each of these authors has expanded our understanding of how to incorporate into the practice of psychotherapy the vast body of knowledge that has accumulated in attachment theory. However, we are just beginning to understand this interface, and many questions remain unanswered. To clinicians, the relevance of attachment is that, in essence, attachment categories tell a story about how emotion has been regulated, what experiences have been allowed into consciousness, and to what degree individuals have been able to make meaningful their primary relationships.

One way of conceptualizing attachment status is that it is a form of affect regulation that occurs in the general context of relationships and in the specific context of how individuals deal with emotions associated with separation, loss, and reunion. Attachment theory therefore seems relevant to one of the most significant areas affecting the work of psychotherapists: the therapeutic alliance.

The Therapist as an Attachment Figure

Bowlby believed that intimate attachments to other human beings form the hub around which a person's life revolves.[29] From these intimate attachments a person draws strength and enjoyment of life. He also believed that one such attachment may be a person's therapist. Bowlby describes the five tasks of attachment-informed psychotherapy.[30] One of those tasks is to explore the relationship with a psychotherapist as an attachment figure. Bowlby believed that the therapist would be viewed as an attachment figure regardless of whether or not the client is aware of this fact. The therapist-client relationship, like the parent-child relationship, will manifest the same four characteristics described earlier – proximity maintenance (the client will seek out the therapist to discuss problems), separation distress (the client will experience some degree of distress if the therapist is needed but not available), safe haven (the client in distress will seek help from the therapist), and secure base (the client will use the therapeutic relationship as a base to explore the inner and outer worlds).

The attachment of the therapeutic relationship, like the attachment of the child-parent relationship, develops in a succession of stages: pre-attachment, attachment-in-the-making, clear-cut attachment, and goal-corrected partnership. And like the childhood patterns of attachment that appear in the stressful Strange Situation procedure, the natural ruptures and reunions of psychotherapy activate the patterns of the attachment behavioural system. For individuals who have had particularly unpleasant experiences in their family of origin, simply walking into the therapist's office is likely to cause anxiety. But in this unusual type of relationship, clients can have these patterns brought to their attention, reappraise their functionality, and learn new methods of regulating affect.

But how does one actually facilitate this process? Schore writes about the non-verbal communication of primary emotions and the importance of "contingent communication" between therapist and client.[31] Contingent communication begins when Person A sends a signal to Person B – these signals are both verbal and non-verbal signals (facial expressions, body movements and gestures, tones of voice, timing and intensity of response, etc.). Person B needs to recognize the signal, interpret it correctly, and send back a signal to Person A. This response is not simply a mirror of what was received but an acknowledgment that Person B has received the original signal and understands it – in other words "We're on the same wavelength." When this occurs, the sender feels able to continue the communication process. Siegel argues that contingent communication is the basis of healthy, collaborative communication and facilitates positive attachments.

In psychotherapy, most communication between the therapist and patient occurs on a non-verbal level. The role of the therapist is to watch for non-verbal signals (a right-brain-to-right-brain process) and work to interpret them and respond to them appropriately. This seems very elementary, and each of us probably remembers a talk in graduate school about the value of non-verbal communication. Yet, if what these writers are telling us is true, then it seems that the ability to read and interpret these non-verbal signals is more than a therapeutic trick we occasionally pull out of our bag.

It is the basis of developing the therapeutic alliance, which in turn is the key to positive therapy outcome.

"Now moments" occur in therapy – flashes of interaction between therapist and client that are rich in potential for change and growth for the client, for the therapist, and for their relationship. Stern describes the process of therapy as moving along in a somewhat spontaneous and sometimes random manner until these moments occur.[32] (Other excellent sources for treating attachment disorders include texts by Stosny and by Clulow.)[33]

Incorporating Treatment for Borderline Traits into CBT for Assaultive Men

A recent editorial in the *American Journal of Psychiatry* argued, referring to borderlines, that "in no other disorder is the therapists' ability to establish a therapeutic alliance so tested."[34] Given the borderline traits in spouse abusers and the unconvinced "precontemplation" phase in which many of them arrive in mandated treatment, this dictum is of the utmost importance.[35] Identification of specific attachment-generated phenomena and concomitant management techniques form another part of attachment therapy. For example, difficulties in reacting to separation (even daily separations and intolerance of lateness) should be chronicled and addressed in group. Abuse cycles, whether addressed as a borderline trait, or as an aspect of ambivalent attachment, need to be addressed. What thoughts does the client have on a daily basis regarding his or her partner and the relationship? Does he or she cognitively express concern over the partner's leaving or dissatisfaction with the partner's closeness? Figure 15.2 shows similarities in CBT applications to four targets.

15.2 Comparison of treatments

CBT anger	DBT borderlines	Attachment	Trauma
Therapeutic bond	Therapeutic consistency	Secure base	Therapeutic consistency
Acceptance of client (empathy)	Radical acceptance attunement (empathy)	Non-judgmental	Empathy
Anger diary	Core skills	Attachment-fear diary	Anxiety/trauma symptom diary
Change anger/abuse	Change impulsivity	Change attachment-anxiety	Lower trauma-based anxiety

Currently, there is no focus on borderline issues in standard CBT treatment for assaultiveness. Dialectical Behaviour Therapy (DBT) has traditionally been used with borderline clients having problems with suicidality.[36] Hence, a well-developed behavioural therapy treatment for borderlines exists, although it has two different foci from CBT for batterers: its focus on self-directed aggression and its adoption of "radical acceptance" as a starting point.[37] According to Linehan, radical acceptance is an acceptance of the client's essential self, used to mitigate an assumed lifetime of non-validation within the family of origin. In the case of abusive clients, a lifetime of shaming may constitute the form of invalidation. Nevertheless, it is a behavioural therapy with many processes similar to those of CBT: both teach such skills as emotion regulation, interpersonal communication, arousal management, and stress tolerance (called "core mindfulness" and involving self-soothing). The integration of CBT-DBT requires simultaneously accepting the client's non-abusive selfhood and contracting with the client to sustain an effort to change abusive behaviours. However, it does not require double the didactic content of the treatment, because there is much overlap between DBT and CBT. A particular strength of the DBT program is careful pre-planning to circumvent obstacles to program completion. DBT requires daily skill practice and diary-keeping.

Even something as apparently complex as management of the transition from the abuse phase to the contrition phase of the abuse cycle can be managed by applying CBT techniques (see Figure 15.3).

15.3 Abuse cycle management: Some techniques

1 If the couple is relatively non-violent and the woman feels safe:
- The man can learn to cue himself *from observing her*. For example: "You are getting withdrawn, is something bothering you?"
- The therapist should role-play these scenarios with the man and explore any feelings he has in response to these cues from his wife.

2 If there is still some violence occurring in the relationship:
- The man must learn to cue himself *from his own thought patterns*. For example, denigrating ("bitch tape") ruminations about his wife have to be recognized, stopped, and replaced with breathing-stretching exercises.
- If any escalation occurs, a call must go to a "buddy" who will assist in tension-reduction via "talking it out," fast walking or jogging, and breathing exercises.

If step two (the buddy) fails, the therapist must be called.

CBT for Trauma

Abusive men in the Dutton studies had elevated levels of trauma symptoms as described above.[38] Hembree and Foa have outlined a variety of treatments for PTSD including psychopharmacological treatment and CBT.[39] (Maiuro and Avery have also suggested that psychopharmacological adjuncts to CBT with abusive clients has promise.)[40] Rothbaum and collegues reviewed CBT for trauma, outlining eight different approaches: exposure therapy, systematic desensitization, stress inoculation training, cognitive processing therapy, cognitive therapy, assertiveness training, biofeedback, relaxation training, and various combinations of the above.[41] From the above outline of CBT with abusive men, it can be seen that assertiveness training, relaxation training, and some forms of stress inoculation training are already in use for abusiveness.

Nevertheless, little is done to address specific anxiety sources (e.g., abandonment fears, jealousy) that Dutton stresses are the motivational basis of the interpersonal controlling behaviours in these clients.[42] Identifying anxiety sources in treatment and then using systematic desensitization, relaxation, and stress inoculation to enable the client to control the anxiety would be the recommended strategy in CBT for PTSD. This would involve construction of anxiety gradients, with relaxation practice to mastery at each increasing level (including breathing retraining). Potential anxiety sources include childhood exposure to physical abuse, lack of a safe haven, and abandonment. Skills would be developed in group with an expectation of their being used in real-world situations. Use of a "24/7 buddy system" (with clients co-contracting to provide haven and support for each other around the clock) as fallback is recommended as a safety device. Again, adding a focus on trauma symptoms to treatment of abusers does not require extensive additional content since many issues are already covered by CBT or DBT. It simply requires a specific focus on the trauma symptoms, their identification, and stress tolerance skills (which are part of DBT training).

CBT for Substance Abuse

Larimer and Marlatt have developed a cognitive-behavioural treatment for addictive behaviours, especially substance abuse.[43] Substance abuse is so closely connected to spouse abuse that many programs require treatment for substance abuse before beginning treatment for spouse abuse.[44] From Dutton's model, substance abuse is connected to Borderline Personality Organization because it provides medication for aversive arousal in a population that cannot self-soothe and therefore both drinks and batters to dissipate tension.[45] Hence substance abuse problems are frequent in spouse abuse populations and require modification. Marlatt's CBT model includes mediation, covert sensitization involving negative imagery, and contingency management (which restructures the addicted individual's environment in such a way that positive behaviours are reinforced and negative behaviours receive negative or neutral consequences).[46] As described above, CBT for spouse abuse also uses contingency management techniques, including the establishment of the "24/7 buddy triads" to act as emergency support for each other. These sources can also supply positive social support for alcohol cessation. Larimer and Marlatt reported success of these procedures in a small-sample outcome study.[47]

Skills training includes training in "drinking skills" (monitoring and cessation), blood alcohol discrimination, interpersonal skills, and vocational skills. Skills training is part of both CBT and DBT, so the concept of skill acquisition is already established in a blended CBT program. In addition, assertiveness and interpersonal skills are part of the core curriculum of both CBT and DBT. Since alcohol abuse is often a dysfunctional form of stress reduction, the stress management skills used in a CBT program (relaxation, stretching, breathing exercises) already aid this aspect of substance management.

One of the stronger aspects of the substance management program is relapse prevention, again an aspect of both CBT and DBT. For substance abuse management, as with anger management, individuals are trained to identify high-risk situations and the discriminative stimuli that signal their approach and to develop coping skills (assertiveness, alternative behaviours, leaving the situation). CBT for spouse abuse also contains all these coping skills, the latter being covered by "time-out" cards that list instructions to be followed when the client is angered (tell your spouse you are taking a time out, leave the house, do not drive or drink, walk until "negative thoughts" subside, remind yourself that you are angry, replace the negative thoughts with positive thoughts, repeat until calm, if unable to calm the self, call a 24/7 buddy). Substance abuse treatment also involves cue exposure where the client is exposed to a sight or smell of a substance without consumption. This is parallel to the role-playing of conflicted argument with the client's spouse in CBT for spouse abuse. Marlatt's outcome studies found that relapse was most likely in clients who lacked effective responses to high-risk situations.[48] Recidivism is an obvious concern for spouse abuse treatment, with recidivism rates of about 21 percent according to police statistics in an eleven-year, nationwide Canadian follow up.[49] The substance abuse treatment literature suggests that increasing role-play practice of conflict skills may be an effective method of reducing recidivism.

CBT for Psychopathy

No area of treatment outcome is more controversial than whether psychopaths are treatable, yet men with antisocial tendencies (some of whom may be psychopathic) are frequently mandated for spouse-assault treatment.[50] Hare and Wong explain what happens:

> The prevailing view is that the attitudes and behaviours of psychopaths are difficult or impossible to modify with traditional forms of treatment, intervention, and management. Indeed, many clinicians will not even attempt to treat psychopaths, and an increasing number of forensic institutions take the position that it is cost-effective to exclude psychopaths from their treatment programs. The reasons for the recalcitrance of psychopaths are not hard to find. Unlike other individuals, including most offenders, psychopaths often appear to suffer little personal distress, seem perfectly satisfied with themselves, see little wrong with their attitudes and behaviour, and seek treatment only when it is in their best interests to do so, such as when attempting to avoid prison or when seeking probation or parole. It is, therefore, not surprising that they appear to derive little benefit from traditional correctional programs, particularly those aimed at the reduction of intrapsychic turmoil and the development of self-esteem, empathy, and conscience.[51]

Several early studies suggested that psychopaths did worse after treatment.[52] However, Wong concluded that we actually know very little about the treatment of psychopaths.[53] He noted that most available studies were deficient in one or more of the criteria considered necessary for a methodologically sound outcome study: (1) the valid and reliable assessment of psychopathy based on clinical tradition and the work of Cleckley and operationalized in the Hare Psychopathy Checklist-Revised (PCL-R), (2) an adequate description of the treatment program, (3) an appropriate treatment evaluation with an adequate follow-up period, and (4) a suitable control group.[54] Out of seventy-four empirical studies of the treatment of psychopathy, sociopathy, and antisocial personality disorder, only two met all criteria.[55]

Losel believed some therapeutic success could be achieved with psychopaths in a highly structured "token economy" environment where acting according to the rules was in their self-interest.[56] However, most court-mandated treatment programs meet once a week and cannot provide this type of 24/7 structure. Mulloy et al. argued that these prior studies were unduly pessimistic since definitions of psychopathy varied from study to study and no longitudinal follow-up was done.[57] The studies used a "multi-modal" program where the predominant treatment modality was CBT and emphasis was placed on the creation of a prosocial group norm and nego-tiation.[58] Recent developments in discovering subcategories of psychopaths also suggest differential treatability, with a category called "pseudo-psychopath" emulating psychopathic indifference but retaining empathic capabilities.[59]

How might assessed psychopaths (using the Psychopathy Checklist – Re-vised, PCL-R) be dealt with in court-mandated treatment?[60] Hare and Wong have recently written a manual for correctional treatment of psychopaths.[61] They stress focusing on: (1) clients' responsibility for their own behaviour, (2) clients' need to learn more pro-social ways to function, (3) consequences of breaking the law (i.e., self-interest), and (4) opportunities for applying clients' strengths and needs to lawful enterprises. Hare and Wong do not attempt to increase empathy or conscience, just to diminish violence and antisocial acts by therapy, showing it is in a client's self-interest to learn to behave in a more prosocial fashion. Effective policing is essential for this model to be convincing, because the criminal justice system rarely resembles a token economy. Also, the Hare and Wong treatment model was designed for institutions; it is not known whether the model would work effectively with an outpatient population treated for a few hours each week.

However, Hervé's finding that idiopathic and secondary psychopathy ex-ists led him to emphasize new possibilities for treatment:

Although additional research is required before applying these results to practical settings, the idea that there may be psychopathic subtypes has certain implications for the criminal justice system. Indeed, if these subtypes have unique etiological histories, these findings would have significant treatment implications; each subtype may require a different treatment approach. For example, idiopathic psychopaths, whose disorder is thought to be rooted in biology, will likely be immune to psychotherapies aimed at "treating" their emotional deficit. While pharmacotherapy may prove to be useful in this regard, the current state of affairs suggests that idiopathic psychopaths require a treat-ment regimen that teaches them how to cope with, not "cure," their unique emotional constitution ... The most successful approach in this respect will likely be one that is heavily behaviorally loaded, supplemented with cognitive interventions to ensure treatment compliance. More cognitive and dynamic therapies, however, may be useful in treating other aspects of the disorder (i.e., interpersonal, lifestyle, and antisocial aspects), especially those features with strong environmental (past or current) underpinnings ... The use of a treatment prototype is akin to a harm reduction approach to therapy; the basic premise would be to reduce the harm associated with psychopathy rather than abolish it altogether. Turning classic and macho psychopaths into manipulative ones might be considered a positive treatment outcome for society in that it is relatively better to lose one's money than one's life. Clearly, the end goal should be to reduce all antisocial manifestation of the disorder, as being defrauded, for example, can have significant adverse consequences for victims, consequences that should not be minimized (e.g., some individuals may commit suicide after losing all of their life savings). Such therapeutic attempts, however, will have to be carefully conducted as to not turn a relatively benign psychopath into a socially devastating one (i.e., turn a manipulative into a classic; e.g., Ogloff et al.[62]).

In contrast to the treatment of idiopathic psychopathy, pseudo-psychopaths may have an emotional constitution that enables them to benefit from traditional treatment programs (i.e., those relying on empathy and responsibility taking); programs that consistently fail (at the very least) with primary psychopaths. Unlike that suggested for idiopathic psychopathy, the treatment regimen of the pseudopsychopath will likely need to focus directly on his/her affective dysfunction and the causal agent(s) responsible for its manifestation.[63]

Court-Mandated Treatment of Female Batterers

Given that Stets and Straus found three times as many women as men used severe violence against a non-violent partner, treatment for female batterers seems a necessity.[64] Curiously, little has been written on it. Dowd and Renzetti both call for a more thoughtful and complex analysis than that offered by the dominant feminist view, which has largely precluded treatment of aggressive women.[65] Nevertheless, the dominant view of male perpetrator/female victim pervades female perpetrator treatment as well. Hamberger and Potente described their court-mandated sample as "battered women who have gotten caught up in a pattern of violence that, most often, they did not initiate and do not control."[66] Hamberger and Potente claim that only three out of sixty-seven women were primary perpetrators. In a later study,

---

15.4 Common features of successful therapeutic approaches

All successful therapies involve the following features:
1 Therapeutic alliance between subject and therapist: consistent, accepting, non-judgmental
2 Acceptance of self along with strategy to change problem behaviour
3 Increased emotional awareness
4 Regulation of emotions via mindfulness
5 Stress management

Hamberger described a sample of fifty-seven female perpetrators as having been in prior abusive relationships and having been exposed to father-to-mother violence.[67] A question is raised about the apparent discrepancy between Hamberger and Potente's data showing so few female instigators and the Moffitt et al. and Stets and Strauss studies cited in Chapter 6, which found that females were even more violent than males in large community samples.[68] Furthermore, the female violence in relationships was predictable by their antisocial behaviour three years prior to entering the relationship. Hamberger and Potente's sample was court-mandated and may represent another example of the criminal justice system's avoiding arresting women. Based on the Moffitt et al. data (and other data reviewed in Chapter 6), we would expect to see more females in court-mandated treatment and many of them being the instigators of aggression.

Busch and Rosenberg found that arrested female perpetrators were just as violent as were males.[69] This study used criminal justice data to compare women and men arrested for domestic violence on their levels of violence, reported victimization, general criminality, and substance abuse. Participants were forty-five women and forty-five men convicted of domestic violence between 1996 and 1998. Results indicate that women were less likely than men to have a history of domestic violence offences and non-violent crimes. They were also more likely to report that they had been injured or victimized by their partners at the time of their arrest. However, in other ways women and men were similar: they were equally likely to have used severe violence, to have inflicted severe injuries on their victims, to have previously committed violence against non-intimates, and to have been using drugs or alcohol at the time of their arrest.

Carney and Buttell evaluated a sixteen-week treatment program for female batterers in South Carolina that was "similar to the national model as it was designed for males."[70] They measured spouse-specific assertiveness, controlling behaviours, and propensity for abusiveness (using the PAS).[71] Of the participants, 85 percent had been arrested for spouse assault. Significant drops post-treatment were found on the PAS scores and use of passive-aggression, but controlling behaviours increased.

Dowd's review seems more motivated to show that men are the worse aggressors than to examine female violence in its own right. If women are getting hurt more than men, why are they using aggression? The statistics reviewed in Chapters 5 and 6 above do not suggest that men always start the fight. In any event, whether male or female clients are treated, a thorough assessment is necessary to evaluate the seriousness and locus of instigation of bidirectional violence. Renzetti found substance abuse, dependency, and jealousy were clinically significant in battering lesbians.[72] Margolies and Leeder found dependency, jealousy, and black-and-white thinking clinically significant in lesbian batterers.[73] All these issues surfaced in male heterosexual perpetrators.

Leisring et al. suggest an important clinical goal for female perpetrators is to stop their violence because it's a predictor of male violence.[74] Again, no one seems worried about male victims getting hurt. The University of Massachusetts treatment program for women has some didactic components in common with men's treatment programs: anger recognition and control, personal responsibility, empathy, time-outs, communication training, reframing cognitions, substance abuse. (The Massachusetts program contains essentially all the components ruled out by the State of Georgia in CBT for men; see Chapter 14.) Leisring et al. modify men's treatment to include increased emphasis on personal safety for the woman client, attention to one's own needs, increased emphasis on PTSD in creating anger control problems, increased attention to conditions that undermine mood stability, less emphasis on power and control. The authors argue, based on the NVAWS data, that men fear their partners less than women do, so power and control issues are not as important for women.[75] I will not revisit the reasons why crime victim surveys misrepresent the larger population. Suffice it to say that Follingstad et al. found power and control issues to be greater for women than for men.[76]

Henning and his colleagues compared female to male domestic violence offenders.[77] Rising numbers of women arrested for domestic violence present many theoretical and practical challenges. At the theoretical level, there is ongoing debate about whether women are as aggressive as men. At the practical level, little research is available to guide how female cases are handled in the criminal justice system. In this study, data were obtained regarding demographic characteristics, mental health functioning, and childhood familial dysfunction for a large sample of male (N = 2,254) and female (N = 281) domestic violence offenders. The women were demographically similar to the men, and few differences were noted in their childhood experiences. Women were more likely than men to have previously attempted suicide, whereas more men had conduct problems in childhood and substance abuse in adulthood. Compared to the male offenders, women reported more symptoms of personality dysfunction and mood disorder. Ninety-five percent of the women offenders had one or more personality disorders above 75 on the MCMI-III, compared to 70 percent of the male offenders. Females were *six times* more likely to have borderline scores above 75, although it is treated as a severe personality pathology on the MCMI.

The fledgling literature on female offenders shows that the issues of focus in male treatment groups are also relevant to female offenders. Control is an issue, and as we saw in Chapter 11, Moffitt et al. found negative emotionality to be a risk factor for abuse in both genders.[78] Negative emotionality consisted of reactions to stress, use of aggressive interpersonal strategies, and negative expectations of other people. All these issues are covered in the CBT treatment focus for males. Henning et al. found borderline personality to be prominent in court-mandated women.[79] Henning et al. reported that an informal analysis of the University of Washington lab's data on self-referred violent couples revealed peaks for borderline on the women in that study (previously unreported).[80] Hence, the focus on identity issues, consistency, and self-soothing described above for borderline male clients may be even more important with women.

15.5 Targets for treatment of female perpetrators of intimate violence

---

1 Female perpetrators are six times as likely as men to be above 75 on the Borderline scale.[1]
2 Female perpetrators tend to have higher rates of personality disorder than male offenders (95 percent vs. 70 percent above 75 on one or more scales of the MCMI – III).[2]
3 Lesbian batterers exhibit dependency, jealousy, black-and-white thinking, and substance abuse at clinically significant levels.[3]

NOTES: **1** K. Henning and L. Feder, "A comparison of men and women arrested for domestic violence: Who presents the greater risk?" *Journal of Family Violence* 19, 2 (2004): 69-80.
2 K. Henning, A. Jones, and R. Holford, "Treatment needs of women arrested for domestic violence: A comparison with male offenders," *Journal of Interpersonal Violence* 18, 8 (2003): 839-56.   **3** C. Renzetti, *Violent Betrayal: Partner Abuse in Lesbian Relationships* (Newbury Park, CA: Sage, 1994), 57; L. Margolies and E. Leeder, "Violence at the door: Treatment of lesbian batterers," *Violence against Women* 1, 2 (1995): 139-57, 153.

Nevertheless, a mystery is presented by the data. As we saw, Stets and Straus found a female-severe/male-non-violent pattern to be three times as likely as the reverse pattern.[81] Archer found females to be only slightly more injured than males by interpersonal violence.[82] So why do the criminal justice system samples of female offenders have such a large subgroup whom many authors deem to be victims of violence?[83] And why does this group of female offenders (who are supposedly victims) nevertheless resemble male offenders in their psychological profiles on the MCMI?

Therapeutic Bonding

Regardless of the gender of the client, therapeutic bonding is essential for treatment success.[84] Schore's landmark work focuses clinical attention on the connection between emotional regulation and attachment disruption during the early years of life (as may occur in abusive families of origin), mediated by right hemisphere development. In light of this connection, Schore has suggested principles of therapeutic treatment (Figure 15.6).[85]

15.6 Schore's principles of therapeutic treatment

---

1 Psychopathology is arrested affect regulation, so the treatment model should be matched to the developmental level of the patient.
2 Right-brain affect regulation is a fundamental process that needs to be addressed in therapy.
3 Therapeutic empathy serves to attune client to therapist via the right brain.
4 Clients' capacity for attachment combines with therapists' facilitating behaviours to generate a therapeutic working relationship.
5 Autonomic states must be synchronized.
6 "Primitive affects" (shame, terror, rage, despair), being unconscious, need to be identified and integrated.
7 Therapy becomes more process-oriented and less skill-oriented.
8 Defences are right-brain non-conscious strategies of emotional regulation for avoiding affect that is too difficult to tolerate and can "traumatically disorganize the self system."
9 The therapeutic process relationship is viewed as "interactive repair."
10 The primary objective of treatment is the restoration of the patient's capacity for self-regulation – to flexibly regulate emotional states through interactions with others and alone (auto-regulation).
11 The long-term objective is to reorganize insecure attachment models into secure models that allow for greater stability in novel situations and a coherent and unified sense of self.

SOURCE: Adapted and condensed from A.N. Schore, *Affect Regulation and the Repair of the Self* (New York: Norton, 2003), 279-81.

These treatment goals re-orient treatment as an enterprise that has affective repair as its goal. This has been largely lost in the CBT orientation of batterer treatment, in which only "anger management," jealousy, and negative emotions are dealt with cognitively. Schore reminds us that in the process of therapy the interactions of therapist and client are at least as important as is the didactic aspect of treatment in generating repair. Of course, Duluth models cannot utilize this remedy, because they are diametrically opposed to the principles of treatment, but then, they were not designed by therapists.

16 Rethinking the Response to Domestic Violence

Chapter 12 presented Linda Mills' thoughtful re-evaluation of criminal justice system policy. Mills argued that mandatory arrest and no-drop policies violate the wishes of many female "victims."[1] As a result, prosecutors find that over 55 percent of women refuse to cooperate in prosecuting their partners.[2] Mills sees this as a systemic dismissal of the wishes of battered women. In the 1970s they were not consulted when police decided not to arrest. Now they are not consulted when police do arrest. Any woman who chooses to stay in an abusive relationship is viewed as trapped rather than as making a choice, even though the abuse may have diminished or abated (one-third of abusive relationships cease without intervention), or for emotional, religious, or cultural reasons. Lesbians, gays, and transgendered persons feel the current policies do not apply to them at all. Many immigrants feel the same, and hence avoid prosecution.

Mandatory arrest has unintended consequences. Changes in social policy require constant re-evaluation based on knowledge of how policy operates in practice. Maiuro et al. (Chapter 14) made this point in the specific context of re-staffing state and county commissions on domestic violence. Grauwiler and Mills examine the "primary assumptions" of feminism, as we have done above in Chapters 5 and 6, and also find them wanting and unsupported. They feel it is a mistake to treat intimate violence as equal to stranger violence and thus deserving of the same severe penalties: "Violence that occurs in intimate relationships is not conducive to a paradigm that assigns all the blame to one party while wholly exonerating the other. Like all intimate relationships, even violent ones have an underlying dynamic that can help illuminate the origins of the violence."[3]

Grauwiler and Mills review much of the data on female violence and the psychological causes of violence in men that we have presented throughout this book because they argue that this helps us to understand the dynamic of violence. An outcome of their review is the possibility of triage of domestic violence calls into three categories. The first and most serious involves extensive injuries to the victim, and incarceration of the perpetrator is warranted for victim protection. The second does not involve serous injury and does not warrant incarceration, but the victim wants the violence to stop, personality disorders seem present, and there is a high risk of repeat violence. With this group the blended behavioural therapy outlined in the previous chapter might be tried.

The third category includes cases in which the violence is bilateral and does not involve serious injury, and the victim does not desire criminal justice proceedings. If the community has the ability to participate, the victim may opt for an Intimate Abuse Circle (IAC) for restorative justice. The IAC is described by Mills and by Grauwiler and Mills,[4] who draw on John Braithwaite's notion of conferences between victims and perpetrators done in the midst of a caring community.[5] Aboriginals in Canada call these "justice circles." By consensus, the group develops a contract that restores to the victim what has been lost (e.g., dignity, property). The contract must be agreed to by both sides and is prepared only after two events have occurred: (1) a full examination of the impact of the violence on those most affected and (2) a genuine expression of remorse by the violent offenders for their actions. Aboriginals call this the "healing process." Conferences can only be formed with the consent of both parties and the participation of the care community. Restorative justice presents a radical alternative to the mainstream "adversarial" justice system where both sides spin the truth to self-advantage. Braithwaite provides considerable empirical evidence that indicates high levels of victim satisfaction from a process that leaves victims feeling empowered by their participation in the conference. The offender's apology offers symbolic reparation and enhanced empathy for the offender (sometimes as a prerequisite for making the apology).

Tolman warns that if restorative justice were to be used, numerous safeguards for women would be necessary.[6] He cautions that "face-to-face contact must not be required" and that "such proceedings must not be used in exchange for dropping charges or orders of restitution in return for restitution."[7] However, according to Grauwiler and Mills, the current mandatory "arrest-no drop" system requires a woman to testify against her abuser and, in some cases, to travel to and from court with him.

There are two other reasons that building this informal aspect into control of abusiveness might work. Dugan found that public housing was a greater deterrent to future abuse than mandatory arrest.[8] She attributed this effect to the public nature of life there. Bringing in a community group has this effect as well. Dutton, Hart, Kennedy, and Williams found that fear of friends' reactions (social condemnation) was more of a deterrent to abusive men than fear of criminal justice system action.[9] Dutton et al. called these "sanction weights" and found that for several groups of men social condemnation was more severe than was criminal justice system action. The only exception was a group of men who had just been arrested. Many abusive men are notoriously isolated, and the community component could correct that. Moreover, the perpetrator is made accountable to the community, either singularly or as a couple, depending on the violence pattern.

Restorative justice is the creation or re-creation of relationships of meaningful social equality. The offender claims responsibility for his choices, his actions, and the consequences of his actions; these are essential components of restorative justice. A Canadian study of "family group conferences" to address child maltreatment and domestic violence found a reduction in indicators of child maltreatment and domestic violence, an advancement of children's development, and an extension of social supports.[10]

Family decision-making conferences were introduced in the Miami-Dade Juvenile Court in 1998. An evaluation study of this project in cases of child maltreatment found an increase in parent and participant satisfaction with the court process, empowerment of families as decision makers, and improved relationships between the family and the government agency in charge.

This raises an important question about conferencing: if it can improve relationships within families and between participants and outside agencies, can it address violence between partners while also improving community relations? As Kay Pranis has observed, a very important value in restorative justice is that of empowering unheard voices.[11] Restorative justice practice in the area of domestic violence can be rooted in a clear set of values and principles that coincide with the concerns of mainstream feminists in serving the needs of battered women: victim safety, victim choice, offender accountability, and system accountability.[12] Restorative conferences as part of a continuum of ongoing services, and even criminal justice intervention in some instances, can help address the violence between individuals and within families, and can facilitate community-wide healing through the participation of friends and community leaders. Historically, intervention in the area of domestic violence has always started at the grassroots level – through experimentation, advocacy, and respect for a diversity of views.

Intimate Abuse Circles

Intimate Abuse Circles, as described by Grauwiler and Mills, are a method of intervention either following an arrest or when no arrest has been made. The IAC is specifically designed for couples who choose to stay together although violence has occurred in their relationship and who seek to understand and deal with the violence rather than lock it away. Intimate Abuse

Circles are especially helpful to immigrant, minority, and religious families, where it is likely that the family will remain intact.[13] IACs may also be used in cases where the partners have children together and would like to separate in a more amicable fashion.

The IAC recognizes as a guiding principle that intimate abuse involves more than just an offender and a victim, which is different from how conferences have been imagined thus far. The IAC process recognizes that the abusive relationship probably involves a dynamic that both parties must acknowledge in order to improve how they relate to each other. The process does not involve victim-blaming but rather the recognition that even the more victimized party maintains some power in the relationship. It provides a forum for the more violent party to take full responsibility for the violence committed in the relationship, while also acknowledging that intimate relationships involve two people with their complex and sometimes conflicting needs. The IAC will enable both parties to choose members of their care communities to participate in the Circle process. Members of the care community help develop concrete and measurable methods for addressing the violent relationship. The role of the care community, including family members and community leaders, will be to participate in creating effective solutions and to help monitor and reduce the violence.

Drawing from principles of restorative justice and family group conferencing, the Intimate Abuse Circle model seeks to honour the partners' choices to remain together despite the violence. The IAC model achieves this goal by establishing within the couple's community circles of support that foster healing within their cultural context. The IAC model addresses the underlying dynamics of abuse while fostering safety for the affected parties through a formalized network of family and community supports; this can be utilized in conjunction with or instead of criminal justice interventions. This model acknowledges the reality that many people seek to end the violence but not the relationship. The circle conferences would be facilitated by professionally trained domestic violence experts who recognize oppressive dynamics and ensure they do not get reproduced in the IAC process. These professionals will guarantee that all parties speak and that the feminist value of parity is actually realized.

Here's how an IAC works. First an Intimate Abuse Assessment Team made up of mental health professionals is assigned to each case.[14] The purpose of this team is to clarify the issues in the relationship and the steps needed to address the abuse. The overall goal is to assess the appropriateness of an IAC for this particular couple. This evaluation has to take into account (1) whether the violence is mainly unilateral or bilateral, (2) the power dynamic in the couple, (3) lethality, and (4) the wishes of the individuals. Once the process is carefully explained to each separately, each is asked whether this how they want to proceed. Mills tries to get victims to move beyond revenge through the IAC process but never advocates that IACs replace criminal justice involvement for victims who wish to take the criminal justice route. Reasons for preferring a criminal justice route include the severity of injury, a desire for government involvement, a desire to end the relationship, and revenge. I emphasize these points because the feminist reaction to IACs may be typified by Tolman's response above.[15] Stubbs, for example, argues that lethality prediction is imprecise.[16] She is correct. The best we can do is to predict who the severe repeat abuser might be. An assessment team would decide against an IAC where the threat is predicted as high. In such cases, individual treatment or incarceration would be recommended. Mills's response is that eventually the couple will re-unite (even when protection orders are in place). Hence, at some point the IAC can be used to work through the anger on both sides.

This radical new model moves intimate abuse beyond the narrow parameters of traditional perceptions, reconceptualizing the issue to incorporate its nuances and dynamics. Doing so provides the opportunity to address the problem holistically and directly. It also provides a culturally specific response that addresses the unique gender dimensions of the problem, including violence by both men and women in heterosexual and homosexual relationships.[17]

The reaction to IACs seems to depend on one's view of abuse causation. Stubbs clearly takes the view that abuse is male-generated and women are victims.[18] This perspective cannot support IACs because the central need is to protect women from men. Mills's view, on the other hand, is that violence is a dynamic process to which both partners contribute, a view like that taken in family or couple therapy. I believe that both kinds of situations exist, as does a third: female-perpetrated IPV.

Strang and Braithwaite report that justice circles in Indianapolis had a 40 percent lower recidivism rate than a control group after six months and 25 percent lower after twelve months.[19] Another quasi-experimental study used with "serious adult offenders" in Winnipeg produced a recidivism rate that was one-third that of the matched control group.[20] A similar improved reduction in recidivism is reported in a study from New Zealand.[21]

Very little exists in the form of outcome evaluation of IACs. The only evaluation available on the application of justice circles to family violence is a study in Newfoundland by Burford and Pennell on "family group conferencing."[22] It was reported by Strang and Braithwaite as finding "marked reduction in both child abuse and neglect and abuse of mothers after the intervention. Thirty-two families who underwent the restorative justice intervention reduced violence by 50 percent in the year after the intervention; thirty-one control families saw it increase."[23]

My reading of this report is less optimistic. The families were from small communities and presented with at least one troubled adolescent and typically general dysfunction including physical and sexual abuse at home. The sample was culturally diverse: Inuit, Micmac, Francophone, and Irish/British. It is questionable whether the study could be replicated in an urban setting. The major treatment measure was case workers' reports of abuse before and after treatment. A set of demographically matched control families was studied as well. The sample was quite small (thirty-two treated, thirty-one control families) and the results not that promising: of the treated families, twenty had a report of child abuse in the year before the study, eleven of these families continued to abuse after the intervention: a 55 percent recidivism rate.[24] It was not made clear what treatment (if any) the control received. Burford and Pennell admit that "a majority of the [treated] and [control] families had reports made about them in both the year before and the year after the project."[25] Not inspiring.

Caution must be employed here. The use of such circles in domestic violence probably requires that participants be screened (by criminal justice system officials) for psychopathy in the perpetrator prior to using this system. Also, the couple has to have access to the "caring community" group that Mills describes. I would add victim veto and careful monitoring of community group composition by the criminal justice system professionals to ensure that no "stacking" of the community group occurs.

There's another caveat. The possibility of a caring community group must exist. Stubbs raises a good point. Is there a community group that is capable of neutrality and compassion? Mills suggested "elders ... church leaders or respected family friends."[26] Yes, where they are available. In a study cited by Stubbs, women in a Manitoba aboriginal community viewed the community-based dispute resolution as partisan and subject to political manipulation. Others were concerned that offenders might stack the process with their supporters or that personal disclosure would be made in a small community where they had to continue to live. With Mills's emphasis on listening to victims, she would have to be cognizant of these concerns.

Triage of Domestic Violence Calls

I think part of the problem we have with domestic violence is that there are multiple models of causation but a "one size fits all" approach to intervention. Regardless of who is arrested on domestic dispute calls, the following needs to be assessed after the arrest: violence severity and frequency by both parties, the power structure of the family, and the instrumental use of violence. This would reveal whether unilateral treatment or couple treatment were warranted. There are cases of "terrorism" where one partner dominates and terrorizes the other. The terrorizing partner may have a personality disorder that would make them act in a similar fashion with any partner. Such people do frequently repeat patterns with different partners. I showed above how male "intimate terrorists" had personality disorders much more frequently than abusers in bilateral or even less violent unilateral abuse situations. I would see the latter as good candidates for Intimate Abuse Circles. I would stay with court-mandated treatment for intimate terrorists regardless of their gender. I do not agree with Stubbs that our ability to assess is severely limited. We can tell whether someone has a personality disorder and can predict the likelihood of recidivist risk. There are still weaknesses, as I described above, with assessing "attachment-panic" cases. However, criminal justice and social policy for IPV has a much broader focus than relatively rare spousal homicides. In general, spousal homicide risk would be decreased by other features of IPV management.

The use of IACs is very new and the type of evaluation that exists for standard treatment has not yet been adequately done. The jury is still out on them. Nevertheless, given Mills's cogent critiques of the criminal justice system problems, IACs are worth a try with certain clients. I would not want to see an IAC trying to deal with a psychopath or some other personality-disordered individual who would attempt to manipulate the proceedings or play the game of restorative justice as they play the game of therapy. Narcissistic personalities, too, would not be amenable to restorative justice, as they feel that there is nothing wrong with them. Borderlines would be perfect if they were in a contrition stage, but what would happen when the inner pressures began to build and they had no way to deal with them?

Essentially it comes down to this: if we cannot cure personality disorders, we cannot stop domestic violence through court-mandated treatment, and they would not be amenable to IACs. There is simply too much evidence that implicates personality disorders as risk factors. See, apart from my work, the research by Ehrensaft et al., Moffitt et al., Hastings and Hamberger, Holtzworth-Munroe and Stuart, among others (all reviewed in this book).[27] Gender analyses have generated a smokescreen that has not helped us deal effectively with domestic violence.

Felony assault calls are probably still best handled through the criminal justice system if the police collect sufficient evidence at the crime scene:

photos of injuries, statements of victim onlookers, medical reports. Police may want to do an initial risk assessment at the scene using either the Hare PCL scan or the DVSI.

I would suggest that the victim's wishes and perceived safety might be more important determinants of police choice than the presence of children or even current employment status (which actually might operate against arrest).[28] The police might get a short-term restraining order and ask the perpetrator to leave or take him or her into custody until the case can be forwarded to a domestic violence committee comprised of professionals. This group would make further interviews and assessments, looking for unilateral versus bilateral abuse, power balance, safety and threat issues, victim willingness to prosecute, and the presence of personality disorder. Based on that assessment either an IAC could be formed (if the requisite criteria were met), or the perpetrator could go through blended behavioural therapy, or couple therapy might be recommended.

Both blended behavioural therapy and IACs have the capability to be adapted to any group. Learning principles are universal, and the concerns of special groups – ethnic or same-sex – can be appended to behavioural treatment. This is not true of psychoeducational groups. Mills also argues that IACs can be used and have been used in a variety of cultural settings.[29]

Research and policy in domestic violence are at a critical crossroads. Present practices are not working: arrest is now overused and misapplied. This is indeed ironic, given how sparsely it was used thirty years ago. Police need discretion to triage cases. Treatment (when it can even be called that) is not working. Psychoeducational groups have zero effect. CBT has some promise if it is more broadly focused to include personality-disorder targets. What is most essential is a changing of the guard or, at least, of the guards' mindset. Activists who really want to diminish the incidence of domestic violence have to abandon outmoded ways of thinking about the problem. To remain closed-minded at this juncture may make one a faithful ideologue but it does no service to victims of intimate partner violence.

The Bottom Line

If we were to summarize the main findings from the research cited in this book they would look like this:

1 The paradigm definition defining the causes of IPV has changed from the nineteenth century, when it was seen as a class problem (exemplified in the writings of John Stuart Mill), to the twentieth century, when

it was seen as a gender problem with males as the perpetrators and females as the victims (see Chapters 1, 4, 5, and 6).

2 The difference between the class and gender paradigms is that the feminist paradigm tried to generate support through scientific studies.

3 This support was mixed or, in many cases, contradictory to the feminist paradigm (see Chapters 3, 5, 6, 8, 11, and 12) despite attempts to "spin" (interpret and report) the data so they were consistent with the paradigm (see especially Chapters 6 and 7).

4 As a result of the feminist paradigm, some criminal justice policies are ill-advised and, in some cases, counter-productive (see Chapter 12). Arrest, for example, decreases recidivist assault with some groups and increases it in others.

5 It is also the case that post-conviction attempts to generate change in those convicted (i.e., psychoeducational models) are not always based on sound therapeutic principles (see Chapters 14, 15, and 16).

6 Important aspects of abusiveness (personality disorder, attachment disorder, trauma in perpetrators, identity disturbance, and shame experiences) have been overlooked because of a feminist ideology that eschews psychological causes (Chapters 4, 5, 14, and 16).

7 All arrests for serious assault (where there is an injury and any risk of repetition) should be followed up by a professional assessment that includes the following: (a) the violence history and potential of both individuals, (b) the power dynamic in the couple, and (c) a short screening for personality disorder, to be followed by more extensive assessment where warranted.

8 This information should be used in deciding how to proceed (i.e., individual therapy, couple therapy, justice circles, or jail time).

9 This information should also be provided to professional therapists (not "facilitators") who work with the individual perpetrator or with the couple.

10 The importance of the early years for neural development is a key finding in most studies cited in this book and early intervention should be a priority. Just how this might be done and in what fashion will be a challenge for twenty-first-century policy makers.

Notes

Chapter 1: The History of Spouse Assault

1 M. Schulman, *A Survey of Spousal Violence against Women in Kentucky* (Washington, DC: US Department of Justice, Law Enforcement, 1979); M.A. Straus, "Measuring intrafamily conflict and violence: The conflict tactics scales," *Journal of Marriage and the Family* 41 (1979): 75-88.

2 G. Steiner, *The Futility of Family Police* (Washington, DC: Brookings Institution, 1981).

3 Ibid.; M. Hunt, *The Natural History of Love* (New York: Alfred A. Knopf, 1959); G.R. Taylor, *Sex in History* (New York: Vanguard Press, 1954); R. Tannahill *Sex in History* (New York: Stein and Day, 1980); A. de Reincourt, *Sex and Power in History* (New York: Delta, 1974); N. Elias, *The History Manners* (New York: Pantheon, 1978); B.W. Tuchman, *The March of Folly* (New York: Alfred A. Knopf, 1984); E. Peters, *Torture* (New York: Blackwell, 1985).

4 M. Summers, *Malleus Maleficarum* (London: Pushkin, 1928); T. Davidson, "Wife beating: A recurring phenomenon throughout history," in M. Roy, ed., *Battered Women: A Psychosociological Study of Domestic Violence* (New York: Van Nostrand, 1977): 1-23; M. Daly, *Beyond God the Father* (Toronto: Fitzhenry and Whiteside, 1973); M. Daly, *Gyn/ecology: The Metaethics of Radical Feminism* (Boston: Beacon, 1978).

5 Davidson, "Wife beating"; Daly, *Beyond God the Father*.

6 P.J. Caplan, "The myth of women's masochism," *American Psychologist* 39, 2 (1984): 130-39.

7 Davidson, "Wife beating."

8 M.J. George, "Invisible touch," *Aggression and Violent Behavior* 8, 1 (2003): 23-60.

9 Davidson, "Wife beating."

10 J.S. Mill, *The Subjection of Women*, rev. ed. (1869; repr., London: Longmans, Green and Co., 1970); Davidson, "Wife beating."

11 P. Goldman, *Violence against Women in the Family* (Montreal: McGill University, Faculty of Law, 1978).

12 E. Pleck, *Domestic Tyranny: The Making of American Social Policy against Family Violence from Colonial Times to the Present* (New York: Oxford University Press, 1987).

13 Ibid.

14 Ibid.

15 W. Blackstone, *Commentaries on the Laws of England (1765-1769)* (Chicago: University of Chicago Press, 1942).

16 Pleck, *Domestic Tyranny*.

17 S. Clave, *Under the Lash: A History of Corporal Punishment in the British Armed Forces* (London: Torchstream Books, 1954).

18 Davidson, "Wife beating."

19 Ibid.

20 Pleck, *Domestic Tyranny*, 119.

21 A. Dworkin, *Pornography: Men Possessing Women* (London: Perigee Books, 1981).

22 E. Pleck, "Criminal approaches to family violence, 1640-1980," *Crime and Justice: A Review of the Research* 12 (1989): 19-58.

23 Goldman, *Violence against Women*.

24 E. Pizzey, *Scream Quietly or the Neighbours Will Hear* (London: Penguin Books, 1971, reprinted 1974).

25 N. Loving and M. Farmer, *Police Handling of Spouse Abuse and Wife Beating Calls: A Guide for Police Managers* (Washington, DC: Police Executive Research Forum, 1980).

26 Ibid.

27 P. Waaland and S. Keeley, "Police decision-making in wife abuse: The impact of legal and extralegal factors," *Law and Human Behavior* 9, 4 (1985): 355-66.

28 Ibid.

29 D.A. Ford, "The impact of police officers' attitudes toward victims on the disinclination to arrest wife batterers," paper presented to Third National Family Violence Conference, Durham, NH, 1987.

30 S.F. Berk and D.R. Loseke, "'Handling' family violence: Situational determinants of police arrest in domestic disturbances," *Law and Society Review* 15, 2 (1980): 317-46.

31 Ibid.

32 Ibid.

33 D.G. Dutton, *The Criminal Justice System Response to Wife Assault* (Ottawa: Solicitor General of Canada, Research Division, 1981); G. Bennett-Sandler, "Structure police organizations to promote crisis management programs," paper presented to Symposium on Crisis Management in Law Enforcement, National Conference of Christians and Jews and California Association of Police Trainers, Berkeley, CA, 1975.

34 D.G. Dutton, "Social psychological contributions to criminal justice policy for wife assault," *Applied Social Psychology Annual* 7, 187 (1986): 238-61.

35 L.G. Mills, *Insult to Injury: Rethinking Our Response to Intimate Abuse* (Princeton, NJ: Princeton University Press, 2003).

36 D. Black, "Dispute Settlement by the Police" (Yale University, 1979).

37 R.E. Worden and A. Pollitz, "Police arrests in domestic disturbances: A further look," *Law and Society Review* 18, 1 (1984): 105-19.

38 D.A. Smith and J.R. Klein, "Police control of interpersonal disputes," *Social Problems* 31, 4 (1984): 468-81.

39 C.H. Kempe, F.N. Silverman, B.F. Steele, W. Droegemueller, and H. Silver, "The battered child syndrome," *Journal of the American Medical Association* 181 (1962): 107-12.

40 R.J. Gelles and M.A. Straus, *Intimate Violence* (New York: Simon and Shuster, 1988).

41 Pleck, *Domestic Tyranny*.

42 Pizzey, *Scream Quietly*.

43 Erin Pizzey, *Prone to Violence* (London: Hamlyn, 1982).

44 H.F. Harlow and M. Harlow, "Psychopathology in monkeys," in H.D. Kinnel, ed., *Experimental Psychopathology* (New York: Academic Press, 1971); R.L. Solomon, "The opponent-process theory of acquired motivation: The costs of pleasure and the benefits of pain," *American Psychologist* 35, 8 (1980): 691–712.

45 L.E. Walker, *The Battered Woman* (New York: Harper and Row, 1979).

46 L MacLeod, *Battered but Not Beaten: Preventing Wife Battering in Canada* (Ottawa: Canadian Advisory Council on the Status of Women, 1987).

47 M.A. Straus and R.J. Gelles, eds., *Physical Violence in American Families* (New Brunswick, NJ: Transaction Publishing, 1992).

48 Dutton, *Criminal Justice System*.

Chapter 2: Nested Ecological Theory

1 R.J. Gelles and M.A. Straus, "Determinants of violence in the family: Toward a theoretical integration," in W. Burt, R. Hill, I.L. Nye, and I. Reiss, eds., *Contemporary Theories about the Family* (New York: Simon and Shuster, 1979).

2 M.A. Straus, "A general systems theory approach to a theory of violence between family members," *Social Science Information* 12, 3 (1973): 105-25.

3 K. Lewin, *Field Theory in Social Science* (New York: Harper and Row, 1951).

4 M.A. Straus, "Violence in the family: How widespread, why it occurs, and some thoughts on prevention" (Family Violence: Proceedings from a Symposium, United Way of Greater Vancouver, Vancouver, BC, 1977); M.A. Straus, "Wife beating: How common and why?" *Victimology: An International Journal* 2, 3-4 (1977): 443-59; R.E. Dobash and R.P. Dobash, *Violence against Wives: A Case against the Patriarchy* (New York: Free Press, 1979).

5 M.A. Straus, R.J. Gelles, and S. Steinmetz, *Behind Closed Doors: Violence in the American Family* (Garden City, NY: Anchor Press/Doubleday, 1980), 219.

6 J. Belsky, "Child mistreatment: An ecological integration," *American Psychologist* 35, 4 (1980): 320-25; D.G. Dutton, *A Nested Ecological Theory of Wife Assault* (Toronto: Canadian Psychological Association, 1981); D.G. Dutton, "An ecologically nested theory of male violence toward intimates," *International Journal of Women's Studies* 8, 4 (1985): 404-13.

7 N. Tinbergen, *The Study of Instinct* (London: Oxford University Press, 1951); U. Bronfenbrenner, "Toward an experimental ecology of human development," *American Psychologist* 32, 6 (1977): 513-31; J. Garbarino, "The human ecology of child maltreatment: A conceptual model for research," *Journal of Marriage and the Family* 39 (1977): 721-36; R. Burgess, "Child abuse: A behavioral analysis," in B. Lakey and A. Kazdin, eds., *Advances in Child Clinical Psychology* (New York: Plenum, 1978).

8 J. Belsky, "Child mistreatment"; Bronfenbrenner, "Toward an experimental ecology"; Tinbergen, *Study of Instinct*.

9 J. Archer, *Cross-Cultural Differences in Physical Aggression between Partners: A Social-Structural Analysis* (Preston, UK: University of Central Lancashire, 2005).

10 Belsky, "Child mistreatment," 321.

11 A. de Reincourt, *Sex and Power in History* (New York: Delta, 1974).

12 D.H. Coleman and M.A. Straus, "Marital power, conflict and violence in a nationally representative sample of Americans," *Violence and Victims* 1, 2 (1986): 141-57.

13 R. Dallaire, *Shake Hands with the Devil: The Failure of Humanity in Rwanda* (Toronto: Random House Canada, 2004); I. Chang, *The Rape of Nanking: The Forgotten Holocaust of World War II* (New York: Basic Books, 1997). Chang attributed the atrocities enacted on the Chinese in Nanking by the Japanese to the "Japanese character" and training methods. Dutton, Boyanowsky, and Bond, "Extreme mass homicide: From military massacre to genocide," *Aggression and Violent Behavior*, 10 (2005): 437-73, showed that similar actions had occurred across historical periods and cultures as disparate as the European Catholic Crusaders, and the twentieth-century Hutu in Rwanda.

14 L. Magdol, T.E. Moffitt, A. Caspi, D.L. Newman, J. Fagan, and P.A. Silva, "Gender differences in partner violence in a birth cohort of 21-year-olds: Bridging the gap between clinical and epidemiological approaches," *Journal of Consulting and Clinical Psychology* 65, 1 (1997): 68-78; M.K. Ehrensaft, P. Cohen, J. Brown, E. Smailes, H. Chen, and J.G. Johnson, "Intergenerational transmission of partner violence: A 20-year prospective study," *Journal of Consulting and Clinical Psychology* 71, 4 (2003): 741-53; T.E. Moffitt, A. Caspi, M. Rutter, and P.A. Silva, *Sex Differences in Antisocial Behavior* (Cambridge: Cambridge University Press, 2001).

15 R.E. Dobash and R.P. Dobash, *Violence against Wives: A Case against the Patriarchy* (New York: Free Press, 1979), 33.

16 J. Archer, "Cross-cultural differences," *Personality and Social Psychology Review* (in press).

17 M.D. Bugenthal, R.L. Kahn, F. Andrews, and K.B. Head, *Justifying Violence: Attitudes of American Men* (Ann Arbor, MI: Institute for Social Research, 1972); R. Stark and J. McEvoy, "Middle class violence," *Psychology Today* 4, 6 (1970): 107-12.

18 T.R. Simon, M. Anderson, M.P. Thompson, A.E. Crosby, G. Shelley, and J.J. Sacks, "Attitudinal acceptance of intimate partner violence among US adults," *Violence and Victims* 16, 2 (2001): 115-26. The Simon study was performed on a huge nationally representative sample and used much better wording of the question (see Chapter 6).

19 B.G. Rule and A.R. Nesdale, "Evidence for a three-factor theory of emotions," *Journal of Research in Personality* 11 (1976): 273-94.

20 D.H. Coleman and M.A. Straus, "Marital power"; T.H. Holmes and R.H. Rahe, "The social readjustment rating scale," *Journal of Psychosomatic Research* 11 (1967): 213-18.

21 R. Parke and C. Collmer, "Child abuse: An interdisciplinary review," in E.M. Hetherington, ed., *Review of Child Development Research* (Chicago: University of Chicago Press, 1975); R.J. Gelles, "Abused wives: Why do they stay?" *Journal of Marriage and the Family* 38 (1976): 659-68.

22 W.S. DeKeseredy and M.D. Schwartz, *Woman Abuse on Campus: Results from the Canadian National Survey* (Thousand Oaks, CA: Sage, 1998).

23 Ibid., 3.

24   Ibid., 42, 54.
25   Moffitt et al., *Sex Differences.*
26   DeKeseredy and Schwartz, "Women Abuse," 56.
27   D.G. Dooley and R. Catalano, "The epidemiology of economic stress," *American Journal of Community Psychology* 12, 4 (1984): 387-409.
28   Belsky, "Child mistreatment," 321.
29   Coleman and Straus, "Marital power."
30   R.J. Blood, and D. Wolfe, *Husbands and Wives: The Dynamics of Married Living* (Glencoe, IL: Free Press, 1960).
31   C.I. Notarius and J.I. Johnson, "Emotional expression in husbands and wives," *Journal of Marriage and the Family* 44 (1982): 483-92; R.W. Levenson and J.M. Gottman, "Marital interaction: Physiological linkage and affective exchange," *Journal of Personality and Social Psychology* 45, 3 (1983): 587-97; N.S. Jacobson, J.M. Gottman, J. Waltz, R. Rushe, J. Babcock, and A. Holtzworth-Munroe, "Affect, verbal content, and psychophysiology in the arguments of couples with a violent husband," *Journal of Consulting and Clinical Psychology* 62, 5 (1994): 982-88.
32   G. Margolin, "Interpersonal and intrapersonal factors associated with marital violence," paper presented at Second National Family Violence Research Conference, Durham, NH, 1984.
33   Ibid.
34   G.R. Patterson, *Families of Antisocial Children: An Interactional Approach* (Eugene, OR: Catalia, 1981); J.B. Reid, G.R. Patterson, and R. Loeber, "The abused child: Victim, instigator or innocent bystander?" in D.J. Bernstein, ed., *Response Structure and Motivation* (Lincoln/London: University of Nebraska Press, 1981); R.G. Wahler, "The multiply entrapped parent: Obstacles to change in parent child problems," in J.P. Vincent, ed., *Advances in Family Intervention, Assessment and Therapy* (Greenwich, CT: JAI Press, 1980).
35   G.R. Patterson, "A performance theory for coercive family interactions," in R. Cairns, ed., *Social Interaction: Methods, Analysis, and Illustrations* (Hillsdale, NJ: Erlbaum, 1979).
36   Patterson, *Families of Antisocial Children.*
37   Wahler, "The multiply entrapped parent."
38   J. Giles-Sims, *Wife Battering: A Systems Theory Approach* (New York: Guilford, 1983).
39   Straus, Gelles, and Steinmetz, *Behind Closed Doors.*
40   Ibid., 100.
41   Ibid., 121
42   Ibid., 173.
43   S.M. Stith, D.B. Smith, C.E. Penn, D.B. Ward, and D. Tritt, "Intimate partner physical abuse perpetration and victimization risk factors: A meta-analysis review," *Aggression and Violent Behavior* 10, 1 (2004): 65-98.
44   Ibid., 72.
45   F. Elliott, "The neurology of explosive rage: The episodic dyscontrol syndrome," in M. Roy, ed., *Battered Women: A Psychosociological Study of Domestic Violence* (New York: Van Nostrand, 1977).
46   N. Shainess, "Psychological aspects of wife battering," in Roy, *Battered Women.*
47   Straus, "Violence in the family"; Straus, "Wife beating," 443-59; and M.A. Straus, "Societal morphogenesis and intrafamily violence in cross cultural perspective," *Annals of the New York Academy of Sciences* 285 (1977): 718-30.
48   N. Caplan and S.D. Nelson, "On being useful: The nature and consequences of psychological research on social problems," *American Psychologist* 28, 3 (1973): 199-211.
49   Straus, "Violence in the family"; Straus, "Wife beating."
50   R.D. Maiuro and D.H. Avery, "Psychopharmacological treatment of aggression," *Violence and Victims* 11, 3 (1996): 239-62.
51   J.E. Snell, P.J. Rosenwald, and A. Robey, "The wifebeater's wife," *Archive of General Psychiatry* 2 (1964): 107-13.
52   E. Hilberman, "Overview: The 'wife beater's wife' reconsidered," *American Journal of Psychiatry* 137, 11 (1980): 1336-47.
53   Reid, Patterson, and Loeber, "The abused child."
54   Ibid., 52.

Chapter 3: Measurement and Incidence of Abuse

1   M.A. Straus, "The controversy over domestic violence by women: A methodological, theo-retical and sociology of science analysis," in X. Arriaga and S. Oskamp, eds., *Violence in Intimate Relationships* (Thousand Oaks, CA: Sage Publications, 1999), 17-44.

2   Solicitor General of Canada, *Bulletin 4: Female Victims of Crime* (Ottawa: Canadian Urban Victimization Survey, 1985).

3   M.A. Straus and R.J. Gelles, "How violent are American families: Estimates from the national family violence resurvey and other surveys," in M.A. Straus and R.J. Gelles, eds., *Physical Violence in American Families* (New Brunswick, NJ: Transaction, 1992), 95-108; M. Schulman, *A Survey of Spousal Violence against Women in Kentucky* (Washington, DC: US Department of Justice, Law Enforcement, 1979).

4   USBO Census, "Social and economic characteristics of the older population, 1978," *Current Population Reports* (Washington, DC: Department of Commerce, US Government Printing Office, 1979), P-23.

5   D.A. Gaquin, "Spouse abuse: Data from the National Crime Survey," *Victimology: An International Journal* 2, 3-4 (1977): 632-42.

6   D.G. Dutton, "The criminal justice response to wife assault," *Law and Human Behavior* 11, 3 (1987): 189-206.

7   P. Tjaden and N. Thoennes, *Prevalence, Incidence and Consequences of Violence against Women: Findings from the National Violence against Women Survey* (Washington, DC: US Department of Justice, 1998).

8   M.A. Straus, R.J. Gelles, and S. Steinmetz, *Behind Closed Doors: Violence in the American Family* (Garden City, NY: Anchor Press/Doubleday, 1980).

9   J. Archer, *Cross-Cultural Differences in Physical Aggression between Partners: A Social-Structural Analysis* (Preston, UK: University of Central Lancashire, 2005).

10 Statistics Canada, *Family Violence in Canada: A Statistical Profile* (Ottawa: Canadian Centre for Justice Statistics, 2000).

11 Ibid., 4.

12 Ibid., 10.

13 Straus, "Controversy over domestic violence."

14 E.S. Buzawa, T.L. Austin, J. Bannon, and J. Jackson, "Role of victim preference in determining police response to victims of domestic violence," in E.S. Buzawa and C.G. Buzawa, eds., *Domestic Violence: The Changing Criminal Justice Response* (Westport, CT: Auburn House, 1992); and G.R. Brown, "Gender as a factor in the response of the law-enforcement system to violence against partners," *Sexuality and Culture* 8 (2004): 1-87.

15 G.R. Brown, "Gender as a factor in the response of the law-enforcement system to violence against partners," *Sexuality and Culture* 8 (2004).

16 Ibid.

17 GSS 1999 Table 3.2; D. LaRoche, *Aspects of the Context and Consequences of Domestic Violence: Situational Couple Violence and Intimate Terrorism in Canada in 1999* (Quebec City: Government of Quebec, 2005).

18 Ibid.

19 G.R. Brown, "Gender as a factor in the response of the law-enforcement system to violence against partners," *Sexuality and Culture* 8 (2004): 1-87; Statistics Canada, *Family Violence in Canada: A Statistical Profile* (Ottawa: Canadian Centre for Justice Statistics, 2000).

20 S. Walby and J. Allen, *2001 British Crime Survey* (London: Home Office, 2004).

21 Ibid.

22 L. Bensley, S. Macdonald, J. Van Eenwyk, K.W. Simmons, and D. Ruggles, *Prevalence of Intimate Partner Violence and Injury, Washington, 1998* (Washington, DC: Washington State Department of Health, 2000).

23 Ibid.

24 A. Eagly, W. Woods, and A.B. Diekman, "Social role theory of sex differences and similarities: A current appraisal," in T. Eckes and H.M. Trautner, eds., *The Developmental Social Psychology of Gender* (Mahwah, NJ: Erlbaum, 2000).

25 Straus, Gelles, and Steinmetz, *Behind Closed Doors.*

26 Ibid., 256.
27 M. Yoshihama, K. Clum, A. Crampton, and B. Gillespie, "Measuring the lifetime experience of domestic violence: Application of the Life History Calendar method," *Violence and Victims* 17, 3 (2002): 297-317.
28 W. Fals-Stewart, G.R. Birchler, and M.L. Kelley, "The timeline followback spousal violence interview to assess physical aggression between intimate partners: Reliability and validity," *Journal of Family Violence* 18, 3 (2003): 131-42.
29 G. Spanier, "Measuring dyadic adjustment: New scales for assessing the quality of marriage and similar dyads," *Journal of Marriage and the Family* 3 (1976) 1; 15-28; D.P. Crowne and D.A. Marlowe, "A new scale of social desirability independent of psychopathology," *Journal of Consulting Psychology* 24 (1960): 349-54.
30 Straus, "Controversy over domestic violence."
31 T.E. Moffitt, A. Caspi, M. Rutter, and P.A. Silva, *Sex Differences in Antisocial Behavior* (Cambridge: Cambridge University Press, 2001).
32 Ibid., 61-62.
33 Straus, Gelles, and Steinmetz, *Behind Closed Doors*; Schulman, *Women in Kentucky*; M.A. Straus and R.J. Gelles, *Is Family Violence Increasing? A Comparison of 1975 and 1985 National Survey Rates* (San Diego, CA: American Society of Criminology, 1985); M.A. Straus and R.J. Gelles, "Societal change in family violence from 1975 to 1985 as revealed by two national surveys," *Journal of Marriage and the Family* 48 (1986): 465-79; L.W. Kennedy and D.G. Dutton, "The incidence of wife assault in Alberta," *Canadian Journal of Behavioural Science* 21, 1 (1989): 40-54.
34 Straus, Gelles, and Steinmetz, *Behind Closed Doors*; Schulman, *Women in Kentucky*; Kennedy and Dutton, "Wife assault in Alberta."
35 Schulman, *Women in Kentucky*; Straus, Gelles, and Steinmetz, *Behind Closed Doors*.
36 Ibid.
37 Straus and Gelles, *Is Family Violence Increasing?* Straus and Gelles, "Change in family violence."
38 Schulman, *Women in Kentucky*.
39 Kennedy and Dutton, "The incidence of wife assault in Alberta."
40 M.V. Kwong, K. Bartholomew, and D. Dutton, "Gender differences in patterns of relationship violence in Alberta," *Canadian Journal of Behavioural Science* 31 (1999): 150-60.
41 K.I. Kim and Y.G. Cho, "Epidemiological survey of spousal abuse in Korea," in E.C. Viano, ed., *Intimate Violence: Interdisciplinary Perspectives* (Washington, DC: Hemisphere Press, 1992), 277-82.
42 Straus, Gelles, and Steinmetz, *Behind Closed Doors*; Kim and Cho, "Epidemiological survey."
43 Schulman, *Women in Kentucky*; Kim and Cho, "Epidemiological survey."
44 F. Kumagai and M.A. Straus, "Conflict resolution in Japan, India and the USA," *Journal of Comparative Family Studies* 14, 3 (1983): 377-92.
45 Archer, *Cross-Cultural Differences*.
46 Schulman, *Women in Kentucky*; Straus, Gelles, and Steinmetz, *Behind Closed Doors*; Kennedy and Dutton, "Wife assault in Alberta."
47 M.A. Straus, "Victims and aggressors in marital violence," *American Behavioral Scientist* 23, 5 (1980).
48 Schulman, *Women in Kentucky*; Straus and Gelles, *Is Family Violence Increasing?*
49 M.A. Straus, "The Conflict Tactics Scale and its critics: An evaluation and new data on validity reliability," in M.A. Straus and R.J. Gelles, *Physical Violence*; M.A. Straus, "Measuring intrafamily conflict and violence: The Conflict Tactics Scale," in Straus and Gelles, *Physical Violence*; M.A. Straus, "The National Family Violence Surveys," in Straus and Gelles *Physical Violence*.
50 Straus, "Conflict Tactics Scale."
51 Ibid.
52 D.G. Dutton and K.J. Hemphill, "Patterns of socially desirable responding among perpetrators and victims of wife assault," *Violence and Victims* 7, 1 (1992): 29-40.
53 B.J. Morse, "Beyond the Conflict Tactics Scale: Assessing gender differences in partner violence," *Violence and Victims*, 4 (1995): 251-71.

54 D.G. Dutton and T.L. Nicholls, "The gender paradigm in domestic violence research and theory: Part 1 - The conflict of theory and data," *Aggression and Violent Behavior*, 10, 6 (2005): 680-714.

55 Moffitt et al., *Sex Differences*; R.E. Dobash and R.P. Dobash, "Wives: The appropriate victims of marital assault," *Victimology: An International Journal* 2 (1978): 426-42.

56 M.A. Straus, S.L. Hamby, S. Boney-McCoy, and D.B. Sugarman, "The revised Conflict Tactics Scale (CTS-2)," *Journal of Family Issues* 17, 3 (1996): 283-317.

57 L.L. Marshall, "Development of the severity of violence against women scales," *Journal of Family Violence* 7, 2 (1992): 103-21.

58 L.L. Marshall, "The severity of violence against men scales," *Journal of Family Violence* 7, 3 (1992): 189-203.

59 J. Briere, *Psychological Assessment of Adult Post-Traumatic States* (Washington, DC: APA Press, 1997); R.M. Tolman, "The development of a measure of psychological maltreatment of women by their male partners," *Violence and Victims* 4, 3 (1989): 159-77.

60 M. Kasian and S.L. Painter, "Frequency and severity of psychological abuse in a dating population," *Journal of Interpersonal Violence* 7, 3 (1992): 350-64.

61 J. Briere and M. Runtz, "The trauma symptom checklist (TSC-33): Early data on a new scale," *Journal of Interpersonal Violence* 4, 2 (1989): 151-62.

62 Ibid.

63 Ibid.

64 J. Briere, "Psychological Assessments."

Chapter 4: Theories of Wife Assault

1 R.E. Dobash and R.P. Dobash, "Wives: The appropriate victims of marital assault," *Victimology: An International Journal* 2 (1978): 426-42; R.E. Dobash and R.P. Dobash, *Violence against Wives: A Case against the Patriarchy* (New York: Free Press, 1979).

2 M. Fields, "Wife beating: Government intervention policies and practices," *Battered Women: Issues of Public Policy* (Washington, DC: US Government Printing Office, 1978).

3 J.E. Snell, P.J. Rosenwald, and A. Robey, "The wifebeater's wife," *Archive of General Psychiatry* 2 (1964): 107-13; M. Faulk, "Men who assault their wives," *Medicine, Science and the Law* 14 (1974): 180-83; F. Elliott, "The neurology of explosive rage: The episodic dyscontrol syndrome," in M. Roy, ed., *Battered Women: A Psychosociological Study of Domestic Violence* (New York: Van Nostrand, 1977); E. Pizzey, *Scream Quietly or the Neighbours Will Hear* (London: Penguin Books, 1974).

4 Faulk, "Men who assault their wives."

5 Snell, Rosenwald, and Robey, "The wifebeater's wife," 109.

6 Ibid., 110.

7 E. Hilberman, "Overview: The 'wife beater's wife' reconsidered," *American Journal of Psychiatry* 137, 11 (1980): 1336-47; E. Hilberman and K. Munson, "Sixty battered women," *Victimology: An International Journal* 2 (1977-78): 460-70.

8 Hilberman, "Overview."

9 American Psychiatric Association, *Diagnostic and Statistical Manual of Mental Disorders*, 3rd ed. (Washington, DC: American Psychiatric Association, 1981); B. Rounsaville, "Theories in marital violence: Evidence from a study of battered women," *Victimology: An International Journal* 3, 1-2 (1978): 11-31; A. Rosenbaum and K.D. O'Leary, "Marital violence: Characteristics of abusive couples," *Journal of Consulting and Clinical Psychology* 41 (1981): 63; A. Ganley and L. Harris, "Domestic violence: Issues in designing and implementing programs for male batterers," *Proceedings*, Eighty-sixth annual convention of the American Psychological Association, Toronto, American Psychological Association, 1978; J.J. Gayford, "Wife battering: A preliminary survey of 100 cases," *British Medical Journal* 301 (1975): 194-97.

10 Elliott, "The neurology of explosive rage."

11 Rounsaville, "Theories in marital violence," 19, Table 4; Gayford, "Wife battering."

12 Rounsaville, "Theories in marital violence," 12.

13 Ibid., 20.

14 Ibid., 22.

15 D.G. Dutton, K. Saunders, A. Starzomski, and K. Bartholomew, "Intimacy anger and inse-cure attachment as precursors of abuse in intimate relationships," *Journal of Applied Social Psychology* 24, 15 (1994), 1367-86; A.J.Z. Henderson, K. Bartholomew, and D.G. Dutton, "He loves me, he loves me not: Attachment and separation resolution of abused women," *Journal of Family Violence* 12, 2 (1997): 169-92; K. Bartholomew, A.J.Z. Henderson, and D.G. Dutton, "Insecure attachment and abusive intimate relationships," in C. Clulow, ed., *Adult Attachment and Couple Psychotherapy: The "Secure Base" Concept in Practice and Research* (London: Routledge, 2001), 43-61.
16 R. Bland and H. Orn, "Family violence and psychiatric disorder," *Canadian Journal of Psychiatry* 31 (1986): 129-37; L.N. Robins, J.E. Helzer, J. Croughan, J.B.W. Williams, and R.L. Spitzer, *The NIMH Diagnostic Interview Schedule, Version III* (Washington, DC: Public Health Service, 1981).
17 L.K. Hamberger and J.E. Hastings, "Personality correlated of men who abuse their partners: A cross-validation study," *Journal of Family Violence* 1 (1986): 323-41.
18 D.G. Saunders, "A typology of men who batter: Three types derived from cluster analysis," *American Journal of Orthopsychiatry* 62, 2 (1992): 264-75; D.G. Dutton and A. Starzomski, "Psychological differences between court-referred and self-referred wife assaulters," *Criminal Justice and Behavior: An International Journal* 21, 2 (1994): 203-22; L.K. Hamberger and J.E. Hastings, "Personality characteristics of spouse abusers: A controlled comparison," *Violence and Victims* 3 (1988): 5-30; L.K. Hamberger and J.E. Hastings, "Counseling male spouse abusers: Characteristics of treatment completers and dropouts," *Violence and Victims* 4 (1989): 275-86; O. Kernberg, "The structural diagnosis of Borderline Personality Organization," in P. Hartocollis, ed., *Borderline Personality Disorders: The Concept, the Syndrome, the Patient* (New York: International Universities Press, 1977), 87-121.
19 S.D. Hart, D.G. Dutton, and T. Newlove, "The prevalence of personality disorder among wife assaulters," *Journal of Personality Disorder* 7, 4 (1993): 329-41; D.G. Dutton and S.D. Hart, "Evidence for long-term specific effects of childhood abuse and neglect on criminal behavior in men," *International Journal of Offender Therapy and Comparative Criminology* 36, 2 (1992): 129-37; D.G. Dutton and S.D. Hart, "Risk markers for family violence in a federally incarcerated population," *International Journal of Law and Psychiatry* 15 (1992): 101-12; D.G. Dutton, "Personality profile of intimate terrorists," *Journal of Interpersonal Violence* (in press).
20 J.M. Lohr, L.K. Hamberger, and D. Bonge, "The nature of irrational beliefs in different personality clusters of spouse abusers," *Journal of Rational Emotive and Cognitive Behavior Therapy* 6 (1988): 273-85.
21 L.K. Hamberger, J.M. Lohr, D. Bonge, and D.F. Tolin, "A large empirical typology of male spouse abusers and its relationship to dimensions of abuse," *Violence and Victims* 11 (1996): 277-92; D.G. Dutton and K.J. Hemphill, "Patterns of socially desirable responding among perpetrators and victims of wife assault," *Violence and Victims* 7, 1 (1992): 29-40.
22 D.G. Dutton, "Treatment of Assaultiveness," in D.G. Dutton and D.L. Sonkin, eds., *Intimate Violence: Contemporary Treatment Approaches* (New York: Haworth Press, 2003).
23 Ibid.
24 D. Goleman, *Emotional Intelligence* (New York: Bantam Books, 1995).
25 B. van der Kolk, *Psychological Trauma* (Washington, DC: American Psychiatric Press, 1987), 55.
26 F. Elliott, "The neurology of explosive rage: The episodic dyscontrol syndrome," in M. Roy, ed., *Battered Women: A Psychosociological Study of Domestic Violence* (New York: Van Nostrand, 1977), 98-109.
27 A.R. Felthous and S. Bryant, "The diagnosis of intermittent explosive disorders in violent men," *Bulletin of the American Academy of Psychiatry and Law* 19, 1 (1991): 71-79.
28 Ibid.
29 F. Elliott, "The neurology of explosive rage," 105.
30 A. Bandura, "The social learning perspective: Mechanisms of aggression," in H. Toch, ed., *The Psychology of Crime and Criminal Justice* (New York: Holt, Rinehart, and Winston, 1979).
31 R.J. Davidson, K.M. Putnam, and C.L. Larson, "Dysfunction in the neural circuitry of emotion regulation: A possible prelude to violence," *Science: American Association for the Advancement of Science* (2000): 591.

32   A.N. Schore, *Affect Regulation and the Origin of the Self: The Neurobiology of Emotional Develop-*
     ment (Hillsdale, NJ: Erlbaum, 1994); A.N. Schore, *Affect Dysregulation and Disorders of the Self*
     (New York: Norton, 2003), 5-89.

33   Ibid., 416; P. Pearson, *When She Was Bad: How and Why Women Get Away with Murder*
     (Middlesex, UK: Penguin, 1998), 343.

34   Schore, *Affect Dysregulation*, 55-91.

35   Ibid., 90.

36   Ibid., 55-91.

37   B. Perry, "Incubated in terror: Neurodevelopmental factors in the 'Cycle of Violence,'" in J.D.
     Osofsky, ed., *Children, Youth and Violence: Searching for Solutions* (New York: Guilford Press,
     1995), 5.

38   E.D. Schwartz and B.D. Perry, "The post-traumatic response in children and adolescents,"
     Psychiatric Clinics of North America 17, 2 (1994): 315.

39   N.D. Volkow and L. Tancredi, "Neural substrates of violent behavior: A preliminary study
     with positron emission tomography," *British Journal of Psychiatry* 151 (1987): 668-73; A.S.
     New, M.S. Novotny, M.S. Bushsbaum, and L.J. Siever, "Neuroimaging in impulsive-aggres-
     sive personality disorder patients," in M. Maes and E.F. Coccaro, eds., *Neurobiology and Clini-*
     cal Views on Aggression and Impulsivity (New York: John Wiley and Sons, 1998).

40   A.D. Raine, J.R. Meloy, S. Bihrle, J. Stoddard, L. Lacasse, and M.S. Bushsbaum, "Reduced
     prefrontal and increased subcortical brain functioning assessed during positron emission
     tomography in predatory and affective murderers," *Behavioral Sciences and the Law* 16 (1998):
     319-32.

41   Schore, *Affect Regulation*, 344.

42   F. Pine, *Drive, Ego, Object and Self* (New York: Basic Books, 1990), 344.

43   Schore, *Affect Dysregulation*, 291-303.

44   A.D. Raine, M. Buchsbaum, and L. Lacasse, "Brain abnormalities in murderers indicated by
     positron emission tomography," *Biological Psychiatry* 42 (1997): 495-508.

45   Ibid., 495.

46   E.F. Coccaro, "Neurotransmitter correlateds of impulsive aggression in humans," *Annals of*
     the New York Academy of Sciences 794 (1996): 82-99; E.F. Coccaro and R.J. Kavoussi, "Neu-
     rotransmitter correlateds of impulsive aggression," in D.M. Stoff and R.B. Cairns, eds., *Ag-*
     gression and Violence: Genetic, Neurobiological and Biosocial Perspectives (Mahwah, NJ: Erlbaum,
     1996).

47   Ibid., 69.

48   B. Stanley, A. Molcho, M. Stanley, R. Winchel, M. Gemeroff, B. Parsons, and J.J. Mann, "Asso-
     ciation of aggressive behavior with altered serotonergic function in patients who are not
     suicidal," *American Journal of Psychiatry* 157 (2000): 609-14.

49   D.M. Stoff and B. Vitiello, "Role of serotonin in aggression of children and adolescents:
     Biochemical and pharmacological studies," in Stoff and Cairns, *Aggression and Violence.*

50   Coccaro and Kavoussi, "Neurotransmitter correlateds."

51   Stoff and Vitiello, "Role of serotonin."

52   Coccaro and Kavoussi, "Neurotransmitter correlateds."

53   J.M. Stolk, R.L. Connor, S. Levine, J.D. Barchas, "Brain norepinephrine metabolism and shock-
     induced fighting behavior in rats," *Journal of Pharmacology and Experimental Therapeutics* 190
     (1974): 193-209.

54   B. Eichelman and J.D. Barchas, "Facilitated shock-induced aggression following antidepres-
     sant medication in the rat," *Pharmacology, Biochemistry and Behavior* 3 (1975): 601-4.

55   J.A. Barrett, H. Edinger, and A. Siegel, "Intrahypothalamic injections of norepinephrine fa-
     cilitate feline affective aggression via alpha-2 adrenoreceptors," *Brain Research* 525 (1990):
     285-93.

56   R.W. Cowdry and D.L. Gardner, "Pharmacotherapy of borderline personality disorder," *Archive*
     of General Psychiatry 45 (1988): 111-19; P.H. Soloff, A. George, R.S. Nathan, P.M. Schultz, and
     J.M. Perel, "Paradoxical effects of amitripyline in borderline patients," *American Journal of*
     Psychiatry 143 (1986): 1603-5.

57   A. Roy, J. de Jong, and M. Linnoila, "Acting out hostility in normal volunteers," *Archive of*
     General Psychiatry 46 (1989): 679-81.

58 Coccaro and Kavoussi, "Neurotransmitter correlateds," 80.
59 D.G. Dutton and G. Kerry, "Modus operandi and personality disorder in incarcerated killers," *International Journal of Law and Psychiatry* 22, 3-4 (1999): 287-300.
60 D.G. Dutton, *The Abusive Personality: Violence and Control in Intimate Relationships* (New York: Guilford Press, 1998).
61 D.G. Dutton, "The traumatic origins of intimate rage," *Aggression and Violent Behavior* 4, 4 (1999): 431-48; and D.G. Dutton, "Trauma symptoms and PTSD-like profiles in perpetrators of intimate abuse," *Journal of Traumatic Stress* 8, 2 (1995): 299-316.
62 Coccaro and Kavoussi, "Neurotransmitter correlateds."
63 P.R. Shaver and M. Mikulincer, "Attachment theory and research: Resurrection of the psychodynamic approach to personality," *Journal of Research in Personality* 39 (2005): 22-45.
64 D.G. Dutton, K. Saunders, A. Starzomski, and K. Bartholomew, "Intimacy anger and insecure attachment as precursors of abuse in intimate relationships," *Journal of Applied Social Psychology* 24, 15 (1994): 1367-86; C. Hazan and P. Shaver, "Conceptualizing romantic love as an attachment process," *Journal of Personality and Social Psychology* 52 (1987): 511-24; N.L. Collins and S.J. Read, "Adult attachment, working models and relationship quality in dating couples," *Journal of Personality and Social Psychology* 58 (1990): 644-63; K.S. Adam, "Suicidal behavior and attachment: Developmental model," in M.B. Sperling and W.H. Berman, eds., *Attachment in Adults: Clinical and Developmental Perspectives* (New York: Guilford, 1994).
65 J. Bowlby, *Attachment and Loss: Attachment* (New York: Basic Books, 1969); J. Bowlby, *Attachment and Loss* (New York: Basic Books, 1973, 1980).
66 Bowlby, *Attachment and Loss: Attachment*; Bowlby, *Attachment and Loss* (1973); M. Ainsworth, M. Blehar, E. Waters, and S. Wall, *Patterns of Attachments* (Hillsdale, NJ: Erlbaum, 1978).
67 J. Bowlby, "The making and breaking of affectional bonds," *British Journal of Psychiatry* 130 (1977): 203.
68 Bowlby, *Attachment and Loss: Attachment*, 27-28.
69 M. Main, N. Kaplan, and J. Cassidy, "Security in infancy, childhood, and adulthood: A move to the level of representation," in I. Bretherton and E. Waters, eds., *Growing Points of Attachment Theory and Research* (Malden, MA: Blackwell, 1985), 66-104, 72.
70 Schore, *Affect Regulation*.
71 Bowlby, *Attachment and Loss: Attachment*, 27.
72 Ibid., 361.
73 C. Hazan and P. Shaver, "Conceptualizing romantic love as an attachment process," *Journal of Personality and Social Psychology* 52 (1987): 511-24; N.L. Collins and S.J. Read, "Adult attachment, working models and relationship quality in dating couples," *Journal of Personality and Social Psychology*, 58 (1990): 644-63.
74 J. Belsky and M. Rovine, "Temperament and attachment security in the strange situation: An empirical rapprochement," *Child Development* 58 (1987): 316-28.
75 Ainsworth et al., *Patterns of Attachments*.
76 Schore, *Affect Regulation*.
77 M. Main, N. Kaplan, and J. Cassidy, "Security in infancy, childhood, and adulthood: A move to the level of representation," in Bretherton and Waters, *Growing Points*, 66-104.
78 R. Karen, "Becoming Attached," *Atlantic Monthly*, Feb 1990, 35-70, 49.
79 Ibid.
80 Ibid.
81 K. Bartholomew, "Avoidance of intimacy: An attachment perspective," *Journal of Social and Personal Relationships* 7 (1990): 147-78.
82 L.A. Sroufe, "Considering the normal and abnormal together: The essence of developmental psychopathology," *Development and Psychopathology* 2 (1990): 335-48.
83 Ainsworth et al., *Patterns of Attachments*; M. Main and D.R. Weston, "Avoidance of the attachment figure in infancy: Descriptions and interpretations," in C.M. Parkes and J. Stevenson-Hinds, eds., *The Place of Attachment in Human Behavior* (London: Tavistock, 1982).
84 R. Karen, "Shame," *Atlantic Monthly* (1992): 42-70, 49.
85 L. Walker, *The Battered Woman Syndrome* (New York: Springer, 1984).
86 D.G. Winter, *The Power Motive* (New York: Free Press, 1973); P. Trachtenberg, *The Casanova Complex* (New York: Poseidon Press, 1988).

87   L.A. Sroufe, "The role of intent-caregiver attachment in development," in J. Belsky and T. Nezworski, eds., *Clinical Implications of Attachment* (Hillsdale, NJ: Erlbaum, 1988).
88   Bowlby, "Making and breaking," 203.
89   H.F. Harlow and M. Harlow, "Psychopathology in monkeys," in H.D. Kinnel, ed., *Experimental Psychopathology* (New York: Academic Press, 1971).
90   Ibid., 206.
91   P.M. Crittenden and M.D.S. Ainsworth, "Attachment and child abuse," in D. Cicchetti and V. Carlson, eds, *Child Maltreatment: Theory and Research in the Cause of Child Abuse and Neglect* (New York: Cambridge University Press, 1989); D. Cicchetti, M. Cummings, M. Greenburg, and R. Marvin, "An organizational perspective on attachment beyond infancy: Implications for theory, measurement, and research," in M. Greenberg, D. Cicchetti, and E.M. Cummings, eds., *Attachment during the Preschool Years: Theory, Research, and Intervention* (Chicago: University of Chicago Press., 1990), 3-51; D. Cicchetti, "The emergence of developmental psychopathology," *Child Development* 55 (1984): 1-5.
92   M.A. Straus, R.J. Gelles, and S. Steinmetz, *Behind Closed Doors: Violence in the American Family* (Garden City, NY: Anchor Press/Doubleday, 1980); D.S. Kalmuss, "The intergenerational transmission of marital aggression," *Journal of Marriage and the Family* 46 (1984): 11-19; C.S. Widom, "Child abuse, neglect, and adult behavior: Research design and findings on criminality, violence and child abuse," *American Journal of Orthopsychiatry* 59 (1989): 355-67.
93   L.H. Silverman and J. Weinberger, "Mommy and I are one: Implications for psychotherapy," *American Psychologist* 40 (1985): 1296-1308, 1297-98.
94   Hazan and Shaver, "Conceptualizing romantic love," 511-24; P. Shaver, C. Hazan, and D. Bradshaw, "Love as attachment: The integration of three behavioral systems," in R.J. Sternberg and M. Barnes, eds., *The Psychology of Love* (New Haven, CT: Yale University Press, 1988).
95   Shaver, Hazan, and Bradshaw, "Love as attachment," 127.
96   N.L. Collins and S.J. Read, "Adult attachment, working models and relationship quality in dating couples," *Journal of Personality and Social Psychology* 58 (1990): 644-63; K. Bartholomew, "Avoidance of intimacy: An attachment perspective," *Journal of Social and Personal Relationships* 7 (1990): 147-78.
97   P.M. Crittenden, "Relationships at risk," in J. Belsky and T. Nezworski, eds., *Clinical Implications of Attachment* (Hillsdale, NJ: Erlbaum, 1988), 136-74, 141.
98   Schore, *Affect Regulation*; Schore, *Affect Dysregulation*; A.N. Schore, *Affect Regulation and the Repair of the Self* (New York: Norton, 2003).
99   Schore, *Affect Regulation* (2003), 278.
100 Schore, *Affect Dysregulation*, 35
101 Schore, *Affect Regulation* (1994), 419, 421.
102 N. Eisenberger, M.D. Lieberman, and K.D. Williams, "Does rejection hurt? An FMRI study of social exclusion," *Science*, 302, 5643 (2005): 290-97.

Chapter 5: Feminist and Sociobiological Explanations for IPV

1   R.E. Dobash and R.P. Dobash, "Wives: The appropriate victims of marital assault," *Victimology: An International Journal* 2 (1978): 426-42; K. Yllo and M. Bograd, eds., *Feminist Perspectives on Wife Abuse* (Beverly Hills, CA: Sage, 1988).
2   Dobash and Dobash, "Wives"; W.G.J. Goode, "Why men resist," *Dissent* (1971): 181-93; M.A. Straus, "Sexual inequality, cultural norm and wife beating," *Victimology: An International Journal* 1 (1976): 54-76; M.A. Straus, "Violence in the family: How widespread, why it occurs, and some thoughts on prevention" (Family Violence: Proceedings from Symposium, United Way of Greater Vancouver, Vancouver, BC, 1977); M.A. Straus, "Societal morphogenesis and intrafamily violence in cross cultural perspective," *Annals of the New York Academy of Sciences* 285 (1977): 718-30; M.A. Straus, "Wife beating: How common and why?" *Victimology: An International Journal* 2, 3-4 (1978): 443-59.
3   M.A. Straus, R.J. Gelles, and S. Steinmetz, *Behind Closed Doors: Violence in the American Family* (Garden City, NY: Anchor Press/Doubleday, 1980).
4   Straus, "Wife beating," 443-59, 455.
5   R.E. Dobash and R.P. Dobash, *Violence against Wives: A Case against the Patriarchy* (New York: Free Press, 1979).

6   M. Bograd, "Feminist perspectives on wife assault: An introduction," in Yllo and Bograd, *Feminist Perspectives*, 11-26.

7   Ibid.

8   G. Serran and P. Firestone, "Intimate partner homicide: A review of the male proprietariness and the self-defense theories," *Aggression and Violent Behavior* 9, 1 (2004): 1-15, 12.

9   Dobash and Dobash, "Wives."

10 V. Goldner, P. Penn, M. Sheinberg, and G. Walker, "Love and violence: Gender paradoxes in volatile attachments," *Family Process* 29, 4 (1990): 343-64.

11 Bograd, "Feminist perspectives," 13.

12 L. Walker, "Psychology and violence against women," *American Psychologist* 44, 4 (1989): 695-702.

13 L. Rosewater, "A critical analysis of the proposed self-defeating personality disorder," *Journal of Personality Disorder* 1 (1987): 190-95.

14 D.G. Dutton and S.L. Painter, "Traumatic bonding: The development of emotional bonds in relationships of intermittent abuse," *Victimology: An International Journal* 6, 1-4 (1981): 139-55.

15 A. Browne and K. Williams, "Exploring the effects of resource availability and the likelihood of female-perpetrated homicides," *Law and Society Review* 23, 1 (1989): 75-94.

16 See the lists of state standards for batterer intervention at http://www.biscmi.org.

17 C.H. Sommers, *Who Stole Feminism? How Women Have Betrayed Feminism* (New York: Touchstone, 1994); P. Pearson, *When She Was Bad: How and Why Women Get Away with Murder* (Middlesex, UK: Penguin, 1998).

18 P. Tjaden and N. Thoennes, *Prevalence, Incidence and Consequences of Violence against Women: Findings from the National Violence against Women Survey* (Washington, DC: US Department of Justice, 1998).

19 D.G. Dutton, *The Domestic Assault of Women: Psychological and Criminal Justice Perspectives*, 2nd ed. (Vancouver: UBC Press, 1995).

20 M.A. Straus and R.J. Gelles, *Physical Violence in American Families* (New Brunswick, NJ: Transaction Publishing, 1992).

21 Ibid., 65-67.

22 J. Archer, "Sex differences in physical aggression to partners: A reply to Frieze (2000), O'Leary (2000), and White, Smith, Koss, and Figueredo (2000)," *Psychological Bulletin* 126, 5 (2000): 697-702.

23 Walby and Allen, *2001 British Crime Survey*; K.A. Malloy, K.A. McCloskey, N. Grigsby, and D. Gardner, "Women's use of violence within intimate relationships," *Journal of Aggression, Maltreatment and Trauma* 6, 2 (2003): 37-59; Statistics Canada, *Family Violence in Canada: A Statistical Profile* (Ottawa: Canadian Centre for Justice Statistics, 2003).

24 Dutton, *Domestic Assault of Women*; Straus and Gelles, *Physical Violence*; M.A. Straus, "The controversy over domestic violence."

25 Brown, "Gender as a factor"; Straus and Gelles, *Physical Violence*; Statistics Canada, *Family Violence in Canada*.

26 J. Archer, "Sex differences in aggression between heterosexual partners: A meta-analytic review," *Psychological Bulletin* 126, 5 (2000): 651-80.

27 J.C. Campbell, "'If I can't have you, no one can': Power and control in homicide of female partners," in J. Radford and D.E.H. Russell, eds., *Femicide: The Politics of Woman Killing* (New York: Twayne Publishers, 1992).

28 S.B. Sorenson and C.A. Taylor, "Female aggression toward male intimate partners: An examination of social norms in a community-based sample," *Psychology of Women Quarterly* 29 (2005): 79-96.

29 D. Levinson, *Family Violence in a Cross-Cultural Perspective* (Newbury Park, CA: Sage Publications, 1989).

30 Campbell, "'If I can't have you.'"

31 J. Archer, *Cross-Cultural Differences in Physical Aggression between Partners: A Social-Structural Analysis* (Preston, UK: University of Central Lancashire, 2005).

32 World Health Organization, *World Report on Violence and Health* (Geneva: World Health Organization, 2002).

33   Archer, *Cross-Cultural Differences*; A. Eagly, *Sex Difference in Social Behavior: Asocial Role Interpertation* (Hillsdale, NJ: Erlbaum, 1987); Eagly, Woods, and Diekman, "Social role theory."

34   A. Eagly and V.J. Steffen, "Gender and aggressive behavior: A meta-analytic review of the social psychological literature," *Psychological Bulletin* 100 (1986): 309-30; Archer, *Cross-cultural differences*.

35   Archer, "Sex Differences in Aggression."

36   E. Pence and M. Paymar, *Education Groups for Men Who Batter: The Duluth Model* (New York: Springer, 1993).

37   K. Corvo and P.J. Johnson, "Vilification of the 'batterer': How blame shapes domestic violence policy and interventions," *Aggression and Violent Behavior* 8, 3 (2003): 259-81, 276.

38   K. Hamberger and T. Potente, "Counseling heterosexual women arrested for domestic violence: Implications for theory and practice," *Violence and Victims* 9, 2 (1994): 125-37.

39   C. Darwin, *The Descent of Man and Selection in Relation to Sex* (London: Murray, 1871).

40   V.C. Wynne-Edwards, *Animal Dispersion in Relation to Social Behavior* (Edinburgh and London: Oliver and Boyd, 1962); E.O. Wilson, *On Human Nature* (Cambridge: Harvard University Press, 1978); E.O. Wilson, *Sociobiology* (Cambridge: Harvard University Press, 1975).

41   R. Bigelow, "The evolution of co-operation, aggression and self-control," in J.K. Cole and D.D. Jensen, eds., *Nebraska Symposium on Motivation* (Lincoln: University of Nebraska Press, 1972).

42   S.J. Gould, "Genes on the brain," *New York Review of Books* (5 June 1983): 5.

43   A. de Reincourt, *Sex and Power in History* (New York: Delta, 1974); T. Davidson, "Wife beating: A recurring phenomenon throughout history," in M. Roy, ed., *Battered Women: A Psychosociological Study of Domestic Violence* (New York: Van Nostrand, 1977), 1-23.

44   W. Simeons, *Man's Presumptuous Brain* (New York: Dutton, 1962).

45   D. Symons, *The Evolution of Human Sexuality* (Cambridge, MA: Cambridge University Press, 1980), 187.

46   Ibid., 189.

47   M. Daly and M. Wilson, *Homicide* (New York: Aldine, 1988).

48   Ibid., 197-99.

49   D. Hawkins, *Homicide among Black Americans* (New York: University Press of America, 1986).

50   Daly and Wilson, *Homicide*, 196-97.

51   Ibid., 208.

52   Ibid., 210.

53   D. Buss, *The Evolution of Desire: Strategies of Human Mating* (New York: Basic Books, 1994).

54   J. Peters, T.K. Shackelfords, and D. Buss, "Understanding domestic violence against women: Using evolutionary psychology to extend the feminist functional analysis," *Violence and Victims* 17, 2 (2002): 255-64.

55   G. Hirshey, *Nowhere to Run* (New York: New York Times Books, 1984).

56   R.P. Dobash, R.E. Dobash, M. Wilson, and M. Daly, "The myth of sexual symmetry in marital violence," *Social Problems* 39, 1 (1992): 71-90.

57   Straus, Gelles, and Steinmetz, *Behind Closed Doors*.

58   M.J. George, "Invisible touch," *Aggression and Violent Behavior* 8, 1 (2003): 23-60; B.J. Morse, "Beyond the Conflict Tactics Scale: Assessing gender differences in partner violence," *Violence and Victims* 4 (1995): 251-71.

59   J. Stets and M. Straus, "The marriage license as a hitting license," in Straus and Gelles, *Physical Violence*; M.A. Straus, "The National Family Violence Surveys," in Straus and Gelles, *Physical Violence*.

60   Dobash et al., "Myth of sexual symmetry," 80.

61   D. Kahneman, P. Slovic, and A. Tversky, *Judgment under Uncertainty: Heuristics and Biases* (London: Cambridge University Press, 1982).

62   Dobash et al., "Myth of sexual symmetry"; D.H. Coleman and M.A. Straus, "Marital power, conflict and violence in a nationally representative sample of Americans," *Violence and Victims* 1, 2 (1986): 141-57.

63   Dobash et al., "Myth of sexual symmetry," 84.

64   D.G. Dutton, "Developing treatment programs for men who assault their wives," *Japanese Journal of Addictions* 9 (2002): 111-26; D.G. Dutton, *The Abusive Personality: Violence and Control in Intimate Relationships* (New York: Guilford Press, 1998); D.G. Dutton, "A scale for

measuring propensity for abusiveness," *Journal of Family Violence* 10, 2 (1995): 203-21; D.G. Dutton, *Accuracy of the Propensity for Abusiveness Scale (PAS) in Assessing Abuse in a Clinical Outpatient Sample* (Vancouver: University of British Columbia, 1994); K. Hamberger and J.E. Hastings, "Personality correlates of men who batter and non-violent men: Some continuities and discontinuities," *Journal of Family Violence* 6, 2 (1991): 131-47; M.K. Ehrensaft, T.E. Moffitt, and A. Caspi, "Clinically abusive relationships in an unselected birth cohort: Men's and women's participation and developmental antecedents," *Journal of Abnormal Psychology* 113, 2 (2004): 258-70; A. Holtzworth-Munroe and G.L. Stuart, "Typologies of male batterers: Three subtypes and the differences among them," *Psychological Bulletin* 116, 3 (1994): 476-97; M.C. Zanarini, E.A. Parachini, F.R. Frankenburg, J.B. Holman, J.P.H. Hennen, D. Reich, and K.R. Silk, "Sexual relationship difficulties among borderline patients and Axis II comparison subjects," *Journal of Nervous and Mental Disease* 191, 7 (2003): 479-82; B. Fortunata and C.S. Kohn, "Demographic, psychosocial and personality characteristics of lesbian batterers," *Violence and Victims* 18, 5 (2003): 557-68.

65 Ehrensaft, Moffitt, and Caspi, "Clinically Abusive Relationships."
66 Dutton, *Abusive Personality*; B. Van der Kolk, A.C. Mcfarlane, and L. Weisaeth, *Traumatic Stress: The Effects of Overwhelming Experience on Mind, Body and Society* (New York: Guilford, 1996); J. Cassidy and P.R. Shaver, *Handbook of Attachment* (New York: Guilford, 1999).

Chapter 6: The Gender Debate and the Feminist Paradigm

1 R.P. Dobash, R.E. Dobash, M. Wilson, and M. Daly, "The myth of sexual symmetry in marital violence," *Social Problems* 39, 1 (1992): 71-90; P. Jaffe, N. Lemon, and S.E. Poisson, *Child Custody and Domestic Violence: A Call for Safety and Accountability* (Thousand Oaks, CA: Sage, 2003).
2 M.A. Straus, R.J. Gelles, and S. Steinmetz, *Behind Closed Doors: Violence in the American Family* (Garden City, NY: Anchor Press/Doubleday, 1980); J. Stets and M. Straus, "Gender differences in reporting marital violence," in M.A. Straus and R.J. Gelles, eds., *Physical Violence in American Families* (New Brunswick, NJ: Transaction Publishers, 1992), 151-66; M.A. Straus and R.J. Gelles, "How violent are American families: Estimates from the national family violence resurvey and other surveys," in Straus and Gelles, *Physical Violence*, 95-108; M. Bograd, "Feminist perspectives on wife assault: An introduction," in K. Yllo and M. Bograd, eds., *Feminist Perspectives on Wife Abuse* (Newbury Park, CA: Sage, 1988), 11-26.
3 D. Kahneman, P. Slovic, and A. Tversky, *Judgment under Uncertainty: Heuristics and Biases* (London: Cambridge University Press, 1982); I.L. Janis, *Groupthink*, 2nd ed. (Boston: Houghton-Mifflin, 1982); C. Lord, L. Ross, and M.R. Lepper, "Biased assimilation and attitude polarization: The effects of prior theories and subsequently considered evidence," *Journal of Personality and Social Psychology* 37 (1979): 2098-109.
4 T.S. Kuhn, *Structure of Scientific Revolutions* (Chicago: University of Chicago Press, 1965).
5 R.J. Gelles and M.A. Straus, *Intimate Violence: The Causes and Consequences of Abuse in the American Family* (New York: Simon and Schuster, 1988).
6 Dobash et al., "Myth of sexual symmetry"; R.E. Dobash and R.P. Dobash, "Wives: The appropriate victims of marital assault," *Victimology: An International Journal* 2 (1978): 426-42; R.E. Dobash and R.P. Dobash, *Violence against Wives: A Case against the Patriarchy* (New York: Free Press, 1979); Yllo and Bograd, *Feminist Perspectives*; L. Walker, "Psychology and violence against women," *American Psychologist* 44, 4 (1989): 695-702; D. Patai, *Heterophobia: Sexual Harassment and the Future of Feminism* (Lanham, MD: Rowman and Littlefield, 1998).
7 K. Corvo and P.J. Johnson, "Vilification of the 'batterer': How blame shapes domestic violence policy and interventions," *Aggression and Violent Behavior* 8, 3 (2003): 259-81; M.J. George, "Invisible touch," *Aggression and Violent Behavior* 8, 1 (2003): 23-60; D.G. Dutton, "Patriarchy and wife assault: The ecological fallacy," *Violence and Victims* 9, 2 (1994): 125-40.
8 Dutton, "Patriarchy and wife assault."
9 Dobash and Dobash, *Violence against Wives*, 24.
10 Bograd, "Feminist perspectives," 13.
11 E. Pence and M. Paymar, *Education Groups for Men Who Batter: The Duluth Model* (New York: Springer, 1993).

12 G. Serran and P. Firestone, "Intimate partner homicide: A review of the male proprietariness and the self-defense theories," *Aggression and Violent Behavior* 9, 1 (2004): 1-15, 12.
13 I. Arias and P. Johnson, "Evaluation of physical aggression among intimate dyads," *Journal of Interpersonal Violence* 4 (1989): 298-307; J. Archer, "Sex differences in aggression between heterosexual partners: A meta-analytic review," *Psychological Bulletin* 126, 5 (2000): 651-80; G.R. Brown, "Gender as a factor in the response of the law-enforcement system to violence against partners," *Sexuality and Culture* 8 (2004): 1-87; M.J. George, "A victimization survey of female-perpetrated assaults in the United Kingdom," *Aggressive Behavior* 25 (1999): 67-79.
14 Stets and Straus, "Gender differences."
15 K. Yllo and M. Straus, "Patriarchy and violence against wives: The impact of structural and normative factors," in Straus and Gelles, *Physical Violence*, 383-99.
16 Yllo and Straus, "Patriarchy and violence," 392.
17 Ibid., 394.
18 Straus, Gelles, and Steinmetz, *Behind Closed Doors*; M. Schulman, *A Survey of Spousal Violence against Women in Kentucky* (Washington, DC: US Department of Justice, Law Enforcement, 1979).
19 M. Smith, "Patriarchal ideology and wife beating: A test of feminist hypothesis," *Violence and Victims* 5, 4 (1990): 257-73.
20 Ibid., 268.
21 D.G. Dutton and A. Starzomski, "Psychological differences between court-referred and self-referred wife assaulters," *Criminal Justice and Behavior: An International Journal* 21, 2 (1994): 203-22.
22 D.J. Bem, "Self-perception: An alternative interpretation to cognitive dissonance phenomena," *Psychological Review* 74 (1972): 183-200.
23 Dobash and Dobash, "Wives."
24 R. Stark and J. McEvoy, "Middle class violence," *Psychology Today* 4, 6 (1970): 107-12.
25 T.R. Simon, M. Anderson, M.P. Thompson, A.E. Crosby, G. Shelley, and J.J. Sacks, "Attitudinal acceptance of intimate partner violence among US adults," *Violence and Victims* 16, 2 (2001): 115-26.
26 Dobash and Dobash, *Violence against Wives*.
27 I. Arias, J. Dankwort, U. Douglas, M.A. Dutton, and K. Stein, "Violence against women: The state of batterer prevention programs," *Journal of Law, Medicine and Ethics* (2002): 157-65.
28 L. Shotland and M. Straw, "Bystander response to an assault: When a man attacks a woman," *Journal of Personality and Social Psychology* 34, 5 (1976): 990-99.
29 Brown, "Gender as a factor," 16.
30 Ibid., 75; Statistics Canada, *Family Violence in Canada: A Statistical Profile* (Ottawa: Canadian Centre for Justice Statistics, 2003).
31 Brown, "Gender as a factor," 74.
32 E.S. Buzawa, T.L. Austin, J. Bannon, and J. Jackson, "Role of victim preference in determining police response to victims of domestic violence," in E.S. Buzawa and C.G. Buzawa, eds., *Domestic Violence: The Changing Criminal Justice Response* (Westport, CT: Auburn House, 1992), 263.
33 Straus and Gelles, *Physical Violence*; M.A. Straus, "The controversy over domestic violence by women: A methodological, theoretical and sociology of science analysis," in X. Arriaga and S. Oskamp, eds., *Violence in Intimate Relationships* (Thousand Oaks, CA: Sage Publications, 1999), 17-44.
34 S.W. Mihalic and D. Elliott, "If violence is domestic, does it really count?" *Journal of Family Violence* 12, 3 (1997): 293-311.
35 Dobash et al., "Myth of sexual symmetry."
36 Straus, "Controversy over domestic violence," 23.
37 Dobash et al., "Myth of sexual symmetry," 74-80.
38 Straus and Gelles, *Physical violence*.
39 Stets and Straus, "Gender differences."
40 Walker, *Battered Woman Syndrome*; D.G. Saunders, "Wife abuse, husband abuse or mutual combat: A feminist perspective on the empirical findings," in Yllo and Bograd, *Feminist Perspectives*, 90-113.

41   Saunders, "Wife abuse," 91.
42   Ibid., 92.
43   Straus, Gelles, and Steinmetz, *Behind Closed Doors*.
44   R. Bland and H. Orn, "Family violence and psychiatric disorder," *Canadian Journal of Psychiatry* 31 (1986): 131, Table 2.
45   J. Stets and M. Straus, "The marriage license as a hitting license," in M.A. Straus and R.J. Gelles, eds., *Physical Violence in American Families* (New Brunswick, NJ: Transaction Publishers, 1992): 155.
46   D.R. Follingstad, S. Wright, S. Lloyd, and J.A. Sebastian, "Sex differences in motivations and effects in dating violence," *Family Relations* 40 (1991): 51-57.
47   M.S. Fiebert and D.M. Gonzalez, "Women who initiate assaults: The reasons offered for such behavior," *Psychological Reports* 80 (1997): 583-90.
48   L.W. Kennedy and D.G. Dutton, "The incidence of wife assault in Alberta," *Canadian Journal of Behavioural Science* 21, 1 (1989): 40-54.
49   M.J. Kwong, K. Bartholomew, and D.G. Dutton, "Gender differences in patterns of relationship violence in Alberta," *Canadian Journal of Behavioural Science* 31 (1999): 150-60.
50   Bland and Orn, "Family violence," 129-37; M.B. Brinkerhoff and E. Lupri, "Interspousal violence," *Canadian Journal of Sociology* 13 (1988): 407-34; DeKeseredy and Schwartz, *Woman Abuse on Campus*; E. Grandin and E. Lupri, "Intimate violence in Canada and the United States: A cross-national comparison," *Journal of Family Violence* 12, 4 (1997): 417-43.
51   K.D. O'Leary, J. Barling, I. Arias, A. Rosenbaum, J. Malone, and A. Tyree, "Prevalence and stability of physical aggression between spouses: A longitudinal analysis," *Journal of Consulting and Clinical Psychology* 57 (1989): 263-68.
52   R. Sommer, G.E. Barnes, and R.P. Murray, "Alcohol consumption, alcohol abuse, personality and female perpetrated spouse abuse," *Personality and Individual Differences* 13, 12 (1992): 1315-23.
53   C.A. Ridley and C.M. Feldman, "Female domestic violence toward male partners: Exploring conflict responses and outcomes," *Journal of Family Violence* 18, 3 (2003): 157-70.
54   M. Kwong and K. Bartholomew, *Gender Difference in Domestic Violence in the City of Vancouver* (San Francisco: American Psychological Association, 1998).
55   Stets and Straus, "Gender differences"; Stets and Straus, "Marriage license."
56   Stets and Straus, "Gender differences."
57   Ibid., Table 9.1
58   Straus and Gelles, *Physical Violence*, 156.
59   Straus, "Controversy over domestic violence."
60   Stets and Straus, "Gender differences," Table 9.1
61   Ibid., 240.
62   Saunders, "Wife abuse"; Dobash et al., "Myth of sexual symmetry"; L. Tutty, *Husband Abuse: An Overview of Research and Perspectives* (Ottawa: Health Canada, National Clearinghouse on Family Violence, 1999).
63   Stets and Straus, "Gender differences"; Stets and Straus, "Marriage license."
64   M.P. Johnson, "Patriarchal terrorism and common couple violence: Two forms of violence against women," *Journal of Marriage and the Family* 57 (1995): 283-94.
65   Stets and Straus, "Gender differences"; Stets and Straus, "Marriage license."
66   Stets and Straus, *Physical Violence*, 118.
67   Canadian General Social Survey (Ottawa: Statistics Canada, 1999); D. LaRoche, *Aspects of the Context and Consequences of Domestic Violence: Situational Couple Violence and Intimate Terrorism in Canada in 1999* (Quebec City: Government of Quebec, 2005); M.P. Johnson and J.M. Leone, "The differential effects of intimate terrorism and situational couple violence: Findings from the National Violence against Women Survey," *Journal of Family Issues* 26, 3 (2005): 322-49; M.P. Johnson, "Patriarchal terrorism and common couple violence: Two forms of violence against women," *Journal of Marriage and the Family* 57 (1995): 283-94; see also D.G. Dutton, "The domestic abuse paradigm in child custody assessments," *Journal of Child Custody* 2, 4 (2005); D.G. Dutton, "On comparing apples to apples deemed non-existent: A reply to Johnson," *Journal of Child Custody* 2, 4 (2005).
68   D.G. Dutton, "The outcome of court-mandated treatment for wife assault: A quasi-experimental evaluation," *Violence and Victims* 1, 3 (1986): 163-75.

69   Walker, "Psychology and violence"; Walker, *Battered Woman Syndrome*; M.D. Pagelow, "Adult victims of domestic abuse: Battered women," *Journal of Interpersonal Violence* 7 (1992): 87-120; K. Yllo, "Political and methodological debates in wife assault research," in Yllo and Bograd, *Feminist Perspectives.*

70   Johnson, "Patriarchal terrorism"; Stets and Straus, *Marriage License,* 234.

71   M.J. Bologna, C.K. Waterman, and L.J. Dawson, "Violence in gay male and lesbian relationships: Implications for practitioners and policy makers," paper presented at Third National Conference of Family Violence Researchers, Durham, NH, 1987; D. Island and P. Letellier, *Men Who Beat the Men Who Love Them* (New York: Harrington Park Press, 1991); G-Y Lie and S. Gentlewarrier, "Intimate violence in lesbian relationships: Discussion of survey findings and practice implications," *Journal of Social Service Research* 15, 1 (1991): 41-59.

72   Bologna, Waterman, and Dawson, "Violence in gay male."

73   Lie and Gentlewarrier, "Intimate violence."

74   G-Y Lie, R. Schilit, J. Bush, M. Montague, and L. Reyes, "Lesbians in currently aggressive relationships: How frequently do they report aggressive past relationships?" *Violence and Victims* 6, 2 (1991): 121-35.

75   D.H. Coleman and M.A. Straus, "Marital power, conflict and violence in a nationally representative sample of Americans," *Violence and Victims* 1, 2 (1986): 141-57.

76   D. Adam, "Treatment models of men who batter: A profeminist analysis," in Yllo and Bograd, *Feminist Perspectives.*

77   M. Kasian and S.L. Painter, "Frequency and severity of psychological abuse in a dating population," *Journal of Interpersonal Violence* 7, 3 (1992): 350-64.

78   K.D. O'Leary, R. Heyman, and P.H. Neidig, "Treatment of wife abuse: A comparison of gender-specific and couple approaches," *Behavior Assessment* 30 (1999): 475-505.

79   D. McClelland, *Power: The Inner Experience* (New York: Halstead, 1975).

80   D.G. Dutton, A. Starzomski, and L. Ryan, "Antecedents of borderline personality organization in wife assaulters," *Journal of Family Violence* 11, 2 (1996): 113-32.

81   D.G. Dutton and C.E. Strachan, "Motivational needs for power and dominance as differentiating variables of assaultive and non-assaultive male populations," *Violence and Victims* 2, 3 (1987): 145-56.

82   E. Fromm, *The Anatomy of Human Destructiveness* (New York: Fawcett, 1973).

83   D.G. Dutton, "A critical review of R. Thorne-Finch's Ending the Silence: The origins and treatment of male violence against women," *Canadian Journal of Family Law* 11, 1 (1992): 179-85.

84   Schulman, *Women in Kentucky.*

85   J.C. Campbell, *Assessing Dangerousness: Violence by Sexual Offenders, Batterers and Child Abusers* (Newbury Park, CA: Sage, 1995).

86   S.L. Feld and M. Straus, "Escalation and desistance from wife assault in marriage," in Straus and Gelles, *Physical Violence.*

87   M.A. Straus, "The National Family Violence Surveys," in Straus and Gelles, *Physical Violence.*

88   Stets and Straus, "Gender differences"; Stets and Straus, "Marriage license."

89   Feld and Straus, "Escalation and desistance."

90   Lie et al., "Lesbians in aggressive relationships"; Archer, "Sex Differences."

91   D. LaRoche, *Aspects of the Context and Consequences of Domestic Violence,* 18.

Chapter 7: The Domestic Assault of Men

1   D. LaRoche, *Aspects of the Context and Consequences of Domestic Violence: Situational Couple Violence and Intimate Terrorism in Canada in 1999* (Quebec City: Government of Quebec, 2005), 16, Table 8.0. The survey sample was $N = 25,876$.

2   J. Archer, "Sex differences in aggression between heterosexual partners: A meta-analytic review," *Psychological Bulletin* 126, 5 (2000): 651-80; J. Stets and M. Straus, "Gender differences in reporting marital violence," in M.A. Straus and R.J. Gelles, eds., *Physical Violence in American Families* (New Brunswick, NJ: Transaction Publishers, 1992), 151-66; LaRoche, *Context and Consequences.*

3   J.M. Watson, M. Cascardi, S. Avery-Leaf, and K.D. O'Leary, "High school students' responses to dating aggression," *Violence and Victims* 16 (2001): 339-48.

4   Ibid., 344.

5   J. Katz, S.W. Kuffel, and A. Coblentz, "Are there gender differences in sustaining dating violence? An examination of frequency, severity, and relationship satisfaction," *Journal of Family Violence* (2002): 247-71.

6   M.A. Straus, "Measuring intrafamily conflict and violence: The Conflict Tactics Scales," *Journal of Marriage and the Family* 41 (1979): 75-88.

7   Katz, et al., "Are there gender differences."

8   M.R. Callahan, R.M. Tolman, and D.G. Saunders, "Adolescent dating violence victimization and psychological well-being," *Journal of Adolescent Research* 18, 6 (2003): 664-81.

9   D.A. Hines and K.J. Saudino, "Gender differences in psychological, physical, and sexual aggression among college students using the Revised Conflict Tactics Scales," *Violence and Victims* 18 (2003): 197-217.

10 D.R. Follingstad, C.M. Bradley, C.M. Helff, and J.E. Laughlin, "A model for predicting dating violence: Anxious attachment, angry temperament and the need for relationship control," *Violence and Victims* 17, 1 (2002): 35-48.

11 Ibid., 42.

12 Ibid., 44.

13 E.M. Douglas and M.A. Straus, *Corporal Punishment Experienced by University Students in 17 Countries and Its Relation to Assault and Injury of Dating Partners* (Helsinki, Finland: European Society of Criminology, 2003).

14 L. Serbin, D. Stack, N. De Genna, N. Grunezweig, C.E. Temcheff, A.E. Schwartzman, and J. Ledingham, "When aggressive girls become mothers," in M. Putallaz and K.L. Bierman, eds., *Aggression, Antisocial Behavior and Violence among Girls* (New York: Guilford Press, 2004), 262-85.

15 Ibid., 266.

16 Ibid., 268.

17 P. Jaffe, N. Lemon, and S.E. Poisson, *Child Custody and Domestic Violence: A Call for Safety and Accountability* (Thousand Oaks, CA: Sage, 2003).

18 L. Magdol, T.E. Moffitt, A. Caspi, D.L. Newman, J. Fagan, and P.A. Silva, "Gender differences in partner violence in a birth cohort of 21-year-olds: Bridging the gap between clinical and epidemiological approaches," *Journal of Consulting and Clinical Psychology* 65, 1 (1997): 68-78; T.E. Moffitt, A. Caspi, M. Rutter, and P.A. Silva, *Sex Differences in Antisocial Behavior* (Cambridge: Cambridge University Press, 2001).

19 Magdol et al., "Gender differences," 69.

20 Moffitt et al., *Sex Differences,* 64-65.

21 Magdol et al., "Gender differences," 69.

22 Moffitt et al., *Sex Differences,* 65.

23 Ibid., 63-65.

24 B.J. Morse, "Beyond the Conflict Tactics Scale: Assessing gender differences in partner violence," *Violence and Victims* 4 (1995): 251-71.

25 Dutton, "The Abusive Personality." See Chapter 11 below.

26 Moffitt et al., *Sex Differences,* 63, 50.

27 M.K. Ehrensaft, T.E. Moffitt, and A. Caspi, "Clinically abusive relationships in an unselected birth cohort: Men's and women's participation and developmental antecedents," *Journal of Abnormal Psychology* 113, 2 (2004): 258-70.

28 J. Stets and M. Straus, "The marriage license as a hitting license," in Straus and Gelles, *Physical Violence.*

29 Ehrensaft, Moffitt, and Caspi, "Clinically abusive relationships," 267.

30 Ibid., 258.

31 F. Elliott, D. Huizinga, and B.J. Morse, *The Dynamics of Delinquent Behaviour: A National Survey Progress Report* (Boulder, CO: Institute of Behavioral Sciences, 1985).

32 Morse, "Beyond the Conflict Tactics Scale," 255.

33 Stets and Straus, "Gender differences."

34 See also D.G. Dutton and T.L. Nicholls, "The gender paradigm in domestic violence research and theory: Part 1—The conflict of theory and data." *Aggression and Violent Behaviour* 10, 6 (2005): 680-714.

35 M.K. Ehrensaft, T.E. Moffitt, and A. Caspi, "Clinically abusive relationships in an unselected birth cohort: Men's and women's participation and developmental antecedents." *Journal of Abnormal Psychology* 113, 2 (2004): 258-70.

36 Ibid., 263.

37 R.C. Kessler, B.E. Molnar, I.D. Feurer, and M. Appelbaum, "Patterns and mental health predictors of domestic violence in the United States: Results from the National Comorbidity Survey," *International Journal of Law and Psychiatry* 24, 4-5 (2001): 487-508.

38 Kessler et al., "Patterns," 500-5.

39 Ibid., 500.

40 Ibid., 492.

41 Stets and Straus, "Marriage license," 234.

42 S.L. Williams and I.H. Frieze, "Patterns of violent relationships, psychological distress, and marital satisfaction in a national sample of men and women," *Sex Roles* 52 (2005): 771-85, 781; see also Stets and Straus, "Marriage license," Table 13.2.

43 D. M. Capaldi, H.K. Kim, and J.W. Shortt, "Women's involvement in aggression in young adult romantic relationships," in Putallaz and Bierman, *Aggression*.

44 Ibid., 233.

45 Ibid., 232.

46 Ibid., 235.

47 Moffitt et al., *Sex Differences*, 69.

48 Archer, "Sex differences in aggression"; see also J. Archer, "Sex differences in physically aggressive acts between heterosexual partners: A meta-analytic review," *Aggression and Violent Behavior* 7, 4 (2002): 315-51.

49 LaRoche, *Context and Consequences*. Effect size is calculated as a fraction of a standard deviation (SD). Hence an effect size of 1 means the two groups are one SD apart. With use of violence, an effect size of -0.05 means women are one-twentieth of an SD more often violent than men across the 85 studies used in the meta-analysis. Similarly, an effect size of 0.08 for injuries means women are injured about one-twelfth of an SD more often than men. In both cases, therefore, the rates by gender are virtually identical.

50 Archer, "Sex differences in aggression."

51 R.E. Dobash and R.P. Dobash, "Wives: The appropriate victims of marital assault," *Victimology: An International Journal* 2 (1978): 426-42.

52 Archer, "Sex differences in aggression," 339.

53 Ibid., 345-51.

54 M.S. Fiebert, "References examining assaults by women on their spouses or male partners: An annotated bibliography," 2004, available online at http://www.csulb.edu/~mfiebert/assault.htm.

55 M.S. Fiebert, "Annotated bibliography: References examining assaults by women on their spouses/partners," in B.M. Dank and R. Refinette, eds., *Sexual harassment and sexual consent* (New Brunswick, NJ: Transaction Publisher, 1997), 273-86.

56 Stets and Straus, "Gender differences."

57 R.B. Felson, "Big people hit little people: Sex differences in physical power and interpersonal violence," *Criminology* 34, 3 (1996): 433-52.

58 M. Cascardi, J. Langhinrichsen-Rohling, and D. Vivian, "Marital aggression: Impact, injury and health correlates for husbands and wives," *Archives of Internal Medicine* 152 (1992): 1178-84.

59 R.B. Felson, *Violence and Gender Re-Examined* (Washington DC: American Psychological Association, 2002; R.B. Felson and A.C. Cares, "Gender differences in the seriousness of assaults on intimate partners and other victims" (in press).

60 Felson and Cares, "Gender differences" (pre-publication copy), 15.

61 Ibid.

62 A.L. Coker, K.E. Davis, I. Arias, S. Desai, M. Sanderson, H.M. Brandt, and P.H. Smith, "Physical and mental health effects of intimate partner violence for men and women," *American Journal of Preventive Medicine* 23,4 (2002): 260-68. See also M.R. Callahan, R.M. Tolman,

D.G. Saunders, "Adolescent dating, violence victimization, and psychological well-being," *Journal of Adolescent Research* 18, 6 (2003): 664-81.
63 LaRoche, *Context and Consequences*, 16, Table 8.
64 C.C. Mechem, F.S. Shofer, S.S. Reinhard, S. Hornig, and E. Datner, "History of domestic violence among male patients presenting to an urban emergency department," *Academic Emergency Medicine* 6 (1999): 786-91.
65 D. Vasquez and R. Falcone, "Cross gender violence," *Annals of Emergency Medicine* 29, 3 (1997): 427-29.
66 D.A. Hines, J. Brown, and E. Dunning, *Characteristics of Callers to the Domestic Abuse Helpline for Men* (Durham, NH: University of New Hampshire, Family Violence Lab, 2003). The helpline, established in 2000, is described at http://www.noexcuse4abuse.org).
67 M.A. Straus and R.J. Gelles, *Physical Violence in American Families* (New Brunswick, NJ: Transaction Publishing, 1992).
68 Hines et al., *Characteristics*, 18; see also D.A. Hines and K.J. Saudino, "Gender differences in psychological, physical, and sexual aggression among college students using the Revised Conflict Tactics Scales," *Violence and Victims* 18 (2003): 197-217.
69 Sophie Goodchild, *The Independent*, Online Edition, 13 November 2005, 1.
70 Hines, Brown, and Dunning, *Characteristics of Callers*; M.J. George, "A victimization survey of female-perpetrated assaults in the United Kingdom," *Aggressive Behavior* 25 (1999): 67-79; E.S. Buzawa and C.G. Buzawa, *Domestic Violence: The Criminal Justice Response* (Thousand Oaks, CA: Sage, 1990), also see 2nd ed. (Thousand Oaks: Sage, 1996); G.R. Brown, "Gender as a factor in the response of the law-enforcement system to violence against partners," *Sexuality and Culture* 8 (2004): 1-87.
71 S. Basile, "Comparison of abuse alleged by same- and opposite-gender litigants as cited in requests for abuse prevention orders," *Journal of Family Violence* 19, 1 (2004): 59-68.
72 Moffitt et al., *Sex Differences*; Morse, "Beyond the Conflict Tactics Scale."
73 S. Pimlott-Kubiak and L.M. Cortina, "Gender, victimization, and outcomes: Reconceptualizing risk," *Journal of Consulting and Clinical Psychology* 71, 3 (2003): 528-39.
74 M.A. Straus, S.L. Hamby, S. Boney-McCoy, and D.B. Sugarman, "The revised Conflict Tactics Scale (CTS-2)," *Journal of Family Issues* 17, 3 (1996): 283-317.
75 P.C. Giordano, T.J. Millhonin, S.A. Cernokovich, M.D. Pugh, and J.L. Rudolph, "Delinquency, identity and women's involvement in relationship violence," *Criminology* 37 (1999): 17-40.
76 L.L. Marshall, "Development of the Severity of Violence against Women Scales," *Journal of Family Violence* 7, 2 (1992): 103-21; L.L. Marshall, "The severity of violence against men scales," *Journal of Family Violence* 7, 3 (1992): 189-203, 200.
77 Buzawa and Buzawa, *Domestic Violence*; Brown, "Gender as a factor."
78 E.S. Buzawa, T.L. Austin, J. Bannon, and J. Jackson, "Role of victim preference in determining police response to victims of domestic violence," in E.S. Buzawa and C.G. Buzawa, eds., *Domestic Violence: The Changing Criminal Justice Response* (Westport, CT: Auburn House, 1992), 263.
79 Ibid., 265.
80 Brown, "Gender as a factor," 1-87.
81 Ibid., 34.
82 Ibid., 37.
83 Ibid., 39.
84 Ibid., 41.
85 Ibid., 47-48.
86 Ibid., 63.
87 Ibid., 64.
88 Ibid., 65.
89 K. Henning and B. Renauer, "Prosecution of women arrested for intimate partner abuse," *Violence and Victims* 20, 3 (2005): 171-89.
90 Straus and Gelles, *Physical Violence*.
91 Brown, "Gender as a factor," 75.
92 S.B. Sorenson and C.A. Taylor, "Female aggression toward male intimate partners: An examination of social norms in a community-based sample," *Psychology of Women Quarterly* 29 (2005): 79-96.

93   D.R. Follingstad, D.D. DeHart, and E.P. Green, "Psychologists' judgments of psychologically aggressive actions when perpetrated by a husband versus a wife," *Violence and Victims* 19, 4 (2004): 435-52.

94   Ibid., 447.

95   P.D. Coontz, C.W. Lidz, and E.P. Mulvey, "Gender and the assessment of dangerousness in the psychiatric emergency room," *International Journal of Law and Psychiatry* 17, 4 (1994): 369-76.

96   Jaffe et al., *Child Custody;* L.S. Bancroft and J.G. Silverman, *The Batterer as Parent: Addressing the Impact of Domestic Violence on Family Dynamics* (Thousand Oaks, CA: Sage, 2002).

97   A.E. Appel and G.W. Holden, "The co-occurrence of spouse abuse and physical child abuse: A review and appraisal," *Journal of Family Violence* 12, 4 (1998): 578-99.

98   N. Trocmé, *Canadian Incidence Study of Reported Child Abuse and Neglect: Final Report* (Ottawa: Health Canada, 2001). Report No. H49-151/2000E.

99   H. Lamm and D. Meyers, "Group induced polarization of attitudes and behavior," in L. Berkowitz, ed., *Advances in Experimental Social Psychology* (New York: Academic Press, 1978).

100 Ibid.

101 Archer, "Sex differences in aggression"; Douglas and Straus, *Corporal punishment*; Magdol et al., "Gender differences"; Moffitt et al., *Sex Differences*; Ehrensaft et al., "Intergenerational Transmission."

102 Pimlott-Kubiak and Cortina, "Gender, victimization, and outcomes."

103 LaRoche, *Context and Consequences.*

Chapter 8: The Social Psychology of the Perpetrator

1   A. Holtzworth-Munroe, L. Bates, N. Smutzler, and E. Sandin, "A brief review of the research on husband violence: Part I—Maritally violent versus non-violent men," *Aggression and Violent Behavior* 2, 1 (1997): 65-99.

2   A. Bandura, "The social learning perspective: Mechanisms of Aggression," in *The Psychology of Crime and Criminal Justice*, ed. H. Toch (New York: Holt, Rinehart, and Winston, 1979).

3   *New York Times Magazine*, 15 January 2006, pp. 46-51.

4   K. Bjorkvist, K. Osterman, and A. Kaukianen, eds., *The Development of Direct and Indirect Aggression Strategies in Males and Females* (San Diego, CA: Academic Press, 1992).

5   L.D. Eron, L.R. Huesmann, M.M. Lefkowitz, and L.O. Walder, "Does television cause aggression?" *American Psychologist* 27 (1972): 253-63.

6   L.R. Huesmann, "An information processing model for the development of aggression," *Aggressive Behavior* 14, 1 (1988): 13-24.

7   M.A. Straus, R.J. Gelles, and S. Steinmetz, *Behind Closed Doors: Violence in the American Family* (Garden City, NY: Anchor Press/Doubleday, 1980); D.S. Kalmuss, "The intergenerational transmission of marital aggression," *Journal of Marriage and the Family* 46 (1984): 11-19.

8   Kalmuss, "Interegenerational transmission"; C.S. Widom, "Child abuse, neglect, and adult behavior: Research design and findings on criminality, violence and child abuse," *American Journal of Orthopsychiatry* 59 (1989): 355-67.

9   G.R. Patterson, R.A. Littman, and W. Brickner, "Assertive behavior in children: A step toward a theory of aggression," *Monographs of the Society for Research in Child Development* 32, 5 (1967): serial no. 133.

10 M.K. Ehrensaft, P. Cohen, J. Brown, E. Smailes, H. Chen, and J.G. Johnson, "Intergenerational transmission of partner violence: A 20-year prospective study," *Journal of Consulting and Clinical Psychology* 71, 4 (2003): 741-53; T.E. Moffitt, A. Caspi, M. Rutter, P.A. Silva, *Sex Differences in Antisocial Behaviour* (Cambridge, UK: Cambridge Unversity Press, 2001).

11 Widom, "Child abuse, neglect."

12 B. Egeland, "A history of abuse is a major risk factor for abusing the next generation," in R.J. Gelles and D.R. Loseke, eds., *Current Controversies on Family Violence* (Newbury Park, CA: Sage, 1993).

13 K.A. Dodge, G.S. Pettit, J.E. Bates, and E. Valente, "Social information-processing patterns partially mediate the effect of early physical abuse on later conduct problems," *Journal of Abnormal Psychology* 104, 4 (1995): 632-43.

14 Egeland, "History of abuse."

15 R. Novaco, *Anger Control* (Lexington: Lexington Books, 1975).

16 R. Novaco, "The functions and regulation of the arousal of anger," *American Journal of Psychiatry* 133 (1976): 1124.

17 Ibid.

18 E. Fromm, *The Anatomy of Human Destructiveness* (New York: Fawcett, 1973).

19 Novaco, "The functions and regulation of the arousal of anger," 1126.

20 J. Pleck, *The Myth of Masculinity* (Cambridge MA: MIT Press, 1981).

21 M. Daly and M. Wilson, *Homicide* (New York: Aldine, 1988).

22 R.P. Dobash, R.E. Dobash, M. Wilson, and M. Daly, "The myth of sexual symmetry in marital violence," *Social Problems* 39, 1 (1992): 71-90.

23 C.E. Strachan and D.G. Dutton, "The role of power and jealousy in anger responses to sexual jealousy," *Journal of Applied Social Psychology* 22 (1992): 1721-40.

24 D.G. Dutton and J.J. Browning, "Power struggles and intimacy anxieties as causative factors of violence in intimate relationships," in G. Russell, ed., *Violence in Intimate Relationships* (Great Neck, NY: PMA Publishing, 1988); D.G. Dutton, "Profiling wife assaulters: Some evidence for a trimodal analysis," *Violence and Victims* 3, 1 (1988): 5-30.

25 C.I. Eckhardt, K.A. Barbour, and G.C. Davis, "Articulated thoughts of maritally violent and non-violent men during anger arousal," *Journal of Consulting and Clinical Psychology* 66, 2 (1998): 259-69.

26 A.T. Beck, *Cognitive Therapy and the Emotional Disorders* (New York: International University Press, 1976).

27 A. Ellis and W. Dryden, *The Practice of Rational-Emotive Therapy* (New York: Springer, 1987).

28 D.G. Dutton, *The Abusive Personality: Violence and Control in Intimate Relationships* (New York: Guilford Press, 1998).

29 B. Rounsaville, "Theories in marital violence: Evidence from a study of battered women," *Victimology: An International Journal* 3, 1-2 (1978): 11-31.

30 Eckhardt, Barbour, and Davis, "Articulated thoughts."

31 H. Arendt, *Eichmann in Jerusalem: A Report on the Banality of Evil* (New York: Viking Press, 1964).

32 Straus, Gelles, and Steinmetz, *Behind Closed Doors*, 108-15.

33 Ibid.

34 A. Rosenbaum and K.D. O'Leary, "Marital violence: Characteristics of abusive couples," *Journal of Consulting and Clinical Psychology* 41 (1981): 63.

35 Kalmuss, "Intergenerational transmission."

36 P. Ulbrich and J. Huber, "Observing parental aggression: Distribution and effects," *Journal of Marriage and the Family* 43 (1981): 623-31.

37 Kalmuss, "Intergenerational transmission," 17.

38 Straus, Gelles, and Steinmetz, *Behind Closed Doors*.

39 E.M. Hetherington, "A developmental study of the effects of sex of the dominant parent on sex-role preference, identification and imitation in children," *Journal of Personality and Social Psychology* 2 (1965): 188-94; A. Bandura, *Aggression: A Social Learning Analysis* (Englewood Cliffs, NJ: Prentice-Hall, 1973).

40 Kalmuss, "Intergenerational transmission."

41 D.S. Kalmuss and J.A. Seltzer, "Continuity of marital behavior in remarriage: The case of spouse abuse," *Journal of Marriage and the Family* 48 (1986): 113-20.

42 Straus, Gelles, and Steinmetz, *Behind Closed Doors*; E.H. Carmen, P.P. Reiker, and T. Mills, "Victims of violence and psychiatric illness," *American Journal of Psychiatry* 141 (1984): 378-79.

43 B.E. Carlson, "Children's observations on interparental violence," in A.R. Roberts, ed., *Battered Women and Their Families* (New York: Springer, 1984).

44 D. Wolfe, P. Jaffe, S.K. Wilson, and L. Zak, "Children of battered women: The relation of child behavior to family violence and maternal stress," *Journal of Consulting and Clinical Psychology* 53 (1985): 657-65.

45 A.N. Schore, *Affect Dysregulation and the Disorders of the Self* (New York: Norton, 2003); A.N. Schore, *Affect Regulation and the Repair of the Self* (New York: Norton, 2003).

46 P. Jaffe, D. Wolfe, S.K. Wilson, and L. Zak, "Family violence and child adjustment: A comparative analysis of girls' and boys' behavioral symptoms," *American Journal of Psychiatry* 143 (1986): 74-77.

47 P. Jaffe, D. Wolfe, S.K. Wilson, and L. Zak, "Similarities in behavioral and social maladjustment among child victims and witnesses to family violence," *American Journal of Orthopsychiatry* 56, 1 (1986): 142-46; P. Jaffe, D. Wolfe, and S.K. Wilson, *Children of Battered Women* (Newbury Park: Sage, 1990).

48 A. Ganley, "Participant's manual. Court-mandated therapy for men who batter: A three-day workshop for professionals" (Washington, DC: Center for Women Policy Studies, 1981).

49 B.E. Carlson, "Children's observations on interparental violence," in A.R. Roberts, ed., *Battered Women and their Families* (New York: Springer, 1984); D.G. Dutton, "Witnessing parental violence as a traumatic experience shaping the abusive personality," in R.A. Geffner, P. Jaffe, and M. Suderman, eds., *Children Exposed to Domestic Violence* (New York: Haworth Press, 2000).

50 E. Hilberman and K. Munson, "Sixty battered women," *Victimology: An International Journal* 2 (1977-78): 460-70.

51 D.G. Dutton, "Trauma symptoms and PTSD profiles in perpetrators of abuse," *Journal of Traumatic Stress* 8 (1995): 299-316.

52 Ibid.

53 Kalmuss, "Intergenerational transmission"; Dutton, *Abusive Personality*.

54 P. Lehmann, "The development of PTSD in a sample of child witnesses to mother assault," *Journal of Family Violence* 12, 3 (1997): 241-57.

55 B. Rind, D. Tromovitch, and R. Bauserman, "A meta-analytic examination of assumed properties of child sexual abuse using college samples," *Psychological Bulletin* 124, 1 (1998): 22-53.

56 D.G. Dutton, C. van Ginkel, and A. Starzomski, "The role of shame and guilt in the intergenerational transmission of abusiveness," *Violence and Victims* 10 (1995): 121-31; D.G. Dutton, "Witnessing parental violence as a traumatic experience shaping the abusive personality," *Journal of Aggression, Maltreatment and Trauma* 3, 1 (2000): 59-67.

57 E.M. Douglas and M.A. Straus, *Corporal Punishment Experienced by University Students in 17 Countries and Its Relation to Assault and Injury of Dating Partners* (Helsinki, Finland: European Society of Criminology, 2003).

58 R.S. Pynoos and S. Eth, "Children traumatized by witnessing acts of personal violence: Homicide, rape, or suicide behavior," in S. Eth and R.S. Pynoos, *Post-traumatic Stress Disorder in Children* (Washington DC: American Psychiatric Press, 1985) 17-44; E.H. Carmen, P.P. Reiker, and T. Mills, "Victims of violence and psychiatric illness," *American Journal of Psychiatry* 141 (1984): 378-83.

59 T.R. Simon, M. Anderson, M.P. Thompson, A.E. Crosby, G. Shelley, and J.J. Sacks, "Attitudinal acceptance of intimate partner violence among US adults," *Violence and Victims* 16, 2 (2001): 115-26, 121.

60 R.E. Dobash and R.P. Dobash, *Violence against Wives: A case against the Patriarchy* (New York: Free Press, 1979).

61 Holtzworth-Munroe et al., "A brief review."

62 S.M. Stith and S.C. Farley, "A predictive model of male spousal violence," *Journal of Family Violence* 8, 2 (1993): 183-201.

63 P.H. Neidig, D.H. Friedman, and B.S. Collins, "Attitudinal characteristics of males who have engaged in spouse abuse," *Journal of Family Violence* 1, 3 (1986): 223-34; G.T. Hotaling and D.B. Sugarman, "An analysis of risk markers in husband-to-wife violence: The current state of knowledge," *Violence and Victims* 1 (1986): 101-24; I. Arias and K.D. O'Leary, "Cognitive-behavioral treatment of physical aggression in marriage," in S. Epstein and S.E. Schlesinger, eds., *Cognitive-Behavioral Therapy with Families* (New York: Brunner and Mazel, 1988), 118-50.

64 M. Smith, "Patriarchal ideology and wife beating: A test of feminist hypothesis," *Violence and Victims* 5, 4 (1990): 257-73.

65 D.J. Bem, "Self-perception: An alternative interpretation of cognitive dissonance phenomena," *Psychological Review* 74 (1967): 183-200.

66 Holtzworth-Munroe et al., "Research on husband violence"; R. Crossman, S.M. Stith, and M. Bender, "Sex role egalitarianism and family violence," *Sex Roles* 22 (1990): 293-303, 299.

67 S.M. Stith, D.B. Smith, C.E. Penn, D.B. Ward, and D. Tritt, "Intimate partner physical abuse perpetration and victimization risk factors: A meta-analysis review," *Aggression and Violent Behavior* 10, 1 (2004): 65-98.

68 Ibid., 89.
69 E. Pence and M. Paymar, *Education Groups for Men Who Batter: The Duluth Model* (New York: Springer, 1993).
70 Straus, Gelles, and Steinmetz, *Behind Closed Doors*; Kalmuss, "Intergenerational transmission."
71 J. Kaufman and E. Zigler, "Do abused children become abusive parents?" *American Journal of Orthopsychiatry* 57 (1987): 186-92.
72 M.A. Straus and C. Smith, "Family patterns and child abuse," in M.A. Straus and R.J. Gelles, eds., *Physical Violence in American Families* (New Brunswick, NJ: Transaction Publishers, 1992).
73 T.E. Moffitt, A. Caspi, M. Rutter, and P.A. Silva, *Sex Differences in Antisocial Behavior* (Cambridge: Cambridge University Press, 2001); M.K. Ehrensaft, T.E. Moffitt, and A. Caspi, "Clinically abusive relationships in an unselected birth cohort: Men's and women's participation and developmental antecedents," *Journal of Abnormal Psychology* 113, 2 (2004): 258-70; M.K. Ehrensaft, P. Cohen, J. Brown, E. Smailes, H. Chen, and J.G. Johnson, "Intergenerational transmission of partner violence: A 20-year prospective study," *Journal of Consulting and Clinical Psychology* 71, 4 (2003): 741-53.
74 M. Ehrensaft, P. Cohen, and J.G. Johnson, "Development of personality disorder symptoms and the risk of partner violence," *Journal of Abnormal Psychology* (In press).
75 D.G. Dutton, *The Domestic Assault of Women: Psychological and Criminal Justice Perspectives*, 2nd ed. (Vancouver: UBC Press, 1995); Dutton, *Abusive Personality*.
76 J. Babcock and D.G. Dutton, "Innocent victims? The personality profiles of females in the University of Washington studies." (2005).
77 M. Zoccolillo, E. Romano, D. Joubert, T. Mazzarello, S. Cote, D. Perusse, and R.E. Tremblay, "The intergenerational transmission of aggression and antisocial behavior," in R.E. Tremblay, W.W. Hartrup, and J. Archer, eds., *Developmental Origins of Aggression* (New York: Guilford Press, 2005); R.C. Bartlett, "Externalizing behavior in children of mothers with borderline personality organization and depressive symptomatology," PhD dissertation, Columbia University, New York, 2001; S. Dickstein, "Impact of maternal psychopathology on family functioning," *Journal of Family Psychology* 12 (1998): 23-40.

Chapter 9: Subtypes of Perpetrators

1 J. Stets and M.A. Straus, "The marriage license as a hitting license," in M.A. Straus and R.J. Gelles, eds., *Physical Violence in American Families* (New Brunswick, NJ: Transaction Publishers, 1992).
2 T.E. Moffitt, A. Caspi, M. Rutter, and P.A. Silva, *Sex Differences in Antisocial Behavior* (Cambridge: Cambridge University Press, 2001)
3 K. Henning, A. Jones, and R. Holford, "Treatment needs of women arrested for domestic violence: A comparison of male offenders," *Journal of Interpersonal Violence* 18, 8 (2003): 839-56.
4 T. Millon, *The Millon Inventories: Clinical Personality Assessment* (New York: Guilford, 1997).
5 D.G. Dutton, *The Abusive Personality: Violence and Control in Intimate Relationships* (New York: Guilford Press, 1998).
6 M. Ehrensaft, P. Cohen, and J.G. Johnson, "Development of personality disorder symptoms and the risk of partner violence," *Journal of Abnormal Psychology* (in press).
7 Ibid., 25
8 D.G. Saunders, "Woman battering," in R.T. Ammerman and M. Hersen, eds., *Assessment of Family Violence: A Clinical and Legal Sourcebook* (New York: Wiley, 1992), 208-35; L.K. Hamberger and J.E. Hastings, "Personality correlated of men who abuse their partners: A cross-validation study," *Journal of Family Violence* 1 (1986): 323-41; L.K. Hamberger and J.E. Hastings, "Personality characteristics of spouse abusers: A controlled comparison," *Violence and Victims* 3 (1988): 5-30; L.K. Hamberger and J.E. Hastings, "Counseling male spouse abusers: Characteristics of treatment completers and dropouts," *Violence and Victims* 4 (1989): 275-86; D.G. Dutton and A. Starzomski, "Psychological differences between court-referred and self-referred wife assaulters," *Criminal Justice and Behavior: An International Journal* 21, 2 (1994): 203-22; O. Kernberg, "The structural diagnosis of Borderline Personality Organization," in P. Hartocollis, ed., *Borderline Personality Disorders: The Concept, the Syndrome, the Patient* (New York: International Universities Press, 1977), 87-121.

9 S.D. Hart, D.G. Dutton, and T. Newlove, "The prevalence of personality disorder among wife assaulters," *Journal of Personality Disorder* 7, 4 (1993): 329-41; D.G. Dutton and S.D. Hart, "Risk markers for family violence in a federally incarcerated population," *International Journal of Law and Psychiatry* 15 (1992): 101-12; D.G. Dutton and S.D. Hart, "Evidence for long-term specific effects of childhood abuse and neglect on criminal behavior in men," *International Journal of Offender Therapy and Comparative Criminology* 36, 2 (1992): 129-37; D.G. Dutton, "Personality profile of intimate terrorists," *Journal of Interpersonal Violence* (2005).

10 G. Groth-Marnat, *Handbook of Psychological Assessment* (New York: Wiley and Sons, 1999), 205.

11 Ibid.

12 G. Hale, J. Duckworth, S. Zimostrad, and D. Nicolas, "Abusive partners: MMPI Profiles," *Journal of Mental Health Counseling* 10, 4 (1988): 214-24.

13 P.S. Flournoy and G.L. Wilson, "Assessment of MMPI profiles of male batterers," *Violence and Victims* 6, 4 (1991): 309-20.

14 L. Else, S.A.M. Wonderlich, W.W. Beatty, D.W. Christie, and M.D. Staton, "Personality characteristics of men who physically abuse women," *Hospital and Community Psychiatry* 44, 1 (1993): 54-58.

15 Millon, *Millon Inventories*.

16 Hastings and Hamberger, "Personality characteristics."

17 Hamberger and Hastings, "Personality correlated."

18 Hart, Dutton, and Newlove, "Prevalence of personality disorder."

19 E.W. Gondolf, "MCMI-III results for batterer program participants in four cities: Less 'pathological' than expected," *Journal of Family Violence* 14 (1999): 1-17.

20 Hamberger and Hastings, "Personality correlated"; Hart, Dutton, and Newlove, "Prevalence of personality disorder"; R. Beasley and C.D. Stoltenberg, "Personality characteristics of male spouse abusers," *Professional Psychology: Research and Practice* 23, 4 (1992): 310-17.

21 Gondolf, "MCMI-III results," 13; D.G. Dutton and A. Starzomski, "Borderline personality in perpetrators of psychological and physical abuse," *Violence and Victims* 8, 4 (1993): 327-37.

22 Dutton, *Abusive Personality*.

23 R.D. Maiuro, T.S. Cahn, P.P. Vitaliano, B.C. Wagner, and J.B. Zegree, "Anger, hostility and depression in domestically violent versus generally assaultive men and non-violent control subjects," *Journal of Consulting and Clinical Psychology* 56 (1988): 17-23; A.T. Beck, C. Ward, M. Mendelson, J. Mock, and J. Erbaugh, "An inventory for measuring depression," *Archive of General Psychiatry* 4 (1961): 561-71.

24 T.W. Julian and P.C. McKenry, "Mediators of male violence toward female intimates," *Journal of Family Violence* 8 (1993): 39-55.

25 H.S. Pan, P.H. Neidig, and K.D. O'Leary, "Predicting mild and severe husband to wife aggression," *Journal of Consulting and Clinical Psychology* 62 (1994): 975-81.

26 J. Babcock and D.G. Dutton, "A re-analysis of women's MCMI scores from the UW spouse abuse sample" (in preparation).

27 R.D. Maiuro, T.S. Cahn, P.P. Vitaliano, and J.B. Zegree, "Anger control treatment for men who engage in domestic violence: A controlled outcome study," paper presented at Annual convention of the Western Psychological Association, Seattle, WA, 1986; A.H. Buss and A. Durkee, "An inventory for assessing different kinds of hostility," *Journal of Consulting Psychology* 21 (1957): 343-49.

28 Maiuro, T.S. Cahn, P.P. Vitaliano, B.C. Wagner, and J.B. Zegree, "Anger, hostility and depression in domestically violent versus generally assaultive men and non-violent control subjects," *Journal of Consulting and Clinical Psychology* 56 (1988): 17-23; T.M. Caine, G.A. Foulds, and K. Hope, *Manual of Hostility and Direction of Hostility Questionnaire (HDHQ)* (London: University of London Press, 1967).

29 O.W. Barnett, R.W. Fagan, and J.M. Booker, "Hostility and stress as mediators of aggression in violent men," *Journal of Family Violence* 6 (1991): 219-41; A.H. Buss and A. Durkee, "An inventory for assessing different kinds of hostility," *Journal of Consulting Psychology* 21 (1957): 343-49.

30 P.C. McKenry, T.W. Julian, and S.M. Gavazzi, "Toward a biophysical model of domestic violence," *Journal of Marriage and the Family* 57 (1995): 307-20; L.R. Derogatis, *SCL-90: Admin-*

istration, Scoring and Procedure Manual for the Revised Edition (Baltimore: Johns Hopkins School of Medicine, 1977).

31 K.E. Leonard and H.T. Blane, "Alcohol and marital aggression in a national sample of young men," *Journal of Interpersonal Violence* 7 (1992): 19-30.

32 K.E. Leonard and M. Senchak, "Alcohol and premarital aggression among newlywed couples," *Journal of Studies on Alcohol* 11 (1993): 96-108.

33 J.M. Siegel, "The multidimensional anger inventory," *Journal of Personality and Social Psychology* 5, 1 (1986): 191-200.

34 D.G. Dutton, K. Saunders, A. Starzomski, and K. Bartholomew, "Intimacy anger and insecure attachment as precursors of abuse in intimate relationships," *Journal of Applied Social Psychology* 24, 15 (1994): 1367-86.

35 D.G. Dutton, "Male abusiveness in intimate relationships," *Clinical Psychology Review* 15, 6 (1995): 567-81.

36 D.G. Dutton and A. Starzomski, "Psychological differences between court-referred and self-referred wife assaulters," *Criminal Justice and Behavior: An International Journal* 21, 2 (1994): 203-22.

37 T. Millon, *The MCMI-II Manual*, 2nd ed. (Minneapolis: National Computer Systems, 1987).

38 Hamberger and Hastings, "Personality correlated."

39 D.G. Dutton, "Profiling wife assaulters."

40 Hamberger and Hastings, "Personality correlated."

41 Hamberger and Hastings, "Personality characteristics."

42 J.M. Lohr, L.K. Hamberger, and D. Bonge, "The nature of irrational beliefs in different personality clusters of spouse abusers," *Journal of Rational Emotive and Cognitive Behavior Therapy* 6 (1988): 273-85.

43 M.A. Straus and R.J. Gelles, "Is family violence increasing? A comparison of 1975 and 1985 survey rates," paper presented to American Society of Criminology, San Diego CA, November 1985.

44 L.K. Hamberger, J.M. Lohr, D. Bonge, and D.F. Tolin, "A large empirical typology of male spouse abusers and its relationship to dimensions of abuse," *Violence and Victims* 11 (1996): 277-92; D.G. Dutton and K.J. Hemphill, "Patterns of socially desirable responding among perpetrators and victims of wife assault," *Violence and Victims* 7, 1 (1992): 29-40.

45 Hart, Dutton, and Newlove, "Prevalence of personality disorder"; Millon, *MCMI-II Manual*; A.W. Loranger, *Personality Disorder Examination (PDE) Manual* (Yonkers, NY: DV Communications, 1988).

46 Gondolf, "MCMI-III results."

47 Hart, Dutton, and Newlove, "Prevalence of personality disorder."

48 D.G. Saunders, "A typology of men who batter: Three types derived from cluster analysis," *American Journal of Orthopsychiatry* 62, 2 (1992): 264-75.

49 C.M. Murphy, S.L. Meyer, and K.D. O'Leary, "Family origin violence and MCMI-II psychopathology among partner assaultive men," *Violence and Victims* 8 (1993): 165-76.

50 Dutton and Hemphill, "Socially desirable responding."

51 A. Holtzworth-Munroe and G.L. Stuart, "Typologies of male batterers: Three subtypes and the differences among them," *Psychological Bulletin* 116, 3 (1994): 476-97.

52 Saunders, "Typology of men."

53 Holtzworth-Munroe and Stuart, "Typologies of Male Batterers."

54 A. Holtzworth-Munroe, J. Meehan, K. Herron, and U. Rehman, "Testing the Holtzworth-Munroe and Stuart typology," *Journal of Consulting and Clinical Psychology* 68 (2000): 1000-19.

55 D.G. Dutton, "Behavioral and affective correlates of borderline personality organization in wife assaulters," *International Journal of Law and Psychiatry* 17, 3 (1994): 265-77; D.G. Dutton, "The origin and structure of the abusive personality," *Journal of Personality Disorder* 8, 3 (1994): 181-91.

56 J. Oldham, J. Clarkin, A. Appelbaum, A. Carr, P. Kernberg, A. Lotterman, and G. Hass, "A self-report instrument for Borderline Personality Organization," in T.H. McGlashan, ed., *The Borderline: Current Empirical Research* (Washington, DC: American Psychiatric Press, 1985), 1-18.

57   D.G. Dutton, *Comparing Assaultive Males with Clinical Outpatients: A Cross Validation of the Propensity for Abusiveness Scale* (Vancouver, BC, 1994).

58   Holtzworth-Munroe et al., "Testing the Holtzworth-Munroe."

59   N.S. Jacobson, J.M. Gottman, J. Waltz, R. Rushe, J. Babcock, and A. Holtzworth-Munroe, "Affect, verbal content, and psychophysiology in the arguments of couples with a violent husband," *Journal of Consulting and Clinical Psychology* 65, 2 (1994): 982-88.

60   R. Tweed and D.G. Dutton, "A comparison of instrumental and impulsive subgroups of batterers," *Violence and Victims* 13, 3 (1998): 217-30.

61   J. Oldham, J. Clarkin, A. Appelbaum, A. Carr, P. Kernberg, A. Lotterman, G. Hass, "A self-report instrument for Borderline Personality Organization," in T.H. McGlashan, ed., *The Borderline: Current Empirical Research* (Washington, DC: American Psychiatric Press, 1985), 1-18; K. Bartholomew and L.W. Horowitz, "Attachment styles among young adults: A test of a four-category model," *Journal of Personality and Social Psychology* 61 (1991): 226-44.

62   Tweed and Dutton, "Comparison of instrumental"; Oldham et al., "Self-report instrument."

63   D.W. Edwards, C.L. Scott, R.M. Yarvis, C.L. Paizis, and M.S. Panizzon, "Impulsiveness, impulsive aggression, personality disorder and spousal violence," *Violence and Victims* 18, 1 (2003): 3-14.

64   L.C. Morey, *The Personality Assessment Inventory: Professional Manual* (Odessa, FL: Psychological Assessment Resources, 1991).

65   Edwards et al., "Impulsiveness, impulsive aggression."

66   M.C. Zanarini, E.A. Parachini, F.R. Frankenburg, J.B. Holman, J.P.H. Hennen, D. Reich, and K.R. Silk, "Sexual relationship difficulties among Borderline patients and Axis II comparison subjects," *Journal of Nervous and Mental Disease* 191, 7 (2003): 479-82; E.F. Coccaro, "Neurotransmitter correlates of impulsive aggression in humans," *Annals of the New York Academy of Sciences* 794 (1996): 82-99; E.F. Coccaro and R.J. Kavoussi, "Neurotransmitter correlateds of impulsive aggression," in D.M. Stoff and R.B. Cairns, eds., *Aggression and Violence* (Mahwah, NJ: Erlbaum, 1996); J.R. Meloy, *Violent Attachments* (Northvale, NJ: Jason Aronson, 1992); Dutton, *Abusive Personality*; Tweed and Dutton, "Comparison of instrumental"; Edwards et al., "Impulsiveness, impulsive aggression."

67   Zanarini et al., "Sexual relationship difficulties."

68   Schore, *Affect Dysregulation.*

69   E. Abel, "Comparing the social service utilization, exposure to violence and trauma symtomatology of domestic violence female victims and female batterers," *Journal of Family Violence* 15, 4 (2001): 401-20.

70   J. Briere and M. Runtz, "The trauma symptom checklist (TSC-33): Early data on a new scale," *Journal of Interpersonal Violence* 4, 2 (1989): 151-62.

71   Holtzworth-Munroe and Stuart, "Typologies of Male Batterers."

72   J. Babcock, S.A. Miller, and C. Siard, "Toward a typology of abusive women: Differences between partner-only and generally violent women in the use of violence," *Psychology of Women Quarterly* 27 (2003): 153-61.

73   K. Henning, A. Jones, R. Holford, "Treatment needs of women arrested for domestic violence: A comparison with male offenders," *Journal of Interpersonal Violence* 18, 8 (2003): 839-56.

74   D.G. Dutton, K. Saunders, A. Starzomski, and K. Bartholomew, "Intimacy anger and insecure attachment as precursors of abuse in intimate relationships," *Journal of Applied Social Psychology* 24, 15 (1994): 1367-86; D.G. Dutton and A. Starzomski, "Psychological differences between court-referred and self-referred wife assaulters," *Criminal Justice and Behavior: An International Journal* 21, 2 (1994): 203-22; D.G. Dutton, "The traumatic origins of intimate rage," *Aggression and Violent Behavior* 4, 4 (1999): 431-48; D.G. Dutton, "Behavioral and affective correlates of Borderline Personality Organization in wife assaulters," *International Journal of Law and Psychiatry* 17 (1994): 265-77; D.G. Dutton, "The origin and structure of the abusive personality," *Journal of Personality Disorder* 8, (1994): 181-91; D.G. Dutton, "Trauma symptoms and PTSD-Like profiles in perpetrators of intimate abuse," *Journal of Traumatic Stress* 8, (1995): 299-316; D.G. Dutton and A. Holtzworth-Munroe, "The role of early trauma in males who assault their wives," in D. Cicchetti and R. Toth, eds., *The Rochester Symposium on Development* (Rochester NY: 1997).

75 D.R. Follingstad, R.G. Bradley, C.M. Helff, and J.E. Laughlin, "A model for predicting dating violence: Anxious attachment, angry temperament and need for relationship control," *Violence and Victims* 17, 1 (2002): 35-47.
76 M. Ehrensaft, P. Cohen, and J.G. Johnson, "Development of personality disorder symptoms and the risk of partner violence," *Journal of Abnormal Psychology* (in press).
77 Ibid., 24.
78 Ibid., 26.
79 Henning, Jones, and Holford, "Treatment needs of women."
80 A. Spidel, G. Vincent, M.T. Huss, J. Winters, L. Thomas, and D.G. Dutton, "Subtyping perpetrators of domestic violence," in H.F.M. Hervé and J. Yuille, eds., *The Psychopath in the 21st Century* (Mahwah, NJ: Erlbaum and Associates, 2006).
81 L. Magdol, T.E. Moffitt, A. Caspi, D.L. Newman, J. Fagan, and P.A. Silva, "Gender differences in partner violence in a birth cohort of 21-year-olds: Bridging the gap between clinical and epidemiological approaches," *Journal of Consulting and Clinical Psychology* 65, 1 (1997): 68-78.
82 Dutton, *Abusive Personality*.
83 Moffitt et al., *Sex Differences*, 65.
84 Zanarini et al, "Sexual relationship difficulties."
85 B. Fortunata and C.S. Kohn, "Demographic, psychosocial and personality characteristics of lesbian batterers," *Violence and Victims* 18, 5 (2003): 557-68.
86 C. Renzetti, *Violent Betrayal: Partner Abuse in Lesbian Relationships* (Newbury Park, CA: Sage, 1992).
87 Babcock and Dutton, "A re-analysis."
88 D.G. Dutton and G. Kerry, "Modus operandi and personality disorder in incarcerated killers," *International Journal of Law and Psychiatry* 22, 3-4 (1999): 287-300.
89 Edwards et al., "Impulsiveness, impulsive aggression."
90 H.F.M. Hervé, "The masks of sanity and psychopathy: A cluster analytical investigation of subtypes of criminal psychopathy," PhD dissertation, Department of Psychology, University of British Columbia, 2002.
91 R.D. Hare, *Without Conscience: The Disturbing World of the Psychopaths among Us* (New York: Pocket Books, 1993), xi.
92 R.D. Hare, *The Hare Psychopathy Checklist: Revised* (Toronto: Multi-Health Systems, 1991).
93 Hare, *Without Conscience*; R.D. Hare, "Psychopathy: A clinical construct whose time has come," *Criminal Justice and Behavior* 23, 1 (1996): 25-54.
94 J. Langhinrichsen-Rohling, M.T. Huss, and S. Ramsey, "The clinical utility of batterer typologies," *Journal of Family Violence* 15 (2000): 37-54.
95 Dutton, *Abusive Personality*; Holtzworth-Munroe and Stuart, "Typologies of Male Batterers."
96 Langhinrichsen-Rohling, Huss, and Ramsey, "Utility of batterer typologies."
97 J. Waltz, J.C. Babcock, N.S. Jacobson, and J. Gottman, "Testing a typology of batterers," *Journal of Consulting and Clinical Psychology* 68 (2000): 658-69.
98 Hervé, "Masks of sanity."
99 Ibid., 109.
100 Ibid., 119-20.
101 Ibid., 133-134.
102 Hervé, "Masks of sanity."
103 S. Porter, "Without conscience or without active conscience? The etiology of psychopathy revisited," *Aggression and Violent Behavior* 1, 2 (1996): 179-89.
104 Hervé, "Masks of sanity."
105 Hare, "Psychopathy"; R.D. Hare, "Psychopathy: Theory, research and implications for society. An introduction," *Issues in Criminological and Legal Psychology* 24 (1995): 4-5.

Chapter 10: The Cycle of Violence and the Abusive Personality

1 L.E. Walker, *The Battered Woman* (New York: Harper and Row, 1979).
2 Ibid., 59.
3 Ibid., 60, my italics.
4 Ibid., 61.

5 D.G. Dutton and S.L. Painter, *Male Domestic Violence and Its Effects on the Victim* (Ottawa: Health and Welfare Canada, 1980).

6 J.G. Gunderson, *Borderline Personality Disorder* (Washington, DC: American Psychiatric Press, Inc., 1984).

7 Ibid.

8 Ibid.

9 O. Kernberg, "The structural diagnosis of Borderline Personality Organization," in P. Hartocollis, ed., *Borderline Personality Disorders: The Concept, the Syndrome, the Patient* (New York: International Universities Press, 1977), 87-121.

10 Gunderson, *Borderline Personality Disorder*.

11 Ibid.

12 Walker, *Battered Woman*.

13 E. Revitch and L.B. Schlesinger, *Psychopathology of Homicide* (Springfield, IL: Charles Thomas, 1981).

14 D.S. Kalmuss, "The intergenerational transmission of marital aggression," *Journal of Marriage and the Family* 46 (1984): 11-19; J. Herman and B. Van der Kolk, "Traumatic antecedents of borderline personality disorder," in B. Van der Kolk, ed., *Psychological Trauma* (Washington, DC: American Psychiatric Assoication Press, 1987), 111-26.

15 D. Westen and J. Shedler, "Revising and assessing Axis II," *American Journal of Psychiatry* 156, 2 (1999): 258-85.

16 D.G. Dutton, "Behavioral and affective correlates of borderline personality organization in wife assaulters," *International Journal of Law and Psychiatry* 17, 3 (1994): 265-77; D.G. Dutton, "The origin and structure of the abusive personality," *Journal of Personality Disorder* 8, 3 (1994): 181-91; D.G. Dutton, K. Saunders, A. Starzomski, and K. Bartholomew, "Intimacy anger and insecure attachment as precursors of abuse in intimate relationships," *Journal of Applied Social Psychology* 24, 15 (1994): 1367-86; D.G. Dutton and A. Starzomski, "Psychological differences between court-referred and self-referred wife assaulters," *Criminal Justice and Behavior: An International Journal* 21, 2 (1994): 203-22; S.D. Hart, D.G. Dutton, and T. Newlove, "The prevalence of personality disorder among wife assaulters," *Journal of Personality Disorder* 7, 4 (1993): 329-41; D.G. Dutton and A. Starzomski, "Perpetrator characteristics associated with women's reports of psychological and physical abuse," *Violence and Victims* 8, 4 (1993): 326-35; D.G. Dutton and M.A. Landolt, *A Cross Validation of the Propensity for Abusiveness Scale* (Ottawa: Ministry of the Solicitor General of Canada, 1995); D.G. Dutton, "Male abusiveness in intimate relationships," *Clinical Psychology Review* 15, 6 (1995): 567-81; D.G. Dutton, "Intimate abusiveness," *Clinical Psychology: Science and Practice* 2, 3 (1995): 207-24; D.G. Dutton, "A scale for measuring propensity for abusiveness," *Journal of Family Violence* 10, 2 (1995): 203-21; D.G. Dutton, "Trauma symptoms and PTSD-like profiles in perpetrators of intimate abuse," *Journal of Traumatic Stress* 8, 2 (1995): 299-316; D.G. Dutton and A. Starzomski, "Borderline personality in perpetrators of psychological and physical abuse," *Violence and Victims* 8, 4 (1993): 327-37.

17 Dutton and Starzomski, "Psychological differences."

18 D.P. Crowne and D.A. Marlowe, "A new scale of social desirability independent of psychopathology," *Journal of Consulting Psychology* 24 (1960): 349-54; D.L. Paulhus, "Two-component models of socially desirable responding," *Journal of Personality and Social Psychology* 46 (1984): 598-609; D.L. Paulhus, "Self-deception and impression management in test responses," in A. Angleitner and J.S. Wiggins, eds., *Personality Assessment via Questionnaire* (New York: Springer, 1986): 142-65; T. Millon, *The MCMI-II Manual*, 2nd ed. (Minneapolis: National Computer Systems, 1987).

19 D.G. Dutton and K.J. Hemphill, "Patterns of socially desirable responding among perpetrators and victims of wife assault," *Violence and Victims* 7, 1 (1992): 29-40; Dutton and Starzomski, "Psychological differences."

20 Dutton and Starzomski, "Psychological differences."

21 Hart, Dutton, and Newlove, "Prevalence of personality disorder," 337.

22 J. Oldham, J. Clarkin, A. Appelbaum, A. Carr, P. Kernberg, A. Lotterman, and G. Hass, "A self-report instrument for Borderline Personality Organization," in T.H. McGlashan, ed., *The Borderline: Current Empirical Research* (Washington, DC: American Psychiatric Press, 1985), 1-18.

23 Dutton, "Behavioral and affective correlates."

24 Oldham et al., "Self-report instrument," 12.

25 D.G. Dutton and A. Starzomski, "Borderline personality in perpetrators of psychological and physical abuse," *Violence and Victims* 8, 4 (1993): 327-37, 329.

26 M.A. Straus, "Measuring intrafamily conflict and violence: The Conflict Tactics Scales," *Journal of Marriage and the Family* 41 (1979): 75-88.

27 Dutton and Starzomski, "Perpetrator characteristics"; R.M. Tolman, "The development of a measure of psychological maltreatment of women by their male partners," *Violence and Victims* 4, 3 (1989): 159-77.

28 R.M. Tolman, "The development of a measure of psychological maltreatment of women by their male partners," *Violence and Victims* 4 (1989): 159-77.

29 D.G. Saunders, "A typology of men who batter: Three types derived from cluster analysis," *American Journal of Orthopsychiatry* 62, 2 (1992): 264-75.

30 A. Holtzworth-Munroe and G.L. Stuart, "Typologies of male batterers: Three subtypes and the differences among them," *Psychological Bulletin* 116, 3 (1994): 476-87; L.K. Hamberger and J.E. Hastings, *Personality Correlates of Men Who Abuse Their Partners: Some Preliminary Data* (Berkeley: Society of Personality Assessment, 1985); R. Tweed and D.G. Dutton, "A comparison of instrumental and impulsive subgroups of batterers," *Violence and Victims* 13, 3 (1998): 217-30.

31 Dutton, "Trauma symptoms."

32 J. Briere and M. Runtz, "The trauma symptom checklist (TSC-33): Early data on a new scale," *Journal of Interpersonal Violence* 4, 2 (1989): 151-62; C. Perris, L. Jacobsson, H. Lindstrom, L. von Knorring, and H. Perris, "Development of a new inventory for assessing memories of parental rearing behaviour," *Acta Psychiatrica Scandinavica* 61 (1980): 265-74.

33 Dutton, "Trauma symptoms," 313.

34 D.G. Dutton, M.A. Landolt, A. Starzomski, and M. Bodnarchuk, "Validation of the PAS in diverse male populations," *Journal of Family Violence* 16, 1 (2001): 59-73.

35 Dutton, "Trauma symptoms"; D.G. Dutton, *The Domestic Assault of Women: Psychological and Criminal Justice Perspectives* (Boston: Allyn and Bacon, 1988).

36 Dutton, *The Domestic Assault* of Women.

37 D.G. Dutton and J.J. Browning, "Concern for power, fear of intimacy, and aversive stimuli for wife assault," in G.J. Hotaling, D. Finkelhor, J.T. Kirkpatrick, and M.A. Straus, eds., *Family Abuse and Its Consequences: New Directions in Research* (Newbury Park, CA: Sage, 1988), 163-75.

38 Walker, *Battered Woman.*

39 Dutton, "Behavioral and affective correlates," 272.

40 D.G. Dutton, A. Starzomski, and L. Ryan, "Antecedents of Borderline Personality Organization in wife assaulters," *Journal of Family Violence* 11, 2 (1996): 113-32.

41 J.L. Herman, J.C. Perry, and B.A. Van der Kolk, "Childhood trauma in Borderline Personality Disorder," *American Journal of Psychiatry* 146 (1989): 490-95; M.C. Zanarini, J.G. Gunderson, M.F. Marino, E.O. Schwartz, and F.R. Frankenburg, "Childhood experiences of borderline patients," *Comprehensive Psychiatry* 30, 1 (1989): 18-25; Kalmuss, "Intergenerational transmission."

42 J. Bowlby, "The making and breaking of affectional bonds," *British Journal of Psychiatry* 130 (1977): 201-35.

43 Dutton and Browning, "Concern for power."

44 K. Bartholomew, "Avoidance of intimacy: An attachment perspective," *Journal of Social and Personal Relationships* 7 (1990): 147-78, 171.

45 D.W. Griffin and K. Bartholomew, "The metaphysics of measurement: The case of adult attachment," in K. Bartholomew and D. Perlman, eds., *Advances in Personal Relationships*, Vol. 5: *Attachment Processes in Adulthood* (London: Jessica Kingsley Publishers, 1994), 17-52.

46 Gunderson, *Borderline Personality Disorder*; Dutton, "Origin and structure."

47 M. Mahler, "A study of the separation-individuation process and its possible application to borderline phenomena in the psychoanalytic situation," *Psychoanalytic Study of the Child* 26 (1971): 403-24.

48 J. Bowlby, *Attachment*, rev. ed. (New York: Basic Books, 1982); K. Bartholomew, A.J.Z. Henderson, and D.G. Dutton, "Insecure attachment and abusive intimate relationships," in

C. Clulow, ed., *Adult Attachment and Couple Psychotherapy: The "Secure Base" Concept in Practice and Research* (London: Routledge, 2001), 43-61.
49 M. Cascardi and D. Vivian, "Context for specific episodes of marital violence: Gender and severity of violence differences," *Journal of Family Violence* 10 (1995): 265-93; C.M. Murphy, S.L. Meyer, and K.D. O'Leary, "Family origin violence and MCMI-II psychopathology among partner assaultive men," *Violence and Victims* 8 (1993): 165-76.
50 Dutton et al., "Intimacy anger"; A. Holtzworth-Munroe, G.L. Stuart, and G. Hutchinson, "Violent versus non-violent husbands: Differences in attachment patterns, dependency, and jealousy," *Journal of Family Psychology* 11 (1997): 314-31.
51 A.J.Z. Henderson, K. Bartholomew, S. Trinke, and M.J. Kwong, "When loving means hurting: An exploration of attachment and intimate abuse in a community sample," *Journal of Family Violence* 20, 4 (2004): 219-31; K. Bartholomew, D. Oram, and M.A. Landolt, "Attachment and abuse in male same-sex relationships," Proceedings of Annual Convention of the American Psychological Association, Washington, DC, 2000.
52 Holtzworth-Munroe, Stuart, and Hutchinson, "Violent versus non-violent husbands"; K. Bartholomew and L.W. Horowitz, "Attachment styles among young adults: A test of a four-category model," *Journal of Personality and Social Psychology* 61 (1991): 226-44; M. Main and R. Goldwyn, *An Adult Attachment Classification System* (Berkeley, CA: 1994).
53 D.G. Dutton and G. Kerry, "Modus operandi and personality disorder in incarcerated killers," *International Journal of Law and Psychiatry* 22, 3-4 (1999): 287-300.
54 J.C. Babcock, N.S. Jacobson, J.M. Gottman, and T.P. Yerington, "Attachment, emotional regulation, and the function of marital violence: Differences between secure, preoccupied, and dismissing violent and non-violent husbands," *Journal of Family Violence* 15 (2000): 391-409; Main and Goldwyn, *Adult attachment*.
55 Henderson et al., "When loving means hurting."
56 S. Bond and M.H. Bond, "Attachment styles and violence within couples," *Journal of Nervous and Mental Disease* 192, 12 (2004): 851-63.
57 J. Bookwala and B. Zdaniuk, "Adult attachment styles and aggressive behavior within dating relationships," *Journal of Social and Personal Relationships* 15 (1998): 175-90.
58 C. Clulow, "Attachment, narcissism and the violent couple," in C. Clulow, ed., *Adult Attachment and Couple Psychotherapy* (London: Brunner-Routledge, 2001).
59 A.M. Mauricio, J. Tein, and F.G. Lopez, "Mediating influences of personality disorder characteristics between attachment and violence," *Violence and Victims* (in press).
60 Bartholomew, Oram, and Landolt, "Attachment and abuse."
61 M.A. Landolt and D.G. Dutton, "Power and personality: An analysis of gay male intimate abuse," *Sex Roles* 37 (1997): 335-58.
62 E.H. Carmen, P.P. Reiker, and T. Mills, "Victims of violence and psychiatric illness," *American Journal of Psychiatry* 141 (1984): 378-79.
63 B. Van der Kolk, *Psychological Trauma* (Washington, DC: American Psychiatric Press, 1987), 31-62.
64 A.N. Schore, *Affect Regulation and the Origin of the Self: The Neurobiology of Emotional Development* (Hillsdale, NJ: Erlbaum, 1994); A.N. Schore, *Affect Dysregulation and the Disorders of the Self* (New York: Norton, 2003); A.N. Schore, *Affect Regulation and the Repair of the Self* (New York: Norton, 2003).
65 Herman and Van der Kolk, *Traumatic Antecedents*, 114.
66 Dutton, "Trauma symptoms."
67 Millon, *MCMI-II Manual*.
68 D.G. Dutton, "Treatment of assaultiveness," in D.G. Dutton and D.L. Sonkin, eds., *Intimate Violence: Contemporary Treatment Approaches* (New York: Haworth Press, 2003).
69 Schore, *Affect Regulation*; Schore, *Affect Dysregulation*; Schore, *The Repair of Self*.
70 A. Starzomski and D.G. Dutton, *Attachment Style, Anger and Attribution in the Intimate Context* (Vancouver: University of British Columbia, Department of Psychology, 1994).
71 Dutton et al., *Intimacy Anger*.
72 F.D. Fincham and T.N. Bradbury, "Assessing attributions in marriage: The relationship attribution measure," *Journal of Personality and Social Psychology* 62, 3 (1992): 457-68.
73 Starzomski and Dutton, *Attachment Style*.

74 Ibid.
75 C.I. Eckhardt, K.A. Barbour, and G.C. Davis, "Articulated thoughts of maritally violent and non-violent men during anger arousal," *Journal of Consulting and Clinical Psychology* 66, 2 (1998): 259-69.
76 K.A. Dodge, G.S. Pettit, J.E. Bates, and E. Valente, "Social information-processing patterns partially mediate the effect of early physical abuse on later conduct problems," *Journal of Abnormal Psychology* 104, 4 (1995): 632-43.
77 J.P. Tangney, "Moral affect: The good, the bad, and the ugly," *Journal of Personality and Social Psychology* 61, 4 (1991): 598-607.
78 Ibid., 599.
79 Tangney, "Moral affect"; J.P. Tangney, P. Wagner, C. Fletcher, and R. Gramzow, "Shamed into anger? The relation of shame and guilt to anger and self-reported aggression," *Journal of Personality and Social Psychology* 62, 4 (1992): 669-75.
80 D.G. Dutton, C. van Ginkel, and A. Starzomski, "The role of shame and guilt in the inter-generational transmission of abusiveness," *Violence and Victims* 10 (1995): 121-31.
81 S. Miller, *The Shame Experience* (Hillsdale, NJ: Erlbaum, 1985); Tangney et al., "Shamed into anger?"; L. Wurmser, *The Mask of Shame* (Baltimore: Johns Hopkins University Press, 1981); S.S. Tompkins, "Shame," in D. Nathanson, ed., *The Many Faces of Shame* (New York: Guilford, 1987); H.B. Lewis, "Shame and the narcissistic personality," in Nathanson, *The Many Faces of Shame*; H.B. Lewis, *Shame and Guilt in Neurosis* (New York: International Universities Press, 1971).
82 Tangney et al., "Shamed into anger?"
83 R. Novaco, *Anger Control* (Lanham, MD: Lexington Books, 1975).
84 Dutton, van Ginkel, and Starzomski, "The role of shame."
85 D.G. Dutton, "Treatment of assaultiveness," in D.G. Dutton and D.A. Sonkin, eds., *Intimate Violence: Contemporary Treatment Approaches* (New York: Haworth Press, 2003).
86 Dutton, *The Domestic Assault of Women*.
87 J. Archer, *Cross-Cultural Differences in Physical Aggression between Partners: A Social-Structural Analysis* (Preston, UK: University of Central Lancashire, 2005).
88 A. Starzomski, *Attachment Style, Affect and the Construal of Interpersonal Conflict* (Vancouver: University of British Columbia: Department of Psychology, 1993), 68.

Chapter 11: Relationship/Interactionist Explanations

1 A.N. Schore, *Affect Dysregulation and the Disorders of the Self* (New York: Norton, 2003).
2 S.L. Williams and I.H. Frieze, "Patterns of violent relationships, psychological distress, and marital satisfaction in a national sample of men and women," *Sex Roles* 52 (2005): 771-85.
3 P.H. Neidig, *Family Advocacy Prevention/Survey Project* (Stony Brook, NY: Behavioral Science Associates, 1993).
4 M.A. Straus, R.J. Gelles, and S. Steinmetz, *Behind Closed Doors: Violence in the American Family* (Garden City, NY: Anchor Press/Doubleday, 1980); M.A. Straus and R.J. Gelles, *Is Family Violence Increasing? A Comparison of 1975 and 1985 National Survey Rates* (San Diego, CA: American Society of Criminology, 1985).
5 S.L. Feld and M. Straus, "Escalation and desistance from wife assault in marriage," in M.A Straus and R.J. Gelles, eds., *Physical Violence in American Families* (New Brunswick, NJ: Trans-action Publishers, 1990).
6 K.E. Leonard, "Alcohol use and husband marital aggression among newlywed couples," in X. Arriaga and S. Oskamp, eds., *Violence in Intimate Relationships* (Thousand Oaks, CA: Sage, 2000).
7 K.E. Leonard and M. Senchak, "Alcohol and premarital aggression among newlywed couples," *Journal of Studies on Alcohol* 11 (1993): 96-108.
8 G.K. Kantor and M.A. Straus, "The 'drunken bum' theory of wife beating," in M.A. Straus and R.J. Gelles, eds., *Physical violence in American Families* (New Brunswick NJ: Transaction Pub-lishers, 1992).
9 D.G. Dutton, R.J.W. Clift, J. Winters, and G. Swihart, *The Abusive Personality: A New "Third Variable" Linking Alcohol and Drug Use amongst Wife Assaulters* (Vancouver: Department of Psychology, University of British Columbia, 2005).

10   Leonard and Senchak, "Alcohol and premarital aggression."
11   Ibid., 106-7.
12   J.A. Schumacher and K.E. Leonard, "Husbands' and wives' marital adjustment, verbal aggression, and physical aggression as longitudinal predictors of physical aggression in early marriage," *Journal of Consulting and Clinical Psychology* 73, 1 (2005), 28-37.
13   C.M. Murphy and K.D. O'Leary, "Psychological aggression predicts physical aggression in early marriage," *Journal of Consulting and Clinical Psychology* 57 (1989): 579-82.
14   K.D. O'Leary, J. Malone, and A. Tyree, "Physical aggression in early marriage: Prerelationship and relationship effects," *Journal of Consulting and Clinical Psychology* 62, 3 (1994): 594b-602.
15   Ibid., 599.
16   N.S. Jacobson, J.M. Gottman, J.M. Gortner, S. Berns, and J.W. Shortt, "Psychological factors in the longitudinal course of battering: When do the couples split up? When does the abuse decrease?" *Violence and Victims* 11, 4 (1996): 371-92.
17   T.E. Moffitt, A. Caspi, M. Rutter, and P.A. Silva, *Sex Differences in Antisocial Behavior* (Cambridge: Cambridge University Press, 2001); L. Magdol, T.E. Moffitt, A. Caspi, D.L. Newman, J. Fagan, and P.A. Silva, "Gender differences in partner violence in a birth cohort of 21-year-olds: Bridging the gap between clinical and epidemiological approaches," *Journal of Consulting and Clinical Psychology* 65, 1 (1997): 68-78.
18   Moffitt et al., *Sex Differences*, 125-34.
19   A. Tellegen, *Brief Manual for the Multidimensional Personality Questionnaire* (Minneapolis: University of Minnesota, 1982); A. Tellegen and N.G. Waller, "Exploring personality through construction: Development of the multidemensional personality questionnaire," in S.R. Briggs and J.M. Check, eds., *Personality Measures: Development and Evaluation* (Greenwich, CT: JAI Press, 2001).
20   Tellegen and Waller, "Exploring personality," 17.
21   J. Stets and M.A. Straus, "The marriage license as a hitting license," in M.A. Straus and R.J. Gelles, eds., *Physical Violence in American Families* (New Brunswick, NJ: Transaction Publishers, 1992).
22   Moffitt et al., *Sex Differences*, 5.
23   G. Margolin, "Interpersonal and intrapersonal factors associated with marital violence," Proceedings of the Second National Family Violence Research Conference, Durham, NH, 1984 (available from Margolin); G. Margolin, R.S. John, and L. Gleberman, "Affective responses to conflictual discussions in distressed and non-ditressed couples," *Journal of Consulting and Clinical Psychology* 56 (1988): 24-33; G. Margolin and B. Burman, "Wife abuse versus marital Violence: Different terminologies, explanations, and solution," *Clinical Psychology Review* 13 (1993): 59-73.
24   G. Spanier, "Measuring dyadic adjustment: New scales for assessing the quality of marriage and similar dyads," *Journal of Marriage and the Family* 3 (1976): 15-28.
25   Margolin, "Interpersonal factors."
26   Ibid., 5.
27   Ibid., 6.
28   Ibid., 9, Table 1.
29   G. Margolin, R.S. John, and L. Glebermen, "Affective responses to conflictual discussions in violent and non-violent couples," *Journal of Consulting and Clinical Psychology* 56, 1 (1989): 24-33.
30   M.S. Forgatch and G.B. Weider, *Parent Adolescent Negotiation Interaction Code (PANIC)* (Eugene, OR: 1981).
31   Margolin, John, and Glebermen, "Affective responses," 31.
32   Ibid.
33   Ibid.
34   D.G. Dutton, "Profiling wife assaulters: Some evidence for a trimodal analysis," *Violence and Victims* 3, 1 (1988): 5-30.
35   B. Burman, G. Margolin, and R.S. John, "America's angriest home videos: Behavioural contingencies observed in home re-enactments of marital conflict," *Journal of Consulting and Clinical Psychology* 61, 1 (1993): 28-39.

36 Ibid., 37.
37 Ibid.
38 Margolin and Burman, "Wife abuse," 60.
39 J.M. Gottman, N.S. Jacobson, R. Rushe, J.W. Shortt, J. Babcock, J.J. La Taillade, and J. Waltz, "The relationship between heart rate reactivity, emotionally aggressive behavior and general violence in batterers," *Journal of Family Psychology* 9, 3 (1995): 227-48; J.C. Babcock, J. Waltz, N.S. Jacobson, and J.M. Gottman, "Power and violence: The relation between communication patterns, power discrepancies, and domestic violence," *Journal of Consulting and Clinical Psychology* 61, 1 (1993): 40-50; N.S. Jacobson, J.M. Gottman, J. Waltz, R. Rushe, J. Babcock, and A. Holtzworth-Munroe, "Affect, verbal content, and psychophysiology in the arguments of couples with a violent husband," *Journal of Consulting and Clinical Psychology* 62, 5 (1994): 982-88.
40 R.W. Levenson and J.M. Gottman, "Marital interaction: physiological linkage and affective exchange," *Journal of Personality and Social Psychology* 45, 3(1983): 587-97.
41 Babcock et al., "Power and violence," 42.
42 Jacobson et al., "Affect, verbal content," 983.
43 Babcock et al., "Power and violence."
44 K. Yllo and M. Straus, "Patriarchy and violence against wives: The impact of structural and normative factors," in M. Straus and R. Gelles, eds., *Physical Violence in American Families* (New Brunswick, NJ: Transaction Publishers, 1990), 383-99.
45 J. Archer, "Cross-cultural differences in physical aggression between partners: A social-structural analysis," *Personality and Social Psychology Review* (in press).
46 J.V. Cordova, N.C. Jacobson, J.M. Gottman, R. Rushe, and G. Cox, "Negative reciprocity and communication in couples with a violent husband," *Journal of Abnormal Psychology* 102, 4 (1993): 559-64.
47 Ibid., 562, Table 2.
48 Ibid., 563.
49 Jacobson et al., "Arguments of couples," 983.
50 Cordova et al., "Negative reciprocity," 562.
51 Ibid., 564.
52 Jacobson et al., "Arguments of couples," 982.
53 Ibid., 986.
54 D.G. Dutton, A.N. Webb, and L. Ryan, "Gender differences in anger/anxiety reactions to witnessing dyadic family conflict," *Canadian Journal of Behavioural Science* 26, 3 (1994): 353-64.
55 Jacobson et al., "Arguments of couples," 986.
56 Ibid., 987.
57 Ibid., 986.
58 Ibid., 987.
59 J. Babcock and D.G. Dutton, "A re-analysis of women's MCMI scores from the UW Spouse Abuse Sample" (in preparation).
60 Gottman et al., "Heart rate reactivity," 227-48.
61 K.E. Leonard and J.J. Roberts, "The effects of alcohol on the marital interactions of aggressive and non-aggressive husbands and their wives," *Journal of Abnormal Psychology* 107, 4 (1998): 602-15.
62 Ibid., 613.
63 Ibid., 614.
64 R. Heyman and K.A. Schlee, "Stopping wife abuse via physical aggression couples treatment," in D.G. Dutton and D. Sonkin, eds., *Intimate Violence: Contemporary Treatment Innovations* (New York: Haworth Press, 2003).
65 P.H. Neidig and D.H. Friedman, *Spouse Abuse: A Treatment Program for Couples* (Champaign, IL: Research Press, 1984).
66 Ibid., 1-7, 11.
67 J. Giles-Sims, *Wife Battering: A Systems Theory Approach* (New York: Guilford, 1983).
68 Ibid., 33.
69 G.R. Patterson, J.A. Cobb, R.S. Ray, "A social engineering technology for retraining families

of aggressive boys," in H.E. Adams and P.J. Unikel, eds., *Issues and Trends in Behavior Therapy* (Springfield, IL: Charles C. Thomas, 1972).
70 M.D. Pagelow, *Family Violence* (New York: Praeger, 1984).
71 Neidig and Friedman, *Spouse Abuse*, 5.
72 H. Richter, *The Family as Patient* (New York: Farrar, Straus, and Giroux, 1974).
73 D.S. Kalmuss and J.A. Seltzer, "Continuity of marital behavior in remarriage: The case of spouse abuse," *Journal of Marriage and the Family* 48 (1986): 113-20.
74 M. Cascardi and D. Vivian, "Context for specific episodes of marital violence: Gender and severity of violence differences," *Journal of Family Violence* 10 (1995): 265-93.
75 D. Vivian and J. Langhinrichsen-Rohling, "Are bi-directionally violent couples mutually victimized? A gender-sensitive comparison," *Violence and Victims* 9 (1994): 107-24.
76 Stets and Straus, "Gender differences," 234, Table 13.2.
77 K.D. O'Leary, D. Vivian, and J. Malone, "Assessment of physical aggression in marriage: The need for a multimodal method," *Behavior Assessment* 14 (1992): 11; M. Ehrensaft and D. Vivian, "Spouses' reasons for not reporting existing physical aggression as a marital problem," *Journal of Family Psychology* 10, 4 (1996): 451.
78 Heyman and Schlee, "Stopping wife abuse," 145.
79 S.M. Stith, K.H. Rosen, E.E. McCollum, and C.J. Thomsen, "Treating intimate partner violence within intact couple relationships: Outcomes of multi-couple versus individual couple therapy," *Journal of Marital and Family Therapy* 30 (2004): 305-18.
80 M. Shepard, "Interventions with men who batter: An evaluation of a domestic abuse program," paper presented at Third National Conference on Domestic Violence, University of New Hampshire, Durham, NH, 1987; M. Shepard, "Predicting batterer recidivism five years after community intervention," *Journal of Family Violence* 7, 3 (1992): 167-78.
81 D.G. Dutton, "The criminal justice response to wife assault," *Law and Human Behavior* 11, 3 (1987): 189-206.; G. Rosenfeld, "Court-ordered treatment of spouse abuse," *Clinical Psychology Review* 12 (1992): 205-26.
82 S.M. Stith, K.H. Rosen, and E.E. McCollum, "Effectiveness of couples treatment for spouse abuse," *Journal of Marital and Family Therapy* 29 (2003): 407-26.

Chapter 12: Failure of Criminal Justice Intervention Policy

1 M. Wanless, "Mandatory arrest: A step toward eradicating domestic violence, but is it enough?" *University of Illinois Law Review* 96, 2 (1996): 533-86; M. Hoctor, "Domestic violence as a crime against the state: The need for mandatory arrest in California," *California Law Review* 85, 3 (1997): 643-700; L.G. Mills, "Killing her softly: Intimate abuse and the violence of state intervention," *Harvard Law Review* 113, 2 (1999): 551-613.
2 M. Bard, "Iatrogenic violence," *Police Chief* 38 (January, 1971): 16-17; M. Bard, J. Zacker, and E. Rutter, *Police Family Crisis Intervention and Conflict-Management: An Action Research Analysis* (New York: US Department of Justice, 1972).
3 I. Illich, *Tools for conviviality* (London: Calder and Boyars, 1973).
4 D.A. Liebman and J.A. Schwartz, "Police programs in domestic crisis intervention: A review," in J. Snibbe and H. Snibbe, eds., *The Urban Policeman In Transition* (Springfield, IL: Charles C. Thomas, 1973).
5 M. Wilt and R. Breedlove, *Domestic Violence and the Police: Studies in Detroit and Kansas City* (Washington, DC: Police Foundation, 1977).
6 D. Lipton, R. Martinson, and J. Wilks, *The Effectiveness of Correctional Treatment* (New York: Praeger, 1975), 186.
7 M. Bard and J. Zacker, "Assaultiveness and alcohol use in family disputes: Police perceptions," *Criminology* 12, 3 (1974): 281-92.
8 R.A. Berk, S.F. Berk, D.R. Loseke, and D. Rauma, "Mutual combat and other family violence myths," in D. Finkelhor, R.J. Gelles, G.T. Hotaling, and M.A. Straus, eds., *The Dark Side of Families: Current Family Violence Research* (Beverly Hills, CA: Sage, 1981): 197-212.
9 P. Jaffe and C.A. Burris, *An Integrated Response to Wife Assault: A Community Model* (Ottawa: Solicitor General of Canada, 1982); G.R. Brown, "Gender as a factor in the response of the law-enforcement system to violence against partners," *Sexuality and Culture* 8 (2004): 1-87; E.S. Buzawa and C.G. Buzawa, *Domestic Violence: The Criminal Justice Response*, 2nd ed. (Thousand Oaks, CA: Sage, 1996).

10 M. Schulman, *A Survey of Spousal Violence against Women in Kentucky* (Washington, DC: US Department of Justice, Law Enforcement, 1979); M.A. Straus, R.J. Gelles, and S. Steinmetz, *Behind Closed Doors: Violence in the American Family* (Garden City, NY: Anchor Press/Doubleday, 1980).

11 L.W. Sherman and R.A. Berk, "The specific deterrent effects of arrest for domestic assault," *American Sociological Review* 49 (1984): 261-72.

12 D. Ford and M.J. Regoli, "The preventive impacts of policies for prosecuting wife batterers," in E.S. Buzawa and C.G. Buzawa, eds., *Domestic Violence: The Changing Criminal Justice Response* (Westport, CT: Auburn House, 1992).

13 D.A. Ford, "Preventing and provoking wife battery through criminal sanctions: A look at the risks," in D.D. Knudsen and J.L. Miller, eds., *Abused and Battered: Social and Legal Responses to Family Violence* (New York: Aldine, 1991), 191-209; D.A. Ford and M.J. Regoli, "The criminal prosecution of wife assaults: Process, problems, and effects," in N.Z. Hilton, ed., *Legal Responses to Wife Assault: Current Trends and Evaluation* (Newbury Park, CA: Sage, 1993), 127-64.

14 Buzawa and Buzawa, *Domestic Violence* (1996), 153.

15 Ibid., 154.

16 P. Jaffe, D. Wolfe, A. Telford, and G. Austin, "The impact of police charges in incidents of wife abuse," *Journal of Family Violence* 1, 1 (1986): 37-49.

17 E.S. Buzawa and C.G. Buzawa, *Domestic Violence* (1996), ix

18 Ibid., 159.

19 Ibid., 161.

20 Ibid., 162.

21 S.L. Williams and I.H. Frieze, "Patterns of violent relationships, psychological distress, and marital satisfaction in a national sample of men and women," *Sex Roles* 52 (2005): 771-85, 772.

22 J. Andenaes, *Punishment and Deterrence* (Ann Arbor, MI: University of Michigan Press, 1974); A. Blumstein, I. Cohen, and D. Nagin, *Deterrence and Incapacitation: Estimating the Effects of Criminal Sanctions on Crime Rates* (Washington, DC: National Academy of Science, 1978); F.E. Zimring and G.J. Hawkins, *Deterrence: The Legal Threat in Crime Control* (Chicago: University of Chicago Press, 1973); I. Ehrlich, "The deterrent effect of capital punishment: A question of life and death," *American Economic Review* 65 (1975): 397-412.

23 National Research Council, *Deterrence and Incapacitation* (Washington, DC: National Academy of Sciences, 1978); J.Q. Wilson, *Thinking about Crime* (New York: Basic, 1983); D.P. Phillips and J.E. Hensley, "When violence is rewarded or punished: The impact of mass media stories on homicide," *Journal of Communication* 34, 3 (1984): 101-16; G. Gibbs, "Deterrence theory and research," Nebraska Symposium on Motivation, University of Nebraska-Lincoln, Lincoln, NE, 1985: 87-130.

24 Wilson, *Thinking about Crime.*

25 Ibid.

26 M.W. Ross, R.L. Campbell, and J.R. Clayter, "New inventory of measurement of parental rearing patterns: An English form of the EMBU," *Acta Psychiatrica Scandinavica* 66 (1982): 499-507.

27 Gibbs, "Deterrence theory and research"; K. Williams and R. Hawkins, *Perceptual Research on General Deterrence: A Critical Review* (Cincinnati: American Society for Criminology, 1984).

28 Wilson, *Thinking about Crime.*

29 Sherman and Berk, "Effects of arrest."

30 The Straus surveys and the Schulman survey reported rates of repeat assault that were two-thirds of the rate for "ever assaulted".

31 Schulman, *Survey of Spousal Violence;* Straus et al., *Behind Closed Doors.*

32 D.G. Dutton and K.J. Hemphill, "Patterns of socially desirable responding among perpetrators and victims of wife assault," *Violence and Victims* 7, 1 (1992): 29-40.

33 J. Fagan, "Cessation of family violence: Deterrence and dissuasion," in L. Ohlin and M. Tonry, eds., *Family Violence* (Chicago: University of Chicago Press, 1989).

34 D.G. Dutton, S.D. Hart, L.W. Kennedy, and K.R. Williams, "Arrest and the reduction of repeat wife assault," in Buzawa and Buzawa, eds., *Domestic Violence.* See also K. Williams and

D. Carmody, *Wife Assault: Perceptions of Sanctions and Deterrence* (University of New Hampshire, Family Relations Lab, 1986); L.W. Kennedy and D.G. Dutton, "The incidence of wife assault in Alberta," *Canadian Journal of Behavioural Science* 21, 1 (1989): 40-54.

35   D.H. Coleman and M.A. Straus, "Marital power, conflict and violence in a nationally representative sample of American couples," in M.A. Straus and R.J. Gelles, eds., *Physical Violence in American families* (New Brunswick, NJ: Transaction, 1992), 287-300.

36   J.C. Babcock, J. Waltz, N.S. Jacobson, and J.M. Gottman, "Power and violence: The relation between communication patterns, power discrepancies, and domestic violence," *Journal of Consulting and Clinical Psychology* 61, 1 (1993): 40-50.

37   Sherman and Berk, "Effects of arrest."

38   Schulman, *Survey of Spousal Violence*; Straus, Gelles, and Steinmetz, *Behind Closed Doors*. See our calculations in Chapter 6, under Patriarchal Violence.

39   R.J. Gelles, "Constraints against family violence: How well do they work?" *American Behavioral Scientist* 36, 5 (1993): 575-86.

40   J.H. Garner and C.D. Maxwell, "What are the lessons of the police arrest studies?" *Journal of Aggression, Maltreatment and Trauma* 4 (2000): 83-114.

41   G. Hotaling and E.S. Buzawa, *Forgoing Criminal Justice Assistance: The Non-Reporting of New Incidents of Abuse in a Court Sample of Domestic Violence Victims* (Washington, DC: National Institute of Justice, National Criminal Justice Reference Service, 2003).

42   P.R. Gartin, *The Individual Effects of Arrest in Domestic Violence Cases: A Re-Analysis of the Minneapolis Domestic Violence Experiment* (Washington, DC: National Institute of Justice, 1991), 92.

43   Bard, "Iatrogenic violence."

44   Sherman and Berk, "Effects of arrest," 268.

45   Dutton et al., "Repeat wife assault."

46   D.G. Dutton, B. Fehr, and H. McEwen, "Severe wife battering as deindividuated violence," *Victimology: An International Journal* 7,1-4 (1982): 13-23; D.W. Edwards, C.L. Scott, R.M. Yarvis, C.L. Paizis, and M.S. Panizzon, "Impulsiveness, impulsive aggression, personality disorder and spousal violence," *Violence and Victims* 18,1 (2003): 3-14; N.S. Jacobson, J.M. Gottman, J. Waltz, R. Rushe, J. Babcock, and A. Holtzworth-Munroe, "Affect, verbal content, and psychophysiology in the arguments of couples with a violent husband," *Journal of Consulting and Clinical Psychology* 62,5 (1994): 982-88; D.G. Dutton, *The Abusive Personality: Violence and Control in Intimate Relationships* (New York: Guilford Press, 1998).

47   R.J. Gelles, "Violence and pregnancy: A note on the extent of the problem and needed services," *The Family Co-ordinator* 24 (1975): 81-86.

48   Sherman and Berk, "Effects of arrest."

49   Fagan, "Cessation of family violence."

50   L.H. Bowker, *Beating Wife Beating* (Lexington, MA: Lexington, 1983).

51   J.D. Hirshel and I.W. Hutchinson, "Female spouse abuse and the police response: The Charlotte, North Carolina experiment," *Journal of Criminal Law and Criminology* 83, 1 (1992): 73-119.

52   L.W. Sherman, J.D. Schmidt, D.P. Rogan, D.A. Smith, P.R. Gartin, E.G. Cohn, D.J. Collins, and A.R. Bacich, "The variable effects of arrest on criminal careers: The Milwaukee domestic violence experiment," *Journal of Criminal Law and Criminology* 83, 1 (1992): 137-69.

53   Ibid., 160.

54   L.G. Mills, *Insult to Injury: Rethinking Our Response to Intimate Abuse* (Princeton, NJ: Princeton University Press, 2003), 38.

55   Garner and Maxwell, "Police arrest studies."

56   F.W. Dunford, D. Huizinga, and D.S. Elliott, "The role of arrest in domestic assault. the Omaha police experiment," *Criminology* 28, 2 (1990): 183-206.

57   J.D. Hirshel and I.W. Hutchinson, "Female spouse abuse and the police response: The Charlotte, North Carolina experiment," *Journal of Criminal Law and Criminology* 83, 1 (1992): 73-119.

58   J.D. Hirschel, I.W. Hutchinson, and C.W. Dean, "The failure of arrest to deter spouse abuse," *Journal of Research in Crime and Delinquency* 29 (1992): 7-33.

59 J.H. Garner, J.A. Fagan, and C.D. Maxwell, "Published findings from the spouse assault rep-
    lication program: A critical review," *Journal of Quantitative Criminology* 11 (1995): 3-28; Gar-
    ner and Maxwell, "Police arrest studies."
60 Garner and Maxwell, "Police arrest studies," 107.
61 L.W. Sherman, "Defiance, deterrence, and irrelevance: A theory of the criminal sanctions,"
    Journal of Research in Crime and Delinquency 30 (1993): 444-73, 471.
62 D. Sugarman and S. Boney-McCoy, "The art of reviewing research," in S.K. Ward and D.
    Finkelstein, eds., *Program Evaluation and Family Violence Research* (New York: Haworth Press,
    1999).
63 Garner and Maxwell, "Police arrest studies"; R.J. Gelles, "Constraints against family vio-
    lence: How well do they work?" in Buzawa and Buzawa, eds., *Domestic Violence*.
64 L. Dugan, "Domestic violence legislation: Exploring its impact on the likelihood of do-
    mestic violence, police intervention and arrest," *Criminology and Public Policy* 2 (2003):
    283-312.
65 Ibid., 300.
66 Ibid., 302.
67 Ford and Regoli, "Preventive impacts of policies."
68 Hotaling and Buzawa, *Forgoing Criminal Justice Assistance*.
69 Ibid., 4.
70 Ibid., 26.
71 Ibid., 28.
72 P. Tjaden and N. Thoennes, *Prevalence, Incidence and Consequences of Violence against Women:
    Findings from the National Violence against Women Survey* (Washington, DC: US Department
    of Justice, 1998).
73 Buzawa and Buzawa, *Domestic Violence*; Garner and Maxwell, "Police arrest studies"; Sherman
    and Berk, "Effects of arrest."
74 E.S. Buzawa, T.L. Austin, J. Bannon, and J. Jackson, "Role of victim preference in determining
    police response to victims of domestic violence," in Buzawa and Buzawa, eds., *Domestic
    Violence*; K. Henning and B. Renauer, "Prosecution of women arrested for intimate partner
    abuse," *Violence and Victims* 20, 3 (2005): 181-97; Hotaling and Buzawa, *Forgoing Criminal
    Justice Assistance*.
75 Mills, "Killing her softly."
76 Ibid., 551.
77 Ibid., 569.
78 Ibid., 608.
79 C. Hanna, "No right to choose: Mandated victim participation in domestic violence pros-
    ecution," *Harvard Law Review* 109 (1998): 1950-70.
80 L. Feder, "Police handling of domestic and non-domestic assault calls: Is there a case for
    discrimination?" *Crime and Delinquency* 44 (1998): 335-47; Hanna, "No right to choose."
81 J. Stets and M. Straus, "Gender differences in reporting marital violence," in Straus and Gelles,
    eds., *Physical Violence*, 151-66.
82 Garner and Maxwell, "Police arrest studies," 109.

Chapter 13: Risk Assessment

1 R. Kropp and S. Hart, *The B-SAFER Manual* (Toronto: Multi-Health Systems, 2005).
2 J. Roehl and K. Guertin, *Current Use of Dangerousness Assessments in Sentencing Domestic Violence Offenders: Final Report* (New York: State Justice Institute, 1998); J.C. Campbell, "Issues
   in risk assessment in the field of intimate partner violence," paper presented at Conference
   on Risk Assessment and Risk Management: Implications for the Prevention of Violence,
   Vancouver, BC, 1999.
3 Roehl and Guertin, *Current Use*.
4 J.C. Campbell, *Assessing Dangerousness: Violence by Sexual Offenders, Batterers and Child Abusers* (Newbury Park, CA: Sage, 1995), 103.
5 J.C. Campbell, "Making sense of the senseless: Women's attributions about battering," paper presented at Third National Family Violence Research Conference, Durham, NH, 1987.

6   A. Browne, *When Battered Women Kill* (New York: Free Press, 1987); R.A. Berk, S.F. Berk, D.R. Loseke, and D. Rauma, "Mutual combat and other family violence myths," in D. Finkelhor, R.J. Gelles, G.T. Hotaling, and M.A. Straus, eds., *The Dark Side of Families: Current Family Violence Research* (Beverly Hills, CA: Sage, 1981): 197-212; J. Fagan, D.K. Stewart, and K.V. Hansen, "Violent men or violent husbands? Background factors and situational correlates," in Finkelhor et al., *The Dark Side of Families,*" 49-68.
7   Campbell, *Assessing Dangerousness*; K.J. Ferraro and J.M. Johnson, "How women experience battering: The process of victimization," *Social Problems* 30 (1983): 325-39.
8   Campbell, *Assessing Dangerousness*; J.C. Campbell, "Nursing assessment for risk of homicide with battered women," *Advances in Nursing Science* 8 (1986): 36-51.
9   Campbell, *Assessing Dangerousness*, 42.
10 G.R. Brown, "Gender as a factor in the response of the law-enforcement system to violence against partners," *Sexuality and Culture* 8 (2004): 12.
11 L.A. Goodman, M.A. Dutton, and L. Bennett, "Predicting repeat abuse among arrested batterers: Use of the danger assessment scale in the criminal justice system," *Journal of Interpersonal Violence* 15, 1 (2000): 63-74.
12 A.N. Weisz, R.M. Tolman, D.G. Saunders, "Assessing the risk of severe domestic violence: The importance of survivors' predictions," *Journal of Interpersonal Violence* 15, 1 (2000): 75-90.
13 J.C. Campbell, D. Webster, J. Koziol-McLain, C. Block, D. Campbell, M.A. Curry, F. Gary, N. Glass, J. McFarlane, C. Sachs, P. Sharps, Y. Utrich, S.A. Wilt, J. Manganello, X. Xi, J. Schollenberger, V. Frye, K. Laughon, "Risk factors for femicide in abusive relationships: Results from a multisite case control study," *American Journal of Public Health* (2003): 1089; M. Daly and M. Wilson, *Homicide* (New York: Aldine, 1988).
14 P.R. Kropp and S. Hart, "The Spousal Assault Risk Assessment (SARA) guide: Reliability and validity in adult male offenders," *Law and Human Behavior* 24, 1 (2000): 101-18.
15 Ibid., 113, Table 8.
16 Ibid., Table 9.
17 K.R. Williams and A.B. Houghton, "Assessing the risk of re-offending: A validational study," *Law and Human Behavior* 28, 4 (2004): 437-52.
18 Ibid.
19 Ibid., 451.
20 Dutton, "Scale for measuring propensity."
21 L.L. Marshall, "Development of the Severity of Violence against Women Scales," *Journal of Family Violence* 7, 2 (1992): 103-21.
22 L. Thomas and D.G. Dutton, "The Propensity for Abusiveness Scale (PAS) as a predictor of affective priming to anticipated intimate conflict," *Journal of Applied Social Psychology* 34, 1 (2004): 1-14.
23 S. Hart and R.D. Hare, "Psychopathy: Assessment and association with criminal behavior," in D. Stoff, J. Breiling, and J.D. Maser, eds., *Handbook of Antisocial Behavior* (New York: John Wiley and Sons, 1997).
24 R.D. Hare, "A research scale for the assessment of psychopathy in criminal populations," *Personality and Individual Differences* 1, 2 (1980): 111-19; R.D. Hare, *The Hare Psychopathy Checklist: Revised* (Toronto: Multi-Health Systems, 1991).
25 Hart and Hare, "Psychopathy"; V.L. Quinsey, G.T. Harris, M.E. Rice, and C. Cormier, *Violent Offenders: Appraising and Managing Risk* (Washington, DC: American Psychological Association, 1998).
26 J.F. Hemphill, R. Templeman, S. Wong, and R.D. Hare, "Psychopathy and crime: Recidivism and criminal careers," in D. Cooke, A. Forth, and R.D. Hare, eds., *Psychopathy: Theory, Research and Implications for Society* (The Netherlands: Kluwer Academic Publishers, 1998).
27 Ibid., 381.
28 D.M. Gottfredson and J.A. Bonds, *A Manual for Intake Base Expectancy Scoring* (San Francisco: California Department of Corrections, 1961); P.B. Hoffman, "Screening for risk: A revised Salient Factor Score," *Journal of Criminal Justice* 11 (1983): 539-47; G.L. Nuffield, *Parole Decision Making in Canada: Research towards Decision Guidelines* (Ottawa: Ministry of Supply and Services Canada, 1982); G.T. Harris, M.E. Rice, and V.L. Quinsey, "Violent recidivism of

mentally disordered offenders: The development of a statistical prediction instrument," *Criminal Justice and Behavior* 20 (1993): 315-35.

29 F.W. Dunford, "The San Diego navy experiment: An assessment of interventions for men who assault their wives," *Journal of Consulting and Clinical Psychology* 68, 3 (2000): 468-76.

30 D.G. Dutton, *The Batterer: A Psychological Profile* (New York: Basic Books, 1995); A. Holtzworth-Munroe and G.L. Stuart, "Typologies of male batterers: Three subtypes and the differences among them," *Psychological Bulletin* 116, 3 (1994): 476-97.

31 Campbell, "Issues in risk assessment."

32 T.E. Moffitt, A. Caspi, M. Rutter, and P.A. Silva, *Sex Differences in Antisocial Behavior* (London: Cambridge University Press, 2003).

33 J. Skeem, C. Schubert, S. Stowman, S. Beeson, E.P. Mulvey, W. Gardner, and C.W. Lidz, "Gender and risk assessment accuracy: Understanding women's potential violence," *Law and Human Behavior* 29, 2 (2005): 173-86.

34 Ibid., 173.

35 Ibid., 181.

36 Ibid., 178.

37 P.C. Robbins, J. Monahan, and E. Silver, "Mental disorder, violence and gender," *Law and Human Behavior* 27, 6 (2003): 561-71.

38 Ibid., 563.

Chapter 14: Treatment Policy Issues

1 R. Gelles, "Standards for men who batter? Not yet," *Journal of Aggression, Maltreatment and Trauma* 5, 2 (2001): 14.

2 D. Levesque, *Violence Desistance among Battering Men: Existing Intervention and the Application of the Transtheoretical Model for Change* (Kingston, RI: Pro-Change Behavior Systems, 1998).

3 R.D. Maiuro, T.S. Hagar, H. Lin, and N. Olson, "Are current state standards for domestic violence perpetrator treatment adequately informed by research? A question of questions," *Journal of Aggression, Maltreatment and Trauma* 5, 2 (2001): 21-44.

4 Ibid., 23.

5 D. Adams, "Treatment models of men who batter: A profeminist analysis," in K. Yllo and M. Bograd, eds., *Feminist Perspectives on Wife Abuse* (Beverly Hills, CA: Sage, 1988).

6 Ibid., 180.

7 Maiuro et al., "Current state standards." See http://www.biscmi.org/other_resources/state_standards.html.

8 K.D. O'Leary, "Conjoint therapy for partners who engage in physically aggressive behavior," *Journal of Aggression, Maltreatment and Trauma* 5, 2 (2001): 145-64.

9 Maiuro et al., "Current state standards," 34.

10 Ibid., 38.

11 Ibid., 37.

12 Cal Pen Code § 1203.097 (2003).

13 http://www.biscmi.org/other_resources/state_standards.html

14 D.G. Dutton and D.J. Sonkin, *Intimate Violence: Contemporary Treatment Innovations* (Binghampton, NY: Haworth Press, 2003).

15 A. Bandura, "The social learning perspective: Mechanisms of Aggression," in H. Toch, ed., *The Psychology of Crime and Criminal Justice* (New York: Holt, Rinehart, and Winston, 1979).

16 A. Ganley, *Court-Mandated Counseling for Men Who Batter: A Three-Day Workshop for Professionals* (Washington, DC: Center for Women Policy Studies, 1981); D.G. Dutton, *The Criminal Justice System Response to Wife Assault* (Ottawa: Solicitor General of Canada, Research Division, 1981).

17 M.J. Eddy and T. Meyers, *Helping Men Who Batter: A Profile of Programs in the U.S.* (Arlington, TX: Texas Council on Family Violence, 1984); J.J. Browning, *Stopping the Violence: Canadian Programmes for Assaultive Men* (Ottawa: Health and Welfare Canada, 1984).

18 J.O. Prochaska, C.D. DiClemente, J.C. Norcross, "In search of how people change: Applications to addictive behaviors," *American Psychologist* 47, 9 (1992): 1102-27.

19   J. Stets and M. Straus, "Gender differences in reporting marital violence," in M.A. Straus and R.J. Gelles, eds., *Physical Violence in American Families* (New Brunswick, NJ: Transaction Publishers, 1992): 151-66.
20   D.G. Dutton, "Treatment of assaultiveness," in D.G. Dutton and D.L. Sonkin, eds., *Intimate Violence: Contemporary Treatment Approaches* (New York: Haworth Press, 2003); E. Pence and M. Paymar, *Education Groups for Men Who Batter: The Duluth Model* (New York: Springer, 1993).
21   M. Bograd, "Feminist perspectives on wife assault: An introduction," in Yllo and Bograd, *Feminist Perspectives*, 11-26; R.E. Dobash and R.P. Dobash, *Violence against Wives: A Case against the Patriarchy* (New York: Free Press, 1979).
22   Levesque, *Violence Desistance*.
23   Pence and Paymar: *Education Groups for Men*, xiii.
24   Ibid., 5.
25   Ibid.
26   Ibid., 7-13.
27   Ibid., 23.
28   Ibid., 41.
29   Ibid., 48.
30   Ibid., 43.
31   Ibid., 49.
32   Ibid., 61-62.
33   Ibid., 63.
34   J.C. Babcock, C.E. Green, and C. Robie, "Does batterers' treatment work? A meta-analytic review of domestic violence treatment outcome research," *Clinical Psychology Review* 23 (2004): 1023-53.
35   Ibid.
36   Dutton, "Treatment of assaultiveness."
37   J. Archer, "Sex differences in aggression between heterosexual partners: A meta-analytic review," *Psychological Bulletin* 126, 5 (2000): 651-80; K. Corvo and P.J. Johnson, "Vilification of the 'batterer': How blame shapes domestic violence policy and interventions," *Aggression and Violent Behavior* 8, 3 (2003): 259-81; D.G. Dutton, "Patriarchy and wife assault: The ecological fallacy," *Violence and Victims* 9, 2 (1994): 125-40.
38   D.H. Coleman and M.A. Straus, "Marital power, conflict, and violence," paper presented at the meeting of the American Society of Criminology, San Diego, CA, 1985; Archer, "Sex differences in aggression"; J. Stets and M. Straus, "The marriage license as a hitting license," in Straus and Gelles, eds., *Physical Violence*; Dutton, "Patriarchy and wife assault"; T.R. Simon, M. Anderson, M.P. Thompson, A.E. Crosby, G. Shelley, and J.J. Sacks, "Attitudinal acceptance of intimate partner violence among U.S. adults," *Violence and Victims* 16, 2 (2001): 115-26; G. Lie, R. Schilit, J. Bush, M. Montague, and L. Reyes, "Lesbians in currently aggressive relationships: How frequently do they report aggressive past relationships?" *Violence and Victims* 6, 2 (1991): 121-35.
39   Dutton, "Patriarchy and wife assault."
40   Archer, "Sex Differences in aggression."
41   Stets and Straus, "Marriage license."
42   Pence and Paymar, *Education Groups for Men*, 9, 105.
43   R.D. Maiuro, T.S. Cahn, P.P. Vitaliano, B.C. Wagner, and J.B. Zegree, "Anger, hostility and depression in domestically violent versus generally assaultive men and non-violent control subjects," *Journal of Consulting and Clinical Psychology* 56 (1988): 17-23, 17.
44   G. Margolin, R.S. John, and L. Glebermen, "Affective responses to conflictual discussions in violent and non-violent couples," *Journal of Consulting and Clinical Psychology* 56, 1 (1989): 24-33.
45   D.G. Dutton and J.J. Browning, "Power struggles and intimacy anxieties as causative factors of violence in intimate relationships," in G. Russell, ed., *Violence in Intimate Relationships* (Great Neck, NY: PMA Publishing, 1988).
46   Dutton and Sonkin, *Intimate Violence*.
47   D.G. Dutton and A. Starzomski, "Psychological differences between court-referred and self-referred wife assaulters," *Criminal Justice and Behavior: An International Journal* 21, 2 (1994):

203-22; J.M. Siegel, "The multidimensional anger inventory," *Journal of Personality and Social Psychology* 5, 1 (1986): 191-200.

48   D.G. Dutton, K. Saunders, A. Starzomski, and K. Bartholomew, "Intimacy anger and insecure attachment as precursors of abuse in intimate relationships," *Journal of Applied Social Psychology* 24, 15 (1994): 1367-86.

49   J. Bowlby, "The making and breaking of affectional bonds," *British Journal of Psychiatry* 130 (1977): 201-10.

50   Dutton et al., "Intimacy anger."

51   N.S. Jacobson, J.M. Gottman, J. Waltz, R. Rushe, J. Babcock, and A. Holtzworth-Munroe, "Affect, verbal content, and psychophysiology in the arguments of couples with a violent husband," *Journal of Consulting and Clinical Psychology* 62, 5 (1994): 983.

52   C.I. Eckhardt, K.A. Barbour, and G.L. Stuart, "Anger and hostility in maritally violent men: Conceptual distinctions, measurement issues and literature review," *Clinical Psychology Review* 17, 4 (1997): 333-58.

53   C.I. Eckhardt, K.A. Barbour, and G.C. Davis, "Articulated thoughts of maritally violent and non-violent men during anger arousal," *Journal of Consulting and Clinical Psychology* 66, 2 (1998): 259-69

54   Eckhardt, Barbour, and Stuart, "Anger and hostility."

55   S.M. Stith, K.H. Rosen, and E.E. McCollum, "Effectiveness of couples treatment for spouse abuse," *Journal of Marital and Family Therapy* 29 (2003): 407-26, 422; K. Hanson, O. Cadsky, A. Harris, and C. Lalonde, "Correlates of battering among 997 men: Family history, adjustment and attitudinal differences," *Violence and Victims* 12, 3 (1997): 191-208.

56   M. Smith, "Patriarchal ideology and wife beating: A test of a feminist hypothesis," *Violence and Victims* 5, 4 (1990): 257-73.

57   D.J. Bem, "Self-perception: An alternative interpretation to cognitive dissonance phenomena," *Psychological Review* 74 (1972): 183-200.

58   Stets and Straus, "Gender differences."

59   L.K. Hamberger and J.E. Hastings, "Personality correlated of men who abuse their partners: A cross-validation study," *Journal of Family Violence* 1 (1986): 323-41; A. Holtzworth-Munroe and G.L. Stuart, "Typologies of male batterers: Three subtypes and the differences among them," *Psychological Bulletin* 116, 3 (1994): 476-97; D.G. Dutton, *The Abusive Personality: Violence and Control in Intimate Relationships*, rev. ed. (New York: Guilford Press, 2002); R. Tweed and D.G. Dutton, "A comparison of instrumental and impulsive subgroups of batterers," *Violence and Victims* 13, 3 (1998): 217-30; D.G. Saunders, "A typology of men who batter: Three types derived from cluster analysis," *American Journal of Orthopsychiatry* 62, 2 (1992): 264-75.

60   Dutton and Sonkin, *Intimate Violence*.

61   Stets and Straus, "Gender differences."

62   M.P. Johnson, "Patriarchal terrorism and common couple violence: Two forms of violence against women," *Journal of Marriage and the Family* 57 (1995): 283-94.

63   Stith, Rosen, McCollum, "Effectiveness of couples treatment"; R. Heyman and K.A. Schlee, "Stopping wife abuse via physical aggression couples treatment," in Dutton and Sonkin, *Intimate Violence*; K.D. O'Leary, R. Heyman, and P.H. Neidig, "Treatment of wife abuse: A comparison of gender-specific and couple approaches," *Behavior Assessment* 30 (1999): 475-505.

64   D. LaRoche, *Aspects of the Consequences of Domestic Violence: Situational Couple Violence and Intimate Terrorism in Canada in 1999* (Quebec City: Government of Quebec, 2005). See also D. LaRoche, *La Violence conjugale envers les hommes et les femmes, au Québec et au Canada* (Quebec City: Government of Québec, 1999).

65   A.N. Schore, *Affect Regulation and the Repair of the Self* (New York: Norton, 2003).

66   L. Luborsky, *Principles of Psychoanalytic Therapy: A Manual for Supportive-Expressive Treatment* (New York: Basic Books, 1984), 162.

67   Ibid., 166.

68   Ibid., 203.

69   D.J. Sonkin and D.G. Dutton, "Treating assaultive men from an attachment perspective," in D.G. Dutton and D.J. Sonkin, eds., *Intimate Violence: Contemporary Treatment Approaches* (New

York: Haworth Press, 2002); A. Schore, *Affect Regulation and the Repair of the Self* (New York: Norton, 2003).

70 M.S. Rosenberg, "Voices from the group: Domestic violence offenders' experience of intervention," in Dutton and Sonkin, *Intimate Violence*, 305.

71 M. Shepard, "Interventions with men who batter: An evaluation of a domestic abuse program," paper presented at Third National Conference on Domestic Violence, University of New Hampshire, Durham, NH, 1987; M. Shepard, "Predicting batterer recidivism five years after community intervention," *Journal of Family Violence* 7, 3 (1992): 167-78.

72 Babcock, Green, and Robie, "Does batterers' treatment work?"

73 L. Feder and D.R. Forde, "A test of efficacy of court-mandated counseling for convicted misdemeanor domestic violence offenders: Results from the Brouward experiment," paper presented at International Family Violence Conference, Durham, NH, 1999.

74 F.W. Dunford, "The San Diego navy experiment: An assessment of interventions for men who assault their wives," *Journal of Consulting and Clinical Psychology* 68, 3 (2000): 468-76.

75 L.W. Sherman, J.D. Schmidt, D.P. Rogan, D.A. Smith, P.R. Gartin, E.G. Cohn, D.J. Collins, A.R. Bacich, "The variable effects of arrest on criminal careers: The Milwaukee domestic violence experiment," *Journal of Criminal Law and Criminology* 83, 1 (1992): 137-69.

76 R.C. Davis, B.G. Taylor, and C.D. Maxwell, "Does batterer treatment reduce violence? A randomized experiment in Brooklyn," *Justice Quarterly* 18 (1998): 171-201.

77 R.C. Davis, B.G. Taylor, and C.D. Maxwell, *Does Batterer Treatment Reduce Violence? A Randomized Experiment in Brooklyn* (Washington, DC: National Institute of Justice, 2000), 122.

78 D.A. Ford and M.J. Regoli, "The criminal prosecution of wife assaults: Process, problems, and effects," in N.Z. Hilton, ed., *Legal Responses to Wife Assault: Current Trends and Evaluation* (Newbury Park, CA: Sage, 1993), 127-64.

79 D.G. Dutton, M. Bodnarchuk, R. Kropp, S. Hart, and J. Ogloff, "Wife assault treatment and criminal recidivism: An eleven year follow-up," *International Journal of Offender Therapy and Comparative Criminology* 41, 1 (1997): 9-23.

80 Babcock, Green, and Robie, "Does batterers' treatment work?"

81 Ibid., 1045.

82 R.C. Davis and B.G. Taylor, "Does batterer treatment reduce violence? A synthesis of the literature," *Women and Criminal Justice* 10 (1999): 69-93.

83 Schore, *Affect Regulation*; I. Yalom, *The Theory and Practice of Group Psychotherapy* (New York: Basic Books, 1975); A.N. Schore, *Affect Dysregulation and the Disorders of the Self* (New York: Norton, 2003).

84 E.W. Gondolf, "Limitations of experimental evaluation of batterer programs," *Trauma, Violence and Abuse* 2, 1 (2001): 79-88.

85 Ibid., 86.

86 Prochaska, DiClemente, and Norcross, "How people change."

87 Levesque, *Violence Desistance*, 32.

88 D.A. Levesque, R.J. Gelles, and W.F. Velicer, "The University of Rhode Island Change Assessment Scale for Domestic Violence (URICA-DV)," *Cognitive Therapy Research* 24 (2000): 175-200.

89 C.M. Murphy and V.A. Baxter, "Motivating batterers to change in the treatment context," *Journal of Interpersonal Violence* 12 (1997): 607-19.

90 C.I. Eckhardt, J. Babcock, and S. Homack, "Partner assaultive men and the stages and processes of change," *Journal of Family Violence* 19, 2 (2004): 81-93.

91 Ibid., 91

92 K. Scott, "Stage of change as a predictor of attrition in a men's batterer program," *Journal of Family Violence* 19, 1 (2004): 37-47.

93 D.T. Campbell, "Reforms as experiments," *American Psychologist* 22 (1968): 169-83.

94 B.R. Cournoyer and G.T. Powers, "Evidence-based social work: The quiet revolution continues," in A.R. Roberts and G. Greene, eds., *The Social Work Desk Reference* (New York: Oxford University Press, 2005), 84.

95 Ibid., 86.

96 A. Holtzworth-Munroe, "Standards for batterer treatment programs: How can research inform our decisions?" *Journal of Aggression, Maltreatment and Trauma* 5, 2 (2001): 165-80.

Chapter 15: Treatment

1   R.J. Lifton, *Thought Reform and the Psychology of Totalism* (Charlotte: University of North Caro-lina Press, 1961, 1989).

2   D.G. Dutton, "Treatment of assaultiveness," in D.G. Dutton and D.L. Sonkin, eds., *Intimate Violence: Contemporary Treatment Approaches* (New York: Haworth Press, 2003).

3   R.D. Maiuro and D.H. Avery, "Psychopharmacological treatment of aggression," *Violence and Victims* 11, 3 (1996): 239-62.

4   Dutton, "Treatment of assaultiveness."

5   R. Wallace and A. Nosko, "Working with shame in group treatment of male batterers," *International Journal of Group Psychotherapy* 43, 1 (1993): 45-61.

6   D.G. Dutton, *The Abusive Personality: Violence and Control in Intimate Relationships* (New York: Guilford Press, 1998; rev. ed., 2002).

7   A. Ellis, "Group rational-emotive and cognitive behavioral therapy," *International Journal of Group Psychotherapy* 42 (1992): 63-80.

8   A.T. Beck, *Cognitive Therapy and the Emotional Disorders* (New York: International University Press, 1976).

9   C.I. Eckhardt, K.A. Barbour, and G.C. Davis, "Articulated thoughts of maritally violent and non-violent men during anger arousal," *Journal of Consulting and Clinical Psychology* 66, 2 (1998): 259-69; C.I. Eckhardt, K.A. Barbour, and G.L. Stuart, "Anger and hostility in mari-tally violent men: Conceptual distinctions, measurement issues and literature review," *Clini-cal Psychology Review* 17, 4 (1997): 333-58.

10   P.A. Miller and N. Eisenberg, "The relation of empathy to aggressive and externalizing/ antisocial behavior," *Psychological Bulletin* 103, 3 (1988): 324-44; S. Stosny, *Treating Attach-ment Abuse* (New York: Springer, 1995).

11   W. Reich, *Character Analysis* (New York: Touchstone/Simon and Schuster, 1945, 1972).

12   J. Kabat-Zinn, *Full Catastrophe Living: Using the Wisdom of Your Body and Mind to Face Stress, Pain and Illness* (New York: Delta, 1990).

13   D.G. Dutton and J. Winters, "Tracking Cyclical Abuse," Department of Psychology, Univer-sity of British Columbia, 1999.

14   D.J. Sonkin and M. Durphy, *Learning to Live without Violence: A Handbook for Men* (Volcano, CA: Volcano Press, 1989); D. Wexler, *Domestic Violence 2000: Group Leaders' Manual* (New York: W.W. Norton, 2000; C.M. Murphy and C.I. Eckhardt, *Treating the Abusive Partner* (New York: Guilford, 2005).

15   D.G. Dutton, M. Bodnarchuk, R. Kropp, S. Hart, and J. Ogloff, "Wife assault treatment and criminal recidivism: An eleven year follow-up," *International Journal of Offender Therapy and Comparative Criminology* 41, 1 (1997): 9-23; D.G. Dutton, M. Bodnarchuk, R. Kropp, S. Hart, and J. Ogloff, "Client personality disorders affecting wife assault post-treatment recidivism," *Violence and Victims* 12, 1 (1997): 37-50.

16   Dutton et al., "Client personality."

17   J.C. Babcock, C.E. Green, and C. Robie, "Does batterers' treatment work? A meta-analytic review of domestic violence treatment outcome research," *Clinical Psychology Review* 23 (2004): 1023-53.

18   See also C.T. Taft, C.M. Murphy, J.D. Elliot, and T.M. Morrel, "Attendance enhancing proce-dures in group counseling for domestic abusers," *Journal of Counseling Psychology* 48, 1 (2001): 51-60.

19   Dutton, *The Abusive Personality* (also rev. ed.); D.G. Dutton, "Developing treatment pro-grams for men who assault their wives," *Japanese Journal of Addictions* 9 (2002): 111-26.

20   J. Bowlby, *Attachment and Loss: Attachment* (New York: Basic Books, 1969).

21   M. Main and R. Goldwyn, *An Adult Attachment Classification System* (Berkeley, CA: 1994); J.C. Babcock, N.C. Jacobson, J.M. Gottman, and T.P. Yerington, "Attachment, emotional regula-tion, and the function of marital violence: Differences between secure, preoccupied, and dis-missing violent and non-violent husbands," *Journal of Family Violence* 15, 4 (2000): 391-409.

22   M. Mikulincer, "Adult attachment style and affect regulation: Strategic variations in self-ap-praisals," *Journal of Personal Social Psychology* 75 (1998): 420-35; Dutton et al., "Client person-ality disorders"; A.N. Schore, *Affect Dysregulation and the Disorders of the Self* (New York: Norton, 2003); A.N. Schore, *Affect Regulation and the Repair of the Self* (New York: Norton, 2003).

23   J. Bowlby, *A Secure Base: Clinical Applications of Attachment Theory* (London: Routledge, 1988).

24   Dutton and Sonkin, *Intimate Violence.*

25   P. Fonagy, *Attachment Theory and Psychoanalysis* (New York: Other Press, 2001); P. Fonagy, M. Target, G. Gergely, and E.J. Jurist, *Affect Regulation, Mentalization and the Development of the Self* (New York: Other Press, 2002).

26   J. Holmes, *In Search of the Secure Base* (London: Routledge, 2001).

27   Schore, *Affect Dysregulation;* Schore, *Affect Regulation.*

28   D.J. Siegel, *The Developing Mind: How Relationships and the Brain Interact to Shape Who We Are,* rev. ed. (New York: Guilford Press, 2001).

29   Bowlby, *Attachment and Loss.*

30   Bowlby, *A Secure Base.*

31   Schore, *Affect Regulation.*

32   D.N. Stern, N. Brushweiler-Stern, A.M. Harrison, K. Lyons-Ruth, A.C. Morgan, J.P. Nahumn, L. Sander, and E.Z. Tronick, "The process of therapeutic change involving implicit knowledge: Some implications of developmental observations for adult psychotherapy," *Infant Mental Health Journal* 19 (1998): 300-8.

33   S. Stosny, *Stop Walking on Eggshells* (New York: Free Press, 2006); C. Clulow, *Adult Attachment and Couple Psychotherapy* (London: Tavistock, 2001).

34   J.H. Gold, "The intolerance of aloneness," *American Journal of Psychiatry* 153, 6 (1998): 750.

35   J.O. Prochaska, C.C. DiClemente, and J.C. Norcross, "In search of how people change: Applications to addictive behaviors," *American Psychologist* 47, 9 (1992): 1102-27.

36   M. Linehan, *Cognitive-Behavioral Treatment of Borderline Personality Disorder* (New York: Guilford, 1993).

37   Ibid.

38   Dutton, *The Abusive Personality* (also rev. ed.); D.G. Dutton, "Profiling wife assaulters: Some evidence for a trimodal analysis," *Violence and Victims* 3, 1 (1988): 5-30.

39   E.A. Hembree and E.B. Foa, "Post-traumatic stress disorder: Psychological factors and psychosocial interventions," *Journal of Clinical Psychology* 61 (2000): 33-39.

40   Maiuro and Avery, "Psychopharmacological treatment."

41   B.O. Rothbaum, E.A. Meadows, P. Resick, and D.A. Foy, "Cognitive behavioral therapy," in E.B. Foa, T.M. Keane, and M.J. Friedman, eds., *Effective Therapy for PTSD* (New York: Guilford Press, 2000).

42   Dutton, *The Abusive Personality* (also rev. ed.).

43   K. Larimer and G.A. Marlatt, "Addictive behaviors," in L.W. Craighead, ed., *Cognitive and Behavioral Interventions: An Empirical Approach to Mental Health Problems* (Boston: Allyn and Bacon, 1994); G.A. Marlatt, "Buddhist philosophy and the treatment of addictive behavior," *Cognitive and Behavioral Practice* 9 (2002): 44-50; K. Witkiewitz and G.A. Marlatt, "Relapse prevention for alcohol and drug problems: That was Zen, this is Tao," *American Psychologist* 59, 4 (2004): 224-35.

44   G.K. Kantor and M. Straus, "The 'drunken bum' theory of wife beating," in M.A. Straus and R.J. Gelles, eds., *Physical Violence in American families* (New Brunswick, NJ: Transaction Publishers, 2002).

45   D.G. Dutton, G. Swihart, J. Winters, R.J.W. Clift, and L. Thomas, "The abusive personality: A new "third variable" linking alcohol and drug use amongst wife assaulters," Department of Psychology, University of British Columbia, 2001.

46   Marlatt, "Buddhist philosophy."

47   Larimer and Marlatt, "Addictive behaviors."

48   G.A. Marlatt, "Relapse prevention: Theoretical rationale and overview of the model," in G.A. Marlatt and J.R. Gordon, eds., *Relapse Prevention* (New York: Guilford Press, 1985), 250-80.

49   Dutton et al., "Client personality disorders."

50   Dutton, *The Abusive Personality,* 6-10.

51   R.D. Hare and S. Wong, *Programme Guidelines for the Institutional Treatment of Violent Offenders* (Toronto: Multi-Health Systems, 2003), 3.

52   J.R.P. Ogloff, S. Wong, and A. Greenwood, "Treating criminal psychopaths in a therapeutic community program," *Behavioral Sciences and the Law* 8 (1990): 181-90; G.T. Harris, M.E.

Rice, and C.A. Cormier, "Psychopathy and violent recidivism," *Law and Human Behavior* 15 (1991): 625-37.

53 S. Wong, *Treatment of Violent Offenders: It Works!* (Orebreo, Sweden: Swedish Correctional Services, 2001).

54 H. Cleckley, *The Mask of Sanity*, 5th ed. (St. Louis, MO: Mosby, 1976); R.D. Hare and S. Wong, *Programme Guidelines*; R.D. Hare, *The Hare Psychopathy Checklist: Revised* (Toronto: Multi-Health Systems, 1991).

55 Hare and Wong, *Programme Guidelines*, 4.

56 F. Losel, "Treatment and management of psychopaths," in D.C. Cooke and R.D. Hare, eds., *Psychopathy: Theory, Research and Implications for Society* (Netherlands: Dordrecht, 1998), 89-113.

57 R. Mulloy, C. Smiley, S. Hart, and D. Dawda, "Psychopathy and cognitive-behavioral treatment success in personality disordered offenders," paper presented to the American Psychological Association, Toronto, 2000.

58 A.T. Beck, *Cognitive Therapy and the Emotional Disorders* (New York: International Universities Press, 1978); Ellis, "Group rational-emotive therapy," 63-80.

59 H.F.M. Hervé, "The masks of sanity and psychopathy: A cluster analytical investigation of subtypes of criminal psychopathy," PhD dissertation, Department of Psychology, University of British Columbia, 2002.

60 Hare, *Hare Psychopathy Checklist: Revised*.

61 Hare and Wong, *Programme Guidelines*.

62 Ogloff, Wong, and Greenwood, "Treating criminal psychopaths."

63 Hervé, "Masks of sanity," 135-36.

64 J. Stets and M. Straus, "Gender differences in reporting marital violence," in Straus and Gelles, *Physical Violence*, 151-66.

65 L. Dowd, "Female perpetrators of partner aggression: Relevant issues and treatment," *Journal of Aggression, Maltreatment and Trauma* 5, 2 (2001): 73-104; C. Renzetti, *Violent Betrayal: Partner Abuse in Lesbian Relationships* (Newbury Park, CA: Sage, 1994).

66 K. Hamberger and T. Potente, "Counseling heterosexual women arrested for domestic violence: Implications for theory and practice," *Violence and Victims* 9, 2 (1994): 125-37.

67 K. Hamberger, "Female offenders in domestic violence: A look at actions in context," *Journal of Aggression, Maltreatment and Trauma* 1, 1 (1997): 117-29.

68 T.E. Moffitt, A. Caspi, M. Rutter, and P.A. Silva, *Sex Differences in Antisocial Behavior* (Cambridge: Cambridge University Press, 2001).

69 A.L. Busch and M.S. Rosenberg, "Comparing women and men arrested for domestic violence: A preliminary report," *Journal of Family Violence* 19, 1 (2004): 49-57.

70 M.M. Carney and F.P. Buttell, "A multidimensional evaluation of a treatment program for female batterers: A pilot study," *Journal of Offender Rehabilitation* (in press).

71 D.G. Dutton, "A scale for measuring propensity for abusiveness," *Journal of Family Violence* 10, 2 (1995): 203-21.

72 Renzetti, *Violent Betrayal*, 57.

73 L. Margolies and E. Leeder, "Violence at the door: Treatment of lesbian batterers," *Violence against Women* 1, 2 (1995): 139-57.

74 P. Leisring, L. Dowd, and A. Rosenbaum, "Treatment of partner aggressive women," in Dutton and Sonkin, *Intimate Violence*.

75 See also P. Tjaden and N. Thoennes, *Prevalence, Incidence and Consequences of Violence against Women: Findings from the National Violence against Women Survey* (Washington, DC: US Department of Justice, 1998).

76 D.R. Follingstad, R.G. Bradley, C.M. Helff, and J.E. Laughlin, "A model for predicting dating violence: Anxious attachment, angry temperament and need for relationship control," *Violence and Victims* 17, 1 (2002): 35-47.

77 K. Henning, A. Jones, and R. Holford, "Treatment needs of women arrested for domestic violence: A comparison with male offenders," *Journal of Interpersonal Violence* 18, 8 (2003): 839-56; K. Henning and L. Feder, "A comparison of men and women arrested for domestic violence: Who presents the greater risk?" *Journal of Family Violence* 19, 2 (2004): 69-80.

78 Moffitt et al., *Sex Differences.*
79 Henning et al., "Treatment needs."
80 J. Babcock and D.G. Dutton, "A re-analysis of women's MCMI scores from the UW Spouse Abuse Sample" (in preparation).
81 Stets and Straus, "Gender differences."
82 J. Archer, "Sex differences in aggression between heterosexual partners: A meta-analytic review," *Psychological Bulletin* 126, 5 (2000): 651-80.
83 Hamberger and Potente, "Counseling heterosexual women"; K. Henning and B. Renauer, "Prosecution of women arrested for intimate partner abuse," *Violence and Victims* 20, 3 (2003): 171-89.
84 Bowlby, *Attachment and Loss*; Schore, *Affect Regulation.*
85 A.N. Schore, *Affect Regulation and the Repair of the Self* (New York: Norton, 2003), 279-81.

Chapter 16: Rethinking the Response to Domestic Violence

1 L.G. Mills, "Killing her softly: Intimate abuse and the violence of state intervention," *Harvard Law Review* 113, 2 (1999): 551-613; L.G. Mills, *Insult to Injury: Rethinking Our Response to Intimate Abuse* (Princeton, NJ: Princeton University Press, 2003).
2 D.J. Rebovitch, "Prosecution response to domestic violence: Results of a survey of large jurisdictions," in E.S. Buzawa and C.G. Buzawa, eds., *Do Arrests and Restraining Orders Work?* (Thousand Oaks, CA: Sage, 1996).
3 P. Grauwiler and L.G. Mills, "Moving beyond the criminal justice paradigm: A radical restorative justice approach to intimate abuse," *Journal of Sociology and Social Welfare* 31, 1 (2004), 55.
4 Mills, *Insult to Injury*; Grauwiler and Mills, "Criminal Justice Paradigm."
5 J. Braithwaite, *Restorative Justice and Responsive Regulation* (Oxford and New York: Oxford University Press, 2002).
6 R.M. Tolman, "Expanding sanctions for batterers: What can we do besides jailing and counseling them," in J.L. Edelson and Z. Eiskovoits, eds., *Future Intervention with Battered Women and Their Families* (Thousand Oaks, CA: Sage, 1996).
7 Ibid., 182.
8 L. Dugan, "Domestic violence legislation: Exploring its impact on the likelihood of domestic violence, police intervention and arrest," *Criminology and Public Policy* 2 (2003): 283-312, 300.
9 D.G. Dutton, S.D. Hart, L.W. Kennedy, and K.R. Williams, "Arrest and the reduction of repeat wife assault," in E.S. Buzawa and C.G. Buzawa, eds., *Domestic Violence: The Changing Criminal Justice Response* (Westport, CT: Auburn House, 1992).
10 G. Burford and J. Pennell, *Family Group Decision Making Project: Outcome Report* (St. John's, NF: Memorial University of Newfoundland, 1998).
11 K. Pranis, "Restorative values and confronting family violence," in H. Strang and J. Braithwaite, eds., *Restorative Justice and Family Violence* (London: Cambridge University Press, 2002).
12 A. Edwards and J. Haslett, "Domestic violence and restorative justice: Advancing the dialogue," Simon Fraser University, 2000. http://www.sfu.ca/cfri/fulltext/haslett.pdf.
13 D.W. Griffin and K. Bartholomew, "Models of the self and other: Fundamental dimensions underlying measures of adult attachment," *Journal of Personality and Social Psychology* 67 (1994): 430-45; D.K. Snyder and N.A. Scheer, "Predicting disposition following brief residence at a shelter for battered women," *American Journal of Community Psychology* 9 (1981): 559-66.
14 Mills, *Insult to Injury*, 104.
15 Tolman, "Expanding sanctions for batterers," 182
16 J. Stubbs, "Domestic violence and women's safety: Feminist challenges to restorative justice," in Strand and Braithwaite, *Restorative Justice.*
17 Grauwiler and Mills, "Moving Beyond," 64-66.
18 Stubbs, "Domestic violence."
19 J. Braithwaite and H. Strang, "Restorative justice and family violence," in H. Strang and J. Braithwaite, eds., *Restorative Justice and Family Violence* (London: Cambridge University Press, 2002), 1-23, 3.

20 Cited in ibid., 3.
21 R. Busch, "Resorative justice and family violence: Who pays if we get it wrong?" in Strang and Braithwate, *Restorative Justice*, 223-46.
22 G. Burford and J. Pennell, *Family Group Decision Making Project.*
23 Braithwaite and Strang, "Restorative justice and family violence," 121.
24 Burford and Pennell, *Family Group Decision Making Project*, 123.
25 Ibid., 84.
26 Mills, *Insult to Injury*, 111-12.
27 M.K. Ehrensaft, T.E. Moffitt and A. Caspi, "Clinically abusive relationships in an unselected birth cohort: Men's and women's participation and developmental antecedents," *Journal of Abnormal Psychology* 113, 2 (2004): 258-70; T.E. Moffitt, A. Caspi, M. Rutter and P.A. Silva, *Sex Differences in Antisocial Behavior* (London: Cambridge University Press, 2003); J.E. Hastings and L.K. Hamberger, "Personality characteristics of spouse abusers: A controlled comparison," *Violence and Victims* 3, 1 (1988): 5-30; A. Holtzworth-Munroe and G.L. Stuart, "Typologies of male batterers: Three subtypes and the differences among them," *Psychological Bulletin* 116, 3 (1994): 476-97.
28 L.W. Sherman, J.D. Schmidt, D.P. Rogan, D.A. Smith, P.R. Gartin, E.G. Cohn, D.J. Collins, and A.R. Bacich, "The variable effects of arrest on criminal careers: The Milwaukee domestic violence experiment," *Journal of Criminal Law and Criminology* 83, 1 (1992): 137-69.
29 Mills, *Insult to Injury*, 111-12.

Index

Page numbers in **bold type** refer to figures.

Printed and bound in Canada by Friesens

Set in Giovanni and Officina Sans by Artegraphica Design Co.

Text design: Irma Rodriguez

Copy editor: Larry MacDonald

Proofreader: Dianne Tiefensee

Indexer: David Luljak